A TEXTBOOK OF ECONOMICS

To
Grace, Shauna, Karen, Susan and St.John
with love

A Textbook of Economics

by Frank Livesey

Senior Lecturer in Management Sciences
University of Manchester Institute of Science and Technology

POLYTECH PUBLISHERS LTD STOCKPORT

First Published 1978
Reprinted 1979

©

Copyright Polytech Publishers Limited
36 Hayburn Road, Stockport SK2 5DB

ISBN 0 85505 024 1

Made and printed in Great Britain by
Butler & Tanner Ltd, Frome and London

CONTENTS

Preface

THIS book is written primarily for students taking Economics at 'A' level or in the first year of a degree course. Although there is a substantial list of books available to such students, the author believes that the present book can be justified by several recent developments.

First there is the increasing emphasis on the incorporation into economics teaching of quantitative data. The desirability of this development was highlighted in 1973 in *The Teaching of Economics in Schools*, a report of a Joint Committee of the Royal Economic Society, the Association of University Teachers of Economics and the Economics Association. Impetus was subsequently given to this development by the introduction by a number of 'A' level Examination Boards of complete or part-papers comprising questions containing quantitative data.

Several people, including the present author, have written books of specimen questions and it is to be hoped that teachers and students have found these books useful in preparing for examinations. Moreover various commentaries utilizing quantitative data, such as the *Economist's* 'Schools Briefs' have been published and again these have no doubt proved helpful. However there would appear to be advantages in having a textbook in which such data is integrated with the theoretical arguments, and this integration has been one of my primary objectives. The main body of the text contains a great deal of material relating to actual economic events and processes, while further material is contained in the exercises which are to be found at the end of each chapter.

Incidentally the use of quantitative data should not be confused with a move towards 'mathematical economics'. There is nothing in this present volume that requires mathematics beyond that taught at 'O' level.

The second development has been the emergence of a certain degree of disenchantment with 'positive economics'. Conversations with teachers of economics at all levels have indicated a frequent (although not universal) desire to re-introduce certain elements of 'political economy', and to recognize the fact that the economic actions of individuals, firms and governments may be influenced by a wide range of motives and objectives. We have taken these diverse motives and objectives into account in our discussion of incomes policies, pricing decisions, alternative economic systems, and indeed wherever it seemed appropriate to do so within the confines of an economics textbook.

Third, there has recently been a revival of 'monetarism' which has led to a challenging of the 'Keynesian conventional wisdom' and to a widespread debate concerning the respective roles of fiscal and monetary policy. One of the most useful outcomes of this debate has been a recognition of the fact that fiscal policy may have very important monetary implications, and we discuss this point at length in Chapter 13.

Finally there has been a tendency in recent years to move away from the rigid distinction between macro and micro economics, and this tendency is reflected to some extent in the present volume. For example, although Chapter 6 is mainly concerned with the macro economic implications of investment expenditure, it also explores the factors which may influence the investment programmes of individual firms. Again macro and micro elements appear in most of the chapters on government policy, and especially in the chapters on regional and manpower policy.

We have, however, retained a broad division between the two areas, the major macro aspects being discussed in the first part of the book, and the major micro aspects in the second. As we point out in Chapter 1, it is hoped that this reversal of the usual order of presentation will enable the student to 'get at' topics of current interest as quickly as possible.

As noted above, the exercises are intended to be an integral part of the book, and to reinforce the parts of the text to which they relate. Some of these exercises have appeared in two of the author's previous publications, *Economics* and *Data Response Questions in Economics*. However the majority are new.

Mrs. Muriel Shingler, together with Miss Mary O'Mohony, my daughter Shauna and my wife Grace, transformed a chaotic manuscript into a typescript fit for presentation to the printer. My thanks are due to the entire team.

The complete manuscript was read by John Oliver and Alan Turner. Both agreed to take on this task despite having work to do on manuscripts of their own, and I am extremely grateful for the numerous improvements which each suggested.

I acknowledge with thanks the material from H.M.S.O. publications which is reproduced with the permission of the Controller of Her Majesty's Stationery Office.

Objective Test Questions

THREE types of objective test questions are included in the book:

Simple completion, where the student chooses one of the five options, A to E.

Multiple completion, where,

A   indicates that all three options are correct
B   indicates that options 1 and 2 are correct
C   indicates that options 2 and 3 are correct
D   indicates that option 1 only is correct
E   indicates that option 3 only is correct.

Double statement, where,

A   indicates that both statements are true, and that the second statement is an explanation of the first
B   indicates that both statements are true, but that the second statement is not an explanation of the first
C   indicates that the first statement is true and the second statement is false
D   indicates that the first statement is false and the second statement is true
E   indicates that both statements are false.

CHAPTER ONE

Introduction: The Nature of Economic Resources

Introduction

ECONOMICS can be divided into two very broad fields of study. Micro economics is concerned with the decisions taken by individual units, e.g. producers, workers and consumers. Macro economics is concerned with the behaviour of aggregates or collections of units, e.g. the output supplied by all producers, the amount spent by all consumers.

Many economic textbooks begin by studying micro economics and then move on to macro economics. There is much to be said for this approach, and indeed the author has himself adopted this approach on other occasions. In this book, however, the process is reversed; macro economic topics are discussed before those of micro economics.

The main reason for adopting this alternative approach is that much of the economic information that the student obtains in everyday life relates to macro economic affairs. Newspapers, radio and television make frequent reference to the rate of inflation, changes in unemployment, the state of the balance of payments, etc., and to macro economic government policy – changes in taxation, attempts to influence the supply of money, borrowing money from, or repaying money to, the I.M.F., etc. It was felt, therefore, that it would be appropriate to discuss at an early stage these matters of daily concern.

The Plan of the Book

We start by considering, in this and the following chapter, the nature of economic resources and the process whereby they are transformed into the goods and services that satisfy the needs and wants of consumers. Economics has become increasingly concerned with measurement. Consequently in Chapter 3 we discuss the various ways in which economic activity, the transformation of resources into goods and services, can be measured.

It is shown in Chapter 3 that one of the most common ways of measuring economic activity is via expenditure on goods and services, and in the following four chapters we examine the four major expenditure flows – consumers' expenditure, government consumption, investment, and international monetary flows which enter into the balance of payments accounts.

Having examined the individual flows in these four chapters, we consider the determinants of total expenditure in Chapter 8. We then examine in Chapter 9 the implications of particular levels of total expenditure. We show that total expenditure may be considered to be too high, being associated with an unacceptable rate of inflation, or too low, being associated with an unacceptable level of unemployment.

The objectives of government economic policy, including those relating to inflation and unemployment, are examined in Chapter 10. This examination forms the background to the discussion in the following ten chapters of the various elements of government policy. The major weapons in the government's armoury are fiscal and monetary policy, which are discussed in Chapters 11 and 12 respectively. Increasing attention has been given in recent years to the monetary implications of fiscal policy and so in Chapter 13 we discuss the interaction between fiscal and monetary policy.

Although fiscal and monetary policy comprise a wide range of measures, they may not always be sufficient to enable governments to meet their economic objectives. When these 'demand management' policies appear to be inadequate, government may place more reliance on prices and incomes policies, as shown in Chapter 14.

Another very important area of government macro economic policy is concerned with our international economic relationships, an area which is discussed in Chapter 15.

We then consider, in Chapters 16 to 20, various components of government policy which have both macro and micro economic implications. These are, in the order in which they are discussed, regional policy, manpower policy, competition policy, nationalization and industrial policy. In these chapters we are, therefore, moving away from macro and towards micro economics, a shift which continues in Chapter 21. In the first part of that chapter we discuss the recent performance of the British economy in terms of the broad aggregates that we have already considered in earlier chapters. In the second part of Chapter 21 we discuss changes in expenditure, output and employment in particular industries – changes which are considered in greater detail in the remaining chapters.

In Chapter 22 we examine the means by which resources may be allocated between various industries. Central to this allocation process is the interaction between demand and supply, concepts which are discussed in greater detail in Chapters 23 and 24. As part of the discussion of supply we consider how prices are determined. Further aspects of price determination in particular types of market are examined in Chapters 25 and 26. In Chapter 27 we apply demand and supply analysis to factor markets and in particular to the labour market. Finally in Chapter 28 we examine some additional aspects of the price mechanism as it applies to areas of current interest, – rent control, minimum wage legislation, price stabilization schemes, the conservation of resources, energy supplies, etc.

The Nature of Economic Resources
Having given a brief outline of the areas covered in the book, we now turn to the main subject of this first chapter, the nature of economic resources. Resources can be divided into two broad categories – human and non-human – and we consider each of these in turn.

Human Resources
The stock of human resources in an economy (in less technical language the size of a country's population) depends upon the birth and death rates and upon international migration flows. In many countries economic development has led to periods of rapid population growth, as improved medical facilities reduced the death rate, followed by periods of less rapid growth as the birth rate declined.

At present there is a tendency for the birth rate, and hence the rate of population growth, to be higher in developing countries than in countries with more fully developed, highly industrialized economies. This is due to several factors, non-economic as well as economic. For example it has been claimed that programmes designed to encourage the use of various contraceptive techniques in under-developed countries would have had a greater measure of success if greater attention had been given to the social structures of the communities and to the role of certain key members in influencing attitudes and behaviour.

While such social factors are no doubt important, economic considerations also help to explain why such programmes have sometimes been less successful than anticipated. The survival of many peasant families depends upon there being sufficient labour to tend the family farm or smallholding. When sickness and disease are common, the birth of additional children may be seen as a form of insurance against the possible future loss of active members of the family. (In more advanced societies families are cushioned to some extent by social security provisions against the loss of income following the death of a breadwinner.)

Economic factors are also an important determinant of migration patterns. People tend to emigrate from less to more developed economies, attracted by the prospect of better employment opportunities and living standards. Sometimes emigration is temporary, the emigrant's motive being to obtain education and training which he can then utilize in his own country. But often it is permanent.

The Flow of Labour Inputs
The flow of labour inputs has two major aspects, quantity and quality. The quantity of labour derived from a given stock or population depends upon several factors. The age and sex structure of the population determine the proportion of the inhabitants who are physically capable of working. Of these people a substantial proportion will not in practice be available for work because of legislation or social conventions.

Legislation reduces the size of the potential work-force by specifying a minimum school-leaving age. At the other end of the age-scale, although compulsory withdrawal from the labour-force is unusual, the provision of state retirement pensions obviously reduces the need for older people to work.

In many countries social convention has decreed that married women, and especially the mothers of young children, should not work. Although, as we show in Chapter 21, attitudes and practice have changed considerably in recent years, 'participation rates' for females remain well below those for males.

The increase that has occurred in the proportion of married women who work is again due to a mixture of economic and non-economic motives. The idea that a woman should be content to act only as wife and mother has been challenged ever more strongly, the most extreme form of this challenge being represented by the 'women's liberation' movement. At the same time economic changes have led to an increase in the opportunities for women to find paid employment. On the one hand there has sometimes been insufficient male workers to fully meet the increasing demand for labour. On the other hand an increase in the availability of domestic labour-saving devices has left women with more time to spend outside the home.

The final important influence on the quantity of labour inputs is the average number of hours worked. This is determined by the average length of the working week and by the number of weeks worked per year, both of which have tended to decline in many countries in recent years. The average hours worked is influenced by legislation, by custom and by negotiations between representatives of employers and workers.

Optimum Population

The optimum population is the size of population at which, given the volume of other resources, the output of goods and services per head of population would be maximized. Since the volume of other resources is constantly changing it follows that the optimum population will also constantly change. As the volume of other resources, and especially of capital, increases, the size of the optimum population will tend to increase. However, increasing concern has been expressed about the continued growth in world population.

There are several reasons for this concern. In some countries the rate of growth of population may outstrip the increase in the availability of certain vital commodities, e.g. staple foodstuffs in India and certain African countries. Elsewhere the growth of population may lead to a deterioration in living conditions, as has occurred in some parts of large cities such as Tokyo, New York and London. Furthermore, rapid population growth may contribute to the early exhaustion of vital resources such as oil, which could cause future living standards to decline. This suggests that our initial definition of optimum population might in some circumstances be inadequate. Rather than confining our attention to the situation at a given point in time, it might be more appropriate to consider the implications of a change in population for both the current and future generations.

THE QUALITY OF LABOUR

In principle, if not always in practice, one can distinguish between workers in terms of inherent (natural) and acquired characteristics. On the one hand some people are naturally more intelligent, energetic, diligent or stronger than others. On the other hand some people have received more education and/or training than others. It follows that the quality of a nation's labour force can be influenced at least to some extent by the education and training facilities provided by the state, employers, etc., and by the willingness and ability of citizens to make use of these facilities.

These facilities are frequently supplied without charge, especially when provided by the state. There is however a very substantial opportunity cost* involved in their provision; if the state spent less on schools, technical colleges and universities, it would be able to spend more on hospitals, roads and prisons. Consequently it is important to consider what benefits may result from this expenditure. The increase in spending on education, and especially on higher and further education, in the post-war period was *partly* due to the belief that this would result in an improvement in the quality of the labour force and thus to an increase in productivity (the ratio of outputs to inputs), and in the rate of economic growth.

The concept of opportunity cost is also involved in a person's decision as to whether or not he or she should undertake further education or training. The opportunity cost of a period of training is the additional income (wages or salary minus any grant received while training) that would have been obtained by working. The loss of this income must be balanced against the potentially higher earnings in future years. (Other non-monetary factors such as the greater freedom enjoyed by students would also be taken into account, i.e. education is both an investment and a consumption good, to use the classification adopted in later chapters).

As we show in Chapter 17 British governments have also attempted, by means

* The opportunity cost of using resources in one way is the maximum benefit that could have been obtained from using them in some other way. Opportunity cost is one of the most important economic concepts.

of legislation and other methods, to increase the resources devoted to training. Here again it was believed that the improvement in the quality of the labour force would result in higher productivity and faster economic growth.

Increased training and education will, of course, pay off in this way only if the skills and abilities acquired and developed are those that are demanded by employers. Technological change means that the most appropriate mix of skills is constantly changing. This implies that part of the training effort should be devoted to the re-training of workers whose skills have become obsolete or less useful in order to increase their occupational mobility. The U.K. has devoted considerably fewer resources to re-training than some other countries, such as Sweden. However, as we show in Chapter 17, there has recently been a substantial improvement in this respect in the U.K., largely as a response to higher levels of unemployment.

Non-Human Resources

We follow the usual convention of distinguishing between two non-human resources, land and capital, although in practice these two resources are normally combined in use.*

Land

If land is defined as the total surface area of the planet, including oceans, lakes and rivers, then its total quantity is fixed. If the definition is restricted to dry land, some increase in quantity may occur as a result of drainage schemes etc., but such increases will clearly be very small in relation to the existing stock.

If we extend our definition of land to include the 'free gifts of nature' – mineral wealth, soil fertility, etc. – it is clear that considerable changes may occur in the quality of land and therefore in the flow of inputs derived from a given quantity or stock. This flow may either increase or decrease over time. In agriculture selective breeding can lead to higher yields. On the other hand over-intensive cultivation can lead to a reduction in the quality of the land and in crop yields, as shown by the creation of huge 'dust-bowls' in the U.S.A. in the inter-war period.

An increase in the flow of inputs from the land often requires the application of capital, sometimes in vast quantities, as illustrated by the development of North Sea oil. In addition labour is also required, of course. In such instances it is clearly impossible to determine the relative contributions to output of the different resources, the different *factors of production*. The significance of this fact is explored during our discussion of the determination of factor prices in Chapter 27.

Although land is immobile geographically, it may be highly mobile as between different uses. This is especially true of agricultural land which can be switched from one crop to another from year to year. Mobility is reduced when land is built on, but even here changes in use do occur.

Capital

Capital is any resource – other than what is defined as land and labour – that is used in the production and distribution of goods or services. Two types of capital are normally distinguished: fixed capital consisting of buildings, plant and machinery, and circulating capital (termed working capital by some writers) consisting of stocks of components, raw materials, etc. The main basis of this

---

* We also continue to speak of the flow of *inputs* derived from a resource, although in another context some of these inputs, e.g. agricultural products and minerals derived from land, might be termed outputs.

distinction is that fixed capital may provide a flow of inputs over a long period – typically ten or so years for machinery and much longer for buildings – whereas circulating capital is used up much more quickly and needs to be constantly re-placed. Another difference between the two is that circulating capital is much the more mobile geographically.

In defining capital we have not made a distinction between those outputs (goods or services) which are marketed and those which are provided free. Thus we would include within capital not only industrial buildings and equipment but also schools, hospitals, roads, etc. Some writers do seek to make a distinction, but the outcome is seldom satisfactory. To take but one example, it would seem to be illogical to include railways within capital because their output is marketed, but to exclude roads because people are not charged directly for their use.

Moreover all capital assets, whether used in the production of marketed or non-marketed outputs, have the important common characteristic that they are physi-cal or 'real' (as opposed to monetary) assets. Furthermore an increase in the output of capital goods is likely to mean that the current consumption of goods and ser-vices is less than it might have been. (The only situation in which this would not be so is if the additional capital goods could be produced by resources which would otherwise have remained idle). The reduction in the current output of consumption goods constitutes the opportunity cost of producing additional capital goods. This cost must be balanced against the benefit that an increased stock of capital goods would enable a greater quantity of consumption goods to be produced in future periods.

If the size of the labour force increases, an increase in the capital stock will be required in order to maintain the existing capital-labour ratio. This process is known as capital widening. In practice most industrialized economies have been characterized by a faster rate of growth in the capital than in the labour stock, i.e. the capital–labour ratio has increased, a process known as capital deepening.

CAPITAL AND ECONOMIC GROWTH
An increase in the capital-labour ratio normally increases labour productivity (out-put per worker), and in many industrialized economies whose labour force is static or growing only very slowly, an increase in the capital–labour ratio is seen as the mainspring of economic growth. However, while there appears to be a link between changes in the capital stock and the rate of economic growth, the connection is by no means straightforward.

The additional capital may be either labour- or capital-saving, or both. For example the introduction in weaving of shuttleless looms made possible an increase in output both per worker and per unit of capital employed. Technological progress may therefore permit economic growth without any increase in the stock of capital. We could define this process as one involving an increase in the *quality* of capital.

A different aspect of the quality of capital has received considerable attention in the less developed countries. In such countries it is often possible to achieve spectacular increases in labour productivity in particular industries by introducing production methods incorporating the latest technical innovations. However since such countries are often characterized by a labour surplus, many of the workers displaced by the new equipment may remain unemployed. If this occurs labour productivity in the country as a whole may be virtually unchanged, while social distress may result from the higher unemployment.

This result is especially likely if the production process 'imported' from more developed countries requires supplies of components, etc., and maintenance facili-

Table 1.1

Growth in Industrial Investment and Production

	1960–70				1967–70			
	U.K.	W. Germany	France	U.S.A	U.K.	W. Germany	France	U.S.A.
Growth of industrial investment (% per annum)	3.2	4.8	8.3	7.4	7.6	8.0	7.3	2.6
Growth in industrial investment ÷ Growth in industrial production	1.03	0.98	1.43	1.35	2.23	1.63	1.22	0.96

Source: O.E.C.D., *The Growth of Output, 1960–1980.*

ties which must also be provided by these countries. Experience of such situations has led to proposals that more of the capital assets of less developed countries should incorporate an 'intermediate technology', less capital intensive than that used in more developed countries. These proposals are discussed further in Chapter 15.

It has often been claimed that one of the main reasons for the U.K.'s slow rate of economic growth in comparison with her main international competitors is a slower rate of increase in her capital stock. So we see from table 1.1 that during the 1960s industrial investment grew much more slowly in the U.K. (3.2 per cent a year) than in other countries. Towards the end of the period the rate of growth in investment increased substantially in the U.K. (to 7.6 per cent a year), becoming similar to the rates of West Germany and France, and well above that of the U.S.A. However this increase in investment was accompanied by an almost identical fall in the yield of the additional investment (shown in the bottom line). This suggests that the link between investment and economic growth may be very weak because the *potential* increase in output from investment may not be achieved.

This fall in the yield of capital was due partly to the fact that the demand for consumption goods did not rise sufficiently to permit the full utilization of the increased capital stock. It is also possible that the increase in output was limited by restrictive practices adopted by some workers in an attempt to maintain or improve employment prospects. It appears that in industries as diverse as newspapers, railways and steel, new equipment is manned by more workers in the U.K. than in many other countries. This increases the cost of producing, and hence the price of, the goods manufactured on this equipment. At these higher prices, fewer goods are bought and therefore the output per unit of capital employed is less than it would otherwise be.

Scarcity and Free Goods

The resources that we have considered so far – labour, land and capital – give rise to flows of inputs each of which has a price. The owners of these resources are able to extract a price because the inputs are used in the production of goods and services for which people are willing and able to pay, either individually or collectively via the state. When a price is paid for an input or a product, scarcity is said to exist.*

People will not normally pay for a product unless they expect to derive from that product satisfaction in one form or another. On the other hand it does not follow that they must always pay for something from which they derive satisfaction. Consider, for example, the person walking in the country who derives deep satisfaction from breathing fresh air and, when thirsty, from drinking from a mountain stream – both obtained at a zero price.

Why is it that these benefits are available free? Part of the explanation is that the 'products' in question are abundant. Indeed this is sometimes given as the sole explanation.† However there is a more fundamental reason, namely that ownership rights in the product or resource have not been established or, if established, have not been exercised. Had the owner of the stream been able to control access he would have been able to make a charge for its use.

* It is clear that this use of the term scarcity differs from the everyday use.

† 'Free goods are goods which are not relatively scarce, and therefore which do not have a price.' G. Bannock, R. E. Baxter, and R. Rees, *The Penguin Dictionary of Economics* (Harmondsworth: Penguin, 1972). We show below that the term 'free good' can be properly applied only to resources.

The importance of property rights – or the lack of them – can be further demonstrated by means of three more examples. First, the 1970s saw the extension of the area of the oceans in which individual countries claimed exclusive fishing rights. This meant that whereas previously ships from any country had been able to fish in these waters at no cost, (apart, of course, from the cost of operating the ships), henceforth foreign ships incurred a cost in terms of the danger of arrest followed by a fine, impounding of their catch, etc.

Second, where no property rights in lakes and inland waterways have been established, or where the owners have chosen not to exercise these rights, anyone has been able to use such waterways without charge for the discharge of effluent. On the other hand where property rights are established and exercised, as by the regional water authorities in the U.K., this free use is often no longer possible. The authorities may forbid the discharge of effluent, in which case the cost to a discharger becomes the risk of punishment if detected. Alternatively the authorities may allow discharge only after appropriate treatment, in which case the cost comprises the installation and operation of the treatment plant. A third possibility, not common in the U.K., is charging a price related to the volume and type of effluent discharged.

The final example, closely comparable to the previous one, is the discharge of smoke and other substances into the air. Parliament has vested property rights in residents if local authorities introduce clean air regulations preventing discharge. The resultant cost to users arises from the need to treat the discharge or change to substitute fuels.

These examples illustrate another important characteristic of a free good, namely that the opportunity cost of utilizing the resource in question is zero – the water that the thirsty man drinks would otherwise have run to waste. On the other hand there *is* an opportunity cost involved in utilizing a river for effluent disposal, namely the loss of amenity, e.g. for swimming or fishing, suffered by other potential users; consequently the river can no longer be treated as a free good. (Although, as we noted above, a charge will be levied only if property rights are established.)

Moreover a product would be free only if *all* the resources required for its supply were free. In practice, as we noted above, even the free gifts of nature can normally be utilized only through the application of additional, scarce resources; to bring mountain water into our homes requires costly capital equipment and considerable man-power. It follows that as a rule the term free good is applied to resources and not to products.*

Summary and Conclusions

In this chapter we have discussed the major economic resources and we have outlined the factors which may cause changes in the quantity and quality of these resources. The inputs derived from these resources have also been discussed. In the next chapter we discuss the process by which these inputs are transformed into outputs.

ESSAY QUESTIONS

1 What are the major determinants of a country's stock of (a) human, and (b) non-human resources?

---

* The walker breathing fresh air and drinking from a stream is a very special case in that the air and the water are resources which could also be seen as products.

2 Explain the significance of the statement that optimum population is a dynamic and not a static concept.
3 'Opportunity cost is a key economic concept.' Discuss.
4 Discuss the relationship between investment and economic growth.
5 Explain what is meant by a 'free good'. What is the fundamental reason for the existence of free goods?
6 'There is no such thing as a free dinner.' Comment.
7 Explain what is meant by the statement that the stock of resources is determined by both economic and non-economic factors.
8 Explain what you understand by the term 'scarcity'.

CHAPTER TWO

The Economic System: The Utilization of Resources

Introduction

HAVING discussed in the previous chapter the major economic resources and the inputs derived from these resources, we now examine the process by which these inputs are transformed into outputs.

Figure 2.1 is a highly simplified representation of a national economy. It shows that the owners of resources supply inputs to producers (flow A) in return for rewards of various kinds – wages and salaries, rent, interest and dividends (flow B). The producers utilise these inputs in the creation of a flow of outputs – goods and

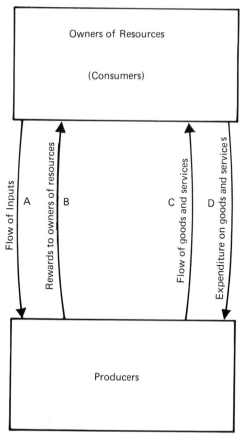

Figure 2.1 A Simple National Economy

services of various kinds (flow C). These goods and services are bought by the owners of resources – now acting as consumers – the expenditure (flow D) being financed out of the rewards (income) received from the producers.

The economy represented in figure 2.1 is a closed economy, i.e. it engages in no international economic transactions. In practice all modern economies are open – to a greater or lesser extent – and the international economic system could be represented by a diagram showing a series of national economies linked by international economic flows. Almost all countries obtain some inputs from abroad and sell goods and services abroad.

No government sector is separately identified in figure 2.1 since we wished to concentrate on the relationships that are common to all economic systems – free market, planned and mixed economies. The role of the government, or the state, in these different systems is explored briefly in the following sections.

Alternative Economic Systems
The Free Market Economy

The two most important characteristics of a free market economy are first that resources are owned by the private sector and not by the government or the state, and second that these resources are allocated via the price mechanism. Allocation of resources via the price mechanism has several implications. First, when the owners of resources decide to which producers they should make inputs available they are influenced by the rewards offered by the various producers. Second, producers, when deciding which goods and services to produce, are influenced by the prices that the various goods and services command and also, of course, by the rewards that they have to offer in order to obtain the inputs required to produce these goods and services. Finally the price mechanism helps to determine which consumers are able to buy particular goods or services and, looking at the matter from a slightly different viewpoint, which goods and services any particular consumer will buy.*

Given the two conditions or characteristics noted above, it is clear that the role of the government in a free market economy must be extremely limited. The private ownership of resources implies a very limited role for the state as a producer (although it could be argued that production by worker co-operatives, a system most highly developed in Yugoslavia, is compatible with a free market economy). The state could however act as a consumer. It could obtain revenue by taxing the rewards accruing to owners of resources, and use this revenue to buy goods and services. An important form of expenditure would probably be on collective consumption goods such as defence, which it is not usually feasible for consumers to purchase individually. In addition the state might buy products for re-sale at a price below the free market price. Such products are known as merit goods – medical and educational facilities being common examples.

An alternative method of influencing the price and availability of merit goods is to subsidize their production (the cost of the subsidies again being met out of taxation). Whether the government chooses this method or whether it enters the market as a consumer, there is some interference with the operation of the price mechanism. It is a matter for debate as to what degrees of interference can be said to be compatible with the existence of a free market economy.

---

*The functions of the price mechanism are sometimes summarized as follows: it helps to determine what should be produced, how it should be produced, and for whom it should be produced.

The Planned Economy

In a fully planned economy, sometimes known as a command economy, resources are allocated by a centralized administrative process. Decisions as to which goods and services should be produced may be influenced by the planning authority's perception of consumers' desires, perhaps as indicated by 'queues' for some products and unwanted stocks of others, indicators which are also important in the free market economy. But the decisions are likely to be heavily influenced by the planners' views of what would be beneficial for the community and the state as a whole. This may involve expanding the output of individual merit goods, and reducing the output of goods deemed to be undesirable. It may also involve the expansion of whole industries or sectors of the economy, e.g. the output of capital goods, of the defence industry, of the agricultural sector.

In a fully planned economy decisions about the desired output of final goods and services are only the start of the planning process. In order to meet this ultimate objective the planners must ensure that the required inputs are available. Thus a series of quotas is established for producers of both final and intermediate goods – components, raw materials, etc. This in turn implies that control must be imposed over the flow of inputs and thus over the allocation of resources.

It is clear that the implementation of the plans will be very much easier if resources are owned by the state. Consequently planned economies are normally characterized by extensive public ownership, as well as by the very limited role accorded to the price mechanism. Indeed in the pure form of the command economy all resources would be publicly owned and the price mechanism would not exist. In practice, even in countries such as the U.S.S.R. and China where central planning is highly developed, some resources are privately owned and the price mechanism continues to operate. In both countries farmers are allowed to own some land and to sell some of their produce in privately-owned shops or markets. Again, although the wage rates for different occupations may be set centrally, wage differentials do exist. (Indeed some observers have claimed that real differentials, taking into account fringe benefits and the tax structure, may be greater in the U.S.S.R. than in many Western countries). One of the functions of these differentials may be to influence people's decisions as to which occupation they should try to enter, i.e. to influence the allocation of human resources.

The existence in planned economies of these elements of the free market system is largely due to three factors. First, the process of planning itself requires resources, and the more detailed the planning procedures the more resources are required. Costs are likely to be especially high when attempts are made to plan the activities of industries in which there are a large number of small producers, widely scattered geographically, as in agriculture and, to a lesser extent, retailing.

Second, although this might in fact be denied by the advocates of planning, experience has shown that complete state control of an industry sometimes leads to a dramatic fall in productivity. The poor performance of the collective farms in the U.S.S.R. in the early years of centralization appears to have been an important factor in the decision to maintain some private ownership of land and indeed to return some land to private owners.

Finally 'ownership' of labour in the sense that labour can be directed into particular occupations and areas, is likely to be highly unpopular politically. (The direction of labour on a temporary basis, as currently practiced in China, is probably due to ideological rather than economic motives, and if the dominant ideology becomes less widespread we would expect the practice to be accepted less readily.)

The less the ability to direct labour centrally, the greater the scope for the operation of the price mechanism.

The Mixed Economy

The mixed economy combines elements of both free market and planned economies. Resources are owned part privately and part publicly and are allocated partly by means of the price mechanism (modified by government intervention) and partly in accordance with a centralized planning mechanism.

As the previous discussion will have indicated, most modern economies are mixed, with differing degrees of state intervention. As a general rule, of the industrialized economies those in Western Europe, North America and Japan have much less state intervention than those of Eastern Europe. Among the less developed nations an equally wide variety of experience can be found.

A Comparison of Alternative Systems

There has been a great deal of discussion about the relative efficiency of free market and planned economies, and of mixed economies that approximate more closely to one or other of these extremes. The major *potential* strengths and benefits claimed for each type of economy are as follows.

The free market economy is more flexible; the reallocation of resources in response to changes in the demands of consumers occurs more quickly via the price mechanism than through a centralized planning procedure. Moreover the private ownership of resources provides an incentive to utilize these resources in order to meet the requirements of consumers as expressed in their desire to purchase goods and services.

In a planned economy centralized planning provides greater opportunities for resources to be concentrated on activities which are felt (by the planners or the government) to be most beneficial to the nation's economic and social well-being. Moreover it gives greater opportunities for the distribution of income and wealth to be modified in ways thought to be desirable (again by the planners or the government).

The relative merits of these two types of economy are discussed at greater length in later chapters. However even this brief outline is sufficient to show that we are unlikely to reach any conclusion that would be universally acceptable about which type of economy is to be preferred, even in principle. There are two basic reasons why agreement is unlikely.

First, there is likely to be considerable disagreement about the role of political processes. Centralized planning tends to be associated with political processes which limit the right of the voter to choose between alternative candidates at elections (if, indeed, public elections are held). Critics might say that in such circumstances it is likely that economic plans will reflect the views and objectives of a small group of officials – who may not be elected at all – rather than of the citizens as a whole. In reply to this argument the supporters of the planned economy might claim that these officials would in practice be very sensitive to the needs of the ordinary citizen. They would also claim that in the extreme form of free market system the allocation of resources is influenced mainly by the distribution of income and wealth, which is unlikely to be ideal.

Second, there are several alternative criteria by which the economic performance of a system might be judged, and different people accord different weight to different criteria. Criteria commonly used are: changes in the volume of output, the range of goods and services and the choices available to consumers, the rate of price increase, the level and stability of employment, the conservation of resources, and the protection of the environment. (It might be an interesting exercise if the reader were to ask a number of his friends to rank these criteria, together with any others thought to be appropriate, in order of importance.)

The fact that different people attach different weight to particular criteria means that even if we are able to refer to evidence concerning the actual performance of economies we are unlikely to reach general agreement as to which economy has performed best overall. Agreement would be possible only in the (very unlikely) event that one economy outperformed another in terms of all the various criteria.

However, although we may be unable to rank economies in terms of their overall performance, we can make meaningful comparisons in terms of individual criteria, such as changes in the level of output or employment. Some comparisons of this kind are presented in later chapters, and especially in Chapter 21. However the main purpose of this book is not to *describe* but to *explain* economic performance, to analyse the factors which influence performance.

This analysis is developed at length in subsequent chapters. By way of introduction we consider in the final sections of this chapter what factors might determine a country's standard of living – obviously an important aspect of economic performance.

The Standard of Living

The standard of living is by no means a simple concept, as we demonstrate below. However we begin with a simple definition, one which would make a great deal of sense to the man-in-the-street: the average standard of living is the volume of goods and services consumed per head in a given time period. (We use the term 'consumed' rather than 'bought' in order to include the goods and services which may be provided free, e.g. medical and educational services, defence.)

If, during that time period, the level of stocks does not change and if the volume of exports equals the volume of imports, the consumption of goods and services will be identical with the output of goods and services for consumption ('consumption goods' for short). Consequently we can represent the standard of living by means of a production possibility boundary or frontier.

The Production Possibility Frontier

In figure 2.2, which makes the simplifying assumption that only two types of product are made, the production possibility frontier AB indicates all the possible output combinations. One possibility would be an output of G food plus Y clothing, another an output of H food plus Z clothing.* Which output is actually produced depends, of course, upon the various factors influencing consumers' demands.

The curve AB is concave to the origin because some resources are better suited to the production of one product and some to the production of another product. As the output of one product is increased it is necessary to employ resources which are less efficient in that use than those previously employed. Consequently the greater the initial output of a product, the more of the other product is foregone for a given increase in the output of the first product. Whereas an increase in the output of food of HG would require a reduction of ZY in the output of clothing,

---

* In discussing any diagram, when we use a single letter to indicate the quantity of any variable, that letter represents a given distance along the axis from the point of origin, O. Thus G, Y, H and Z are the simplified forms of OG, OY, OH and OZ.

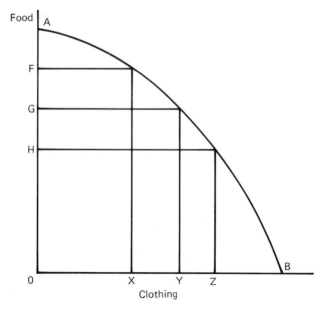

Figure 2.2   A Production Possibility Frontier

a further increase of GF (=HG) in food would require a larger reduction (YX) in clothing.

Although the concept of a concave production possibility frontier has general applicability, the exact shape of the frontier will depend upon the nature of the

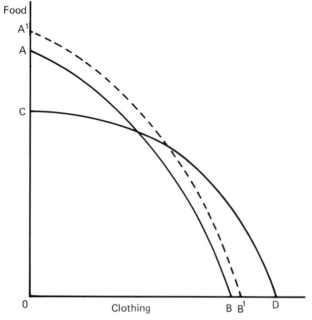

Figure 2.3   Alternative Production Possibility Frontiers

resources in the economy concerned. In figure 2.3 we show two alternative frontiers. AB might refer to a country with an abundance of fertile agricultural land and farming skills, CD to a country whose terrain and climate were more suited to manufacturing and whose workers had the manual dexterity required for manufacturing processes. Differences of this kind are an important determinant of international trade, as we shall see in Chapter 7.

Turning now to the *position* of the frontier, the most important question is how the frontier might be shifted outward, i.e. what factors might cause curve AB in figure 2.3 to move to A^1B^1. One obvious possibility is that the volume of resources, and hence the flow of inputs, may increase over time. As we showed in Chapter 1 an increase in the capital stock is likely to be especially important. Indeed in countries in which the size and structure of the population are constant, capital is the only resource in which significant changes are possible. Consequently we will concentrate our attention on this factor. (Another reason for emphasizing changes in capital is that although an increase in labour input may cause the frontier to shift outwards, this may not result in an increase in average living standards if the additional labour results from an increase in population.)

THE EFFECT OF CHANGES IN THE STOCK OF CAPITAL

In figure 2.4 AB indicates the various combinations of consumption and capital goods that could be produced in a given period. In terms of our initial definition, the highest standard of living in this period would be represented by an output of L consumption goods. However this would imply that all resources would be utilized in the consumption goods industries and that the output of capital goods

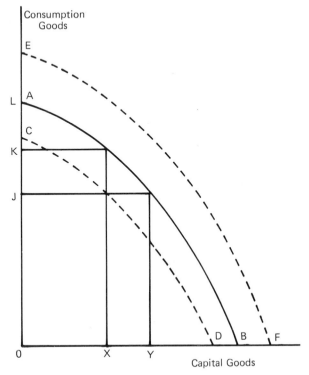

Figure 2.4   Investment and the Production Possibility Frontier

would be zero. Since some of the existing capital stock would be used up in current production (a process known as capital consumption) economic or productive capacity in future periods would fall, i.e. the production possibility frontier would shift to CD.

If we assume that the quality of capital is given, and the amount of investment, the output of capital goods, required to balance capital consumption is X, then the maximum output of consumer goods consistent with maintaining the existing economic capacity is K. If economic capacity is to be increased, i.e. if the production possibility frontier is to be shifted outwards, the output of capital goods must exceed X. For example output Y might be required to shift the frontier to EF. This shift would enable the output of both consumption and capital goods to be increased in the subsequent period. However this would require a sacrifice in consumption of KJ in the current period. This is the opportunity cost of investment to which we referred in Chapter 1.

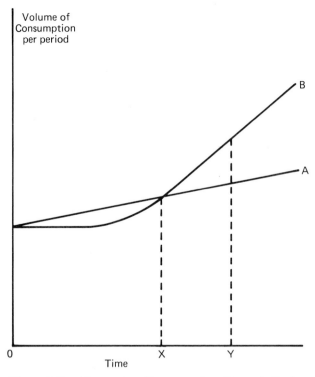

Figure 2.5 Alternative Consumption Growth Paths

The effect of diverting resources from the consumption to the capital goods industries is represented in a slightly different way in figure 2.5. Line A shows the rate of increase in consumption that could be achieved with a given rate of investment. Line B shows the rate of increase with a higher rate of investment, i.e. when, in each period, a higher proportion of resources is devoted to the capital goods industries. Consumption grows more slowly at first and subsequently more quickly. In period X the volume of consumption is identical for the two growth paths; thereafter the volume of consumption per period is greater for path B. However the total volume of consumption since period 0 becomes identical only in period Y; thereafter it is greater for path B.*

Given the importance of the time dimension, the choice of investment rate is not an easy one. It has been argued that planned or command economies have frequently depressed current levels of consumption more than was justified, i.e. have directed too many resources into the capital goods industries. One's reaction to this argument will clearly depend partly upon one's view about the relationship between successive generations of citizens. It will also depend upon the current level of consumption. A reduction in current consumption is far more feasible in highly industrialized countries than in underdeveloped countries where many people are living at subsistence level.

In free market economies the allocation of resources as between the capital and consumption goods industries is the result of the decisions of a large number of individuals. These decisions are influenced by many factors, but especially important are the rewards offered to savers, i.e. to people who defer consumption, and the potential yield to investment in capital goods. These points are discussed in detail in Chapter 6.

AN IMPROVEMENT IN THE QUALITY OF INPUTS
In the above section we assumed that the quality of capital was unchanged. In practice, as we showed in Chapter 1, research and development is likely to lead to an improvement over time in the average quality of the capital stock, and thus to an outward shift in the production possibility frontier. The same argument applies to an improvement in the quality of other inputs. Indeed some commentators, when discussing expenditure on education and training facilities, have used the phrase 'investment in human capital'.

CHANGES IN INDUSTRIAL ORGANIZATION
Finally we should note that economic efficiency may increase, i.e. the production possibility frontier may shift outward, because of a number of factors that we can group loosely under the heading of changes in industrial organization.† These changes may apply at the level of: (1) the individual plant, e.g. when an improved layout leads to an improved flow of work through the factory; (2) the firm, e.g. when the production of different products is rearranged so as to enable each factory to devote itself to a single product and thus to reap the advantages of specialization in both labour and capital; (3) two or more firms, e.g. when a merger permits the redeployment of facilities that were duplicated; (4) the industry, e.g. when a central organization is established to undertake research and development that could not be financed by individual firms.

A Reduction in Economic Capacity
We showed above that technological progress is likely to result in an outward shift in the production possibility frontier, but that the frontier might contract, i.e. economic capacity might decline, if a country devoted too high a proportion of its resources to production for current consumption. Fears have been expressed, most notably by the 'Club of Rome'.‡ that the economic capacity of individual nations,

* Even then we cannot conclude that path B is to be preferred, since society may value consumption in one period more highly than consumption in a later period.

† Some of these factors could also be classified as changes in the quality of the 'managerial' input.

‡ D. H. Meadows et al., The Limits to Growth (London: Earth Island, 1972).

and of the world as a whole, may contract in the future because of a shortage, and even the exhaustion, of certain vital raw materials, including sources of energy. Furthermore it is argued that even if total economic capacity does not contract, average living standards may fall as the rate of population growth outstrips the rate of growth of production.

This is far too big a topic to be adequately discussed here, but three brief points may be made. First, potential shortages of raw materials may require more attention to be given to the recycling of materials that have already been used and which are currently treated as waste. Second, the time scale and the capital required to unlock new sources of raw materials e.g. mineral deposits in sea water, solar energy, may necessitate an increase in state intervention and international co-operation. Finally, the impact of shortages may be more easily withstood by the highly developed than by the underdeveloped nations. This implies that the economic obligations of the former group towards the latter may need to be reconsidered.

The Production Possibility Frontier and Economic Growth
Economic growth is virtually synonymous with an outward shift in the production possibility frontier. So in figure 2.6 the increase in output from Y to Z, associated with the shift in the frontier from AB to A¹B¹, could properly be designated as economic growth. On the other hand an increase in output from X to Y, the frontier remaining at AB, should not be so designated (although the increase in living standards would be none the less welcome). The move from X to Y represents an increase in the degree of utilization of the existing economic capacity. Such a process is essentially short-term; it must come to an end when capacity has become fully utilized, i.e. when the frontier is reached.

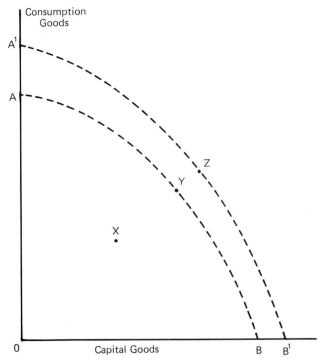

Figure 2.6   Economic Growth and Increases in Output

Other Aspects of the Standard of Living
We initially defined the standard of living in terms of the average level of consumption. We subsequently qualified this definition to take account of the need to devote resources to the production of capital goods in order to protect future consumption levels. In this final section we make some further qualifications.

The Production of Economic Bads
First, as noted in Chapter 1, an economic system may produce both economic goods and economic 'bads', such as pollution of various kinds, traffic congestion and the destruction of recreational areas. If an increase in the output of goods is accompanied by an increase in the output of bads, then any measure which takes the former into account but ignores the latter will overstate the increase, or improvement, in the standard of living. Conversely, if, in a given period, there is a reduction in the output of bads, as happened when legislation led to the introduction of smokeless zones, the improvement in living standards will be greater than indicated by the change in consumption of goods and services.

In the following chapter we give some measures, in relation to the U.K., of what would be commonly accepted as economic bads. However we should emphasize that it is not *always* clear what constitutes a bad. Aircraft noise is normally considered to be a nuisance, as the makers of Concorde have discovered to their cost. However it is quite conceivable that the citizens of a developing nation may take great pride in the noise made by the aircraft of their national airline, which symbolizes the progress made by the nation.

Deviations from the Average
Second, an increase in average consumption does not imply an increase in consumption by all citizens, as recent experience in the U.K. indicates. Moreover it appears that the incidence of bads may be very unevenly distributed so that even if all citizens become better off materially it will almost certainly be possible to find some people whose welfare, defined more widely, falls. For example, road-widening schemes, the building of motorways, the extending of airport runways, although undertaken 'in the public interest', almost always affect some individuals adversely.

An Extension of Consumer Choice
Before leaving this discussion about the connection between consumption and welfare we should refer to one final point, already briefly mentioned above. The satisfaction of consumers is influenced not simply by the volume of goods and services that they buy, but also by the degree of choice that they are offered. Choice refers here both to the range of different products and to differences in style and quality within a given product. A large amount of research and development effort in highly developed countries is devoted to the widening of the consumer's choice in both respects.

The increase in welfare that results from this activity is sometimes very great, as when a new life-saving drug is discovered. In other instances the benefits may appear to be negligible as, for example, when another brand of toothpaste is marketed. However, appearances can be deceptive; the new toothpaste might well have a distinctive characteristic – colour, flavour or texture – that encourages teeth-cleaning, (especially by young children).

Consumption, Work and Leisure

We justified putting emphasis on a change in the capital stock as the determinant of a shift in the production possibility frontier on the grounds that (a) it is easier to change the quantity of capital than of other inputs when the population is stable, and (b) changes in labour input are usually accompanied by changes in population, so that consumption per head changes less than total consumption, and may not even change at all. However the relationship between changes in consumption and in working patterns has important economic and social implications which deserve consideration.

First, output can be increased by increasing the average number of hours worked per worker, in particular by the introduction of overtime working.* Since workers undertake this additional work voluntarily we can conclude that the additional income, and thus the additional output, more than compensates for the reduction in leisure. Nevertheless the increase in working hours would normally be considered as a cost which should be taken into account in assessing the *net* benefit of the additional output. It is not of course, possible to put a precise figure on this cost, which is likely to vary from person to person depending upon such factors as the length of their normal working week and the importance they attach to leisure activities.

The same arguments apply to an increase in output that results from an increase in the proportion of the population in work. We mentioned in Chapter 1 that there has been a substantial increase in the number of women, and especially married women, working. For many of these women the loss of leisure must be counted as a cost. However for some women employment, including unpaid employment, e.g. for charitable institutions, may have a positive benefit in relieving the monotony and boredom which might beset them at home. This latter consideration may apply even more strongly to men because of their traditional role as the 'breadwinner'. For many men work fulfils deep psychological and social needs.

In many industries there has been in the post-war period an increase in shift-working and a transference of labour from one part of the country to another. These developments can again give rise to costs which should be offset against the benefit of higher output. Shift-working may prevent a person from following his preferred pattern of leisure activities, while labour mobility may involve a weakening of social ties, including moving away from relatives. Moreover some observers claim to have identified a connection between labour mobility and the break-up of community on the one hand and delinquency and vandalism on the other. (It must be said, however, that little hard evidence has been produced on this last point.)

Summary and Conclusions

In this chapter we have examined the main characteristics of alternative economic systems, and the factors which are most likely, in any system, to affect the efficiency of the process whereby economic inputs are transformed into outputs. We have seen that the performance of an economic system has many aspects,† and further

---

* An increase in output from a higher labour input derived from a *given* population might be represented either as a movement nearer to an existing production possibility frontier or alternatively as an outward shift of the frontier. Which representation is appropriate depends upon the precise definition of the frontier.

† Other writers may give other names to these different aspects of economic performance or efficiency. For example, in Chapter 11 of *Economics of the Market* (London: Fontana, 1976), Gordon Hewitt identifies three aspects: (i) Productive efficiency, which is maximized

that one of these aspects, the standard of living, has itself many facets. This leads to problems in measuring and assessing the performance of any economy. Nevertheless some measurement is required in order to give substance to our analysis, and in the following chapter we present data relating to economic activity in the United Kingdom.

ESSAY QUESTIONS

1 What are the major characteristics of free market, planned and mixed economies?
2 'Merit goods cannot exist in a free market economy,' Discuss.
3 To what extent do you agree with the view that the needs of consumers are more likely to be satisfied in a planned than in a market economy?
4 How would you explain the increasing importance of mixed economies?
5 Why is it often difficult to obtain agreement about which type of economy is preferable?
6 What factors might cause a change in (a) the shape, (b) the position, of a production possibility frontier?
7 Explain what you understand by the term 'standard of living'.
8 'An increase in the output of goods and services always indicates that economic growth is taking place.' Comment.
9 Discuss and illustrate the statement that one person's economic good may be another person's economic bad.
10 Discuss the factors which may affect the efficiency with which economic inputs are transformed into outputs.

---

when an economic system operates at the limit of the production frontier. (As we have shown, maximum production efficiency is consistent with many possible combinations of goods and services.) (ii) Allocative efficiency, which implies producing the combination of goods and services which maximizes the welfare of consumers. (iii) Distributive efficiency, which is concerned with the way in which the goods and services produced in an economy are shared among consumers.

EXERCISES

2.1 'Whatever a nation's goals – more help for the poor countries of the world, stronger defences, a larger public sector, a larger share of output for under-privileged persons at home – they can most easily be achieved by providing more resources through the growth of available output per head.' (Professor M. Lipton.)

'The continued pursuit of economic growth by western societies is more likely on balance to reduce rather than increase social welfare.' (Professor E. J. Mishan.)

Comment on the two views expressed in the above quotations.

2.2 Figure 2.7 shows the production possibility frontier (boundary) for an economy at a given point in time. (i) Account for the shape of the curve. (ii) Compare positions A and B in terms of (a) current living standards and (b) future living standards. (iii) Why might the combination of goods represented by point X be produced? (iv) Show the effect of a change in technology which resulted in the country becoming less efficient in the production of consumption goods and more efficient in the production of capital goods.

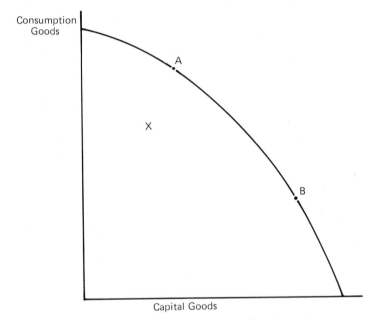

Figure 2.7 A Production Possibility Frontier

CHAPTER THREE

The Measurement of Economic Activity

Introduction
IN the previous chapter we presented, in figure 2.1, a highly simplified representation of a national economy. We showed that the owners of resources supply inputs to producers in return for rewards or income of various kinds, and that these resources are transformed into a flow of outputs supplied to consumers in exchange for payment. In many countries, including the U.K., economic statisticians measure three of these four flows. They measure the level of economic activity in terms of the value of: incomes (flow B), output (flow C) and expenditure (flow D). We begin this chapter by examining the flow of expenditure.

The Flow of Expenditure and the Gross Domestic Product
Figure 3.1 shows the flow of expenditure among four sectors: households (consumers), U.K. producers, the government and the overseas sector (producers and consumers). Seven major flows are identified and the value of each of these in 1976 is given in table 3.1. The total of the seven flows gives the value of gross domestic product (GDP). The significance of this total is discussed below, but first we briefly examine each of the components, beginning with the most important, consumers' expenditure.

Consumers' Expenditure
Accounting in 1976 for 60 per cent of GDP at market prices, this category includes almost all the items which consumers buy – food, drink, heat and light, consumer durable goods, travel, entertainment, etc. There is one exception, one item which one might expect to be included under this heading but is not; that is consumers' expenditure on the purchase of new dwellings, which is classified as part of gross fixed capital formation.

General Government Final Consumption
This category is similar to consumers' expenditure insofar as it refers mainly to goods or services that are 'consumed' by households.* However there is an important difference between the two categories. Whereas the items classified under consumers' expenditure are sold at prices designed to cover production costs and yield producers a profit, most of the government's current expenditure consists of goods or services which are provided either free or below cost, e.g. national defence, medical and educational services, etc. Expenditure by consumers on these products is clearly not a meaningful measure of their value. Consequently they are valued in the national accounts at their cost of production – the amount paid

* About 3 per cent comprises imputed consumption of non-trading capital. See Chapter 5.

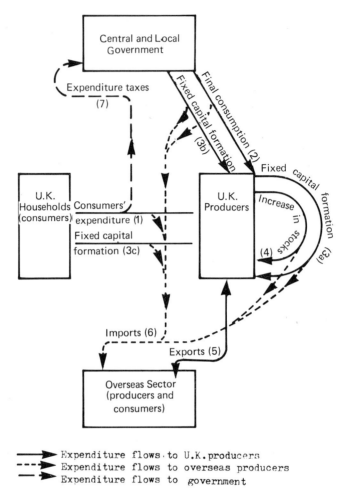

Figure 3.1 The Flow of Expenditure

Table 3.1

Gross Domestic Product, U.K. (1976)

	£ millions
(1) Consumers' expenditure	73,656
(2) General government final consumption	26,562
(3) Gross domestic fixed capital formation	23,427
(4) Value of physical increase in stocks and work in progress	359
(5) Exports of goods and services	34,837
(6) *Minus* Imports of goods and services	−36,564
Gross domestic product at market prices	122,277
(7) *Minus* Taxes on expenditure (net of subsidies)	−13,197
Gross domestic product at factor cost (G.D.P.)	109,080

Source: *National Income and Expenditure* (H.M.S.O., 1977).

by the public authorities for materials, wages, salaries, etc. Incidentally, one should not think of the government as meaning only the central government. In 1976 about 40 per cent of government final consumption was accounted for by the expenditure of local authorities.

Gross Fixed Capital Formation
This is the major component of investment expenditure, which approximates to the 'capital' input identified in Chapters 1 and 2. It can be seen from figure 3.1 that fixed capital formation comprises three separate flows. Producers are responsible for most fixed capital formation, followed by the government and by households. Major items include buildings of various kinds – factories, offices, shops, hospitals, schools, dwellings – plant and equipment, vehicles, ships, transport and communication facilities. The importance of capital formation in preserving future living standards was emphasized in Chapter 2, and we can see that in 1976 this category accounted for 19 per cent of GDP at market prices.

Value of the Physical Increase in Stocks and Work in Progress
The second component of investment expenditure, this is much less important than fixed capital formation. Changes in both categories may occur in line with producers' plans. However changes in stocks may also be unplanned. For example, if firms produce to meet a level of demand greater than actually occurs, stocks are likely to rise, at least until producers have had time to revise their production levels.

Exports and Imports of Goods and Services
One of the main purposes of measuring the flow of expenditure is that it provides an indication of the pressure of demand on the country's resources. Consequently we include exports, i.e. the expenditure by overseas residents on British goods and services, since this involves the utilization of our resources. Conversely we deduct the value of imports, i.e. expenditure by U.K. residents on goods and services supplied from abroad, since this involves the utilization of the resources of other countries.

Table 3.1 shows that the flows of expenditure on exports and imports are very important in the U.K., coming second only to consumers' expenditure. However it is the net balance of these two items that affects the level of utilization of domestic resources, and this is relatively small. In 1976 the excess of imports over exports amounted to only $1\frac{1}{2}$ per cent of GDP.

Gross Domestic Product
The sum of the above items gives the gross domestic product at market prices, amounting to £122, 277 millions in 1976. However of this figure £13,197 millions represented expenditure taxes (net of subsidies). When we subtract this figure we arrive at gross domestic product at factor cost (£109, 080 millions). GDP at factor cost measures the rewards accruing, to factors of production, and thus is a better indicator of the utilization of the nations resources.

The Usefulness of Measures of Expenditure
The classification of expenditure presented in table 3.1 has several advantages. It makes it possible to monitor changes in consumption, the most important element of the current standard of living, and in investment, a primary determinant of future living standards. It also helps in the analysis of the likely effects of changes

in the many factors, including government policies, which influence expenditure, since a change in a given factor will have different effects on different forms of expenditure. For example a change in the rate of tax on personal incomes is likely to have the greatest effect on consumers' expenditure, whereas the introduction of investment grants would be most likely to affect fixed capital formation. This point has become more important as the involvement of government in economic management has increased, and will be discussed at length in future chapters.

Finally, as we said above, the total of the various expenditure flows, GDP at factor cost, indicates the overall utilization of the nation's resources in the period in question. We also pointed out above that statisticians provide measures of other flows, i.e. measure economic activity in other ways. In the following sections we briefly examine these alternative measures.

The Flow of Output and the Gross Domestic Product

Table 3.2 shows the contribution to GDP of the various sectors of the economy. Manufacturing is the most important sector as one would expect in a highly industrialized country such as the U.K. However experience shows that beyond a

Table 3.2
Gross Domestic Product by Industry (1976)

	£ millions
Agriculture, forestry and fishing	3,116
Mining and quarrying	2,458
Manufacturing	30,464
Construction	7,793
Gas, electricity and water	3,905
Transport	6,624
Communication	3,691
Distributive trades	10,379
Insurance, banking, finance and business services	7,717
Ownership of dwellings	6,723
Public administration and defence	8,458
Public health and educational services	8,055
Other services	13,417
Adjustment for financial services	−4,702
Residual error	982
Gross domestic product at factor cost	109,080

Source: *National Income and Expenditure* (H.M.S.O., 1977).

certain point in a country's development the fastest rate of growth of output tends to occur in the service sector. Manufacturing's share of GDP fell from 33 to 28 per cent between 1966 and 1976, while over the same period the share of public health and educational services rose from 4.7 per cent to 7.4 per cent, and that of insurance, banking, finance and business services from 5.8 per cent to 7.1 per cent.

The Flow of Incomes, Gross National Product and National Income

Table 3.3 presents the final method of classifying GDP, namely in terms of the types of income received by the owners of resources. This table also shows the various adjustments to GDP that are required in order to arrive at a measure of the *national income*. These adjustments could, of course, be made to the GDP

Table 3.3

National Income, U.K. (1976)

	£ millions
Income from employment	78,639
Income from self-employment	10,208
Gross trading profits of companies	12,445
Gross trading surplus of public corporations and government enterprises	4,580
Rent	7,771
Imputed consumption of non-trading capital	1,012
Minus Stock appreciation	−6,557
Residual error	982
Gross domestic product at factor cost	109,080
Net property income from abroad	1,179
Gross national product	110,259
Minus Capital consumption	−13,583
National income	96,676

Source: *National Income and Expenditure* (H.M.S.O., 1977).

figures in tables 3.1 or 3.2, but it is conventional to make them to the incomes table.

The first adjustment is for net property income from abroad. This represents rent, interest, profits and dividends received by U.K. residents from abroad, minus the corresponding payments made abroad. Since in 1976 the U.K. had, on balance, a surplus on these items, the gross national product (GNP) exceeded the gross domestic product. GNP is yet another possible indicator of the standard of living, although it is inferior to GDP as a measure of the utilization of domestic resources.

Second, a substantial sum is deducted for capital consumption. As we noted in Chapter 2 the nation's capital stock – factories, machines, roads, hospitals, etc. – gradually wears out with use. If our productive or economic capacity is to be maintained, this capital consumption has to be made good. In other words part of the gross capital formation that takes place in any year is required to maintain the existing productive capacity; only the remainder (net investment) represents an addition to capacity. A comparison of tables 3.1 and 3.3 shows that in 1976 capital consumption amounted to over a half of gross fixed capital formation.*

Since capital consumption is allowed for in the calculation of national income, changes in national income provide a good indicator of *sustainable* changes in living standards. However, since resources are utilized by all capital formation, including that required to balance capital consumption, national income is a less good measure of resource utilization that either gross domestic product or gross national product.†

A Composite Measure of Gross Domestic Product

It will be noticed that although the estimates of GDP arrived at by the three methods are identical, this happens only because a 'residual error' figure is included

* The figure for capital consumption is based upon depreciation allowances made by firms in their accounting records. Depreciation is discussed in Chapter 25.

† Some writers prefer to use the term 'net national income' when referring to national income as defined in the national accounts. They use the term national income, or sometimes gross national income, as being equivalent to gross national product. See the further discussion of this point in Chapter 8.

Table 3.4

Index Numbers of Gross Domestic Product and National Disposable Income U.K. (1970=100)

	1966	1967	1968	1969	1970	1971	1972	1973	1974	1975	1976
Gross domestic product at constant factor cost	90.5	92.4	96.0	98.0	100	101.8	104.3	110.3	109.8	107.6	108.9
Gross national disposable income at constant market prices	90.2	92.0	94.9	97.3	100	102.2	105.3	110.1	104.9	104.7	106.2

Source: *Economic Trends* (H.M.S.O., Sept. 1977).

in tables 3.2 and 3.3. This reflects the fact that the methods of data collection are imperfect. These errors can assume considerable significance when changes in GDP between one year and the next are being measured. However over a longer period the discrepancies become much less important, tending to be self-cancelling. Furthermore the statisticians provide a composite measure, an estimate of GDP which is an average of the three separate estimates.

Index numbers showing average changes in GDP for the period 1966 to 1976 are presented in the top line of table 3.4.* Since adjustments have been made for changes in prices the data indicates changes in real GDP. It can be seen that GDP rose each year until 1973. Thereafter a decline occurred and although 1976 saw a slight recovery, GDP remained below the level attained three years earlier.

GDP and the Supply of Labour

We noted in the previous chapter that GDP may rise because of an increase in the flow of labour inputs, i.e. in the supply of labour. This has not, however, been an important factor in the U.K. in recent years. In the period covered by table 3.4 the total working population and the employed labour force remained virtually static. Furthermore the average number of hours worked per week (full time adult males), after increasing from 48 in 1950 to 49 in 1955 has fallen steadily to less than 44 today. Moreover workers' holiday entitlement has increased markedly. In 1960 97 per cent of adult male workers were entitled to two weeks' holiday or less. By 1975 this figure had fallen to 1 per cent. There had been a corresponding increase in the percentage entitled to four weeks or more holiday from zero to 30 per cent.

Gross National Disposable Income

Table 3.4 also includes average estimates (again in index number form) of gross national disposable income. These estimates are derived from gross national product at market prices. An adjustment is made to GNP to allow for changes in the *terms of trade*, i.e. the ratio of the average price of our exports to the average price of our imports. In 1973 and 1974 the terms of trade moved strongly against the U.K. because of a substantial increase in the prices of many imported commodities, and in particular oil. This increase in the price of imports relative to exports meant that in order to maintain the previous relationship between the value of imports and exports, an increase in the *volume* of our exports relative to the volume of imports would be required. In other words we would need to divert resources into exports, leaving fewer resources available for the production of goods for the home market.

This explains why, while GDP fell only slightly in 1974, a much greater fall occurred in gross national disposable income. We have given a detailed, rather technical, explanation of this data because, as we shall see subsequently, the fall in gross national disposable income in this period had very important implications for government economic policy.

The Output of Economic Bads

We have presented in this chapter several alternative measures of economic activity, one measure being most useful for one purpose and another for another. These measures have one common characteristic, namely that they do not take into account the output of what we designated in the previous chapter as economic

---

* The bottom line of this table is discussed below.

bads. Since, as we showed in that chapter, the existence of economic bads ought to be taken into account in an assessment of living standards, we now briefly discuss some of the data relating to this point.

RIVER POLLUTION

Table 3.5 indicates that Britain's rivers are tending to become less polluted on the whole. Since, during the period covered by table 3.5, the level of economic

Table 3.5

River Pollution, U.K.

	Per Cent of Total Mileage	
Chemical classification	1958	1973
Unpolluted	69.6	74.4
Doubtful	16.4	16.0
Poor	7.1	5.3
Grossly polluted	6.9	4.3

Source: *Social Trends* (H.M.S.O., 1977).

activity increased, this reduction in pollution must be due to improved methods of pollution control. On the whole these methods are likely to have added to the costs of production of the firms concerned. The benefits comprise improved leisure facilities for walkers, anglers etc. There may also be some benefit in reduced cost of treatment of water used for drinking purposes from rivers such as the Thames.

AIR POLLUTION

The amount of air pollution has also been steadily reduced, especially in terms of the emission of smoke (table 3.6). Cleaner air is a universal benefit in terms

Table 3.6

Air Pollution, U.K.
(mn. metric tons)

	1952	1962	1971	1973	1975
Emission of smoke	2.39	1.51	0.61	0.49	0.39
Emission of sulphur dioxide	4.74	5.89	5.83	5.87	5.11

Source: *Social Trends* (H.M.S.O., 1977).

of comfort, reduced costs of washing and laundering, and improved health.

Progress on another form of air pollution, the emission of pollutants from road vehicles has occurred much more recently, emission levels falling for the first time

Table 3.7

Pollutants from Road Vehicles, U.K.
(mn. tonnes)

	1969/70	1970/1	1971/2	1972/3	1973	1974
Carbon dioxide	6.40	6.81	7.11	7.61	8.12	7.92
Other pollutants	.70	.74	.69	.79	.80	.78

Source: *Social Trends* (H.M.S.O., 1977).

in 1973 (table 3.7). One reason for this slower progress has been the increase in the number of vehicles on the roads.

ROAD CASUALTIES

An increase in the number of road vehicles might also be expected to lead to an increase in the number of road accidents. In fact, as can be seen from table 3.8,

Table 3.8

Number of Road Casualties, Great Britain (000's)

Number of people	1961	1966	1971	1972	1973	1974	1975
Killed	6.9	8.0	7.7	7.8	7.4	6.9	6.4
Seriously injured	82	100	91	91	89	82	77
Slightly injured	259	285	253	261	257	236	241
Total	348	392	352	360	353	325	325

Source: Social Trends (H.M.S.O., 1977).

the reverse has tended to occur since 1966. This is due to a combination of circumstances – the building of motorways, improved safety standards in cars, the imposition of heavier penalties for 'drinking and driving', etc.

This indicates that improved road safety involves additional costs on almost all sectors of the community – the manufacturers and drivers of cars, taxpayers and ratepayers. Virtually all sectors of the community should also benefit, either as drivers, passengers or pedestrians.

The above evidence would seem to suggest that the output of economic bads has tended to decrease rather than increase in the U.K. in recent years. The picture that we have presented is by no means comprehensive, of course. There may well be other aspects of our environment, such as the amount of noise and the availability of natural recreational areas, that would present a less satisfactory picture if valid measures were available.

The other point that emerges clearly from the above discussion is that a reduction in the output of economic bads involves both costs and benefits. Cost-benefit analysis has emerged as an important area of economics in recent years, and is discussed at greater length in Chapter 28.

Summary and Conclusions

The main purpose of this chapter has been to relate the theoretical analysis of the previous chapters to the economic system of the U.K. We have done this by presenting various measures of economic activity – expenditure, output and incomes – as found in the national accounts.

In general we have discussed the level of activity in a single year. However we looked briefly at changes in activity over a decade. This data suggested that in most years the U.K. achieved modest increases in material living standards. Furthermore it appears that there was a trend towards a reduction in the output of at least some economics bads.*

Of the various measures that we outlined, we discussed the flow of expenditure in the greatest detail. This discussion will act as a preparation for the following four chapters, each of which is devoted to an examination of one of the four major expenditure flows – consumption, general government current expenditure on goods and services, investment, and payments for exports and imports.

* The performance of the U.K. economy is discussed in greater detail in Chapter 21.

ESSAY QUESTIONS

1 Outline three different methods of measuring the level of economic activity and explain why they should in principle give the same answer.
2 Explain why a change in the value of consumers' expenditure may be an imperfect indicator of a change in the standard of living.
3 'Since an increase in our consumption of imports means an increase in our living standards, imports should not be excluded from the calculation of national income.' Comment.
4 Define capital consumption and explain its significance.
5 Explain what each of the following terms measures: (a) gross domestic product; (b) gross national product; (c) (net) national income.
6 Explain why it is possible, between one year and another, for gross national product and gross national disposable income to move in different directions.
7 Explain why it may be important but difficult to measure the incidence of economic bads.
8 'Changes in national income are a poor indicator of a country's economic progress'. Discuss.

EXERCISES

3.1 Calculate from table 3.9 each of the following: (a) gross domestic product at market prices, (b) gross domestic product at factor cost, (c) gross national product at factor cost, (d) (net) national income.

Table 3.9

The National Accounts of Brittanica

	£ billions
Consumers' expenditure	70
General government final consumption	10
Gross domestic fixed capital formation	15
Value of physical increase in stocks and work in progress	5
Exports of goods and services	9
Imports of goods and services	11
Taxes on expenditure	6
Subsidies	2
Net property income from abroad	3
Capital consumption	5

3.2 Explain the relationships among the three variables shown in figure 3.2.
3.3 At the beginning of 1978, Mr. A. L. L. Go, a senior economist in Europa, a prominent Western industrialized nation, paid a visit, for cultural and educational purposes, to a number of under-developed nations.

One evening found him engaged in an informal after-dinner discussion with a group of officials who were anxious to benefit as much as possible from the experience of Mr. Go and his colleagues. They said they understood that 1977 had on the whole been a good year for Europa. 'It certainly has,' replied Mr. Go, 'last year expenditure went up by around 7 per cent in real terms. Almost all sectors of the economy expanded, but the leader was construction. You know, some of our cities have become pretty snarled up with traffic – workers always arriving late, goods often delayed and so forth, and several

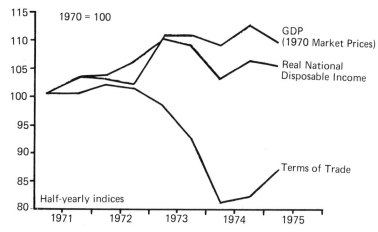

Figure 3.2   Changes in GDP, RNDI and the Terms of Trade

of the big companies have wanted to move to the outskirts for some time. However the government had always refused to release any green-belt land for building. It reversed this policy in 1976 and the building boom got under way in 1977.

Of course we are putting more into our buildings these days. Double glazing and air-conditioning are standard in new houses – although I must admit that with the rise in prices, new houses are getting beyond the reach of most people.'

At this point Mr. Go's host interrupted him to ask why they needed air-conditioning and double-glazing.

'Well, I suppose that when people have sufficient of the necessities of life – food, shelter and so forth – they are willing to pay more for comfort, and these things certainly make life more comfortable. I know that the climate in our two countries isn't all that different, but one seems to notice the extremes more, and especially the heat, in large cities. Also we can't just just open a few windows, as you do, because of the noise. This is getting an increasing problem, especially with the growth of jet travel. I reckon that the building of our new airport was worth at least £2 million in sales to the double-glazing manufacturers.'

'Your cities do not seem to be particularly pleasant places in which to live,' said his host. 'Oh, I don't know. There's plenty by way of entertainment. I could go to a different cinema or theatre every night of the week and never see the same film or play twice. All the same, most people do seem to feel the need to get away from the city fairly often. The second cottage in the country is becoming increasingly common, and of course most families have a car (three or four in some families), and they get away for the day whenever they can.

'I suppose that the vehicles industry is also doing well,' asked his host. 'They have expanded considerably during the past decade, but 1977 was rather a flat year. Money expenditure was up by about 10 per cent, but this was almost entirely due to higher car prices – the manufacturers seem to have gone in for chrome in a big way this year. Also they have had to meet the cost of engine modifications to reduce pollution, and safety modifications to cut down on the number of accidents.'

'Do your drivers have a bad safety record then?'

'I don't think that we are any worse than any other country with the same number of cars as ourselves. Certainly the number of accidents has gone up much less than the number of cars on the road. However, what with road accidents and the increasing number of deaths from bronchitis and cancer – it seems fairly clear that these are connected with the increasing consumption of cigarettes and with air pollution – we have had to expand the medical services generally, and in particular the number of hospital beds available.'

'And that, I suppose, gives another boost to the construction industry,' said his host, neatly completing the circle of the conversation.

Discuss the meaning of an increase in the national income with particular reference to the above passage.

3.4 What can be deduced from table 3.10 about changes in the standard of living?

Table 3.10
Number of Minutes of Work* Required to Pay for Selected Items

	1950	1976
Weekly rent of a three-bedroomed council house	312	266
Weekly mortgage payments – interest and principal – in the first year after buying a house at the average price for 'second hand' houses assuming 72 per cent of price advanced. (Net of tax relief)	600	750
3 lbs of beef sirloin	128	215
2 lbs of fresh cod fillets	60	79
14 lbs of potatoes	35	86
Large loaf per 1¾ lb	9	11
½ lb of tea	33	15
1 quart of fresh milk	17	10
5 cwts of coal (high quality)	461	529
5 gallons of petrol	308	212
1 monthly season ticket Surbiton to Victoria	805	826
Postage on five letters	21	19
1 telegram of twelve words	25	89
20 cigarettes	66	24
1 pint of beer	23	12
1 bottle of whisky	659	209

* Married man, two children, average manual wage.
Source: *Department of Employment.*

OBJECTIVE TEST QUESTIONS: SET I

1 All the following are part of a country's stock of capital except

   A   factories
   B   hospitals
   C   machinery
   D   stocks of components
   E   money.

2 Economic capacity is likely to increase in all of the following situations except

   A   capital consumption exceeds gross investment
   B   the quality of the labour force increases
   C   the size of the labour force increases
   D   the quality of capital increases
   E   the quality of land increases.

3   In the national income accounts consumers' expenditure includes expenditure on all of the following except

A   school fees
B   private legal services
C   consumer durables
D   new houses
E   travel.

4   In an economy whose resources are fully utilized, the most likely effect on the output of consumption goods of an increase in the current output of capital goods is

A   a reduction in both the current and subsequent periods
B   an increase in both the current and subsequent periods
C   a reduction in the current and an increase in subsequent periods
D   an increase in the current and a reduction in subsequent periods
E   no change in the current and an increase in subsequent periods.

5   The opportunity cost of a free course of training to the person undertaking the course is the

A   cost of the lecturers' salaries
B   cost of the lecturers' salaries plus the depreciation of the buildings
C   fees charged for a comparable course by a private educational institution
D   additional income that the person could have earned during the period of the course
E   additional income that the person could have earned during the period of the course and in all subsequent periods.

6   The optimum population is that level of population at which the

A   average cost of production is minimized
B   total output is maximized
C   output per person employed is maximized
D   output per unit of capital employed is maximized
E   output per head of population is maximized

Questions 7 to 10 relate to the table below.

	£ millions
Consumers' expenditure	1,300
General government consumption	300
Gross domestic fixed capital formation	250
Change in the value of stocks	0
Exports of goods and services	350
Imports of goods and services	400
Taxes on expenditure (net of subsidies)	150
Net property income from abroad	100
Capital consumption	200

7   Gross domestic product at factor cost (£ millions) is

A   1,600
B   1,650
C   1,800
D   1,900
E   1,950.

8 Gross domestic product at market prices (£ millions) is

   A   1,650
   B   1,700
   C   1,800
   D   1,900
   E   1,950.

9 Gross national product at factor cost (£ millions) is

   A   1,650
   B   1,750
   C   1,850
   D   1,900
   E   1,950.

10 (Net) National income (£ millions) is

   A   1,550
   B   1,600
   C   1,650
   D   1,700
   E   1,750.

11 Which of the following directly affects a country's terms of trade? A change in the

   1   volume of that country's exports
   2   volume of that country's imports
   3   prices of that country's imports.

12 A country's terms of trade would improve as a result of

   1   an increase in the prices of that country's exports
   2   a fall in the prices of that country's imports
   3   a fall in the volume of that country's imports.

13 In order to obtain an estimate of national income, one would subtract from the gross national product at factor cost

   1   expenditure taxes
   2   net property income from abroad
   3   capital consumption.

14 The flow of labour inputs in a given period is likely to be influenced by the

   1   age structure of the population
   2   sex structure of the population
   3   average number of hours worked per worker

15 Fixed capital includes

   1   stocks of raw materials
   2   stocks of work in progress
   3   machinery

16 The optimum population is likely to change over time.
     The quantity of resources other than labour is likely to change over time.

17 Capital is used in the production of marketed but not non-marketed products.
     Only products which are marketed contribute to the standard of living.

18 A free good is a resource in which no property rights have been established.
    The absence of property rights in a resource implies that the resource is available in unlimited quantities.

19 Provided that the distribution of income does not change, an increase in the average standard of living implies an increase in the living standards of every citizen.
    A change in the distribution of income is likely to affect the relative living standards of different citizens.

20 An increase in expenditure on U.K. exports implies an increase in the U.K.'s national product.
    The gross national product is defined as the gross domestic product plus exports minus imports.

TRUE/FALSE

1 Gross domestic product at market prices must always exceed gross domestic product at factor cost.
2 Gross national product at market prices must always exceed gross domestic product at market prices.
3 National income can never exceed gross national product.
4 Gross national product can never exceed gross national disposable income.
5 Other things remaining equal, an improvement in a country's terms of trade implies an increase in its gross national disposable income.
6 Education and training can be considered as either investment or consumption.
7 Land is immobile as between different uses.
8 An increase in the capital–labour ratio is known as capital widening.
9 If gross investment is greater than zero, productive capacity will increase.
10 Gross domestic product is usually a better indicator than gross national product of the level of utilization of domestic resources.

CHAPTER FOUR

Consumers' Expenditure

Introduction

WE saw in the previous chapter that consumption, or consumers' expenditure, is the most important element of total expenditure, accounting for 60 per cent of gross domestic product and 59 per cent of gross national product.* It is therefore appropriate that we should begin our detailed examination of the behaviour of expenditure by considering consumption.

The Determinants of Consumption

The Level of Income

Numerous studies have shown that the most important single determinant of consumption is income. For the individual, income in this context usually means the husband's or the family income. For the economy as a whole various measures of income exist, as we saw in the previous chapter. One of the most commonly used measures is gross national product and we shall use this here. (Gross domestic product would also be a suitable measure, and we consider in the appendix to this chapter the implications of using yet another alternative, personal disposable income).

Using symbols we express the relationship between consumption and our chosen measure of income as follows:

$$C=f(Y)$$

where C   denotes consumption
     Y   denotes gross national product
     f   indicates that consumption is a function of, depends upon, gross national product

THE MARGINAL PROPENSITY TO CONSUME

In order to analyse the operation of the economy it is especially useful to know by how much consumption changes as GNP changes, i.e. to be able to estimate the value of the marginal propensity to consume, defined as follows:

$$MPC=\frac{\Delta C}{\Delta Y}$$

where, as before, C and Y denote consumption and gross national product, and Δ denotes a small change in these variables.

Studies undertaken in a number of countries and covering different time periods have, not surprisingly, revealed different values for MPC. But a value of 0.7 would be typical for the U.K. in the post-war period. A hypothetical consumption sche-

* At market prices ($=68$ per cent of GDP and 67 per cent of GNP at factor cost).

Table 4.1
A Hypothetical Consumption Schedule: C=0.7 GNP

GNP (£ millions)	Consumption (£ millions)
1,000	700
2,000	1,400
3,000	2,100
4,000	2,800
5,000	3,500
6,000	4,200

dule which yields a value for MPC of 0.7 at all levels of income is presented in table 4.1 while figure 4.1 presents the data in graphical form. (The dotted 45° line indicates what consumption would be if it always equalled GNP.)

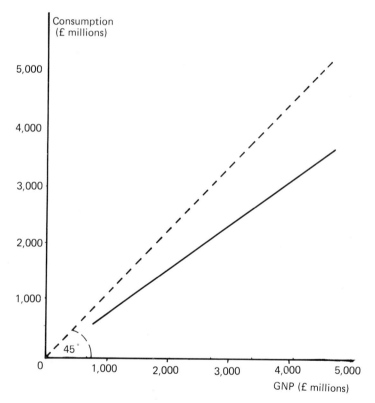

Figure 4.1 A Hypothetical Consumption Function: C=0.7 GNP

THE AVERAGE PROPENSITY TO CONSUME

The average propensity to consume relates total consumption to GNP. It is defined as follows:

$$APC = \frac{C}{Y}$$

where, as before, C denotes total consumption and Y denotes gross national product. Applying this formula to the data in table 4.1 we find that APC has the same value as MPC, namely 0.7.

The Behaviour of Average and Marginal Propensity to Consume
Some studies have found APC and MPC to be equal, as in the above hypothetical example, and also that their value tends to remain constant over a long time period. The results of other studies, however, suggest that APC may fall as a nation becomes richer.   This situation is depicted in figure 4.2. The consumption function

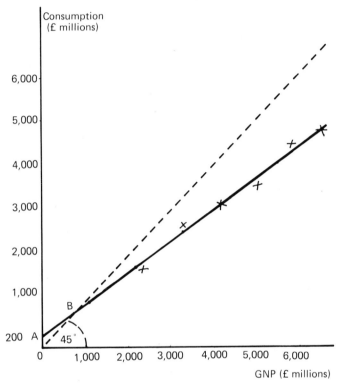

Figure 4.2   A Hypothetical Consumption Function: C=200+0.7 GNP

CC is a straight line, indicating that MPC is constant. However APC is *not* constant; it falls as GNP rises. Algebraically this situation is expressed thus:

$$C=a+b(Y)$$

where a is a constant and b is the marginal propensity to consume. In this instance a=£200 millions and b=0.7 (the gradient of CC). The value of APC at various levels of GNP is shown in table 4.2.

THE ESTIMATION OF APC
Observations from which estimated values of APC have been empirically derived relate to levels of GNP at which APC is less than unity, such as indicated by the scatter of points marked X in figure 4.2. The segment of the curve at which APC is unity or greater than unity, i.e. the segment BA, is hypothetical, representing an extrapolation from the observed values.

Table 4.2

GNP (£ millions)	Consumption (£ millions)	APC	MPC
colspan continued	*Average and Marginal Propensity to Consume: C=200+0.7 GNP (£mn.)*		
1,000	900	0.90	0.7
2,000	1,600	0.80	0.7
3,000	2,300	0.77	0.7
4,000	3,000	0.75	0.7
5,000	3,700	0.74	0.7
6,000	4,400	0.73	0.7

It is in fact extremely unlikely that a situation would arise in which consumption was equal to or greater than GNP (although it might exceed personal disposable income – see the appendix to this chapter). We have seen that by definition total expenditure equals GDP, which has usually been less than GNP. Consequently consumption can exceed GNP only if some other element of expenditure is heavily negative. This could only be net exports, and it seems inconceivable that the government would permit a deficit in net exports of such a magnitude.

In figure 4.3 we illustrate the situation where both APC and MPC fall as GNP increases. As noted above, the value of MPC is indicated by the gradient of the

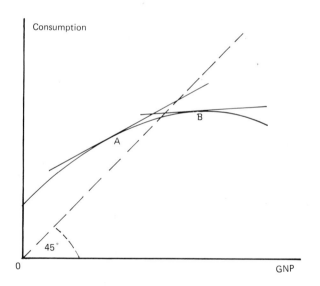

Figure 4.3 Falling Average and Marginal Propensity to Consume

consumption function. Drawing tangents to the curve shows clearly that the gradient is steeper at point A than at B. Some studies appear to have identified situations in which MPC declined as income rose. This might represent a long run change as indicated in figure 4.3. Alternatively it might indicate a short-run reaction to the change in income.

Milton Friedman has advanced the hypothesis that consumption is mainly influenced by consumers' permanent income. Consequently when income changes, the effect on consumption is likely at first to be slight, since consumers are uncertain as to whether or not the change is permanent. Subsequently if the change does prove to be permanent, consumption responds more fully. The implication of the 'permanent income hypothesis' is that the value of the short-run MPC may be considerably below the long run value.

In figure 4.4 C_S and C_L represent the short and long run consumption functions

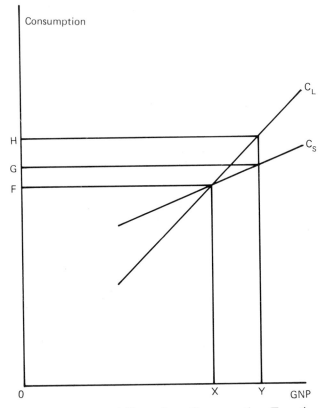

Figure 4.4   Long and Short Run Consumption Functions

respectively. When GNP increases from X to Y consumption at first increases from F to G in accordance with the short-run consumption function. Subsequently, as the higher level of GNP persists, consumption increases further to H. Similarly if GNP were to fall the decline in consumption would be greater in the long than in the short run.*

It is difficult to test the permanent income hypothesis empirically since the hypothesis involves income expectations, a concept which is impossible to measure accurately, at least at the national level. However the hypothesis appears plausible a priori, and the evidence relating to the U.K. is certainly consistent with the hypothesis.

* For an extended discussion of the permanent income hypothesis see R. G. Lipsey, *An Introduction to Positive Economics* (London: Weidenfeld and Nicolson, 1975, 4th edn.), p. 526 ff.

Other Determinants of Consumption

Although we have shown that consumption is strongly related to GNP, it is also subject to a number of other influences, some of which may be more important than GNP in the short run.

Taxation and Government Expenditure

An increase in taxation or a fall in government expenditure usually leaves less money in consumers' pockets, and so reduces consumption. Conversely consumption is likely to rise following a reduction in taxation or an increase in government expenditure. The magnitude of the change in consumption will depend not only upon the magnitude of the change introduced by the government but also on the form of the change. Consumption is likely to be particularly sensitive to changes in taxation on personal incomes, and to changes in forms of expenditure that affect the lowest income groups, e.g. unemployment benefit.

Availability and Price of Credit

A high proportion of certain forms of consumption, e.g. the purchase of consumer durables, is financed by credit of one kind or another – hire purchase, bank loans, etc. Consequently these forms of consumption may be curtailed when credit becomes more expensive and/or difficult to obtain. Another aspect of a rise in the cost of credit is that financial institutions may offer higher rates of interest to savers. This may persuade some people to reduce their consumption in order to take advantage of the higher rewards to saving.

Price Expectations

When consumers experience a very rapid rate of price increases such as happened in Germany after the first world war (a situation known as hyperinflation), they increase consumption in order to try to beat future price rises. When the U.K.'s annual rate of inflation approached 25 per cent in 1975 fears were expressed that the propensity to consume might rise and thus add to the inflationary pressure. In fact the reverse happened. The fall in APC that had characterized the U.K. economy in the post-war period not only continued, but actually accelerated. If there was a tendency for people to increase consumption in order to beat rising prices, this must have been outweighed by a desire to increase their savings in case economic conditions worsened, and in particular in case unemployment continued to rise.

Long Term Influences

Any of the above factors may have an appreciable impact on consumption in both the short and the long term. In the long term consumption may also be influenced by changes in the distribution of income and wealth. This is especially likely if income and wealth are redistributed in favour of the poorer members of the community, since their propensity to consume is often above average.

Finally the propensity to consume may fall as income rises simply because people have satisfied a higher proportion of their needs. However this tendency is offset insofar as producers continue to introduce new goods and services and thus extend consumers' purchasing horizons.

THE PROPENSITY TO SAVE

Just as the marginal propensity to consume relates a change in consumption to a change in GNP, so the marginal propensity to save relates a change in saving to a change in GNP:

$$MPS = \frac{\Delta S}{\Delta Y}$$

If we make the simplying assumption that all income is either consumed or saved, it follows that the marginal propensity to consume plus the marginal propensity to save must equal one.

Similarly the average propensity to save is a relationship between total saving and GNP:

$$APS = \frac{S}{Y}$$

It follows that $APC + APS = 1$.

Appendix   Personal Disposable Income and the Propensity to Consume

One of the advantages of choosing personal disposable income as the independent variable in analysing the propensity to consume is that it allows a wider range of empirical investigations to be employed. For example cross-section studies of the consumption of families with different levels of disposable income have been undertaken. This wider range of studies has certainly increased our understanding of the factors influencing consumption.

However, personal disposable income is less easily integrated than GNP into the model of national income determination that we develop in Chapter 8. On balance we feel that for the students for whom this book was written, the disadvantages of using personal disposable income would outweigh the advantages, although the reverse might apply for other students.

As an indication of the differences that result from the choice of one measure rather than the other, let us consider the consumption functions estimated by Professor Ford for the U.K. during the period 1958—68. These were:

Consumption $= 1,739 + 0.69$ GNP
Consumption $= 1,498 + 0.85$ disposable income
(Each expressed in £ millions at 1958 prices).*

MPC is lower when related to GNP (0.69) than to disposable income (0.85).

Summary and Conclusions

We have shown that the most important determinant of consumption, especially in the long term, is the level of income. Consumption changes in line with, although usually by a smaller absolute amount than, GNP. However different studies have yielded different values for the propensity to consume, and one reason for these differences is probably the effect on consumption of factors other than income. The fact that the average and marginal propensities to consume do not have unique values that apply at all times and in all countries does not mean that the concepts are not useful. We shall in fact see that they are extremely useful in the construction of models of income determination such as are presented in Chapter 8.

ESSAY QUESTIONS

1   Discuss the major determinants of the aggregate level of consumption.

* A. G. Ford, *Income, Spending and the Price Level* (London: Fontana, 1971), p. 35.

2 Explain what is meant by the term 'consumption function' and show why the value of the function in the short run may differ from that in the long run.
3 Discuss the possible effects of inflation on the propensity to consume.
4 'Since it is impossible to test the permanent income hypothesis it is not a useful concept.' Discuss.

EXERCISES

4.1 (i) Assuming that the country referred to in table 4.3 has a constant marginal propensity to consume, calculate the level of consumption when GNP is (a) zero, (b) £6 billions.

Table 4.3
A Hypothetical Consumption Schedule

GNP (£ billions)	Consumption (£ billions)
1	1.5
2	2.0
3	2.5

(ii) Calculate the average propensity to consume when GNP is £5 billions.
(iii) Substitute the appropriate values of a and b in the following equation: C=a+b (GNP).
(iv) What economic concept does the term b denote?
(v) What is the marginal propensity to save in this economy?

4.2 Sketch consumption functions having the following properties: (a) constant average and marginal propensities to consume, (b) falling average, and constant marginal propensities to consume, (c) falling average and marginal propensities to consume.

CHAPTER FIVE

Government Consumption

Introduction

THE term 'General government final consumption' was first introduced in the National Income and Expenditure Blue Book published in 1977. The category differs from that used previously, 'Public authorities' current expenditure on goods and services', in two ways. First the current expenditure of the public corporations is now excluded. Second, an 'imputed charge for consumption of non-trading capital' is now included. This latter item is, however, of minor importance, and final consumption mainly comprises central and local government current expenditure on goods and services. This is a form of spending whose relative importance has tended to increase over time, as shown in table 5.1.

Table 5.1
Government Current Expenditure on Goods and Services
(percentage of GDP at factor cost)

1966	1970	1971	1972	1973	1974	1975	1976
19.1	20.0	20.1	20.5	20.1	21.7	23.7	23.6

Source: *National Income and Expenditure* (H.M.S.O., 1977).

Determinants of the Level of Government Expenditure

The Level of Gross National Product

In the long term a limit to government expenditure is set by the revenue that can be raised by taxation of one form or another.* The community's taxable capacity is closely connected with its living standards – the higher the standard of living the greater the absolute amount of taxes that individuals and institutions can afford to pay. Consequently when we consider a long period the most important influence on the expenditure of the government is the level of GNP. The higher the level of GNP the higher their level of expenditure.

Indeed there has been a tendency in many countries for increases in GNP to be associated with even bigger increases in the demand for services which are often provided by the government e.g. medical and educational facilities. This parallels the increasing demand for services provided by the private sector, to which we referred in Chapter 3.

Political Factors

Since decisions on public expenditure are taken by politicians (advised by public officials) political considerations inevitably have an influence on these decisions.

* The government can borrow to cover the gap between expenditure and tax receipts in any one year. However the interest on borrowing has to be paid from taxation in subsequent years. See Chapters 11 and 12.

In broad terms left-wing governments tend to be more in favour of public expenditure than right-wing governments, and the increased expenditure in the mid 1970s to which we drew attention above owed something to the ideology of the Labour government in power.

However, table 5.1 indicates that government expenditure has shown a tendency to rise under governments of differing political persuasions, and a change in government seldom leads to a substantial change in public expenditure measured as a proportion of GNP.

This is particularly true of reductions in expenditure, for several reasons. First, much public expenditure would be agreed to be desirable by politicians, and indeed by most citizens, of any political persuasion. Second, many public sector employees – servicemen, policemen, teachers etc. – have terms of service which make it difficult to effect substantial reductions in labour costs in the short term. Third, about 40 per cent of government current expenditure on goods and services is accounted for by local authorities, many of whom may be influenced by different considerations than the central government. As we show in Chapter 11, local authorities have responded very slowly to pressure from the central government to restrict their spending.

Determinants of the Pattern of Government Expenditure

Factors which influence the level of government expenditure are likely to influence its pattern, and vice versa. However there are certain factors which are especially important in relation to the pattern. Table 5.2 shows the relative importance, in

Table 5.2
U.K. Government Expenditure on Goods
and Services (percentage at 1970 prices)

	1966	1976
Military defence	34.5	22.6
National health service	19.8	21.3
Education	17.2	21.3
Other	28.4	34.8
Total	100	100

Source: National Income and Expenditure.
(H.M.S.O., 1977).

1966 and 1976, of the major items of the current expenditure of central and local government.

The fall in the relative importance of defence spending reflects the reduction in Britain's overseas military commitments, and also, perhaps, the substitution of capital equipment (more sophisticated military hardware) for labour – table 5.2 excludes capital expenditure.

The increase in the relative importance of spending on education is partly a reflection of rising incomes, as noted above. It is also due to a rise in the birth rate which led to an increase in the number of children in the 'educable' age bracket. Finally the width of this age bracket increased, when the minimum school-leaving age rose.

A rise in the birth rate also required an increase in spending on health. Another important factor was the discovery and development of new, very potent, but often expensive, drugs. We see here a parallel with the introduction of new products which provides a stimulus to consumption expenditure, referred to in the previous chapter.

Incidentally one of the consequences of improved medical care has been an increase in the number of people surviving into old age. Such people often put heavy demands on the social services. This illustrates the complex inter-relationship which may exist within this category of expenditure.

Summary and Conclusions

We have discussed the major components of the government's current expenditure on goods and services, and outlined the major influences, economic and non-economic, on the level and pattern of expenditure. The discussion has been brief for two reasons. First we go into more detail in the later chapters on government economic policy. Second, we have excluded two important forms of public expenditure. The first is capital expenditure which is discussed along with other forms of investment expenditure in the next chapter. The other is transfer payments. Although these are a form of current expenditure they do not directly require an increase in output, and are treated differently in the national accounts from current expenditure on goods and services. Consequently we defer their discussion until Chapter 11.

ESSAY QUESTIONS

1 What are the major determinants of government current expenditure on goods and services?
2 Why has the government current expenditure on goods and services tended to grow more rapidly than consumers' expenditure in the post-war period?
3 'The increase in the relative importance of government current expenditure on goods and services is to be welcomed as indicator that society is becoming more responsible.' Discuss.

EXERCISES

5.1 Discuss the reasons for the change in the relative importance of government expenditure, as shown in table 5.1, and assess the implications of this change.
5.2 (i) Discuss the reasons for the changes in the pattern of government expenditure, shown in table 5.2. (ii) What future changes in the pattern would you expect to occur?

CHAPTER SIX

Investment

Introduction

INVESTMENT expenditure, which in 1976 accounted for 19 per cent of GDP,* comprises two components. These are gross domestic fixed capital formation and the value of the physical increase in stocks and work in progress. Of these two components fixed capital formation is by far the larger in value and will be discussed first.

Gross Domestic Fixed Capital Formation

In Chapter 3 we showed that fixed capital formation is undertaken by producers, households and the government. In table 6.1 a slightly different breakdown is presented, a distinction being made between the private and public sectors. The

Table 6.1
Gross Domestic Fixed Capital Formation, by sector
and type of asset, U.K. (1976)

	£ millions
Private sector:	
Vehicles, ships and aircraft	1,933
Plant and machinery	5,260
Dwellings	2,320
Other new buildings and works, etc.	3,589
Net purchases of land and existing buildings	213
Total private sector	13,315
Public sector:	
Vehicles, ships and aircraft	435
Plant and machinery	2,856
Dwellings	2,312
Other new buildings and works, etc.	4,022
Net purchases of land and existing buildings	487
Total public sector	10,112
Total gross domestic fixed capital formation	23,427

Source: *National Income and Expenditure* (H.M.S.O., 1977).

private sector comprises private sector producers and households. The public sector comprises central and local government and the public corporations (public sector producers), e.g. the National Coal Board, British Rail. We examine the major determinants of the expenditure of each of these four groups in turn. But most attention will be paid to expenditure by private sector producers.

* At market prices (=21 per cent of GDP at factor cost).

Expenditure by Private Sector Producers

The major items of expenditure are plant and machinery, new buildings and works, vehicles, ships and aircraft. As we pointed out in Chapters 2 and 3 expenditure on these items leads to an increase in economic capacity. However part of this expenditure is required to replace existing plant, equipment, etc. that wears out or becomes obsolete. As we saw in Chapter 3 this estimated reduction in capacity is entered in the national accounts as capital consumption. (As noted in that chapter the term depreciation may also be used, especially with reference to the activity of individual firms). We denote the amount of investment required to compensate for capital consumption as *replacement investment*, and the remainder, which represents an increase in the capital stock, as *net investment*. Summarizing:

$$\text{gross investment} = \text{replacement investment} + \text{net investment}$$

In examining the determinants of expenditure we shall occasionally distinguish between replacement and net investment. When we simply use the term investment (or fixed capital formation) it should be understood to refer to both together, i.e. to gross investment.

The Motives for Investment

Businesses may invest for many reasons – to increase capacity and thus facilitate an increase in sales, to improve the quality of the product and thus improve its market share, to reduce the cost of production, etc. Most of these reasons have as a common element a desire to increase profitability, (including preventing the fall in profitability that might occur if the investment were not undertaken, a motive which is especially important in relation to replacement investment). Consequently it is appropriate to relate the volume of desired investment to the expected profitability or, more precisely, rate of return. (The rate of return is defined in the appendix to this chapter). This relationship can be expressed by means of an investment demand schedule.

The Investment Demand Schedule

If we consider private sector producers as a whole there will be, for any given period, a range of investment opportunities with differing potential rates of return. There will be a few projects that appear likely to yield very high returns and far more with potentially lower yields. This situation is illustrated in figure 6.1.

The investment projects within the range OQ_1 have prospective yields of at least R_1. The projects within the range Q_1Q_2 have lower yields, between R_2 and R_1. The prospective yield continues to fall until finally, if investment were pushed to Q_3, no further project with a positive rate of return would remain. (As we shall see in the appendix, investment would only be pushed to this point if investment funds were available at zero cost).

Factors Influencing the Yield from Investment

The potential yield from any given volume of investment is likely to change from one period to another. Such changes would be represented by shifts of the investment demand schedule. If the potential yields from investment increased, the schedule would shift to the right; if they decreased it would shift to the left. The factors most likely to cause such shifts are discussed in the following sections.

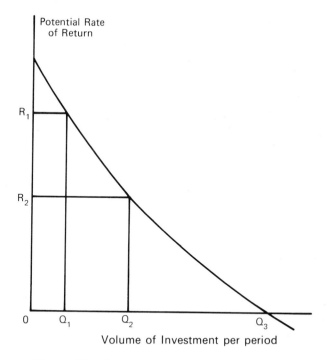

Figure 6.1   An Investment Demand Schedule

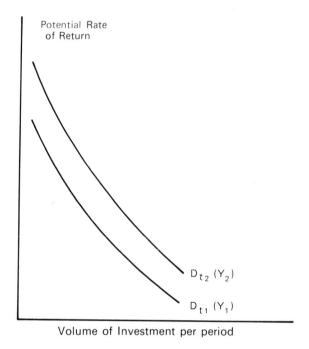

Figure 6.2   The Investment Demand Schedule at Different Levels of GDP

THE LEVEL OF GROSS DOMESTIC PRODUCT

As we showed in Chapters 2 and 3 a higher GDP implies higher expenditure, incomes and output. Consequently the higher the GDP the greater will tend to be the volume of investment with any given prospective yield. In other words the higher the GDP the further to the right the investment demand schedule will tend to be. This is illustrated in figure 6.2 which shows demand schedules relating to two time periods. In period t_1 GDP is Y_1. In period t_2, GDP is higher at Y_2.

THE EFFECT OF A CHANGE IN GDP: THE ACCELERATION PRINCIPLE

Figure 6.2 simply indicates that investment demand is higher the higher the level of GDP. It says nothing about the effect of a change from one level of GDP to another. There is, however, reason to believe that the process of change itself has an effect on investment. This response of investment to a change in the level of GDP is known as the acceleration principle.

The operation of this principle can be illustrated by means of a simple example. Let us assume that for a number of years consumers purchase 20,000 kitchen tables a year. These tables are produced on ten machines, each having a capacity of 2,000 tables a year. These machines have an average life of ten years and the producers have to replace one machine each year.

Consider now the effect of a 10 per cent increase in consumers' demand as part of a 10 per cent increase in GDP between year t_1 and year t_2. In year t_2 consumers wish to buy 22,000 tables. In order to meet this demand producers require eleven machines. In this year they will therefore buy two machines, one for replacement, as in year t_1, and one to increase their capacity (net investment). A 10 per cent increase in GDP and in consumers' expenditure has led to a 100 per cent increase in investment expenditure.

The accelerator is the link between the change in consumption (or, more generally, the change in output or sales) and the change in investment. The acceleration principle can be expressed formally as follows:

$$\Delta I = a(\Delta C)$$

where I is investment
      C is consumers' expenditure
      a is the accelerator coefficient
      Δ denotes a small change in the variable.
A more general formulation of the principle is

$$\Delta I = a(Y_{t_2} - Y_{t_1})$$

where $Y_{t_2} - Y_{t_1}$ is the change in output, sales or, more generally, GDP, between one period and another.

The value of the accelerator depends upon the desired ratio of the capital stock to output. (Indeed the 'incremental capital-output ratio' is another term for the accelerator coefficient). Let us assume that for the economy as a whole £5 of capital is required to produce £1 of output a year. In this instance the accelerator coefficient would be five. If the 'kitchen table industry', considered above, was representative of the economy as a whole, this would mean that the additional machine would cost five times as much as the 2,000 tables which it could produce each year. For example if each table sold at £5, the machine would cost £50,000; $(5 \times £10,000)$.

Note that the value of the accelerator may not be the same for decreases as for increases in GDP. This can be illustrated by developing the above example.

Assume that in year t_3 GDP fell to its level in year t_1 and that consumers' demand for tables fell to 20,000. Since producers now have eleven machines they would not need to replace the one that wears out. The required output of 20,000 tables could be made on the remaining ten machines. Consequently investment in year t_3 would be zero.

Furthermore the acceleration principle may continue to cause fluctuations in investment even in periods when consumption does not change. If GDP in year t_3 had remained at the same level as in year t_2, and consumers had continued to buy 22,000 tables, producers would have needed to buy only one (replacement) machine. Investment would be 50 per cent less than in year t_2.

It would be impossible adequately to represent these dynamic effects on a diagram. However it is appropriate to examine briefly their implications with reference to figure 6.2. As noted above, the two investment demand schedules simply reflect two different levels of GDP. If GDP changed from Y_1 to Y_2 the accelerator effect (ignored in figure 6.2) would cause the investment demand schedule to fluctuate around D_{t_2} – the fluctuations becoming less the longer the time period considered.

A DAMPENED ACCELERATOR

The acceleration principle may not operate in quite so violent a manner as indicated in the above section, for a number of reasons. First, the producers of consumer goods (tables) may have some excess capacity which enables them to meet at least modest increases in demand without further (net) investment. Second, if they are working at full capacity they may be cautious in their response to increases in demand. At least some producers may refuse to increase capacity until they are convinced that the increase in demand is permanent. In the meantime they may ration their customers by one means or another, including raising the prices of tables. Finally, even if the manufacturers of tables do wish to increase their capacity immediately they may not be able to do so if there is a shortage of capacity in the capital goods sector – in those firms which make the wood-working machines.

The possibility of such lags occurring reduces the simplicity of the principle. Nevertheless experience shows that investment expenditure is more volatile than other forms of expenditure, and it seems likely that this is at least partly due to the acceleration principle.

The development of North Sea oil provided a good example of the operation of the principle. The initial discovery of oil reserves led to increases in capacity in a wide range of capital goods industries in order to meet the demand for platforms, drilling rigs, well casing, tubing, etc. While this increase in activity was on the whole extremely welcome, there were some less favourable developments. Even before the first oil was pumped ashore there were signs that there had been too great an increase in capacity in some sectors. Order books for platforms and rigs began to shorten, and the prospects of redundancies appeared. Eventually substantial redundancies occurred, and in 1976, the British National Oil Corporation, with the help of government finance, ordered a rig for stock, in the hope that they might subsequently find a buyer, perhaps operating in another part of the world. In 1977 it was announced that two construction yards, developed with considerable government assistance to produce concrete platforms, were to close without having obtained a single order.

SUBSTITUTION: THE COST AND AVAILABILITY OF OTHER INPUTS

When deciding which method of production to adopt, producers take into account the costs of the various inputs that they might use. A change in the relative cost of these inputs will change the desirable mix of inputs. More fixed capital is likely to be employed, i.e. the investment demand schedule is likely to shift to the right, as the costs of other inputs rise relative to the cost of capital. Conversely a fall in the relative costs of other inputs will lead to these other inputs being substituted for capital.

The widespread introduction of vending machines, both within and outside factories, offices, shops etc., is a good example of the substitution of capital for labour. Another familiar, if less visible, example is the introduction of automatic telephone equipment which reduces the number of operators required.

TECHNOLOGICAL CHANGE

The above examples indicate that technological change may be stimulated by changes in the relative costs of inputs. In other instances technological change has resulted in better and more efficient machines that have been capital-saving rather than labour-saving. This again influences the rate of investment, although the exact nature of the effect is not easy to predict.

One possibility is that the introduction of more highly productive machines may lead to a fall in the total capital employed. On the other hand it may enable the cost of production, and hence the price of the final product, to be reduced to such an extent that the quantity bought of that product increases substantially. Thus although the capital–output ratio falls, the total capital employed may increase. Moreover, even if the total capital employed does not increase, gross investment may rise – at least for some time – as producers accelerate the installation of new machinery in order to reduce the cost of production.

As we have noted in earlier chapters, technological change is also important in product markets, in terms of the introduction of new or improved products. If additional capacity is required to manufacture these products, investment is again likely to rise.

BUSINESS EXPECTATIONS

Although producers may attempt to make accurate estimates of the yield from investment, the future is always subject to uncertainty. Consequently subjective factors invariably have some influence. Since an investment demand schedule relates investment to the prospective or expected yield, a change in business expectations will cause the schedule to shift. If producers become more optimistic the schedule will shift to the right. If they become less optimistic it will shift to the left.

The Availability and Cost of Finance

So far we have considered the factors which influence the *desired* expenditure on investment and thus the demand for investment funds. The amount of investment undertaken in a given period depends also upon the supply of investment funds, and we now turn our attention to the supply side, i.e. we examine the factors influencing the availability and cost of finance.

THE LEVEL OF GROSS DOMESTIC PRODUCT

In Chapter 4 we saw that the balance of evidence from a number of studies suggests that (except during a hyperinflation) average propensity to consume either remains constant or declines as GNP and GDP increase. If we continue to make the assumption that income not spent on consumption is saved, it follows that the volume of savings will rise in line with, or perhaps faster than, GDP. This parallels the increase in the demand for investment funds that normally accompanies a rise in GDP. We discuss below the various processes by which these savings are made available to the firms who wish to undertake investment, but first we discuss briefly other determinants of the volume of savings.*

GOVERNMENT ECONOMIC POLICY

In many modern economies, including the U.K., the government's fiscal and monetary policies have an important influence on the supply of money. Since these policies are discussed in detail in Chapters 11 and 12 it is sufficient here to outline the policies that have especially important implications for the supply of finance for investment. Policies which would tend to lead to an increase in the supply of such finance include:

1. A reduction in taxation – especially important would be a reduction in the taxation of company profits.
2. The operation of a budget deficit, i.e. the government spends more than it raises in taxation. (There could clearly be a connection here with the previous point).
3. Making it easier for banks and other financial institutions to create money to lend – this might be achieved by various forms of monetary policy.

CHANGES IN THE DISPOSITION OF SAVINGS

Private sector producers are only one of several groups of institutions seeking investment funds. The success of these producers in obtaining funds will be influenced by the attractiveness of the prospective returns they offer to savers – in terms of yield, security and liquidity – by comparison with what is offered by other institutions such as building societies, local authorities and the central government.

As we noted above, a budget deficit would normally tend to increase the supply of money. However the investment funds available to private producers may not increase if the government, in order to borrow sufficient money to cover its deficit, offers a rate of return that private producers find difficult to match (see Chapter 12).

Having discussed the factors that influence the volume of savings likely to be made available to finance investment by private sector producers, we examine the ways in which this finance might be transferred from savers to investors.

The Sources of Finance

There are two main routes by which the savings of households are made available to producers. First, savers can directly supply finance to producers in the form of either long-term loans (by buying debentures) or permanent, equity, capital (by buying shares). Second, households can deposit their savings with banks and other financial institutions who in turn make the money available to producers, again in the form of either loans (short, medium and long term) or permanent capital.†

In addition the government may provide financial assistance of various kinds. The government itself obtains the money either by taxation – which could be seen as a form of forced saving – or by borrowing from households, and thus acting as a financial intermediary.

Finally, firms themselves save, i.e. retain and plough back earnings which could

---

* As we shall see, saving is undertaken by other institutions, in addition to households.

† The role of the banks in the process of credit creation is discussed in detail in Chapter 12.

otherwise have been distributed to shareholders and thus been available for consumption. This is known as internal finance.

Sources of External Finance

We now examine the sources of external finance in greater detail. First we look at the various sources available to different legal forms of business.

Unincorporated Businesses: Sole Traders and Partnerships

There are about $2\frac{1}{4}$ million unincorporated businesses in the U.K., making this the most important form numerically. However they are mainly very small, and together account for only about one-third of the income generated by all private sector businesses.

External finance for one-man businesses (sole traders), which are particularly common in retailing, farming and the building trades, is largely short-term, comprising bank loans, trade credit, hire-purchase finance, etc. Longer-term credit may sometimes be obtained by means of a mortgage on land or buildings. Permanent capital is restricted to the savings of the owner and the earnings retained in the business.

Sources of finance for partnerships, which are very common in the professions – law, accountancy, medicine etc. – are similar to those for the one-man business. But a partnership usually has more permanent capital since it can have up to twenty partners – more for solicitors and accountants.

Joint Stock Companies

There are almost 600,000 companies registered in Great Britain. They are of two types, private companies, which are the more important numerically, and public companies (not to be confused with public corporations), which are more important in terms of aggregate size. In addition to having access to all the sources of finance available to unincorporated businesses, joint-stock companies are able to raise permanent capital by the issue of shares.

The two main types of share are preference and ordinary shares. Preference shares usually attract a fixed rate of dividend which is paid in full before holders of ordinary shares receive anything. (Preference shareholders are, however, paid after the holders of debentures – issued in return for long-term loans – and usually receive a slightly higher payment in compensation.) Ordinary shares generally do not carry a fixed rate of dividend, and holders receive a share of profits only after all other claims have been met. Similarly ordinary shareholders have the last claim upon the assets of the firm following bankruptcy or liquidation. Consequently ordinary shares constitute a risky form of investment. On the other hand, ordinary shareholders tend to receive the greatest rewards when the business flourishes and profits are high.

The maximum number of shareholders in a private company is limited by law to fifty, which can limit the amount of permanent finance that such firms can raise. No such limitation is imposed on the public company. Moreover the securities issued by public companies, unlike those issued by private companies, can be freely traded. This provides an additional incentive to make funds available to public companies.

THE STOCK EXCHANGE

Most transactions in the securities issued by public companies take place on the stock exchange. A potential buyer or seller of securities puts his order through a stockbroker, who acts as his agent. The actual markets in the securities are made by stock jobbers, who hope to make profits by selling at prices above those at which they buy. Since buying and selling orders seldom coincide, and since prices fluctuate from day to day, and indeed from hour to hour, the jobber's trade is inherently risky, and his profit is mainly a reward for risk-taking.

Several points may be noted concerning the operation of the stock-exchange. First it is a market in existing, 'second-hand' securities and is not directly involved in raising new capital. Nevertheless without a second-hand market, savers would be more reluctant to make finance available for investment since stocks and shares would then be a much less liquid form of asset. Second, the stock exchange authorities permit the quotation of institutions such as investment trusts whose assets comprise the securities issued by other companies. In this way companies are able to draw upon the savings of people who might be reluctant to invest directly in an industrial or commercial company.

Finally it should be mentioned that the efficiency of the stock exchange has recently been questioned. In particular it has been asserted that the commission charged by brokers on large deals was higher than could be justified by the work involved. Consequently in 1976 Ariel, a computerized securities-transfer system financed by, and intended for the use of, large financial institutions began operations. This system is designed to bring potential buyers and sellers into closer contact, and to reduce the costs of transactions.

THE NEW ISSUE MARKET

As noted above, transactions on the stock exchange are confined to securities that have already been issued. New issues, i.e. the raising of additional finance by companies, may take several forms.

PUBLIC ISSUE BY PROSPECTUS

Here the company offers, directly to the general public, a fixed number of shares or debentures at a stated price. A prospectus must be issued, setting out the nature of the company's business, and giving details of its past turnover, profits, etc.

OFFER FOR SALE

This is similar to the public issue, but the company sells the securities to an issuing house (usually a merchant bank), which in turn offers them to the general public.

PLACING

The securities are again acquired by an issuing house, which now places them with its clients and with jobbers. In order to reduce the possibility that the institutions with whom the securities are placed may make substantial profits when the securities are subsequently traded on the stock exchange, the authorities stipulate that a minimum quantity be initially placed with jobbers.

OFFER FOR SALE BY TENDER

This, the only method whereby the amount of money to be raised by a new issue is not known in advance, tends to be used when investors' attitudes are very volatile, making it difficult to assess the appropriate issue price. A minimum price at which a tender will be accepted is stated. If investors believe that the securities are worth more than this minimum they will put in a higher offer in order to try to secure an allocation.

RIGHTS ISSUE

Rights issues are confined to existing shareholders who are offered additional shares in proportion to their holdings. The new shares are issued at a price below the current market price, and this can be seen as a reward to shareholders. A compensating benefit to the company is that the administration costs are substantially lower than for alternative methods.

Rights issues should not be confused with bonus or scrip issues. These also involve the issue of additional shares to existing shareholders, but since they are issued free, no new finance is raised.

UNDERWRITING

Since companies issuing securities normally plan in advance the uses to which they will put the funds raised, it is important that they should obtain these funds. Although they set a price for the securities at which they expect the public to buy, it is difficult to predict reactions, since conditions in the market may change during the period between setting the price and the day of issue.

To insure against the consequences of the issue not being fully subscribed, it is arranged that one or more underwriters – substantial financial institutions such as insurance companies – will take up any securities not bought by the general public. Where an issue is undersubscribed it is probable that trading in the securities will open at a price below the market price. In order to compensate for this risk the underwriters charge a small commission related to the total value of the issue.

The Shareholders

A feature of modern capitalism is that an increasing proportion of company securities tends to be held by institutional investors – insurance companies, pension funds, investment trusts, unit trusts, etc. This trend was highlighted by data produced by the Diamond Commission, and presented in table 6.2. This trend has

Table 6.2

The Pattern of Ownership of Quoted Ordinary
Shares, U.K. (percentage)

	1963	1973
Persons, executors, trustees	58.7	42.0
Charities	2.6	4.4
Insurance companies	10.6	16.2
Pension funds	7.0	12.2
Investment trust companies	6.7	6.5
Unit trusts	1.2	3.4
Banks, other financial institutions	2.3	3.3
Non-financial companies	4.8	4.3
Public sector	1.6	2.5
Overseas holders	4.4	5.2
Total	100	100

Source: *Report of the Royal Commission on the Distribution of Incomes and Wealth.*

continued since the Commission reported, and it is estimated that the U.K. personal sector now holds less than 40 per cent of the shares issued by quoted companies.

As noted above, institutional investment has the advantage that it enables the individual saver or investor to spread his risks. However there may also be disadvantages. It has been suggested that institutional investors prefer not to become involved in the formulation of company policy. They may even be reluctant to intervene in order to influence policy in companies whose financial or economic performance is poor, preferring either to sell their holdings for reinvestment elsewhere or, if the holdings are so large that they could sell only at an unattractive price, simply to wait in the hope that the companies' performance will eventually improve. When large shareholders, which increasingly means institutions, behave in this way, it is said that a divorce has occurred between ownership and control. One result of this divorce may be that Boards of Directors become less concerned to increase profits than they would be if they were themselves major shareholders.

The second aspect of institutional shareholding to which increasing attention has recently been given is the increase in the volatility of share prices that may result when buying or selling orders are large. A vicious circle may emerge here; the volatility may deter potential small investors, which will result in a further increase in the relative importance of institutional investors, and thus to further increases in volatility.

The Relative Importance of the Various Sources of Finance
The relative importance of the various sources of finance changes from year to year. Moreover it is impossible to obtain comprehensive data on all sources at the national level. Consequently it is difficult to present an adequate picture of the relative importance of the various sources available. However taking the postwar period as a whole, the following broad conclusions can be drawn.

First, internal sources of finance – depreciation allowances and undistributed profits – have been considerably more important than external sources. Internal funds have accounted for more than two thirds of funds from all sources.

Second, the principal components of external funds have been long-term loans and bank borrowing, each accounting for more than 10 per cent of total funds from all sources.

Third, cash issues of ordinary shares are not a very important source of finance in terms of size. Even for large public companies whose shares are listed on the stock exchange, they account for less than 5 per cent of total funds. However, new issues of ordinary shares have an importance greater than indicated by the amount of money raised. As noted above, there are limits to the amount of money that a company can raise by borrowing, especially important being the company's *gearing*, that is the ratio of loan capital to equity. Issuing shares lowers this ratio and so facilitates the issue of more debt capital in the future.

Fourth, the number of new issues in a given year is strongly influenced by existing share prices – rising share prices are usually felt to be conducive to the success of new issues. This is mirrored to some extent by bank borrowing – the less favourable the conditions for issuing shares, the more reliant companies become on bank borrowing.

Finally, the State has become a more important source of capital for private sector producers (see Chapters 16 and 20).

The Needs of Small and Medium-Sized Firms
If the outcome of every proposed investment project were certain, the ability of the firm to raise sufficient funds to finance any project would depend upon the prospective yield from that project and not upon the size of the firm. In practice

the yields of all investment projects are uncertain, a factor which militates against the small firm with respect to a given project.

To see why this is so, consider the following simple example. Assume that a firm has accumulated reserves of £1 million and that it is considering investing this in a project whose profitability, i.e. the excess of total revenue over total cost, is estimated as shown in table 6.3. The most likely outcome (probability 0.5) is a profit of £200,000. There is a reasonable chance (probability 0.25) that a profit of £500,000 may result, but an equal probability that a loss of £100,000 may be incurred. The weighted probable outcome is: $(£500,000 \times 0.25) + (£200,000 \times 0.5) + (-£100,000 \times 0.25) = £125,000 + £100,000 - £25,000 = £200,000$

Table 6.3
Estimated Profitability of a Hypothetical Investment Project

Profit (£)	Probability
500,000	.25
200,000	.5
−100,000	.25

If the firm were certain that it could obtain a profit of £200,000 it would undertake the project. However the presence of uncertainty requires it to consider the implications of outcomes other than the most probable and in particular the possibility of making a loss. Since the whole of the firm's reserves would be required for this project, a loss might lead to bankruptcy. This is a danger that would not be thought to be compensated by the chance of obtaining a profit of £500,000.

A firm with larger reserves, on the other hand, would be able to take the risk. It it considered that the weighted probable profit of £200,000 represented an adequate return it would go ahead with the investment. For this firm the possibility of a loss, which would *not* now involve bankruptcy, would be counterbalanced by the possibility of a larger profit.

When firms rely on external finance the situation becomes more complex, but the same principle applies. Investors, and especially those buying ordinary shares, are likely to steer clear of companies which may go bankrupt if things go badly, even if those same companies might do very well under more favourable conditions. Investors are likely to believe that such situations are more characteristic of small than large companies.

In order to compensate for the additional risk, investors may require higher returns, (interest or dividends) from small companies, i.e. the cost of capital will be higher for small than for large companies. (Furthermore, administrative costs tend to be higher for small than for large *issues*.) Some small companies may be unable to offer the returns required to elicit sufficient finance from the usual sources (including such institutions as merchant banks), especially if they wish to expand rapidly. In order to overcome these problems a number of institutions catering for the needs of small and medium size firms have been established.

Specialist Sources of Finance

The first group of institutions, including Charterhouse Industrial Development and Credit for Industry, were established following the report of the Macmillan Committee on Finance and Industry, published in 1931. The resources of these early institutions were very modest and met only part of the needs of the smaller firms. Since it was anticipated that the end of the war would lead to an increase in these needs, in 1945 the clearing banks, with the support of the Bank of England, established the Industrial and Commercial Finance Corporation. I.C.F.C. had initial resources of £45 millions, with a remit to provide long-term loans and subscribe equity capital within the range £5,000 to £200,000. In 1959 the Radcliffe Committee identified a need for additional finance to facilitate the commercial exploitation of technical innovations. To meet this need I.C.F.C. established a subsidiary, Technical Development Capital Ltd.

These and other institutions have continued to expand the scale of their operations, and in 1975 I.C.F.C., along with the Finance Corporation for Industry, which supplied finance to large companies, became a subsidiary of Finance For Industry. F.F.I., whose shareholders are the clearing banks (85 per cent of shares) and the Bank of England (15 per cent), has access to funds of £1,000 millions, intended mainly for medium-term lending.

The activities of F.F.I. are complemented by two other institutions established more recently. Equity Capital for Industry was established in 1976 with a capital of £50 millions, provided by various institutional investors. As suggested by the name of the institution, these funds are intended as a source of permanent capital, and E.C.I. acquired its first shares, at a cost of £1.75 million, early in 1977.

The National Enterprise Board was established primarily as a vehicle through which the state could acquire a stake in large public companies, and its assets mainly consist of holdings in large companies – British Leyland, Rolls Royce etc.* However it has also developed as a significant source of finance for small and medium size companies. In its first year of operation it acquired assets in more than a dozen such companies, its smallest investment costing only £50,000, and it announced the intention of increasing the number of such companies to around seventy within the following twelve months.

The Volume of Investment

As we noted above, the volume of investment undertaken in a given period depends upon both the demand for investment funds and the supply of such funds. (Remember that we have assumed there to be adequate capacity in the capital goods industries). The interaction of these two sets of forces is illustrated in figure 6.3.

As before, the investment demand schedule, D, indicates the demand for investment funds. The supply of funds, S, is positively related to the rate of interest. At the equilibrium point the return, R, from the last unit of investment undertaken equals the cost of the funds required for that investment. The total amount of investment undertaken is Q. The yield from any further investment would be less than the cost of the funds required for that investment.

As will be clear from the discussion in the preceding sections, figure 6.3 is based on two simplifying assumptions. The first is that there is a single market for investment funds, and the second is that all these funds attract a fixed return, designated as the rate of interest. By making these assumptions the analysis of the behaviour of aggregate investment can be simplified.

In figure 6.4 the supply and demand curves of figure 6.3 are reproduced as S_1 and D_1. The initial equilibrium rate of interest is A and X investment is undertaken. If the supply of funds increased, as indicated by the shift in the supply schedule to S_2, the equilibrium rate of interest would fall to B and the volume of investment would increase to Y. If now the investment demand schedule were to shift to D_2, the volume of investment would increase to Z and the equilibrium rate of interest would rise to C.

Investment is a 'real' variable while the rate of interest is a monetary variable.

*See Chapter 20.

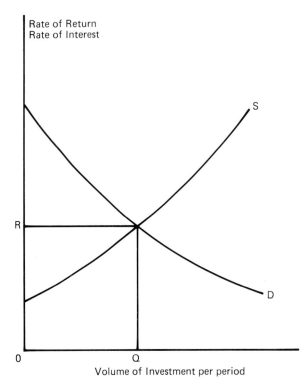

Rate of Return
Rate of Interest

S

R

D

0

Q

Volume of Investment per period

Figure 6.3 The Market for Investment Funds

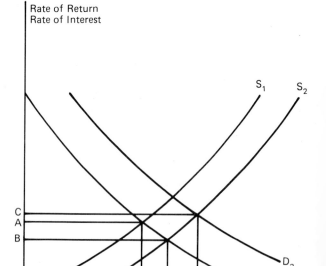

Rate of Return
Rate of Interest

S₁ S₂

C
A
B

D₂

D₁

Figure 6.4 Changes in the Market for Investment Funds

X Y Z

Volume of Investment per period

Figure 6.4 indicates that these variables interact, a change in either implying a change in the other.

Expenditure on other forms of investment can also be explained in terms of the interaction of the demand and supply of investment funds, although each form of investment is particularly sensitive to certain factors which may be less important for other forms. We now briefly examine these remaining forms, beginning with the second element of fixed capital formation, investment in dwellings, almost all of which is undertaken by households.

Expenditure by Households on New Dwellings

Taking one year with another the most important determinant of the demand for new dwellings is the rate of change in population and, more specifically, the formation of new households. Other factors which may be important in the long term are changes in multiple occupancy (the sharing of a dwelling by two or more households) and in the ownership of second homes, e.g. for holidays. Finally, demand

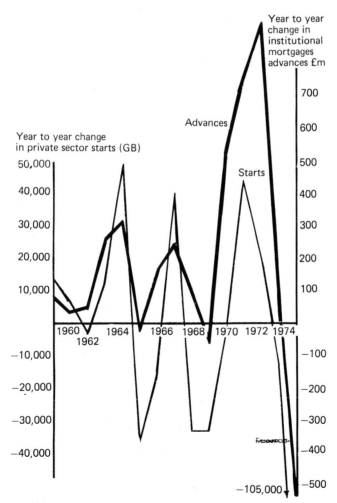

Figure 6.5 Changes in Mortgage Advances and Private Sector Building Starts

is influenced by the relationship between people's ideas of what constitutes an adequate standard of housing and the quality of the existing housing stock. Expectations normally rise as average incomes rise, and this causes an increased reluctance to live in old houses or houses without such amenities as indoor sanitation.

The most important influence on demand in any particular year is the availability of mortgage funds. A high proportion of house purchase transactions are partly financed by money borrowed from institutions, and in particular from the building societies. Figure 6.5 shows the very close relationship between changes in institutional mortgage advances and changes in the number of dwellings started in a given year.

The number of dwellings started (and completed) in any year could also be affected by the capacity of the construction industry. When the demand for new houses is very high, potential buyers may have to wait longer before obtaining possession. Supply constraints have occurred from time to time in the U.K. However in general the number of dwellings built has been determined primarily by demand conditions.

Public Sector Investment

Table 6.1 shows that in 1976 the public sector accounted for £10,112 million, or 43 per cent of total gross fixed capital formation. Most public sector investment is undertaken by the local authorities and the public corporations, the central government's share being relatively minor.

Although investment decisions in this sector can be analysed in terms of the demand for and the supply of funds, these concepts now have a different interpretation, as we can see from a brief examination of the main items of expenditure. (The investment expenditure of central and local government is discussed in greater detail in Chapter 11, and that of public corporations or nationalized industries in Chapter 19.)

The investment expenditure of the public corporations probably comes nearest to that of the private sector in that much of the expenditure (a) is on plant, equipment and vehicles, and (b) can be ranked in terms of the prospective rate of return. The major difference from the private sector is that the public corporations do not usually have to compete for funds on the open market. If they are unable to finance their operations out of retained earnings, the shortfall is made good by the government. It has sometimes been suggested that the government should charge a rate of interest comparable to the open-market rate. In practice the public corporations have obtained funds more cheaply.*

As far as the local authorities are concerned the demand for investment funds tends to be governed not by considerations of the prospective financial return, but by a concept of social need – for schools, houses, etc. Furthermore the bulk of the funds are again not raised on the open market. They are obtained either from the ratepayers, or as grants or loans from the central government. (See Chapter 11.)

However this does not imply that the cost of finance has no significance in the public sector. Even though the cost may be less than the open-market level it is still positive. Since there are invariably alternative projects for which these funds might be used, ranking in terms of their prospective rates of return is still required, especially in public corporations. Even in local authorities whose spending, as noted above, may be strongly influenced by social considerations, economic factors

* See also the section in the appendix on the test discount rate.

cannot be ignored. The use of scarce funds implies that the authorities should try to ensure that a given level of service, a given output, should be provided at minimum cost. Hence the saving in costs likely to arise from investment should be carefully considered.

Pressure on public authorities to use resources efficiently has increased as a reaction occurred against the rising shares of resources utilized by the public sector. This point is discussed in greater detail in Chapter 11.

Value of the Physical Increase in Stocks and Work in Progress

This second element of investment expenditure is much smaller than fixed capital formation and hence will be treated very briefly.

This item is more important in the private than the public sector and changes in stocks are often due to the same factors as affect expenditure on fixed capital by private producers. On the demand side many of the forces which stimulate expenditure on fixed capital – an increase in GDP, the introduction of new products, etc., lead to an increase in the value of stocks. Similarly, the acceleration principle can again be applied to investment in stocks. The major difference between the two elements is that whereas fixed capital formation is always planned, an increase in stocks may sometimes be unplanned, as when production takes place in anticipation of a demand that does not arise.

Levels of stocks and work in progress are again sensitive to changes in the cost and availability of funds; indeed some studies have found that one of the earliest reactions to an increase in interest rates is a reduction in stock levels.

Appendix   The Measurement of the Rate of Return and of the Cost of Investment Funds

The Rate of Return

When calculating the yield of an investment project, firms may use one of several methods. The method that has probably the most to commend it in terms of its underlying economic logic is the internal or discounted cash flow (DCF) rate of return method. This method takes account of the fact that a given sum of money received at different points in time has different values. It is better to receive money this year than next year, because the money can be put to work for a year in one way or another. In order to take this into account, a discount factor is applied to money which is expected to be received in future years. The use of a discount factor explains why this method is usually known as the discounted cash flow method.

In order to calculate the expected rate of return of a project the firm must be able to estimate first the initial cash outflow required (CO) – this will usually consist of expenditure on plant, equipment, etc. – and second the net cash inflows (NCI) arising in future years as a result of the initial expenditure – these inflows will usually comprise revenue from additional sales, minus other costs incurred e.g. for labour, materials and power. (However note that the net cash inflow can also be increased by an investment which simply leads to a reduction in the costs of production). Having obtained these estimates the firm can calculate the rate of return by applying the following formula:

$$CO = \sum \frac{NCI}{(1+r)^n}$$

In the above formula r is the internal rate of return, sometimes known as the marginal efficiency of capital. n indicates the number of years over which the return is calculated. If the investment relates to the purchase of an additional machine the firm might expect this to yield revenue for, say, ten years. In this instance, 'exploding' the formula gives us:

$$CO = \frac{NCI_1}{(1+r)^1} + \frac{NCI_2}{(1+r)^2} + \frac{NCI_3}{(1+r)^3} + \cdots + \frac{NCI_{10}}{(1+r)^{10}}$$

where NCI_1 refers to the cash inflow in year 1, NCI_2 to year 2, and so forth.

A more simple example, but one which applies exactly the same principle, would be the purchase by a farmer of young beef cattle for fattening and subsequent resale in a year's time. This gives us the simplest possible form of the formula:

$$CO = \frac{NCI_1}{(1+r)}$$

If the cattle cost the farmer £100,000 and he estimates that, after meeting all his other costs, he will receive £120,000 when he sells them in a year's time, the rate of return is 0.2 or 20 per cent. This can easily be seen by substituting the relevant values in the formula:

$$£100,000 = \frac{£120,000}{1.2}$$

This means that if the farmer obtained finance at a cost of 20 per cent per annum and invested it in the purchase of cattle he would be just as well off as if he had not done so. (Technically, the net present value of the project equals zero). If he could obtain finance for less than 20 per cent the investment would leave him better off; if he had to pay more than 20 per cent he would be worse off and should not undertake the investment.

We consider in a moment how the cost of finance might be calculated, but first, in order to consolidate understanding of the discounting procedure, let us assume that our farmer has to keep his cattle for two years before reselling them at a price which leaves him with £120,000 after meeting all his other costs. The rate of return would now be approximately 0.095 or $9\frac{1}{2}$ per cent. (We make the simplifying assumption that all the farmer's other costs are incurred in year 2.)

$$CO = \frac{NCI_2}{(1+r)^2} \qquad £100,000 \simeq \frac{£120,000}{(1.095)^2}$$

It would now pay the farmer to invest only if he could obtain finance at a cost of $9\frac{1}{2}$ per cent a year or less. This example shows why it is so important to take the time pattern of cash flows into account.

The Cost of Investment Funds
If one considers firms' investment programmes over a number of years one normally finds that the expenditure is funded by three broad types of finance – money borrowed, for example by the issue of debentures, permanent (equity) capital obtained by the issue of shares, and retained earnings. The cost of these three types of finance will vary over time and also, as noted earlier, from one firm to another. However the general rule is that, after taking tax considerations into account, borrowed money is cheapest and equity capital the most expensive, with retained earnings coming in between. (Attaching a cost to the use of retained earnings can be justified in terms of the concept of opportunity cost – if these earnings were not

used to finance investment within the firm they would be available for use in some other way, e.g. to be loaned at interest.)

One might expect firms to finance as much of their investment as possible by the cheapest type of finance, borrowed money. In practice, however, considerations of risk, both to borrower and lender, will limit the use made of this source of funds.

In order to calculate its cost of capital the firm must estimate the cost of each type of finance and the amounts of each type that it would expect to use, taking one year with another. If it estimated the costs to be: borrowing 8 per cent, permanent (equity) capital 12 per cent, and retained earnings 10 per cent, and it planned to finance investment thus: 25 per cent borrowed money, 25 per cent new permanent capital, 50 per cent retained earnings, then its overall cost of capital would be:

$$(.25 \times 8\%) + (.25 \times 12\%) + (.5 \times 10\%) = 10\%$$

The Rate of Return and the Cost of Finance Compared

Calculating the rate of return and the cost of finance in the ways described in this appendix makes it easy to compare the two. As we have said, the guideline is that investment should be undertaken only where the rate of return is at least equal to the cost of finance, i.e. where the net present value of the project is zero or (preferably) positive. In practice it has been found that firms usually prefer to work with a 'safety net', i.e. they invest only if they expect the rate of return to exceed the cost of capital, often by several percentage points. This allows for the possibility that their estimates of costs and revenue may turn out to have been too optimistic.

Furthermore, it is known that other methods of 'investment appraisal' are used. For example projects may be ranked in terms of the length of time likely to elapse before the sum of the net cash inflows equals the initial cash outflow. The shorter the 'payback' period, the higher the project is ranked. The payback method has most to recommend it when future economic conditions are very uncertain and the firm wishes to limit its risks. (When the DCF method is used, a very high discount factor becomes appropriate in such circumstances.)

The Test Discount Rate

A government White Paper issued in 1967 advocated that proposed investment by public corporations should be undertaken only if it promised to yield more than the test discount rate (TDR). The TDR was initially set at 8 per cent in real terms, in line with the current average expected rate of return on low risk projects in the private sector. However the proposed procedure has in practice had very limited application, as noted in a N.E.D.O. report: 'For example, the major part of the investment programme in the Post Office and British Gas is determined by prior strategic decisions to maintain a certain standard for telecommunications services or to purchase the output of North Sea gas fields. Investment cannot in these cases be disaggregated for appraisal purposes because it relates to a total system – the telephone network or gas distribution grid – and consequently most of the investment programme becomes classified as inescapable or essential.'*

Summary and Conclusions

In this chapter we have examined the relative importance of the main forms of investment expenditure. We have also discussed the factors influencing each of these forms. Although the determinants may vary somewhat as between one form

*N.E.D.O., *The Nationalised Industries* (London: H.M.S.O., 1976), p. 31.

and another, a common thread is the desire to increase efficiency and, in the private sector, profitability.

One of the most important determinants of investment expenditure is the cost and availability of finance. For many producers retained earnings constitute the major source of finance, so that the liquidity of the private sector is a key factor. The implications of this for government policy are discussed in later chapters, especially those concerned with fiscal policy and prices and incomes policy. There are many sources of external finance, including specialist institutions established to meet the needs of small firms, and we reviewed the relative importance of these various sources.

Investment expenditure has been discussed at considerable length because of its significance for economic growth and the standard of living. This significance has been discussed in earlier chapters, and will again occupy our attention at a later stage.

ESSAY QUESTIONS

1 What are the major determinants of investment spending by (a) private sector producers, (b) public sector producers, (c) central and local government?
2 Assess the relative contribution to economic growth of the investment expenditure of (a) private sector producers, (b) public sector producers, (c) central and local government.
3 Explain the statement that the amount of investment undertaken is determined by the interaction of the demand for and the supply of investment funds.
4 Discuss the factors which might cause a change in the demand for investment funds.
5 Explain why the value of the accelerator is unlikely to be the same for an increase as for a decrease in GDP.
6 'The operation of the accelerator may amplify but not initiate fluctuations in economic activity.' Discuss.
7 What factors would tend to reduce the supply of investment funds?
8 What do you understand by the term 'divorce between ownership and control'? Discuss the factors encouraging this 'divorce' and assess their implications.
9 'An increase in the demand for investment funds causes a rise in the rate of interest.' 'At higher rates of interest less investment is undertaken.' How may these apparently conflicting statements be reconciled?
10 Show how the rate of return may be calculated and explain the relationship between the rate of return and the investment demand schedule.

EXERCISES

6.1 For a number of years a company has produced 50,000 grummets a year on 10 machines, each having a capacity of 5,000 grummets a year. Each machine lasts for 5 years, and the company has replaced 2 machines each year. An export drive then leads to an increase in sales of grummets to 60,000 a year, for each of the next two years. However in the following year an increase in international competition causes sales to fall back to 50,000.

(i) On the assumption that the company wishes to keep its capacity in line with the demand for its products, calculate the number of machines bought in each of the three years. (ii) Comment briefly on the value of the accelerator coefficient.

6.2 What factors might explain the pattern of new issues shown in table 6.4?

Table 6.4
Money Raised by New Issues by Companies
(£mn, *constant prices*)

1966	623
1967	422
1968	656
1969	572
1970	353
1971	664
1972	956
1973	211
1974	162
1975	1,578
1976	1,161

Source: *Midland Bank Review*, February 1977.

6.3 The information below relates to four pairs of hypothetical companies. Say, in each case, for which company you would expect the cost of finance to be higher, and briefly justify your answers.

(i) Company A has assets of £3 millions and manufactures a wide range of foodstuffs.

Company B has assets of £200,000 and manufactures components for the vehicles industry.

(ii) The profits of the two companies, which have the same volume of assets, over the past 5 years have been as follows:

	Company A (£000)	Company B (£000)
1973	500	500
1974	550	700
1975	450	300
1976	500	700
1977	500	300

(iii) The profits of the two companies over the past 5 years have been as follows:

	Company A (£000)	Company B (£000)
1973	200	30
1974	220	50
1975	160	90
1976	220	130
1977	200	180

(iv) Company A plans capital expenditure of £500,000 and will obtain the necessary finance by the issue of debentures.

Company B plans capital expenditure of £3 millions and will obtain the necessary finance by an equity rights issue.

OBJECTIVE TEST QUESTIONS: SET 2

1 An investment demand schedule shows, for a given period, the

   A amount of investment undertaken
   B amount of investment expected to yield given rates of return
   C number of shares demanded by investors
   D number of shares and other securities demanded by investors
   E relationship between the demand for investment funds and the cost of capital.

2 Which of the following would be least likely to cause an investment demand schedule to shift to the right?

   A an increase in GDP
   B the development of a large number of new products
   C a rise in the price of labour
   D a fall in the productivity of labour
   E a rise in the cost of investment funds.

3 A public company can raise additional finance by all of the following methods except

   A a public issue by prospectus
   B an offer for sale
   C a stock exchange placing
   D a bonus issue
   E a rights issue.

Questions 4 to 7 refer to figure 6.6. The initial demand and supply schedules, relating to funds for investment by private sector producers, are indicated by the unbroken lines. New demand and supply schedules, which might result from the

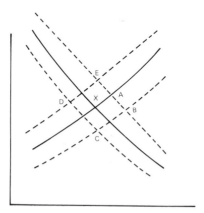

Figure 6.6

various changes listed below, are indicated by the broken lines. Starting each time from the initial point of equilibrium X, and assuming no other changes than those specified, indicate the new points of equilibrium A, B, C, D or E. (Each letter may apply once, more than once, or not at all).

4 Businessmen become more optimistic about future economic conditions.

5 Technological progress results in new products being introduced on to the market; the rates offered to depositors by building societies increase.

6 Gross domestic product falls substantially.

7 New institutions are established to supply funds for investment by medium-sized companies; technological progress leads to the introduction of more labour-saving equipment.

8 Figure 6.7 indicates that
   1 APC falls as GNP rises
   2 MPC falls as GNP rises
   3 APC=1 at point X.

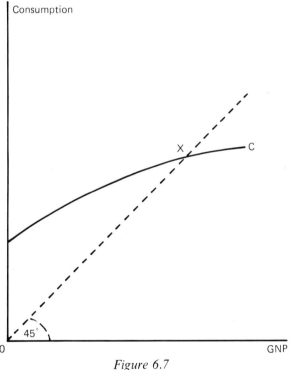

Figure 6.7

9 The permanent income hypothesis implies that
   1 when income rises the long run MPC exceeds the short run MPC
   2 when income falls the short run MPC exceeds the long run MPC
   3 MPC can never equal APC.

10

GNP (£ millions)	Consumption (£ millions)
1,000	850
2,000	1,350
3,000	1,850
4,000	2,350

From the above table we can deduce that

1 within the income range £2,000 millions to £3,000 millions, MPC=0.5
2 when GNP is £2,000 millions, APC=0.5
3 as income rises APC and MPC decline.

11 The government's current expenditure on goods and services includes
1 the payment of teachers' salaries
2 expenditure on building a new school
3 transfer payments.

12 The effect of the accelerator will tend to be dampened if
1 producers of consumer goods have excess capacity
2 producers of capital goods are working at full capacity
3 some producers feel that the increase in demand is temporary.

13 Which of the following sources of finance is/are available to private companies?
1 bank loans
2 shares, which can be traded on the stock exchange
3 debentures, which can be traded on the stock exchange.

14 Assume a consumption function of the form $C=a+b(Y)$, where Y represents GNP. If a is positive and $b=0.5$ we can conclude that
1 APC=MPC
2 the change in total consumption will be less than the change in GNP
3 MPS=0.5.

15 Fixed capital formation is undertaken by
1 producers
2 government
3 households.

16 A fall in the marginal propensity to consume implies that the average propensity to consume also falls.
Average and marginal propensity to consume are always equal.

17 Redistribution of income and wealth from the poorer to the richer members of a community is likely to cause a fall in the overall propensity to consume.
The propensity to consume of richer people tends to be less than that of poorer people.

18 The rate of change in investment will be greater than the rate of change in GDP whenever the accelerator coefficient exceeds zero.
The accelerator coefficient is the incremental capital-output ratio.

19 The level of fixed capital formation and of stocks of work in progress always rise when GDP rises.
Both fixed capital formation and stocks of work in progress are forms of investment.

20 A change in the productivity of labour may affect the demand for both labour and capital.
An increase in the demand for one factor of production implies a fall in the demand for other factors.

TRUE/FALSE

1   If we assume that all income is either consumed or saved it follows that APC + APS = 1.

2   The amount of investment required to compensate for capital consumption is known as net investment.

3   The acceleration principle states that the higher the level of GDP the higher is the level of investment.

4   Stock jobbers act as agents for investors in the buying and selling of securities.

5   If the rate of return of an investment project is greater than the cost of capital the net present value of the project is positive.

6   The marginal propensity to consume denotes the proportion consumed of a small increase in income.

7   The average propensity to save denotes the change in saving that occurs as a result of a small change in income.

8   The value of the marginal propensity to consume is indicated by the gradient of the consumption function.

9   In the national accounts only some transfer payments are included in the government's expenditure on goods and services.

10 Expenditure on new houses forms part of investment.

CHAPTER SEVEN

International Trade and the Balance of Payments

Introduction

In Chapter 3 we identified four major flows of expenditure which give rise to the utilization of domestic resources. Chapters 4 to 6 have each been concerned with one of these flows, and in this chapter we discuss the fourth and final flow – expenditure on exports (and also on imports) of goods and services.

We begin by considering why international trade might arise. We then examine some of the major implications of international trade – and in particular of an imbalance between imports and exports. Finally we discuss changes in the U.K.'s overseas trade and balance of payments in recent years. The starting point, the key to international trade, is the principle of comparative advantage.

The Principle of Comparative Advantage

We saw in Chapter 2 that an economy can be considered as a bundle or collection of resources which can be transformed into alternative combinations of products, and that these alternative combinations can be represented by a production possibility frontier.

Figure 7.1 shows the production possibility frontiers for two hypothetical countries. Country A could allocate its resources so as to produce, in a given period, either 10,000 units of food or 5,000 machines or any combination of food and machines lying on the line AA. The fact that the production possibility frontier is a straight line indicates that the opportunity cost of producing one product, in terms of the other, is constant. The opportunity cost of one machine is two units of food, i.e. for every additional machine produced, two units of food must be sacrificed. (As we showed in Chapter 2 the opportunity cost ratio may often not be constant. Production possibility frontiers are more likely to be concave to the origin. We have assumed a straight line frontier merely in order to simplify the analysis.)

The resources with which country B is endowed would permit it to produce 5,000 units of food or 10,000 machines, or any combination lying on the line BB. For B the opportunity cost of producing one additional machine is 0.5 units of food, i.e. for every additional machine produced, 0.5 units of food must be sacrificed.

To summarize, the opportunity cost ratios as between machines and food are 1:2 in country A and 1:0.5 in country B. In these circumstances it is easy to see that total production will be greater if each country specializes in that product in which it has a comparative advantage, i.e. country A in food and country B in machines. A can produce 10,000 units of food and B 10,000 machines, whereas if there were no specialization, if each country allocated half its resources to each product, total production would be 7,500 (5,000 + 2,000) units of food and 7,500 (2,500 + 5,000) machines.

We examine below the conditions which must be fulfilled in order for specializa-

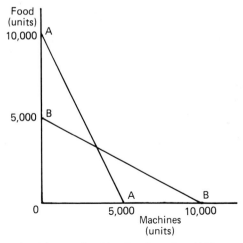

Figure 7.1 Alternative Production Possibility Frontiers

tion to occur, but first let us consider the situation represented in figure 7.2. In contrast to the previous situation, country A has an *absolute* advantage in the production of both food and machines. However the opportunity cost ratios as between machines and food still differ (1:2 in country A, 1:1 in country B). This again indicates that production can be increased if each country specializes in that product in which it has a *comparative* advantage, i.e. country A in food and country B in machines.

If each country were to allocate half of its resources to each product, total output would be 7,000 (5,000+2,000) units of food and 4,500 (2,500+2,000) machines. On the other hand if A devotes 75 per cent of its resources to the production of food and the remaining 25 per cent to machines, while B specializes entirely on machines, total output will be 7,500 units of food and 5,250 (1,250+4,000) machines. The output of both food and machines has increased.

Only if opportunity costs were identical, i.e. only if a situation of compara-

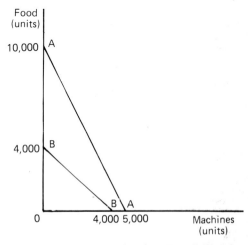

Figure 7.2 Alternative Production Possibility Frontiers

tive advantage did not exist, would specialization fail to lead to a greater total output.*

The Conditions For International Trade

As we have seen, if international specialization and trade is to lead to increased production, opportunity cost ratios in different countries must differ. Given that this condition is fulfilled trade will take place provided that the countries can agree on a rate at which the products should exchange. This rate of exchange must lie between the two domestic opportunity cost ratios.

In the second situation considered above, the rate of exchange of machines for food must lie between 1 : 1 and 1 : 2. The countries might, for example, agree that one machine should exchange for 1.5 units of food. Country A, which specializes in the production of food, would then obtain one machine in exchange for each 1.5 units of food sold, whereas to produce one more machine it would have to sacrifice the production of two units of food. Conversely country B would obtain 1.5 units of food for each machine it sold whereas if it produced its own food it would obtain only one unit of food for every machine foregone.

Today most international trade does not, of course, take place on a barter basis as in the above example. Instead transactions are undertaken in terms of internationally accepted currencies. In these circumstances the condition for international trade can be specified as follows. Specialization and trade will occur provided that the exchange rates of currencies lie between the limits set by the international (non-trading) price ratios for different products.

In order to demonstrate this point let us re-cast in monetary terms the data relating to the second situation considered above. The opportunity cost ratio within a country will be reflected in the domestic price ratio. This is illustrated in the first line of table 7.1.** Since country A can produce, with a given quantity of

Table 7.1

Alternative Exchange Rates and International Trade

| | Price in Country | | | |
| | A | | B | |
	Food	Machines	Food	Machines
Domestic prices	$2	$4	£1	£1
Import prices at exchange rate:				
£1 = $3	$3	$3	£0.67	£1.33
£1 = $5	$5	$5	£0.4	£0.8
£1 = $1	$1	$1	£2	£4

resources, twice as many units of food as machines, the price of food ($2 per unit) is half that of machines ($4). In country B, with an opportunity cost ratio of 1 : 1, food and machines have the same price (£1).

The international, non-trading, price ratios are £1 = $2 (for food) and £1 = $4 (for machines). Provided that the exchange rate is between these limits, trade will occur. If, for example, the exchange rate were £1 = $3 import prices would be as shown in the second line of table 7.1. At these prices producers in country B would

---

* If specialization leads to greater economies of scale (see Chapter 24) production may increase even if the *initial* opportunity cost ratios are identical. However following specialization the *final* ratios will differ.

** In practice the correspondence between the two ratios may not be as exact as assumed here.

be able to sell machines (but not food) in A, and producers in A would be able to sell food (but not machines) in B.

Table 7.1 also illustrates the situation where the exchange rate lies outside the limits set by the international, non-trading, price ratios. In line 3 we assume an exchange rate of £1 = $5. At this rate producers of both food and machines in country A would be able to export to country B at prices below those charged by domestic producers. However producers in B would be unable to sell either food or machines in A. In line 4, with an exchange rate of £1 = $1, the situation is reversed. Producers in B would be able to sell both food and machines in country A, but producers in A would be unable to sell either in country B.

This simple example illustrates the significance of exchange rates for international trade and the implications of changes in exchange rates are discussed in greater detail below.* But for the moment we continue to examine the conditions that must be fulfilled if international specialization and trade are to occur.

In the above example we made no reference to transport costs. In fact transport costs should not be so high as to outweigh the price advantage enjoyed by exporters over domestic producers. In table 7.1, with an exchange rate of £1 = $3 international trade would cease if transport costs were more than $1 (or £0.33) per unit. In practice transport costs differ from one product to another, tending to be highest in relation to the price of the product for products with a low price–volume ratio. Consequently they inhibit trade in some products (e.g. bricks, cement) far more than others (e.g. watches, jewellery).

The second condition is that international trade should not be seriously inhibited by artificial barriers to trade. Especially important barriers are tariffs, which in effect are taxes on imports, and quotas, which regulate the volume or total value of imports. These barriers are imposed by governments and are therefore examined during our discussion of international economic policies in Chapter 15.

To conclude this outline of the conditions for international specialization and trade, one final point should be made. The example above related to a two-product, bilateral (two-country) trading situation, whereas in practice international trade is conducted on a multi-product multilateral basis. The wider the basis for trade, the greater is likely to be the scope for the application of the principle of comparative advantage, and thus for an increase in total economic welfare.

Gross Domestic Product and International Trade
Provided that the conditions for international trade, outlined above, continue to be fulfilled we would expect an increase in GDP to be accompanied by higher levels of both imports and exports. If we were to consider a single country the higher level of imports would be attributed to the increase in expenditure, by both consumers and producers, some of which is satisfied by importing goods from abroad. On the export side, the increase in exports would reflect the increase in that country's economic capacity, not all of which is absorbed by additional domestic expenditure.

In practice we cannot, of course, confine our attention to a single country when we are considering international trade. Part of the explanation of the increase in imports is that overseas countries have expanded their economic capacity and are therefore able to satisfy part of our increased demands. Similarly the ability to increase exports depends upon the increase in the GDP, and hence the expenditure, of overseas countries. In fact experience shows that as the world economy expands,

---

* The determination of exchange rates is discussed in the appendix to this chapter.

international trade tends to expand more rapidly, reflecting a greater degree of specialization between countries.

The Interaction between Product and Currency Markets

We have identified the exchange rate as one of the major influences on international trade. However it is important to recognize that this relationship is a two-way one. The pattern of international trade can be influenced by, but can also influence, the exchange rate. For example consider an increase in the volume of a country's exports relative to imports. This relative increase in exports may occur for various reasons.

First, technological progress may be faster than in other countries, leading to a more rapid rate of innovation. The introduction of new or improved products may cause an increase in the demand for exports, and a fall in the demand for imports. Second, costs of production, and hence prices, may fall in relation to those in other countries, increasing the attractiveness of this country's products vis-a-vis those of other countries. Finally, the emergence of unfavourable domestic economic conditions may induce producers to put more resources into exporting. The changed conditions may be short-term, e.g. a government may freeze domestic prices and thus cause a reduction in domestic profit margins if costs rise. A longer-term change in conditions would be implied by a reduction in the growth rate of GDP relative to growth in other countries. This should also induce exporters to put more resources into exporting. (However it is possible that factors which may cause a slow rate of growth – a lack of innovation, outdated working methods, etc. – may also inhibit exports.)

Whatever the cause this increase in the volume of exports relative to imports is likely to cause a rise in the external value of the country's currency, i.e. in the exchange rate. Moreover the interaction between the two types of market is unlikely to end there. If a change in the pattern of trade causes the exchange rate to alter, this will in turn cause a change in the relative profitability of importing and exporting, and hence in the pattern of trade.

Again, consider a change in the exchange rate arising from an international monetary flow not directly connected with trade flows. For example an increase in domestic interest rates may lead to an inflow of investment funds from abroad and hence in a movement of the exchange rate. This movement will influence the pattern of international trade and changes in this pattern may cause further movements in the exchange rate.

International Trade and the Utilization of Resources

The exports of goods and services means that domestic resources are utilized to satisfy the demands of overseas customers. Conversely, imports involve the utilization of resources overseas in order to satisfy the demands of U.K. residents. If, at a given level of prices, the volume of exports equals the volume of imports, the net effect on the utilization of domestic resources is zero. A surplus (expenditure on exports exceeds expenditure on imports) implies a higher level of utilization of resources. Conversely, a deficit implies a lower level of resource utilization.

This can be illustrated by reference to figure 7.3, in which AA indicates the production possibility frontier. Let us assume that the total planned domestic expenditure, i.e. planned consumption plus investment (both private and public) is indicated by point X. If output exactly matches planned expenditure, and if, at a given level of prices, the volume of exports equals the volume of imports, resource

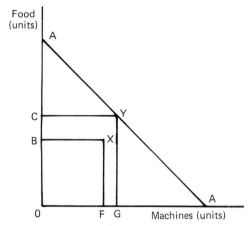

Figure 7.3 Resource Utilization with a Trade Surplus

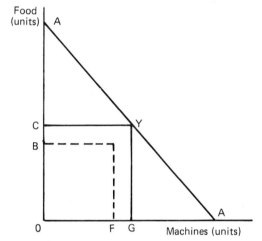

Figure 7.4 Resource Utilization with a Trade Deficit

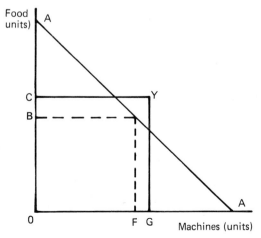

Figure 7.5 Expenditure Beyond the Production Possibility Frontier

utilization can be represented by OB plus OF.* If however, exports exceed imports, resource utilization will increase, say to OC plus OG.

Figure 7.3 also demonstrates the fact that if planned domestic expenditure were Y this would not be compatible with a surplus of exports over imports, since no combination of outputs to the right of line AA is possible.

The impact of a deficit (imports exceed exports) is demonstrated in figure 7.4. Domestic expenditure is represented by point Y. However domestic resource utilization is (again using shorthand) only OB plus OF. BC plus FG represents the trade deficit.

In this instance a deficit on foreign trade involves the underutilization of resources. However this is not a necessary consequence of a foreign trade deficit. Consider figure 7.5. Here domestic expenditure plans, represented by Y can be fulfilled only by means of such a deficit. Domestic resources are fully utilized (OB plus OF), and BC plus FG indicates the foreign trade deficit.

In the short-run a country may be able to finance such a deficit either by attracting an inflow of currency from abroad or by running down its reserves of international currencies. However no country can continue such a policy indefinitely. In the longer-term a country's expenditure has to conform more closely to the limits set by its economic capacity. (The implications of this point for the U.K. are discussed in the section below on the balance of payments.)

THE IMPACT OF A CHANGE IN RELATIVE PRICES
In the previous section we examined the implications of an imbalance between expenditure on exports and imports at a given level of prices. When changes occur in relative prices the analysis is more complicated. It is no longer possible to draw such firm conclusions about the impact of an imbalance (whether surplus or deficit) on resource allocation.

For example, let us examine the possible consequences of an increase in the relative price of imports. This increase is likely to cause some switching of expenditure from imported goods to domestic substitutes, and thus an increase in the utilization of domestic resources. However although total expenditure on imports may fall, this is by no means certain to happen. Indeed, as we show below, large increases in the prices of fuels and basic materials have resulted in a substantial increase in the U.K.'s expenditure on imports and in the gap between expenditure on imports and exports.

We can see, then, that when there is a change in relative prices, the simple rule that we annunciated above may no longer apply. A deficit (or an increase in the deficit) in payments for imports over exports need not imply a lower level of domestic resource utilization in that period.

The International Economic Transactions of the United Kingdom
Having discussed the factors which exert a major influence on international economic transactions (including, of course, the flow of trade), we now examine the pattern of transactions of the U.K. We shall mainly concentrate on the record since 1972, the year in which sterling was allowed to float. (See Chapter 15.) However it is appropriate to begin by considering a longer period in order to demonstrate the relationship between changes in GDP and international trade. Table 7.2 shows that as GDP increases, the *volume* of both exports and imports of goods

---

* This is a shorthand expression. Since the two axes measure outputs and not inputs, and since international trade occurs we should really say that resource utilization is equivalent to that required to produce OB food and OF machines.

Table 7.2
Changes in GDP and International Trade (U.K., constant prices)

	Index of GDP factor cost (1970=100)	Exports as % of GDP	Imports as % of GDP
1964	87	21.2	22.5
1966	91	22.1	22.3
1968	96	23.5	24.0
1970	100	26.0	25.2
1972	104	27.9	28.7
1974	110	31.5	30.9
1976	109	32.5	30.5

Source: *National Income and Expenditure* (H.M.S.O., 1977).

and services usually increases as a proportion of GDP. This is in line with the trend towards increasing international specialization and trade that we noted above.

The Pattern of Trade
The industrial pattern of the U.K.'s foreign trade indicates a considerable degree of specialization. If we consider the broadest categories first we see from table 7.3 that the value of our imports of goods exceeds the value of our exports, whereas the reverse applies in services. The fact that the surplus on trade in services is so

Table 7.3
International Trade in Goods and Services (U.K., £m., current prices)

	1973	1974	1975	1976
Exports of goods minus imports	−2,334	−5,221	−3,195	−3,592
Exports of services minus imports	689	914	1,100	1,940

Source: *Economic Trends* (H.M.S.O., Sept. 1977).

Table 7.4
Pattern of the External Visible Trade of the United Kingdom (percentage)

	1973	1974	1975	1976
Exports				
Food, beverages and tobacco	7.0	6.5	7.2	6.6
Basic materials	3.5	3.5	2.8	3.0
Fuels	3.0	4.7	4.1	4.9
Manufactures	84.0	83.0	82.6	82.8
Other	2.5	2.3	3.3	2.7
Total	100	100	100	100
Imports				
Food, beverages and tobacco	19.5	16.3	18.0	16.0
Basic materials	12.4	11.2	9.1	10.3
Fuels	10.9	20.0	17.8	18.1
Manufactures	56.2	51.6	53.0	54.2
Others	1.0	0.9	2.0	1.3
Total	100	100	100	100

Source: *Monthly Digest of Statistics* (H.M.S.O., Sept. 1977).

much smaller than the deficit on trade in goods reflects the fact that the total trade is much greater in goods than in services. It is also partly due to the fact that the government sector has a deficit on trade in services; the surplus earned by private sector producers is roughly twice as big as the surplus shown in table 7.3. Important surplus-generating activities include insurance, banking, brokerage and other financial and allied services.

Within the goods category (visible trade) there is again considerable specialization, as shown in table 7.4. Although manufactures are the largest component of both exports and imports, their relative importance is much greater for exports. This reflects both Britain's status as an industrial nation, and her lack of many foodstuffs, basic materials and fuels. The increase in the relative importance of imports of fuels during the period covered by table 7.4 stems from the increase in the price of O.P.E.C. oil. As the output of North Sea oil increases we will find that fuels become a less important import and a more important export.

There is further evidence of specialization within the 'manufacturers' category. Industries in which we earn a healthy surplus include chemicals and engineering, while deficit industries include paper manufactures, clothing and footwear.

THE TERMS OF TRADE

We noted above that the volume and pattern of international trade is influenced by changes in relative prices. The prices of one country's products, in relation to those of another country, may change because of a change in either the ratio of the costs of production in the two countries or in the exchange rate. The terms of trade is a summary measure which takes into account both of these factors. It expresses the relationship between the average price of our exports of goods and of our imports of goods. In each case the average price is a weighted average, the weights being the relative importance of different categories of goods in the base year.

The terms of trade are expressed as an index with a value of 100 in the base year. If the average price of our exports increases in relation to the price of our imports the index rises; if the average price of our exports falls in relation to the price of our imports the index falls.

Table 7.5 shows that between 1970 and 1972 the average price ('unit value') of

Table 7.5

Export and Import Unit Value Index Numbers, United Kingdom (1970=100)

	1971	1972	1973	1974	1975	1976
Exports	105.6	111.1	126.0	162.7	198.5	240.6
Imports	104.7	109.7	139.6	216.7	245.0	299.4
Terms of Trade	100.9	101.3	90.3	75.1	81.0	80.4

Source: *Economic Trends* (H.M.S.O., Sept. 1977).

our exports rose slightly more than the price of imports, causing an improvement in our terms of trade. Thereafter very sharp increases in the price of imports caused adverse movements in the terms of trade in 1973 and 1974. The depreciation of the pound led to an increase in the prices of all imports. In addition, world prices of many commodities, including oil, increased sharply. The combination of these two factors led to an almost four-fold increase in the prices of imported fuels between 1972 and 1974 and to a doubling of the prices of imported basic materials. The adverse movement in the terms of trade was reversed in 1975, but the index remained about 20 per cent below the 1971 figure.

The Balance of Payments

We have concentrated so far on exports and imports of goods and services, and the corresponding monetary flows, because they directly involve the utilization of resources, and so are comparable with the expenditure flows discussed in the previous three chapters. However we have also mentioned other international monetary flows, which do not correspond to flows of goods and services. Since these other flows also have important implications, albeit indirect, for the utilization of resources, it is appropriate that they should be examined in somewhat greater detail.

These various types of international financial flows are brought together in the U.K. balance of payments accounts, a summary version of which is presented in table 7.6. For all items a net figure is presented, i.e. a flow of money into the U.K. is offset against any corresponding outflow.

Table 7.6

Summary Balance of Payments Accounts of the United Kingdom (£mn)

	1973	1974	1975	1976
Visible trade	−2,334	−5,221	−3,195	−3,592
Invisible trade	1,582	1,841	1,560	2,169
Current balance	−752	−3,380	−1,635	−1,423
Investment and other capital flows	26	1,681	360	−1,938
Balancing item and other capital flows[1]	−45	53	−190	−267
Total currency flow – balance for official financing	−771	−1,646	−1,465	−3,628
Drawings on/additions to official reserves	−228	−105	655	853
Other transactions[2]	999	1,751	810	2,775
Total official financing	771	1,646	1,465	3,628

[1] Capital transfers and EEA loss on forward commitments.

[2] Includes transactions with overseas monetary authorities and other foreign currency borrowing by H.M. Government and by the public sector.

Source: *Economic Trends* (H.M.S.O., Sept. 1977).

The first two items relate to the flows to which we gave most attention above. The *visible balance* comprises expenditure on goods. This balance is almost always negative, there having been a surplus in only seven years since 1800. However the deficits in the period covered by table 7.6 were unusually heavy, being mainly due to the steep increases in the prices of fuels and materials, referred to earlier.

Services and transfers – which include trade in services, discussed above, and transfers such as military and economic assistance provided by the government to other countries – together with interest, profits and dividends, comprise the *invisible balance*. This is invariably positive, the size of the surplus frequently being sufficient to outweigh the deficit on visible trade. We had, for example, a surplus on *current account* for each of the four years 1969 to 1972. However this was followed, as can be seen, by four years of deficits, including the record deficit of 1974.

The behaviour of the current account receives a great deal of attention and publicity. This is partly due to the fact that details of the current balance are published monthly, more frequently than any other component of the balance of payments. But it is mainly due to the fact that the current balance is the best indicator of the extent to which the U.K. is 'paying her way' internationally. If the current balance is seriously in deficit for any length of time, the government will be obliged to take remedial action. (The various policies which might be adopted are discussed in subsequent chapters and especially in Chapter 15.)

On the other hand a current deficit, even of the size incurred in 1974, does not imply immediate national bankruptcy. It may be possible to cover the deficit from funds obtained from overseas. Table 7.6 shows that the balance of *investment and other capital flows* was strongly positive in that year. These flows are of various types, including overseas investment in the U.K. private sector – either by buying shares in existing companies or establishing subsidiaries from scratch – deposits with banks and other financial institutions, purchases of U.K. government securities, etc.

Adding together the current balance and the net investment and other capital flows (and also the balancing item which refers to transactions not recorded directly) gives the *total currency flow*. This indicates the total outflow or inflow of money that must be balanced by *official financing*.

In principle official financing may consist entirely of a *change in the official reserves*. However if the total currency flow is strongly negative there may be considerable reluctance to allow the official reserves to take all the strain. For example almost a quarter of the total reserves would have been required to meet the outflow in 1974. Such a reduction might have entailed a further loss of confidence in sterling. Consequently the government preferred to resort to *foreign currency borrowing* (included within *other transactions*). It borrowed sufficient money abroad to cover the outflow and indeed to enable £105 millions to be added to the official reserves. Similarly, when the total currency flow is positive, as in the second part of 1977, the surplus may be used partly to bolster the reserves, and partly to repay money previously borrowed abroad.

THE COSTS OF A CURRENT DEFICIT

As we said above, a substantial current deficit does not imply immediate national bankruptcy. However it does involve substantial costs, not all of which can be deduced from table 7.6. Some of the more important of these costs are as follows.

First, the increased long-term investment in the U.K. that occurred during this period implies an increased outflow in subsequent periods in the form of interest, profits and dividends.

Second, there has already been a substantial increase in interest payments to holders of short-term debt. This is due partly to the fact that a larger volume of debt was issued and partly to the need to offer increased rates of interest in order to attract funds on the scale required.

Third, despite the capital inflows the sterling exchange rate fell dramatically. At the end of 1976 it was some 40 per cent below the level ruling at the end of 1971, and only a partial recovery has occurred since then. The implications of a fall in the exchange rate have already been briefly touched upon and are discussed further in the appendix.

Finally, the unsatisfactory state of the current balance led to a level of economic activity, a degree of resource utilization, lower than might otherwise have occurred. Since government policy had an important role here a full discussion of this point is deferred until later chapters. However we may note here that this particular cost could have been much greater had overseas institutions, both private and public, been less willing to supply funds, short and long-term, to the U.K. A very important factor here was the prospect that North Sea oil would, in the foreseeable future, enable the U.K. to earn a sufficient surplus on current account to considerably reduce her level of indebtedness.

Appendix The Determination of Exchange Rates
The behaviour of exchange rates has received increasing attention in the 1970s as a move has occurred away from fixed and towards floating rates. In this appendix we present a more rigorous analysis of the determination of exchange rates than was given in the main body of the chapter.

The basic determinant of the rate at which one currency exchanges for another is the balance between the demand for and the supply of the two currencies. We can illustrate this by considering the position of sterling in relation to the dollar.

The Demand for Sterling
Pounds are demanded by American importers to pay for products purchased from the U.K. The lower the value of sterling in relation to the dollar, the greater will be the volume of our exports, and so the greater the number of pounds demanded.

To understand why this is so, consider a British company exporting bicycles which it sells on the domestic market for £50. If it wishes to obtain the same revenue per unit from export sales, and the current rate of exchange is £1 = $2, it will set a price of $100. If now the exchange rate falls to £1 = $1.50 it need set a price of only $75 in order to obtain a revenue per unit of £50. As the price is reduced the volume of sales, and therefore the demand for sterling, is likely to rise. If, for example sales increase from 1,000 bicycles to 1,200 a month, the monthly demand for sterling from U.S. importers will rise from £50,000 to £60,000.

Changes in exchange rates are not always fully reflected in export prices. Nevertheless there is usually some effect on prices, and consequently on the volume of exports. The relationship between the exchange rate and the quantity of the currency (sterling) demanded can therefore be represented by a demand curve, of the form shown in figure 7.6. (In the very unlikely event that no change occurred in the quantity of exports demanded, the demand schedule for sterling would be vertical).

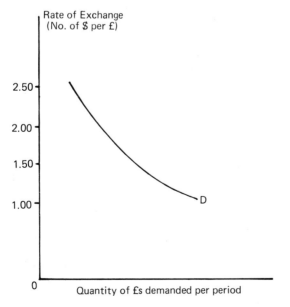

Figure 7.6 The Exchange Rate and the Demand for Sterling

The Supply of Sterling
The change in the exchange rate will also be reflected in the price of our imports from the U.S.A. For example assume that an American manufacturer of golf balls which sell at $1.50 in the U.S.A., sells these for 75 pence in the U.K. when the exchange rate is £1 = $2. If now the exchange rate alters to £1 = $1.50 he will have to adjust the U.K. price to £1 if he is to continue to obtain $1.50 per ball from U.K. sales.

The effect of this price change on the sterling revenue of this firm, and thus on the supply of sterling to the international currency market, will depend upon the price elasticity of demand for golf balls. The price elasticity of demand (PED) is defined as follows:

$$PED = \frac{\Delta Q}{Q} \div \frac{\Delta P}{P}$$

where Q is the (initial) quantity demanded
P is the (initial) price
Δ denotes a small change in the variable.*

The significance of the price elasticity of demand is discussed at length in chapter 23. It is sufficient to note here that there are three alternative situations, three alternative responses to the increase in import prices. First, if demand is elastic, (PED > 1) the revenue of the exporter, and hence the supply of sterling to the currency market, will fall. This situation is represented by the supply curve S_E in figure 7.7. Second, if demand is of unitary elasticity, (PED = 1) revenue and hence the

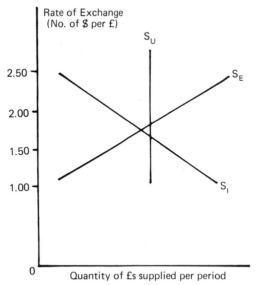

Figure 7.7   The Exchange Rate and the Supply of Sterling

supply of sterling will be unchanged (supply curve S_U). Finally, if demand is inelastic, (PED < 1) the revenue and hence the supply of sterling will increase (supply curve S_I).

* This formula defines the *point* elasticity of demand. The formula for arc elasticity is more complicated.

The Equilibrium Exchange Rate
The equilibrium rate of exchange is the rate at which the demand for sterling equals the supply, i.e. the rate at which the demand and supply curves intersect. In figure 7.8, which assumes that the supply curve is upward sloping, the initial equilibrium rate is A, the quantity of sterling traded being Q.

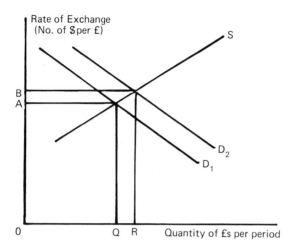

Figure 7.8 The Equilibrium Rate of Exchange

A Change in the Equilibrium Exchange Rate
The equilibrium rate of exchange may alter for various reasons. We consider first an increase in exports of British goods to the U.S.A. This might occur because of an increase in GDP in the U.S.A., an improvement in the quality of British goods, a change in tastes in favour of British goods, and so forth.
    This increase in the volume of our exports implies an increase in the demand

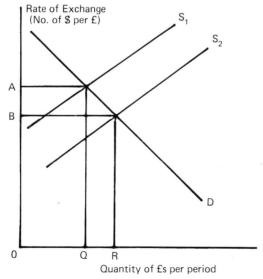

Figure 7.9 An Increase in Imports and the Rate of Exchange

for sterling, as indicated by the shift of the demand curve to D_2 in figure 7.8. The new equilibrium rate of exchange is B, the quantity of sterling traded being R. Note that this increase in the exchange rate implies a rise in the dollar price of U.K. goods. Consequently although the level of exports, and thus the volume of sterling traded, is higher than it was initially, it is not as high as it would have been had the exchange rate not risen. (We can say that the initial income or quality effect is partly offset by the price effect.)

The converse of this situation is illustrated in figure 7.9. Here the U.K.'s demand for imports is assumed to rise because of an income or quality effect. This causes the supply curve of sterling to shift to the right, from S_1 to S_2, and the equilibrium exchange rate to fall from A to B. This fall in the exchange rate implies a rise in the price of imports and a fall in the price of exports. These price effects will partly offset the initial income or quality effect.

We now turn to the situation where the initial change represents a price and not an income or quality effect. Let us assume that the rate of inflation is higher in the U.K. than in the U.S.A. with the result that the prices of British goods rise, relative to the prices of American goods, in both markets. In fact we can assume, for the sake of simplicity, that the rate of inflation in the U.S.A. is zero.

As the U.K.'s exports become dearer, their volume falls. The effect on the total value of exports, and thus on the demand for sterling, depends upon the elasticity of demand for exports. If demand is elastic the value of exports *at any given exchange rate* will fall, i.e. the demand curve for sterling will shift to the left (from D_1 to D_2 in figure 7.10). If demand for exports is inelastic, the demand curve for sterling will shift to the right (D_3). Finally, if demand for exports is of unitary elasticity, the demand curve for sterling will remain at D_1.

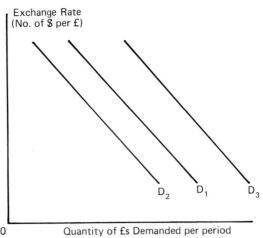

Figure 7.10   The Elasticity of Demand for Exports and the Demand for Sterling

We have assumed that the rate of inflation in the U.S.A. is zero; consequently there will *initially* be no tendency for the price of imports to change. Nevertheless the volume of imports is likely to rise as expenditure is switched from the dearer domestically produced goods. Consequently the total value of imports, and thus the supply of sterling, *at any given exchange rate*, will rise, i.e. the supply curve for sterling will shift to the right.

The possible effects on the exchange rate, via changes in both exports and imports, are illustrated in figure 7.11. With the initial demand for and supply of

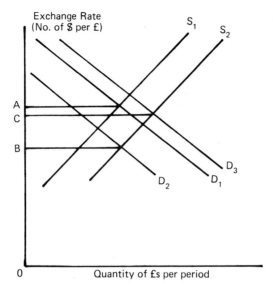

Figure 7.11 The Elasticity of Demand for Exports and the Exchange Rate

sterling represented by D_1 and S_1, the equilibrium exchange rate is A. As U.K. prices rise, the supply curve shifts to S_2. If the demand for U.K. exports is elastic, the demand curve shifts to D_2 and the exchange rate falls from A to B. If the demand for exports is inelastic the demand curve shifts to D_3. This implies a smaller fall in the exchange rate, to C. Indeed the exchange rate may be unchanged, or it could even rise.

Of these three possibilities, the most likely reaction to a rise in the prices of U.K. goods is a fall in the sterling exchange rate. Indeed the *purchasing power parity theory* suggests that the exchange rate would alter so as to compensate exactly for the change in relative prices. Although experience has shown that an exactly compensatory change seldom occurs, the change is certainly likely to be in the direction predicted by this theory.

The exchange rate may also change as a result of a change in the balance of the other monetary flows that we considered above. These flows may themselves be indirectly influenced by changes in imports and exports, or they may change independently of trade flows. There is insufficient space to demonstrate the effects of such changes. But in principle they can all be explained in terms of the demand-supply analysis presented in this appendix. For example, overseas investment in the U.K., e.g. the buying of shares by overseas residents, implies an increase in the demand for sterling. Conversely overseas disinvestment, e.g. the selling of shares, implies an increase in the supply of sterling.

Summary and Conclusions

In this chapter we have examined the reasons for, and potential advantages of, international specialization and trade. We have shown that specialization in ac-cordance with the principle of comparative advantage is likely to lead to an increase in the total output of goods and services. In so far as economic welfare can be equated with the consumption of goods and services we can say that total economic welfare will also be increased. However we should remember that this does not necessarily imply that the economic welfare of every country will increase – a point to which we return in Chapter 15.

We have also explored the implications of international trade for several important aspects of the domestic economy, including the level of resource utilization and the behaviour of prices. This exploration was undertaken partly in general terms and partly with reference to the U.K. economy. This discussion of the U.K. economy completed our examination of the major expenditure flows. Having examined each flow in turn we discuss, in the following chapter, the inter-relationships and interactions among these flows.

ESSAY QUESTIONS

1 Discuss the conditions which are favourable to international specialization and trade.
2 Show by means of a numerical example how economic welfare can be increased by means of international specialization and trade in accordance with the principle of *comparative* advantage. Indicate what factors might prevent trade taking place in accordance with this principle.
3 'The pattern of international trade can be influenced by, but can also influence, the exchange rate.' Discuss.
4 Discuss the implications of a balance of payments deficit for the utilization of domestic resources.
5 What costs might be incurred by a country which experienced a substantial deficit on the balance of payments current account.
6 Explain what factors would determine a country's exchange rate in the absence of government interference.
7 Define the equilibrium rate of exchange and explain what might cause a change in its value.
8 Discuss the possible effects of a substantial rise in the price of United Kingdom exports.
9 How might a marked fall in import prices affect the U.K. economy?

EXERCISES

7.1 Alternative Production Possibilities

Situation	Country X	Country Y
A	100 fish, or	60 fish, or
	10 rabbits	12 rabbits
B	120 fish, or	60 fish, or
	24 rabbits	20 rabbits
C	100 fish, or	50 fish, or
	20 rabbits	10 rabbits

(i) In which of these three situations could total output be increased as a result of international specialization and trade? (ii) In situation B, calculate the difference in output between the following alternatives: (a) each country allocates half its resources to fishing, and half to hunting; (b) X allocates eleven twelfths of its resources to fishing and one twelfth to hunting, while Y specializes completely in hunting. (iii) Assume that domestic costs are as follows: in X one fish costs one 'single' (s), one rabbit costs 5s; in Y one fish costs one 'double' (d), one rabbit costs 3d. At which of the following exchange rates would international specialization and trade take place: 1s = 0.5d, 1s = 0.8d, 1s = 1.5d?

7.2 **Estimated Income and Price Elasticities in Foreign Trade**

Country	Income Elasticities:		Price Elasticities:	
	Exports	Imports	Exports	Imports
Great Britain	0.86	1.51	−0.44	ns
France	1.53	1.62	−2.27	ns
Denmark	1.69	1.31	−0.56	−1.66
Japan	3.55	1.23	−0.80	−0.72

The above estimates were derived by H. Houthakker and S. Magee, and published in the Harvard Review of Economics and Statistics, May 1969. Import, income and price elasticities were calculated by regressing the volume of each country's imports on the growth in its GNP and import prices relative to domestic wholesale.prices. Export elasticities were calculated by regressing export volume on GNP growth in other countries and export prices relative to competitors' prices. (ns indicates that the calculated price elasticity was not statistically significant).

In the light of the above data, comment on the likely relationship between growth in the world economy and the foreign trade of the four countries listed, and on the ease or difficulty with which each country would be able to cure any balance of payments deficit that might arise.

7.3 Indicate which of the factors listed below would cause a change in (a) the visible trade account, (b) the invisible trade account, (c) the investment and other capital flows account, and whether each factor would have a favourable or unfavourable effect on the U.K.'s balance of payments.
   (i) I.C.I. increases its exports of chemicals to Belgium.
   (ii) Encouraged by the success of this venture, I.C.I. builds a factory in Belgium from which to supply the Belgian market.
   (iii) Having lost some of its Belgian market to I.C.I., German chemical manufacturers retaliate by stepping up exports to Britain.
   (iv) A British shipping line wins a contract to transport these chemicals from Hamburg to London.
   (v) In order to try to reduce political unrest, Britain makes a long-term loan to three underdeveloped countries.
   (vi) The initial interest payments on these loans are made by the three countries.
   (vii) A U.S. company buys out the minority British holding in its U.K. subsidiary.
   (viii) The number of British troops stationed in Europe is reduced.
   (ix) Increasing unemployment in the U.S. leads to a reduction in the number of American tourists visiting Britain.
   (x) Elton John and the London Symphony Orchestra both have successful American tours.

7.4 Calculate, from the data contained in table 7.7, the following items: (a) the visible balance, (b) the invisible balance, (c) the balance on current account, (d) the total currency flow. Given the additional information that Brittanica added £500 millions to the official reserves, calculate (e) other transactions.

Table 7.7
The Balance of Payments Accounts of Brittanica

	£mn
Exports of goods	3,000
Exports of services	1,600
Imports of goods	4,500
Imports of services	800
Investment and other capital flows (net)	1,700

7.5 'Since March, 1975, the pound has depreciated by more than a quarter against the U.S. dollar and by over 20 per cent against the weighted average of leading trading currencies.

Following the fall in the pound's value last week, *Financial Times* correspondents in London and overseas asked companies what effect the fall in the pound was having on the pricing and volume of their business.

The principal conclusions are that:

1. Most exporters either cannot, or do not want to, reduce foreign currency prices to reflect the decline in sterling.

2. Companies do, however, feel that they can hold foreign prices for some time to come and this should make them progressively more competitive.

3. Almost all industries fear that increased raw material import prices could cancel out what competitive advantage has been gained.'

The above passage was extracted from the *Financial Times*, 26.4.76. (i) How would you explain companies' pricing policies? (ii) Given the conclusions presented in the passage, discuss the probable effects of the depreciation of sterling.

CHAPTER EIGHT

Total Expenditure Revisited

Introduction

THE title of this chapter refers to the fact that we have already discussed, in Chapter 3, the total flow of expenditure in the U.K. Following this discussion we examined, in the following four chapters, the determinants of each of the four major expenditure flows. We now put together the pieces and consider once more the overall picture, i.e. we are again concerned with total expenditure. However the focus of our attention in this chapter is quite different from what it was in Chapter 3. We shall be concerned here with the concept of the equilibrium level of national income and with changes in that level. We shall also explore, towards the end of the chapter, the concept of the optimum level of expenditure.

A NOTE ON DEFINITIONS

In Chapter 3 we presented several alternative measures of economic activity. We showed that one of these measures, national income, as officially defined in the national accounts, is a good indicator of the standard of living that is sustainable in the long term. However, better indicators of current living standards are gross domestic product and gross national product, with GNP probably being the more reliable indicator of future levels of consumption.

Consequently we shall use GNP as our measure of economic activity. However we shall follow the convention, long-established in the economics literature, of using the terms gross national income and national income as being synonymous with GNP (as we noted in Chapter 3, some writers refer to national income as defined in the national accounts – i.e. GNP minus capital consumption – as net national income).

Equilibrium National Income

An equilibrium situation is said to exist when *planned* expenditure in one period $(t+1)$ equals (gross) national income in the previous period (t). This is illustrated in figure 8.1. From a national income (Y) of £100 million in period t, expenditure (E) of £100 million in period $t+1$ is planned. Assuming that producers are able to supply the goods and services required, these expenditure plans will be fulfilled. Consequently national income in period $t+1$ will again be £100 million and the process, the circular flow of income, will continue at this level. Furthermore, provided that the price level is unchanged, the real level of economic activity will be unchanged.

A Changing Level of National Income

What happens when the conditions for equilibrium are not fulfilled, i.e. where E_{t+1} does not equal Y_t? Let us consider first the situation where planned expenditure is less than the national income of the previous period. In figure 8.2 planned

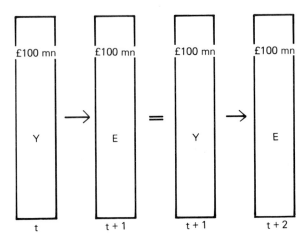

Figure 8.1 Equilibrium National Income

expenditure is assumed to be 80 per cent of national income in the previous period. It can be seen that national income declines from £100 million in period t to £80 million in period t + 1 and to £64 million in period t + 2. (With an unchanged price level a corresponding decline in the real level of economic activity would occur).

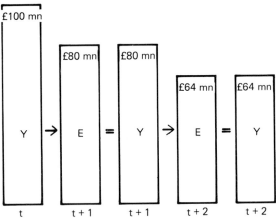

Figure 8.2 Decreasing National Income

If, on the other hand, planned expenditure exceeds national income in the previous period – as it may if consumers plan to draw on past savings – national income will rise. However as we pointed out in Chapter 7, once expenditure reaches the limit set by economic capacity, a further rise in real expenditure can be achieved only by running a deficit on international trade.

The three alternative situations that we have examined here can be summarized by means of a 45° diagram. In figure 8.3 the 45° line indicates the points at which planned expenditure in period t + 1 and national income in period t are equal. The levels of planned expenditure at various levels of income are indicated by the expenditure function, E. It can be seen that the only level of income at which planned expenditure (t + 1) and income (t) are equal is Y_E; i.e. this denotes the equilibrium level of income. If planned expenditure is above national income, e.g. at income

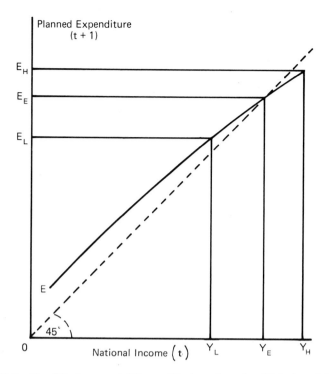

Figure 8.3 Equilibrium and Disequilibrium Levels of National Income

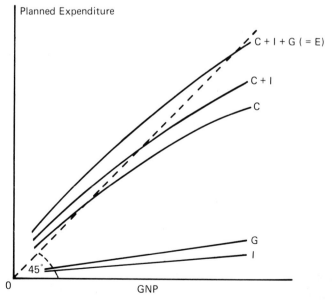

Figure 8.4 The Derivation of the Planned Expenditure Function

Y_L, income will rise. If planned expenditure is below national income, e.g. at Y_H, national income will fall.

The Shape of the Expenditure Function

In order to explain the shape of the expenditure function shown in figure 8.3 we can draw upon the analysis presented in Chapters 4 to 7.

In Chapter 4 we showed that a change in GNP is normally accompanied by a smaller absolute change in consumers' expenditure, and that the consumption function could take the form indicated by line C in figure 8.4. In Chapters 5 and 6 we showed that both government consumption and total investment expenditure were likely to increase with GNP. These forms of expenditure are represented in figure 8.4 by G and I respectively. For the sake of simplicity we have assumed that both G and I grow at a constant rate as GNP increases.

In order to obtain the total expenditure function we simply aggregate the three curves vertically. In figure 8.4 we have done this in stages, first adding I to C, and then G to (C + I). The resulting (planned) expenditure function E, corresponds to that in figure 8.3.

It will be noticed that we have not included in figure 8.4 a schedule relating to expenditure on exports, even though this has been identified as one of the four components of total expenditure. This is because, as we saw in Chapter 3, when GNP is calculated, expenditure on imports is offset against expenditure on exports, a net figure being included in total expenditure. We cannot say a priori whether this figure is likely to be positive or negative. We have therefore assumed that the net flow is zero (as it would be for the world economy).*

With our present approach, if we wished to depict the situation for a particular economy which had a surplus, i.e. whose exports of goods and services exceeded imports, we would include this as a fourth positive expenditure flow. This would cause the total expenditure function to shift upwards. Conversely a deficit, an excess of imports over exports, would shift the function downwards.

Autonomous and Induced Expenditure

Let us now examine what happens to GNP when a change occurs in one of these expenditure flows. For example, assume that the discovery of vast mineral reserves increases the prospective profitability of investment, and thus the volume of investment expenditure. Since the increase in investment is *not* the result of an increase in income we define it as an *autonomous* change in investment.

The initial results of an autonomous increase in investment in period t are shown in figure 8.5. The additional expenditure increases the incomes of households (in their roles as suppliers of labour), firms (who supply other inputs), and the government (in the form of taxation). The additional income obtained by these three groups is shown in the first column. In the second column we show the change in planned expenditure which results from the change in income.

Some of the money accruing to households and firms is saved – this is designated as S. The rest is spent; spending by households on consumption goods is designated as C, and spending by firms (investment spending) as I. Again, of the money received by the government, some is spent (G), and the rest (T) is retained. The

---

* An alternative approach would be to interpret C, G and I as referring to expenditure on domestically produced goods only – this would be equivalent to subtracting imports from these expenditure flows. Exports could then be added as a fourth flow. However this approach simply complicates the diagrammatic presentation of the analysis.

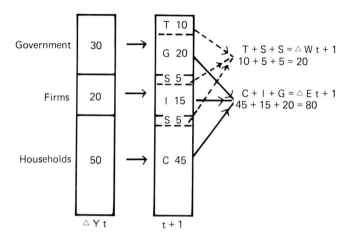

Figure 8.5 The Consequences of an Autonomous Increase in Investment

additional spending resulting from the autonomous investment expenditure is known as *induced* expenditure.

The Marginal Propensity to Spend

If we add together the amounts spent $-C+I+G-$ and express this as a proportion of the initial increase in GNP we obtain the marginal propensity to spend (MPE). Of the additional 100 units of income received, 80 are spent, i.e. MPE$=0.8$. (Note that we have assumed here that the additional spending on exports equals the additional spending on imports. If exports had exceeded imports by 5, MPE would have been 0.85; conversely if imports had exceeded exports by 5, MPE would have been 0.75). These expenditure flows are fed back into the circular flow of income and together with the continuing autonomous expenditure, give rise to further induced expenditure.

This is shown in figure 8.6. Starting with an increase in investment of 100 in period t, and with MPE$=0.8$, induced expenditure in period $t+1$ is 80. Since the continuing autonomous expenditure is 100, total expenditure in period $t+1$ is 180

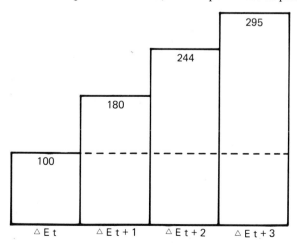

Figure 8.6 The Continuing Effect of an Autonomous Increase in Investment

units greater than in period $t-1$. In period $t+2$ the total induced expenditure is 144 $(=0.8 \times 180)$, and in period $t+3$ it is 195.2 $(=0.8 \times 244)$.

The series could be continued indefinitely. Fortunately there is an easy method of calculating what the eventual outcome would be at the end of the process. This involves the concept of the multiplier.

The Multiplier
The multiplier is defined as the ratio of the final change in GNP resulting from an autonomous change in expenditure, to that autonomous change in expenditure. Using symbols:

$$K = \frac{\Delta GNP}{\Delta E}$$

where K is the multiplier
     Δ GNP is the final change in GNP
     Δ E is the autonomous change in expenditure.

Here the autonomous change occurred in investment. Exactly the same analysis would apply to an autonomous change in any of the expenditure flows.

The value of the multiplier is given by the expression

$$K = \frac{1}{1 - MPE}$$

In the above example, with a marginal propensity to spend of 0.8, we have:

$$K = \frac{1}{1 - MPE} = \frac{1}{1 - 0.8} = \frac{1}{0.2} = 5$$

Applying this value of the multiplier to the autonomous change in expenditure of 100 tells us that the eventual change in GNP would be 500 $(=5 \times 100)$, of which 400 would be induced expenditure. This is illustrated in figure 8.7, in which t_n denotes the period in which the multiplier effect would be completed.

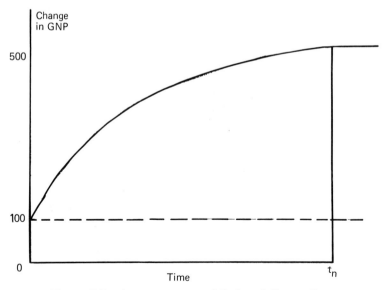

Figure 8.7   Autonomous and Induced Expenditure

AN ALTERNATIVE METHOD OF CALCULATING THE VALUE OF THE MULTIPLIER

An alternative, simpler, method of calculating the value of the multiplier involves the concept of withdrawals. Withdrawals are simply those parts of an increase in GNP that are *not* passed on into the circular flow. Figure 8.5 shows that with an initial increase in income of 100 total withdrawals, comprising saving (S) and taxation (T) equal 20. This means that the marginal propensity to withdraw $= 0.2$ (20/100).*

The simpler form of the multiplier is:

$$K = \frac{1}{MPW} = \frac{1}{0.2} = 5.$$

Again, therefore, we arrive at the result that expenditure would eventually rise by 500, comprising the autonomous increase of 100 plus the induced expenditure of 400. At this point the process would cease, i.e. equilibrium would be re-established.

An Alternative Definition of Equilibrium National Income

Earlier in this chapter we defined equilibrium national income as the level at which planned expenditure equals income. We are now able to provide an alternative definition. We showed in the above example that equilibrium is re-established when induced expenditure equals 400. When this occurs total withdrawals will equal 100. This is illustrated in figure 8.8, in which t_n has the same meaning as in figure 8.7, i.e. in period t_n the total additional income (ΔY) is 500. In the following period, with $MPE = 0.8$, induced expenditure (IE) is 400; consequently withdrawals are 100.

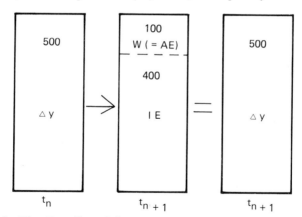

Figure 8.8   The Equality of Autonomous Expenditure and Withdrawals

This situation is on of equilibrium because total planned expenditure (and income) in period t_{n+1} is 500. This occurs because withdrawals are exactly balanced by the autonomous expenditure (AE). Consequently we can say that if the equilibrium national income is disturbed by a change in autonomous expenditure,

---

* It must again be remembered that we have assumed the change in exports and imports to be equal. As we noted above, if the change in imports had exceeded exports by 5, MPE would have been reduced to 0.75. The other way of looking at this is that this deficit in foreign trade would represent a third type of withdrawal from the circular flow. Total withdrawals would then amount to 25, and the MPW to 0.25.

equilibrium will be re-established at the level of income at which the change in autonomous expenditure equals the change in withdrawals.

A DIAGRAMMATIC REPRESENTATION OF THE MULTIPLIER PROCESS
The operation of the multiplier process is illustrated in figure 8.9. The initial expenditure schedule E_t gives rise to an equilibrium national income Y_t. Subsequently the investment schedule rises from I_t to I_{t+1}, and the expenditure schedule from E_t to E_{t+1}. This causes a rise in the equilibrium level of national income from Y_t to Y_{t+1}.

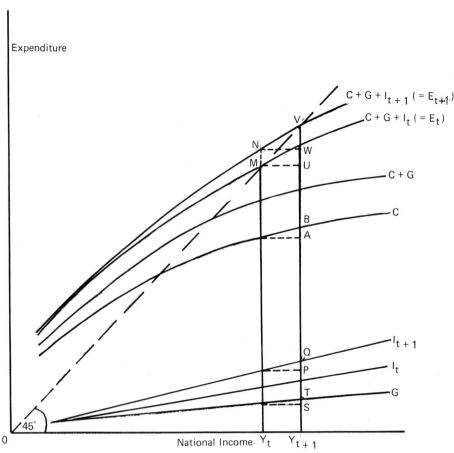

Figure 8.9 The Multiplier

It can be seen that the rise in national income $(Y_t Y_{t+1})$ is greater than the initial increase in expenditure (MN). The ratio of these two quantities, i.e.

$$\frac{Y_t\ Y_{t+1}}{MN}$$

is the value of the multiplier. The final increase in GNP, $Y_t Y_{t+1}$ ($= UV$), comprises the autonomous increase in expenditure, MN, plus the induced expenditure WV, comprising expenditure on: consumption (AB), investment (PQ) and government current expenditure on goods and services (ST).

The Optimum Level of Expenditure

In Chapter 2 we suggested that the desirability of any level of expenditure could be determined only in relation to the country's economic capacity; the higher that capacity the higher the optimum level of expenditure. In that chapter we adopted as our main criterion the utilization of resources. The implication of our analysis was that the highest possible level of resource utilization should be sought. We must now widen our frame of reference. While continuing to recognize resource utilization as an important criterion we must also look at the implications of expenditure for the behaviour of prices (which in turn has implications for the behaviour of the balance of payments).

In order to show the effect of a change in expenditure on prices we use a 45° diagram, which shows the total *value* of income and expenditure, in conjunction

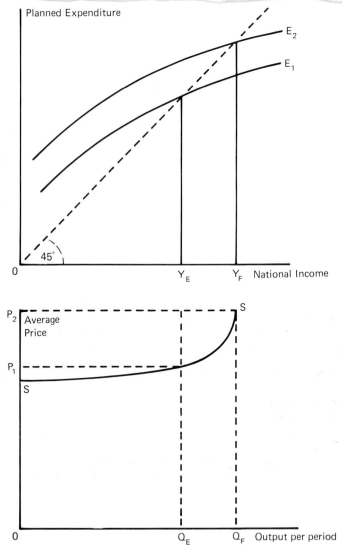

Figure 8.10 The Effect of an Increase in Expenditure on Price and Output

with a second diagram plotting price and output. In figure 8.10 the equilibrium level of income is Y_E. This corresponds to output Q_E in the bottom diagram, which is supplied at an average price level P_1.

Since Q_E is below the full employment level of output Q_F, i.e. since some resources are unemployed, we might think it desirable that expenditure should increase. An upward shift in the expenditure function from E_1 to E_2 would result in income reaching equilibrium at the full employment level Y_F, (the corresponding output being Q_F). However, the increase in expenditure would also result in the average price level rising from P_1 to P_2. (In other words the increase in real national income would be less than the increase in money national income Y_E Y_F). In evaluating the desirability of the increased expenditure the increase in resource utilization has to be weighed against the disadvantage of an increase in the price level.

This 'trade-off' is a consideration fundamental to a wide range of government policies designed to influence the level of expenditure. It is therefore important that the conditions of the trade-off should be specified as carefully as possible. The major aspects to be considered are as follows:

(i) Most obviously, by how much would the rate of inflation be likely to increase in response to a given increase in capacity utilization? (We do not suggest that the increase would necessarily be as dramatic as suggested by figure 8.10).

(ii) What would be the effects, both internal and external, of an increase in the inflation rate?

(iii) What mix of policies might be adopted in order to increase expenditure, and what would be the implications of these policies for other possible objectives such as the redistribution of income and wealth?

We shall examine these questions in succeeding chapters. We shall also consider the argument that there is in fact no long-term trade-off between full employment and inflation – that a policy which sacrifices price stability for a short-term increase in employment will eventually lead to a situation where both unemployment and the rate of inflation are higher than they would otherwise have been.

ESSAY QUESTIONS

1 Define equilibrium national income and discuss the factors which might cause the equilibrium level of national income to change.

2 Explain how equilibrium is re-established when planned expenditure in a given period differs from national income in the previous period.

3 Draw a diagram to show an expenditure function and explain why it assumes that shape.

4 Distinguish between autonomous and induced expenditure and discuss the significance of the distinction.

5 Examine the significance of the multiplier in the determination of national income.

6 Discuss the relationships between consumption and investment.

7 Explain what you understand by the term 'the optimum level of expenditure'.

EXERCISES

8.1 (i) Calculate on the basis of the data in table 8.1, the average propensity to consume when national income is (a) £2,000 mn., (b) £8,000 mn.

Table 8.1
A Hypothetical Schedule of Income and Consumption

National Income (£000 mn)	Consumption (£000 mn)
0	1.00
1	1.75
2	2.50
3	3.25
4	4.00
5	4.75
6	5.50
7	6.25
8	7.00
9	7.75

(ii) Calculate the marginal propensity to consume when national income is
    (a) £3,000 mn., (b) £6,000 mn.
(iii) What would be the equilibrium level of income in a closed economy with
     no government sector if investment were (a) zero, (b) £1,000 mn?
(iv) Calculate the value of the multiplier.

8.2 An investment project generates an additional 100 units of gross income, of
which 80 per cent comprises income from employment and 20 per cent income
from profits.
    Tax is levied at the following rates:

on earned income	25%
on profits	50%
on expenditure (except imports)	20%

The marginal propensity to consume is $\frac{2}{3}$ of disposable income. One quarter
of expenditure comprises imports, (which are not subject to tax). Companies
distribute all their after-tax profits as dividends, (not subject to further taxation).

(i) What proportion of the gross income derived from the initial investment
   is (a) paid as taxation (b) saved, (c) spent on imports?
(ii) By how much will income eventually rise following the additional in-
    vestment?
(iii) Describe in a few sentences why the operation of the accelerator might
     be expected to lead to a rise in income different from that calculated
     above.

8.3 The personal savings ratio measures the proportion of total personal disposable income that is not spent by the consumer.
   (i) How would you account for the trend in the ratio, shown in figure 8.11?
   (ii) Would you say that this trend was desirable or undesirable?
   (iii) Why is it desirable that the government should be able to forecast the
   behaviour of the savings ratio?

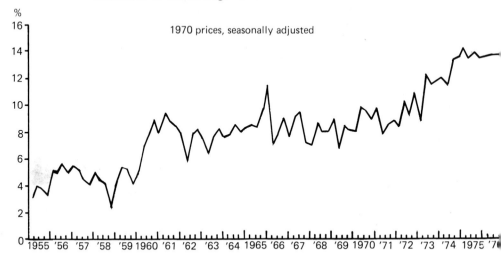

Figure 8.11   U.K. Personal Savings Ratio

CHAPTER NINE

The Relationship between Unemployment and Inflation

Introduction

WE demonstrated in the previous chapter that a 'trade-off' may exist between unemployment and inflation, i.e. the higher the level of unemployment the lower the rate of inflation; the lower the level of unemployment the higher the rate of inflation. We suggested that one of the reasons for an increase in the level of prices might be that total planned expenditure, (sometimes known as aggregate monetary demand) might be too high in relation to the country's productive capacity. We begin this chapter by exploring in greater detail the mechanisms whereby an increase in planned expenditure may lead to a rise in prices. (We assume that the money supply expands sufficiently to permit expenditure plans to be fulfilled, i.e. the increase in planned expenditure is transformed into an increase in aggregate monetary demand. The money supply is discussed in detail in Chapter 12.)

Total Expenditure and Inflation

Three processes can be identified whereby an increase in expenditure may lead to an increase in the rate of inflation. First, producers, taking advantage of the increased demand, may increase the prices of goods and services. Subsequently suppliers of inputs may react by demanding, and obtaining, higher rewards. For example, workers may demand higher wages in order to compensate for the higher prices of the products that they buy, i.e. to prevent their real income from falling.

Second, in order to obtain the additional resources required to meet the increased demand for goods and services, producers may bid more vigorously for these resources – offering higher rates of pay to labour, being willing to pay more for raw materials, and so forth. They are willing to do this because they believe that they can pass on the additional costs in the form of higher prices. (In the intervening period these additional costs may be financed out of reserves or by borrowing.)

Finally, suppliers of inputs – labour, materials, etc. – realizing that the demand for goods and services has increased, may demand higher rewards. They believe that these demands will be met because producers are able to recoup their higher costs by increasing product prices.

Although separable in principle, in practice all of these processes may occur more or less simultaneously when expenditure increases, one process being prominent in one sector of the economy, another process in another sector. Although prices may react more quickly with the first process than the other two, all three result in higher costs to producers and higher prices to consumers.

It is possible that an increase in costs and prices will be the only effect of the increase in expenditure. Indeed if there is no spare capacity in the economy, no unused resources which can be utilized in order to increase the volume of output, an increase in prices is the only way in which plans for an increase in the total value of expenditure can be fulfilled.* We usually denote such a situation as one of full employment. Referring back to the previous chapter, the full employment level of output is designated Q_F in figure 8.10.

However it is more likely that an increase in expenditure will be associated – at least in the short term – with an increase in costs and prices and in output, and hence a reduction in unemployment. Indeed some economists have claimed to have discovered a clear relationship between the level of unemployment on the one hand and the rate of change in costs and prices on the other hand.

The Relationship between Unemployment and Inflation

The best known attempt to quantify the trade-off, i.e. to measure the sensitivity of the inflation rate to changes in unemployment, is that made by the late Professor A. W. Phillips. In a study of the British economy between 1862 and 1958, Phillips found that a close relationship existed between the level of unemployment and the rate of change of money wages. Since, when a long period is considered, there is a strong correlation between money wages and prices, Phillips's findings can be related to the trade-off between unemployment and inflation. The nature of the relationship found by Phillips is illustrated in figure 9.1.

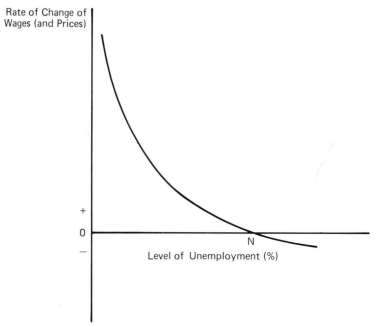

Figure 9.1   The Relationship between Unemployment and Inflation

There is a level of unemployment, indicated by point N, at which prices are stable. At higher levels of unemployment prices fall. At lower levels of unemployment – the situation with which we are concerned – prices rise. Moreover the lower the level of unemployment the more sensitive are prices to a given fall in unemployment; the Phillips curve becomes steeper as it approaches the point

* Some increase in the volume of output may occur via an increase in productivity, especially over a long period. This would, of course, tend to reduce the inflationary impact of the increase in expenditure (as would an increase in imports).

of origin. Putting the relationship in a more general form we can say that the higher the existing level of capacity utilization, the greater will be the rate of increase in prices for a given increase in capacity utilization.

Shifts in the Phillips Curve
It appears that the relationship between unemployment and changes in wage rates or prices, suggested by Phillips, underwent a substantial change in the early 1970s. Phillips's results implied that at an unemployment rate of $5\frac{1}{2}$ per cent wage rates would be stable, whereas when unemployment reached this level during 1976, wage increases well into double figures were being registered.

It may be possible to explain this apparently contradictory evidence in one of two ways. First, the Phillips curve might have shifted to the right, so that a given level of unemployment has become associated with a higher rate of inflation than previously (figure 9.2). This shift could occur as a result of increasing imperfections

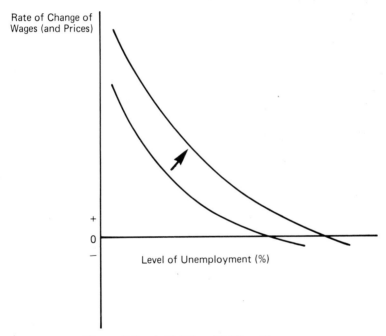

Figure 9.2   A Shifting Phillips Curve

in the labour market – greater bargaining power by trade unions, higher unemployment and other social security benefits, redundancy pay which enables workers to be rather more 'choosy' when considering new jobs, etc.

The second explanation, which is in fact quite consistent with the first, is that when negotiating pay increases, workers now give more weight to the behaviour of prices. If they begin to take into account price increases that have occurred in past periods this will in itself be sufficient to shift the curve to the right. We can say that the 'money illusion' has ceased to operate, i.e. workers have begun to bargain in real, rather than money, terms.*

* Since we now have two independent variables – the level of unemployment and prior changes in prices, the situation cannot be adequately represented by a two-dimensional diagram. Figure 9.2 should be seen as a simplified illustration of this situation.

The ultimate stage in this process of bargaining in real terms is reached when workers take into account, not only past price increases but also anticipated increases, i.e. increases expected to occur. The increasing importance of price anticipations could certainly explain the shift in the Phillips curve, but in fact the whole situation can now become unstable, with the curve continually shifting at each stage of the wage-bargaining process, i.e. an inflationary spiral may arise.

Before we leave this question we should point out that the analysis has been at a highly aggregated level – we have talked in terms of unemployment and capacity utilization as a whole. In practice the degree of capacity utilization may vary considerably between different sectors of the economy. Shortages of some types of labour or equipment may occur while the stock of other types remains adequate to meet the demand. The term 'bottleneck' is sometimes used to describe a shortage of capacity in a particular sector. The greater the number of bottlenecks the more likely it is that prices will rise in response to a given increase in expenditure.

The Effects of Inflation

We showed in the previous section that if expectations of price increases become built into the wage bargaining process an inflationary spiral may result. Such a situation is obviously very serious. However even if the rate of inflation does not accelerate in this way, even if prices rise by a constant percentage each year, the consequences both internal and external, may be undesirable. We start by examining the consequences internal to an economy.

The Internal Effects of Inflation

Two sets of internal effects can be identified. The first is the undesirable psychological effects of rising prices. These effects have been neglected by many economic commentators, who argue that if psychological effects are sufficiently important they will result in economic responses. For example as noted above, wage-earners will demand higher wages to compensate for higher prices; or, as noted in Chapter 4, rising prices or the fear of unemployment may affect the community's propensity to consume.

However we would argue that inflation does have psychological costs for which it is not possible to obtain economic compensation. In particular, some psychological discomfort may be felt by housewives because of rising prices, regardless of whether they are receiving a higher housekeeping allowance in compensation.

The second set of effects arises from the fact that not all prices, and perhaps even more important not all incomes, adjust to inflation at the same rate. Even if price expectations do not lead to an increase in the rate of inflation overall, some groups of workers, e.g. those with very strong unions, may be better able than others to protect and improve their real incomes. (This might also, of course, apply in the absence of inflation.) Again, public sector employees have sometimes, although not always, found it difficult to protect their real incomes under inflationary conditions, because of the role of the state or the government as an employer. Finally, the incomes of some groups of non-wage earners, such as pensioners, may lag behind prices.*

It is sometimes said that borrowers (debtors) benefit and lenders (creditors) suffer from inflation. The reasoning behind this statement can be easily illustrated by means of a simple example. If a man borrows from his bank £1,000 for a period of a year, and during this year prices rise by 10 per cent, then when the money

* Some occupational pensions may not be adjusted at all for changes in the price level.

is repaid it is 'worth' 10 per cent less than when it was borrowed, i.e. it will buy 10 per cent fewer goods.

The lender will, however, have suffered only insofar as he failed to anticipate and adjust to inflation. If he knew that prices were likely to rise by 10 per cent, then he should have charged the borrower a rate of interest, say 15 per cent, that took this into account. (If the borrower realized that the real rate would be reduced considerably by virtue of rising prices, he should be willing to pay a higher nominal rate.)

Of course people's expectations concerning the rate of inflation may prove to be inaccurate. But in principle this is just as likely to benefit lenders as borrowers, since inflation may be higher or lower than anticipated. The fact that lenders have tended to suffer from the high rates of inflation in the 1970s is due less to errors in prediction than to a failure of the financial system to adjust to the higher rates. Lenders, and especially individuals with private savings, have had to lend at negative real rates of interest because of a lack of better alternatives. The highest yielding savings medium for the private individual in the mid 1970s was the index linked bond (and its equivalents) issued by the government. Since the yield was tied to changes in the index of retail prices the real rate of interest was zero.

Although one can find numerous examples of groups who have suffered as a result of inflation, these internal effects are clearly very dependent upon institutional arrangements, e.g. retirement pensioners in the U.K. are now better protected than they were previously, by virtue of a government commitment to review pension rates twice a year in the light of changes in prices and earnings. It is possible in principle to evolve a set of arrangements whereby the disadvantageous internal effects of inflation are largely eliminated. However inflation also has external effects which may be very damaging to a country's economy.

The External Effects of Inflation

If prices are rising at a higher rate in one country than in other countries the volume of that country's exports is likely to fall, and of its imports to increase. (This assumes that the prices of internationally traded products change in roughly the same way as the prices of all other products and also that these changes are not fully offset by movements in exchange rates.) It is also likely that the *value* of exports will fall in relation to the value of imports, although this will depend upon the elasticities of demand (see Chapter 15). Since trade in goods and services is an important element in our balance of payments, a deficit in this trade will tend to lead to a worsening of our balance of payments position. This tendency will be strengthened insofar as other international financial flows are influenced by the balance of our trade in goods and services. As we pointed out in Chapter 7, a country whose inflation rate is significantly above those of its main competitors does not find it easy to attract the funds of overseas investors.

Furthermore, even if the effect of inflation on the volume of trade and on the balance of payments was not adverse, the consequences for employment would still be unfavourable. A fall in the volume of exports implies less employment in export industries. Similarly a rise in the volume of imports implies less employment in domestic industries competing with these imports.

This implies that, in evaluating the trade-off between inflation and unemployment, the scales will be balanced more heavily against inflation than they would if only the internal effects were considered. This is not only because inflation may lead to balance of payments problems but also because, even in the absence of such problems, it can lead to a reduction in employment.

Favourable Effects of Inflation

Are there any considerations that we have not yet taken into account which might tilt the balance more in favour of inflation? It is sometimes claimed that mildly inflationary conditions are desirable since they provide a stimulus to producers to increase their capacity, without giving rise to serious problems of the kind discussed above.

Gently rising prices may indeed be preferable to falling prices accompanied by reductions in output and employment, as has occurred in some periods in the (rather distant) past. But will mild inflation in fact provide a stimulus to producers? It seems that this will occur only if rising prices are not accompanied by costs rising at the same rate. In this situation the stimulus is really a prospective increase in profitability. Moreover the other side of this coin is a prospective fall in the real income of wage earners. It is therefore doubtful whether we can conclude that, overall, gently rising prices are to be preferred to stable prices.

The Effects of Inflation: Summary

Although inflation may have undesirable internal consequences, the internal economic effects have normally been less serious than the external effects, at least as far as the U.K., is concerned. The U.K. has repeatedly encountered balance of payment difficulties in the post-war years and these have often, although not always, been associated with a rate of inflation in excess of those of our competitors.

The Long-term Trade Off between Unemployment and Inflation

While all economists would agree that governments can usually reduce unemployment in the short term by policies designed to increase expenditure, there has been a considerable amount of controversy as to whether the reduction can be sustained in the longer-term, given that it is likely to be accompanied by an increase in the rate of inflation.

Two possible reasons for doubting the efficacy of such a policy have been suggested in earlier sections. First, if price expectations (or even simply a desire to obtain compensation for past price increases) become built into the wage bargaining process, an inflationary spiral may result which eventually forces the government to take steps to reduce the level of expenditure.

A formal model of this process has been developed by two American economists, Milton Friedman and Edward Phelps. They have argued that there is in any economy a 'natural' rate of unemployment (termed the 'normal' rate by some other commentators). If unemployment is at this level the rate of inflation will be constant (but not necessarily zero). If unemployment is below this level, the rate of inflation will accelerate. This situation is illustrated in figure 9.3, where U is the natural rate of unemployment. The vertical line drawn through U indicates that any (constant) rate of price change, positive, zero or negative, could be associated with the natural rate of unemployment.

We discuss in the appendix to this chapter what might be involved in the empirical testing of the concept of the natural rate of unemployment. It is sufficient to note here that the way in which the concept is formulated makes it difficult to provide strong empirical support. On the other hand recent experience, especially in the U.K., does suggest that the concept has some validity. Attempts by successive U.K. governments to reduce unemployment by increasing expenditure have usually been unsuccessful, except for very short periods, and have, moreover, led to (or at least been accompanied by) accelerating inflation.

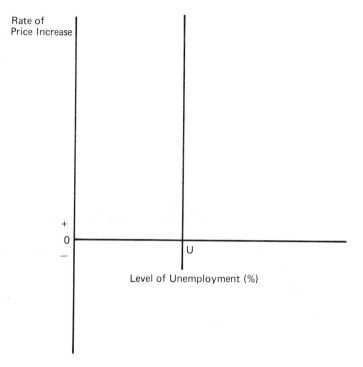

Figure 9.3   The Natural Rate of Unemployment

We have noted a second reason why it may not be possible to permanently reduce unemployment by increasing expenditure. We have pointed out that even if it does not accelerate, inflation may have undesirable external consequences, in that it may lead to a balance of payments deficit which requires a reduction in expenditure. At one time it was believed that a reduction in expenditure for this reason would be required only if a country had adopted a policy of fixed exchange rates. However recent experience suggests that even if exchange rates are allowed to float, governments may still be forced to adopt expenditure-reducing policies. (This is discussed further in Chapter 15.)

Alternative Expenditure-inducing Policies
Since we discuss in the following chapters the various policies that the government might adopt in order to effect an increase in expenditure, it is not appropriate to discuss these policies in detail here. However it will be useful to make a few general points concerning the choice between alternative policies, since different policies may have different consequences which should be taken into account in considering the trade-off between inflation and unemployment.

First, there may be differences in the long-term effects of different policies. For example consider the choice between policies designed to increase either investment or consumption expenditure. Although the short-term effects may be very similar, investment expenditure is much more likely than consumption to lead to an increase in the country's economic capacity and hence reduce the likelihood of inflationary pressures arising in the future.

Second, different policies may be viewed differently by the community, and these differences in view may themselves have important economic implications.

For example, in order to increase the level of private consumption the government may reduce taxation, whereas an alternative policy involving an increase in government expenditure is unlikely to allow tax reductions and indeed may even involve an increase in taxation. Some members of the community, and in particular those who benefit least from the public expenditure, are likely to favour the first alternative. This preference might find economic expression in terms of less militancy in pursuing wage claims should this alternative be adopted.

Finally, we should remember that whichever policy governments might *prefer* to adopt, they may be forced by circumstances to adopt other policies. For example, while the government might prefer to encourage exports it may instead place greater reliance on changes in government expenditure, simply because its influence on this form of expenditure is more direct and immediate. Again it may wish to increase tariffs in order to reduce the volume of imports, but be afraid to do so because of the danger of retaliation by other countries, or because of its treaty commitments.

Altering the Terms of the Trade-off

The analysis of the preceding section would suggest that the terms of the trade-off between unemployment and inflation may be influenced by the choice made by the government among alternative expenditure-inducing policies. The terms of the trade-off may, perhaps, be influenced to an even greater extent by quite different types of policies. We now outline two such policies; first those involving the control of prices and incomes; second policies designed to increase economic capacity.

Prices and Incomes Policies

These policies represent an attempt to intervene directly in the inflationary process. The intervention is most direct when controls are exercised on prices. Intervention is somewhat less direct if controls are exercised only on income, but controls on wages, the most important form of income, can be expected quickly to affect the rate of price change. In practice policies have normally attempted to control both prices and incomes.

The attractions of such policies are clear. The modification of inflationary pressures allows a higher level of employment to be maintained. Balance of payments problems are less likely to arise since the price competitiveness of our goods improves – this in itself contributes to improved employment prospects. Finally, since the reduction in the rate of increase in incomes is balanced by a reduction in the rate of price increase, the policies should not adversely affect *real* incomes.

Despite these attractions, prices and incomes policies have been criticized for a number of reasons. First, some of those who are affected by the policies – including both wage-earners and employers – complain that the policies operate unfairly in the sense that some people suffer more than others as a result of the imposition of controls.

Second, quite apart from these undesirable effects, the policies have been criticized as interfering with what is seen as the 'right' to engage in free collective bargaining between representatives of employers and employees. This right is usually claimed most vociferously by employees' representatives, and this can be seen as an ideological argument. However the argument may affect the response to the policy and therefore should not be ignored.

The third argument is connected with the second, although it is normally advanced by people having a different ideological viewpoint. It is that interference with the free working of the labour market gives rise to inefficiencies, in particular by impeding the changes in relative wages that allocate resources (labour) among various employers and occupations.

Finally it is claimed that the introduction of prices and incomes policies may draw attention away from the need to control other variables – in particular the level of government expenditure and the supply of money – which have important effects, especially in the long-term, on the rate of inflation.

We defer a fuller evaluation of the efficacy of prices and incomes policies until Chapter 14, where evidence on the actual operation of the policies is presented. However we have probably given a sufficient indication here as to why such policies have not had as much success as might be expected in view of their apparent attractions.

Policies Designed to Increase the Country's Economic Capacity
We showed in Chapter 4 that economic capacity depends heavily upon investment expenditure. Consequently any policies designed to increase investment expenditure – and we shall see in subsequent chapters that there is quite a wide range of such policies – will contribute to an increase in economic capacity.

Although the additional investment will, via the increase in capacity, tend to reduce inflationary pressures in the long term, it may add to inflationary pressures in the short term. This is illustrated in figure 9.4 where the full employment income in period t is designated Y_{Ft}. It may be possible to shift the full employment income,

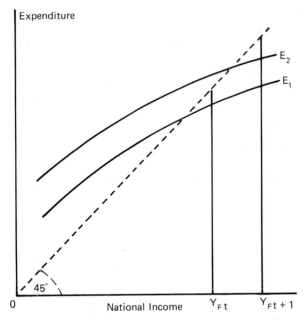

Figure 9.4 The Impact of an Increase in Expenditure

i.e. to increase economic capacity, in period $t+1$ to Y_{Ft+1}. However the increase in investment expenditure required would shift the total expenditure schedule from E_1 to E_2. This could clearly add to inflationary pressures in the transitional period before the increased capacity is installed.

There may appear to be a simple answer to this problem. If other forms of expenditure can be reduced, then the resources that are released can be utilized for investment. Unfortunately, such a simple solution may not be feasible for two reasons.

First it may not be easy, especially in the short-term, to transfer resources in this way. Buildings and machines may not be fully adaptable. Workers may be reluctant to transfer from one occupation or industry to another. Even if they are willing to transfer they may need retraining.

Second, the reduction in other forms of expenditure required to accommodate the increased investment expenditure implies a sacrifice by at least some members of the community. Since balance of payments considerations makes it unlikely that the government would wish to discourage exports, the reduction must occur in consumption (consumers' expenditure and/or the government's current expenditure).*

Finally we should note the suggestion that governments should intervene to encourage investment in particular sectors of the economy whose capacity and efficiency is felt to be crucial to the process of economic growth. Selective policies of this kind are discussed in Chapter 20.

An Automatic Adjustment Mechanism?

As we noted above there is no guarantee that, in the absence of government intervention, the economy would settle at an equilibrium point at which there was full employment. The demonstration of this point was seen as one of the most important contributions made to economic analysis by Lord Keynes. Previously the classical school of economists had believed that full employment would eventually be attained. At less than full employment, interest rates would fall and so investment expenditure would increase. Similarly the excess of workers over the number of jobs available would lead to a fall in wages which would encourage firms to increase employment.

Keynes refuted both of these propositions. He showed tht it was quite possible that interest rates would not fall to the level required to call forth a 'full employment level' of investment expenditure. Again he demonstrated that wages were often extremely sticky downwards, so that the required boost to employment need not occur. Furthermore the reduction in wages might lead to a fall in consumption by wage earners, which might discourage firms from increasing employment.

How do things look today? Do these points remain valid in the changed circumstances of the 1970s?

As far as interest rates are concerned we can say that the experience of the 1970s was entirely consistent with Keynes's views. High rates of inflation meant that at times *real* rates of interest were actually negative. Despite this fact investment, as a share of GNP, tended to fall rather than increase. Evidently if interest rates are an important determinant of investment, their influence was outweighed by other factors during this period.

Second, Keynes was clearly correct in claiming that money wages were sticky downwards, and indeed this stickiness is probably even greater today. However, insofar as a money illusion exists, rapid rates of inflation may lead to a fall in real wages; money wages may fail to rise as rapidly as prices. This fall in real wages should in principle encourage employment. However in practice this does not appear to have happened. This may be partly due to the fact noted above, that a reduction in wages may lead to a reduction in consumption, and partly to other factors, e.g. government policies towards company taxation.

* This point was discussed in Chapter 2, and illustrated in figure 2.5.

It appears then that there is no evidence to suggest that, in the absence of government intervention, the economy would reach equilibrium at the full employment level. It is therefore almost inevitable that governments should intervene in order to influence the level of expenditure. In this chapter we have concentrated on those circumstances in which expenditure-inducing policies might be felt to be desirable. In other circumstances, namely if the rate of inflation is felt to be too high and/or if the country encounters balance of payments problems, the government might be concerned to reduce total expenditure.

In the succeeding chapters we examine in detail the various government policies which we have outlined in this chapter. We will again be particularly concerned with the ways in which these policies effect the balance between expenditure and economic capacity. However we shall see that many policies have additional objectives and consequences.

Appendix   The Natural Rate of Unemployment

The evidence concerning the natural rate of unemployment is conflicting. If we consider the U.K. we find that the rate of inflation began to accelerate from about the middle of the 1960s, the acceleration being especially marked in the first half of the 1970s. This could be interpreted as an indication that the rate of unemployment was below the natural level. On the other hand unemployment during this period was higher than in the period 1945–65 when inflation showed no tendency to accelerate. Although this would appear to throw doubt on the concept of a natural rate of unemployment, it cannot be said to disprove it, since the proponents of the concept allow that the value of the natural rate is not necessarily fixed. Indeed they argue that it is likely to change if changes occur in certain factors, especially those which affect the working of the labour market.

Of these factors, one of the most important is probably the relation between a worker's income while in employment and when unemployed. (We mentioned this factor when discussing the proposition that the Phillips curve might have shifted to the right.) This relation will obviously vary from person to person, being affected not only by the worker's job but also by his family circumstances, tax liability, etc. Nevertheless there is no doubt that in general the gap between employment and unemployment incomes has been reduced. For example J. S. Flemming presents data relating to an unemployed man with a wife and two children. The ratio of his (after-tax) income to what his income would have been if he had earned the average for all workers varied between 36 per cent and 46 per cent for most of the period 1950–65. It then rose sharply to exceed 70 per cent in 1967 and has remained above 70 per cent since then.* When we also take account of the fact that redundancy payments were increased under the Redundancy Payments Act of 1965, we can see that the economic penalties attached to unemployment are considerably lower than previously.

Another factor mentioned in connection with our analysis of the Phillips curve was trade union power. It seems that if unions are 'stronger' the natural rate of unemployment may be higher. There are in fact several ways of measuring union strength; of these the existence of a closed shop, whereby only members of a union are employed, appears to be an especially important determinant of wage levels, and this might also have particular significance for the natural rate of unemployment.

A different aspect of union power is the willingness to take industrial action in support of wage claims. There certainly appears to have been increased militancy

* J. S. Flemming, *Inflation* (London: Oxford University Press, 1976), p. 50.

on the part of many unions in recent years (although this may be partly due to a heightened perception of the need to gain compensation for increased prices).

Finally the process of finding new employment may be hindered by several factors, including a lack of information, a lack of the requisite skills and geographical immobility. The more important these hindrances, or imperfections, the greater the natural rate of unemployment is likely to be, and it is interesting that in recent years governments have applied more resources to the task of trying to remove such imperfections. (See Chapter 17.)

One final feature of the natural rate of unemployment remains to be discussed. As we showed above, this natural rate may be associated with any (constant) rate of inflation. If this is so it means that we are unable to specify a precise trade-off between unemployment and inflation, as was possible with the original formulation of the Phillips curve.

This also raises the question as to what factors will influence the rate at which inflation will settle if unemployment is maintained at the natural rate. A detailed explanation of this question is outside the scope of this book. However, central to this explanation is the fact that a constant rate of inflation is deemed to be an equilibrium situation because it allows accurate price expectations. These expectations will be strongly influenced by people's experience of inflation, especially in the recent past. Consequently it follows that the higher the rate of inflation during periods of disequilibrium, the higher is likely to be the rate in equilibrium. This fact should be taken into account when one is trying to evaluate the long-term trade-off between inflation and unemployment.

Summary and Conclusions

In this chapter we have explored several aspects of the trade-off between unemployment and inflation. We have shown that the nature of the trade-off, i.e. the rate of price change associated with a given level of unemployment, may be influenced by various factors, including imperfections in the labour market, attempts by workers to obtain compensation for past price increases, and expectations about the future behaviour of prices.

We have discussed the effects of inflation, making a distinction between internal and external effects. We showed that many of the internal effects are due less to inflation itself, than to a failure of individuals and institutions to predict the rate of inflation or to adjust their behaviour in accordance with their predictions. The external effects, on the other hand, are likely to be adverse, whether or not inflation is predicted accurately.

We discussed the view expressed by some economists that the notion of a trade-off between unemployment and inflation is in fact an illusion, and that there is a normal or natural rate of unemployment towards which the economic system tends. We showed, in the appendix, that it is extremely difficult to test this proposition empirically. Nevertheless U.K. experience would certainly be compatible with this view.

Returning again to our previous assumption that there may be a trade-off between inflation and unemployment we briefly considered what policies might be adopted in order to influence the nature of the trade-off; under this heading we examined prices and incomes policies and policies designed to increase the country's economic policy.

Finally we explored briefly the possibility that there might be an automatic mechanism whereby full employment at an acceptable rate of inflation would be achieved without government intervention. We concluded that there was little evidence that such an outcome was likely, and that positive action by government is required. This leads on to the discussion, in the following chapter, of the objectives of economic policy.

ESSAY QUESTIONS

1 Examine the possible relationships between the level of expenditure and the rate of inflation.
2 Explain how an increase in expenditure may affect (a) the price level, (b) the level of output.
3 Outline the relationships embodied in the Phillips curve and explain why these relationships appear to have changed in recent years.
4 Discuss the statement that inflation is undesirable only if it runs at a higher rate than in other countries.
5 'Higher prices mean higher profits which encourage producers to expand. Inflation is, therefore, good for employment.' Discuss.
6 Why might one expect to find a trade-off between employment and inflation? What policies might be adopted in order to try to alter the terms of trade-off?
7 Discuss the proposition that in the absence of government intervention the economy would be unlikely to reach a full employment level of equilibrium.
8 Explain what you understand by the term 'the natural rate of unemployment' and suggest what factors may influence its value.
9 Is full employment compatible with stable prices?
10 Explain how knowledge of the numerical values of the accelerator and the multiplier could assist the government in its formulation of economic policy.

OBJECTIVE TEST QUESTIONS: SET 3

1 An increase in investment expenditure when there is a high level of capacity utilization is most likely to
   A increase inflationary pressures in the long term without having any effect in the short term
   B increase inflationary pressures in the short term without having any effect in the long term
   C increase inflationary pressures in both the short and the long term
   D reduce inflationary pressures in the short term but increase them in the long term
   E increase inflationary pressures in the short term but reduce them in the long term.

2 If the marginal propensity to spend is 0.6 the multiplier is
   A 6
   B 4
   C 2.5
   D 1.67
   E none of the above.

3 With an equilibrium national income of £10 millions an autonomous increase in investment of £1 million occurs. If the new equilibrium national income

is £14 millions, we can conclude that the marginal propensity to spend is

A 0.25
B 0.4
C 0.6
D 0.75
E none of the above.

4

	Country X		Country Y	
	Food	Machines	Food	Machines
Price per Unit	£1	£2	$2	$3

Given the above prices of food and machines in countries X and Y we can conclude that

A X will produce food only and Y will produce machines only
B X will produce machines only and Y will produce food only
C X will produce both food and machines, and Y will produce machines only
D both X and Y will produce both food and machines
E we can conclude nothing about the pattern of production because we do not know the exchange rate.

5 If the terms of trade change from 105 to 110 we can conclude that
A the total value of exports has risen
B the total value of imports has risen
C the total value of exports has risen more than the total value of imports
D the average price of imports has risen relative to the average price of exports
E none of the above.

Questions 6 and 7 relate to figure 9.5, in which an autonomous change in expenditure causes the expenditure function to shift from E_1 to E_2.

6 The value of the multiplier is

A AB÷IG
B AB÷HG
C FG÷HG
D HG÷BH
E IG÷BI.

7 The level of induced expenditure is

A FI
B FG
C IH
D IG
E HG.

8 The level of aggregate demand is likely to increase as a result of all of the following factors except

A a reduction in taxation of company profits
B a reduction in personal taxation
C a reduction in tariff barriers
D an increase in unemployment benefit
E an increase in investment.

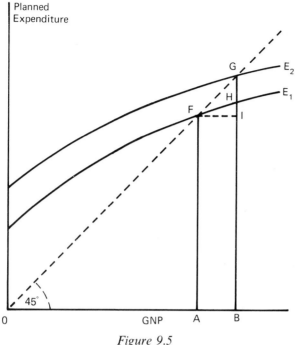

Figure 9.5

9 *Export Prices* *Import Prices*

	Year 1	Year 2		Year 1	Year 2
	100	120		100	80

The terms of trade in year 2 are

A 67
B 80
C 120
D 150
E none of the above.

Questions 10 and 11 are based on the following table

	£ millions
Exports of goods	1,500
Imports of goods	2,000
Exports of services	1,000
Imports of services	500
Interest, profits and dividends received from abroad	750
Interest, profits and dividends paid abroad	300

10 The current balance (£millions) was

A zero
B 450
C 950
D 1,450
E 2,500.

11 We can deduce from the above table that
   1 the total currency flow was positive
   2 a surplus was earned on visible trade
   3 a surplus was earned on invisible trade.

12 The volume of food and machines that could be produced by countries X and Y if all their resources were allocated to either one product or the other are as follows:

	Country X		Country Y	
Situation	Food	or Machines	Food	or Machines
1	5,000	8,000	10,000	16,000
2	6,000	6,000	6,000	8,000
3	2,000	4,000	4,000	2,000

In which of the above situations would the principle of comparative advantage suggest that economic welfare would be increased by international specialization and trade?

13 The Phillips curve would be likely to shift outwards, i.e. away from the point of origin, if
   1 rates of unemployment benefit were reduced
   2 an improved system of notification of job vacancies was introduced
   3 in wage negotiations more weight was given than previously to past price increases.

14 The opportunity cost ratios, as between food and machines, are as follows

Country X		Country Y	
Food	Machines	Food	Machines
1	4	1	2

At which of the following exchange rates would international trade occur?
   1 1 unit of food=1 machine
   2 2 units of food=9 machines
   3 3 units of food=8 machines

15 The U.K.'s balance of payments on current account would benefit from
   1 an increase in the value of U.K. sales of cars in the U.S.A.
   2 an increase in spending by Japanese tourists in London
   3 the purchase of shares in a U.K. property company by Kuwait.

16 The principle of comparative advantage states that a country should specialize in the production of any product which it can make more efficiently than any other country.
   Total production is increased if countries specialize in accordance with the principle of comparative advantage.

17 The demand for sterling will fall following a rise in the prices of British exports.
   A rise in the prices of British exports will cause the volume of exports to fall.

18 Other things remaining equal the depreciation of a currency will cause a worsening of the terms of trade.
   The terms of trade is an index denoting the ratio of export prices to import prices.

19 When planned expenditure in one period equals national income in the previous period, the national income is said to have reached the equilibrium level.

  When planned expenditure in one period equals national income in the previous period, there is no tendency for the level of national income to change.

20 The natural or normal rate of unemployment refers to the level of unemployment at which prices would be stable.

  If unemployment is below the natural or normal rate there is a tendency for the rate of inflation to accelerate.

TRUE/FALSE

1 Total production will increase following international specialization and trade provided that the opportunity cost ratios are the same in all countries.
2 The visible balance represents expenditure on the exports of goods minus expenditure on imports of goods.
3 The invisible balance represents expenditure on exports of goods and services minus expenditure on imports of goods and services.
4 Other things remaining equal the depreciation of a currency will cause an improvement in the terms of trade.
5 If in a given period national income equals total expenditure, national income is said to have reached an equilibrium level.
6 If planned expenditure in one period exceeds national income in the previous period the level of national income will tend to rise.
7 An autonomous change in expenditure is one that is caused by a prior change in income.
8 If the equilibrium level of national income is disturbed by an autonomous change in expenditure, equilibrium will be re-established when the change in withdrawals equals the autonomous change in expenditure.
9 The Phillips curve indicates the relationship between the level of unemployment and changes in wage levels.
10 The natural or normal rate of unemployment may be associated with any (constant) rate of change in prices.

CHAPTER TEN

The Objectives of Government Economic Policy

Introduction
DURING our examination of the economic system in preceding chapters we made numerous references to possible objectives of government economic policy. In this chapter we draw together these references, summarize the objectives mentioned previously and introduce additional objectives which might be considered important by at least some governments. This chapter thus provides a bridge leading to the discussion, in subsequent chapters, of specific economic policies.

The Major Policy Objectives
Looking first at the objectives mentioned in previous chapters, four major objectives can be identified:

(1) An increase in the nation's economic capacity and thereby in its material living standards.
(2) A high level of capacity utilization, and in particular a low level of unemployment.
(3) Price stability or, at worst, an increase in prices no higher than that of our major competitors in overseas countries.
(4) A balance on our international transactions which, over the long term, is not in deficit.

The preceding discussion has demonstrated that these objectives may not be compatible. In particular there may be a conflict between the second objective on the one hand the third and fourth objectives on the other. The first objective may also conflict with the third and fourth in the short run, although not in the long run.

This suggests that it may be extremely difficult for the government to devise a universally acceptable economic policy, especially if different members of the community attach different degrees of importance to particular objectives – as is likely to happen. So for example, unemployed workers will be most concerned that the government shall adopt policies designed to increase the level of capacity utilization, whereas people whose jobs are secure will attach more importance to policies designed to maintain stable prices.

The difficulty of devising an acceptable policy is compounded when one takes into account other possible objectives. These include:

(5) To minimize the production of economic 'bads'. As we saw in Chapter 2, there may be a tendency for an increase in the output of goods to be accompanied by an increase in the output of bads with important implications for the standard of living.
(6) Equality is a concept which has many aspects, often non-economic. Neverthe-

less it does have an important economic dimension. Government policy has often been influenced by the desire to reduce inequalities, in terms of job opportunities and income levels, as between one part of the United Kingdom and another. There has also been some attempt to prevent an increase in the gap in real incomes as between the United Kingdom as a whole and the underdeveloped countries.

Again it is generally accepted that the inequalities of income and wealth that would emerge in the absence of government intervention would be too great. Consequently a reduction in inequality, a redistribution of wealth and income, has been an important government objective.

Another aspect of equality is equality of opportunity. This might appear to be consistent with – and indeed to require – redistribution of wealth and income. However equality of opportunity might be felt by some people to include the right to enjoy the fruits of one's labour. This right could obviously conflict with an objective of income redistribution and it is therefore, not surprising to find constant controversy concerning the extent to which income redistribution should proceed.

(7) An extension of ownership by the state of the means of production and distribution. This objective, which would be rejected by many people, has an important political or ideological dimension. The most marked increase in state ownership in the U.K. occurred with the nationalization programme of the first post-war Labour government, and subsequent discussions about the extension or contraction of state ownership have tended to be conducted along party political lines.

Nevertheless, the fact that relatively few changes in the overall level of state ownership have occurred since 1950, despite frequent changes in political control, suggests that economic considerations are also important.

As we shall see in Chapter 19, the economic arguments in favour of state ownership are linked with the equality objective, discussed above, and with the next objective, an increase in economic efficiency.

(8) An increase in economic efficiency may often involve an increase in economic capacity, listed above as our first objective. However, it goes beyond this, to encompass the structure of industry. Thus it is especially relevant to two areas of economic policy – direct invention by the government (including nationalization) and policies relating to competition. Furthermore, since economic efficiency includes the meeting of the needs of consumers, policies designed to protect consumers are also relevant. Finally an increase in economic efficiency is an important objective of many of the measures taken by government as part of its regional and manpower policy.

Summary and Conclusions

We have listed eight objectives that will often find expression in government economic policy. We would not claim that this list is necessarily comprehensive – readers may be able to add other objectives which they feel governments have, or ought to have. Nevertheless, the list enables us to explain the major economic measures adopted by governments.

It is clear that we cannot equate one objective with one type of policy. Indeed each type of policy will have implications for several objectives. Consequently we shall constantly refer back to this list as we discuss the major types of policy in the succeeding chapters.

ESSAY QUESTIONS

1 Explain why it may be difficult for the government to devise a universally acceptable economic policy.
2 Explain what you understand by the term 'equality' and indicate what economic policies might be adopted in order to increase the degree of equality.
3 'The only reason why disagreements occur concerning government economic policies is ignorance concerning the likely consequences of these policies.' Discuss.
4 Evaluate the proposition that the main objective of government economic policy should be to increase economic efficiency.
5 Discuss the reasons why the priority given to different objectives of government economic policy may change over time.

EXERCISES

10.1 Explain why it may be difficult for the government to simultaneously pursue the following objectives:

(a) An increase in the nation's economic capacity and thereby in its material living standards.
(b) A high level of capacity utilization.
(c) Price stability.
(d) A balance on our international transactions which is not in deficit.

10.2 Table 10.1 presents an index of the GDP, together with *some* of its components, for two hypothetical countries. (The index in the base year is 100 in both instances.) Given that the GDP of the two countries was identical in the base year, comment on the proposition that the data suggests that country A's economic policies were more successful than those of country B.

Table 10.1
Index of Changes in Gross Domestic Product

	Country A	Country B
Consumers' expenditure	150	140
of which:		
food	120	130
consumer durables	160	140
jewellery, watches, etc.	200	120
Government consumption	140	150
of which:		
defence	160	130
health services	130	160
education services	140	150
Gross fixed capital formation	150	160
Gross domestic product	150	145

10.3 The following data is taken from the third report of the Royal Commission on the Distribution of Income and Wealth (H.M.S.O. 1976).

'In 1974–5 the number of persons receiving total employment incomes before tax of £10,000 a year or more we estimate to be 65,000, or about three in every thousand of all recipients of employment incomes. We estimate further that these 0.3 per cent of all recipients received about 2.1 per cent of the employment income received by all persons.

We have found that there has been compression in the dispersion of employment incomes before tax since 1959 at the higher levels. The highest decimillile (the level above which the top ten thousandth of incomes lie) for males, which in 1959–60 was 21 times the median (the income level above which half the incomes lie), moved to 15 times the median in 1972–3. Over the same period the highest millile (the level above which the top thousandth of incomes lie), moved from nearly ten times to nearly eight times the median.

When the levels of before-tax remuneration are adjusted to allow for income-tax and changes in the value of money since 1959, we estimate that the median employment income increased by 34 per cent between 1959–60 and 1973–4. In the same period the highest millile decreased by 2 per cent and the highest decimillile decreased by 15 per cent.

Between 1969 and 1975 the ratio in before-tax incomes of full time directors to foremen was reduced from 8.75 : 1 to 7.05 : 1. The after-tax ratio was reduced from 5.11 : 1 to 3.88 : 1.

When allowance is made for cost of living differences and tax, salaries for managers are substantially lower in the U.K. than in most other developed countries. U.K. remuneration for comparable jobs is about the same as in Australia, but about 70 to 75 per cent of that in Germany, and about 50 to 60 per cent of that in France, Canada, and the U.S.A.'

(i) Would you say that the level of 'top incomes' in the U.K. is too high, too low, or just about right? (You should justify your answer on economic grounds).

(ii) Economic theory suggests that employment incomes are determined by employees' marginal revenue productivities. To what extent is this conclusion consistent with the above data?

(iii) Show how the combination of an increase in the cost of living and a progressive tax system can lead to differential changes in the real incomes of high and lower income earners. Illustrate your answer both by reference to the above data, and by providing additional hypothetical data.

(iv) Discuss the case for equating the real incomes of U.K. managers with those of managers in other countries.

10.4 The third report issued by the Royal Commission on the Distribution of Income and Wealth contained an addendum written by three members of the Commission. Part of the addendum reads as follows:

'The major question raised by the level of top salaries is the relationship between economic efficiency and social justice. We have seen that during the past 40 years there has been a steady trend in the direction of a rise in the standard of living of the majority of wage and salary earners and that this has been accompanied by a substantial fall in the differentials between the highest paid and the manual and lower supervisory grades. This has been possible mainly because of the rise during that period in gross national product, but also because of a general concern for greater social justice.

However, the evidence gathered for this report shows that recently this process has greatly accelerated. While the median earnings of all men have risen faster in the past five years than the retail price increase, salaries after tax at constant prices had fallen between July 1969 and July 1975 by 17 per cent at the £10,000 a year level and 25 per cent at the £20,000 a year level, most of this decline occurring in the past two years. Because of the freeze on salaries of £8,500 and above since then, this decline is steadily increasing as retail prices continue to rise.

The total after-tax earnings of the small group of 65,000 earning £10,000 or more from employment amounts to only 1.2 per cent of the total after-tax income of all employment incomes. An improvement in the standard of living of the lower paid cannot be achieved by further redistribution of earnings from the higher salary earners. It can only come from the creation of more income resulting from new capital investment and greater productivity.'

Comment upon, and discuss the implications of, the conclusions expressed in the passage.

CHAPTER ELEVEN

Fiscal Policy

Introduction

FISCAL policy, which has been the major form of demand management in the U.K. in the post-war period, encompasses government expenditure on the one hand and taxation on the other. A very important aspect of fiscal policy is the balance between these two elements. This is discussed at some length towards the end of the chapter. But first we examine the two elements separately, beginning with government expenditure.

The Purposes of Government Expenditure

The Provision of Public Goods

If we took a very long historical perspective, the provision of public, or collective consumption, goods would probably emerge as the primary purpose of government expenditure. These goods have two essential characteristics. First, if the good is provided to one citizen, it is provided to all. This is known as non-excludability. Second, the consumption of the good by one person does not impede its consumption by others. This is known as non-rivalness.

The best example of a public good is probably national defence. If the government raises an army to prevent an invasion of its territory, all citizens benefit from this protection. I am made no less safe because my neighbour is made more safe. The services of a police force may also be taken as an example of a public good. However, the growth in recent years of private security organizations such as Securicor suggests that the condition of non-rivalness may not always be met. Presumably the firms who hire Securicor to protect their property feel that the police are so occupied in other duties that they may not be able to offer them sufficient protection.

Other examples of public goods include water purification plants, barrages and dams to control flooding, and street lighting. The fact that such products are consumed collectively means that it is very difficult to finance their supply through the market. Take as an example the construction of a barrage to reduce the danger of flooding, such as the proposed Thames barrage. Let us assume that everyone likely to be affected by the scheme agrees that the project would be desirable, i.e. that the total benefits would exceed the costs of construction and operation.

On this basis a private firm might hope to raise sufficient money to finance the scheme. However, if it tried to raise the money in advance of the construction it would probably find that many of the potential beneficiaries would refuse to subscribe, even if they felt that their share of the costs would be less than the benefit of the project to them. They might argue that since their contribution was so small a part of the total cost, the project would be likely to go ahead even without their support; this would allow them to benefit from it without incurring any cost. (This is a particular example of a general problem sometimes known as the 'free-rider' problem.)

Faced with this reaction the firm would not undertake the construction of the barrage, since it would have no power to charge individuals for the benefits conferred by the barrage when built. A public authority on the other hand could undertake construction since it would be able to recoup the cost by imposing a tax of one kind or another on the beneficiaries.

The Provision of Products at a Price Below the Cost of Production
This objective might be met by giving subsidies to private producers, as in the case of food subsidies whose value was increased for a while during the mid 70's. More commonly the products are supplied by public sector producers, either nationalized industries or government departments.

In general the intention is that the nationalized industries should operate without subsidies, and the subsidies – of one kind and another – that they have required, could be classified on the whole as 'unplanned'. On the other hand it is a matter of deliberate policy that the output of government departments, such as many educational and medical services, should for the most part be provided free or at nominal prices.

An important purpose of subsidies is to encourage the consumption of products that are felt by the government to be desirable (so-called 'merit goods'). The policy is also likely to bring about a redistribution of real income. Subsidies are mainly financed out of taxation; therefore, given the existence of a system of progressive taxation (discussed below), poorer people will tend to obtain the greatest benefit from subsidies in relation to their share of the cost.

The Redistribution of Income
A more important method of redistributing income is by the use of transfer payments. Indeed these are called transfer payments because they transfer money from some members of the community, through taxation, to other members in the form of a range of benefits. The benefits include unemployment benefit, sickness benefit, retirement pensions, and child benefits. Since they are paid without the recipient providing any service in exchange, they are excluded from the calculation of the national income, and therefore from government expenditure (G) as defined in our earlier analysis of income determination.

An Increase in Economic Efficiency
This may involve either an extension of public ownership – undertaken in the belief that the efficiency of the production process will thereby be increased – or public expenditure designed to increase the efficiency of the private sector. Both processes are discussed in detail in later chapters.

The Forms of Government Expenditure
The major categories of government expenditure in 1976 are shown in table 11.1.*
It can be seen that over half of the total expenditure comprises *expenditure on goods and services*. Most of this spending was on current account, the category of expenditure discussed in Chapter 5. The major items of current expenditure by the central government were military defence (£6,090 millions) and the national health service (£5,734 millions), while around half of the current spending of the local authorities was accounted for by education (£5,253 millions). Of these three

* The term 'general government' refers to central plus local government.

Table 11.1

U.K. General Government Expenditure (1976)

	£ mn	Per cent
Current account:		
Goods and services	25,742	44.0
Non-trading capital consumption	820	1.4
Subsidies and grants	17,077	29.2
Debt interest	5,446	9.3
Total current expenditure	49,085	83.9
Capital Account:		
Goods and service	5,382	9.2
Increase in value of stocks	39	0.1
Grants and other transfers	1,421	2.4
Total capital expenditure	6,842	11.7
Net lending to public corporations, private sector and overseas	2,579	4.4
Total expenditure	58,506	100

Source: *National Income and Expenditure* (H.M.S.O.; 1977).

items, which together account for more than one third of total current expenditure, the first is a public good provided at zero price while the other two comprise facilities and services provided at zero price or at prices well below cost.

By far the largest item of capital expenditure on goods and services is spending on housing by local authorities. Other items include the building of roads, hospitals, and schools. This category of expenditure was discussed, along with other forms of investment, in Chapter 6.

Subsidies and grants, the most important types of transfer payment, have become increasingly important in recent years, and now account for almost one third of total government expenditure.

The grants made by the public authorities in 1976 are listed in table 11.2. It

Table 11.2

U.K. Government Grants (1976)

	£mn	Per cent
Retirement pensions	5,493	36.5
Sickness benefit	1,083	7.2
Unemployment benefit	569	3.8
Widows benefit/guardians allowance	434	2.9
Supplementary benefits	1,525	10.1
Family allowances	563	3.7
Other social security benefits	837	5.6
Total social security benefits	10,504	69.9
Scholarships, grants to universities, colleges, etc.	1,097	7.3
Rent rebates and allowances	140	0.9
Current grants overseas	792	5.3
Other current grants	1,081	7.2
Capital grants and transfers	1,421	9.5
Total Grants	15,035	100

Source: *National Income and Expenditure* (H.M.S.O., 1977).

can be seen that social security benefits account for a high proportion of the total. This indicates that this form of expenditure is especially important in relation to the objectives of the redistribution of income and greater equality.

These two objectives are also met to a limited extent by subsidies. However, as can be seen from table 11.3, producers receive a much higher proportion of the total expenditure on subsidies than of the expenditure on grants. This suggests that an increase in economic efficiency may be a *relatively* more important objective of subsidies than of grants. (However, it must be remembered that total expenditure on grants is far greater than on subsidies.)

Table 11.3
U.K. Government Subsidies (1976)

	£mn	Per cent
Housing	1,334	38.5
Agriculture, forestry, fishing, food	851	24.6
Publicly owned transport undertakings	701	20.2
Employment premiums	234	6.8
Other	343	9.9
Total	3,463	100

Source: *National Income and Expenditure* (H.M.S.O., 1977).

Debt interest, also treated as a transfer payment, accounted in 1976 for 9.3 per cent of general government total expenditure as shown in table 11.1, and for 5 per cent of GNP at factor cost. These percentages increased during the mid 1970s, largely because of the government's need to borrow large sums of money at high interest rates following the disturbance to the economy caused by the rise in oil prices. This trend caused some concern, not least because interest payments to overseas holders of debt adversely affect our balance of payments on current account.

On the other hand an increase in the national debt may have some compensating advantages, especially in the longer term. If some of the money that is borrowed is used to finance projects which increase the level of economic capacity, this will facilitate an increase in GNP. This increase in GNP would make a given level of interest payments less burdensome – indeed the real burden of the debt, the share of GNP accounted for by interest payments, might fall.*

The remaining major item in table 11.1 is *net lending* to the private sector, public corporations and the overseas sector. Expenditure under this heading would be expected to give rise to a future flow of interest and dividends to the government.

The Receipts of the Government

Taxation

Table 11.4 shows that the receipts of the general (central and local) government comprise four major categories. We discuss each of these categories in turn, beginning with the most important, taxation, which in 1976 accounted for 62 per cent of total receipts.

---

* The total nominal value of the national debt (as opposed to the interest payments) as a percentage of GDP fell from 84.6 per cent in 1963 to 41.5 per cent in 1976.

Table 11.4

The Receipts of the U.K. General Government (1976)

	£mn	*Per cent*
Revenue from taxation	36,269	62
Contributions to National Insurance Fund, etc.	8,426	14
Rent, interest, dividends, etc.	4,494	8
Imputed consumption of non-trading capital	820	1
Borrowing and other financial transactions	8,497	15
Total receipts	58,506	100

Source: *National Income and Expenditure* (H.M.S.O., 1977).

The Functions of Taxation

TO RAISE REVENUE

Given the overwhelming importance of taxation within the sum total of the receipts of the government, the primary function of taxation, must be to raise revenue. As we shall see below this function influences both the level and structure of taxation.

Other important functions of taxation may include any of the following:

TO INFLUENCE THE LEVEL OF TOTAL EXPENDITURE

The higher the level of taxation the lower the level of real expenditure is likely to be.* In the case of direct taxation, i.e. taxes on income and wealth, expenditure is reduced simply because the disposable income of individuals and firms is reduced. When indirect taxes, i.e. taxes on expenditure, are imposed, *money* disposable income is unchanged. However, its real value falls because of the increase in prices, and this fall causes a fall in real expenditure.

TO INFLUENCE THE PATTERN OF EXPENDITURE

The quantities of various products purchased can be influenced by the imposition of high expenditure taxes on some products and low or zero taxes on others. The pattern of expenditure may also change due to changes in disposable income as a result of direct taxation and wealth.

TO REDISTRIBUTE INCOME

A system of differential expenditure taxes can be used – in conjunction with public expenditure – to redistribute real income. Redistribution in favour of poorer members of the community requires that low or zero taxes should be imposed on products that account for a greater proportion of the expenditure of poorer than of richer people. Conversely higher taxes should be imposed on products that account for a greater proportion of the expenditure of richer than of poorer people.

More important in the U.K., however, is redistribution by means of a progressive system of direct taxation. Direct taxation is said to be progressive when the *proportion* of income paid in tax increases as the level of income increases. (The opposite situation is known as a regressive system.) As we show below, direct taxation in the U.K. is highly progressive.

Measures which redistribute income will also, in the long term, influence the distribution of wealth. In addition the distribution of wealth may be directly affected by taxes on wealth or capital.

---

* Unless the effects of higher taxation are balanced by higher government expenditure.

Having identified the main functions of taxation, let us now examine the main features of the structure of taxation in the U.K.

The Structure of Taxation

Table 11.5 gives a broad breakdown of revenue from taxation in 1976. It can be seen that direct taxes, i.e. taxes on income and capital, accounted for 54 per cent of total revenue, with personal income taxes being the single most important source

Table 11.5
U.K. Government Revenue from Taxation (1976)

	£mn	Per cent
Taxes on income:		
personal sector	16,635	45.9
companies and public corporations	1,398	3.9
non-residents	691	1.9
Total taxes on income	18,724	51.6
Taxes on capital:	885	2.4
Taxes on expenditure:		
value added tax	3,982	11.0
alcoholic drinks	1,889	5.2
tobacco	1,808	5.0
hydrocarbon oils	1,941	5.4
protective duties	659	1.8
motor vehicle duties	820	2.3
other central government taxes	1,021	2.8
Local authority rates	4,540	12.5
Total taxes on expenditure	16,660	46.0
Total revenue from taxation	36,269	100

Source: *National Income and Expenditure* (H.M.S.O., 1977).

of revenue. Since the structure of personal taxation is highly progressive and the income distribution is skewed, the tax structure as a whole is progressive.

Expenditure or indirect taxes accounted for 46 per cent of total tax revenue. Value added tax, a general expenditure tax, is the most important source of central government revenue, but considerable sums are raised from the taxes levied on three groups of products – alcoholic drinks, tobacco and hydrocarbon oils. Local authority rates, although now accounting for less than one third of the total revenue of local authorities, remains the most important single source of revenue from indirect taxation.

Having outlined the main features of the structure of taxation we now examine each of the major forms of taxation. We first examine the various forms of direct taxation, and then we discuss indirect taxation.

Direct Taxation

We begin our examination of direct taxation by considering personal taxation. This is the most important form of direct taxation – indeed in 1976 taxes on personal incomes accounted for 46 per cent of total revenue from all forms of taxation.

Personal Taxation

The structure of personal taxation in 1977–8 is outlined in table 11.6. It can be seen that there is a wide spread of tax rates between the basic rate of 34 per cent

Table 11.6

The Structure of Personal Taxation, U.K. 1977–8

Band of taxable income (£)	Tax rate (per cent)
0– 6,000	34
6,001– 7,000	40
7,001– 8,000	45
8,001– 9,000	50
9,001–10,000	55
10,001–12,000	60
12,001–14,000	65
14,001–16,000	70
16,001–21,000	75
Over 21,000	83

The above rates refer to earned income. Investment income incurs a surcharge as follows:

Bands of investment income (£)	Tax rate
1,5001–2,000	10
Over 2,000	15

and the highest rate of 83 per cent (plus the investment surcharge of up to 15 per cent). An individual's taxable income, and hence the amount paid in tax, is reduced by various allowances. The value of these allowances depends mainly upon whether the taxpayer is married or single, and the number and ages of children in the family.

In table 11.7 we show the amounts that would have been paid, under the Budget proposals, by a 'typical' family at different levels of income.* It should be noted

Table 11.7

*Income Tax Payable 1977–8, Budget Proposals
(married couple with 2 children not over 11, all income earned, £ per annum)*

Income Before Tax	Income Tax	Net Income	Increase in net income over 1976–7
1,500	—	1,500	52
2,000	135	1,865	73
4,000	795	3,205	113
8,000	2,144	5,856	283
15,000	5,996	9,004	717
25,000	13,529	11,471	882

that net income is defined here to include family allowances or child benefit, but that no allowance is made for any deductions from income other than income tax. We may take the ratio of net income to gross income as a measure of the average propensity to (income) taxation. We can deduce from table 11.7 that this varies from zero at an annual income of £1,500 through 27 per cent at £8,000 to 54 per cent at £25,000. (We refer to the final column in this table in a later section).

THE EFFECT ON REVENUE OF A CHANGE IN PERSONAL TAXATION

In most instances an increase in the rates of personal taxation will lead to an increase in revenue. To understand why on occasions this may *not* be so, we need to realize that (a) for many people, earning a given income is not an end in itself

* As shown below, these proposals were subsequently modified.

but a means to obtaining a certain standard of living, and (b) that leisure is also an important element in the standard of living.

Each person has some idea of the amount of leisure he is prepared to give up in order to increase his income and hence his consumption. We can represent the preferences of any individual by means of an indifference curve. In figure 11.1 we

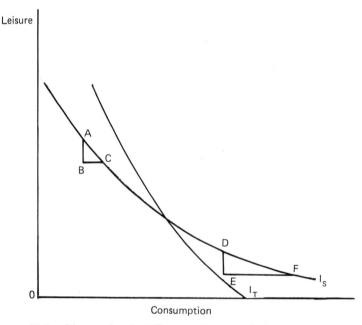

Figure 11.1 Alternative Indifference Curves – Leisure and Consumption

have two curves representing the preference of two different individuals. Each curve indicates combinations of leisure and consumption with which that individual would be equally satisfied (is indifferent between).

It will be noticed that both curves are convex to the origin. This occurs because the marginal rate of substitution of one good for another is lower the less of the first good, and the more of the second good, the individual has to begin with. The operation of this *law (or hypothesis) of the diminishing rate of substitution* can be illustrated by reference to the curve I_s. If the individual were at point A he would be willing to sacrifice AB of leisure in order to increase his consumption by BC. At point D he is enjoying a much higher level of consumption but much less leisure than at A. Consequently he is willing to give up the same amount of leisure as before (DE=AB) only if the increase in consumption is much greater than previously (EF > BC).

Although, due to the operation of this law, both indifference curves are convex to the origin, they have quite different shapes, indicating the different preferences, as between leisure and consumption, of the two individuals. These differences can be crucial in influencing people's reactions to a change in direct taxation.

In figure 11.2 line AB indicates the combinations of leisure and consumption that might be available to an individual. The two extremes are indicated by points A and B. If a person were willing to forego all his leisure, his consumption would be Y. At the other extreme an unemployed man, drawing unemployment benefit, could consume only X.

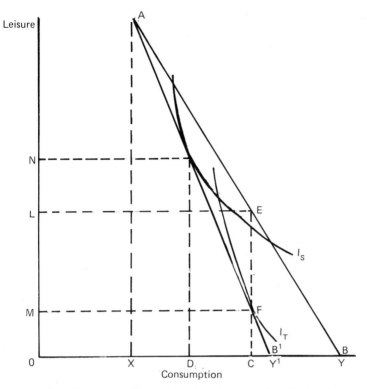

Figure 11.2 The Effect of a Change in Taxation on the Choice between Leisure and Consumption

Let us consider the effect of a change in taxation on an individual who chooses point E, representing a combination of C consumption and L leisure. The imposition of a higher rate of direct taxation means a change in the combinations of consumption and leisure available to this individual. For any given level of work (and thus for any given level of leisure), his disposable income, and therefore his consumption, is less than previously. The curve AB pivots to AB^1, the maximum possible consumption now being Y^1.

The effect of this change will depend upon the individual's preferences as between consumption and leisure. Some members of the community may be willing to work longer hours than before in order to maintain their consumption. A typical indifference curve of such a 'thruster' is I_T. This person's new equilibrium position is where I_T is tangential to AB^1, i.e. at point F, representing an unchanged level of consumption C, but a reduction in leisure to M.

On the other hand, since the rewards from work have been reduced some people may decide to work less. I_S would be the indifference curve of such a 'sleeper'. At his new equilibrium position G, (where I_S is tangential to AB^1), his consumption is reduced to D, but he enjoys more leisure, N.*

This demonstrates that it is possible in principle for an increase in personal taxa-

* Note that although the two individuals react in different ways they must both be worse off than previously. In order to simplify the diagram we have not drawn the original indifference curves passing through E. However it is clear that each individual must move to a lower curve.

tion to lead to a fall in total tax revenue. If the proportion of 'sleepers' in the community is high enough and if they are able to exercise their preferences, a reduction in the number of hours worked could cause the total yield from personal taxation to fall. Even if this did not occur, total tax revenue could still fall since the yield from indirect direction would be reduced if the level of consumption fell.

In the short term the ability of workers to reduce their hours of work may, due to the existence of negotiated agreements, be confined to a reduction in overtime hours. Over a longer period pressure might arise for a reduction in the length of the standard working week. In addition some people might leave the work force entirely, either by emigrating or by retiring earlier than they would otherwise have done. (On the other hand there might be an increase in the number of housewives seeking work from the households of thrusters). Finally, as the rewards for working decline, and more specifically as point Y in figure 11.2 moves closer to X, there will be less incentive for people drawing (untaxed) unemployment benefit to seek work yielding a (taxable) income.

OTHER EFFECTS OF PERSONAL TAXATION

We have explored the effect of an increase in personal taxation on tax revenue in some detail because the analysis also throws light on other possible effects of taxation. In so far as high rates of taxation deter people from working as hard, or cause them to leave the work force completely, the overall level of economic efficiency is likely to suffer. This is perhaps especially likely to occur if workers have skills that are in demand in other countries which can offer higher real rewards. The emigration of senior managers and of professional people such as doctors would be good examples.

These disincentive effects of high tax rates were referred to by the Chancellor in his speech introducing the 1977 budget – a budget which proposed substantial increases in net incomes, as shown in table 11.7. While these increases were naturally welcomed by taxpayers, they should be assessed in the light of two very important considerations.

First, under a progressive tax system, a rise in aggregate money incomes automatically leads to an increase in the total tax revenue, a process known as fiscal drag. If the increase in money incomes represents an increase in real incomes, one could conclude that the increase in tax revenue was a justified and intended consequence of the progressive system of taxation. If, on the other hand, the increase in money incomes is accompanied by an increase in prices, real incomes may increase very little or not at all. In these circumstances the increased tax revenue may appear to be unintended and unjustified.

In the early and mid 1970s the combination of inflation and a progressive system of personal taxation led to a substantial increase in the tax burden falling on many individuals in the U.K. especially those earning high incomes. The Commissioners of Inland Revenue reported that between 1972–3 and 1976–7 the amount of income tax collected trebled, despite the fact that real incomes rose very little during these four years. Some of the increase was due to higher tax rates, but fiscal drag was far more important.

A specific example of this process is given in figure 11.3* which shows the decline in the real value of personal and dependent allowances. This decline occurred despite several increases in their nominal values – indicated by the peaks in the curves.

---

* This figure originally appeared in D. Morgan, *Overtaxation by Inflation* (London: Institute of Economic Affairs, 1977).

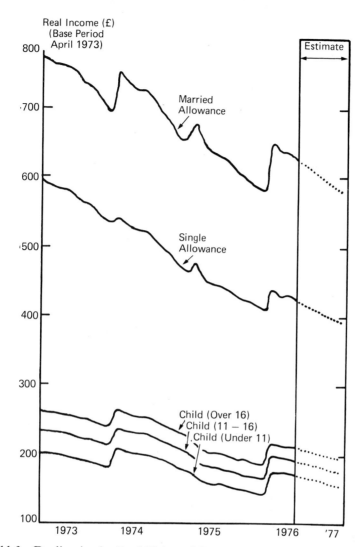

Figure 11.3 Decline in the Real Value of Personal and Dependent Allowances
(The dotted lines are estimates of the further fall in real values that would have occurred in the absence of the changes introduced by the 1977 Budget.)

The changes proposed in the 1977 Budget were therefore only a partial readjustment of the trend to a higher tax burden during the preceding years, and in fact pressures within Parliament induced the Chancellor to modify his proposals and to introduce bigger increases in allowances than he originally intended. On the other hand a failure to obtain the agreement of the unions to continued wage restraint led him to reduce the basic rate of personal tax from 35 to 34 per cent, and not to 33 per cent as he had initially proposed.*

* These modifications meant, of course, that the overall pattern of increases in net incomes was somewhat different from that indicated in table 11.7. Another important amendment accepted by the Chancellor meant that allowances would be changed annually in line with the index of retail prices unless the Budget proposed – and Parliament accepted – that this should not happen.

The second factor that should be borne in mind when assessing the structure of personal taxation, is that although average tax rates are no doubt important, they may be less important than marginal rates when individuals are deciding how long or how hard to work. This is why attention has frequently been drawn to the fact that marginal rates of tax on higher income earners are higher in the U.K. than in most other countries (see figure 11.4).

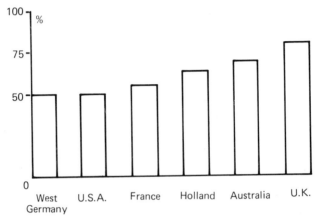

Figure 11.4 Top Marginal Rates of Income Tax, Various Countries, 1975

While there is a general acceptance of a measure of income redistribution via progressive taxation, very high rates of tax can be felt by tax payers to be unfair. The increases in net incomes introduced by the 1977 budget were justified by the Chancellor in terms of equity as well as increased economic efficiency. However one could also understand why some people might consider the pattern of increases shown in the final column of table 11.7 to be inconsistent with an objective of equality, and why pressure arose to modify the proposals so as to increase the relative benefit accruing to the lower income groups.

Capital Transfer Tax
This tax which was introduced in 1975, was intended as a more effective means of distributing wealth than the estate duty it replaced. C.T.T. applies to all gifts ('gratuitous transfers of personal wealth') whether they take place during a person's lifetime or on his death.

The first £15,000 transferred is not taxed. Thereafter the tax rate varies between 10 and 75 per cent, depending upon the amount of the total wealth transferred by one donor. The top rate of 75 per cent is paid when transfers exceed £2 millions. There are certain exemptions, such as gifts between husband and wife, and those relating to the assets of family firms.

When C.T.T. was introduced it was announced that the government intended to supplement it by means of an annual tax on wealth. However plans for the introduction of a wealth tax have been deferred, and wealth as such is still not taxed in the U.K.

Corporation Tax
Companies pay direct taxes in the form of corporation tax, which in 1976 yielded £1,398 millions. The tax is levied on the profits of companies at a rate of 52 per cent (reducing to 42 per cent on annual profits of less than £30,000). The taxation

of company income can again be justified in terms of revenue raising, although the yield is much less than from income tax. There may also be an element of income redistribution if the average shareholder has a higher income than the average non-shareholder. (Such differences in income have to some extent been eroded by the increase in the proportion of shares held by pension and insurance funds, discussed in Chapter 6.)

Another very important factor to be borne in mind when assessing the rate of company taxation is the need of companies to retain sufficient funds, after the payment of taxes, to finance investment. As we showed in Chapter 6 a substantial proportion of companies' capital spending is financed from retained earnings. Consequently a fall in retained earnings – whether due to a fall in pre-tax profits or to an increase in the rate of taxation – may reduce the rate of growth of productive capacity.

We can measure profitability in terms of the rate of return on the assets employed by companies, these assets being valued at their original or historic cost. Measured in this way profitability shows no clear trend since 1960. However, a more meaningful measure takes into account the fact that when prices are rising the cost of maintaining companies' assets increases. The replacement cost – of both fixed assets and stocks – tends to exceed historic cost. Consequently some of the profits that have been earned are required to meet this additional cost of continuing in business. When an allowance is made for this fact, profitability showed a dramatic decline, falling from about 13 per cent in 1960 to about 4 per cent in 1975. The behaviour of these two series is shown in figure 11.5, which appeared in the Economic Progress Report, February 1977.

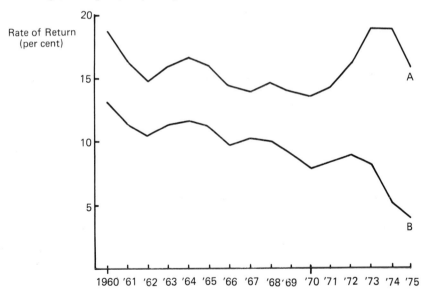

Figure 11.5   Rate of Return of Industrial and Commercial Companies

It is not surprising to find that profits have also fallen as a percentage of GDP. This is shown in figure 11.6 where profits are measured after deductions have been made for stock appreciation and for capital consumption at replacement cost; i.e. the definition of profits corresponds to that in series B in figure 11.5.

It might be thought that this downward trend in pre-tax profits would have led to a reduction in company taxation. In fact the rates of corporation tax are now

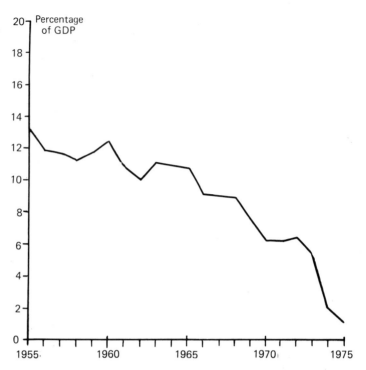

Figure 11.6   Company Profits as a Proportion of Gross Domestic Product

higher than when the tax was introduced. On the other hand increased allowances have considerably reduced the tax burden. Especially important has been the provision whereby companies can offset the full cost of capital investment against the profits earned in the year in which the investment is undertaken, instead of the cost being spread out over the life of the asset (the so-called free depreciation provision). Also important has been the provision whereby profits arising from stock appreciation are ignored in calculations of tax liability.

Such provisions are designed to encourage investment in two ways. First by reducing the burden of taxation they leave more money in the hands of companies and therefore make it easier for them to invest (the liquidity effect). Second, if the allowance is tied to the purchase of plant and equipment it encourages companies to increase their capital inputs rather than other inputs (the incentive effect).

Indirect Taxation: Taxes on Expenditure
The current structure of indirect taxation in the U.K., outlined in table 11.5 and already discussed briefly, is examined in more detail below. But we first discuss three of the functions of taxation listed above which help to explain this structure.

TO RAISE REVENUE
Since raising revenue is the primary purpose of taxation, one might conclude that the heaviest taxes should be imposed on the products with the lowest demand elasticities. A low elasticity implies that the quantity demanded would decline only slightly in response to the increase in price that would follow the imposition of an indirect tax. Conversely the lightest taxes should be imposed on products with

a high elasticity in demand, since for these products a much greater fall in the quantity demanded would follow a price rise.*

This is illustrated in figure 11.7, where we assume that producers are willing to supply an unlimited quantity of each of two products A and B at price P. The demand curves for the two products are D_A and D_B respectively. For the sake of simplicity we assume that for each product the initial equilibrium position is X, Q of each product being bought at price P.

The government now imposes an indirect tax of PC per unit on both products. At the higher price, C, the quantity bought of A falls only slightly to R, and the tax revenue is PCBA. The demand for B is, however, for more elastic. The quantity bought falls to T and the tax revenue is PCDE. This demonstrates the fact that for a given rate of tax, the less elastic the demand the greater will be the tax revenue.

Indeed there may be a point at which an increase in the tax rate on a product with a highly elastic demand would cause a decline in tax revenue. In figure 11.8, Q is bought at price P. After the imposition of a tax per unit of PC, R is bought and tax revenue is PCEF. However, a further increase in the tax rate to PD would lead to a reduction in the quantity bought to T, and to a fall in the tax revenue (PDHI < PCEF).

TO REDISTRIBUTE REAL INCOME

When one considers the products whose price elasticity of demand is relatively low, one finds that many are so called necessary goods on which low income groups spend a higher proportion of their income than high income groups, e.g. basic foodstuffs, public transport, fuel. Consequently the imposition of high rates of taxation on these products would have a regressive effect. In other words the objectives of revenue raising and the redistribution of real income are in conflict.

TO INFLUENCE THE PATTERN OF EXPENDITURE

Indirect taxation offers considerable scope for influencing the pattern of expenditure, and differential rates of taxation can usually be at least partly explained in these terms. For example, high rates of taxes have been imposed on products considered to be dangerous to health, those having a high import content, etc. However a proliferation of rates adds to the cost of tax collection, both on the part of the government department collecting the taxes and the firms responsible for making payment. Consequently there has been a tendency in the U.K. since the war to reduce the number of tax rates.

Having identified the major influences on the structure of indirect taxation, let us now examine that structure in the U.K.

The Structure of Indirect Taxation

The main general expenditure tax imposed by the central government is *value added tax*. When first introduced in 1973 the standard rate of tax was 8 per cent. However, a range of products, including foodstuffs, gas, electricity and public transport services were zero-rated. Subsequently, a rate of $12\frac{1}{2}$ per cent was imposed on 'less essential' goods, mainly consumer durables, e.g. television sets, washing machines (petrol is taxed at 25 per cent, and cars bear an additional tax). Overall the structure of VAT appears to have been strongly influenced by a desire not to have a regressive effect rather than by an objective of maximizing revenue.

As shown in Table 11.5 about one third of the total revenue from indirect taxa-

* A formal definition of price elasticity of demand was given in Chapter 7. See also Chapter 23.

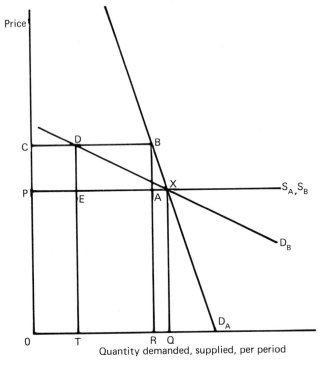

Figure 11.7 Elasticity of Demand and Tax Revenue

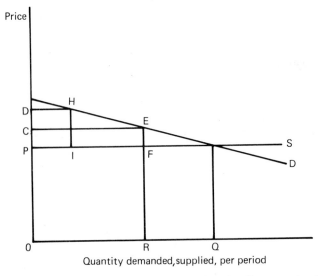

Figure 11.8 A Fall in Tax Revenue Following An Increase in the Tax Rate

tion is obtained from *customs and excise duties* on three groups of products: alcoholic drinks, tobacco, and hydrocarbon oils (petrol, diesel oil, etc.). The main purpose of these taxes is undoubtedly revenue maximization – experience suggests that their demand elasticities have been fairly low.

There may be a further justification for taxing these products heavily. Their consumption gives rise to social costs – road accidents, pollution, a need for more hospital beds, etc. If the taxes deter consumption these social costs will thereby be reduced.

Value added tax is an ad valorem tax, i.e. for any given rate of tax the amount of tax paid changes in line with the price of the product. Consequently, in inflationery conditions the tax yield automatically increases. By contrast most other customs and excise duties are specific, i.e. the tax is levied at a given absolute rate per unit quantity sold, e.g. 50 pence per gallon of petrol. The yield from specific duties does not increase as a result of inflation. Indeed the real burden of such taxes falls with inflation – the tax accounts for a smaller proportion of the selling price. Consequently in order to maintain a constant real burden of taxation the rates of specific taxes should be adjusted upwards. This contrasts with the need to reduce nominal rates of direct taxes (assuming direct taxation to be progressive) in order to maintain a constant real burden of taxation.

Table 11.5 shows that the revenue raised by *protective duties* (tariffs) is relatively small. This reflects the fact that the trend in the post-war period has been to reduce the level of protection afforded to U.K. industries by tariffs. Between 1960 and 1972 U.K. tariffs on manufactured goods imported from a wide range of countries were reduced by roughly two fifths, with even bigger reductions on a high proportion of finished goods, including machinery and vehicles. Further reductions in tariffs on manufactured goods resulted from the U.K.'s membership of the E.E.C., although tariffs on some agricultural products bought from non-E.E.C. countries were raised (see Chapter 15).

The final major form of indirect taxation is *local authority rates*, which in 1976 accounted for 12.5 per cent of total revenue from indirect taxation. The rates paid by any household or business depend partly upon the rateable value of the premises and partly upon the rate poundage levied in the local authority area in which the premises are situated. Rates can be seen as being equivalent to an expenditure tax. There is a rough relationship between the value of the local authority services 'consumed' and the rateable value. Consequently for any given area there is a rough relationship between 'consumption' and the amount paid in rates.

However, this relationship is so rough that numerous suggestions have been made for alternative methods of financing local authorities. The increasing reliance of local authorities on assistance from the central government has also been questioned. In view of the increasing attention being given to these questions, the expenditure and finance of the local authorities are discussed in a separate section below. But first we consider the remaining sources of government receipts, beginning with contributions to the National Insurance Fund.

Contributions to the National Insurance Fund, etc.
As shown in table 11.4 contributions to the National Insurance Fund, the National Health Service and the Redundancy Fund amounted in 1976 to £8,426 millions, or 14 per cent of total government receipts. Of this amount over half was paid by employers, the remainder being paid by employees and the self employed. This item can therefore be seen as yet another type of tax, falling partly on employers and partly on employees.

Taking one year with another these contributions are roughly balanced by national insurance benefits. However, this does not mean that the overall economic effect is neutral. The contributions increase the costs of labour and so encourage employers to substitute other inputs and especially, perhaps, machinery, for labour. On the other side the employee's share of the contribution may have some slight effect on the supply of labour, especially now that the contribution includes an income-related element. This element in effect raises the marginal rates of personal taxation, a process whose dangers were outlined above.

Rent, Interest and Dividends

This is a miscellaneous group of receipts, emanating from several sources. Most of the 'rent' item refers to the imputed rent income in respect of houses owned by the local authorities. The bulk of the 'interest and dividends' were received by the central government, mainly in respect of loans made to the nationalized industries. Finally a small surplus was earned on the trading activities of the local authorities, e.g. municipal markets.

Borrowing and Other Financial Transactions

This item amounted to £8,497 millions in 1976, of which £7,921 millions was *borrowing by central and local government*. This borrowing figure amounted to 13.5 per cent of total government expenditure. The significance of this fact is discussed at length in the following section and also in Chapter 12.

The Balance between Expenditure and Receipts

A comparison of tables 11.1 and 11.4 reveals that government expenditure was exactly balanced by its receipts. The reason for this balance is, of course, the inclusion within the receipts of an item for borrowing. Borrowing must be undertaken whenever the government fails to cover its expenditure by the revenue derived from other sources. Conversely, should the revenue from other sources exceed expenditure, the government would repay money previously borrowed.

Considerable economic significance attaches to the percentage of government expenditure that has to be covered by borrowing or, putting the matter the other way round, to the relationship between expenditure and revenue from sources other than borrowing. For ease of expression we shall henceforth call revenue from these sources 'taxation', since this is by far the most important of these sources.

The Balance between Government Expenditure and Taxation

It will be useful to begin this discussion by referring to the 45° diagram introduced during our discussion of total expenditure in Chapter 8. In figure 11.9 the expenditure function $C+I$ indicates what planned expenditure would be, at various levels of national income, in the absence of government expenditure and taxation.

Government spending on goods and services (G) shifts the expenditure function upwards to $C+I+G$, having a direct effect on expenditure. Transfer payments, on the other hand, do not have a direct effect on expenditure. However, they do have an indirect effect. They increase the real disposable income of individuals and/or firms, and therefore increase the propensity to spend, i.e. the amount spent from any given level of national income. This is shown in figure 11.9 by a further upward shift of the expenditure function to C^1+I^1+G.

The precise effect of a given level of transfer payments depends, of course, upon their composition. Grants to individuals will increase consumption spending and grants to firms investment spending. The effect of a subsidy may be more compli-

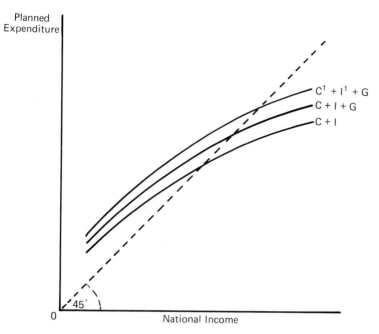

Figure 11.9   Government Spending and Total Expenditure

cated. If it results in lower prices, real consumption will increase. In addition it may lead to increased company profits and therefore, via the liquidity effect, to higher investment spending.

Taxation has the reverse effects. By reducing the disposable income of individuals and firms, direct taxation (and we can include here national insurance contributions) reduces consumption and investment. Moreover indirect taxation, although not affecting disposable income, will, via higher prices, reduce the level of real expenditure.

These changes will, of course, cause the expenditure function to shift downwards. What is crucial is the net effect on the expenditure function of these two conflicting sets of forces, one tending to increase expenditure and the other to decrease it. In order to understand what the net effect is likely to be, let us first examine the situation in which expenditure and taxation are equal.

THE BALANCED BUDGET

The term balanced budget implies that government expenditure is exactly matched by taxation (widely defined), i.e. that government borrowing is zero. It might be felt that a balanced budget would leave total expenditure unchanged, the forces tending to increase expenditure being exactly offset by those tending to decrease it. However this will be so only if the marginal propensity to consume or spend (MPE) of taxpayers equals the marginal propensity to spend of the government, including the recipients of transfer payments.

This situation is illustrated in table 11.8, where we assume that government expenditure consists entirely of transfer payments and that the MPE of the recipients is 0.85. Since this equals the MPE of the taxpayers, the net effect on total expenditure is zero.

However, it is extremely unlikely that MPEs will be equal. Since many of the

Table 11.8
A Balanced Budget: Equal Propensities to Spend

	£mn
Amount paid in taxation	100
Reduction in expenditure of taxpayers	85
Government expenditure (transfer payments)	100
Expenditure of recipients of transfer payments	85

recipients have incomes below average, e.g. the unemployed, retirement pensioners, their MPE is likely to be well above average. So, if in the above example, the average MPE of recipients were 0.95, the initial impact of the balanced budget would be an increase in total expenditure of £10 millions (£95 − 85 millions).

Furthermore, we have seen that in practice more than one half of government expenditure comprises spending on goods and services. This can be seen as analogous to an MPE of 1.0. Consequently the overall 'MPE of the government' is likely to be very high, say 0.98. In the above example this would imply, for a balanced budget of £100 million, an initial increase in expenditure of £13 million (£98 − 85 millions). Moreover, this would subsequently be extended by the operation of the multiplier and accelerator effects. Consequently the effect of a balanced budget will almost certainly be expansionary.*

A BUDGET SURPLUS

It is sometimes claimed that a budget surplus, where revenue from taxation exceeds government expenditure, will cause the economy to contract. However, the analysis of the previous section suggests that this need not be so. Since the MPE of the government exceeds that of taxpayers, a modest budget surplus may leave total expenditure unchanged. However, there clearly must come a point at which the surplus is so great as to cause total expenditure to fall, and the economy to contract.

A BUDGET DEFICIT

If a balanced budget is likely to be expansionary, then clearly a budget deficit, where public expenditure exceeds revenue from taxation, is even more likely to be expansionary. Moreover, in addition to the effects on total expenditure, as outlined above, there are other important implications of a budget deficit. As we have seen, a deficit involves borrowing by the government, and this may have a significant effect on the money supply. This effect is discussed in the following chapter.

The Relationship between Government Expenditure and the Gross Domestic Product
Even if the relationship between government expenditure and taxation, i.e. the size of the budget deficit or surplus, is considered appropriate, it might still be felt that public expenditure was too large, (or too small), in relation to GDP. In other words it might be felt that both government expenditure and taxation should be reduced, (or increased). There might be several possible reasons for this.

First, it might be felt that levels of taxation had been pushed to the point at which they were causing adverse economic consequences. As we pointed out above, high rates of personal taxation may have disincentive effects, while high rates of company taxation may lead to a reduction in investment. High rates of indirect

* The term 'balanced budget multiplier' is sometimes used to denote the overall effect of a balanced budget. For a highly simplified example, see G. Stanlake, *Macro-economics: an Introduction* (London: Longman 1974).

taxation may cause prices to increase to the extent that employees demand higher wages in compensation.

Other arguments relate to the expenditure side of the equation. It has been pointed out that an increase in government expenditure may lead to so high a proportion of resources being absorbed by the public sector that there are insufficient resources to meet the needs of the private sector. This argument has been developed furthest by Eltis and Bacon, whose views are considered in Chapter 20.

We should recognize that some people may feel that government expenditure and taxation should be increased for one reason or another, e.g. because they want to see more money spent on specific areas such as education or health or because they wish to see further changes in the distribution of income and wealth. However the more common view in the U.K. was that by the mid-1970s government expenditure was taking too large a share of total expenditure and that this share should be reduced.

The upward trend in spending that had given rise to concern is shown in figure 11.10. Line A expresses government expenditure on goods and services as a per-

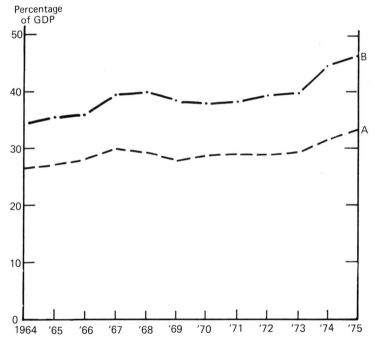

Figure 11.10 Government Expenditure as a Proportion of Gross Domestic Product

centage of GDP at factor cost. This is therefore a measure of the utilization of resources resulting directly from government expenditure. Line B relates government expenditure, including transfer payments, to GDP at market prices. Both measures show a substantial increase in the relative importance of government expenditure, especially in the first half of the 1970s.

At the beginning of 1977 a White Paper (Cmnd. 6721) was issued in which the government outlined its plans for restraining and indeed reversing the upward trend in the share of resources and of total expenditure accounted for by the public sector. A summary of past changes and of the plans contained in the White Paper are presented in table 11.9.

Table 11.9
Public Expenditure as a Proportion of Gross Domestic Product

	1965–6	1975–6	1978–9
Expenditure on goods and services as % of GDP at factor cost	24	30	27
Expenditure, including transfer payments, as % of GDP at market prices	35.5	46	42–3

Source: Financial Times, 31.1.77.

The White Paper showed not only a planned decline in the share of the public sector during the second half of the 1970s, but also a decline in absolute terms (after allowing for inflation). The change in trend implied by this plan is illustrated in figure 11.11, in which government expenditure (including transfer payments) is expressed in constant (1975) prices. The percentage figures in the diagram show the change in expenditure from the previous year.

It is not, of course, unknown for government's financial plans to go astray – especially when they involve reductions in expenditure! In an attempt to exert a greater degree of financial discipline the government has placed increasing reliance

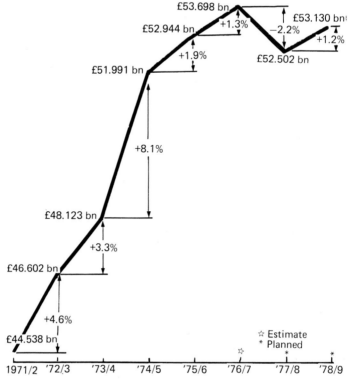

Figure 11.11   Changes in Public Spending

on cash limits on the expenditure of government departments. Cash limits have also been imposed on the loans made by central government to finance the capital expenditure of local authorities, and on the amount of rate support grant which helps to finance current spending by those authorities.

The Expenditure and Finance of Local Authorities

In much of the earlier discussion we have included the expenditure and finance of the local authorities along with that of the central government. However the activities of the local authorities (L.A.s.) raise a number of important issues which require separate attention.

Local authority expenditure in real terms tended to increase at a rate far in excess of the growth of the economy as a whole, especially in the first part of the 1970s. In fact real expenditure increased by about one quarter in the first half of the decade. This increase in expenditure no doubt resulted in improvements in some of the services provided by L.A.s. – education, welfare services, recreational facilities, etc. However it has been suggested that the increase in expenditure was also an indication of a reduction in efficiency in the local authority sector as a whole.

Whatever the merits of that argument, it appears that L.A.s. felt unable to ask ratepayers to increase their payments in line with the increase in expenditure. The percentage of the L.A.s'. current expenditure covered by rates revenue fell from about 40 per cent in the mid-1960s to about 30 per cent in the mid-1970s. (There was a corresponding fall in the percentage of total expenditure covered from about 30 per cent to about 20 per cent.)

One consequence of the failure of rates revenue to rise in line with expenditure was an increasing reliance on central government finance. This trend was strengthened by the fact that the current expenditure of the L.A.s. frequently turned out to be greater than indicated when the amount of the annual rate support grant was agreed. Since the amount of rates revenue is fixed at the beginning of the year, an excess of current expenditure over that intended invariably implies that the central government must supplement the rate support grant. (The use of cash limits, referred to above, was intended to eliminate or substantially reduce such supplementary payments.)

The result of these factors was that by the mid-1970s almost two thirds of the current expenditure of the L.A.s. was being financed by means of grants from the central government. Consequently when the central government announced plans to halt the expansion of public expenditure it was able to put pressure on the L.A.s. to bring them into line. The need to ensure that the spending of the L.A.s. was curbed can be seen from the fact that they account for almost one third of the combined spending of central and local government.

The pattern of local authority spending and revenue in 1976 is shown in tables 11.10 and 11.11. Although some discretion is exercised at the local level, the pattern of expenditure is mainly determined by policies adopted by the central government, and approved by Parliament. (A good example is the large amount of money spent by the L.As. in financing a system of education whose basic structure is determined centrally.)

This factor has led to suggestions that the central government should take a more direct responsibility for financing these services, rather than channeling support through the L.As. in the form of grants and loans.

On the other hand, suggestions have been made that were designed to reduce the dependence of the L.As. on central government – one effect of this might be to increase interest in local political affairs. Since the present burden of rate

Table 11.10
Local Authoritties' Combined Current and Capital Expenditure (1976)

	£mn	Per cent
Expenditure on goods and services:		
education	5,851	30.7
housing	2,246	11.8
environmental services	1,279	6.7
roads and public lighting	1,018	5.3
police, justice, fire service	1,441	7.6
personal social services	1,117	5.9
school meals and milk	436	2.3
other expenditure on goods and services	858	4.5
Total expenditure on goods and services	14,246	74.8
Non-trading capital consumption	555	2.9
Subsidies (mainly housing and passenger transport)	483	2.5
Grants (scholarships, rent rebates, etc.)	727	3.8
Net lending (mainly for house purchase)	144	0.8
Debt interest	2,894	15.2
Total Expenditure	19,049	100

Source: *National Income and Expenditure* (H.M.S.O., 1977).

Table 11.11
Local Authorities' Revenue, Combined Current and Capital Account. (1976)

	£mn	Per cent
Rates	4,540	23.8
Trading surplus	81	0.4
Rent from dwellings, etc.	1,879	9.9
Interest, etc.	611	3.2
Imputed consumption of non-trading capital	555	2.9
Central government grants	9,647	50.6
Borrowing from central government (net)	481	2.5
Other borrowing (net)	1,327	7.0
Total	19,049	100

Source: *National Income and Expenditure* (H.M.S.O., 1977).

payments is generally considered to be sufficiently high, this implies the introduction of new sources of finance. The most common suggestions are for local income and sales taxes, such as are found in the U.S.A. There is no indication so far of any official support for these suggestions, perhaps because of the administrative problems that might arise.* For example when residential areas and areas of work are far apart, it is not easy to determine appropriate boundaries for the taxing authorities.

Summary and Conclusions
Government expenditure may have various purposes, including the provision of public goods, the provision of goods (including public goods) at prices below the costs of production, the redistribution of income and an increase in economic efficiency. Although different governments may have different views about the relative

* In 1977 the Conservative Party announced that it would abolish household rates when it returned to power, without specifying what alternative it favoured.

importance of these purposes, there is a great deal of common ground among the major political parties. Consequently major changes in the pattern of government expenditure are rare, and tend to occur only over a long period.

Government expenditure may take different forms, and the 'mix' of expenditure has implications both for the various purposes noted above and for the eventual change in total expenditure that follows from a given level of government expenditure.

Of the various sources of funds from which government expenditure might be financed, we concentrated our attention on taxation. We considered the various functions of taxation, including raising revenue. We also examined the current structure of taxation in the U.K. and discussed some of the possible consequences of this structure.

We demonstrated that a particularly important aspect of fiscal policy is the balance between government expenditure and revenue from taxation, and we discussed the likely effect, first of a balanced budget and then of a budget surplus and deficit.

We noted the increasing concern shown about two aspects of fiscal policy. The first was the increase in the relative important of the budget, i.e. of both public expenditure and revenue from taxation. The second was the tendency in the mid-1970s for budget deficits to become larger. We showed that this concern had been shared by government, and that plans to halt, and indeed reverse, these trends had been announced.

We shall further evaluate the role of fiscal policy in Chapter 13. But first we examine the other major form of demand management – monetary policy.

ESSAY QUESTIONS

1 Discuss the major characteristics of public goods and explain why such goods are normally supplied by the government.
2 Assess the role of fiscal policy in relation to any three economic objectives.
3 Discuss the major functions of taxation and show how these functions have influenced the structure of taxation in the U.K.
4 Discuss the major functions of government expenditure and show how these functions have influenced the pattern of U.K. government expenditure.
5 Discuss the possible effects on total tax revenue of a reduction in the rates of personal taxation.
6 Discuss the possible effects on the supply of labour of changes in (a) direct (b) indirect taxation.
7 Analyse the possible effects of a reduction in the rates of corporation tax combined with an increase in the rates of capital transfer tax. (Assume that the effect on total tax revenue is neutral.)
8 Analyse the possible effects of an increase in the rates of direct taxation combined with a reduction in the rates of indirect taxation. (Assume that the effect on total tax revenue is neutral.)
9 Analyse the possible effects on total expenditure of a balanced budget.
10 'A budget surplus will cause a reduction in the level of economic activity.' Discuss.
11 Explain what you understand by the term 'the burden of the national debt'. Under what circumstances if any, might an increase in the burden of the debt be justified?

EXERCISES

11.1 If between one year and another the following changes occurred:

(i) The prices of all manufactured goods rose by 10 per cent,
(ii) the price of food rose by 15 per cent,
(iii) the prices of raw materials rose by 5 per cent,
(iv) all wages rose by 10 per cent,
(v) all types of government expenditure rose by 10 per cent, which of the following groups would be most likely to (a) suffer and (b) benefit?
(i) Wage-earners.
(ii) Share-holders.
(iii) Retirement pensioners.

11.2 In 1977 exemption from all payment for a wide range of medical and dental services was granted to the following groups: children under 16, men over 65, women over 60, expectant and nursing mothers, families in receipt of supplementary benefit or family income supplement.

Say why you think these exemptions might have been made, and discuss their implications.

11.3 'Public spending roughly divides into four broad categories:

'First, there is the direct expenditure of resources on services, many of which contain a large social service element – the NHS, the personal social services, housing investment, and the rest.

'Secondly, there are transfers. Transfers redistribute money from original income recipients to pensioners and social security beneficiaries, to consumers of subsidized services such as public transport, and to holders of Government debt.

'Thirdly, there is public spending designed to increase productive capacity, whether in the form of investment in the nationalized industries, or in the form of grants to private industry.

'Fourthly, there is public spending on the acquisition of assets, for example the extension of public ownership in industry, or the municipalization of privately rented housing.

'Spending between these categories differs fundamentally in its economic and social effect.'

The above passage was taken from an article by Anthony Crosland, then Minister of the Environment, and published in *The Guardian* (24.3.76).

Comment on the conclusion that 'Spending between these categories differs fundamentally in its economic and social effect', discussing especially the implications of each type of spending for (a) economic growth, (b) inflation, (c) the reduction of inequality.

11.4 'In the last three years public expenditure has grown by nearly 20 per cent in volume, while output has risen by less than 2 per cent. The ratio of public expenditure to gross domestic product has risen from 50 per cent to 60 per cent. Fifteen years ago it was 42 per cent. The tax burden has also greatly increased. In 1975–6 a married man on average earnings is paying about a quarter of his earnings in income tax, compared with a tenth in 1960–1. At two-thirds average earnings, he is paying about a fifth compared with less than a twentieth. ... Tax thresholds have fallen sharply in relation to average earnings, and people are being drawn into tax at income levels which are below social security benefit levels ...'

The above passage was taken from the White Paper *Public Expenditure 1979–80* (H.M.S.O., 1976). Discuss the significance of the changes referred to in the passage.

11.5 The estimates of changes in real disposable income at various levels of gross income, shown in figure 11.12, were contained in an article in the *Financial Times* (30.3.77). Discuss the possible consequences of these changes.

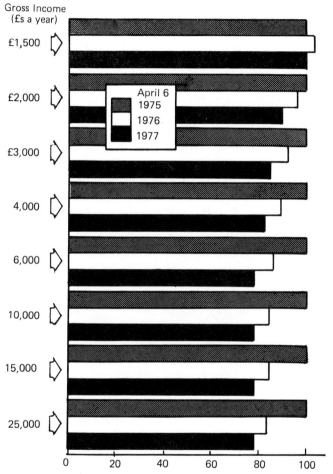

Figure 11.12 Changes in Real Disposable Income since 1975

11.6 At the beginning of 1977 the proportion of income taken by income taxes in various countries was as follows:

U.K.	43 per cent
Germany	33 per cent
Italy	21 per cent
France	20 per cent

How would you respond to the suggestion that these figures indicate that the rate of taxation was too high in the U.K.?

11.7 Discuss the proposition that table 11.12 shows clearly that in 1973 taxation was too high in the Netherlands and too low in Japan.

Table 11.12
Ratio of Total Tax Receipts to GNP (1973)

Netherlands	43.7
Sweden	43.5
Belgium	36.6
Germany	37.3
France	36.9
United Kingdom	32.8
Italy	29.2
United States	28.0
Japan	22.6

Source: *O.E.C.D.*

11.8 When discussing in March 1972 the value added tax, to be introduced in 1973, the Chancellor of the Exchequer announced that there would be a single standard rate of tax, but with certain exceptions, as follows:

(i) Food, other than those foods then subject to purchase-tax, would be zero-rated (i.e. would not be taxed).
(ii) Newspapers, periodical and books would be zero-rated.
(iii) All new construction, whether of houses or other buildings, would be zero-rated.
(iv) Exports of all goods would be zero-rated.
(v) Fuel – gas, electricity and coal – and fares would be zero-rated.
(vi) There would be, in addition to the standard rate of VAT, a special tax on new cars at the rate of 10 per cent of the wholesale value.
(vii) There would be a general exemption from VAT of all businesses whose taxable turnover does not exceed £5,000 a year: this would exclude from tax about 500,000 traders.

How would you justify these exemptions?

11.9 Table 11.13 shows the composition of the tax burden (including national insurance contributions but excluding taxes on capital) in the U.K. in various years. (i) What factors do you think might account for the changes as between

Table 11.13
U.K. Government Tax Revenue (per cent)

	1969/70	1976/77 (provisional)	1977/78 (estimated)
Direct central government taxes on income	39	44	41
Indirect central government taxes on expenditure	39	27	29
Rates	8	10	11
National Insurance contributions:			
Employers	7	11	11
Employees	7	8	8
Total taxation	100	100	100

Source: *Economic Progress Report*, September 1977.

(a) 1969–70 and 1976–77, (b) 1976–77 and 1977–78? (ii) Discuss the possible implications of these changes.

11.10 'Table 11.14 indicates that the burden of the national debt has steadily fallen.' Discuss.

Table 11.14
Nominal Value of the National Debt

End–March	£mn	As % of GDP
1964	21,630	78.4
1966	22,040	69.5
1968	24,479	69.1
1970	23,424	58.3
1972	26,619	52.6
1974	27,716	43.1
1976	40,407	41.5

Source: Bank of England Quarterly Bulletin, September 1977.

OBJECTIVE TEST QUESTIONS: SET 4

1   Transfer payments include all of the following except

A salaries of school teachers
B interest on the national debt
C retirement pensions
D sickness benefit
E child benefit.

2   The best definition of a progressive tax system is that

A all taxpayers pay the same absolute amount in taxation
B all taxpayers pay the same proportion of their income in taxation
C high income earners pay more in taxes than low income earners
D high income earners pay a higher proportion of their income in taxes than low income earners
E there is a bigger absolute range in pre-tax than in post-tax incomes.

3   Assume that in a closed economy public expenditure and taxation are both £100 millions. 60 per cent of the public expenditure consists of spending on goods and services, and 40 per cent of transfer payments. The marginal propensity to consume of taxpayers is 0.8. Ignoring any multiplier or accelerator effects, the net effect of fiscal policy will be an increase in total expenditure of (£ millions)

A   100
B   60
C   25
D   17
E   zero

4   'Any excess of public expenditure over revenue must increase the real burden of the national debt.' This statement is incorrect because

A   most of the national debt is held by U.K. citizens
B   rates of interest may fall
C   public expenditure may cause an increase in GNP

D the gap between expenditure and revenue can be filled by borrowing abroad

E an excess of expenditure over revenue re-distributes income in favour of the poorer member of the community.

5 The characteristics of public goods include
  1 non-rivalness
  2 non-excludability
  3 zero opportunity cost.

6

		Income before tax £	Income after tax £
1	X	10,000	9,000
	Y	5,000	4,000
2	X	10,000	8,000
	Y	5,000	4,000
3	X	10,000	5,000
	Y	5,000	3,000

Which of the above situations indicate(s) the existence of a progressive system of taxation?

7 Under a regressive tax system
  1 there is a bigger absolute range in post-tax than in pre-tax incomes
  2 all taxpayers pay the same absolute amount in taxation
  3 all taxpayers pay the same proportion of their income in tax.

8 Direct taxes include
  1 personal (income) tax
  2 corporation tax
  3 capital transfer tax.

9 In figure 11.13 AB indicates all the possible combinations of leisure and consumption available to an individual. The movement of the curve to AB^1 could be due to a fall in
  1 direct tax rates
  2 indirect tax rates
  3 unemployment benefit.

10 In order to maintain a constant real burden of taxation under inflationary conditions it is usually necessary to increase the rates of
  1 direct taxes
  2 ad valorem expenditure taxes
  3 specific expenditure taxes.

11 The effect of a balanced budget on total expenditure is likely to depend upon the
  1 marginal propensity to consume of taxpayers
  2 marginal propensity to consume of the recipients of transfer payments
  3 composition of public expenditure.

12 The capital transfer tax
  1 applies to all capital transfers
  2 is a tax on wealth
  3 is a progressive tax.

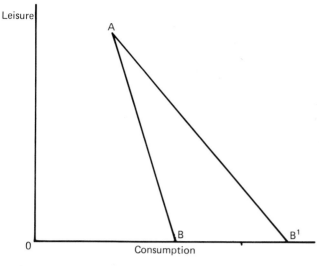

Figure 11.13

13 Indirect taxes include
  1 value added tax
  2 local authority rates
  3 capital gains tax.

14 Personal tax, as currently levied in the U.K., is progressive because
  1 no tax is payable on incomes below a minimum figure
  2 on incomes beyond a certain figure the rate of tax increases
  3 the maximum rate of tax is less than 100 per cent.

15 Transfer payments are not included in the calculation of national income.
    Transfer payments are made without any productive service being provided in exchange.

16 An increase in the rates of direct taxation may cause a fall in total tax revenue.
    The amount of revenue from both direct and indirect taxation may fall following an increase in the rates of direct taxation.

17 The greater the elasticity of demand the greater is the tax revenue for any given rate of tax.
    Elasticity of demand measures the responsiveness of the quantity demanded to a change in price.

18 A balanced budget does not affect total expenditure.
    A balanced budget implies that net borrowing by the public authorities is zero.

19 A budget surplus always causes total expenditure to fall.
    A budget surplus implies that net borrowing by the government is positive.

20 Inflation is more likely to lead to an increase in tax revenue under a progressive than a regressive system of taxation.
    Tax rates are higher under a progressive than a regressive system of taxation.

TRUE/FALSE

1 When applied to public goods, non-excludability denotes that if a good is supplied to one citizen it must be supplied to all.

2 The fee charged by a solicitor for effecting the transfer of ownership of property is an example of a transfer payment.

3 Indirect taxation is most likely to lead to a redistribution of income in favour of poor people if the highest taxes are imposed on those products which account for a greater proportion of the expenditure of rich than of poor people.

4 Under a progressive tax system all taxpayers pay the same proportion of their income in tax.

5 Fiscal drag refers to the fact that with a progressive tax system the proportion of income paid in taxation automatically increases in inflationary conditions.

6 Fiscal policy encompasses both taxation and public expenditure.

7 The 'free-rider problem' refers to the difficulty of preventing someone who has not contributed to the cost of a project, from deriving benefits from that project.

8 Housing is the major item of local authorities' current expenditure.

9 The government provides subsidies and grants to both companies and private individuals.

10 Interest on the national debt is treated in the national accounts as a transfer payment.

CHAPTER TWELVE

Monetary Policy

Introduction

As we noted at the end of the previous chapter, monetary policy has been used along with fiscal policy in order to influence the level of economic activity. Policy designed to influence the supply of money* is implemented via a wide range of institutions, both public and private, and we discuss these institutions in some detail.

Monetary policy is also concerned with the cost of money, which is influenced not only by supply, but also by demand conditions Before discussing the supply side, we examine the major determinants of the demand for money.

The Demand for Money

Keynes specified three types of demand for money: the transactions, precautionary and speculative demand. These three types of demand may be related to three basic reasons why individuals or firms may wish to hold money rather than use it to acquire assets, such as shares, goods, property, etc., which would yield a positive return.

The Transaction Demand

The transactions demand reflects the fact that the pattern of income – of household or firm – seldom coincides with the pattern of expenditure. The worker is paid every week or month, while he (or his wife), makes payments for food, travel, etc., every day. Firms have to pay workers, suppliers of materials, etc., at times different from that at which they receive payment for goods sold. Consequently, both households and firms maintain a stock of money out of which they can make payments in those periods during which their current income is inadequate.

The most important determinant of the size of the transactions demand is the value of the transactions which the household or firm expects to make in a given period, which itself depends upon the income of the household or firm. If we aggregate these individual demands we can say that the main determinant of the total transactions demand is the level of GDP or national income. Other influences include the flexibility of the financial system – and in particular the ability of an individual or firm to acquire money at short notice when required – and the penalty for non-payment of bills on the due date. The opportunity cost of holding money, i.e. the benefit foregone by not spending money, may also be important.

The Precautionary Demand

The precautionary demand reflects the fact that uncertainty may exist concerning

---

* Official definitions of money are given later in the chapter. For the moment it is sufficient to note that anything which is generally acceptable in exchange for goods and services and which acts as a measure and store of value can be regarded as money.

future financial obligations. The size of the precautionary demand is subject to very similar influences as the transactions demand, and the difference between the two is probably best explained by means of a simple example.

A family setting off for a day's car ride would take a given amount of money to pay for any meals, petrol, etc., that they planned to buy. This would constitute their transactions demand. They would also, if they were sensible, take an additional amount to cover the possibility of a breakdown or accident requiring expenditure on repairs, train fares, etc. This would constitute their precautionary demand.

The Speculative Demand

In its simplest form, as formulated by Keynes, the speculative demand for money is related to the current rate of interest on fixed interest government stock or bonds. Keynes suggested that the speculative demand would be inversely related to the rate of interest for two reasons. The first reason is that the higher the rate of interest the greater is the opportunity cost of holding money, and consequently the less money will be held.

The second reason is connected with the fact that the rate of interest is inversely related to the price of bonds. For example if a £100 bond bearing a 'coupon' of 5 per cent is issued at par, i.e. at a price of £100, then the actual rate of interest is, of course, 5 per cent. The purchaser of a bond for £100 would receive £5 a year interest. (We ignore taxation). If the price of that bond were subsequently to fall to £50, a purchaser could now obtain an annual return of £5 for an outlay of £50, i.e. the actual rate of interest to new purchasers would be 10 per cent, double the nominal rate. Conversely at a price of £125 the actual rate of interest would be 4 per cent $(=5\% \times 100/125)$.

Although the price of bonds is influenced by many factors, and although different investors may take different views about the relative importance of these factors, a general feeling is likely to emerge about what the correct or normal rate of interest should be in the prevailing economic circumstances. If the current rate is actually greater than what is adjudged normal, a decline in the rate, i.e. a *rise* in the price of bonds would be expected. Such an expectation would encourage investors to switch from money to bonds. That is to say a high rate of interest tends to give rise to a low speculative demand for money. Conversely a low rate of interest would induce an expectation of a future fall in bond prices (a rise in the rate of interest) and would therefore encourage a switch from bonds to money, i.e. a low rate of interest tends to give rise to a high speculative demand.

Consequently these two factors, the current return on bonds and expectations about changes in future prices, combine to make the speculative demand sensitive to the rate of interest, i.e. to make demand interest elastic.

As we mentioned above, Keynes's original formulation of the speculative demand referred to government stock. Government stock is not, of course, the only form of investment. One alternative is the purchase of debentures issued by companies. But since the prices, and hence rates of interest, of government stock and company debentures tend to move together, the analysis can easily be extended to cover the latter. The analysis cannot, however, be extended so easily to encompass investment in shares, since the prices (and yields) of shares and of fixed interest securities frequently move in opposite directions. This limitation of the analysis should be borne in mind.

Figure 12.1 summarizes the above analysis of the determinants of the demand for money. The transactions and precautionary demands have been combined in

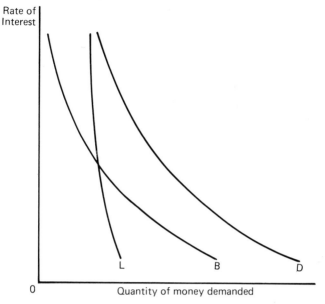

Figure 12.1   A Demand Function for Money

curve L, which is only slightly sensitive to the rate of interest. The speculative demand, B, is much more interest elastic. The total demand function for money, D, is obtained by aggregating horizontally the two separate demand functions.

Figure 12.1 represents the situation with a given level of national income. As we noted above the transactions and precautionary demands and therefore, of course, the total demand for money, will be positively related to the level of

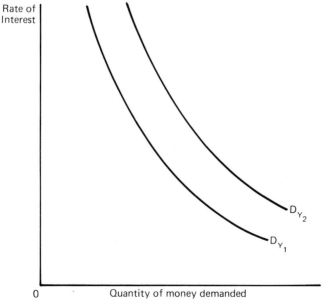

Figure 12.2   A Change in the Demand for Money

national income. This is shown in figure 12.2 where the demand function shifts to the right as the level of national income rises from Y_1 to Y_2.

The Supply of Money

Before we can examine the factors affecting the supply of money we must briefly discuss the definition of money, since several alternative definitions might be used.

Alternative Definitions of the Money Supply

Money was defined above as anything which is generally acceptable in exchange for goods and services and which acts as a measure and store of value. While this definition has the advantage of being comprehensive, it is not of much help when we are attempting to discover the effect of changes in the supply of money. In order to do this we must be able to measure the money supply, and consequently a more precise definition is required.

In the U.K. two official definitions of the money supply exist. M_1 comprises notes and coin in circulation plus current bank accounts held in sterling by private sector residents. Since current account holders have the option of paying for almost all purchases by notes and coin or by cheques, it is clearly sensible to treat all three as money, and indeed M_1 is probably the definition which comes closest to the ordinary citizen's idea of money.

M_3 consists of notes and coins in circulation, plus all bank deposits – in both current and deposit accounts, in sterling and non-sterling, including certificates of deposit – held by U.K. residents in both the private and public sectors. The components of M_3 that are not included in M_1 are slightly less liquid assets. For example holders of deposit accounts do not have cheque books, and are formally required to give notice, often seven days, of withdrawal. Even though this formal requirement may be waived it remains less convenient to make payments by drawing on a deposit than a current account. However, although M_3 is slightly less liquid overall than M_1 it is probably a better measure of aggregate domestic purchasing power.

Whichever of these two definitions we adopt, bank deposits constitute the greater part of the money supply, as can be seen from table 12.1. It is therefore appropriate to discuss next the functions of the banking system.

Table 12.1
The Money Supply (U.K., April 1977)

	£mn
Notes and coin	6,540
Private sector sterling current accounts	12,636
M1	19,176
Private sector sterling deposit accounts	19,747
U.K. public sector deposits	1,188
U.K. residents' deposits in other currencies	4,234
M3	44,345

Source: Bank of England Quarterly Bulletin, June 1977.

The Functions of a Banking System

The basic functions of a banking system are to accept deposits and to make loans of one kind or another. Deposits are the major item on the liabilities side of most banks' balance sheets, and loans the major item on the assets side. Liabilities must always equal assets. Nevertheless banks are able to extend loans in excess of the amount of money *initially* deposited with them.

Credit Creation in a Single Bank System
This can be explained with reference to table 12.2 which relates to the simplest form of banking system with just a single bank. We start from the point at which,

Table 12.2
Credit Creation in a Single Bank System

Liabilities (£)		Assets (£)	
Stage 1 Initial deposits	100,000	Coin	100,000
Stage 2 Initial deposits	100,000	Coin	100,000
Created deposits	900,000	Loans	900,000
	1,000,000		1,000,000

since beginning operations, the bank has succeeded in attracting *initial deposits* of coin to the value of £100,000. At this stage, designated Stage 1, the coin lies idle in the bank's vaults. If the bank expects depositors to withdraw their deposits at short notice it will be prudent to retain all the money deposited.

On the other hand if experience elsewhere suggests that depositors will not withdraw all their deposits at any one time, the bank will be able to lend the money that is not required. For example if it believed that depositors would not call upon more than one tenth of their deposits, it would be able to lend the remaining nine tenths.

When people borrow money from a bank they normally do so because they wish to buy something. Consequently, this money (coin) loaned by the bank will be used for payment for goods and services. The suppliers of these goods and services will deposit the money received with the same bank as made the loans, since this is the only bank in existence. This money we call *created deposits*.

The coin that is redeposited with the bank can be loaned out again and again provided that the bank continues to hold coin equal to 10 per cent of its total deposits or total assets. The limit to this process of credit creation is represented by Stage 2 in table 12.2. The bank has coin to the value of £100,000 but this now represents only 10 per cent of its assets. The bank has created credit of nine times the level of its initial deposits.

Credit Creation in a Multi-Bank System
Although the arithmetic is slightly different, the principle of credit creation is exactly the same in a multi-bank system. Let us consider the simplest form of multi-bank system, i.e. one comprising two banks. In table 12.3 we again begin with initial deposits of £100,000, but these are now split equally between the two banks, (Stage 1).

If each bank could be sure that for every £100 of loans that it made it would receive a further £100 of (created) deposits, then it could operate on the same cash assets ratio as previously. However in practice each bank may feel obliged to keep a slightly higher cash ratio in case it loses potential deposits to the other bank. If each bank operates with a $12\frac{1}{2}$ per cent cash ratio and lends money up to this limit, the final position will be as at Stage 2 in table 12.3. Each bank has created credit of seven times its initial deposits. We have assumed here that neither bank is more successful than the other in attracting deposits. If one bank were more

Table 12.3
Credit Creation in a MultiBank System

	Bank A			
	Liabilities (£)		Assets (£)	
Stage 1 Initial deposits	50,000		Coin	50,000
Stage 2 Initial deposits	50,000		Coin	50,000
Created deposits	350,000		Loans	350,000
	400,000			400,000

	Bank B			
	Liabilities (£)		Assets (£)	
Stage 1 Initial deposits	50,000		Coin	50,000
Stage 2 Initial deposits	50,000		Coin	50,000
Created deposits	350,000		Loans	350,000
	400,000			400,000

successful, the final distribution of deposits and loans would be different. However the totals for the system would be the same, provided that both banks continued to work to the same cash ratios.

The U.K. Banking System
In the U.K., as in most industrialized economies, by far the greater part of the total value of transactions is settled by payment by cheque. Similarly the loans made by the banks mainly comprise accounts against which payment can be made by cheque, rather than coin or notes. However the principle of credit creation remains the same. The base to which credit creation is related today is discussed below. But first we discuss the assets of the banking system.

The distribution of the sterling assets of the U.K. banks is shown in table 12.4. It will be noticed that almost half of the assets are held by the London clearing

Table 12.4
The Sterling Assets of United Kingdom Banks (May 1977)

	All Banks		London Clearing Banks	
	£mn	Per cent	£mn	Per cent
Notes and coin	1,124	2.1	706	2.8
Reserve assets	5,026	9.4	2,654	10.4
Special and supplementary deposits	1,047	2.0	601	2.4
Other market loans and bills	15,760	29.5	3,713	14.6
Advances	27,314	51.1	15,772	61.9
Investments	3,233	6.0	2,027	8.0
Total*	53,504	100	25,491	100

*Excludes miscellaneous assets in sterling and other currencies.
Source: *Monthly Digest of Statistics*, June 1977.

banks. These comprise the 'big four' – National Westminster, Barclays, Midland and Lloyds – and the smaller Williams and Glyns, Coutts and the Co-operative Bank. The share of the London clearers used to be considerably greater than this, and has declined as other banks, including branches of foreign banks, have been established and have competed for deposits. (The branches of foreign banks have an even greater share of non-sterling deposits and assets, and the London clearing banks now account for only about a quarter of the total assets – sterling and other currencies – of the U.K. banking system.)

The distribution of sterling assets shown in table 12.4 reflects a number of influences, in particular the need for profitability, for liquidity, and for compliance with government policies. (As we shall see, these last two requirements coincide to some extent.)

Profitability

In order to cover their operating costs, and to earn profits from which to pay dividends to shareholders, the banks must use their deposits in ways which, in total, yield a surplus over the payments made to depositors. The most profitable type of asset is normally advances – mainly loans and overdrafts. The rate of interest charged on advances is fixed in relation to the bank's *base rate*. The margin charged above base rate varies according to the nature and status of the customer but is normally within the range 1 to 5 per cent. (The rate paid to depositors might be 3 to 4 per cent below base rate, depending upon the amount deposited and the length of notice of withdrawal required.)

Investments, which mainly comprise government stocks, also tend to provide a high yield. However, if the banks wish to sell the stock before the date of maturity, there is always the possibility that they will make a capital loss, i.e. that they will obtain a lower price than they paid for the stock. This possibility means that investments must be seen as a relatively illiquid type of asset.

Liquidity

In the hypothetical banking systems discussed earlier, the banks' need for liquidity was met by ensuring that reserves of coin were always at least 10 per cent, ($12\frac{1}{2}$ per cent in the multi-bank system) of total liabilities or total assets. Precisely the same procedure applies in practice today, in that the banks maintain a certain reserve of notes and coin. (It will be noticed in table 12.4 that the London clearing banks keep relatively higher reserves of notes and coin than do other banks. This reflects the more extensive branch network and the much greater number of depositors of the clearers.)

These reserves of notes and coin are intended to meet the day to day requirements of the banks' depositors. The fact that the percentage of assets backed by cash is relatively small can be partly explained by the increasing tendency to make payments by cheque. Some of these payments relate to transactions between customers of the same bank. However, many involve customers of different banks, e.g. a firm with an account at Barclays pays a supplier with an account at the Midland; an individual who banks at the Midland makes a cheque out to an account holder at Lloyds; and so on.

These latter (inter-bank) transactions lead to a set of claims and counter-claims among the clearers. Many of these claims simply offset each other. But at the end of the day, when all cheques have been cleared at the clearing house, some banks emerge as net creditors and others as net debtors. These debts are settled by making transfers between the balances that each bank holds at the Bank of England. These balances are therefore almost as liquid as the reserves of notes and coin.

COMPLIANCE WITH GOVERNMENT POLICY

In 1971 the government introduced a new system of competition and credit control (C.C.C.) An important part of this system was the designation of a category of reserve assets and a requirement that the banks' holdings of reserve assets should equal at least $12\frac{1}{2}$ per cent of eligible liabilities. (Eligible liabilities include private sterling deposits, net deposits and certificates of deposit owed to other banks, and net foreign currency liabilities.)

RESERVE ASSETS

Reserve assets comprise balances with the Bank of England (other than special deposits), money at call with the London money market, Treasury bills, British government stocks with one year or less to maturity, local authority bills eligible for rediscount at the Bank of England and (up to a maximum of 2 per cent of eligible liabilities) commercial bills eligible for rediscount at the Bank of England.

We noted above that the need for liquidity and the need to comply with government policy tend to coincide. As we shall see below reserve assets tend to be more liquid than other assets (except notes and coin of course). However, the corollary of this greater liquidity is that reserve assets tend to have a lower yield that other assets, and in the absence of government intervention, the banks' need for liquidity *might* be satisfied by a lower reserve assets ratio. In other words, the coincidence between these two requirements *may* be only partial.

THE RESERVE ASSETS STRUCTURE

The reserve assets held by the banks are shown in table 12.5. Balances at the Bank of England can be seen as a form of money available for specific purposes – the settling of inter-bank indebtedness, and making payments to the authorities.

Table 12.5

U.K. Banks' Reserve Assets (May 1977)

	£mn
Balances at the Bank of England	323
Money at call	2,008
Treasury bills	1,411
British government stocks, not more than one year to maturity	555
Local authority bills eligible for re-discount of the Bank of England	92
Commercial bills eligible for re-discount at the Bank of England	637
Total reserve assets	5,026
Eligible liabilities	35,826
(Reserve assets ratio)	(14 per cent)

Source: *Monthly Digest of Statistics*, June 1977.

The next most liquid asset is money lent 'at call and short notice' to the London money market. If, on a given day, a bank finds that it has more than enough money to meet its immediate requirements, it may lend the surplus to the various institutions which comprise the London money market, of which the discount houses are the most important. All of this lending is short term, some of it for as little as twenty-four hours. Money loaned on this basis is known as money 'at call' since the banks can call in these loans, i.e. re-convert them into money, as required. (We show below how the money market finances the repayment of the loans that are called in by the banks.)

Treasury bills constitute short term borrowing by the government. A certain quantity of bills, normally with a period to maturity of ninety days, is offered each week. (The quantity offered depends upon the Government's borrowing requirement.) The banks do not bid for bills when they are offered initially, but subsequently buy them in the market, the bills then having less than the initial ninety days to maturity. The banks normally keep Treasury bills until maturity, and arrange their purchases so that some of their holdings mature each week, i.e. the banks have a regular inflow of money from this source. The same principles apply to their holdings of eligible local authority and commercial bills.

The final type of reserve asset is British government stocks with not more than one year to maturity. Although on the whole this item represents longer-term lending than the other reserve assets, it is still more liquid than advances and investments (not included within reserve assets).

The Bank of England

The major areas of responsibility of the Bank of England are similar to those of most other central banks, namely:

(1) Supervising the activities of the institutions comprising the country's banking and financial system so as to ensure the stability and efficient functioning of the system. This is a responsibility that is often taken for granted, and indeed we say little about it here, since it is relatively unimportant in the context of monetary policy. However in a wider sense it is clearly extremely important. This was illustrated when the collapse of several 'fringe' or secondary banks in the mid 1970s threatened the stability of the entire financial system of the U.K. The Bank of England was able to organize the support required to counter this threat. Under the 'lifeboat' scheme instigated by the Bank, the major banks – predominantly the clearing banks – who were presumed to be the recipients of deposits withdrawn from the secondary banks, agreed to recycle these funds back to those banks in order to try to prevent further collapses. The major banks agreed to this scheme despite the risk that they might lose some of these funds – as indeed some banks did.*

(2) Acting as banker to the government. The Bank must ensure that the government has at all times sufficient money to meet its planned expenditure. Since, as we saw in the previous chapter, public expenditure frequently exceeds revenue from taxation, this implies that the Bank is responsible for managing the government's borrowing programme.

(3) Implementing the government's monetary policy. There is clearly a connection between this area of responsibility and the previous one. However they do not necessarily coincide.

The role of the Bank of England as the government's banker can be explained with reference to the Bank's balance sheet, as shown in table 12.6.

Looking first at the Issue Department we see that its main liability comprises notes in circulation. These notes are held by persons, firms and other institutions. Its main assets are government securities. Consequently, an increase in the note issue generally implies an increase in the department's holding of government securities. Or, putting the matter the other way round, the borrowing requirements of the government can be (partly) met by obtaining notes from the Issue Depart-

---

*This indicates that the Bank's actions designed to maintain stability was not an unmixed blessing. Moreover some commentators have suggested that in the long term stability is more likely to be achieved by making each bank fully responsible for the consequences of its actions.

Table 12.6

The Balance Sheet of the Bank of England (June 1977, £mn)

Issue Department			
Liabilities		*Assets*	
Notes issued:			
In circulation	7,166	Government securities	6,229
To Banking Dept.	9	Other	946
	7,175		7,175

Banking Department			
Liabilities		*Assets*	
Deposits:			
Public	19	Government securities	1,599
Bankers	310	Advances and other accounts	269
Special deposits	1,055	Premises, equipment and other	
Reserves and other accounts	561	securities	85
		Notes and coins	9

Source: *Monthly Digest of Statistics*, July 1977.

ment in exchange for securities. (These notes are not, of course, held by the government, but are used to finance its expenditure.)* Conversely, when the government has excess cash it will, in effect, exchange this for securities. In practice this normally means not issuing new securities to replace those that mature.

Turning to the Banking Department, the liabilities that are of the greatest interest to our present discussion are bankers' deposits and special deposits. Bankers' deposits belong to the London clearing banks, the Scottish banks, other banks, accepting houses and the discount market. The importance of these deposits to the commercial banks was discussed above.

Special deposits also belong to the commercial banks. They have an important role in monetary policy, and are discussed at some length below. For the moment we can simply note that they do *not* constitute part of the banks' reserve assets.

Like the Issue Department, the Banking Department holds a substantial part of its assets in the form of government securities. These include Treasury bills, government stocks and Ways and Means Advances, made overnight to the Exchequer if it finds itself short of funds at the end of the day. The basic effect of purchases by the department of securities from the government is, via government spending, to increase the volume of bankers' deposits. Conversely, sales reduce the volume of these deposits.

Other securities include bills purchased by the Bank in order to check on the quality of bills circulating in the London Market. The Bank will not purchase bills of which it disapproves, and this acts as a deterrent to their issue and circulation. Notes correspond to the similar item in the Issue Department. Finally advances and other accounts include discounts and advances to the discount houses and are discussed in the following section.

The Discount Houses

The discount houses operate at the shorter end of the financial market. As can be seen from table 12.7 most of their borrowed funds are obtained from the banks –

---

*The quantity of notes issued also changes in accordance with the public's requirements. For example at Christmas time the note circulation is approximately 4 per cent above the annual average. (See I. L. Buchanan, *Topical Economics* (London: Oxford U.P., 1975).)

Table 12.7

Sterling Liabilities of the Discount Market (May 1977)

	Per cent
Funds borrowed from:	
Bank of England	3.3
Other U.K. banking sector	85.3
Other U.K. sources	9.8
Overseas	1.6
Total	100
Of which:	
Borrowed at call and overnight	81.4
Other	18.6

Source: *Monthly Digest of Statistics.*

Table 12.8

Sterling Assets of the Discount Market (May 1977)

	Per cent
Treasury bills	38.6
Other bills	34.3
Loans	12.1
British government stocks	6.4
Local authority securities	8.1
Other sterling assets	0.5
Total	100

Source: *Monthly Digest of Statistics*, June 1977.

these funds usually being loaned at call or short notice. Table 12.8 shows that these funds are invested in assets which are again essentially short-term, including a substantial proportion of bills.

We saw above that money loaned to the discount houses is often treated by the banks as a first line of defence, the first asset to be realized if they need to replenish their reserves of money. When the repayment of these loans is demanded, if the discount houses cannot borrow elsewhere, they turn to the Bank of England which makes funds available to them against suitable collateral – which must include a minimum proportion of Treasury Bills.

The Bank of England is said here to act as the lender of last resort to the monetary and financial system, via the discount houses, who are the only institutions to have automatic access to the Bank in this way.

This privilege is extended to them on the understanding that the discount houses apply each week for the full amount of the Treasury bill issue. (Other institutions also apply, of course, so that the discount houses normally take up only part of each issue.) In this way the government is assured that its short-term borrowing needs will, via the issue of Treasury bills, always be met. The cost of borrowing may, however, vary from week to week in accordance with changes in the balance between the demand for bills and the quantity issued.

Government Policy and the Supply of Money
We discuss *why* the government might wish to influence the supply of money in the following section. In this section we discuss *how* they might seek to do so. Since bank deposits form such an important part of the money supply, much of

this discussion will be concerned with the effects of official policy on the volume of bank deposits and the structure of the banks' assets.

THE MINIMUM RESERVE ASSETS RATIO

We showed above that the banks are required to maintain a certain proportion of their assets as reserve assets. Reserve assets must equal at least $12\frac{1}{2}$ per cent of a bank's eligible liabilities – defined as all private sterling deposits, net deposits owed to other banks and net foreign currency liabilities. If the banks had expanded their assets to the maximum extent consistent with observing this requirement, the situation would be as shown, in a simplified form, at Stage 1 in table 12.9.

Table 12.9

The Multiple Contraction of Deposits

	Liabilities (£mn)		Assets (£mn)		Reserve assets ratio
Stage 1	Deposits	100,000	Reserve assets	12,500	
			Other assets	87,500	
				100,000	$12\frac{1}{2}\%$
Stage 2	Deposits	80,000	Reserve assets	10,000	
			Other assets	70,000	
				80,000	$12\frac{1}{2}\%$

If the authorities were now to cause a reduction in the reserve assets of the banks of £2,500 million, then in order to maintain the required reserve assets ratio the banks would have to reduce their other assets by no less than £17,500 millions. In total assets, and hence deposits, would fall by £20,000 millions, i.e. by eight times the fall in reserve assets. (It will be noticed that eight is the reciprocal of the reserve assets ratio.) This process, shown at Stage 2 in table 12.9, is known as the *multiple contraction of deposits*. (The reverse process, when total assets and deposits increase by more than the increase in reserve assets, is known as the multiple expansion of deposits.)

The authorities can reduce the banks' reserve assets in several ways.

OPEN MARKET OPERATIONS

Open market operations refers to the buying and selling of government stock in the open market. If it is desired to reduce the bank's reserve assets, additional stock will be issued. The banks may themselves buy some of this stock, but most is likely to be bought by the general public, including the large institutions. Whether bought by the banks or by their depositors, who draw upon their deposits, the purchase of stock causes a fall in the level of the banks' balances at the Bank of England, which are, of course, part of the banks' reserve assets.

FUNDING

Funding is the process of converting short-term to longer-term debt. Given the desired level of government borrowing, an increase in the sales of stock (long term debt) implies less need to issue Treasury bills (short term debt). Consequently it is possible that open market sales of government stock may have an effect on the banks' reserve assets additional to that outlined above. If the banks are unable to compensate for the reduced supply of Treasury bills by acquiring other types of reserve assets, e.g. government stock with less than a year to maturity, their total reserve assets will fall.

A CHANGE IN THE MINIMUM RESERVE ASSETS RATIO

The minimum reserve assets ratio has been maintained at $12\frac{1}{2}$ per cent since its introduction in 1971. However it could well change in the future, just as, in earlier years, the liquidity ratio was reduced from 30 to 28 per cent. Any change would have important implications for the money supply.

For example if, following Stage 1 in table 12.10, the authorities were to stipulate an increase in the minimum reserve assets ratio to 15 per cent and the banks were unable to increase their volume of reserve assets, a contraction in other assets would be required, as shown at Stage 2.

Table 12.10
A Change in the Minimum Reserve Assets Ratio

	Liabilities (£mn)	Assets (£mn)		Reserve assets ratio
Stage 1	Deposits 100,000	Reserve assets	12,500	
		Other assets	87,500	
			100,000	$12\frac{1}{2}\%$
Stage 2	Deposits 83,333	Reserve assets	12,500	
		Other assets	70,833	
			83,333	15%

SPECIAL DEPOSITS

From time to time the Bank of England has called upon the banks for deposits amounting to a certain proportion of the banks' eligible liabilities. These 'special deposits' do not form part of the banks' reserve assets ratio. Consequently if the banks, in order to meet the call for special deposits, have to reduce their reserve assets, and if they are initially operating at the limit imposed by the ratio, e.g. at Stage 1 in table 12.9, a multiple contraction of deposits will follow.

On occasion the special deposits scheme has been buttressed by a call for non-interest bearing or supplementary special deposits. This scheme is different from all the others considered in this section since it operates directly on the liabilities of the banks rather than on their assets.

The essence of the scheme (which is sometimes known as the 'corset'), is that the authorities specify a maximum rate at which a bank's interest-bearing eligible liabilities (IBELS) may grow in a given period. Any bank whose IBELS grow at a faster rate than that specified is required to make special deposits, which in this instance do not attract interest, with the Bank of England. The fact that such deposits attract no interest, whereas the banks pay interest to their depositors, clearly acts as a disincentive to expand their deposits at a faster rate than that specified by the authorities. This reduction in the rate of growth of deposits in turn implies a reduction in the rate of growth in bank lending.

THE RATE OF INTEREST

The authorities may use any of the above measures in order to influence the supply of money. Changes in the money supply have implications for the behaviour of interest rates, as we shall show below. In addition the authorities may attempt to directly influence interest rates. However the intention of C.C.C. was that such direct influence should be exercised less frequently than hitherto.

Before the introduction of the new policy, the rates on bank deposits and loans were tied to the Bank Rate. Consequently when the Bank of England changed the Bank Rate these other rates changed automatically; moreover these changes in turn affected other lending and borrowing rates.

Under the new policy the Bank Rate was replaced by the Minimum Lending Rate (MLR), which is the minimum rate at which the Bank of England will provide money to the discount houses, either by rediscounting bills or by making loans against the security of such bills. Much more than a change in name was involved here, for it was intended that MLR should follow market rates of interest rather than seek to lead or influence them. Indeed the usual formula for calculating MLR is to add $\frac{1}{2}$ per cent to the average discount rate at the most recent Treasury bill tender and to round up to the nearest $\frac{1}{4}$ per cent.*

However the Bank of England retained the right to depart from this procedure, to attempt to influence market rates, if this was thought to be appropriate. So, for example, when the government wished to see short-term interest rates rise in October 1976, MLR was raised by 2 per cent to a record 15 per cent. Again, when rates subsequently began to decline, MLR did not follow the market down exactly as would have been required by adherence to the formula.

QUALITATIVE GUIDANCE AND INSTRUCTIONS
The general intention of C.C.C. was that the decision of the banks should be less subject to detailed intervention by the authorities. Nevertheless, the authorities retained the right to 'provide the banks with such qualitative guidance as may be appropriate'. The first important exercise of this right occurred in 1973 when the Chancellor of the Exchequer announced that a limit of $9\frac{1}{2}$ per cent was to be placed on the rate of interest that the banks could pay on smaller deposits – up to £10,000 – in order to reduce the upward pressure on the rates offered to depositors by Building Societies and hence on the rates charged on mortgages. At the same time it was announced that the Bank of England had requested the banks to restrain their lending to the personal sector.

Another example of the influence of the authorities was the instigation by the Bank of England of the 'lifeboat' scheme following the collapse of the secondary banks, referred to above.

The Effect of Changes in the Supply of Money

Having discussed the various measures by means of which the authorities might seek to influence the supply of money, we now examine the possible consequences of changes in the money supply. In our earlier discussion we examined the operation of particular measures in hypothetical situations in which we assumed that the government wished to *restrict* the money supply. In practice monetary policy may be either restrictive or expansionary. As we shall see when we review recent British experience, particular concern has been caused by expansionary policies. Therefore we concentrate on the consequences of expansionary policies, i.e., the consequences of an increase in the money supply.

The Quantity Theory of Money
One approach to the effects of a change in the supply of money is via the quantity

---

* The rates on bank deposits and loans are now tied to Base Rate which is determined by the banks independently of the authorities.

theory of money. In its simplest version this theory can be expressed as follows:

$$MV = PT$$

where M is the supply or stock of money

    V is the velocity of circulation of money

    P is the price level

    T is the volume of transactions

The equation states that an increase in the supply of money will, unless balanced by a fall in the velocity of circulation, cause an increase in the price level and/or the volume of transactions. (The velocity of circulation can be measured in various ways, depending upon the definitions of expenditure and money supply adopted. But all the measures suggest that velocity has tended to increase in the U.K. in the post-war period – or at least until the 1970s – thereby reversing the previous trend.)

The quantity theory does not allow us to say whether the impact of a change in the money supply will be on the price level, on the volume of transactions, or on both. However, it seems extremely likely that where there is a substantial reserve of unemployed resources, at least part of the impact will take the form of an increase in transactions, i.e. in the level of economic activity.

The quantity theory has some fairly obvious defects. It has been pointed out that the equation given above does not embody any functional relationship. It is in fact a tautology. The two sides of the equation simply represent different ways of measuring total expenditure. Following on from this it is argued that although the theory may describe what is likely to happen following a change in the money supply it does not provide an *explanation* of such consequences.

This argument raises questions about the role of economic theory. Since these questions are very important we return to them in the following chapter. Here we consider an explanation that *has* been given of the effects of a change in the money supply.

The Supply of Money and the Level of Economic Activity

In Figure 12.3, D indicates the demand schedule for money at a given level of national income, and S_1 and S_2 represent the supply of money in periods t_1 and t_2.* In period t_1 the equilibrium rate of interest is R_1. The increase in money supply causes the equilibrium rate of interest to fall from R_1 to R_2. A change in one financial or monetary variable has caused a change in another monetary variable.

However the repercussions of the increase in the money supply are unlikely to end there. There may also be an effect on real variables, i.e. on the level of economic activity. The classical economists believed that one of the most important stimuli to economic activity, to an increase in real national income, was an increase in investment expenditure following a reduction in the rate of interest.

Incidentally it should be pointed out that if an increase in national income did occur this would cause an increase in the demand for money and hence would exert upward pressure on interest rates, thus modifying the initial expansionary effect of the increased money supply. This is indicated in figure 12.3 by the shift of the demand schedule to D^1, and the establishment of an equilibrium rate of interest between R_1 and R_2. (As we show in the next chapter, some contemporary economists emphasize the fact that an increase in the money supply may cause

* In order to simplify the analysis we assume that supply is not sensitive to the rate of interest.

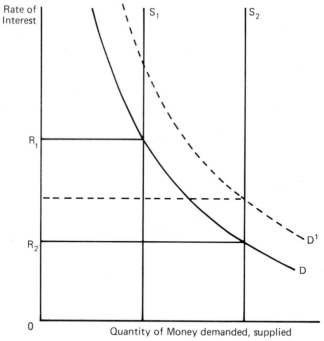

Figure 12.3 A Change in the Money Supply and the Rate of Interest

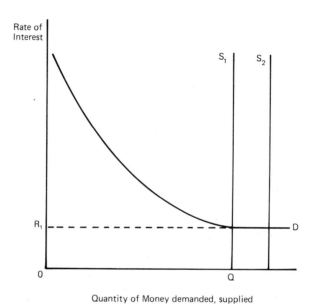

Quantity of Money demanded, supplied

Figure 12.4 The Liquidity Trap

an increase in consumption, and hence in aggregate monetary demand. It is possible that this will cause an increase in interest rates.)

However, Keynes argued that an increase in money supply might not lead to an increase in investment, and hence in national income, for two reasons. First, once the rate of interest has fallen to a certain level the demand for money may become perfectly interest elastic. In figure 12.4, with the rate of interest at R_1, people are willing to hold any addition to the money supply. Consequently any increase in the money supply beyond Q, such as from S_1 to S_2, would leave the rate of interest unchanged. (This phenomenon has been named the liquidity trap.)

Second, even if the demand for money is not perfectly interest elastic, i.e. even if an increase in the money supply causes the rate of interest to fall, investment may not respond. The cost of finance is only one of numerous factors which influence investment spending, and these other factors may operate so as to make investment unresponsive to changes in interest rates. For example, if companies are very pessimistic concerning future economic prospects, their investment expenditure may not increase at all in response to a fall in interest rates, i.e. investment may be perfectly interest inelastic.

The implication of a possible failure of investment to respond to an increase in the money supply is that national income may also be unchanged. It was this possibility that led Keynes to advocate an increase in government expenditure as the surest way of increasing national income and reducing the level of unemployment. He argued that even if there was a tendency for the system to move towards full employment via an increase in investment (or in consumption or exports) the process would proceed at a far slower rate than was required in view of the massive unemployment experienced by the U.K. and many other countries in the inter-war period.

Controversy continues concerning the efficacy of different types of economic policy. However, in the post-war period the context has been somewhat different, with a much greater emphasis being given to the need to prevent prices from rising too rapidly. The role of both monetary and fiscal policy in these circumstances is discussed in the following chapter. To conclude the present chapter we briefly discuss a final monetary variable that has had an important bearing on government policy.

Appendix – The Money Supply and Domestic Credit Expansion

The relationship between an increase in the money supply and domestic credit expansion (DCE) is rather complex. Briefly the main adjustments that have to be made to the change in M_3 in order to arrive at a measure of DCE are the increase in sterling bank deposits of overseas residents, bank lending in foreign currency to the public sector and sales of public sector debt to overseas holders. The main significance of these adjustments is as follows. Whereas a deficit on the balance of payments current account would lead to a reduction in M_3, DCE would not be affected insofar as the surplus of the overseas sector was utilized in the ways listed above.

We have given this somewhat technical explanation because when the U.K. applied in 1976 for a loan to the International Monetary Fund, we had to give certain undertakings to the Fund that both the public sector borrowing requirement and the volume of DCE would be reduced in future years. Moreover it was announced that in future the Fund would monitor the U.K.'s progress mainly in terms of the target for DCE.

Summary and Conclusions

Monetary policy may affect the level of economic activity – and also other variables such as the rate of inflation – by influencing the supply and the cost of money. Consequently, after a relatively brief discussion of the factors affecting the demand for money, most of this chapter has been concerned with the various components of the financial system – the system that supplies money to householders and firms. (Some of these components were also discussed in Chapter 6.)

We have seen that the banks have an especially important role in the supply of money since they are able to create credit. However, this ability to create credit is circumscribed by a wide variety of measures which may be adopted by the authorities – and in particular by the Bank of England, acting on behalf of the government.

There has been considerable controversy about the efficacy of monetary policy. The main lines of the debate were presented and discussed briefly. However it is impossible adequately to evaluate monetary policy in isolation. Consequently in the following chapter we consider the role of monetary policy vis-a-vis fiscal policy which, as we pointed out in Chapter 11, has been the major form of demand management in the U.K. in the post-war period.

ESSAY QUESTIONS

1 Discuss the factors which might cause a change in the demand for money and examine the possible implications of such a change.
2 Discuss the factors which might cause a change in the supply of money and examine the possible consequences of such a change.
3 Explain how banks can create credit and discuss the factors which limit their ability to do so.
4 'The pattern of bank assets reflects the need for profitability, liquidity and for compliance with government policy.' Discuss.
5 Explain why the authorities might wish to restrict the supply of money and discuss the measures which they might adopt.
6 Discuss the role within the financial system of (a) the Bank of England, (b) the London clearing banks, (c) the discount houses.
7 Explain what you understand by the term 'the rate of interest' and show what factors might cause the rate to change.
8 Evaluate the major changes that have occurred in monetary policy since 1971.
9 'Monetary policy is more useful when the authorities wish to expand the level of economic activity than when they wish to restrict it.' Discuss.
10 Explain, using a numerical example, the multiple expansion of deposits, and discuss its significance.

EXERCISES

12.1 Given the initial situation shown in table 12.3, show the likely effects of the receipt by each bank of additional deposits of £50,000, assuming that the banks maintain a cash ratio of (a) $12\frac{1}{2}$ per cent, (b) 10 per cent.
12.2 Given the position as shown in table 12.4, discuss the changes in the pattern of the banks' assets that would be likely to occur if the authorities increased the minimum reserve assets ratio.
12.3 Discuss, with reference to table 12.11, the statement that the rate of interest is determined by the demand for, and the supply, of money.

Table 12.11

Local Authority Bond Table (Jan. 1976)

Authority	Annual gross interest %	Minimum sum £	Life of bond Years
Barking	11	1,000	2.5
Belfast	12	500	2.3
Greenwich	$12\frac{1}{2}$	1,000	4.7
Liverpool	12	500	3.4
Liverpool	$12\frac{1}{2}$	500	5.7
Redbridge	12	1,000	3.5
Sandwell	$12\frac{1}{4}$	1,000	3.5
Thurrock	$10\frac{3}{4}$	300	1.2
Wandsworth	$12\frac{3}{4}$	5,000	5.7
Wandsworth	$12\frac{1}{2}$	1,000	5.7
West Yorkshire	$12\frac{1}{4}$	1,000	3.4

Table 12.12

Rates of Interest (May 1977)

	%
Bank of England's minimum lending rate to the market	8
Treasury Bills: average tender rate of discount	7.43
Clearing bank base rate for lending	$8\frac{1}{2}$
Clearing bank deposit rate for sums at seven days notice	4
Sterling certificates of deposit (3 months)	$7\frac{3}{4}$
Local authority deposits (3 months)	$7\frac{3}{4}-7\frac{7}{8}$
Building society: shares	7
Building society: new mortgages to owner occupiers	$11\frac{1}{4}$
Finance house base rate	$9\frac{1}{2}$

Source: *Financial Statistics.*

12.4 Discuss the pattern of interest rates shown in table 12.12.

12.5 'At its simplest, the monetarist view is based upon an observed close connection between the rise in the money supply in one year and the rate of price inflation a year or 18 months later. They say that cost-inflation is possible only if the government allows the money supply to grow fast enough to finance it....

'Monetarists are sceptical of the government's ability other than over a very short period of time, to push the rate of unemployment below its "natural" level as dictated by structural and institutional forces. The longer the government goes on feeding cost-inflation in an effort to secure over-full employment, the higher will be the ultimate level of unemployment needed to cure inflation.'

The above passage was extracted from 'Keynes and the monetarists' (*The Economist*, 15.3.75). (i) Why do the monetarists assert that 'cost-inflation is possible only if the government allows the money supply to grow fast enough to finance it'? (ii) What might happen if the money supply did not grow fast enough? (iii) Indicate what you understand by the term the 'natural level of unemployment', and indicate what structural and institutional forces dictate this level.

CHAPTER THIRTEEN

The Interaction between Fiscal and Monetary Policy

Introduction

IN this chapter we draw together the arguments presented in the previous two chapters. We do this with two main purposes in mind. First, since all governments have both a fiscal and a monetary policy, we wish to consider what their respective roles might be, and to examine the relative advantages of particular policy 'mixes'. Second, we wish to explore the inter-relationships between the different types of policy, and in particular the monetary implications of fiscal policy.

Although we shall make a distinction between Keynesian and monetarist views, the reader should be aware that 'Keynesian' and 'monetarist' are labels of convenience, that differences of opinion exist within both schools of thought, and that there is some common ground between the two. The distinction is justified partly by the fact that 'Keynesian' economists tend to advocate the use of fiscal policy, while 'monetarists' would place greater reliance on monetary policy. Perhaps an even more important reason for distinguishing between the two schools of thought is that monetarists have been very critical of the level of aggregate demand that has been generated by the use of fiscal policy in the U.K. at certain periods since 1945. In principle these criticisms could also have been applied to monetary policy if it had operated so as to generate the same level of aggregate demand. In other words the distinction lies in the use, as much as in the choice, of policy.

We take as our starting point the argument outlined towards the end of the previous chapter, namely that monetary policy was inadequate to deal with the economic problems facing the U.K. in the inter-war years, and that fiscal policy should have a much more important role. These arguments gained increasing acceptance, and post-war economic policy in the U.K. has placed greater reliance on fiscal policy. Moreover this shift in policy appeared to be justified by the fact that the U.K.'s economic performance in the post-war period was much more satisfactory, especially in terms of maintaining a high level of employment, than in the inter-war years.

However, as we indicated in Chapter 11, fiscal policy also has its drawbacks and the views of critics of the policy began to gain more attention as the performance of the U.K. economy became less satisfactory in the 1970s. It was argued that the effectiveness of fiscal policy was severely limited by the conditions ruling in the U.K. in the post-war period, or at least in the 1970s. Moreover, it was claimed that the effectiveness of fiscal policy had been further reduced by some of the policy decisions that had been taken. It was suggested that decisions to change the level of government expenditure and taxation were often badly timed and resulted in wider swings in the level of economic activity than would otherwise have occurred. A great deal of evidence has been produced relating to this point. But much of it is inconclusive and we shall not consider it here. We do however examine a further argument, namely that the policy makers often ignored, or at least underestimated, the monetary implications of fiscal policy. But first we outline the major differences in economic circumstances between the inter-war and the post-war periods, differences which should be taken into account in any evaluation of the appropriateness of particular economic policies.

Some Characteristics of the Post-War Economy

First, governments of all political persuasions attach greater priority to full employment than did most pre-war governments. In much of the post-war period unemployment has been below the figure of 3 per cent, chosen by Beveridge as his definition of full employment in *Full Employment in a Free Society*, published in 1944 and taken as a reference point for government policy. Furthermore, although unemployment in the 1970s has been higher than in the rest of the post-war period, it is well below the levels experienced in much of the inter-war years.

Second, an increase has occurred in the power of organized labour. This is partly the result of the greater priority attached by government to full employment, since workers now feel that there is less likelihood of high wage increases leading to reduced employment opportunities.

Third, some loss of flexibility in the labour market might have occurred as a result of higher unemployment benefit and other social security payments. While such payments may be desirable of themselves, they may slow down the movement of workers to those sectors of the economy where labour is in short supply.

Fourth, international specialization and trade have increased. This has two implications. On the one hand the U.K. economy is more subject to disturbances originating in other economies, although 'imported' disturbances were by no means unknown before the war. On the other hand changing trends in the U.K. economy are more likely than previously to result in changes in our balance of payments.

Finally we should note an important change – not in the economy as such – but in our knowledge of economic relationships. Some economists claim to have identified a clear link between changes in the money supply and in the rate of inflation. Especially important has been the work undertaken by Friedman and Schwartz, who have demonstrated that in the U.S.A. a change in the money supply is followed, after a lag of 12 to 18 months, by a change in the rate of price increase. Although such a clear link does not appear to exist in the U.K., most economists would accept that changes in the money supply have important implications for the rate of inflation.

A link between the money supply and prices is, of course, consistent with the quantity theory of money and at this point we can refer back to the controversy concerning the role of economic theory. The 'positivist' approach to economics, associated most closely today with Professor Friedman, suggests that the most important characteristic of a theory is the extent to which it enables useful predictions to be made. In terms of this criterion the quantity theory might be considered to perform well, despite the fact that it does not offer a detailed explanation of the mechanism and relationships underlying economic change.

The explanation that is offered is general in nature. Briefly it is argued that money is subject to the laws of supply and demand in much the same way as any other commodity. The community's preferences lead to a balance between holdings of money and of other commodities. If this balance is disturbed by an increase in the quantity of money, expenditure will be increased in order to restore the balance.*

* For an exposition and critique of the quantity theory, see J. M. Flemming, *Inflation* (London: Oxford University Press, 1976), chapters 1–3.

The Role of Fiscal and Monetary Policy
Having examined some of the major features of the post-war economic scene we can now reconsider the role of fiscal and monetary policy and, more generally, the approach of the Keynesians and the monetarists to economic policy. It is convenient for this purpose to refer to figure 13.1.

With the initial expenditure function E_1 the equilibrium national income is Y_1. Since the full employment national income would be Y_F a considerable volume

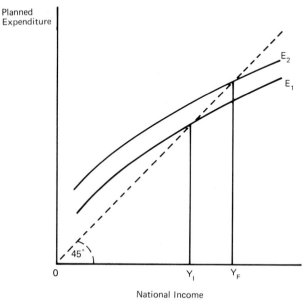

Figure 13.1   Expenditure and National Income

of resources remains unemployed. In order to absorb these resources an increase in expenditure to E_2 is required.

The first point to note is that it would in principle be possible to bring about the required increase in expenditure by the use of either fiscal or monetary policy, although the composition of the additional expenditure may differ. Fiscal policy (a budget deficit) is more likely to entail an increase in government expenditure, while monetary policy (an increase in the money supply) is more likely to entail an increase in consumption.* Although Keynes was probably right to insist on a greater reliance on fiscal policy in the inter-war years, this does not imply that the same mix of policies would be the most appropriate today.

Second, there would be some measure of agreement between Keynesians and monetarists about the likely effect of the increased expenditure on the price level. Keynesians would expect a budget deficit to lead to an increase in prices, and monetarists would agree with this insofar as the deficit involved an increase in the money supply. (The connection between a budget deficit and the money supply is explored below).

As far as monetary policy is concerned, the quantity theory does not itself imply that an increase in M will necessarily result in an increase in P – the entire impact

* We stress 'more likely'. Clearly a budget deficit due to a reduction in taxation would tend to lead to an increase in consumption.

could be on T. However, as noted above, empirical work suggests that a rise in price invariably follows an increase in the money supply. Furthermore, as we pointed out in Chapter 9, Professor Friedman and other economists have claimed that if unemployment is at the natural or normal level, the entire impact of an increase in expenditure – however engendered – will in the long run be on prices.

It seems, then, that both fiscal and monetary policies have disadvantages, and this might suggest that the degree of success attained by economic policy depends less on the choice of policy than on the skill with which that policy is applied. In this context it is worth briefly re-examining fiscal policy, on which post-war governments have relied heavily, and in particular the impact of budget deficits.

The impact of a budget deficit is twofold. There is the direct (sometimes known as the physical) effect on total expenditure. Since government expenditure exceeds revenue from taxation, total expenditure is increased. (This effect was discussed in detail in Chapter 11). Second, there is the indirect or monetary effect.* The gap between expenditure and revenue from taxation must be filled by borrowing, and this may cause an increase in the money supply. Let us consider this second effect in a little more detail.

The Monetary Implications of a Budget Deficit
The precise effect of a given public sector borrowing requirement (P.S.B.R) depends mainly upon the way in which it is financed.† Consider the situation illustrated in figure 13.2 where the excess of government expenditure over revenue from taxation results in the net outflow of money designated A. The important issue is how the government obtains the funds required to balance this outflow. We consider the various alternatives in a moment, but first notice that it is extremely likely that some of this additional expenditure will be spent on imports, leading to a current account deficit – flow B.‡

There are basically three sources of funds upon which the government can draw in order to finance its deficit. First it can sell stock to individuals and firms in the U.K. private sector – the flow of funds obtained from this source is designated 1 in figure 13.2. We showed in the previous chapter that selling stock tends to cause a reduction in the banks' balances at the Bank of England (a reserve asset) and so in the supply of money. In the present context the emphasis is slightly different. The sale of stock serves to *moderate the increase* in the banks' balances at the Bank of England – the larger is flow 1, the smaller is flow C.

Second, the public sector may borrow funds from the overseas sector in two ways. If the overseas sector wishes to hold its current account surplus in sterling it may buy government stock. Alternatively, if it wishes to obtain foreign currencies these will be provided by the Exchange Equalization Account. The sterling received

* In addition to these macro-economic effects, a budget deficit is likely to have specific micro-economic effects. For example some sectors of the economy may benefit more than others from government spending. (Some of these effects are considered in later chapters, and especially in Chapters 16 and 20.)

† The public sector borrowing requirement is related to, but larger than, the budget deficit because it includes some loans made by the central government to other parts of the public sector. It is the net difference between the income and expenditure of the whole public sector. We introduce the term P.S.B.R. here because it is commonly used in official statements and publications.

‡ It is conceivable that if the excess expenditure took a form which led to an increase in economic efficiency a balance or even a surplus on current account might occur in the longer term.

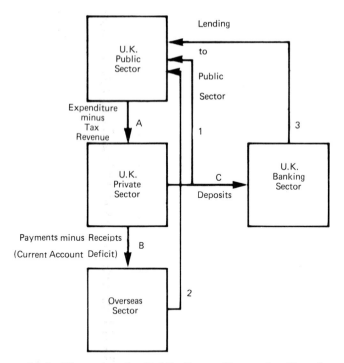

Figure 13.2 Financing the Public Sector Borrowing Requirement

in exchange is invested in government securities. These two flows are designated as 2 in figure 13.2. (Incidentally if part of the overseas sector's current surplus is deposited with U.K. banks this does not increase the money supply.)

If the P.S.B.R. is not fully met from these two sources the government is obliged to issue additional Treasury Bills. It is likely that at least some of these bills will be taken up by the banking sector and will thus increase the reserve assets of the banks – the banks are able to finance the purchase of these bills out of the additional deposits received from the private sector (flow C). As we saw in the previous chapter, an increase in the banks' reserve assets permits a multiple expansion of deposits and assets. Consequently we can say that the higher the proportion of a given deficit financed by the issue of Treasury bills, the more expansionary that deficit tends to be. But we should note that two other factors influence the impact of government borrowing. First, there is the extent to which the banks are able to take advantage of the increase in their reserve assets. Their ability to do so may be inhibited by a lack of demand for additional finance from credit-worthy customers. However, it is unlikely that there will be *no* increase in demand for credit, especially if greater availability of finance leads to a reduction in the cost of borrowing.

Second, the government may take steps to neutralize the potentially expansionary effects of the increase in reserve assets. They may call for special deposits and thus reduce the level of reserve assets. Alternatively they may impose a target rate of growth on IBELS, the so-called corset. Both of these measures were discussed in the previous chapter.

It is clearly not easy to predict what the precise effect of government borrowing will be, since this is influenced by so many factors. However it is likely to cause the money supply to increase to some extent and this increase means that government borrowing arising from a budget deficit will have an expansionary effect in addition to the direct physical effects discussed above. This means that if the government takes into account only the physical effects it will underestimate the overall effect of a deficit.

This has implications of the utmost importance which can be demonstrated very easily by reference to figure 13.1. If E_2 is the total expenditure required to bring about full employment, the planned budget deficit should be such that the *physical* effects will leave total expenditure less than E_2. The gap will be filled by the additional expenditure – consumption and investment – arising from the increase in the money supply.

An important part of the monetarist case against the fiscal policies adopted by U.K. governments is that they have frequently neglected the secondary monetary effects and so have over stimulated the economy. For example, in 1972 the money supply was allowed to expand at an annual rate of about 30 per cent, which contributed to the subsequent acceleration of the inflation rate. This excessive growth in the money supply was due partly to the introduction of C.C.C. – since the reserve assets ratio of the banks was well in excess of the minimum $12\frac{1}{2}$ per cent they were able to substantially increase their lending. It was also due to a succession of budget deficits.

THE IMPLICATIONS OF A BUDGET DEFICIT FOR THE RATE OF INTEREST
For the reasons explained above, the government will usually try to meet a high proportion of its borrowing requirement by the issue of long-dated stock. However, sales of a large volume of stock tends to depress the price and thus increase the rate of interest. The increase in the rate of interest associated with the increase in the borrowing requirement in the mid 1970s is shown in figure 13.3. This implies,

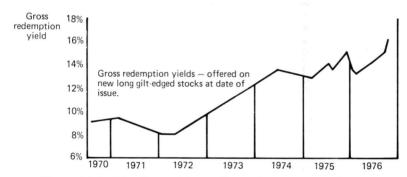

Figure 13.3   The Cost of Long Term Government Finance

of course, an increase in government expenditure on interest payments in future years. Moreover the rate of interest on government stock (gilts) influences other rates, and especially the rates that have to be offered by companies who wish to borrow long term. Consequently a policy of borrowing long by the government, while having the advantage that it reduces the potentially inflationary effects of a budget deficit, may have the disadvantage that it reduces company liquidity and thus the level of investment.

Summary: The Effectiveness of Monetary and Fiscal Policies

The use of monetary and/or fiscal policies in order to influence the level of demand or expenditure, is known as demand management. The objective of demand management policies has been to combine a high level of capacity utilization with a low rate of inflation (and hence a satisfactory balance of payments).

The U.K., together with most other industrialized nations, has been much more successful in achieving these objectives in the post-war period than in the inter-war years. However during the 1960s and more especially the 1970s it appeared that demand management policies were increasingly becoming less successful, and in the mid 1970s the U.K. experienced the highest rates of both inflation and un-employment of the post-war period (see Chapter 21).

Reactions to this situation have varied, differences often, although not always, being between 'Keynesian' economists on the one hand, and 'monetarists' on the other hand. Whereas the Keynesians continued to think of there being a trade-off between unemployment and inflation some monetarists denied that such a trade off existed, at least in the long term. Any attempt to permanently reduce the level of unemployment below the natural or normal level was doomed to failure. In the long-run unemployment would revert to the higher level, but this time accom-panied by a higher rate of inflation. Moreover it is claimed that the reliance on fiscal policy was accompanied by a failure to recognize the importance of changes in the money supply. (In fact there is now general agreement among economists that increases in the money supply on the scale that occurred in 1972–3 are exces-sive.)

It is further claimed that demand management policies have sometimes been counter-productive, i.e. have accentuated the problem they were designed to solve. This was due to frequent changes in policy which were undertaken in an attempt to 'fine tune' the economy. Much more consistency in policy is desired. For example monetarists, who naturally tend to favour the use of monetary policy, suggest that the authorities should allow the money supply to grow at a constant rate – say 5 per cent a year. If the underlying rate of growth in productivity was 3 per cent a year this would result in an acceptable inflation rate of 2 per cent a year. This does not, of course, imply that the government should not have a fiscal policy – indeed the existence of a public sector entails such a policy – but that the balance between government expenditure and taxation should be consistent with the monetary target.

It is impossible to draw upon British experience in order to evaluate this argu-ment since the proposed policy has not been followed by any post-war British government. However, it is worth considering briefly the counter-arguments that have been advanced.

First, it has been pointed out that technical problems may arise in the imple-mentation of the policy. There are several alternative ways of measuring the money supply, and it is not clear to which of these measures the target rate of growth should apply. Since considerable differences sometimes occur in the growth rates of M_1 and M_3 this problem may be very important. Another technical problem is that unforeseen changes may occur in the velocity of circulation, whose impor-tance was discussed in Chapter 12.

Second, it claimed that a rigid target for the growth of the money supply may lead to an unacceptedly high level of unemployment. For example let us assume that the money supply is to increase at a rate that would accommodate a 2 per cent rise in prices, but that wage costs rise by 10 per cent. Since wages are by far the most important cost in the economy as a whole, the rise in wage costs will be reflected fairly closely in a change in prices. But if prices rise by 10 per cent the result will be an increase in unemployment of around 8 per cent.

Many monetarists would argue that if workers were convinced that the government was determined to keep to its stated target of monetary growth, they would not be so foolish as to negotiate wage increases which they knew would result in a loss of jobs. This hypothesis is extremely difficult to test. On the one hand, one can point to a country such as Germany where a stricter control of the money supply than in Britain has been accompanied by lower wage increases (although this does not, of course, prove the existence of a causal relationship). On the other hand one can think of reasons why the possible effect of wage increases on employment may not have the weight suggested in wage negotiations. Especially important is the fact that the composition of the labour force is constantly changing. Some workers retire and others enter the labour force for the first time. Consequently the main burden of the reduction in employment opportunities often falls on new entrants, and in particular on people who have just completed their education. While one would not suggest that the needs of such people are ignored in negotiations, it seems likely that the effects on employment would be given greater weight if the jobs of the negotiators were themselves at risk!

Moreover, as an open economy the U.K. is especially vulnerable to cost increases arising from higher import prices. If the target rate of monetary growth remains unchanged these cost increases will lead to unemployment in the same way as domestic cost increases.

Finally, even those economists who advocate a greater role for monetary policy recognise that very considerable problems would arise in making the transition from a rate of inflation of, say, 15 per cent to one of 5 per cent or less. Indeed in the mid 1970s several prominent monetarists highlighted the dangers to employment prospects of too rapid a reduction in the rate of growth of the money supply, and advocated a more gradual policy than that undertaken by the U.K. government at that time.

Having examined the major weapons of demand management we next discuss prices and incomes policies. These policies tend to be adopted at times when demand management policies have been least successful. Prices and incomes policies have found the greatest measure of support among Keynesian economists, who advocate their use in conjunction with fiscal policy.

ESSAY QUESTIONS

1 'The debate between Keynesians and monetarists is a debate about the use rather than the choice of policy.' Discuss.
2 'The economic conditions of the 1970s make reliance on fiscal policy less appropriate than in the 1930s.' Discuss.
3 Discuss the view that the most valuable contribution made by the monetarists to the theory of economic policy is concerned with the monetary implications of fiscal policy.
4 Compare and contrast the probable effects of government measures designed to increase the level of economic activity by means of (a) monetary and (b) fiscal policy.
5 Explain why it is important to distinguish between the direct (physical) and indirect (monetary) effects of a budget deficit.
6 'The precise effect of a given public sector borrowing requirement depends mainly upon the way it is financed.' Discuss.
7 Why may it be considered advantageous for the government to finance as high a proportion of its deficit as possible by the issue of stock to individuals?

8   Under what circumstances is the financing of a budget deficit by the issue of Treasury bills most likely to be inflationary?
9   Analyse the possible effects of a budget deficit on the level of fixed capital formation.
10 Evaluate a policy designed to permit the money supply to grow at a constant rate.

EXERCISES

13.1 Question 13.1 refers to table 13.1. (i) Why do you think the rise in public expenditure planned for the period 1975/6 to 1979/80 is so much smaller than the actual rise for the period 1971/2 to 1975/6? (ii) What additional informa-

Table 13.1

Public Expenditure (£mn 1975 prices)

	1971/2	1975/6	1979/80
Defence	4,593	4,538	4,541
Overseas aid and services	646	734	1,085
Agriculture, fisheries and forestry	718	1,438	612
Trade, industry and employment:			
investment grants	635	63	1
other	1,234	2,618	2,113
Nationalized industries' capital expenditure	2,554	3,358	2,907
Roads and transport	1,727	2,316	1,852
Housing	2,492	4,018	4,090
Other environmental services	1,888	2,217	1,981
Law, order and protective services	1,175	1,444	1,438
Education (inc. libraries and arts)	5,434	6,164	5,995
Health and personal social services	4,405	5,285	5,548
Social security	7,646	9,463	9,963
Other public and common services	1,042	1,395	1,288
Northern Ireland	802	1,321	1,258
Debt interest	4,048	5,000	7,500
Contingency reserve (minus shortfall)	—	− 200	1,150
	41,122	51,172	53,322

Source: Public Expenditure to 1976/80 (H.M.S.O., 1976).

tion would you require in order to assess whether the expenditure planned for 1979/80 was likely to be inflationary? (iii) Comment briefly on 'the burden of the national debt' in the light of the above figures. What factors would help to explain the rise in the expected debt interest?
13.2 Discuss the significance of the changes in government financing shown in table 13.2.
13.3 (i) What factors might have caused the changes in the P.S.B.R., shown by the unbroken lines in figure 13.4? (ii) What are the implications of these changes? (iii) How might the planned changes in P.S.B.R., shown by the broken lines, be achieved? (iv) In what circumstances might it be difficult to fulfil these plans?
13.4 'By late June and early July a prospective conflict was emerging between public and private borrowing. To guard against an excessive growth in the money supply, to contain interest rates and to maintain confidence at home and abroad it was judged that there was a need to reduce the P.S.B.R. to £9 billion

Table 13.2

The Financing of Government Expenditure

	1970	1975
Percentage of government expenditure financed by		
Taxes on income	33.9	29.9
Taxes on capital	33.1	1.5
Taxes on expenditure	38.5	26.0
National insurance contributions, etc.	12.1	12.6
Gross trading surplus of public corporations	7.3	5.4
Rent, interest, dividends, etc.	7.0	5.7
Other	−1.9	−0.5
Borrowing	0.0	19.4
	100	100

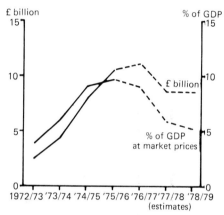

Figure 13.4   The Public Sector Borrowing Requirement

in 1977–8. This was £1.5 billion less than the forecast for that year as it then stood. The main features of the measures announced for this purpose were a reduction of £1 billion in plans for public expenditure, and a surcharge on employers' national insurance contributions to yield a further gross £1 billion in a full year. Both would take effect in 1977–8.'

The above passage appeared in the Financial Statement and Budget Report, 1977–8. (i) Explain the connection between the P.S.B.R. and (a) the money supply, (b) interest rates and (c) public confidence. (ii) Compare the probable effects of the two measures designed to reduce the P.S.B.R.

13.5 'The link between the size of the borrowing requirement and the growth in the quantity of money is very erratic. It depends on the size of *the balance-of-payments deficit on current account*, which determines the extent to which foreigners finance the borrowing requirements; it depends on the *private sector's appetite for gilt-edged securities* and on the *policy of the government and the Bank about interest rates*. In any case, with modern methods of control by the Bank of the banking system, the financing of the borrowing requirement by the banks can be largely prevented from enabling the banks to expand credit by more than is regarded as desirable.'

The above passage was taken from an article by Lord Kahn in *Lloyds Bank*

Review. (i) Explain why the factors listed in italics influence the relationship between the public sector borrowing requirement and the growth in the quantity of money. (ii) In what ways may the undesirable consequences of the financing of the borrowing requirement by the banks be prevented?

CHAPTER FOURTEEN

Prices and Incomes Policies

Introduction

As suggested in the previous chapter, prices and income policies are most likely to be adopted when conventional demand management policies are least successful. Their basic rationale is that by reducing inflationary tendencies or pressures they permit a higher level of expenditure, and hence a higher degree of resource utilization, than would otherwise be possible.

A comprehensive policy involves controls on both prices and incomes. However, since the costs of implementing such a policy are high, governments have sometimes preferred to adopt a less comprehensive approach, seeking to control either prices or incomes. In examining the principles on which policies might be formulated it is convenient to start with the less comprehensive approach. We consider first a policy designed to control prices only.

The Control of Prices

If we were to adopt a very simple definition of inflation, namely an increase in the level of prices, the immediate effect of successfully controlling prices would be to reduce the rate of inflation. However a wider definition of inflation would take account of the underlying forces which have led, or might lead, to rising prices. According to this view the control of prices modifies inflation only if it modifies these underlying inflationary forces.

This throws us right back to the controversies concerning the operation of the economy that we discussed in earlier chapters. If the crucial factor is the balance between demand and supply of goods and services, price controls will do nothing to modify inflationary tendencies. They will simply cause open inflation to be replaced by suppressed (or repressed) inflation.

Suppressed Inflation

In figure 14.1, D and S represent aggregate demand and supply for the economy as a whole. In the absence of government intervention an equilibrium price level P_E would be established, at which the quantity demanded would be Q_E. If the government set a maximum price P_M the quantity demanded at this price, R, would exceed the quantity supplied, T. This excess demand is an indication of suppressed inflation.

Given the excess demand, TR, the question arises as to how products are to be allocated among consumers. One possibility is that an official system of rationing may be introduced. Alternatively, in order to avoid the costs of administering such a scheme, the government may leave decisions about allocation to the suppliers of the various products.

The suppliers may choose any of the following methods of allocation. First they may supply products to customers on a first-come first-served basis. This method

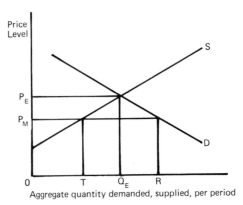

Figure 14.1 The Effect of a Maximum Price

is likely to lead to the formation of 'queues', e.g. lines of shoppers, lengthening waiting lists. A second method is to allocate supplies on the basis of past purchases. This is clearly most feasible for those products for which records of past purchases have been maintained. Third, a ballot may be held among prospective purchasers of such products as tickets for concerts and football matches. Finally suppliers may arbitrarily allocate products in accordance with their perceptions of consumers' needs or in accordance with the suppliers' own interests.

One's evaluation of any of these methods of allocating products is likely to depend very much upon how one is personally affected by it. The person who is at the front of the queue, is lucky in the ballot or is on good terms with suppliers, will be much more favourably disposed towards the method than the person at the back of the queue, whose name does not come out of the hat, or who is on less good terms with suppliers.

Given the element of chance inherent in all these methods, one cannot conclude that the welfare of consumers as a whole will increase as a result of the control of prices. The benefit to those consumers who obtain supplies at lower prices than they would otherwise have paid, could in principle be outweighed by the loss of satisfaction on the part of those consumers whose consumption is forcibly reduced.

As we noted above the government may institute an official rationing scheme. By issuing 'tokens' giving the right to purchase a certain quantity, the government would try to ensure that total effective demand matched supply at the maximum price (quantity T at price P_M in figure 14.1). It is claimed that this reduces the element of chance inherent in unofficial rationing schemes and that a 'fair' allocation of products results. On the other hand it has been pointed out that all administrative methods of allocating resources – as opposed to allocation by market mechanisms – provide opportunities for corruption, or at least for the exercise of the administrators' preferences. Moreover, these opportunities may be just as great when a scheme is administered by public officials as by suppliers.

Furthermore, even if the allocation of the tokens giving a right to purchase is fair, there is no guarantee that all trading will take place through officially approved channels and at official prices. 'Black markets' may arise in which products are traded at prices above the official maximum and indeed possibly above the equilibrium price that would have been established in the absence of controls.

Another important aspect of a system of price controls is the proportion of prices to which controls are applied. Clearly the more products covered by the controls the greater will be the cost of administering the system. On the other hand if only some products are covered the result is likely to be that the price of the remaining products will rise even faster than they would have done in the absence of controls. This is due to the 'real income' effect, i.e. to the fact that since less money is spent on products whose prices are controlled consumers are left with more money to spend on non-controlled products.

The Long term Implications of Price Controls
In the above discussion we assumed a time period sufficiently short as to enable the analysis to be conducted in terms of given demand and supply curves. This was obviously a simplification, since price controls and rationing schemes frequently extend over a period of months and even years. In this section we extend the time horizon and consider whether effective price controls are likely to cause the aggregate demand and supply curves to shift, and if so, why.

THE EFFECT OF PRICE CONTROLS ON AGGREGATE DEMAND
When the control of prices is not accompanied by the control of incomes, important changes in real incomes are likely to occur. The real income of wage and salary earners is likely to rise, and the real income of companies – and thus of shareholders – to fall.

This change in the distribution of income is likely to be reflected in the pattern of expenditure – with consumption rising and investment falling. The effect on aggregate expenditure of these changes depends upon the magnitude of the changes and the propensities to spend of the various groups concerned. It is very difficult to predict what the overall effect will be, but the fact that consumption is by far the major form of expenditure suggests that aggregate demand is more likely to increase than to decrease.

A further boost to aggregate demand may also occur if imported goods are exempt from price controls – as is likely. In these circumstances there is likely to be some switching away from (non-controlled) imports to (controlled) domestic products.

THE EFFECT OF PRICE CONTROLS ON AGGREGATE SUPPLY
Some producers may react to controls on domestic prices by switching supplies to export markets. This would cause the aggregate supply curve shown in figure 14.1 to shift to the left. This might also occur if company profits, and therefore investment, were squeezed to the extent that a reduction in economic capacity resulted.

THE OVERALL EFFECT OF PRICE CONTROLS ON INFLATIONARY
PRESSURES
We suggested above that price controls are likely to cause aggregate supply to fall. Since there is unlikely to be a corresponding fall in aggregate demand it appears that price controls, unaccompanied by controls on incomes, are likely to accentuate rather than moderate the underlying inflationary pressures.*

The only circumstances in which this conclusion might not apply is if supply conditions are modified as a result of changing expectations about the behaviour of prices. As we showed in Chapter 9, wage claims may take into account both past changes in prices and expected future changes. If price controls have an

* We have shown that aggregate demand is likely to increase in the initial stages. Eventually aggregate demand must fall if economic capacity shrinks. However there would still be no reason to believe that the balance between aggregate demand and supply would be rendered any less inflationary by the imposition of price controls.

appreciable impact on the rate of price increases this may lead to a moderation of wage claims and to wage costs being lower than they would otherwise be. This would cause the supply curve to shift to the right, indicating that producers would be willing to supply more at any given price. This increase in supply would, of course, tend to reduce the underlying inflationary pressures.

If expectations are very important, the reduction in the rate of price increases in one period may lead to a reduction in the pressure for higher wages in succeeding periods, and hence establish a 'virtuous circle'. Given the disadvantages involved in price controls many economists have concluded that they can be justified only if they operate on expectations in the way outlined here.

The Control of Incomes

We now consider the likely effects of a policy which controls incomes but which does not *directly* control prices. Such a policy is most likely to be adopted if it is felt that the basic cause of inflation is a rise in factor costs, and in particular in the cost of domestic inputs. (It is extremely difficult to control or combat increases in the prices of imported factors, although a method that may be appropriate in some circumstances is a revaluation of the currency, a policy discussed in Chapter 15.) Inflation which is believed to arise from this cause is sometimes termed cost-push inflation.

It is argued that if the rise in factor costs can be checked or moderated, price increases will also be moderated. This will occur because producers typically set their prices by adding a fixed markup to their costs. The implication of this argument is that it is not necessary to control prices, and thus incur additional administrative costs.

If this reasoning is valid (and this point is discussed further below), this might appear to be the ideal method of preventing or halting inflation. However, to be successful an incomes policy requires the co-operation of all members of the community and especially, perhaps, of employees. Many employees may not accept the markup theory of pricing outlined above. They may not believe that the rate of price increases will respond to the rate of wage increases in the way suggested here. They may feel that prices will rise faster than money wages.

Should this happen, real wages would of course fall. (The only circumstances in which this may not happen is if the rise in domestic prices is balanced by a fall in import prices.) Furthermore company profits and therefore dividend payments are likely to rise. (Even if dividends are controlled as part of the incomes policy, shareholders are likely to benefit in the long run if higher profits cause share prices to rise.) The belief that the control of incomes may result in a redistribution of income away from employees, suggests that they are unlikely to accept controls on incomes unless accompanied by price controls.

Policies to Control Prices and Incomes

Although a policy which controls both prices and incomes is likely to find a greater degree of public acceptance than a policy which seeks to control only one or the other, it may still be very difficult to devise and implement a suitable policy. Conflicts are likely to arise among the various groups affected by the policy, since universal agreement does not exist concerning the principles on which the policy should be based.

Perhaps the most obvious source of potential conflict is between the requirement of workers for an increase in their real income and the need for firms to maintain and if possible, increase their profits in order both to increase the level of investment and to satisfy the requirements of their shareholders. This conflict is likely to be most serious when the level of real disposable national income fails to grow, since it is then impossible to meet both of these requirements. As we showed in Chapter 3 such a situation arose in the U.K. following the steep rise in the price of oil that occurred in the first half of the 1970s.

As far as the wages/salaries part of the policies is concerned, experience suggests that there is likely to be a conflict between the interests of skilled and less skilled workers. Partly connected with this is the conflict between the need to protect the lowest-paid workers and the need to maintain incentives for more highly paid workers.

A different type of conflict is that between the need for a rigid policy which, if accepted, is relatively easy to implement, and the need for flexibility in order to allow some scope for the operation of market forces.

Other aspects of the policies could be mentioned, but the above examples are sufficient to explain many of the changes in incomes policies that have occurred in the U.K. and elsewhere. As an example of these policies, let us consider the round of policies operated in the U.K. in the 1970s.

Prices and Incomes Policies in the United Kingdom

Under the Counter-Inflation Act, passed towards the end of 1972, the government was given the power to freeze prices, pay, dividends and rents, for a period of ninety days – subsequently extended for a further sixty days. These drastic powers were intended to provide an immediate check on prices and incomes and to give the government time to prepare more comprehensive legislation.

This legislation, the Counter-Inflation Act 1973, came into force in April 1973. The Act provided for two new agencies – a Price Commission and a Pay Board – which had responsibility for implementing the new policy. The main provisions of this policy were as follows:

Manufacturers were permitted to increase their *prices* only when they incurred unavoidable costs increases. Even then only part of the increase could be recovered, the intention being that companies should try to make good the shortfall by increasing productivity – the so-called productivity deduction. This requirement was buttressed by a limitation of net profit margins as a percentage of sales (in the home market). If these exceeded the average level in the best two of the previous five years, price reductions were required. A comparable limitation of profit margins was applied to distributors (wholesalers and retailers), and in addition their gross margins were held at the level of a recent base period.

Pay increases were limited to £1, plus 4 per cent of the average weekly pay received by a group of workers in the previous year. There was also an overriding limitation that no individual should receive an increase of more than £250 a year.

Finally, no company was allowed to increase its *dividends* by more than 5 per cent of the previous year's payments. These three sets of limitations comprised 'stage 2' of the policy.

Subsequently, under 'stage 3', the prices policy was modified somewhat in order to reduce the danger that the controls might discourage investment. Increases in depreciation costs could henceforth be taken into account in prices, and dividend increases of more than 5 per cent might be allowed where new capital had to be raised for investment.

There was also some relaxation of the limitations on pay. Annual increases of up to 7 per cent were allowed or, if the negotiators preferred, a flat rate increase of £2.25 a week. The individual ceiling was raised to £350 a year. In addition a 'threshold safeguard' was introduced whereby pay could be increased by up to 40p. a week if the increase in the retail price index reached 7 per cent above its level at the beginning of stage 3, and by up to another 40p. a week for every 1 per cent rise above that level.

The return to power of a Labour government heralded the demise of the Pay Board. Henceforth increases in incomes were to be agreed between the government and the T.U.C. as part of the 'Social Contract'. The Price Commission was retained. However, further relaxations in the Price Code followed at the end of 1974, in the light of the dramatic fall that had occurred in company profits (discussed in Chapter 11). Provision was made for an increase in allowable costs (including $17\frac{1}{2}$ per cent of fixed capital investment in 1975–6) and for a reduction in the productivity deduction.

The Social Contract did little during this period to moderate the rate of wage increases. Wages and prices continued to rise alarmingly, both reaching an annual rate of increase of more than 25 per cent in 1975. These increases put the government in a dilemma. Because of the past increases in costs and continuing increases in the price of imported commodities, including oil, it was certain that prices would continue to rise rapidly for some time. Thus controls on money incomes implied that real incomes were likely to fall. On the other hand it seemed that without controls the rate of inflation was likely to accelerate.

The government's response was to impose, with the agreement of the T.U.C., a limit to pay increases during the year from August 1975 of £6 a week, and to specify that no increases would be payable for those with earnings above £8,500 a year. As an incentive to employers to observe the policy, it was announced that where an employer broke the pay limit the whole pay increase would be disallowed for the purpose of any application to the Price Commission for a price increase.

The following year, 1976, saw an interesting innovation in incomes policy. In his budget statement the Chancellor of the Exchequer announced that certain tax concessions would be introduced if the trade unions agreed to a lower rate of pay increases than they were then demanding. This was accepted by the unions, who agreed to wage increases within the range £2.50 to £4.00 a week. This was expected to result in an average increase in wages and salaries of around $4\frac{1}{2}$ per cent in the year from August 1976 (although the outcome proved to be an increase in *earnings* of 8.8 per cent). It was also agreed that further modifications should be made to the Price Code in order to encourage investment and reduce unemployment.

In the 1977 budget the Chancellor again offered tax concessions that were partly dependent upon the outcome of the impending wage negotiations. However the T.U.C., influenced no doubt by the fact that during the period covered by phase 2 – August 1976 to July 1977 – prices rose twice as fast as earnings, refused to support the government's proposals and 1977 saw the virtual abandonment of controls over incomes. The unions demanded a return to free collective bargaining from the beginning of August, and the only element of the previous policy for which the government was able to obtain the support of the T.U.C. was that there should be a gap of at least twelve months between successive wage increases.

In the absence of any further agreement with the unions the government attempted to restrain incomes by putting pressure on firms which entered into wage settlements giving increases in earnings above the Chancellor's guideline of 10 per cent a year. One form of pressure was that government departments and nationalized industries would be advised to discriminate against such firms in their purchasing policies. Furthermore the revised Price Code contained a provision whereby any company breaking the 'twelve month rule' would have its statutory profit margin ceilings reduced by an amount corresponding to the increase in the wage bill.

Controls on profit margins and on dividends (dividend increases were limited to 10 per cent of the previous year's payments) were continued for a further year. Since wage controls had been virtually abandoned, these limitations were opposed by employers; however it appeared that they would have only a slight impact overall since the current profit margins of most companies were well inside the statutory limits.

Detailed control of prices was relaxed in the sense that the Price Commission was henceforth to spend less time administering a detailed Price Code and to concentrate its attention on a much narrower range of industries. In particular it would examine highly concentrated industries in which it was felt prices might be higher than was desirable, either because profits were too high or because, in the absence of keen competition, the incentive to restrain costs had been weakened. (See also Chapter 18). However this implied that for the industries chosen for investigation by the Commission control would be *more* detailed. Moreover the Commission was given the power to freeze prices – a more stringent control than it had previously been able to exercise.

The Effects of Prices and Incomes Policies

We have examined U.K. policy in the period 1972 to 1977 in some detail because this was the longest period of comprehensive controls over prices and incomes in the post-war period. The many policy changes that were made during this period illustrate the point made earlier about the difficulty of devising a policy that is universally acceptable. Indeed the fact that the policy was accepted for so long was probably due mainly to the perilous economic situation faced by the U.K. in the first part of the 1970s.

It is extremely difficult to evaluate the effects of prices and incomes policies (and indeed other types of economic policy) since such an evaluation would require knowledge of what would have happened in the absence of the policy.

Considering the period 1952 to 1966, during part of which an incomes policy operated, *The Economist* (5.4.75) concluded that during periods in which an incomes policy was 'full on', wages were lower than would have been expected. This was seen as 'prima facie evidence that a short-lived freeze works'. However in subsequent periods, when policy was only 'half on' or had been completely abandoned, 'wages soon catch up again – prima facie evidence that the ground gained in the freeze is subsequently lost'.

It is even more difficult to measure the effect of the policy as it applied during the 1970s. The rate of increase in prices (and wages) continued to accelerate for a considerable time after the introduction of the policy at the end of 1972. The rate dropped thereafter – by 1976 the annual rate of price increase had stabilized (for a time) at around 15 per cent as compared to annual rate of 26 per cent in June 1975. However 15 per cent was substantially in excess of the rates being experienced by most of our major competitors, including those countries without an incomes policy.

Moreover the rate of increase in prices might well have fallen in the absence of an incomes policy. The prices of several major commodities fell in 1976. Furthermore monetarist economists had predicted that the overall rate of price increase would decline. As noted in Chapter 12, monetarists believe that the major influence on the rate of inflation is the growth of the money supply, and not changes in factor prices. In 1975 and 1976 the increase in M_3 was below the rate of price increase, implying a fall in the real supply of money.

We said at the beginning of this chapter that a major objective of an incomes policy is that, by reducing inflationary pressures, it permits a higher level of expenditure, and hence a higher level of resource utilization. And yet unemployment was higher in 1976 than in 1972, indicating that this objective was not achieved.

Finally we should point out that an incomes policy may give rise to substantial costs. Most obviously, costs are incurred in administering the policy. Perhaps more important are the costs that may arise when the operation of market forces is impeded.

These considerations have led some economists, such as Professor Friedman, to deny that an incomes policy can make aany contribution to the management of the economy. Other economists, such as Samuel Brittan, have been willing to concede that an income policy might make a limited contribution in certain circumstances.

These circumstances are (a) that the policy is adopted together with, and not as an alternative to, policies designed to control the level of expenditure, (b) that it has an effect on expectations which leads to a moderation of wage claims and hence to a reduction in the pressure on costs and prices, and (c) that it is not enforced for such a long period of time as to seriously impede the operation of market forces.

Summary and Conclusions
An incomes policy (and we include within the term the control of prices) differs from many other forms of economic policy in that it specifies in some detail the likely consequences for different members of the community. This means that potential conflicts are brought into the open, which makes it difficult to devise a universally acceptable policy. The major areas of conflict were outlined above.

Moreover, quite apart from the practical problems of implementation, which we illustrated by a brief account of British experience, it appears that an incomes policy may have economic disadvantages, and in the previous section we considered the circumstances in which the disadvantages might be minimized.

The evaluation of any economic policy must take account not only of the disadvantages of the policy, which are usually easy to see, but also of the advantages, which may be less easily identified. We saw that in many respects the economic performance of the U.K. was far from satisfactory during those periods in the 1970s in which an incomes policy operated. However it is quite possible that without such a policy we would have fared even worse. The rate of inflation might have continued to increase, with adverse consequences for the utilization of domestic resources and the balance of payments. (Although monetarist economists believe that the tighter control that was exercised over the money supply would have caused the rate of inflation to decline).

One final point is relevant to a discussion of the role of an incomes policy. As we showed in earlier chapters, the public sector (central and local government and the nationalised industries), is now a major employer. Consequently, the overall rate of change in wages is strongly influenced by the changes in wages in this sector. In one sense, therefore, the government is obliged to have an income policy.

ESSAY QUESTIONS

1 'In situations where incomes policies are effective they are not required, whereas in situations where they are required they are not effective.' Discuss.
2 Explain the statement that the basic rationale of an incomes policy is that by reducing inflationary tendencies or pressures it permits a higher degree of resource utilization than would otherwise be possible.
3 Examine the relative advantages and disadvantages of controlling both prices and incomes as compared with controlling only one or the other.
4 Explain what you understand by the term 'suppressed inflation', and describe its characteristics and consequences.
5 'Although producers may suffer as a result of price controls, consumers must benefit.' Discuss.
6 Discuss the proposition that price controls unaccompanied by controls on incomes are likely to accentuate rather than moderate inflationary pressures.
7 Explain why it is sometimes claimed that prices and incomes policies are successful only insofar as they influence expectations.
8 Why have governments found it difficult to sustain prices and incomes policies over long periods?
9 Evaluate prices and incomes policies with particular reference to U.K. experience in the 1970s.
10 Under what circumstances are prices and incomes policies most likely to contribute usefully to the management of the economy?
11 'It is easier to identify the benefits than the costs of incomes policies.' Discuss.

EXERCISES

14.1 'The reaction of a businessman to an increase in the demand for his product is well known. He will not immediately increase the price. First he will wish to make sure that the increase in demand is permanent and not a flash in the pan. Thus the first reaction is to produce more from existing resources. Any slack is taken up, stocks are run down, short-time working is eliminated, and the quantity of output of the firm is increased and sold readily at the existing prices. Thus it seems that there is an increase in the rate of growth without any increase in the price level. It seems, therefore, that one can have unusually high growth without inflation. And it is tempting to end the story at this point; but we must face the consequences and go on.

'The businessmen who have run down their stocks and eliminated part-time working will be induced to attempt to hire more labour and to buy more stocks of raw materials to keep the higher rate of production going. But, of course, all businessmen will be there trying to buy labour and commodities. The price of such raw materials would be increased, and one would find that the wage rates of labour, particularly those of skilled workers in short supply, would rise quickly. The businessman will then say that "costs have risen", and so he must put up his prices; he will agree that it was not the rise in demand that gave rise to his need to increase prices; on the contrary the higher demand kept down costs because of the greater throughput. It was the cost-push that caused it all. The corollary is that if we could only keep down the prices of raw materials and commodities and the wages of labour, then we would beat inflation.'

Source: A. A. Walters, *Money and Inflation* (Aims of Industry, 1974).

Comment on the conclusion presented in the final sentence of this passage.

14.2 'A flat rate approach has the advantages of focusing increases on the low paid and preventing unduly large cash increases being obtained by the high paid. It is clear and simple, emphasizes the General Council's view about the gravity of the economic and industrial situation, and cuts through the complication of separate provisions for particular groups which, via comparability claims, had helped to weaken the previous policy. The General Council therefore conclude that there should be a universal application of the figure of £6 per week. The T.U.C. will oppose any settlement in excess of this figure.

'The General Council fully appreciate the problems which may arise from interfering with differentials based on skill and responsibility, and emphasize that this is a temporary policy put forward for the coming year to arrest the inflationary process, prevent massive unemployment and enable the Labour Government to carry out its industrial programme.'

The above passage is an extract from a T.U.C. document published as an annex to the White Paper *The Attack on Inflation* (H.M.S.O., 1975). (i) Why did the T.U.C. consider that a policy of pay restraint was necessary to 'prevent massive unemployment'? (ii) Why might 'comparability claims' weaken a policy designed to restrain incomes? (iii) What problems 'may arise from interfering with differentials based on skill and responsibility'? (iv) In view of these problems comment on the proposal contained in the T.U.C. document, that 'those with incomes over £7,000 a year should forego any increase in their incomes in the present period of difficulties'.

14.3 The third report issued by the Royal Commission on the Distribution of Income and Wealth contained an addendum written by three members of the Commission. Part of the addendum reads as follows:

'The major question raised by the level of top salaries is the relationship between economic efficiency and social justice. We have seen that during the past 40 years there has been a steady trend in the direction of a rise in the standard of living of the majority of wage and salary earners and that this has been accompanied by a substantial fall in the differentials between the highest paid and the manual and lower supvervisory grades. This has been possible mainly because of the rise during that period in gross national product, but also because of a general concern for greater social justice.

'However, the evidence gathered for this report shows that recently this process has greatly accelerated. While the median earnings of all men have risen faster in the past five years than the retail price increase, salaries after tax at constant prices had fallen between July 1969 and July 1975 by 17 per cent. at the £10,000 a year level and 25 per cent. at the £20,000 a year level, most of this decline occurring in the past two years. Because of the freeze on salaries of £8,500 and above since then, this decline is steadily increasing as retail prices continue to rise.

'The total after-tax earnings of the small group of 65,000 earning £10,000 or more from employment amounts to only 1.2 per cent. of the total after-tax income of all employment incomes. An improvement in the standard of living of the lower paid cannot be achieved by further redistribution of earnings from the higher salary earners. It can only come from the creation of more income resulting from new capital investment and greater productivity.'

Comment upon, and discuss the implications of, the conclusions expressed in the passage.

14.4 'The aims of the Price Code are: (1) to limit the extent to which prices may be increased on account of increased costs and to secure reductions as a result of reduced costs; (2) to reinforce the control of prices by a control on profit margins while safeguarding and encouraging investment; (3) to reinforce the effects of competition and to secure its full benefits on the general level of prices. With certain exceptions the Code covers the prices of all goods and services supplied to the UK home market. In the main prices may only be raised if justified by certain "allowable" cost increases, which include rises in the cost of labour, materials, fuel, rent and rates, and under the "productivity deduction" a proportion of any increase in labour costs has to be absorbed out of profits. There are also strict controls on net profit margins and on distributors' gross margins.

In his Budget speech in November the Chancellor announced certain modifications, and the revised Price Code embodying these has been in force since 20 December 1974. The main changes affect investment relief, the productivity deduction, and safeguards for profits. Firms are now entitled to recover, through higher prices and profit margins, $17\frac{1}{2}$ per cent of firmly budgeted capital expenditure on certain investment for the home market, mainly investment in plant and machinery, industrial buildings and warehouses. Firms are required to absorb a certain proportion of cost increases due to wage rises – the so-called productivity deduction, originally fixed at 50 per cent. It has now been reduced to a standard 20 per cent, extending upwards to a maximum of 35 per cent for the least labour-intensive products and processes, and falling to a minimum of 10 per cent for the most labour-intensive. Nationalised industries may, subject to certain ministerial controls, raise prices in order to make a modest surplus.'

The above passage was taken from an article in the Economic Progress Report, March 1975. (i) Assess the likely effects of the Price Code in terms of its three aims. (ii) Why do you think it was felt desirable to amend the Code in 1974?

CHAPTER FIFTEEN

International Economic Policies

Introduction

IN Chapter 7 we discussed international economic transactions as they might influence, and be influenced by, the economy of the United Kingdom. We made no reference to specific government policies. Indeed we assumed that the government allowed international trade to be determined by the free interplay of economic forces.

We now examine government policies which influence international economic transactions and relationships. Policies in this sphere can be broadly divided into those relating to the exchange rate, those which involve the imposition, or the removal, of barriers to trade, and those relating to membership of international economic organizations. As far as possible we shall discuss each of these three sets of policies separately, although, as we shall see, there is a considerable degree of overlap.

Policies Relating to the Rate of Exchange

The first distinction to be made here is between a policy of allowing exchange rates to float, i.e. to move to a level determined by the free interplay of market forces, and a policy of fixed exchanged rates – or more precisely the stabilization of the exchange rate for long periods of time. It is convenient to discuss floating rates first, since this provides a useful frame of reference within which we can subsequently evaluate government intervention designed to stabilize the exchange rate.

Floating Exchange Rates: the Effects of Depreciation

In Chapter 7 we discussed the factors that influence the rate of exchange in the absence of government intervention. We now consider the effects of a change in the exchange rate. The exchange rate may, of course, float either up or down. However since 1972, when sterling was allowed to float, its value in relation to most other currencies has declined, i.e. sterling has depreciated. Consequently we concentrate on the effect of the depreciation of a currency. We discuss the effects on resource utilization, the rate of inflation and the balance of payments.

DEPRECIATION AND RESOURCE UTILIZATION

Depreciation implies a fall in the price of our exports and therefore an increase in their volume, and a rise in the price of our imports and hence a fall in their volume. Consequently depreciation will increase the level of utilization of domestic resources. (The reverse would apply if the currency were to appreciate, i.e. the exchange rate moved upwards.)

DEPRECIATION AND THE RATE OF INFLATION

As we have shown in earlier chapters, an increase in resource utilization may give rise to inflationary pressures. For this reason alone depreciation tends to be inflationary. In addition the fall in the exchange rate affects the level of prices. We have already seen that imports become dearer. The prices of domestic producers are also likely to rise for three reasons. First, those producers who use materials and components bought from abroad suffer increased costs. Second, suppliers whose products are in competition with imported goods may take advantage of the increase in the prices of these competitive goods to raise their own prices. Finally, since prices in the U.K. have risen, workers may press for and achieve wage increases, thus putting up the costs of all domestic producers.

There is a danger that, due to these various factors, the costs and prices of domestic producers may rise so much that the initial price effect of the fall in the exchange rate is cancelled out. Indeed it is possible for a vicious circle of increasing costs and prices to arise, which may cause resource utilization to be *lower* than it would have been had the currency not depreciated.

DEPRECIATION AND THE BALANCE OF PAYMENTS

The efffect of depreciation on the balance of payments depends upon the price elasticities of demand for exports and imports. The balance of payments, or more strictly the balance in relation to trade in goods and services, will improve following the depreciation of a currency if the sum of the demand elasticities is greater than one. (It is conventional to ignore the negative signs.) For example the balance of payments will improve if the elasticity of demand for imports is (negative) 0.4 and the elasticity of demand for exports is (negative) 0.7. The balance will worsen if the sum of the demand elasticities is less than one.

In most instances one would expect the sum of the demand elasticities to exceed one, and hence a depreciation to lead to an improved balance of payments, at least in the long term. However the short term effect may be less favourable. The shorter the time period, the more difficult it is for purchasers to modify their purchasing patterns. In particular, manufacturers may find it difficult to change their sources of supply for materials and components because of technical specifications and requirements. This means that demand may be highly inelastic in the short term, i.e. a currency depreciation may worsen the balance of payments in relation to trade in goods and services.

The effect on the balance of payments as a whole will depend also upon the behaviour of the remaining currency flows, discussed in Chapter 7. There is a danger that international investors, observing the initial weakening of the balance of payments, may lose confidence in the currency. For example if sterling begins to weaken investors may sell pounds and buy safer currencies such as German marks. Similarly U.K. importers, observing the weakening of sterling, may anticipate a further fall in the exchange rate. This will be an incentive to pay for their imports as quickly as possible, before the value of their sterling falls further. Conversely, purchasers of U.K. exports may delay payment in the hope of eventually being able to obtain a larger number of pounds for their own currency.* Finally the pressure on the exchange rate may be increased by the speculative selling of sterling – although the reverse effect could also occur if speculators felt that the weakness in the currency was temporary.

It is difficult to identify the precise effect of these various sets of factors. Nevertheless British experience in the mid 1970s strongly suggests that the initial effect of a fall in the exchange rate on the current account (and therefore on the balance of payments) may well be adverse. This effect and the subsequent improvement

*These actions by importers and exporters are known as 'leads and lags'.

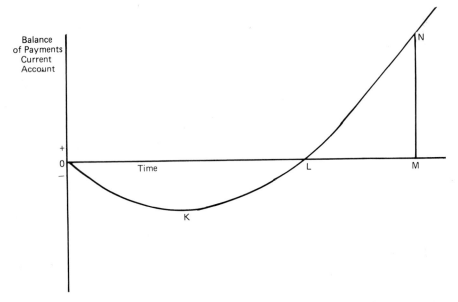

Figure 15.1 Depreciation and the Current Account

in the current balance is illustrated in figure 15.1. In this figure the plus and minus signs on the vertical axis indicate an improvement or a worsening of the current balance in relation to its level before the currency depreciated. If, for the sake of simplicity, we assume that the current balance was initially zero, a plus indicates a current account surplus, and a minus indicates a deficit.

A most important consideration is obviously the length of time that elapses before the current account moves back into surplus, i.e. period OL, and also the period at which the accumulated surpluses equal the accumulated deficits, i.e. period OM (area LMN=OLK). Following the devaluation (i.e. depreciation by government action) of sterling in November 1967, more than a year elapsed before a current account surplus was achieved, and considerably longer before the accumulated deficits were eliminated.

Fixed Exchange Rates
Although many currencies have been allowed to float during the 1970s, this was a reversal of the previous situation. For most of the post-war period the major international trading nations had operated a system of fixed exchange rates. We now examine the major implications of such a system, beginning again with resource utilization.

THE IMPLICATIONS OF FIXED EXCHANGE RATES FOR RESOURCE UTILIZATION
We showed above that a fall in the exchange rate leads, via a change in the relative prices of products, to an increase in the volume of exports and a decline in the volume of imports, both of which imply an increase in the level of resource utilization. It follows, therefore, that when the authorities intervene to support a currency at a level above that which would be established in a free market, the result is likely to be a lower level of resource utilization. In addition, if the market forces which are causing the pressure on the currency are strong, the government may

take positive steps (via fiscal and/or monetary policy) to reduce the level of domestic expenditure. U.K. governments have frequently felt obliged to adopt such policies when in balance of payments difficulties. Such action will, of course, lead to a further fall in resource utilization.

On the other hand, if the authorities intervene to prevent a currency rising to the free market level it will thereby increase, or at least prevent a fall in, the level of utilization of domestic resources.

FIXED EXCHANGE RATES AND THE RATE OF INFLATION
We can again refer to our earlier discussion, where we showed that a depreciation of the currency tends, for several reasons, to be inflationary. It follows that intervention to prevent a fall in the exchange rate will result in prices increasing less than they would otherwise have done.* Conversely, preventing an upward movement in the exchange rate will lead to a relatively higher rate of domestic price increase.

FIXED EXCHANGE RATES AND THE BALANCE OF PAYMENTS
We showed above that the depreciation of a currency would lead to an improvement in the current balance, and hence probably in the overall balance of payments, provided that the sum of the elasticities of demand for imports and exports exceeded unity. (One should add the further condition that sufficient spare capacity should exist to meet the increased demand.) Conversely an (upward) appreciation of the currency would lead to an improvement in the balance of payments provided that sum of the demand elasticities is less than unity. It follows that the effect on the balance of payments of intervention to prevent a change in the exchange rate will depend on the values of the demand elasticities.

DEVALUATION AND REVALUATION
When a country feels unable to sustain the existing parity of its currency because there is a fundamental persistent disequilibrium in its international trading position, it will devalue. The extent of the devaluation will depend mainly upon how serious the disequilibrium is felt to be, and in particular how much the prices of its products which are traded internationally are out of line with competitive products. In practice devaluations tend to be substantial. For example sterling was devalued against the dollar by 14 per cent in 1967.

The effects of a devaluation are similar to those of a currency depreciation, discussed above. However since the international value of the currency is changed by a substantial amount literally overnight the impact is more dramatic.

The effects of a revaluation (or upvaluation) are similar to the appreciation of a currency. A currency is most likely to be revalued when the country has a persistent balance of payments surplus, especially if this is accompanied by significant inflationary pressures. Since a revaluation has a potentially adverse effect on resource utilization, revaluations tend to be more modest than devaluations. For example the German mark has been revalued several times by around 5 per cent.

FIXED EXCHANGE RATES AND SPECULATION
There has been considerable controversy concerning the role of speculation – the buying and selling of currencies in the hope of profit rather than for use in settling trading transactions. It is especially difficult to identify the effect of speculation

* This will tend to counterbalance the adverse effect of intervention on resource utilization, discussed in the previous section.

when currencies are floating. However when currencies are fixed speculation is almost certain to add to whatever pressures on a currency may already exist. For example if a country is suffering balance of payments difficulties then any change in the value of its currency will be downward. Speculators will, therefore, move out of this currency and into currencies whose relative value is likely to increase. This selling of the troubled currency will make it more difficult and expensive for the authorities to support the existing value of the currency.

THE COMMITMENT TO FIXED EXCHANGE RATES: THE BRETTON WOODS AGREEMENT

The basis for the post-war system of fixed exchange rates was an agreement signed at a conference held at Bretton Woods in 1944. Members of the *International Monetary Fund* (the I.M.F.), which actually came into operation in 1947, agreed to set the value of their currencies in terms of either the dollar or sterling (and hence ultimately gold), and not to allow a deviation of more than one per cent from these rates or 'parities'. This meant that if a currency came under pressure on the foreign exchange market the country had to use its reserves of dollars, sterling or gold to buy foreign currencies and thus to stabilize the exchange rate.

It was recognized that a particular currency might occasionally come under such severe pressure that the country's reserves would be depleted by a support operation. Faced with this prospect the country might attempt to improve its balance of payments by restricting its expenditure, in order to reduce its volume of imports. Such a policy might, however, simply transfer the problem to other countries whose exports, and therefore balance of payments, would be adversely affected.

To reduce the danger of such 'beggar-my-neighbour' policies being adopted it was decided to set up a second line of defence in the form of additional reserves. Each member of the I.M.F. was given a quota which it paid into the Fund in the form of gold (25 per cent) and its own currency (75 per cent). Each member was then allowed to borrow from the Fund up to 125 per cent of its quota.

Money borrowed from the I.M.F. must be repaid within three to five years, by the end of which time the borrowing country is expected to have introduced measures to counteract the factors which necessitated the borrowing. Although this usually implies policies designed to reduce total expenditure, it is recognized that in some instances these measures may include a change in the exchange rate. However, countries agreed that such changes would be 'orderly', i.e. on a once-and-for-all basis.

The various domestic disadvantages which may follow from fixed exchange rates – in particular the need by deficit countries to introduce expenditure-reducing policies – gradually made more governments seriously consider a move to floating rates. Although in most instances the change was made during the 1970s, these changes can be fully understood only within the context of earlier developments in the international economy.

THE MOVE TO FLOATING RATES

In the 1950s, as countries such as Germany and Japan emerged as major international competitors, the U.S.A. and the U.K. began to run into balance of payments problems and the dollar and the pound came under pressure. Partly in order to reduce the danger that the U.K. might be forced into a devaluation which would destroy the existing stability of currency parities, and partly to accommodate the substantial increase in international trade that had occurred, a series of steps were taken to increase the level of international liquidity.

I.M.F. quota subscriptions were more than doubled between 1959 and 1975. By the General Arrangements to Borrow, adopted in 1962, the 'Group of Ten' industrial nations* provided the I.M.F. with an extra $6 billion worth of currencies. In 1969 Special Drawing Rights were established. The S.D.R. is in effect an entry in a member's bank balance with the I.M.F., and is available for settlements between central banks and with the I.M.F.

Steps to increase international liquidity have also been taken outside the I.M.F. For example under the auspices of the Bank for International Settlements central bankers have made 'swop arrangements' – agreements to exchange each other's currencies for a limited period in order to relieve the pressure on one currency or the other.

Despite these various attempts to shore up the international financial system, it gradually began to collapse. The first crack appeared with the devaluation of sterling in 1967. This was followed by speculative attacks on other currencies including the franc, which was devalued, and the dollar, which was allowed to float down.

THE SMITHSONIAN AGREEMENT

An attempt to restore stability was made at a meeting held at the Smithsonian Institution in 1971. A new pattern of fixed exchange rates was agreed, with a wider range of fluctuation ($2\frac{1}{4}$ per cent either side of the parity) than previously. However the new arrangement did not last long. In June 1972 sterling was allowed to float and many other countries were soon to follow.

One of the effects of this change was some loss of authority on the part of the I.M.F. However the Fund remains an important source of international liquidity. Indeed the U.K. turned to the I.M.F. in 1976 for support in halting the prolonged slide in the value of sterling.

Dirty Floating

Today most exchange rates are floating. However they are all subject, to some degree, to government intervention designed to steady the rate. Thus although the rates are allowed to respond to market forces, governments reserve the right to intervene. For instance a government might intervene to counteract a movement which it feels is due purely to speculative activity, or which is inconsistent with its economic strategy, e.g. a rapid depreciation of the currency which would be reflected in a rapid rise in import prices and hence in domestic costs and prices. Governments may also have in mind, when acting to steady the exchange rate, that rapid fluctuations create added uncertainties for traders – although these uncertainties can, at a cost, be overcome by buying or selling currencies in forward markets.

Barriers to Trade

We said above that a country faced with balance of payments difficulties can attempt to overcome these difficulties either by changing its exchange rate or by reducing the level of domestic expenditure. A third alternative is to erect barriers designed to reduce imports. Any country which benefits from the imposition of trade barriers obviously does so at the expense of other countries, and invites retaliation. Furthermore, barriers to trade are recognized as interfering with the process of international specialization and trade in accordance with the principle of comparative advantage. Consequently the post-war period has seen a general

* U.S.A., U.K., W. Germany, France, Belgium, Netherlands, Italy, Sweden, Canada, Japan.

reduction in barriers, at least until recently (see below). The main types of barrier are as follows:

Tariffs

Tariffs are taxes imposed on imports. They may be levied on an ad valorem basis, i.e. as a certain percentage of value, or on a specific basis, i.e. as an amount per unit. By increasing the price of the product, a tariff reduces the quantity demanded.

Quotas

Quotas are quantitative restrictions on imports. A quota may relate to the total quantity or value of a commodity that can be imported in a given period, or it may relate to the quantity or value that can be imported from a particular source, e.g. a certain country or group of countries.

Other Barriers to Trade

Importers may be required to deposit with the government for a certain period of time a percentage of the value of the products imported. If no interest is paid on the money deposited – as happened with the import deposit scheme introduced in the U.K. in the 1960s – the importer loses a potential source of income. Moreover some importers may suffer liquidity problems. The combined effect is therefore to discourage imports.

Imports may also be discouraged by instituting a restrictive system of licensing, by insisting on technical specifications for products which may be difficult or costly to meet, or by limiting the funds available for importing. Finally, governments may discriminate against imports in their purchasing policies, e.g. the U.K. government has usually 'bought British' in the field of armaments, computers, etc.

CONDITIONS FAVOURING TRADE BARRIERS

Trade barriers are least likely to invite retaliation if certain conditions are fulfilled. A developed country should seek to indicate that the restriction is intended to be temporary and that other steps are also being taken to solve the problem that made the restriction necessary. For example the U.K. would be in a better position to justify the protection of the textile industry if it could show that, during the period of protection, it had planned an orderly run-down of the industry, including an accelerated programme of re-training employees for work in other industries.

There tends to be greater tolerance of restrictions imposed by less developed countries because of their lower living standards. However even here temporary restrictions are likely to be viewed most favourably. An argument frequently advanced by these countries is that an industry that is just developing in that country may be inherently as efficient there as in any other country, but that it requires protection in order to allow it to gain the advantages that come only with experience and larger-scale production. This so-called infant industry argument is particularly appealing since it implies that once the industry has matured, and the restrictions on competition from imports are removed, specialization and trade will take place in accordance with the principle of comparative advantage. However it should be pointed out that protection from competition can breed inefficiency, and that many infant industries take much longer to grow up than one might expect!

Finally, retaliation is less likely for the less 'visible' forms of protection, such as technical specifications, than for quotas and tariffs. This no doubt helps to explain the growth in the importance of such forms in recent years.

THE GENERAL AGREEMENT ON TARIFFS AND TRADE

The advantages to be derived from international specialization and trade were the main reason for the establishment in 1947 of the General Agreement on Tariffs and Trade, an international organization based in Geneva. The members of G.A.T.T. are pledged to the expansion of multinational trade, and to the removal or at least a reduction of measures which distort the pattern of trade, such as import restrictions and export incentives.

Under G.A.T.T. negotiations, preferential arrangements can now be made for imports from developing nations, without these arrangements being extended to all the contracting parties of G.A.T.T. This departure from the normal G.A.T.T. principle of non-discrimination in trade policy was again justified in terms of the need to aid the development, and raise the living standards, of the less developed nations.

REGIONAL TRADE GROUPINGS

Membership of G.A.T.T. implies some limitation of the freedom of members to adopt policies which they consider to be in their own interest. This restriction is also inherent in membership of a regional trade grouping, the most important forms of which are the free trade area and the customs union.

FREE TRADE AREAS

In a free trade area all restrictions on trade between members are removed. But each member remains free to decide upon its policy in relation to non-members. Examples of this type of grouping include the European Free Trade Association, of which the U.K. was formerly a member, and the Latin American Free Trade Area, which currently comprises ten South American countries.

CUSTOMS UNIONS

As in a free trade area, all restrictions on trade between members are abolished. However a member of a customs union also gives up the right to decide upon its policy towards non-members. Instead a common external tariff, observed by all members, is established.

A customs union may also oblige its members to adopt common policies in other spheres. So, for example, the European Economic Community (the Common Market) has a Common Agricultural Policy which determines the prices of foodstuffs within the Community. The E.E.C. is also moving towards the harmonization of a wide range of economic policies relating, for example, to the movement of labour, retraining, assistance designed to correct regional imbalances, etc.*

The Economic Effects of Regional Groupings

Regional groupings can be evaluated in terms of their effects on the total welfare of all countries, the welfare of their members as a whole, and the welfare of individual members. It might be thought that total welfare would be increased by the formation of a regional grouping since the abolition of barriers to trade among members encourages, within that grouping, specialization and trade in accordance with the principle of comparative advantage. However, on a wider international scale, regional groupings – and especially customs unions – may be inconsistent with that principle. One member of the grouping may have a comparative advantage in a particular product when compared to other members, but not when

*One of the reasons for harmonization is that differences in national economic policies can interfere with international trade.

compared to non-members. To put the matter slightly differently, a low cost producer may be excluded from a market, leaving it to be supplied by a relatively high cost producer.

The total welfare of all the nations in the world may not, therefore, increase as a result of the formation of a regional grouping. Moreover, even when we confine our attention to the members of the grouping it is not inevitable that total welfare should increase. The high-cost producer will benefit by being sheltered from the competition of low-cost non-members, but this is at the expense of consumers, who have to pay higher prices.

Finally the producers of some member countries may benefit at the expense of producers in other member countries. There is some evidence to suggest that on the whole U.K. manufacturing industry has lost rather than gained sales as a result of our entry into the European Economic Community (see table 15.1).

Table 15.1

U.K. Trade Balance* (£mn)

	1970	1975	1976
With the 'E.E.C. Six'	195	−992	−1,090
With the rest of the world	1,186	3,220	3,521

* Excluding food and petroleum products. Line 1 refers to the original six members of the E.E.C. The 1976 figure is an estimate, based on trade during the first nine months.
Source: *Financial Times*, 27.1.77.

Other International Economic Organizations
We now consider some of the other organizations which influence international trade and payments, beginning with the clutch of institutions associated with the E.E.C.

The *European Investment Bank* was created by the Treaty of Rome, and came into force in 1958. Its principal role is to make loans within member countries for projects that:

(a) benefit less developed regions; or
(b) are concerned with developments of such a size or nature that they cannot be entirely financed by the means available in individual member countries; or
(c) are of common interest to several member countries and cannot be financed entirely by the means available in individual countries.

U.K. projects that have attracted funds from the E.I.B. include the construction of steel plants, a nuclear power station and a second Thames tunnel.

The *Regional Development Fund* was established in 1975 to provide assistance to the less developed regions in member countries. The scope of the Fund's activities has gradually extended as illustrated by the proposed increase in its budget from 400 million units of account (£263 million) in 1977 to 750 million units of account (£492 million) in 1978. The national quotas are set in the light of the Commission's views about each country's needs. Italy's 40 per cent share is largely due to the heavy unemployment in the south of that country. The U.K. has the second highest quota with 28 per cent, and the money which we receive supplements the various forms of government assistance which we consider in the following chapter.

The *European Social Fund* was set up under the auspices of the E.E.C. to assist the redeployment of redundant workers (especially where the redundancy was caused by the creation of the Community). For example, finance was offered by the Fund to meet the cost of retraining workers whose jobs in the U.K. newspaper industry were threatened by technological change.

Not all European institutions are concerned only with the interests of their own members. The *European Development Fund* was established in 1971 to provide loans and non-repayable credits for specific development projects in the developing countries, such as the building of roads and bridges and radio and telecommunications networks.

Of the international institutions the best known, apart from the I.M.F. whose role was described earlier, is probably the *International Bank for Reconstruction and Development*, also known as the *World Bank*. Established like the I.M.F. as a result of the Bretton Woods conference, the I.B.R.D. began operations in 1946. Its primary purpose is to encourage capital investment for the reconstruction or development of its member countries. It seeks to fulfil this purpose both by acting as a channel for private funds and by drawing on its own resources. These resources comprise partly the subscriptions of member countries and partly money raised by selling bonds on the world market. Today nearly all the Bank's lending is to the less developed countries.

The *International Finance Corporation*, an affiliate of the I.B.R.D., was established in 1956 mainly to stimulate the provision of aid from private sources to the less developed countries. In addition to providing loans, the I.F.C. can hold shares in companies. Also affiliated to the I.B.R.D., the *International Development Association* provides loans at little or no interest for projects in developing countries that would not be feasible if finance had to be obtained at normal commercial rates. These projects often have a long life and are capital intensive, e.g. roads, power supplies, etc.

International Aid and Economic Development
The primary purpose of many of the institutions listed above is to encourage the economic development of the less developed countries. In addition individual governments have been encouraged by bodies such as the United Nations to increase the level of their international aid. However not all commentators see an increase in international aid as contributing to a solution of the problems of the underdeveloped countries.

Some economists, such as Professor Bauer, claim that international aid may sap local initiative, so that the net effect of aid on economic growth is very small and possibly even negative. Others, such as the late Dr. Schumacher, criticize the nature rather than the scale of the aid, claiming that many of the projects that are supported are unsuitable for less developed countries.

Schumacher has argued that more projects should use 'intermediate technology'. Since it is less sophisticated than the more advanced technology employed in highly industrialized economies, intermediate technology is more readily absorbed by underdeveloped countries without the help of experts from the industrialized nations. Moreover, since it normally involves a higher labour–capital ratio than more advanced technology, it meets one of the primary needs of many developing nations – the need for additional employment.

AID VERSUS TRADE
Whether the present scale of aid is too little, too great or just about right, will continue to be a matter for debate. What is generally accepted, however, is that

the less developed countries would benefit if they were allowed greater freedom in their international trading relationships.

One method of increasing freedom is to reduce the proportion of aid that is tied, i.e. where the recipient is required to spend a certain percentage (which may be 100 in extreme instances), of the aid in the purchase of products from the donor country.

Another method is, of course, to reduce the various barriers that might be raised against products exported from the less developed countries. In 1970, following negotiations conducted under the auspices of G.A.T.T., an agreement was reached whereby the developed nations of E.F.T.A., the E.E.C. and the U.S.A. gave preferential treatment in specified manufactured goods to the developing countries.

In 1975 negotiations were conducted between the E.E.C. and a group of forty-six African, Caribbean and Pacific states (the A.C.P. countries), which resulted in the Lomé Agreement. Under this agreement the E.E.C. and the A.C.P. countries comprise a preferential trading area in which the E.E.C. has relinquished the right of reciprocity. It was estimated that henceforth 94 per cent of the agricultural products of the A.C.P. states would enter the Community free of duty.

The United Nations Conference on Trade and Development has stressed the benefits, including a greater degree of price stability, to be obtained from international commodity agreements. Products which are now subject to such agreements, of varying degrees of comprehensiveness, include bauxite, iron ore, phosphates and bananas. (Several alternative stabilization policies are examined in Chapter 28.)

Summary and Conclusions

In the first part of the chapter we considered the advantages and disadvantages of fixed and floating exchange rates. The choice between these two systems must take into account the implications for other government policies, considered in earlier chapters. One of the most obvious disadvantages of a fixed exchange rate is that if a currency is overvalued there will be a persistent tendency towards a balance of payments deficit, which will force the government to adopt measures to restrict total expenditure. The overvaluation of sterling was a major cause of the 'stop–go' policies adopted by successive British governments, especially in the 1960s.

The disadvantages of fixed exchange rates eventually led to the adoption of floating rates by many countries. When sterling was allowed to float in 1972 it was argued that the strain imposed by any disequilibrium in our international trading relationships would henceforth be taken by the exchange rate and not by changes in expenditure, enforced by the government. However subsequent experience showed that allowing the exchange rate to take the strain can itself have undesirable consequences. We examined in Chapter 7 the factors that influence the rate of exchange and we saw that in some circumstances a fall in the exchange rate may be self-reinforcing. In this chapter we explored the consequences of the fall in the exchange rate of sterling, which appears to have entered a downward spiral in the mid 1970s. We saw that this depreciation contributed to the rise in domestic costs and prices, and that it might well have affected the balance of payments adversely, especially in the short term.

In the second part of the chapter we discussed the major institutional aspects of the international economy. We examined barriers to trade and outlined the circumstances in which these barriers are likely to be least objectionable – perhaps the single most important factor here is whether the barrier is intended to be temporary or permanent. We also outlined the role of the major international economic institutions. We saw that the major purpose of many of these institutions is either to increase the level of international liquidity or to aid the economic growth of the less developed nations.

We noted that while the post-war period has seen an increase in international economic co-operation there have recently been signs that the world recession in the mid 1970s had led some countries to adopt protectionist measures. In 1977 the I.M.F. identified several areas in which curbs had become more prevalent, including quantitative controls, the use of import surcharges and taxes, and advance import deposit schemes. A later report issued by G.A.T.T. confirmed this trend to greater protectionism and suggested that the uncertainty generated by the spread of protectionism was seriously inhibiting investment at a time when it was needed both as a stimulus to demand and to promote structural adjustment in the industrial countries.

ESSAY QUESTIONS

1 Discuss the relative advantages and disadvantages of fixed and floating exchange rates.
2 Analyse the possible effects of the appreciation of a currency's external value.
3 'Devaluation is more likely to have a favourable effect on resource utilization than on the balance of payments.' Discuss.
4 'As a result of inflation Belgradia's currency depreciated.' 'The depreciation of Belgradia's currency increased the inflationary pressures.' Comment.
5 Analyse the circumstances under which devaluation is likely to result in an improvement in the balance of payments.
6 'A deficit on the balance of payments current account has favourable short-run, but unfavourable long-run consequences.' Discuss.
7 Analyse the relationship between a fixed exchange rate and the rate of inflation.
8 Discuss the proposition that the move towards floating exchange rates in the post-war period indicates that they are to be preferred to fixed rates.
9 Explain the meaning of the term 'dirty floating' and why it occurs.
10 'Since barriers to trade inhibit international specialization in accordance with the principle of comparative advantage they must reduce the overall level of economic welfare.' Discuss.
11 Compare and contrast the characteristics and objectives of customs unions and free trade areas.
12 'Although a customs union increases the economic welfare of each of its members, this is at the expense of non-members.' Discuss.
13 Describe the major objectives of the following: the International Monetary Fund, the World Bank, the European Investment Bank.
14 'Trade is always to be preferred to aid.' Discuss.

EXERCISES

15.1 'Since July 1974, despite the unprecedented rate of deficit to which the current balance has descended, there has been no downward trend in the sterling exchange rate. In May 1973, the effective overall depreciation of sterling compared with the Smithsonian level of December 1971 was around 10 per cent.

Largely because of interest rate differentials, sterling came under pressure in June and July, and fell to approaching 20 per cent depreciation. It was for this reason that the authorities enforced the sudden sharp rise in short-term interest rates in the United Kingdom, and with the aid of some official support the decline was halted. Thereafter it has continued at much the same overall level, fluctuating around a level of about 18 per cent depreciation.'

Source: *Midland Bank Review*, May 1975, p. 16.

(i) Why would you expect a deficit on the U.K.'s current balance to lead to a downward trend in the sterling exchange rate? (ii) Why did this not occur on this occasion? (iii) How may the authorities enforce a rise in short-term interest-rates? (iv) Do you consider a policy of trying to prevent a fall in the sterling exchange rate to be sensible when there is a deficit on current account?

15.2 (i) How would you account for the movements in the U.K.'s terms of trade shown in table 15.2? (ii) Were these movements favourable or unfavourable? (iii) The weights used in calculating the terms of trade are the values

Table 15.2
U.K. Terms of Trade (1970 = 100)

1964	95.2
1965	97.6
1966	99.6
1967	100.8
1968	97.1
1969	97.3
1970	100.0
1971	100.8
1972	101.3
1973	90.2
1974	74.9
1975	84.1
1976	83.2

Source: *Economic Trends*, Sept. 1977.

of trade for each commodity in the base year. From October 1973, the base year was changed from 1961 to 1970. Why do you think this change was required?

15.3 (i) Discuss the elasticity of demand for imports and exports with reference to the data in table 15.3. (ii) Do you think that the increase in the price of our exports that occurred between 1973 and 1974 was desirable? (iii) Compare the rise in import prices that occurred in the period 1970 to 1973 with that in the period 1973 to 1974. How would you account for the differences in the rate of price change?

15.4 'Under a fixed exchange rate a persistent deficit on current account implies a tendency for the money stock of the country to decline unless this effect is deliberately neutralized by the actions of the central bank. The loss of reserves implies an excess demand for foreign exchange, matched by an excess supply of the domestic currency absorbed by the central bank as a result of its intervention in the foreign exchange market.'

(i) Why does a persistent deficit on current account imply a tendency for the money stock of the country to decline? (ii) How might the central bank neutralize this tendency? (iii) Would this process of neutralization be likely to contribute to or impede a solution of the current account deficit?

Table 15.3
Export and Import Volume and Unit Value Index Numbers, U.K. (1970=100)

| | Volume | | Unit Value (Price) | |
	1973	1974	1973	1974
Exports				
Food, beverages, tobacco	135	142	126	148
Basic materials	114	115	143	181
Fuels	107	101	166	381
Manufactures	128	135	124	155
Total	126.9	132.9	125.5	160.7
Imports				
Food, beverages, tobacco	102	99	150	193
Fuels	112	106	164	468
Industrial materials	125	129	131	190
Finished manufactures	186	189	128	152
Total	132.7	133.4	138.1	210.3

Source: *Annual Abstract of Statistics* (H.M.S.O., 1977).

15.5 Which of the following conditions are likely to make devaluation (a) more and (b) less effective?
   (i) The elasticity of demand for our exports is high.
   (ii) Our elasticity of demand for imports is high.
   (iii) The economy is working at full capacity.
   (iv) The economies of our overseas competitors are working at full capacity.
   (v) Our exports have a high import content (i.e. contain a high proportion of imported raw materials and components).

15.6 The 1967 devaluation of sterling was accompanied by the following measures: cuts in planned government expenditure of £200 million a year, a moderate increase in hire-purchase restrictions, an increase in Bank Rate (now replaced by Minimum Lending Rate) from $6\frac{1}{2}$ per cent to 8 per cent, and a ceiling upon bank lending.

(i) Why was it thought desirable to introduce at the time of devaluation the measures listed above?

After the devaluation the sterling price of tea, (some one half of whose exports are bought by Britain) remained virtually unchanged. The sterling price of most other commodities rose, although not by the full extent of the devaluation.

(ii) How would you explain the pattern of price changes that occurred following devaluation?

15.7 In the light of the data contained in table 15.4, would you consider the U.K.'s balance of payments to have been more satisfactory in 1964 or 1973? Explain your answer by reference to the behaviour of the major currency flows.

15.8 'Britain's official reserves rose by $512m. last month to $10.13bn. – about $6bn. higher than at the start of the year. But the rate of inflow is now expected to slow down.

'This is the first time the reserves have been more than $10bn. The large increase so far this year is the result of both official borrowing abroad of around $2.2bn. – with no new drawings in April – and a continuing heavy underlying inflow of foreign currency. The underlying inflow since the beginning of December when confidence started to recover now totals $4.26bn., offsetting a large part of last year's unprecedented outflow.

Table 15.4

Balance of Payments, United Kingdom (£mn)

	1964	1973
Visible balance	−500	−2,295
Invisible balance	+145	+1,460
1. CURRENT BALANCE	−355	−835
2. Capital transfers (payments under Sterling Agreements)	—	−59
Long-term investment flows	−357	−178
Short-term investment flows	+56	+1,084
3. TOTAL INVESTMENT AND OTHER CAPITAL FLOWS	−301	+906
4. Balancing Item	−39	+198
5. TOTAL CURRENCY FLOW (=1+2+3+4)	−695	+210
Official Financing:		
Net transactions with I.M.F.	+357	—
Net transactions with other overseas monetary authorities	+216	—
Drawings on (+)/additions to (−) official reserves	+122	−210
TOTAL OFFICIAL FINANCING	+695	−210

Source: Annual Abstract of Statistics 1975, table 309. N.B. Long-term investment flows comprise items 3 to 6 of the *original* table; short-term investment flows comprise items 7 to 15 of the *original* table.

'However, the authorities believe that the underlying inflow could soon be smaller. Indeed, last month's rise was around half the increase in March. The once-and-for-all commercial inflow from the unwinding of last year's adverse pattern of commercial payments (known as leads and lags) and from the ban on the use of sterling for financing third country trade was still an important factor last month, but may now have been largely completed. The rise in the reserves last month probably owed rather more than earlier in the year to an increase in the so-called hot money deposits by foreigners in the U.K. The authorities now expect that this inflow could soon stop, with possibly some reversal of the flows, and they would apparently not be too disturbed if this happened. There was a similar expectation a month ago, but this prospect now seems more likely in view of the further fall in U.K. interest rates, narrowing the gap with U.S. rates.

'Uncertainty about the continuation of the pay policy after July could unsettle the foreign exchange market during the next few weeks. The Bank of England's only real period of support for the pound last month occurred after a speech by Mr. Jack Jones on this topic.'

The above article appeared in the *Financial Times*, 4.5.77. (i) Explain the phrase 'the unwinding of last year's adverse pattern of commercial payments (leads and lags). (ii) Why might the authorities 'not be too disturbed' if the inflow of hot money stopped? (iii) Why should the flow of hot money be influenced by the gap between U.K. and U.S. interest rates? (iv) Why might uncertainty about the continuation of the pay policy have unsettled the foreign exchange market? (v) Comment on the fact that official borrowing abroad during January to March amounted to $2.2bn.

OBJECTIVE TEST QUESTIONS: SET 5

1 The M3 definition of the money supply includes all of the following types of bank deposit except

A sterling deposit accounts held by U.K. residents
B sterling current accounts held by U.K. residents
C sterling current accounts held by overseas residents
D non-sterling deposit accounts held by U.K. residents
E non-sterling current accounts held by U.K. residents.

2 All of the following are part of the banks' reserve assets except

A notes and coins
B balances at the Bank of England
C money at call with the London money market
D Treasury Bills
E British government stocks with less than one year to maturity.

3 Assume a banking system with ten banks each having total assets of £10 millions, of which £1 million comprises cash. If each bank now obtained an additional £1 million of cash and wished to continue operating with a cash/ assets ratio of 10 per cent, the total amount of *additional* assets that the system could support would be (£millions).

A 9
B 10
C 90
D 100
E 110.

4 In which of the following situations will the appreciation of the currency cause an improvement in the balance of payments?

	Elasticity of Demand for Exports	Elasticity of Demand for Imports
A	0.5	0.5
B	0.2	0.8
C	0.6	0.8
D	0.0	1.1
E	None of the above.	

5 The formation of a customs union must lead to an increase in

A the welfare of every country in the world
B the total welfare of all countries in the world
C the welfare of each member of the union
D the total welfare of all members of the union
E none of the above.

6 The main difference between a customs union and a free trade area is that in a customs union, but not a free trade area,

A floating exchange rates are allowed
B specialization and trade take place in accordance with the principle of comparative advantage
C a common external tariff must be observed by all members

D tariffs on trade between members are permitted
E quotas on trade between members are permitted.

7 Special Drawing Rights are assets of the members of the
A International Bank for Reconstruction and Development
B European Investment Bank
C International Monetary Fund
D European Social Fund
E International Finance Corporation.

8 Which of the following is/are included within the M_1 definition of the money supply?
1 notes and coin in circulation
2 bank current accounts held in sterling by private sector residents
3 bank deposit accounts held in sterling by private sector residents.

9 Which of the following would tend to cause a reduction in the supply of money?
1 purchases by the Bank of England of government stock held by the public
2 an increase in the minimum reserve assets ratio
3 an increase in the required volume of special deposits.

10 According to the quantity theory of money an increase in the price level may be caused by an increase in the
1 supply of money
2 velocity of circulation of money
3 volume of transactions.

11 The national income may fail to rise following an increase in the money supply if
1 the demand for money is perfectly interest elastic
2 investment expenditure is perfectly interest inelastic
3 all economic resources are fully utilized.

12 In which of the following situations would the depreciation of a currency be likely to result in an improvement in the balance of payments in relation to trade in goods and services?

	Elasticity of Demand for Imports	Elasticity of Demand for Exports
1	0.4	0.6
2	0.0	1.2
3	0.2	0.9

13 For which of the following reasons would the depreciation of a currency be likely to a result in an increase in the domestic price level?
1 the prices of imports would rise
2 the costs of domestic producers would rise
3 domestic producers would meet less competition from overseas producers

14 Which of the following constitute quantitative controls on imports?
1 quotas
2 tariffs
3 import deposit schemes.

15 Membership of G.A.T.T. involves a commitment to
1 a reduction in import restrictions
2 a reduction in export incentives
3 an expansion of multilateral trade.

16 Keynes suggested that the speculative demand for money is inversely related to the price of bonds.
If the price of bonds falls below the issue price the rate of interest also falls.

17 If government controls prevent the prices of some products from increasing, this may lead to greater increases in the prices of other products.
Price controls may result in the real incomes of consumers being higher than they would otherwise have been.

18 Any policy which causes prices to rise less than they would otherwise have done reduces inflationary pressures.
Rising prices are a symptom of inflationary pressures.

19 The balance of payments will improve following the depreciation of the currency provided that the elasticity of demand for exports is greater than that for imports.
If the elasticity of demand for exports exceeds unity the value of exports will increase following a fall in their price.

20 Devaluation is likely to lead to an increase in domestic resource utilization.
Devaluation will cause the value of exports to rise and the value of imports to fall.

TRUE/FALSE

1 If a bond with a nominal value of £100 and a nominal rate of interest of 6 per cent can be bought for £50, the actual rate of interest is 12 per cent.
2 If the banks initially have reserve assets equal to 12½ per cent of eligible liabilities and these reserve assets fall by £100,000, in order to restore the reserve assets ratio to its previous level a further reduction in assets of £800,000 is required.
3 The quantity theory of money states that an increase in the quantity of money will always lead to an increase in the price level.
4 The term 'suppressed inflation' indicates that the government has eliminated all inflationary pressures in the economy.
5 The minimum lending rate is the minimum rate at which the Bank of England provides funds to the discount houses.
6 Devaluation of the currency will always lead to an improvement in the balance of payments in the long term.
7 If the foreign exchange value of a currency is tending to fall, this tendency will be counter-balanced by the operation of leads and lags in international payments.
8 If the authorities intervene to prevent a currency from rising to its free market level, this would have a favourable effect on the level of domestic resource utilization.
9 If the authorities intervene to prevent a currency from rising to its free market level this will moderate the rate of inflation.
10 The 'infant industry' argument provides justification for granting an industry permanent protection from foreign competition.

CHAPTER SIXTEEN

Regional Policy

Introduction

IN the discussion of government policies in earlier chapters we have been mainly concerned with the consequences of policy for the economy as a whole, and with the behaviour of broad aggregates such as the change in GDP and in the overall level of unemployment. In this chapter we take a rather less aggregative view, examining the effects of policies not at the national but at the regional level.

One of the objectives of government policy listed in Chapter 10 was an increase in equality, which many people would consider should include equality of opportunity between people living in different regions. The aspects of equality of opportunity normally stressed in this context are employment opportunities and the standard of living, aspects which are, of course, interrelated.

Regional Unemployment

It is useful to consider first the pattern of regional unemployment in periods during which there were no, or at most very weak, regional policies in operation. For the U.K. this implies examining data for the inter-war period. Dr. McCrone has shown that 'whereas London and the South East had unemployment rates of around 5 or 6 per cent in the 1920s which rose to 15 per cent in 1932–3, Scotland, Wales, Northern England and Northern Ireland had unemployment rates of 12 to 15 per cent in the 1920s and these rose to between 25 and 35 per cent in 1932'.*

These differences in unemployment rates were associated with differences in average incomes per head and in average living standards. We can therefore conclude that there were serious regional inequalities in the U.K. in the inter-war period. The next question to ask is whether the government should act so as to try to reduce these inequalities or whether we might expect the operation of market forces to do so.

The Free Market Approach

The ideological view underlying this approach is that economic units should be free to make their own decisions. The argument is advanced that if workers are dissatisfied with the employment opportunities, and the associated standard of living, in a given area they will seek work in other areas. In this way the unemployment differentials will be reduced and eventually disappear. If workers do not move, this would be taken as an indication that the area has advantages which outweigh the limited employment opportunities, so that again, it is argued, there is no case for government intervention.

Similarly if firms are left free to make their own location decisions they will establish plants in areas of high unemployment in order to take advantage of the excess labour supply, and of the lower wage rates with which (in the absence of union monopoly power) this will be associated. If firms do not establish plants

*G. McCrone, *Regional Policy in Britain* (London: Allen and Unwin, 1969), p. 91.

in these areas it indicates that they consider the advantages of a plentiful labour supply to be outweighed by other economic disadvantages, and so again there is no case for government intervention.

To summarize, this suggests that market forces are likely to lead to the elimination of unemployment differentials; furthermore if this does not occur it indicates that workers and firms consider that the costs involved in eliminating the differentials would outweigh the benefits. Hence, the government should not attempt to influence the location decisions of workers and firms.

An Evaluation of the Free Market Approach

An evaluation of the free market approach must take into account institutional factors, the nature of the costs and benefits involved in decisions, and the time-scale likely to be involved in the solution. It should also, of course, take into account the costs of alternative solutions, a point considered later in the chapter.

INSTITUTIONAL FACTORS

An important plank in the free market platform is the assumption that the labour market is subject to market forces, and in particular that differential rates of unemployment will be reflected in differential wage rates. In practice the spread of collective bargaining, often on an industry or occupation-wide basis, has reduced the sensitivity of wage rates to local unemployment rates. (Incidentally, even if wage rates are lower in some areas than others it does not follow that labour costs will be lower, since differences in wage rates may be balanced or even outweighed by differences in labour productivity.)

Another important institutional factor is the availability of unemployment and other social security benefits. As we saw in Chapter 9 the gap between these benefits and average post-tax earnings has been steadily reduced, i.e. these factors (which are not primarily related to regional policies) interfere with the operation of market forces. We are not concerned with whether this interference is or is not desirable. We merely point out that a 'pure' free market solution to the regional problem is in fact ruled out.

THE COSTS AND BENEFITS

It is impossible to identify and measure all the costs and benefits associated with location decisions, if only because subjective judgements are involved, at least on the part of workers. Nevertheless the free market approach can be challenged on the grounds that it ignores two important types of cost.

First, the approach takes account only of internal or private costs, and ignores external costs – costs incurred by people not party to the decision. When a firm considers the cost of establishing a plant in alternative locations it is likely to take account only of the costs which affect its own profitability; it does not consider how its decision may affect the profitability of other firms. And yet it is not difficult to show that external costs are likely to arise. The arrival of a firm of any size in an area adds to the pressure in the labour market which may make it more difficult and/or expensive for other employers to attract and retain labour. Similarly, added pressure will be put on the transport network, which may result in more congestion, delays in the delivery of goods, etc.

Again, the movement of workers into an area is likely to put additional pressure on communal facilities – medical, educational, recreational, etc. – to the detriment of people already living in that area.

It should be said that external effects, or externalities, are not always adverse. External benefits (external economies) may also arise. The establishment of one firm may reduce the costs of other firms in the area, either directly or indirectly. The new firm may be able to supply components at a lower price than alternative suppliers located in other, more distant, areas. An indirect benefit may arise if the establishment of new firms justifies the creation or development of facilities, such as an airport or a technical college, that benefit all firms in the area. Similarly the migration of workers to an area may justify the development of social facilities such as a theatre or sports complex. (However this migration is equally likely to reduce the viability of such enterprises in their 'home' areas.)

We cannot therefore conclude that the external effects of every location decision will on balance be adverse. However the fact remains that total welfare is affected by external effects, and any approach which neglects such effects is to some extent inadequate.

An allied but slightly different point concerns what we may call removal costs. These are simply the costs incurred when people move their residence or firms change their location – the costs of searching for a new home or site, of moving furniture or machines, etc. Although existing 'residents' – firms or families – may be adversely affected by an inflow of firms or workers, they may still be better off than they would be if they uprooted themselves and moved to another area, because of the removal costs that they would then incur. However the fact that they stay does not mean that they have not suffered additional costs on account of the inflow.

A final set of costs which should be mentioned here, and which are partly internal and partly external, might be classed as social costs. These include the disruption of family life that may occur when workers move, the increase in vandalism and crime that may result when people move into an area whose recreational facilities are inadequate, and mental illness suffered by people living alone in large cities. There has been a considerable debate concerning the extent to which economists should be concerned with social costs, and indeed precisely where the line between social and economic costs should be drawn. In fact the debate is, we believe, rather sterile, since many 'social costs' have an economic dimension, i.e. they give rise to monetary costs – such as the cost of preventing or repairing the effects of vandalism, and an increase in expenditure on social services.

THE TIME SCALE

Advocates of the free market approach seldom indicate how long they believe it would take for the problem to be solved – for regional unemployment differentials and differences in income to be eliminated. We clearly could not expect a precise time-scale to be provided, but an approximation would be useful since there is a danger that any solution which required a long period for its implementation would be unacceptable.

There are in fact several reasons for believing that the free market approach *would* require a long period. First, the differential rates of unemployment have arisen mainly because of the decline in long-established industries – coal mining, slate quarrying, shipbuilding, cotton textiles, etc. – which were highly concentrated geographically. The areas affected had a comparative advantage in these industries. On the other hand they may have a comparative disadvantage in many of the new industries that have become established more recently – light engineering, electronics, etc. The requirements of these newer industries for labour, factory sites and access to markets were often met more easily in the South of England than in the more traditional industrial areas in the North of England, Scotland and Wales.

The second reason is the operation of the 'local multiplier'. We saw in Chapter 8 that an increase in spending in one time period results in additional spending in subsequent periods. (The same effect, but in reverse, follows an initial reduction in spending.) In concrete terms this means that an increase in employment in an area will lead to more money being spent in the local shops, pubs, etc. Immense technical problems arise in the estimation of the value of the local or regional multiplier, but a range of 1.5 to 2.0 appears to be plausible.

The implications of this mechanism are clear: prosperous areas, to which workers move, become even more prosperous; depressed areas, from which workers move, become even more depressed. In terms of unemployment, the emigration of workers can be self-defeating. As some unemployed workers leave an area, additional unemployment may result from the loss of their purchasing power. These changes in the purchasing power of particular areas may also influence the subsequent location decisions of some firms. Other things being equal, the bigger the market the more attractive the area.

Third, of the workers who emigrate, a relatively high proportion tend to be, for obvious reasons, young and potentially more adaptable. These are the types of workers who are required by many employers, and their loss may make the area less attractive to potential new employers.

Finally, the free market approach will take longer to eliminate regional inequalities the less sensitive firms are to these inequalities, and especially to cost differentials. The approach assumes that firms undertake an extensive evaluation of alternative locations in order to discover the location at which profitability will be maximized. (This evaluation will take into account both costs and revenue.) In fact numerous studies have shown that the degree of search undertaken by firms is often very limited. Firms tend to set certain minimum requirements and to choose the first location which meets these requirements.

It would appear then that we may not be justified in leaving a solution of the regional problem to the operation of market forces, and that the case for intervention should be considered. This conclusion is strengthened by the fact that substantial differentials in regional unemployment rates may make it more difficult to achieve other government objectives. Governments may feel unable to plan for the level of expenditure required to reduce unemployment in depressed regions because this might lead to inflationary pressures in prosperous areas. Conversely governments may feel unable to reduce expenditure in order to counteract inflationary pressures in prosperous areas because of the implications for unemployment in depressed areas.

Let us now therefore examine the policies that governments might adopt in order to modify the operation of market forces.

Government Intervention
The first distinction is between policies designed to induce workers, and especially the unemployed, to move to areas of relatively low unemployment and those designed to induce firms to move to areas of high unemployment.

The first of these approaches implies the provision of incentives – financial assistance, training facilities – and/or information. The second approach may involve incentives of various kinds and/or restrictions, e.g. on where a new plant can be built. Restrictions are likely to represent the greatest degree of interference with the free play of market forces, although this depends, of course, upon the nature and scale of the incentives offered.

We discuss below the actual policies in force in the U.K. As a preliminary to

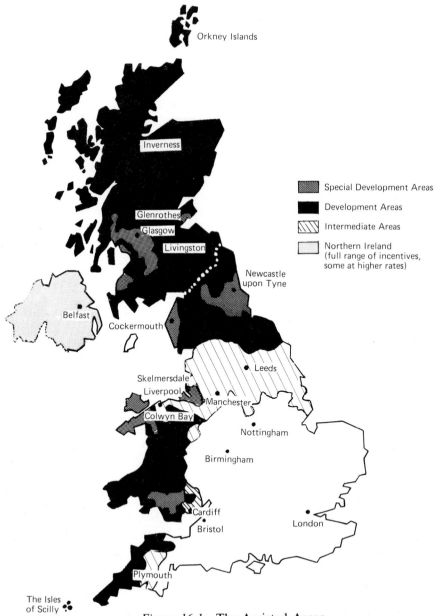

Figure 16.1 **The Assisted Areas**

this discussion we present a classification of the types of incentive that might in principle be offered to firms which create employment in areas of high un-employment.

Government Incentives to Firms
1   Subsidies related to the total costs and/or revenue of the firm.
2   Subsidies related to the cost of capital inputs – buildings, plant and equipment.
3   Subsidies related to the cost of labour.
4   The provision of facilities, especially factories, for individual firms. Factories may be made available to rent or purchase. If they are provided at less than the market price, this measure is very similar to number 2.
5   The provision of facilities that might benefit more than one firm, e.g. central training facilities, an improved communications network.

The term subsidy, as used above, may refer to: tax relief (1), a low-cost loan (2) or a grant (2 and 3). A further distinction can be made between assistance available only to firms which move to an area and assistance available to all firms in an area, including those already established there. Finally other conditions may be specified for the provision of assistance e.g. that the assisted project creates a certain amount of additional employment.

Having examined the types of incentive that might be offered, we now outline the pattern of assistance in the U.K. We shall see that all the above types of incentive, except the first, are available.

The Pattern of Assistance in Great Britain
As can be seen from figure 16.1 there are three categories of 'Areas for Expansion' in which firms qualify for government assistance – Special Development Areas, Development Areas and Intermediate Areas. The major forms of assistance available in these areas are listed in table 16.1. (We have omitted Northern Ireland from this table, since the incentives available there are slightly different. Overall, Northern Ireland offers greater incentives than the Special Development Areas.)

The present pattern of assistance was established by the Industry Act 1972, although this built on previous legislation introduced over a period of almost forty years. Regional Development Grants are available under Part 1 of the Act, and various forms of selective financial assistance under Section 7.

The range of incentives offered has gradually increased. Moreover the 'mix' has changed in various ways. One important change was the introduction in 1967 of the Regional Employment Premium – an employment subsidy paid to any employer with a manufacturing establishment in a Development or a Special Development Area. Before the introduction of R.E.P. the pattern of incentives was heavily biased towards subsidies to capital inputs. Probably as a result of this, the assisted areas attracted some highly capital intensive units which employed relatively few workers, e.g. heavy chemical plants in North East England. The introduction of R.E.P. was intended to create a more 'neutral' set of incentives, which might have a greater appeal than hitherto to labour-intensive firms.

R.E.P. was first introduced for a period of seven years. This was subsequently extended. However it was announced in 1976 that it was to be phased out. As an incentive available to any manufacturer in the relevant areas, it did not fit well with the move towards a more selective pattern of assistance that occurred in the mid 1970s (a move which is examined further during our discussion of industrial policy in Chapter 20). However the withdrawal of R.E.P. probably means a return

Table 16.1

The Major Government Incentives for Industry in the Areas for Expansion

Incentive	Special development areas	Development areas	Intermediate areas
Regional development grants: New buildings and works (other than mining works) and adaptations	22%	20%	20%
New machinery, plant and mining works	22%	20%	Nil

Incentive	
Selective financial assistance: Loans	On favourable terms for general capital purposes for projects which provide additional employment*; on broadly commercial terms for other projects that maintain or safeguard employment if the finance required cannot reasonably be obtained from commercial sources.
Interest relief grants*	As an alternative to loans on favourable terms, grants towards the interest costs of finance provided from non-public sources for projects which provide additional employment.
Removal grants*	Grants of up to 80% of certain costs incurred in moving an undertaking into one of these Areas.
Service industry grants*	To help offices, research and development units and other service industry undertakings moving into the Areas. Employees transferred: A grant of £1500 for each employee moving with his work (within a limit of 50% of new jobs created). A grant for each job created: £1,500 £1,000 Rent: Grant to cover the cost of approved rent of premises in the new location for: Up to 7 years Up to 5 years Up to 3 years
Government factories	For rent: standard factories. Two-year rent-free period* For sale: standard and custom-built factories. Payment spread over a period.

*Incentives are subject to the provision of sufficient additional employment to justify the assistance sought.

to the earlier situation, with the pattern of incentives again biased towards capital inputs.*

Another important change in the mix of incentives occurred in 1973 when for the first time substantial assistance was provided towards the cost of employment

*At a public enquiry held in 1977 it was stated that the cost of building two proposed petro-chemical plants on the east coast of Scotland was £400 millions. Of this, £280 millions would be paid by the Government in development grants. This would represent about £1 million per permanent job created.

in offices, research and development units and all undertakings in service industries – transport and communications, the distributive trades, insurance, banking,
business services, etc.

Changes have also been made from time to time in the areas qualifying for assistance. The general effect of these changes has been to increase the geographical
coverage of the assisted areas. As can be seen from figure 16.1, the Areas for
Expansion now cover well over half of the United Kingdom, and about 40 per
cent of the population lives in these areas.

Controls on Developments
Despite the extensive coverage of the assisted areas, governments have felt unable
to rely entirely on incentives; consequently these have been supplemented by controls on developments in other areas. The basic weapon of control is the Industrial
Development Certificate which is required for any industrial development above
a certain size – 5,000 sq. ft. in the South East Planning Region, 10,000 sq. ft. in other
non-assisted areas, and 15,000 sq. ft. in Intermediate Areas. (I.D.Cs. are not required in Development and Special Development Areas.)

In 1965 a comparable form of control on office building was introduced; Office
Development Permits are now required in the South East and the Midlands. This
corrected a curious anomaly in that while industrial employment was strictly controlled, office employment had been allowed to expand rapidly. The effect of the
new controls can be judged from the fact that it was announced in 1977 that the
Location of Offices Bureau, established in the 1960s to encourage firms to move
their offices out of city centres and especially out of London, was to be asked to
encourage overseas companies to establish offices in inner London.

Incentives to Workers
Financial assistance to workers who are prepared to move to find work include
a rehousing grant (of up to £600), lodging allowances and the payment of fares.
Non-financial incentives are considered as part of our discussion of manpower
policy in Chapter 17.

The Effects of Government Intervention
As we said when discussing the free market approach, it is important to try to
identify and measure the costs of government intervention. Before attempting that
task we consider the equally important question of what the effects of intervention
have been. We have emphasized in the preceding discussion the possible effects
of government policy on the regional rates of unemployment, and it might seem
logical to look first at changes in unemployment. In fact unemployment statistics
are probably *not* the best indicator. Not all people who wish to work register as
unemployed, and there is some evidence to suggest that the number of unregistered
unemployed may fall as regional policy becomes effective. If this is so, the fall
in the number of registered unemployed would underestimate the success of
regional policy in stimulating employment. Therefore changes in *employment* are
probably a better indicator of the policy's effectiveness.

Changes in Employment
In order to assess the effectiveness of regional policy we need to know how actual
changes in employment differ from those that would have occurred in the absence
of that policy. An estimate of what the growth in employment would have been
in certain Development Areas was obtained by Moore and Rhodes by applying

the *national* growth rates to the industries represented in these D.As. A comparison of these 'expected changes with actual changes in employment is presented' in figure 16.2, which first appeared in the *Economic Journal*, 1973.

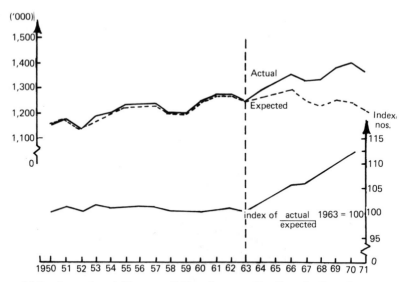

Figure 16.2   Actual and 'Expected' Employment in Certain Development Areas

Between 1950 and 1963 there was little difference between the two series. Thereafter actual employment grew more quickly than expected, the gap steadily widening until in 1971 actual employment in manufacturing in the D.As. was about 12 per cent higher than the expected figure. The total additional jobs created between 1963 and 1970 was estimated at 220,000.

The change in behaviour since 1963 seems highly significant since that year saw the introduction of a much more 'active' regional policy. For the first time financial assistance in respect of capital expenditure became available as of right to both incoming and established firms in Development Areas. The geographical coverage of these areas was also extended at this time. Largely as a result of these measures the estimated cost of regional policy was increased sixfold. A further increase in cost followed the introduction of the Regional Employment Premium in 1967. Finally the Industrial Development Certificate policy was applied more stringently in the 1960s than it had been in the 1950s.

Some of the additional employment was in overseas firms which established branches or subsidiaries in the U.K. But the Development Areas also benefited at the expense of non-assisted areas. Moore and Rhodes found that employment in the Midlands and the South East grew more rapidly than 'expected' during the period 1950–63, but much less rapidly than expected during 1963–70.

Unemployment in the Development Areas
Despite the diversion of employment from non-assisted to assisted areas, considerable differentials in unemployment remain. In April 1977 when Great Britain as a whole had an unemployment figure of 5.5 per cent, the corresponding figure in Development Areas was 8.4 per cent, and in the Special Development Areas 9.4 per cent. (The position was even more serious in Northern Ireland, where 10 per cent of workers were unemployed.)

Regional Inequalities

Since the Development and Special Development Areas are concentrated in the northern and western parts of the U.K. there are considerable differentials in regional unemployment rates. Table 16.2 shows that unemployment has tended

Table 16.2

Regional Unemployment Rates (%s)

	1970	1971	1972	1973	1974	1975	1976	1977
South East	1.6	2.0	2.2	1.5	1.5	2.8	4.2	4.3
East Anglia	2.1	3.2	2.9	1.9	1.9	3.5	4.9	5.3
East Midlands	2.2	2.9	3.0	2.0	2.2	3.6	4.8	4.9
West Midlands	1.9	2.9	3.6	2.2	n.a.	4.1	5.8	5.5
Yorkshire/Humberside	2.8	3.8	4.2	2.8	2.6	4.0	5.6	5.3
South West	2.8	3.3	3.4	2.4	2.6	4.7	6.5	6.8
North West	2.7	3.9	4.8	3.5	3.5	5.3	7.0	6.8
North	4.6	5.7	6.3	4.6	4.6	5.9	7.6	7.7
Wales	3.9	4.4	4.8	3.4	3.7	5.6	7.5	7.5
Scotland	4.2	5.8	6.4	4.5	4.0	5.2	7.2	8.1
Northern Ireland	6.8	7.9	8.0	6.1	5.7	7.9	10.3	10.4
United Kingdom	2.6	3.5	3.8	2.7	2.6	4.1	5.8	5.9

N.B. The data for 1970–6 are annual averages, the 1977 figures refer to April.
Source: Department of Employment.

to be lowest in the South East and the Midlands (the four regions in the first block) and highest in the northern and western areas (the five regions in the third block).

There are also considerable disparities in average incomes in different regions. Especially noticeable in table 16.3 is the much higher incomes in the South East

Table 16.3

Income per Head, by Regions (1974)

	Personal Income	Disposable Income	Social Security Benefits
	(U.K. = 100)	(U.K. = 100)	(% of Income)
South East	113.7	111.6	7.6
West Midlands	99.2	99.5	8.6
South West	97.0	97.7	9.7
North West	96.0	97.6	11.5
East Midlands	95.4	96.4	9.3
Yorkshire/Humberside	94.2	95.0	10.5
East Anglia	94.4	94.9	9.7
Scotland	93.0	93.1	10.5
North	91.9	92.4	10.5
Wales	88.0	89.7	12.1
Northern Ireland	74.9	78.1	16.4

Source: Regional Statistics (H.M.S.O., 1976).

than in the rest of the U.K. The data on disposable income shows that a substantial gap exists even after the payment of taxes. Also noticeable is the fact that the lowest incomes are found in the northern and western regions.

These differences in income are, of course, partly a reflection of differences in unemployment, and without regional policy the differences would no doubt be even more pronounced. Moreover the differences in income, substantial though they are, would also be increased in the absence of unemployment and other social security benefits. The final column in table 16.3 shows that social security benefits form a considerably higher proportion of the average income in poorer than in richer regions.

The Costs of Regional Policy

As we have seen, regional policy has had some effect in that regional inequalities today are less than they would have been had there been no regional policy. However the success of that policy must also be judged in terms of its costs.

These costs are of various kinds, some of which are much easier to measure than others. In our discussions of the free market approach we drew attention to the fact that government intervention may prevent firms from developing at the locations at which their private costs would be minimized. (The other way of expressing this is that areas may be prevented from specializing in the production of those goods and services in which they have the greatest comparative advantage.) Even if firms receive financial assistance in compensation, their real efficiency will still be reduced. For firms in the so-called 'foot loose' industries, costs appear to be influenced very little by location. In other industries, costs may be significantly higher at some locations than at others. For example Sir Donald Stokes, when chairman of British Leyland, said that the cost of each tractor produced at Bathgate in central Scotland, was £40 more than the equivalent cost in the Midlands, where the company would have preferred to locate. However it is impossible to make even a rough estimate of the overall importance of this type of cost, which is clearly unfortunate in view of the attention given to it by the advocates of the free market approach.

It is much easier to estimate the financial costs incurred by the government in administering the policy. In 1974 firms received over £400 millions in assistance, of which about 95 per cent was non-returnable, i.e. grants and Regional Employment Premiums. The creation of employment may be quite an extended process so that we cannot compare this figure with the additional jobs created in that year. However the work of Moore and Rhodes suggests that since 1963 an average of something over 30,000 jobs had been created in the Development Areas each year, indicating an average cost per job in 1974 of around £1,250.

It should be emphasized that this refers to the cost of providing additional jobs in the Development Areas. Since many of these jobs were diverted from non-assisted areas, the cost per new job created in the country as a whole would be higher than this. On the other hand, there would be some compensating savings in respect of those jobs that were additional in the U.K. as a whole, e.g. the jobs created in the subsidiaries of overseas companies which were encouraged to establish units in the U.K. by regional policy. This additional employment would result in savings in unemployment benefit and in additional government revenue in the form of the taxes paid by the newly employed workers and the employers.

Summary and Conclusions

Differences in the economic characteristics of different regions inevitably result in regional inequalities, including differential rates of unemployment. These inequalities have been reduced but by no means eliminated by the government's regional policies.

The disadvantages attached to the free market approach ensure that governments will continue to intervene in order to influence the location decisions of firms and workers. However the policy will no doubt be modified in the future, as it has on many occasions in the past. This will happen partly because of changes in the country's economic circumstances and partly because of the difficulties that arise in trying to identify the cost and benefits associated with any particular set of measures.

ESSAY QUESTIONS

1 'Since businessmen know most about the costs and benefits of alternative locations governments should not attempt to influence their location decisions.' Discuss.
2 'There are several different regional problems which require different solutions.' Discuss.
3 Evaluate the free market approach to the problem of regional inequalities.
4 Discuss the view that the objective of government regional policy should be to take workers to the work rather than work to the workers.
5 Discuss the major components of the government's current regional policy and explain the objective of each component.
6 Discuss the various criteria by which regional policy might be evaluated.
7 What difficulties arise in trying to measure the success of regional policy?
8 'Regional policy inhibits the allocation of resources in accordance with the principle of comparative advantage and should therefore be abandoned.' Discuss.
9 Explain what information would be required in order to enable the costs of regional policy to be measured.
10 'Regional policy may redistribute the nation's wealth, but it cannot increase it.' Discuss.

EXERCISES

16.1 'The essence of the free market approach to the "regional problem" is that firms and individuals should be allowed to make their own decisions. Firms' location decisions should not be subject to government interference either in the form of inducements to locate in certain areas or the imposition of controls on development in other areas. Similarly individuals should have a free choice, again "unbiased" by government inducements, as to where they seek work.

'Under these conditions the forces of demand and supply will operate so as to bring about an efficient allocation of resources. If the costs of congestion in high-growth areas cause firms' costs to become higher than they would be in other areas, this will prove a disincentive to further growth in the former areas. If social costs bear so heavily on workers in high-growth areas as to outweigh the advantages of working on those areas, workers will be more ready to look for work in other areas. To counteract this tendency employers in high-growth areas will have to increase wages in order to retain workers.

'Conversely if, in the low-growth areas, the costs to workers, in terms of poor employment prospects, are greater than the advantages of living in those areas, workers will move to other areas to find employment. Thus eventually the "excess" unemployment will disappear.'
Critically evaluate the arguments advanced in this passage.

16.2 What factors might account for the differences in GDP per head, shown in

16.13

table 16.4? To what extent is this data likely to be an indicator of differences in living standards in different regions?

Table 16.4

Index of Gross Domestic Product per head (factor cost, current prices, U.K. = 100)

Region	1967	1971	1974
North	84	85	90
Yorkshire/Humberside	96	93	93
East Midlands	97	96	96
East Anglia	96	94	93
South East	115	117	117
South West	93	91	93
West Midlands	106	103	99
North West	95	94	95
Wales	86	89	84
Scotland	90	91	94
Northern Ireland	69	73	74

Source: Regional Statistics (H.M.S.O., 1976).

16.3 Table 16.5 shows the amount of assistance received by various regions in the form of regional development grants and selective regional assistance (under Section 7 of the Industry Act) during the period August 1972 to March 1975. It also shows the average unemployment percentage in those two years. (i) Comment on the pattern of regional assistance in the light of the unemployment rates in those two years. (ii) What additional information would you require in order to make a better assessment of the effectiveness of the government's regional economic policy?

Table 16.5

Regional Assistance under the Industry Act

Region	Assistance (£mn)	Unemployment 1972 (%)	Unemployment 1975 (%)
North	104	6.4	6.3
Yorks/Humberside	21	4.2	4.2
East Midlands	5	3.1	3.7
East Anglia	—	2.9	3.6
South East	—	2.2	2.9
South West	9	3.4	4.9
West Midlands	2	3.6	4.3
North West	77	4.9	5.6
Wales	60	4.9	6.0
Scotland	120	6.5	5.3
Great Britain	397	3.8	4.3

16.4 (i) Discuss, in the light of the data in table 16.6, the success of government regional policy. (N.B., the two years chosen were both years of relatively low unemployment.) (ii) What other information would you have found helpful in answering question (i)?

Table 16.6

Regional Disparities

	Unemployment rate (Ratio to U.K. av.)		Net migration (Annual av., 000s)		GDP (Share of U.K. total)	
	1965	1973	1951–61	1971–3	1966	1973
South East	0.60	0.59	55	−35	35.7	35.8
West Midlands	0.60	0.77	8	−4	9.8	9.2
East Midlands	0.60	0.82	7	15	5.9	6.0
Yorks/Humberside	0.73	1.05	−8	−5	8.4	7.9
East Anglia	0.86	0.73	4	22	2.8	2.9
North West	1.06	1.32	−8	−16	11.8	11.6
South West	1.07	0.95	12	38	6.2	6.4
North	1.73	1.77	−6	−6	5.0	5.2
Wales	1.73	1.36	−3	8	4.2	4.3
Scotland	2.00	1.68	−28	−19	8.5	8.6
N. Ireland	4.07	2.41	−9	−10	1.7	2.0

CHAPTER SEVENTEEN

Manpower Policy

Introduction

THE main objective, particularly in recent years, of the set of measures that we consider under the heading of manpower policy, has been to reduce the level of unemployment, and this is the first objective that we discuss in this chapter. However, as we show later in the chapter, other objectives are also important, including an increase in economic efficiency and the protection of workers' rights.

In order to demonstrate the role of manpower policy in reducing the level of unemployment it is useful to classify the different types of unemployment that may arise.

The Main Types of Unemployment

Cyclical Unemployment

A number of economists have claimed to have found evidence, from observation of statistical data, of fairly regular cycles in economic activity. One aspect of this cyclical activity has been fairly regular changes in the level or rate of unemployment. Such cycles are far less pronounced today than they were previously. Nevertheless it seems worth retaining the term cyclical unemployment to denote unemployment which results from a general deficiency in demand affecting virtually all industries.

This characteristic implies that cyclical unemployment can be most appropriately countered by general demand management policies, and in particular by fiscal and monetary policy. However as we show below, there has been an increased tendency to supplement demand management policies by measures intended to provide a temporary stimulus to employment. Especially important in this context has been the provision of subsidies to employers.

Structural Unemployment

Structural unemployment arises when there is a long-term decline in the demand for the products of a particular industry, and other industries are unable to absorb the redundant workers. If the declining industry is concentrated geographically, structural unemployment may be associated with regional unemployment, as we saw in the previous chapter.

General demand management policies are clearly less appropriate here. Greater attention is given to methods of increasing labour mobility – retraining in new skills, providing information about alternative employment opportunities and offering financial assistance to unemployed workers who move to find employment. (Incentives are also offered to firms which set up or expand in regions of high unemployment, as shown in the previous chapter.)

Technological Unemployment

Technological unemployment is due to the introduction of new machines or processes which reduce the need for workers of a given type. There is obviously an analogy with structural unemployment – although technological unemployment tends to be concentrated among particular occupations rather than industries* – and similar policies are required to counteract the unemployment.

Frictional Unemployment

Frictional unemployment arises when a worker leaves one job and finds another, not immediately, but after a short period of time. Although considered less serious than the previous types of unemployment, frictional unemployment may constitute a significant proportion of the total. Consequently governments have tried to reduce frictional unemployment by providing better information concerning vacancies, and by extending worker placement services.

Seasonal Unemployment

As the term suggests, seasonal unemployment occurs when the demand for workers is seasonal, as in tourism, catering and parts of agriculture. Governments have not taken any specific measures to deal with seasonal unemployment; nor is it clear that they should do so. Although the establishment of new firms would reduce the seasonal peaks of unemployment, they would, of course, also add to the pressure on the labour market at other times, to the disadvantage of employers in the 'seasonal' industries.

The Measurement of Unemployment

While it is useful to classify unemployment in this way in order to clarify the contribution of the various policies, it is not possible to measure precisely the relative importance of each type of unemployment. The various types exist side by side and each is constantly changing. So, for example, it would be very difficult to determine how much of the rise in registered unemployment that occurred in the early and mid 1970s was cyclical and how much structural. There is, moreover, the problem of the unregistered unemployed who have been estimated by the Department of Employment to number around a quarter of a million, but about whose employment experience little is known. (The biggest group of unregistered unemployed are probably those married women who would not qualify for unemployment benefit.)

However some broad indicators are available. It is known that of the unemployed on the register at any one time about one quarter have been on for less than four weeks, and that the *average* length of a completed spell on the register has been between six and ten weeks. This suggests that frictional unemployment may be substantial, as noted above. The Department of Employment makes a seasonal correction to the published employment rate, which implies an ability to estimate the level of seasonal employment. Regular statistics are published on regional unemployment rates, as shown in the previous chapter, while data published on an industrial and occupational basis may be a *broad* indicator of the level of structural and technological unemployment. Finally, data on the age distribution of the unemployed has highlighted the increase in unemployment among younger people, and influenced policies intended to provide a temporary stimulus to the employment of such people (see table 17.1).

* For example, new production processes have reduced the number of weaving jobs in both textiles and carpet manufacturing.

Table 17.1

Unemployment by Age (Great Britain)

Age group	Registered unemployed (000s) Jan. 1971	Jan. 1977	Index 1977 (1971 = 100)
Under 18	44.8	122.4	273
18/19	57.7	129.9	225
20–29	185.3	433.0	234
30–39	110.8	219.3	198
40–49	109.6	171.2	156
50–59	112.2	174.7	156
60 and over	107.6	140.0	141
Total	727.9	1390.5	191

Source: *Department of Employment Gazette.*

Measures to Combat Unemployment

Of the various *manpower* policies mentioned during the above discussion of unemployment, the two most important are those designed to (a) increase the amount of training and (b) provide a temporary stimulus to employment. We discuss each of these in turn.

Policies Designed to Increase the Amount of Training

The government may seek to influence training for several reasons. First, as noted above, training in new skills makes unemployed workers more mobile occupationally, and perhaps geographically. This benefits not only workers but also employers, since the match between the pattern of supply of labour and the pattern of demand is improved. Moreover the nation as a whole benefits, since this improved match in the labour market increases overall economic efficiency.

Second, the government may intervene in order to re-distribute the cost of training among employers. Some employers may not train sufficient workers to meet their requirements, hoping to meet the shortfall by recruiting workers trained by other firms. This implies, of course, either that these other firms must train a 'surplus', and thus incur additional costs, or that the total requirement for trained workers is not met.

Third, the government may seek to improve the efficiency of training. This may involve disseminating information about training methods and/or providing central training facilities that would be too expensive for individual employers to provide.

THE INDUSTRIAL TRAINING ACT

These objectives led to the passing in 1964 of the Industrial Training Act, under which a number of Industrial Training Boards were established, each having the responsibility of increasing the quantity and quality of training undertaken in a particular industry. In order to carry out this responsibility, each I.T.B. was empowered to operate a levy and grant system. Each employer above a certain size paid a levy based on its payroll, and in turn received a grant whose value depended upon the Board's assessment of its training performance. Grants of up to 150 per cent of the levy were payable, but in total a surplus of levy over grant was required in order to pay the administrative costs incurred by the Boards.

THE EMPLOYMENT AND TRAINING ACT

Although the levy-grant system had the worthy aim of a fairer distribution of the costs of training, it was a rather cumbersome and costly mechanism and under the Employment and Training Act 1973 employers (except in the construction industry) were allowed to opt out of the scheme, provided they could prove that their training was satisfactory. This Act also provided some £35 millions a year to cover the Boards' administrative costs, and created the Training Services Agency, an offshoot of the new Manpower Commission, to oversee the Boards' operations.

There are now twenty-four I.T.Bs. covering 63 per cent of Britain's industrial workforce, plus six non-industrial Boards. Despite this extensive coverage, there is little firm evidence concerning their impact on training. For example, although the proportion of boy school-leavers starting apprenticeships rose from 36 per cent in 1963 to 43 per cent in 1968, it had fallen back to 39 per cent by 1972, and shortages of skilled workers continue to occur – shortages which may inhibit economic growth.

Government Training Facilities

The government has itself played an increasingly important part in training, especially in Skillcentres (previously known as Government Training Centres). In so far as employed workers are retrained in skills that are in demand, the main effect is likely to be an increase in economic efficiency. But in practice many of the trainees were previously unemployed (52 per cent in a study conducted by the author in 1967). In this case the main purpose of training is to improve the trainees' chances of obtaining employment, and thus to reduce unemployment. At the beginning of 1977 there were sixty Skillcentres in operation with a further twelve due for completion by 1979. The growth in the numbers trained in these and other institutions is shown in table 17.2.

Since 1973 the Skillcentres have come under the control of the Training Services Agency, as part of its responsibility for the implementation of the Training Opportunities Scheme. Although the growth of the Skillcentres has continued under TOPS, the main expansion has occurred in training undertaken in other institutions, and especially in colleges of further education (see table 17.2). This expansion has meant a significant change in the mix of trainees. While the engineering occupations remained most important, accounting for 40 per cent of TOPS trainees in 1975, 26 per cent were being trained for clerical occupations. Again, 36 per cent of trainees were females, as compared to only 3 per cent in 1971. This suggests a much more widespread training effort than previously, in line with the more widespread unemployment.

Table 17.2

Training Opportunities Scheme: Numbers Trained

Year	Skillcentres	Colleges of Further Education	Employers' establishments	Residential Training Centres	Total
1962	3,336				—
1971	16,575				—
1973	16,897	16,009	6,163	861	39,930
1974	17,117	21,692	5,809	798	45,416
1975	18,737	33,698	7,490	799	60,724
1976	22,692	51,998	14,241	720	89,651

N.B. 1973 was the first full year in which the Training Opportunities Scheme operated.
Source: Training Services Agency.

Measures Intended to Provide a Temporary Stimulus to Employment

The *Temporary Employment Subsidy* was introduced in 1975 to persuade employers to defer impending redundancies affecting ten or more workers. Employers are paid £20 a week for each worker kept on the payroll who would otherwise have been dismissed.

The *job creation programme* was launched in 1975 to provide temporary jobs for the unemployed. The Manpower Services Commission provides grants to cover the wages of those involved in community projects – intended to be biased towards young workers and to give priority to urban renewal.

The *youth employment subsidy*, which replaced an earlier scheme in 1976, pays employers a subsidy of £10 a week, for up to twenty-six weeks, for every youth recruited who had been unemployed for at least six months.

The *job release scheme*, which was introduced for one year in 1977 offered workers £23 a week tax-free to give up work one year before retirement, provided that their jobs were made available to younger, unemployed workers.

The Cost of the Measures

All the above measures involve a subsidy of one form or another, paid to either employer or employee. At the beginning of 1977 *The Economist* estimated that since April 1975 the government had spent £500m on these measures, and that about 500,000 jobs had been saved or created. This implied a cost of about £1,000 a job. Since the stimulus to employment was temporary, the reduction in employment at any one time was less than the total saving – probably about 150,000, or roughly 10 per cent of the total unemployed.

The net cost to the taxpayer would, of course, be much less than £500m, since an allowance has to be made for savings on unemployment benefit and social security payments, and for receipts from taxation. In addition, non-quantifiable benefits and costs should be considered. It will have been noticed that the measures are particularly intended to help school-leavers and other young workers and thus, presumably, to avoid the harm that a sustained spell of unemployment can cause to people at this impressionable age.

On the other hand it has been argued that the measures, and especially the T.E.S., served to featherbed over-manned, low-productivity industries. It appears that most of the money made available under this measure went to industries in long-term decline, such as textiles and footwear, rather than to industries such as engineering whose support was considered to be vital to industrial recovery.

We now switch our attention to consider briefly policies relating to two other aspects of manpower policy, those relating to property rights in jobs and to industrial relations.

Property Rights in Jobs

This technical term refers to the idea that when a worker takes up employment he makes an investment in his job, the return to which should not be entirely at the employer's discretion. In other words, if the employer wishes to terminate the worker's employment, the worker should be either compensated or protected.

THE REDUNDANCY PAYMENTS ACTS

Compensation is provided by the Redundancy Payments Acts of 1965 and 1969, under which any worker who has been with his present employer for at least two years is given a tax-free lump sum. Since this sum is related to the worker's length of service with that employer, his age, and his normal weekly earnings, the property rights concept is clearly relevant. Protection is afforded by the Employment Protection Act.

This Act requires firms to consult the appropriate trade unions about proposed redundancies, and to note and reply to any representations made by the unions. If the unions are not consulted as required, they can apply to an industrial tribunal which may make a protective award the effect of which is that the employer has to continue to pay for a specified period those affected by redundancy.

In addition, firms which lay-off employees or put them on short-time because work cannot be provided, must continue to pay them their normal daily earnings up to a maximum of £6 a day, for up to twenty days in any year. Furthermore if they are being made redundant they must be allowed time off to look for a new job or arrange training if they so require. Finally, the protection against unfair dismissal, provided by the 1974 Trade Union and Labour Relations Act, was strengthened by the 1975 Act.

Industrial Relations Legislation

Legislation on industrial relations has several objectives, most of which are outside the scope of this book. However there is an important economic element, in that legislation may help to reduce the incidence of strikes and thus lead to an increase in economic efficiency. An example of what can be accomplished is provided by the Advisory, Conciliation and Arbitration Service which was put on a statutory basis by the Employment Protection Act. This Act also established a Central Arbitration Committee.

The C.A.C. has nine offices spread around the country and in its first year handled well over 3,000 disputes, covering such matters as trade union recognition, and the implementation of the Equal Pay Act which is designed to ensure that both sexes obtain equal pay for work of a comparable nature.

Summary and Conclusions

Manpower policy has a number of objectives, including a reduction in unemployment, an increase in economic efficiency, a more equitable distribution of training costs among employers, and the protection of workers' rights. The relative importance attached to these various objectives may be influenced by economic conditions. In the 1960s attention was concentrated on the need to increase the supply of labour having those skills that were in great demand, and thus to increase economic efficiency. In the 1970s, as the rate of unemployment rose, more attention was given to employment-creation measures. Political factors may also be important – the spate of legislation in the mid 1970s designed to protect workers' rights can be at least partly explained by the return to power of a Labour government supported by the T.U.C.

In many instances the different objectives of manpower policy are compatible. For example re-training is likely to contribute to both a reduction in unemployment and an increase in economic efficiency. But conflicts may sometimes arise. As we noted above, it is possible that maintaining employment by means of the Temporary Employment Subsidy may also lead to a loss in efficiency in some sections of the economy.

ESSAY QUESTIONS

1 Define the major forms of unemployment. Why may it be useful to be able to distinguish between one form and another?
2 'Different forms of unemployment require different measures for their relief.' Discuss.
3 Discuss the view that if aggregate demand were always maintained at a sufficiently high level there would be no need for a manpower policy.
4 'All unemployment arises because of inadequate demand.' Discuss.
5 'Left to his own devices, every employer will train as many people as he requires. There is, therefore, no need for government assistance with training.' Discuss.
6 Discuss the advantages and disadvantages of government subsidies to employment.
7 Explain what you understand by the term 'property rights in jobs' and show how the concept might influence government policy.
8 Discuss the major objectives of manpower policy and describe the measures taken in order to achieve each of these objectives.
9 Write a short essay on the costs and benefits of manpower policy.
10 Why may governments wish to increase (a) the occupational and (b) the geographical mobility of labour? Discuss recent government policies in relation to *one* of these.

EXERCISES

17.1 Outline the factors which might have contributed to the pattern of changes in unemployment, as shown in the final column of table 17.1, and discuss the implication of these changes.
17.2 What factors might account for the differences in the ratio of unemployed to vacancies for the occupations listed in table 17.3?

Table 17.3
Numbers of Registered Unemployed and Notified Vacancies (Great Britain, March 1977)

Occupation	Registered unemployed	Notified vacancies
Managerial and professional	87,968	14,225
Clerical and related	181,008	21,387
Other non-manual occupations	68,958	11,950
Craft and similar occupations	161,972	39,427
General labourers	441,513	6,495
Other manual occupations	313,883	49,038

Source: *Department of Employment Gazette.*

17.3 'Continuation and extension of the temporary employment subsidy, generally regarded as the most successful of the government's job protection measures, forms the centre of its latest plans to alleviate unemployment problems. The £20 per week subsidies which employers receive if they agree to defer redundancies were due to close for applications at the end of next month. It will now be continued until March 1978, at an estimated gross cost of £172m.

'The intention of the subsidy, payable for a year, is to give employers a breathing space in which to improve their industrial base rather than simply to defer redundancies which then take place when the subsidised year ends. But it has now become apparent that for some firms a year has not proved long enough and jobs remain at risk. To help companies which are still experiencing difficulties when the year ends the government now proposes to introduce a new subsidy of £10 per worker per week payable for a further maximum of six months.

'The subsidy is calculated to be protecting the jobs of about 180,000 workers at present and a total of 224,000 redundancies have been avoided at a cost of £212m since the scheme began in August 1975. Mr. Albert Booth, Employment Secretary, hopes that the continuation and extension of the subsidy for another year will mean that between one-quarter and one-third of employees whose jobs would have been at risk will be kept in work.

'On a quite opposite principle to the temporary employment subsidy, the government is, under a modest but significant scheme, experimenting with the idea of paying subsidies to employers who agree to take on new labour. This is an approach which the Department of Employment has until now been reluctant to pursue.

'Under a scheme announced today, small firms – those with less than 50 workers – will qualify for grants of £20 a week for every new job created during a six-months experimental period between July 1 and December 31. It will apply only to private manufacturing industry in special development areas and the base line for new jobs created will be employment levels yesterday. The government estimates that under the scheme 5,500 people can be found work at a cost of less than £3m.

'The Government is also looking at ways of giving special attention to the problems of the long-term unemployed – those who have been out of work for 12 months or more. This form of unemployment has become an increasing problem recently with the proportion of long-term unemployed rising from 14 per cent of total unemployment in July 1975, to 20 per cent in January of this year.'

The above passage was extracted from an article in the *Financial Times*, 30.3.77. (i) Discuss the advantages and disadvantages of (a) the Temporary Employment Subsidy, and (b) the Small Firms Employment Subsidy. (ii) Why do you think the latter subsidy was initially confined to small firms? (iii) Outline and evaluate measures which might help to solve the problem of long-term unemployment.

CHAPTER EIGHTEEN

Competition Policy

Introduction

IN explaining the basis of competition policy it is useful to begin by briefly examining three important aspects of an industry or a market – structure, conduct and performance.

Market Structure

Market structure has a number of elements, but the most important in terms of competition policy are the number of firms in the industry or market, and their relative market shares. It is generally believed that highly concentrated industries, i.e. those in which a relatively few firms account for a high share of total output, are more likely to give rise to undesirable conduct than are less concentrated industries. Consequently competition policy has often attempted to prevent industries from becoming highly concentrated.

Market Conduct

Market conduct refers to the behaviour of firms, especially important aspects of behaviour being

(a) whether or not existing firms seek to prevent new firms from entering the industry;
(b) how sensitive prices are to changes in the balance between supply and demand.

Market Performance

The most important elements of market performance are first the level of *productive efficiency*, i.e. the extent to which firms minimize their costs, and second a group of elements which together indicate the *allocative efficiency* of the system – the rate of profitability, the rate of innovation, in terms of both new products and new processes, and the ratio of advertising expenditure to sales revenue. (This last factor is sometimes classified as a conduct element.) When we look at the economy as a whole, the level of productive efficiency and the level of allocative efficiency together determine the level of *economic efficiency*.

Since the primary objective of competition policy is to increase the level of economic efficiency, the ultimate concern of policy must be with market performance. However since market performance may be heavily influenced by market structure and conduct, competition policy has been concerned as much with these two aspects as with performance.

Indeed if it could be demonstrated that a certain structure was likely to give rise to a certain pattern of conduct and eventually to a certain pattern of performance, policy could concern itself only with structure and conduct, or even perhaps only with structure. In fact this approach underlies much 'anti-trust' legislation in the U.S.A. In the U.K., however, a more pragmatic approach has been adopted. We have been unwilling to base policy on the presumption of a clear relationship between structure, conduct and performance, preferring instead to adopt a case-by-case approach in which attention has been given to all three elements. The advantages of adopting this approach can be demonstrated by considering briefly the position of a highly concentrated industry.

The Conduct and Performance of a Highly Concentrated Industry

We suggested above that highly concentrated industries tend to be associated with undesirable forms of conduct, one of which is that larger firms may be in a better position to prevent potential new entrants from entering the industry. Furthermore, if existing firms are protected from new entry they may earn abnormally high profit margins, i.e. their performance would, in this respect, be judged undesirable.

On the other hand the concentration of output in the hands of only a few firms may enable these firms to enjoy economies of scale (see Chapter 24) and so lower costs of production, i.e. productive efficiency would be high. Even if the profitability of these firms is above average, their prices could actually be lower than if the industry were less concentrated. Furthermore these firms may use at least some of their additional profits to invest in research and development, which may result in a high rate of innovation. In these respects, therefore, the performance of the industry could be considered to be satisfactory.

The fact that performance may be satisfactory in some respects but not in others clearly makes it difficult to evaluate performance overall. This difficulty is increased by the fact that some aspects of performance are more satisfactorily measured than others. On the one hand the profitability of the firms in one industry can be readily compared with the average profitability in other industries. On the other hand comparisons of price levels, or even of changes in these levels, are less meaningful. Again, although the rate of innovation in an industry might be considered to be satisfactory, we cannot say that it would not have been even more satisfactory had new firms been able to enter the industry more freely.

These problems of evaluating performance clearly make it difficult to specify a clear link *in principle* between structure, conduct and performance, and therefore, it is argued, justify the adoption of a pragmatic, case-by-case approach.

We shall see in the following sections how the pragmatic approach has influenced policy in the U.K., as we look first at legislation and then at the effects of this legislation. We then consider whether the existing policy is satisfactory or whether changes – for example a move nearer to the U.S. system – might be desirable.

We consider the legislation in the order in which the various Acts were passed. In this way we can bring out most clearly the interactions between market structure, conduct and performance.

THE MONOPOLIES AND RESTRICTIVE PRACTICES ACT 1948

This Act established a Monopolies Commission with the responsibility for investigating and reporting on monopoly situations, defined as markets or industries in which one third of a class of goods was supplied in the U.K. by a single firm, or a group of firms acting together so as to restrict competition. (This proportion was subsequently reduced to one quarter.)

This Act clearly had a structural dimension in that it referred to single-firm monopolies having a minimum market share. But it also had an important conduct element, first because it included a reference to 'a group of firms acting together' and partly because of the responsibility laid on the Commission to investigate the behaviour of firms (acting either independently or together). Finally the Commission's responsibility to present a report on the industry it investigated implied that it would concern itself with the performance of that industry.

As it turned out the investigations and reports of the Commission served to focus attention on market conduct more than on structure. The Commission found evidence that collective restrictive practices (i.e. practices involving agreements among two or more firms that restricted competition in one way or another) were widespread in British industry, and the need to reduce the incidence of such practices emerged as the most important aspect of competition policy at that time.

This emphasis on the conduct of a group of firms acting together also appeared appropriate in the light of economic theory. Theory suggests that highly concentrated industries may give rise to both adverse and favourable consequences, as indicated above. But the adverse consequences are less likely to be balanced by favourable ones when a group of firms acts together than when larger firms act independently. In particular the maintenance of high profit margins may not be balanced by lower costs, since the economies of scale enjoyed by a large firm are not available to a group of smaller firms.

The conclusions from economic theory about the undesirability of collective restrictive agreements, together with the evidence provided by the report of the Monopolies Commission of their widespread existence, led to legislation designed to combat such agreements.

THE RESTRICTIVE TRADE PRACTICES ACT 1956

This act required all restrictive agreements to be registered with the Registrar of Restrictive Trading Agreements. A restrictive agreement is defined as any agreement between two or more persons carrying on business in the production or supply of goods, under which restrictions are accepted by the parties in respect of the prices to be charged, the terms or conditions of sale, quantities or types to be produced, the process of manufacture, the persons or areas to be supplied, or the persons or areas from which goods are to be acquired.

The emphasis here is clearly on conduct, and the Act was based on the presumption that certain types of conduct were undesirable. However the Act also recognized that performance was important, and it made provision for these potentially undesirable forms of conduct to be continued, provided that it could be shown that in practice they led to an improvement in performance.

The decision as to whether or not an agreement should be permitted is made by the Restrictive Practices Court, also established by the 1956 Act. The parties to an agreement can attempt to justify it only on certain specific grounds. These 'gateways' are

(a) that the restriction is reasonably necessary to protect the public against injury;
(b) that the removal of the restriction would deny to the public, as purchasers, consumers or users of any goods, specific and substantial benefits;
(c) that the restriction is reasonably necessary to counteract measures taken by a person, not party to the agreement, with a view to restricting competition;
(d) that the restriction is reasonably necessary to enable fair terms to be negotiated with a large supplier or purchaser;
(e) that the removal of the restriction would be likely to have a serious and persistent adverse effect on unemployment in areas in which the industry is concentrated;

(f) that the removal of the restriction would be likely to cause a substantial reduction in export business;

(g) that the restriction is reasonably required for the purpose of supporting other restrictions in the agreement which are in the public interest;

(h) that the restriction does not directly or indirectly restrict or discourage competition to any material degree in any relevant trade or industry and is not likely to do so. (This last clause was added by the Restrictive Trade Practices Act, 1968.)

The three gateways that have received most prominence in the cases heard by the Court are (b), by far the most important, (e) and (f), all of which refer to aspects of an industry's performance. The improvements in performance which the Court has considered to be sufficiently important to outweigh the detriments inherent in a restrictive agreement, and thus to justify the agreement, include the following:

(1) The agreement results in lower prices, one of the benefits included under clause (b). The Cement Makers Federation argued that restricting price competition reduced member firms' risks and led them to accept lower prices than they would in more competitive conditions. The Distant Water Vessels Development Association claimed that although without the agreement prices would fall in the short run, this would lead to a reduction in investment and therefore in capacity, which in turn would result in higher prices in the long run. Similarly it was argued that if the Net Book Agreement were abandoned, price competition would lead to a reduction in the number of stockholding booksellers, a rise in the price of books and a fall in the number of published titles.

(2) Co-operation on research and the dissemination of research results lead to product improvement and/or a reduction in costs – also benefits under clause (b).

(3) The maintenance of export orders was enhanced by co-operation in overseas markets, (clause (f)).

In addition to considering the strength of these specific arguments, the Court takes into account other, more general, performance indicators. For example, one of the factors persuading it to accept the arguments of the Cement Makers Federation was that the industry had been efficient and that excessive profits had not been earned.

In this instance these various performance indicators were all favourable. In other instances some were favourable and others adverse, e.g. the agreement made by members of the Yarn Spinners Association. The Court accepted the arguments advanced under clause (e), that the abandoning of the agreement would have a serious and persistent adverse effect on unemployment in certain areas. Nevertheless they decided that the agreement should not be permitted since in many other ways the performance of the industry had been unsatisfactory. The agreement had made it easier for high-cost firms to survive, i.e. productive efficiency was low. Furthermore the industry was absorbing too many resources in relation to the demand for its products, as indicated by the high level of short-time working, i.e. allocative efficiency was unsatisfactory.

Since the passing of the 1956 Act around 3,000 agreements have been registered. However the vast majority were ended by the parties themselves. During the first 20 years of this legislation only 37 agreements were contested before the Court, and of these only 11 were upheld as being in the public interest. The very high rate of abandonment can be explained mainly by the fact that the Court approved of very few of the early agreements that it considered – only one of the first seven.

THE RESALE PRICES ACT 1964

The 1956 Act, while making it much more difficult for firms to sustain collective price agreements, strengthened the legal position of those manufacturers who wished to specify the prices at which distributors could sell their products. This situation was reversed in 1964 when the Resale Prices Act laid down that a manufacturer was allowed to enforce or maintain resale prices only if he could convince the Restrictive Practices Court that this would be in the public interest. The background to this Act was a rapid increase in the market share of multiple retailers, largely due to their policy of reducing prices in order to achieve a higher volume of turnover. The ability of manufacturers to prevent distributors from reducing prices inhibited the growth of such firms. The 1964 Act was, therefore, seen as a way of trying to improve market performance and economic efficiency in retailing.

Specific grounds for the justification of an agreement were again laid down, namely that in the absence of resale price maintenance the public would suffer in one of the following ways:

(a) the quality and variety of goods available for sale would be substantially reduced;
(b) the number of retail establishments in which the goods were sold would be substantially reduced;
(c) the retail prices of the goods would increase;
(d) goods would be sold under conditions likely to cause danger to health in consequence of their misuse by the public;
(e) any necessary services provided in connection with the sale of the goods would cease to be provided, or would be substantially reduced.

Even if a manufacturer succeeds in justifying r.p.m. on one of these grounds, he has then to show that this advantage of r.p.m. outweighed the disadvantage of restricting the freedom of distributors. Only the manufacturers of books, maps and certain medicaments have satisfied the Court in this respect.

Another consequence of the 1956 Act was an increase in the rate of merger activity. This consequence was fairly predictable, since if firms are denied the opportunity of collaborating with their rivals they will seek alternative methods of achieving the objective of that collaboration. Specifically, if they can no longer enter into agreements with rivals to set prices, their ability to maintain prices will be enhanced by mergers which reduce the number of rivals.

Other developments in the early 1960s served to increase disquiet about the absence of legislation specifically designed to influence the structure of industry. I.C.I. launched a take-over bid for Courtaulds which, had it succeeded, would have resulted in the formation of a giant firm with a dominant position in a number of markets. The bid failed because of the opposition of Courtaulds, not because of any legislation. Round about the same time several mergers in the newspaper industry raised the spectre of a 'monopoly of the press'. The fact that the lost papers might have failed in any case did little to allay the disquiet. Eventually, such considerations found expression in the introduction of the Monopolies and Mergers Act.

THE MONOPOLIES AND MERGERS ACT 1965

This Act represented the first serious attempt in the U.K. to control the non-collective activities of independent firms. Where it appeared from an investigation by the Monopolies Commission that a merger was likely to operate against the public interest, the Board of Trade (later the Department of Prices and Consumer Protection) was empowered to stop the merger, break up the merger if it had already taken place or lay down certain conditions on which the merger could proceed.

Any proposed merger could be referred to the Commission for investigation if it would result in at least one third (later reduced to one quarter) of the market being in the hands of a single supplier or if the assets acquired would exceed £5 million. In other words the criteria laid down in the act – market share and size of firm – related to the structure of the industry. However reference to conduct and performance is also involved at two stages of the implementation of the legislation.

The first stage is the decision as to which proposed mergers should be referred to the Commission. The criteria laid down in the Act, and especially the size of assets acquired, were such that a very large number of mergers came within the scope of the legislation – well over a thousand during the period 1965–75. Because of the size and composition of the Commission – most members serve in a part-time capacity – it could not be expected to investigate more than a small fraction. Of the first 1,150 only 31 were referred.

In deciding which mergers to refer, it is inevitable that conduct and performance variables should be taken into account. Indeed the Office of Fair Trading, which in 1973 was given responsibility for administering policy (see below), indicated that product sectors would probably be considered most worthy of investigation if they achieved 'high marks' in terms of four conduct and four performance indicators.

The four conduct indicators were: complaints, from both trade and consumer sources, evidence or accusation of either price leadership or parallel pricing (see Chapter 25), the ratio of advertising expenditure to sales (sometimes treated as a performance indicator as noted above), and the degree of merger activity in the field concerned. The four performance indicators were the ratio of capital employed to turnover (a high ratio possibly indicating inefficiency), changes in profit margins, return on capital employed and the movement of prices in a particular product sector relative to the general rate of inflation.

The importance of this initial decision, and thus of the criteria taken into account, can be seen from the fact that whereas about 97 per cent of proposed mergers have been allowed to proceed without reference to the Commission, only about 30 per cent of those referred have subsequently come to fruition. Some proposed mergers are abandoned following an adverse report by the Commission, others before an investigation gets under way.

This takes us to the second stage of the implementation of the legislation, namely the findings of the Monopolies Commission, and the action taken following those findings. The Commission is invariably asked to consider proposed rather than past mergers, and thus has to predict what the effect of the merger is likely to be. In its prediction, while the Commission takes into account what economic theory has to say about the effects of an increase in the level of market concentration, it also considers the facts appertaining to a particular merger, and its conclusions are likely to be strongly influenced by its findings about the past conduct and performance of the firms concerned.

For example there is a general theoretical presumption that the larger the number of firms the greater the degree of price competition. However the extent to which a reduction in the number of firms affects price competition will depend upon the degree of competition that previously existed between firms which propose to merge. Proposed mergers between serious rivals which were not approved by the Commission have included Ross/Associated Fisheries and British Sidac/ Transparent Paper.

When no clear conclusions can be drawn from economic theory, even more weight is likely to be placed on past conduct and performance. One of the central issues in the proposed merger between Boots and Glaxo was the need for firms in the pharmaceutical industry to maintain a high level of research and development. Economic theory suggests that economies of scale may apply in R. & D., as was claimed by Boots. However there are also grounds for believing that, provided that the firms have attained a certain minimum size, the total R. & D. effort and the rate of innovation will be greater the greater the number of independent R. & D. units. In the absence of clear theoretical prescriptions, the Commission considered past performance. It was presumably impressed by the performance of Boots and Glaxo as independent units, since it declared against the merger.

When considering the proposed merger between Barclays, Lloyds and Martins Banks, the Commission was able to refer to the actual cost savings that had followed previous mergers in the industry. Since the majority of the members of the Commission declared against the merger they presumably felt that the potential cost savings were outweighed by the disadvantages of a substantial increase in the level of concentration.

When the Commission considers existing monopolies it must clearly be concerned with past conduct and performance. In its report, 'Building Bricks', issued in 1976, the Commission noted that the profits of London Brick Company were not excessive and that its prices were reasonable. Indeed one of the reasons for the company's monopoly position was that its prices were so low that other, less efficient producers, had left the market. The only change in policy recommended by the Commission was that L.B.C.'s policy of subsidizing the cost of transport to its more distant customers should be abandoned, since it represented unfair competition.

On the other hand the Commission has sometimes felt that monopolists have earned excessive profits. In such situations one 'solution' would be to split the company concerned into a number of smaller units having less market power, i.e. to change the structure of the industry. The disadvantage of this approach is that it might lead to an increase in costs, because of the disruption caused and because of the loss of economies of scale.

In fact the Commission has never recommended this approach, preferring instead that prices and profits should be controlled by the appropriate government department, i.e. that action should be taken relating to conduct and performance. Industries in which price controls have been recommended include detergents (Unilever and Procter and Gamble), breakfast cereals (Kelloggs) and pharmaceuticals (Hoffmann–La Roche).

The basic structure of U.K. competition policy was established by the Acts of 1956, 1964 and 1965, and the next major piece of legislation in 1973 built upon this structure.

The Fair Trading Act 1973
This Act contains provisions relating both to collective restrictive practices and to monopolies and mergers and we consider these two sets of provisions in turn. It also contains provisions relating to consumer protection, discussed later.

PROVISIONS RELATING TO RESTRICTIVE PRACTICES
The Act established the Office of the Director General of Fair Trading to whom were transferred the powers of the Registrar of Restrictive Trading Agreements.

It also extended the provisions of the 1956 Act to cover firms supplying commercial services, such as hairdressers, estate agents and travel agents. Registration with the Office of Fair Trading is required for agreements relating to:

(a) the charges made, quoted or paid for services;
(b) the terms or conditions on which services are supplied or obtained;
(c) the extent or scale on which services are supplied or obtained;
(d) the form or manner in which services are supplied or obtained;
(e) the persons, areas or places to, in, or from which services are supplied or obtained.

If the Director General of Fair Trading considers that a registered agreement restricts competition he may refer it to the Restrictive Practices Court. Thus the distinction between goods and services, which was introduced by the 1956 Act, but which made little economic sense, was swept away.

As an example of the impact of the Act we can note that when the first batch of agreements were registered it was found that the Association of British Travel Agents had dropped its recommendation to members to charge a standard 10 per cent commission on holidays sold, and that it had withdrawn its advice on minimum charges to be made for other services such as the sale of travellers cheques.

PROVISIONS RELATING TO MONOPOLY AND MERGERS

The increase in the scope of legislation on restrictive practices was paralleled by changes in the monopoly and mergers legislation. First, the market-share criterion for reference to the (renamed) Monopolies and Mergers Commission was reduced from $33\frac{1}{3}$ to 25 per cent. Moreover export monopolies and local (geographical) monopolies can now be investigated. Furthermore *monopoly* references to the Commission can now be made either by the relevant Minister (the Secretary of State for Prices and Consumer Protection), or by the Director-General of Fair Trading. (Merger references can be made by the Minister only.)

PROVISIONS RELATING TO CONSUMER PROTECTION

Policies to control restrictive practices, monopolies and mergers are intended ultimately to benefit the consumer. The 1973 Act also contained a number of provisions designed to directly protect consumers' interests. It gave the Director General a duty to keep under review commercial activities relating to the supply of goods and services that might adversely affect the economic interests of U.K. consumers. If he identifies a practice which he considers to be against the public interest, he may propose that an order of Parliament be made to regulate or prohibit the practice.

The Director General may also propose changes in the law if he considers that a 'consumer trade practice':

(a) misleads customers as to their rights and obligations;
(b) is otherwise misleading or confusing to customers;
(c) subjects customers to undue pressure; or
(d) contains 'inequitable' terms or conditions.

In practice, rather than invoke the force of law, the Director General has preferred to obtain a voluntary undertaking that a practice he considers to be unsatisfactory will be changed. Voluntary codes of conduct have been agreed which cover a wide variety of industries, including electrical servicing, laundries and dry cleaning, motor traders and travel agents. A common feature of these codes is that the industry should set minimum standards of conduct and establish an independent arbitration service for complaints.

The Effectiveness of Competition Policy
Restrictive Practices
We saw above that only a small proportion of registered agreements have survived, and this is an indication that legislation designed to influence this form of conduct and hence improve performance has been effective. It might be possible to extend this influence in two ways.

First, restrictive practices could be declared illegal, regardless of their effect on performance. There would be no practical obstacle to adopting this 'per se' rule, as has been done in the U.S.A. However it contains the danger that the (few) agreements with potentially beneficial effects would have to be abandoned along with the others.

Second it would be possible to strengthen the enforcement of the legislation to reduce the number of unregistered agreements which undoubtedly exist. However stronger enforcement would require increased costs of administration.

Monopoly and Mergers
Here the policy appears to have been much less effective. Despite the passing of the Monopolies and Mergers Act in 1965 the concentration of industry has continued to increase, and industry is now more highly concentrated in the U.K. than in many other countries, including the U.S.A., France and West Germany.*

Alternative Approaches
In view of the evidence of increasing concentration, several alternative methods of control have been suggested.

One possibility is that the prices of very large firms should be subject to control. This suggestion was overtaken by the passage of events which brought more general price controls, but was revived in 1977 as part of the changes in the prices and incomes policies. Another suggestion is that a policy should incorporate non-discretionary rules. For example it might be stipulated that no merger would be allowed which involved the biggest twenty-five firms, or which would bring the combined market share of the merging firms above a certain level – say 25 per cent. The term non-discretionary refers to the fact that the rules are applied automatically, and not at the discretion of any body such as the Monopolies and Mergers Commission or a government department.

The main advantage of this approach is that it would substantially reduce the cost of administering the policy. Moreover the approach tends to be favoured by those economists who feel that policy should be strengthened, although such a consequence would, of course, occur only if the limits were set at an appropriate level.

Two main objections have been raised to this approach. First, it assumes a much more distinct link between structure and performance than exists in practice. This means that it would rule out changes in structure which, even if they could be shown to be *generally* undesirable, might be desirable – e.g. in leading to lower costs or a higher rate of innovation – in particular instances.

Second, there are technical problems which make it difficult to apply the policy.

* See S. J. Prais, 'The Evolution of Giant Firms in Britain' (Cambridge: Cambridge U.P. 1976).

For example even if it were possible to agree on an appropriate limitation on market share, say 25 per cent, it might not be possible to obtain a satisfactory definition of 'the market'. When the proposed merger between British Sidac and Transparent Paper was referred to the Monopolies Commission it was decided that the relevant market was cellulose film and that, had the merger proceeded, the resulting company would have been a monopoly in terms of the 1965 Act. However had the market been defined as 'all flexible packaging materials' no monopoly would have been found to exist. Other problems of definition exist, such as the inclusion or non-inclusion of imports and exports, the time period over which market shares should be measured, etc.

A somewhat different, although still contentious, point would arise if it were decided to ban mergers involving any of the largest firms. Such firms normally supply many different markets, and some of the proposed mergers in which they might be involved might have little economic significance. It is possible that these mergers could be banned while others of greater significance were allowed.

Although these arguments against the application of non-discretionary rules have considerable force, one still has to face the fact that the level of concentration is high in the U.K. and continues to increase. It was recently suggested by Dr. Prais that there is a connection between the U.K.'s relatively high level of concentration and our relatively poor economic performance in recent years.*

If there is any truth in such assertions, we cannot conclude that the existing policy is satisfactory. A possible improvement which would represent a compromise between the existing pragmatic and the non-discretionary approach would be that mergers falling into certain categories should be forbidden unless the parties to the merger could convince an independent body that the net effect of the merger was likely to be beneficial. This would put the control of mergers on a basis roughly similar to that applying to restrictive practices which, as we noted above, is generally considered to have worked well.

ESSAY QUESTIONS

1 Explain the meaning of market structure, conduct and performance and discuss the possible relationships among them.
2 Outline the major elements of market structure and discuss the possible implications of each element.
3 Explain how competition policy may influence the level of economic efficiency.
4 'Since high levels of concentration facilitate undesirable conduct, competition policy should try to prevent any increase in concentration.' Discuss.
5 Outline the main provisions of U.K. legislation concerning (a) monopolies, (b) mergers, (c) collective restrictive practices, and discuss the major objectives of this legislation.
6 Why have U.K. governments adopted a much tougher line towards collective restrictive practices than towards mergers?
7 Outline the main provisions of the 1973 Fair Trading Act and explain how these provisions might benefit consumers.
8 Discuss the view that the most effective form of competition policy would be to control the prices of large firms.
9 Discuss the view that the most effective form of competition policy would be to control the profits of large firms.

*S. J. Prais, op. cit.

10   Discuss the advantages and disadvantages of a competition policy which incorporates non-discretionary rules.

EXERCISES

18.1 All of the following company policies have been found in operation at some time in the past, either in the U.K. or the U.S.A. Say which of these policies you think ought to be permitted, which ought to be forbidden, and why.

(i)   Selective price discrimination in certain geographical areas or to certain customers, perhaps by means of a 'fighting company', e.g. a subsidiary of the British Match Corporation reduced its prices to prevent the loss of sales to independent companies.

(ii)   Monopolization of the supply of inputs, e.g. the acquisition by Alcoa over a period of more than 30 years of most of the available deposits of bauxite and of uncommitted hydro-electricity sites.

(iii) The supply of materials or products by a vertically integrated company on discriminating terms, e.g. Alcoa, a finisher as well as a supplier of aluminium ingots, sold ingots at very high prices to non-integrated finishers; e.g. American makers of cinema films allowed non-integrated cinemas to show these films only a considerable period after they had been shown in their own cinemas.

(iv)   The control of a vital process by means of a patent, for 16 years in the U.K., 17 in the U.S.A., with the possibility of extensions.

(v)   Full-line forcing: when a firm has control over a much sought after article, it may use this as a bargaining point to push the sales of its other products, e.g. American Can hired its can-closing machinery only to the purchasers of its cans.

(vi)   Collective boycotts: the large British makers of gramophone records threatened to cut off supplies to retailers who stocked the records of new companies, and to stop advertising in magazines which accepted advertisements from these companies.

18.2 In 1965 B.M.C., the largest producer of cars and commercial vehicles in Great Britain, made an offer for the shares of Pressed Steel, the only remaining independent British supplier of car bodies. Pressed Steel's major customers for car bodies were B.M.C. and Rootes, each taking about 40 per cent of its output by value. Other customers were Rover, Jaguar, Rolls Royce, Triumph and Volvo for car bodies, and Ford for commercial vehicle bodies.

Of these customers, Rootes, Rover and Jaguar were almost entirely dependent upon Pressed Steel for supplies of bodies, while B.M.C. bought about one third of its bodies from Pressed Steel.

Pressed Steel produced car bodies in three plants, located at Cowley, Swindon and Linwood. A substantial proportion of the output of each plant went to nearby assembly plants. For example the Cowley plant supplied B.M.C.'s Oxford factory, while bodies from Linwood went to the Scottish assembly plants of Rootes and B.M.C. However all plants supplied assembly units located at greater distances; indeed over half of the total output of bodies went to various assembly units, (of which the most important were those owned by Rootes and B.M.C.) in Birmingham and Coventry, where Pressed Steel did not have a plant.

During the previous twenty years there had been a tendency for most car assemblers to build or acquire their own body-making capacity. Moreover a policy had been adopted whereby specialist production of various parts of motor vehicles had been undertaken, and specialist plants set up for the production of these parts, a policy which was also applicable to body manufacture.

  (i) What advantages would a merger offer to (a) B.M.C., (b) Pressed Steel?
  (ii) The bid was referred to the Monopolies Commission. What factors do you think the Commission should have taken into account in its evaluation of the bid?

18.3 'The Monopolies Commission were satisfied that the Company had not used its monopoly position to make excessive profit out of fletton brickmaking. The report showed that in terms of capital employed on an historic basis, at no time over the last 20 years had the return exceeded 30 per cent and that the average level of Group profit had been 23 per cent. In a significant passage the Commission stated that they were struck by the consistency of the Company's profit record.

'This suggests that the risks attached to L.B.C. brickmaking activities are less than might be inferred from the vagaries of the brickmaking industry. The evidence indicates that L.B.C. has not exploited its market power to raise prices at times when demand for bricks has been strong but has been able to use its market power to raise its prices in a recession so as to recover its profitability. Use of market power in this way is, I would contend, wholly legitimate. Not only does it safeguard the livelihood of those engaged in the industry and protect the interests of stockholders, but it ensures that the industry remains viable and that the customer continues to receive an efficient service in the supply of fletton bricks.

'The one practice operated by the Company which was felt by a majority of the Commission to be against the public interest lay in the field of distribution. The practice related to the treatment of delivery charges in the compilation of the Company's delivered prices for bricks at distant points and whilst rather unimportant in commercial terms, is interesting in the broader context of seeking to decide where the common interest lies.

'Before the war when London Brick was seeking to expand its markets throughout the country, a policy was adopted of seeking a lower return on the price of bricks delivered longer distances from the works from those delivered nearer home. This was unashamedly designed to establish wider markets for the fletton brick at a time when the "fletton" was not nationally accepted and when a few pence off the price could mean the difference between winning or losing an order. Those days have long since gone and for some years the sale of L.B.C. bricks has been firmly established throughout the country at prices considerably below those of its competitors. The practice however of accepting some lower margin on bricks delivered over longer distances and balancing this by rather higher margins in bricks delivered nearer home has been maintained for rather different reasons. It was believed that, as fletton bricks are a basic material for building and particularly used in low cost housing, it was in the interest of both our builder and local authority customers engaged in brick construction to apply some element of levelling in the prices charged throughout the country. Secondly, it was felt that through maintaining a large volume of business at distant points we would gain the same additional benefit of economy of scale, both in our production and perhaps more important in our methods of distribution.'

The above passage was taken from the statement circulated to shareholders by the chairman of the London Brick Company. Discuss the chairman's comments concerning (i) the policy of raising prices in a recession, and (ii) the policy of accepting lower margins on bricks delivered over longer distances.

18.4 The following data was taken from the Monopolies Commission Report on Household Detergents (H.M.S.O., 1966). It refers to the activities of Unilever and Procter and Gamble, whose sales of household detergents in 1964 were roughly equal, and who together accounted for some 90 per cent of total supplies.

Breakdown of Retail Price of 'Typical' Packet of Detergent (Index Nos.)

	Unilever	P. & G.
Factory cost	46	43.5
Research, administration, distribution	7.5	7
Selling cost	23	23
Total manufacturer's cost	76.5	73.5
Manufacturer's profit	7.5	10.5
Manufacturer's price	84	84
Retailer's margin	16	16
Retail price	100	100

Indices of Sales, Manufacturer's Prices and Costs: all Detergents 1964 (1954 = 100)

	Unilever	P. & G.
Sales tonnage	115	148
Manufacturer's price	118	105
Costs other than selling expenses (per ton)	113	97
Selling expenses (per ton)	88	99
Total costs (per ton)	103	97

Profits as a Percentage of Capital Employed (replacement cost basis)

	Unilever	P. & G.	Manufacturing Industry Average
1959	n.a.	29.3	12.2
1960	34.3	36.2	13.1
1961	12.9	34.8	11.1
1962	14.8	42.4	9.9
1963	26.9	40.3	10.8
1964	17.6	36.9	n.a.
1965	16.4	37.0	n.a.

n.a. = not available.

In the light of this data, evaluate the heavy selling expenses incurred by the manufacturers of detergents from the viewpoint of (a) the two manufacturers, (b) consumers.

18.5 Exercise 18.5 is based on arguments presented before the Restrictive Practices Court in connection with various agreements. Assess the validity and strength of each argument.

(i) Gateway (a) of the 1956 Act, 'that the restriction is reasonably necessary ... to protect the public against injury in connection with the consumption or use of goods,' was quoted by the Chemists Federation, an association of manufacturers of and dealers in proprietary medicines, to justify their policy of supplying these only to those retailers who employed a registered pharmacist on the premises.

Note: (a) The list of medicines included cod liver oil and barrier creams.
(b) Legislation prohibits the sale of most dangerous drugs unless they have been prescribed by a doctor. (c) The agreement did not

require that the persons buying the listed preparations should be served by the pharmacist.

(ii) The Black Bolt and Nut Association claimed that their Agreement conferred two specific and substantial benefits on the public and hence could be justified under gateway (b) of the 1956 Act.

The first benefit comprised the exchange of technical information and joint research, which depended upon the existence of a price agreement.

Second, uniformity of prices saved the buyers of black bolts from the expense of 'going shopping' for the cheapest source of supply.

Note: The members of the Association made several thousand types of nuts and bolts.

(iii) The Cement Makers' Federation also claimed that their price agreement kept prices to the consumer down. They claimed that the price restriction made the industry less risky, and that producers were therefore able to borrow money, for the construction of new plants, etc., at a lower rate of interest than could many firms of comparable size in other industries. Given that capital costs are a very important part of total costs in this industry, cheaper finance would enable the industry to keep prices lower than they would otherwise be.

18.6 The following arguments were advanced by Cadbury Bros. Ltd. in an attempt to justify to the Restrictive Practices Court a policy of enforcing the resale prices of chocolate and sugar confectionery.

'(1) In the absence of resale price maintenance on confectionery some retailers will cut prices. Price cutting will not be confined to supermarkets, but they will start the cutting. Price cutting in these shops will be of two types: (a) regular cuts on a small number of leading lines, for example, $\frac{1}{2}$ lb Cadbury's dairy milk chocolate, and (b) special cuts lasting for not more than one to two weeks on a succession of leading lines including those in (a), some of which may be deep cuts. In general, supermarkets will sell other lines at manufacturers' recommended prices, particularly because a substantial part of the trade is at round prices of 3d, 6d and 1s. (This point would be rather less important since decimalization. Only the last price, 1 shilling, has a decimal equivalent (5 pence) which is a round price.) The overall effect on the price level of confectionery sold in supermarkets will, therefore, be less than the impression created by the price cuts made.

(2) A trader who stocks a wide variety of products is in a better position to cut prices on a particular product than is a trader who specializes in that product, because he can expect to draw people into his shop to buy other goods.

'(3) Overall demand for confectionery is static. Total demand is not significantly price or income elastic in our affluent society. Thus, any increase in sales by any one class of distributor will be at the expense of the sales of the other distributors.

'(4) The outlets most seriously affected will be the large and medium sweet shops (particularly those near supermarkets), which offer a wide variety of confectionery and act as the "shop window" for the industry. The trade of such sweet shops will also be adversely affected by the impression created by supermarkets' price cuts. Widespread closure of such shops would: (a) result in a fall of total consumption because of the loss of many sales which are made on impulse or are otherwise dependent upon the existence of these shops, and (b) result in a fall in variety available because these are the distributors who stock the variety and upon whom manufacturers depend for its distribution.

'(5) Cadbury, and we believe other manufacturers, will not acquiesce in the disappearance of important outlets for confectionery and will seek to increase the percentage margin realized by sweet shops, so that their businesses remain viable on a smaller turnover. We consider that our trade will be harmed less by our increasing trade margins (or other display incentives) to the extent of, say 2–3 per cent of consumer prices, than by the demise of outlets which this extra margin might help to save. I believe that in this affluent society the consumer would be prepared to pay and that the effect on the total demand would be relatively small.

'(6) It may be thought that this increased margin will only encourage the supermarket to cut to a greater extent, and therefore, fail in its purpose; but two points must be remembered: (a) retailer price cutting is relative, and the supermarket is anxious mainly to establish the impression of a differential between its prices and those of traders in general, and (b) competition at the retailer level is imperfect and many shops will be able to realize the increased margin.

'(7) The long term position which I envisage is, therefore, one in which: (a) a larger proportion of confectionery sales is sold through supermarkets. There will be a considerable expansion of special discounts and trade deals; I believe that in the final event the costs of these discounts are passed on to the consumer; (b) manufacturers' recommended prices will be higher than they would otherwise be. A narrow range of lines will be price cut, but in general, confectionery will be sold at those higher recommended prices. On average, prices will be higher than they would otherwise be; (c) there will be some reduction in the number of outlets and in the variety of confectionery available since the higher margins will not be sufficient to maintain all the present day outlets in business; (d) there will be a reduction in the sales and availability of seasonal lines.

'(8) I have considered what would be the position if manufacturers did not increase realizable margins, so that the court may be able to see the seriousness to the industry of those consequences. However, I do not believe that manufacturers will allow this situation to occur.

'(9) The Resale Price Act (of 1964) provides for exceptions to the general abolition of resale price maintenance. We do not support resale price maintenance as a generality, and do not practise it for our grocery lines. However, we believe that confectionery is different from grocery products. I have given the reasons why I forecast that the consumer of confectionery would suffer detriment as a result of higher average consumer prices in the long run, fewer retail outlets, and a reduction in variety, all of which are "gateways" provided for in the Act. I have had to forecast because no other method is available.

'(10) Facts are, of course, preferable to forecasts and I can only conclude by reminding the court that in the present situation with resale price maintenance: (a) The industry is competitive and efficient, and (b) that we undermine this satisfactory situation at our peril and to the detriment of the consumer.'

(i) Why was it claimed that retailers would be most likely to cut the price of 'leading lines'? (ii) Why are lines with 'round prices' least likely to be sold at reduced prices? (iii) Comment on the statement that total demand for confectionery is not significantly price or income elastic? (iv) Comment on the argument presented in paragraph (4). (v) Do you see any contradictions in the arguments presented in paragraphs (4) and (6)? (vi) Comment on the conclusion presented in paragraph (10). (vii) Do you believe that manufacturers should be allowed to enforce the resale price of chocolate and sugar confectionery? Explain your answer in a few sentences.

CHAPTER NINETEEN

Nationalization

Introduction

THE essential feature of nationalization is that the assets of an industry or industries are publicly owned. In the United Kingdom, as in many other countries, these assets are vested in a number of 'public corporations' whose boards of directors are appointed by the government, but who are not civil servants.

A study published by the National Economic Development office showed that in 1975 public corporations accounted for 11 per cent of the country's output, 8 per cent of employment and 19 per cent of fixed investment. The relative importance of the various nationalized industries depends upon which of these three measures is used, but overall the 'big 6' are the Post Office (the biggest on all measures), the Electricity industry, the National Coal Board, the British Steel Corporation, British Rail and British Gas.

Given the significant proportion of economic activity accounted for by the nationalized industries, it is important to consider the possible reasons for nationalization.

The Reasons for Nationalization

Nationalization occurs as much for political or ideological as for economic reasons and we shall be obliged to refer to these political considerations. However in each of the following sections the analysis is presented primarily in economic terms.

To Control Monopoly Profits

We saw in the previous chapter that it would generally be considered undesirable if the firms in any industry were to earn profits persistently in excess of the average earned by industry as a whole (unless it could be shown that the excess was due solely to superior efficiency). We also saw that various measures might be adopted in order to try to control excess profits. An alternative to such measures is to nationalize the industry concerned.

From the point of view of allocative efficiency, excess profits are still undesirable, even if the industry is nationalized. However it is obviously easier for the government to ensure that excess profits are *not* earned if the industry is nationalized.

To Redistribute Income

There may be a connection here with the previous objective. If, following nationalization, prices are reduced in order to eliminate excess profits, the real income of consumers will be increased. Alternatively, if wages are increased, income will be redistributed from (former) shareholders to workers. (Note that if, as often happens, profits before nationalization are not excessive, an increase in wage costs following nationalization must be recouped either by higher prices or by government subsidies. In these instances income is redistributed from the consumers of the product or from taxpayers to workers in the industry.)

Countries in which assets are owned or controlled from overseas may nationalize these assets in order to ensure that profits are retained within the country. This entails some redistribution of income at the international level. (This is a specific example of a general desire to control the use of assets that were formerly foreign-owned.)

To Increase Economic Efficiency
Clause 4 of the Labour Party's constitution calls for 'the public ownership of the means of production, distribution and exchange'. This has not been interpreted as implying complete nationalization, but rather as requiring control over the 'commanding heights' of the economy. This may be required partly as a means of controlling monopoly profits and redistributing income, as already mentioned. But it also implies an objective of increasing economic efficiency.

Bringing the assets of an industry under unified control may make it easier to organize production in such a way that economies of scale can be enjoyed. Economies of scale are discussed in detail in Chapter 24, and it is sufficient to note here that two particular types of economy may *in principle* be expected to follow from nationalization. The first is the reduction in cost per unit of output that can often be obtained by concentrating production in fewer and bigger plants.* The second is the reduction in cost that can arise from the closer integration of different operations. So, for example, in the steel industry the siting in close proximity of plants producing ingots and plants rolling those ingots allows savings in fuel and transport costs.

Economic efficiency can also be increased by eliminating the overlapping activities of competing suppliers. The supply of such services as gas, electricity and water requires the provision of physical 'channels of supply' – pipes, conduits, etc., and it is clearly more economical to provide one set of channels for a given area than several.

To Ensure an Adequate Supply of Goods and Services
This objective has several different, although inter-related, aspects. First, it is argued that the capital requirements of an industry may be so great that it would be difficult to raise sufficient finance from the private capital market. If the finance must be provided by the state, it is sensible to ensure by nationalization that the state obtains the resulted rewards.

As indicated by the figures quoted in the opening section, the nationalized industries are on the whole capital intensive. They accounted in 1975 for almost one fifth of total fixed capital formation. Nevertheless there is no hard evidence to prove that private capital markets would in principle be unable to meet these requirements,† especially when account is taken of the fact that industry normally finances the greater part of its investment out of retained profits.

A far more tenable argument is that the private capital market might be *unwilling* to provide finance to industries whose prospects it judged to be unsatisfactory, because of the risk involved. It might, for example, be felt that falling demand increased the risk of investing in the railways or the postal service. (Adverse demand conditions also make it difficult for an industry to finance investment from internal sources.) In other words, the justification for the provision of state finance in such circumstances is that in its absence investment would fall, and consequently

* Economies *may* also arise from the concentration of production in larger *firms*.

† Note, for example, the purchase by private investors of around £564 million of shares in B.P. offered for sale by the U.K. government in 1977.

the supply of goods and services would become inadequate. On what grounds might such a conclusion be reached, what does 'inadequate' mean in this context?

One important argument is that relating to merit goods – goods whose consumption the government wishes to encourage. Since this argument was explored in Chapter 5 it need not be repeated here.

A second, quite different, argument relates to the concepts of linkages and bottlenecks. This argument may be illustrated by reference to the steel industry. The demand for steel tends to be highly cyclical. Consequently if the industry were in private hands producers might play safe by restricting the expansion of capacity so as to ensure, as far as possible, a high degree of capacity utilization. They might risk a loss of potential profits should demand turn out to be higher than expected, in order to minimize the possibility of losses due to demand turning out to be less than expected.

While such a policy might be sensible from the steel producers' point of view, it might mean that producers in other industries are unable to meet the peak demand for such products as cars and washing machines, because of a shortage of steel.

In other words linkages between industries may mean that a bottleneck, a limitation on supply, in one industry can have important consequences for other industries. If frequent bottlenecks occur in certain 'strategic' industries, i.e. those which supply products used in a wide range of other industries, economic efficiency and indeed the rate of economic growth, may suffer. In these circumstances, where 'incorrect' decisions are taken by the private sector because of imperfect knowledge of the future, the state may be justified in overriding these decisions. However there is, of course, no guarantee that the balance struck following state intervention will be correct. The economy might be left with too much capacity of certain kinds.

The strategic nature of the industries that have been nationalized in the U.K. can be judged from their share of the output in a number of very important markets. They accounted in the mid 1970s for more than half of the total energy supplied, one quarter of the freight traffic, approximately 90 per cent of the total tonnage of steel, and virtually the entire 'output' of the communications industry – the telephone and letter services.

Finally under this heading we should note the possibility that private sector producers might be unwilling to supply certain parts of the market, e.g. remote geographical areas, because of the high costs involved. This is especially likely to happen where substantial costs have to be incurred before supply can take place, e.g. in electricity distribution. Under nationalization, supplies to these areas can be subsidized out of the revenue derived from the more profitable parts of the market, or out of general taxation.

To Maintain Employment

Not surprisingly this objective of public ownership received increasing attention during the 1970s. Since much of the debate concerned the extension of public ownership outside the framework of the nationalized industries it is considered in the following chapter. However it is appropriate to make the point here that maintaining employment at a level above that determined by the operation of market forces implies that compensating costs, in the form of a subsidy of one type or another, are likely to be incurred.

Other Objectives

The nationalization of particular industries has sometimes been justified by reference to objectives additional to those listed above. For example industries supplying defence products may be nationalized on grounds of national security. The balance of payments may benefit by nationalizing industries previously controlled from overseas (as noted above) or which require subsidies in order to be able to compete with imported products.

The Objectives of Nationalization: Summary
The economic objectives of nationalization can be summarized as being (a) to reduce the level of real costs, i.e. to increase productive efficiency, and (b) to redistribute costs – for example as between consumers or employees and taxpayers; this objective implies the redistribution of real income. With these two summary objectives in mind, let us briefly discuss the performance of these industries.

The Performance of the Nationalized Industries
If we consider first the objective of increasing efficiency, a good starting point is the change in productivity. Data on eight industries is presented in table 19.1. This

Table 19.1
Changes in the Output, Employment and Productivity of the Nationalized Industries (per cent per annum)

		Output	Employ-ment	Capital stock	Output per head	Total productivity
British Airways	1960–74	11.0	3.6	3.4	7.1	7.2
British Gas	1960–73	7.4	−1.4	6.2	8.9	5.1
British Rail	1963–75	0.0	−5.5	n.a	5.8	n.a.
B.S.C.	1968–75	−3.9	−2.5	3.3	−1.4	−3.4
Electricity	1960–75	4.7	−1.6	5.0	6.3	1.7
N.C.B.	1960–75	−4.3	−5.9	n.a.	1.7	n.a.
Post office						
posts	1960–75	0.5	0.1	n.a.	0.4	n.a.
telecommunications	1960–75	9.9	2.1	6.1	7.7	6.4
Total manufacturing	1960–75	2.7	−0.7	3.5	3.4	2.3

Source: National Economic Development Office.

table shows that the different nationalized industries faced a range of different economic conditions and produced different economic performances. Consequently it is difficult to make satisfactory generalizations about the success, or lack of success, of the nationalized industries.

Furthermore it appears that the economic conditions faced by a particular industry have an important influence on the performance of that industry. Industries which experienced a healthy growth in demand, such as airways, gas, electricity and telecommunications were able to increase labour productivity much more rapidly than those industries in which output was stagnant or declined – the railways, steel, coal and the postal service.

Of the eight industries listed in table 19.1, five achieved an increase in labour productivity greater than that achieved by manufacturing industry as a whole, and performance in this respect must be considered to be satisfactory. However this favourable record is partly due to the fact that the capital stock grew more quickly in most nationalized industries than in manufacturing as a whole. When an allowance is made for this there is probably very little to choose between changes in total productivity in the national industries and in the private sector.

(Unfortunately data on changes in capital stock were not available for three of the industries listed in table 19.1.)

An evaluation of the performance of the nationalized industries in the light of the second summary objective, the redistribution of costs and income, requires us to consider changes in wages or earnings, prices and the financing of the industries.

Earnings
Table 19.2 compares changes in the earnings of manual employees in four national-ized industries with changes in manufacturing and in all industries. It can be seen

Table 19.2
Changes in Average Weekly Earnings in the Nationalized Industries
(per cent per annum)

	Gas	British Rail	Elec-tricity	N.C.B.	Nat. Inds*	Manufac-turing	All Inds.
1960–70	109	110	75	72	86	91	93
1970–75	130	128	137	176	152	107	124

* Average of four listed industries.
Source: National Economic Development Office.

that in the period 1960–70 the average changes in earnings in these nationalized industries was slightly below that in other industries. However after 1970 the posi-tion was reversed. The increase in earnings in coal-mining and, to a lesser extent, the electricity industry, outstripped the average increase in all industries. Since workers in gas and rail continued to obtain above average increases, the group of nationalized industries as a whole achieved increases substantially in excess of manual workers in all industries.

The result of these changes was that by 1975 average weekly earnings for manual employees in the nationalized sector as a whole were 12 per cent (6 per cent exclud-ing coal-mining) above the average for all industries. There is, of course, no golden rule that says that earnings in all sectors of the economy should be equal. Dif-ferences in earnings may arise for many reasons, including differences in the pro-portions of skilled and unskilled workers, differences in shift work and overtime working, etc. But during the 1970s *changes* in such factors do not appear to have been an important determinant of the changes in earnings in the nationalized indus-tries relative to earnings in other industries.

A more important determinant appears to be the fact of nationalization itself. Particularly significant were the above-average increases obtained in coal-mining and the railways, despite the fall in the demand for the products of these industries. It appears that these industries felt that they were sheltered to some extent from the operation of market forces, believing that they would be able to recoup the additional wage costs by charging higher prices for their products or alternatively that the government would meet any financial deficit that they might incur.

*Prices**
Figure 19.1 indicates that since 1960 those products of the nationalized industries that enter into the retail price index have witnessed an increase in prices above that for all items entering into the index. Taking the period since 1960 as a whole the excess has been about 1.2 per cent a year. The only years during which the
* See also Chapter 26.

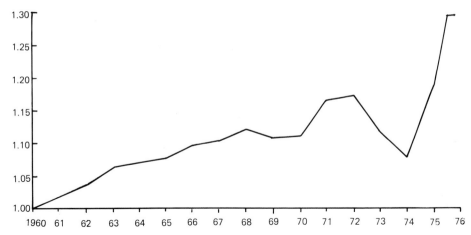

Figure 19.1   Ratio of Nationalized Industries' Retail Price Index to Total Retail

relative prices of the nationalized industries fell were in 1973 and 1974. This reversal of the trend was due to government instructions to the nationalized industries to moderate price increases – a policy intended to help in the fight against inflation. Unfortunately, but inevitably, this policy entailed an increase in financial assistance from the government, an increase which the government decided it was unable to sustain. Eventually the nationalized industries were told to charge prices that would increase their profitability and thus reduce the burden on the government. This change in policy was reflected in the very large increase in relative prices after 1974.

Financing
We showed in Chapter 6 that private sector producers normally finance about two thirds of their investment from internal sources. Internal financing has been much less important for the nationalized industries. During the 1960s internal sources accounted for between 25 per cent and 45 per cent of investment spending. The two external sources of finance available to the nationalized industries are borrowing (mainly from the government) and government subsidies, grants and compensation payments, which in the 1960s accounted, in very broad terms for 50 per cent and 10 per cent respectively of investment.

The fact that the nationalized industries relied more heavily than the private sector on borrowing might mean that the nationalized industries were *unable* to generate a sufficient surplus of revenue over costs. Alternatively it might mean that they *preferred* to borrow more. Investment expenditure undertaken now benefits future generations of consumers. Borrowing means that these future consumers help to meet the cost of the investment by paying prices which cover the interest charges on the borrowed money. In other words the primary effect of differences in borrowing is on the allocation of cost between consumers over time.

On the other hand government subsidies and grants represent a re-allocation of costs today. The consumers of the products pay less and taxpayers pay more. (Or alternatively the taxpayers may in effect help to subsidize earnings.) It was therefore a matter of considerable concern when in the early 1970s the relative importance of internal financing fell, and there was a substantial increase in government subsidies. (As we saw above, this change was due partly to government controls on prices. As the controls were relaxed in the mid 1970s, the relative importance of internal financing increased, as shown in figure 19.2.)

Moreover, government revenue support (as distinct from loans) has been much greater than an analysis of subsidy payments would indicate. During the period 1963–74 over £2,700 millions of capital debt was written off for the nine major

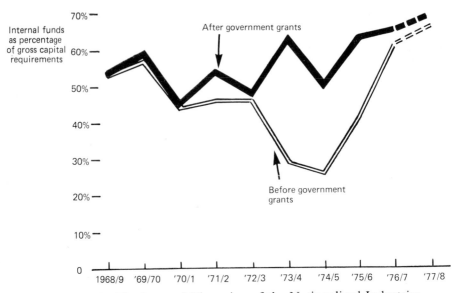

Figure 19.2 The Internal Financing of the Nationalized Industries

public corporations – only the electricity and gas industries did not benefit in this way. This cancellation of debt resulted in substantial reductions in interest payments.

As we said earlier, it is extremely difficult to generalize about the performance of the nationalized industries. However, trying to briefly summarize performance in terms of the second objective noted above, we can say that there is some evidence of a redistribution of income in that the general taxpayer has subsidized both the consumers of the products of the nationalized industries and the employees of those industries. The industries which received by far the greatest benefit were the railways and coal-mining. Incidentally, although employment in these two industries has steadily declined, the decline would undoubtedly have been more severe in the absence of financial support from the government.

Summary and Conclusions
Having examined the various reasons which might lead governments to embark upon a programme of nationalization, we considered the performance of the nationalized sector of the U.K. economy. We saw that different industries have had very different experiences in terms of changes in demand, productivity, prices, etc.

Overall, productivity appears to have risen at about the same rate as in manufacturing as a whole, although some nationalized industries have performed much better, and others much worse than this average.

At least some industries, most notably the railways and coal-mining, have received substantial financial support from the government in the form of subsidies and the writing-off of capital debt. The result of this policy is that prices have probably been maintained at a level below what they would otherwise have been – which in turn has led to higher sales and employment. There is also some evidence to suggest that workers have benefited from increases in average earnings in excess of those in the private sector.

We should add that the process of events outlined in the previous paragraph can be challenged. Critics of nationalization would claim that granting a public corporation monopoly rights in an industry or market, and making provision for government assistance if deficits are incurred, is a sure way to breed inefficiency. Consequently prices may not be lower than if the industry had been left in private hands, even after taking account of subsidies.

Some critics of nationalization may disagree with some of its objectives. Others may be more sympathetic towards these objectives but point out alternative methods of attaining these objectives. For example a system of licencing might be adopted whereby the right to supply a given product was granted to a limited number of producers. This would reduce the danger of the duplication and sub-sequent under-utilization of resources, especially fixed assets.* The issuing of licences might be dependent upon certain conditions being fulfilled, e.g. that a certain frequency or level of service would be provided, or that excessive profits would not be earned. (Such conditions applied to many 'public utility' companies which supplied water, gas and electricity in the U.K. before nationalization.)

An alternative method of trying to ensure that an adequate supply of goods or services is forthcoming is to provide subsidies to private sector producers. Such a policy was, of course, adopted for many years for agricultural products. More recently support has been given to firms in certain key sectors of the economy, one objective of this support being to reduce the possibility that bottlenecks in supply may occur. This form of support, together with the introduction of planning agreements, constitute part of the government's industrial policy, considered in the following chapter.

ESSAY QUESTIONS

1 What do you think should be the objectives of nationalized industries? How (if at all) do you think these objectives should differ from those of non-nationalized concerns?

2 'All commercial institutions should be subject to discipline of one kind or another, either the discipline of the market-place, or discipline imposed by higher authority. The trouble with nationalization is that it removed the first source of discipline, without introducing the second.' Discuss.

3 Outline the various objectives which nationalization might be designed to achieve, and show why conflicts may arise between these objectives.

4 'Although nationalization may in principle contribute to an increase in economic efficiency, the performance of the nationalized industries indicates that it does not do so in practice.' Discuss.

5 To what extent are the financial results of the nationalized industries an indicator of their efficiency?

6 Show how nationalization may lead to a redistribution of real income.

* One of the most extensive licensing exercises undertaken by the U.K. government in recent years related to North Sea oil exploration; the rights to explore specific blocks of the ocean bed were granted to a single company or group of companies.

7 Outline the major objectives of nationalization and discuss what alternative measures (if any) might enable these objectives to be achieved.

8 What factors should be considered by (a) a private sector producer and (b) a public corporation in making an investment decision?

9 Discuss the relative merits of the public regulation of, and the public ownership of, a monopoly.

EXERCISES

19.1 Below is a list of policies each of which may be assumed to result in a loss to the nationalized industry adopting that policy. State in each case whether you think that the policy should be adopted, and if so, who should bear the loss. Explain the reasoning underlying your answers.

(i) The provision of air services to the Highlands and Islands of Scotland.

(ii) The building of an underground railway line in London, which would reduce the amount of rush-hour congestion.

(iii) The operation of unprofitable coal mines in areas of high unemployment.

(iv) The purchase of coal produced in the U.K., rather than cheaper imported coal, to fuel electricity-generating stations.

(v) The movement of steel by rail rather than by road transport, which would be less expensive.

19.2 In the light of the data presented in table 19.1, table 19.2 and figure 19.1, evaluate the performance of the nationalized industries.

19.3 (i) In the light of the data presented in table 19.1 how satisfactory do you consider the change in the productivity of the nationalized industries to have been? (ii) What other information would you have found helpful in answering (i)?

19.4 Evaluate the changes in the internal financing of the nationalized industries shown in figure 19.2. (N.B. The data refers to the eight major nationalized industries other than British Rail. The estimates for 1977/8 were taken from the Financial Statement and Budget Report, 1977.)

CHAPTER TWENTY

Industrial Policy

Introduction
In this final chapter on government economic policy we consider elements of policy that would not fit easily into previous chapters. We shall be particularly concerned with a group of measures that can be classified as industrial policy or strategy. But before examining specific measures it is useful to consider the overall pattern of government assistance to industry.

The Pattern of Government Assistance to Industry
In table 20.1 we show the assistance provided by the government in 1975–6 and

Table 20.1
Government Assistance to Trade, Industry and Employment (£mn, constant prices)

	1975–6	1976–7	1977–8	1978–9
Regional support and regeneration	671	743	475	532
Industrial innovation	373	281	224	214
General support for industry	621	532	515	519
Support for nationalized industries (excl. transport)	165	138	94	66
International trade	653	556	367	331
Functioning of the labour market	405	695	842	677
Miscellaneous	94	99	−400	97
Total	3,008	3,074	2,152	2,469

Source: *Public Expenditure to 1978–9*, H.M.S.O., February 1977.

the planned assistance in subsequent years. In considering the totals it is important to recognize that the White Paper from which these figures are taken was issued in 1977, at a time when the government was committed to reducing the public sector borrowing requirement. This explains why the total assistance was planned to fall in subsequent years.

Looking at the individual categories, we see that during the first two years most money was spent on regional support and regeneration, an area of assistance that we discussed in Chapter 16. The major items within this category were regional development grants and the regional employment premium, and the planned decline in this category of assistance is largely due to the phasing-out of the R.E.P.

Another category in which assistance is planned to decline is international trade. Almost all of this assistance comprises the refinancing of fixed rate export credits, which is virtually the only direct method of assisting exports available to the government in the light of its international obligations.

The planned decline in support for the nationalized industries is mainly due to the greater freedom given to these industries to price their output at commercial rates, and hence to a reduction in the payments made by the government to compensate the industries for revenue lost due to price restraint.

As we showed in Chapter 17 the government has recently given more attention to manpower policies, and this is reflected in the growth in assistance designed to improve the functioning of the labour market. Whereas it is intended that the increase in the level of industrial training should be permanent, much of the assistance designed to create new jobs was introduced on a temporary basis, which explains why total assistance in this category was expected to fall in 1978–9.

The last two major categories, industrial innovation and general support for industry, which are the categories of most concern to us in this chapter, accounted for about one third of total assistance during the period as a whole. Industrial innovation covers the sponsorship of general research and development and assistance to certain 'technologically oriented' industries such as the aircraft, aerospace and nuclear power industries. General support for industry includes the selective investment scheme, industry aid schemes and the activities of the National Enterprise Board. Both of these categories of assistance are discussed in the following sections.

Industrial Strategy

The use of the term industrial strategy became widespread in the mid 1970s. However, various elements of policy included under this heading had been introduced in earlier years, and it is useful to begin this section with a brief historical survey, highlighting the objectives of the various policy measures. These measures fall into two broad groups, those concerned with indicative planning and those concerned with industrial restructuring.

Indicative Planning*

The first attempt at indicative planning was undertaken by the National Economic Development Council, set up in 1962 with a brief to study the country's economic performance, and to suggest how the country's resources might best be used to further economic growth. In a number of reports N.E.D.C. explored the implications, for the economy as a whole and for seventeen selected industries, of an annual growth rate from 1961 to 1966 of 4 per cent. It was hoped that this exploration would enable firms to forecast demand more accurately and thus to plan their future operations more efficiently. This would in turn reduce the chances that bottlenecks in production might occur.

The success of such an exercise depends heavily on the choice of an appropriate growth rate, and it soon became clear that the economy was not going to grow at 4 per cent a year. Any plans made on this basis were, therefore, invalidated.

Despite the failure of this initial exercise, a much more extensive version was undertaken with the publication in 1965 of a National Plan. This fared no better than its predecessor. Indeed only ten months after the publication of the plan, an economic 'freeze' ensured that the economy would not reach the projected growth rate.

Since then planning has been concerned with key sectors of the economy rather than with the economy as a whole. We consider some of these more recent planning

---

*Indicative planning can be distinguished in principle from central planning in that the former may not involve executive action by the state. In practice, however, the dividing line between the two may not be clear cut.

exercises below, but first we discuss the other major component of industrial strategy – industrial restructuring.

Industrial Restructuring

Assistance to specific industries has been made available by legislation such as the Cotton Industry Act of 1959 and the Shipbuilding Industry Act of 1967. These Acts attempted to increase the efficiency of the industries by encouraging investment and rationalization, the ultimate aim being the concentration of production in fewer but more efficient units. (The introduction of such legislation implies a belief on the part of the government that market forces could not be relied upon to bring about the desired degree of concentration.)

THE INDUSTRIAL REORGANIZATION ACT 1967

This Act represented a more general attempt to promote industrial efficiency. It established the Industrial Reorganization Corporation, which was given the function of promoting or assisting the reorganization or development of any industry or industrial enterprise. It was envisaged that in some instances the I.R.C. might simply act as a 'marriage broker' helping to arrange mergers, and that in other instances it would make loans or acquire shares in companies.

While the primary objective was to increase economic efficiency, it was hoped that the operations of the I.R.C. would help in achieving other objectives. In a White Paper preceding the Act it was stated that 'the Corporation will give priority to schemes of rationalization and modernization which offer good prospects in terms of increased exports or reduced import requirements, and will have regard to the regional aspects of the Government's policies for economic development'.

Of the loans made by the I.R.C. between 1967 and 1971 almost a third went to the automobile industry, other major recipients of funds being computers, aircraft, instrument engineering and ball bearings. One of the monuments of the merger activity sponsored by the I.R.C. is British Leyland Ltd. The troubles subsequently experienced by this company indicate that the impact of the I.R.C. on economic efficiency cannot necessarily be considered to be beneficial.

THE INDUSTRIAL EXPANSION ACT 1968

This Act also made general provision for assistance for projects designed 'to promote efficiency, to support technological advance; or to create, expand or sustain productive capacity'. Projects which were assisted included: a merger in the computer industry creating I.C.L., thought to be necessary to combat the challenge offered by I.B.M. and other multi-national concerns; building a major aluminium smelter in the U.K. with favourable implications for the balance of payments; and the Concorde project which received initial loans and credit guarantees up to £100 million, a figure subsequently increased on several occasions.

THE INDUSTRY ACT 1972

As we noted in Chapter 17 the pattern of regional assistance was partly established by the Industry Act. The Act also empowered the government to provide finance for companies for other purposes, e.g. to increase efficiency and to protect employment. The Act was introduced by a Conservative government which had declared itself to be less interventionist than its predecessor and which had dissolved the I.R.C. Consequently there seemed to be little prospect of large amounts of assistance being provided under the Act. However, the flow of assistance increased markedly after the return to power of a Labour government in 1974. The provisions of the Act were used to enable the government to take control, either partially or fully, of a number of companies in financial difficulty, including British Leyland and Alfred Herbert, the producer of a wide range of machine tools.

THE INDUSTRY ACT 1975
This Act established the National Enterprise Board as a publicly owned industrial holding company. The N.E.B. took over assets that the government had acquired under the provisions of several previous Acts, including holdings in British Leyland, Rolls Royce (1971) Ltd., and Ferranti. This part of the Act could be seen as a tidying-up operation. However the fact that the N.E.B. was given access to funds up to £1,000 million indicates that it is a potential vehicle for a substantial expansion of government influence and control over industry, outside the framework of the Nationalization Acts.*

We noted in Chapter 6 that the Board bought a stake in thirteen small companies during its first year of operation, and that it planned to substantially increase its activities in this area. It also announced that it was considering how it might aid rationalization and improved efficiency in several sectors, e.g. electrical engineering, office equipment, electronics.

The Act also provided for 'voluntary planning agreements', whereby companies would discuss (and presumably agree) with the government plans concerning their future operations. Progress on this front has been extremely slow, reflecting the fact that the government's enthusiasm for planning was not on the whole shared by industry.

The Resurgence of Planning
In addition to the specific provisions of the 1975 Act, the government took steps to reactivate the planning mechanism, working through the National Economic Development Council, a tripartite body representing the government, the trade unions and management. A number of sector working parties were established to consider what obstacles to an increase in economic efficiency and growth might exist. They identified a number of potential production bottlenecks, in steel, electric motors, diesel engines etc., which were felt likely to inhibit the revival of industry once demand expanded.

More than £300 million was made available through the Industry Act 1972 to accelerate investment projects which would increase efficiency and remove such bottlenecks. For example it was announced at the beginning of 1977 that £40 million was to be made available to support the modernization of the electronic components industry and non-ferrous foundries. Grants of up to 25 per cent of costs might be made for projects submitted before the end of July 1978.

The working parties also suggested means whereby production in particular industries might be rationalized, e.g. by mergers, and government support for these schemes has also been made available. This indicates that the two components of industrial strategy – planning and industrial restructuring – are complementary.

De-Industrialization
This term was given prominence as a result of work undertaken by two economists, Eltis and Bacon who showed in a recent book† that a substantial change had

---

* Similar responsibilities are exercised in Scotland and Wales by the Scottish and Welsh Development Agencies.

† R. Bacon and W. Eltis, Britain's Economic Problem – Too Few Producers (London: Macmillan, 1976).

occurred in the distribution of the U.K. labour force. While the number employed in manufacturing had declined, the number employed in the service sector, and especially in public services, had increased very considerably.

An increase in the relative importance of the service sector commonly occurs as countries develop and living standards rise, and this element of Eltis and Bacon's analysis was in no sense new or significant. What was significant was their demonstration that there had been a substantial shift in employment, not matched in most other industrialized nations, towards the 'non-market' sector, i.e. towards industries whose output was not sold in the market (see figure 20.1). There is obviously

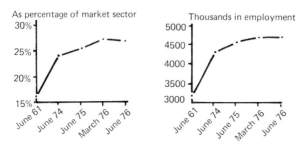

Figure 20.1 Employment in the Non-Market Sector in Great Britain

a close connection between this shift and the expansion of public services referred to above.

This shift has some extremely important implications. First, manpower absorbed by the non-market sector is not available for employment in the market sector. Consequently if employment in the non-market sector is increased to reduce the level of unemployment during a recession, this may make it more difficult for the market sector to acquire the labour resources it requires when demand subsequently increases. This could be seen as a giant, economy-wide, bottleneck.

Second, there may be a corresponding maldistribution of physical resources. For example, if resources are employed in building offices and manufacturing office machinery for the non-market sector, fewer resources will be available for producing factories, offices and machinery for the market sector.

Third, even if there were ample resources to meet the requirements of both sectors, the expansion of the non-market sector might still have undesirable repercussions. Since, by definition, the output of the non-market sector is not sold (or is provided at prices well below cost), an expansion of that sector implies that government's revenue from taxation must increase. More important, an increase in the share of output accounted for by the non-market sector implies an increase in tax revenue as a proportion of GDP. If the government, or the taxpayers, are unwilling to see this happen, the public sector borrowing requirement will expand. The impact of higher taxation and of a larger borrowing requirement were discussed in Chapters 12 and 13, and there is no need to repeat the arguments here. We merely emphasize that the result of such fiscal and monetary factors may be that the market sector will be unwilling or unable to expand even when sufficient *physical* resources are available. Such a result would, of course, run contrary to the objectives of industrial policy.

The major conclusion drawn by Eltis and Bacon is that the increase in employment in the public sector, or at least employment in the provision of public services, should be reversed. This would remove a major potential bottleneck to expansion. However they recognize that there may also be a place for more direct assistance to the market sector of the kinds discussed in this chapter.

An Evaluation of Industrial Strategy

Industrial strategy comprises so many different aspects that it is impossible to do more than suggest a few guidelines as to what factors should be taken into account in evaluating the policy.

As always it is useful to start with the objectives of the policy. As with nationalization, political considerations cannot be ignored. A more positive or interventionist policy tends to be adopted under Labour than Conservative governments. This may partly reflect differences between the two parties in their perception of the likely economic consequences of a free market system, but it also indicates a feeling within the Labour party that an extension of public ownership and control is ideologically desirable. However we confine our attention here to economic objectives, beginning with economic efficiency.

Economic Efficiency

Under this heading let us first consider productive efficiency as applied to the individual firm. A good example is provided by the operations of British Leyland, since a justification for using large amounts of taxpayers' money to support the company was attempted in the Ryder Report.* The Report considered that massive public support was required mainly to instal more modern and efficient plant and also to restore working capital to a more satisfactory level. Basically the Report said that state assistance was required to solve problems caused by the mismanagement of the previous owners or directors.

Three comments can be made concerning this diagnosis. First, it is possible that the previous owners did not undertake more investment because they felt that it would not produce an acceptable return on ploughed back profits and/or new money raised from the capital markets.

One of the factors which can reduce the return on capital is a high incidence of strikes, as had occurred at British Leyland. Commenting on this the Report said: 'We do not subscribe to the view that all the ills of B.L. can be laid at the door of a strike-prone and work-shy labour force. Nevertheless, it is clear that if B.L. is to compete effectively there must be a reduction in the man-hours lost through industrial disputes.'

Working practices are also important: 'More productive use must also be made both of B.L.'s existing capital investment and the planned additional capital investment and this must mean more realistic manning levels and more mobility and interchangeability of labour.'

Second, even if the diagnosis is correct, the future implications of the proposed solution should be considered. If it is felt that inefficient companies will be rescued by the state the incentive to remain efficient is weakened.

Finally, as always, the opportunity cost of the funds used – in this instance some £900 millions in the first three and a half years alone – should be considered.

The second aspect of economic efficiency with which industrial strategy has been concerned is the savings in costs that might be made following mergers. There is no doubt that some officially sponsored mergers have resulted in the creation of more efficient and profitable units, such as I.C.L. However the question arises as to why potentially profitable mergers might not occur in the absence of government intervention. If the crucial factor is financial assistance, we must again con-

* British Leyland: the next decade, London: H.M.S.O. 1975.

sider the opportunity cost of providing this assistance. (We might also reflect that, as shown in Chapter 18, an Act was passed in 1965 designed to make it more diffi-cult for firms to merge.)

The next aspect of increased efficiency is the reduction in cost that follows from rationalization – the concentration of production in fewer and more efficient units – not, in this instance, as a consequence of mergers. Here again one should consider the alternative to spending public money in this way. Might not the operation of market forces produce the same result? The more efficient firms would drive out the less efficient and thus gain their share of the market. While this may be a realistic scenario, experience in industries such as cotton textiles indicates that the process may operate only very slowly, and that in the meantime the casualties may include more, as well as less, efficient firms. Consequently government inter-vention might be justified if it significantly speeds up the process of rationalization, and increases the chances of survival of the more efficient units.

Finally, advantages may arise if potential bottlenecks can be removed. As we have shown earlier, uncertainty concerning the future is one cause of bottlenecks, and the government may play a valuable role by reducing the degree of uncertainty.

Other Objectives

Although increased efficiency is the major objective of industrial strategy, particu-lar measures have often been justified on other grounds, such as preventing a deterioration in the balance of payments or an increase in unemployment. So when Mr. Wilson, as Prime Minister, addressed the House of Commons on the Ryder Report, he noted that in the absence of government support, 'There would have been a risk of massive increases in imports and in redundancies on a very large scale, a good number of them in areas of high unemployment.'

Critics might suggest that the country would have benefited by allowing some resources to leave this industry to seek employment in other, more profitable, indus-tries, including those supplying products for export. The merits of these opposing viewpoints can be judged only in the light of all the circumstances pertaining to a particular decision. In this instance the relevant circumstances would include the existing balance between the demand for and supply of resources, especially labour, the nature of the resources released (the skills of the workers, the types of machinery, etc.), the trend in demand for the product concerned, the geographi-cal location of the plants in danger of closure, and so forth.

Again the National Enterprise Board has a number of major objectives. It was asked by the government to concentrate on:

1. Preparing for growth by action to increase longer-term capacity in key sectors of manufacturing industry;
2. Increasing exports or saving imports;
3. Where there was a choice of location, creating new jobs in areas of high un-employment.

In addition the Board seeks to obtain a 'commercially acceptable' return on the assets it controls.

Summary and Conclusions

The two major components of industrial policy or strategy are indicative planning and industrial restructuring.

The earliest attempts at indicative planning, in the 1960s, met with a marked lack of success. This was probably due partly to the adoption of an over-optimistic target rate of growth, and partly to a lack of depth in the plans. An attempt was made to remedy this latter fault in the planning exercises undertaken in the 1970s. In these exercises a number of sectors were explored in some depth. Markets which appeared to offer the greatest scope for expansion were identified, and suggestions were made as to how obstacles to expansion might be overcome.

Industrial restructuring has involved more positive assistance to industry. This assistance has taken two forms – direct assistance from the government to private industry, and assistance provided via intermediaries, in particular by the I.R.C. and the N.E.B.

Although the mechanisms and procedures involved in these two components of industrial policy are quite distinct, the two would generally be considered to be complementary. Indeed this complementarity can be seen from the fact that some of the recommendations emerging from the planning exercises of the 1970s have implied the provision of government assistance.

As we noted in the introduction, the mid 1970s saw a change in emphasis away from the provision of aid on a non-selective basis in the assisted areas, towards selective assistance of the kinds discussed in this chapter. One aspect of this change is the distribution of assistance provided under the government's accelerated projects scheme. (This scheme which ended in July 1976 was succeeded by a similar selective investment scheme.) It was estimated that the assistance, which approached £100 millions, would result in the creation of 12,800 new jobs. Of these 8,300 were in the non-assisted areas, and 1,800 in the assisted areas, with the remaining 2,700 being spread over both types of area.

ESSAY QUESTIONS

1 Outline what you understand by the term 'industrial policy' and explain why this policy was given increasing emphasis during the mid 1970s.
2 Evaluate the role of indicative planning in a mixed economy.
3 Discuss the ways in which the activities of the National Enterprise Board might affect economic efficiency.
4 Explain the meaning and significance of 'de-industrialization'.
5 'The best method of achieving industrial restructuring is to allow the free operation of market forces.' Discuss.
6 Should the government seek to promote or to prevent mergers?

EXERCISES

20.1 'Nothing shows up the differences between the West German and the British economic systems like a comparison of the Volkswagen, British Leyland, and British Steel Corporation affairs. In Germany the country's biggest car company ran with misguided momentum into a loss of £100m. for a single year. The Socialist–Liberal Government therefore supported a new chairman in his plan to make 25,000 people redundant over two years. The biggest British car company courted a similar degree of financial disaster and a Socialist Government promptly nationalized it at a cost of £1.5bn. The chairman of B.S.C. suggested that he must make "considerable" reductions in the workforce to keep the Corporation viable and was taken to task by Mr. Anthony Wedgwood Benn, the Secretary for Industry, with "I do not accept that a publicly owned industry can behave as though it was some private concern of the Board of management."

'What Mr. Benn does not accept is exactly what the Bonn Government has insisted on. The Volkswagen affair demonstrates a remarkable commitment to the "market" aspect of the "Social Market economy". Even in the middle of a recession, with unemployment high and important elections approaching, the Government refused to bail Volkswagen out of its troubles. "I will have no British Leylands here", said the Economics Minister, Herr Hans Friederichs.

'Although 40 per cent of the company's stock is in the hands of the State, the Government maintained continually that Volkswagen was a private company whose affairs should not be interfered with. When the long expected blow fell and it became clear that 10,000 workers would be fired, the Government agreed to put up DM105m. for the creation of new jobs. Yet the sum was directed not towards specific projects in the affected areas. It was simply made available as a subsidy to any entrepreneur who could think of a profitable way of employing people. Even in the "rescue operation" market forces were given the final say.'

The above passage was taken from an article in the *Financial Times* (30.4.75). Comment on the relative merits of the British and German economic policies discussed in the passage.

20.2 In 1975 the government agreed to provide support of £127.5m. to Chrysler (U.K.), a subsidiary of the U.S. Chrysler Corporation. The support comprised a guarantee of £72.5m. towards possible losses over the following four years and a loan – at interest – of £55m. to finance capital expenditure. The government estimated that the provision of this support would reduce the number of redundancies at Chrysler from 25,000 to 8,000.

What factors should be taken into account in deciding whether this government support was justified?

20.3 Figure 20.2 shows changes in, A: total employees in employment, B: employees in manufacturing. Outline the possible reasons for these changes and discuss their implications.

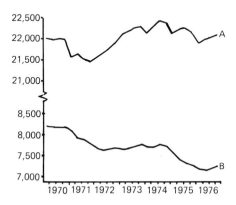

Figure 20.2 Employees in Employment, Great Britain (000s)

20.4 What information would help you to evaluate the desirability of the changes in the number of public sector employees, shown in figure 20.3?

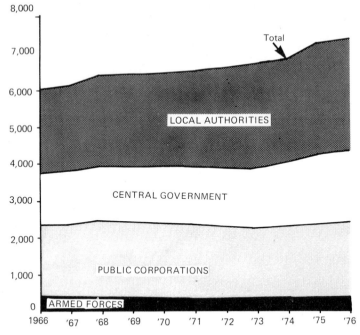

Figure 20.3 Number of Public Sector Employees (000s)

OBJECTIVE TEST QUESTIONS: SET 6

1 A collective restrictive agreement may be justified before the Restrictive Practices Court on any of the following grounds except that the removal of the restriction would

   A lead to an increase in merger activity
   B deny to the public specific and substantial benefits
   C cause a substantial reduction in export business
   D have a serious and persistent adverse effect on unemployment
   E reduce protection to the public against injury.

2 In Great Britain all of the following types of regional incentive are available except

   A subsidies related to the total cost of the firm
   B subsidies related to the cost of capital inputs
   C subsidies related to the cost of labour
   D the provision of factories to rent
   E the provision of factories to purchase.

3 The proportion of the population living in the Assisted Areas is

   A more than 50 per cent
   B about 50 per cent
   C about 40 per cent
   D about 30 per cent
   E about 25 per cent.

4 The Industrial Training Boards were established under the

   A   Industry Act
   B   Employment and Training Act
   C   Industrial Training Act
   D   Employment Protection Act
   E   Industrial Relations Act.

5 An increase in government subsidies to a nationalized industry implies a redistribution of real income

   A   from consumers to employees
   B   from employees to consumers
   C   from employees to taxpayers
   D   from consumers to taxpayers
   E   from taxpayers to consumers.

6 Changes in the unemployment statistics are not the best indicator of the effectiveness of the government's regional policy because

   A   unemployment differentials are associated with income differentials
   B   the local multiplier may affect unemployment differentials
   C   some workers who lose their jobs do not register as unemployed
   D   local wage rates are not sensitive to local unemployment rates
   E   companies do not always seek the area in which their production costs would be minimized.

7 Unemployment resulting from a general deficiency in demand affecting virtually all industries is known as

   A   structural unemployment
   B   cyclical unemployment
   C   technological unemployment
   D   regional unemployment
   E   frictional unemployment.

8 The 1956 Restrictive Trade Practices Act made it more difficult for

   1   firms to sustain collective restrictive agreements
   2   individual manufacturers to enforce resale price maintenance
   3   firms to merge.

9 Resale price maintenance may be justified under the Resale Prices Act on the grounds that in its absence the

   1   retail prices of the goods would increase
   2   number of retail establishments in which the goods were sold would be substantially reduced
   3   quantity and variety of goods available for sale would be substantially reduced.

10 Regional development grants towards the cost of new buildings and works are available in

   1   Special Development Areas
   2   Development Areas
   3   Intermediate Areas.

11 The free market approach to the regional problem takes account of
   1   social costs
   2   external costs
   3   internal costs.

12 Examples of external economies include
   1   central training facilities available to all the firms in the area
   2   improved public transport facilities
   3   the take-over by a firm of a supplier.

13 Which of the following Acts was intended to facilitate the restructuring of industry?
   1   The Monopolies and Restrictive Trade Practices Act, 1956
   2   The Shipbuilding Industry Act, 1967
   3   The Industry Act, 1975.

14 Which of the following bodies has/have encouraged mergers?
   1   The Industrial Reorganization Corporation
   2   The National Enterprise Board
   3   The Monopolies Commission.

15 Measures intended to provide a temporary stimulus to employment include the
   1   Temporary Employment Subsidy
   2   Youth Employment Subsidy
   3   Job Release Scheme.

16 A pragmatic, case-by-case approach to competition policy is most likely to be adopted when a clear link can be established between market structure, conduct and performance.
   Market performance may be affected by either market structure or conduct.

17 Under the 1956 Restrictive Trade Practices Act collective restrictive agreement are forbidden.
   The 1956 Restrictive Trade Practices Act is based on the presumption that collective restrictive agreements are against the public interest.

18 Absolute differences in regional unemployment rates are less today than in the inter-war period.
   The local multiplier operates to reduce regional inequalities.

19 A fall in the profits of an industry following nationalization indicates that consumers have benefited from nationalization.
   The nationalization of an industry may result in a redistribution of real income.

20 An increase in the number of people trained in government Skillcentres would tend to increase occupational mobility.
   Skillcentres admit only unemployed workers.

TRUE/FALSE

1   The spread of collective bargaining has reduced the sensitivity of wage rates to local unemployment rates.

2   Regional development grants towards the cost of new buildings and works are available in all the Assisted Areas.
3   The same pattern of regional incentives now applies to both manufacturing and service industries.
4   The external effects of the movement of a firm to an overcrowded area must be adverse.
5   The phasing out of the Regional Employment Premium made the pattern of regional incentives more capital-biased.
6   Costs are less influenced by location in foot-loose than in other industries.
7   Frictional unemployment is short-term.
8   A change in the proportion of an industry's capital investment financed by borrowing implies a change in the allocation of cost in different time periods.
9   Resale price maintenance is forbidden under the Resale Prices Act.
10 Collective restrictive agreements in all service industries must be registered with the Restrictive Practices Court.

CHAPTER TWENTY-ONE

Recent Changes in the U.K. Economy

Introduction

In this chapter we present and discuss two sets of data. The first relates to the various economic aggregates that have been discussed in previous chapters, and gives some indication of the extent to which the government has succeeded in achieving the various objectives discussed above. The second set of data is at a lower level of aggregation, being concerned, for example, with changes in output and employment in particular industries. This data provides an introduction to topics discussed in subsequent chapters. Thus this chapter provides a link between the two areas of economics, macro economics and micro economics.

Gross Domestic Product

Since the major economic objective of most governments has been to increase the standard of living it is appropriate to begin by considering changes in gross domestic product, which we have suggested is a good measure of living standards. As we explained in Chapter 3 there are three alternative ways of calculating GDP, and the measure used in figure 21.1 is an average of the three. It is calculated at constant market prices, i.e. in real terms, and expressed in index number form.

It can be seen that GDP rose throughout the period 1965 to 1973. However in the next two years some of the earlier gains were lost, and the rise in 1976 still left GDP at a level below that of 1973.

Gross National Disposable Income

The lower graph in figure 21.1 shows the behaviour of gross national disposable income, which forms an alternative measure of living standards. To obtain a measure of GNDI from GDP we must make an allowance for (a) net property income from abroad and net current transfers abroad, and (b) changes in the terms of trade. Changes in GNDI indicate the extent to which domestic expenditure could change without any change in the current external balance.

The two series normally move very closely together. However, national disposable income fell far more sharply than gross domestic product between 1973 and 1974. This was due to the adverse movement in the terms of trade caused by the steep rise in the price of oil and other commodities, and to the fall in the external value of sterling.

The Standard of Living

During the period covered by figure 21.1, living standards rose by about 20 per cent, so at least the economy moved in the right direction. Whether we moved fast enough in this direction is another matter. International comparisons reveal that many other countries did better than the U.K., as shown in table 21.1.

Returning to the period since 1973, while the decline in living standards is obvi-

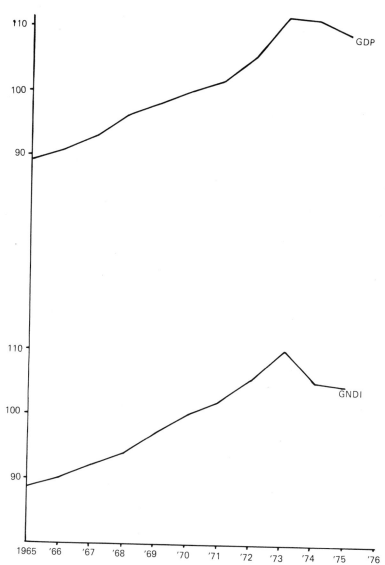

Figure 21.1 Gross Domestic Product, Gross National Disposable Income

Table 21.1

Change in GDP, Selected Countries (constant prices
and exchange rates)

Country	Increase in G.D.P., 1965–76 (%)
Japan	144
France	66
West Germany	45
U.S.A.	39
Sweden	38
U.K.	24
O.E.C.D. Total	50

Source: O.E.C.D.

ously undesirable, it represents a loss of only a small part of the ground gained in previous years. Perhaps the main problem arising from this reversal is that people's expectations are not so easily reversed. If people expect a continuation of the rise in living standards that cannot be achieved in the current economic circumstances, severe strains are likely to arise – especially, perhaps, in wage negotiations.

The behaviour of the main components of GDP is shown – in real terms and in index number form – in figure 21.2. Since consumers' expenditure accounts for more than 60 per cent of GDP, the two series must obviously move fairly closely together, and we see that consumers' expenditure grew each year to reach a peak in 1973, and then declined.

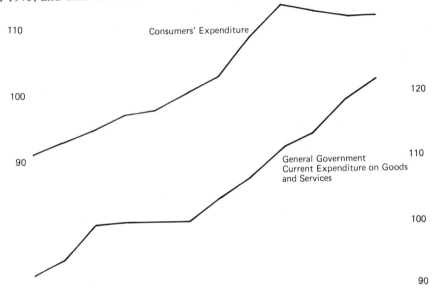

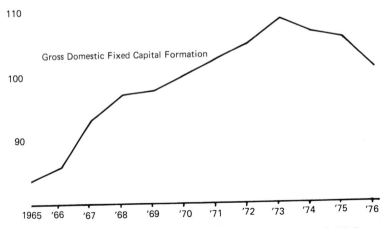

Figure 21.2   Changes in the Components of GDP

Future changes in expenditure are strongly influenced by changes in economic capacity, and thus by investment spending, the most important element of which is fixed capital formation. As can be seen from figure 21.2, fixed capital formation also declined after 1973, which did not bode well for future changes in living standards.

General government final consumption has a pattern quite different from the other two series, indicating that it is subject to a somewhat different set of influences. The continued growth in government expenditure beyond 1973 reflected the ideology of the governing political party, as noted in chapter 11.

The Production of Economic Bads
We examine below what the rise in living standards has meant in terms of changes in expenditure on, and the output of, various goods and services. However, as we argued in Chapter 2, a comprehensive measure of changes in living standards should also take account of the production of economic 'bads'. We showed in Chapter 3 that the quantity of the most easily measurable bads has tended to decline, but we suggested that the reverse may apply to some bads which are less easily measurable, such as noise.

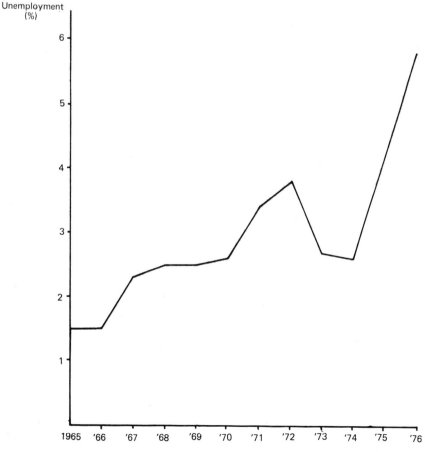

Figure 21.3 Percentage Unemployed, U.K.

Unemployment

Figure 21.3 shows that the unemployment situation was very much worse at the end than at the beginning of the period. The rise in unemployment which occurred after 1974 and which culminated in record post-war unemployment in 1976 clearly reflects the fall in GDP. The lag in the rise in unemployment is partly due to the fact that when output falls many employers do not lay off workers immediately. Apart from the social distress caused by unemployment, dismissing workers costs money in terms of redundancy payments. Moreover additional training costs may be incurred if demand revives and new workers are recruited.

Figure 21.4 compares the number unemployed with the number of unfilled vacancies. It can be seen that unemployment remained well above the number of vacancies, even when unemployment fell in 1973. Since both unemployment and vacancies are understated by the statistics of registrations, the gap between the two may not be an entirely accurate measure of the overall shortage of jobs (or of workers) at a given point in time. However, changes in the relationship between the two series do indicate changes in the pressure of demand for labour, and there

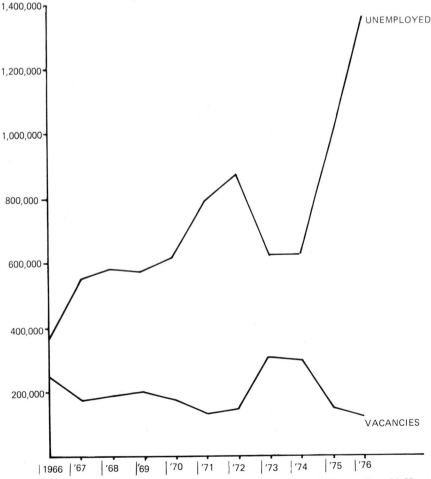

Figure 21.4 Number of Registered Unemployed and Vacancies, U.K.

can be no doubt that this pressure fell, i.e. jobs became more difficult to obtain, after 1974.

International comparisons of unemployment are made difficult by differences in the ways in which the data is collected. However estimates are made by the Department of Employment which seek to adjust for these differences. Figure 21.5, which is based on these adjusted figures, indicates that although unemployment in Great Britain has beeen lower than in U.S.A. and Canada, it has usually been

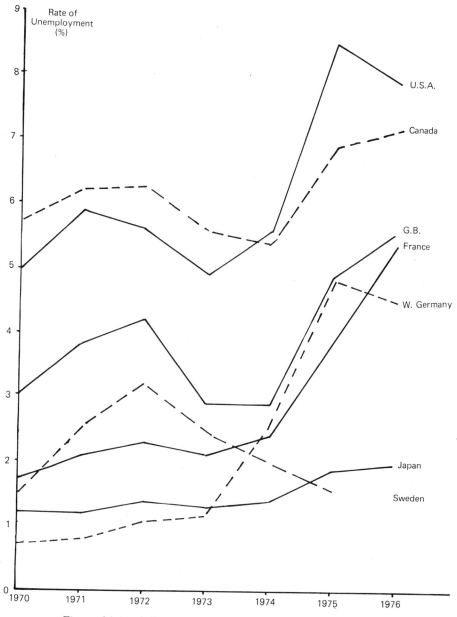

Figure 21.5   Adjusted International Unemployment Rates

higher than in many other industrialized nations, including Japan, France, West Germany and Sweden.

Prices
Of the various price indices that are published, greatest attention is usually paid to the index of retail prices, which shows the 'average' change in the price of a

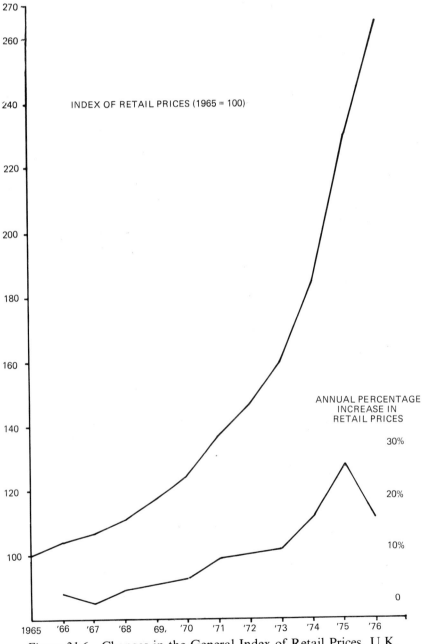

Figure 21.6 Changes in the General Index of Retail Prices, U.K.

given 'basket' of goods and services. The weights (i.e. the relative importance) attached to the various products included in the basket are based on the pattern of consumers' expenditure in the previous year. For example in 1975, with an overall weighting for all items of 1,000, food accounted for 232, fuel and light for 53 and transport and vehicles for 149. The importance of this index to the man in the street is indicated by the fact that it is often referred to as the 'cost of living index' – although it would in fact be an exact measure of the cost of living only for those people whose pattern of expenditure matched the weights used in compiling the index.

In figure 21.6 we show in the top line changes in the index, taking 1965 as our base year. It can be seen that prices rose each year, and that the rise was much greater in the later than in the earlier part of the period. This increase in the rate of inflation can be seen very clearly in the lower line, which shows the change in prices from one year to the next. Although this increase was checked in 1976, the rate of inflation remained much higher than it was in the earlier part of the period.

We have discussed in earlier chapters the reasons for the increase in the rate of inflation, and we drew particular attention to the effects of the increase in the price of oil and other raw materials. These price increases affected all countries, and inflation rates were higher virtually throughout the world in the 1970s than in previous decades. Nevertheless, the rate of inflation was higher in the U.K. than in most other countries, and almost double the average for other O.E.C.D. countries, as shown in table 21.2.

Table 21.2
Increases in Retail Prices, Selected Countries

	Increase in Price 1970–6 (per cent)
Japan	88
France	52
West Germany	41
U.S.A.	46
Sweden	62
U.K.	115
O.E.C.D. Total	63

Source: O.E.C.D.

Balance of Payments
Before considering the balance of payments as a whole we examine the behaviour of the major components, beginning with exports and imports of goods and services, i.e. visible trade.

Visible Trade
Table 21.3 shows that over the period as a whole the U.K. ran a very substantial deficit on visible trade. A visible deficit is by no means unusual – indeed the surplus earned in 1971 was only the seventh since 1800. What was alarming, however, was the size of the deficits incurred since 1971. The main reason for these huge deficits was the steep rise in the price of our oil imports. About two thirds of the record visible deficit incurred in 1974 was accounted for by petroleum and petroleum products.

Table 21.3

Visible Trade of the United Kingdom (£mn)

	Imports	Exports	Visible balance
1965	5,071	4,848	−223
1966	5,342	5,276	−66
1967	5,796	5,241	−555
1968	7,100	6,433	−667
1969	7,425	7,269	−156
1970	8,146	8,121	−25
1971	8,781	9,061	+280
1972	10,151	9,449	−702
1973	14,449	12,115	−2,334
1974	21,671	16,450	−5,221
1975	22,574	19,379	−3,195
1976	28,886	25,294	−3,592

Source: *Economic Trends* (H.M.S.O., Sept. 1977).

Terms of Trade

The impact of dearer oil can be seen in the unit value (or price) index numbers shown in table 21.4. Up to 1972 the prices of our exports tended to edge ahead of the prices of imports, as shown by the movement of the terms of trade figure. (The check to this movement imposed by the devaluation of November 1967 proved to be both modest and temporary.) However in 1973 and 1974 the terms of trade moved sharply against the U.K.

Table 21.4

The Terms of Trade of the United Kingdom

	Unit value index numbers		Terms of trade
	Imports	Exports	
1965	81.3	79.3	97.6
1966	82.6	82.2	99.6
1967	82.8	83.4	100.8
1968	92.7	90.0	97.1
1969	95.6	93.0	97.3
1970	100.0	100.0	100.0
1971	104.7	105.6	100.9
1972	109.7	111.1	101.3
1973	139.7	126.0	90.2
1974	218.0	162.7	74.6
1975	245.7	198.5	80.8
1976	299.4	240.6	80.4

Source: *Economic Trends* (H.M.S.O., Sept. 1977).

The volume index figures of imports and exports make interesting reading in view of the assertion that is sometimes made that Britain's economic troubles are due to a failure to compete in world markets. It is true that Britain's trade in many markets has fallen. Nevertheless we can see from table 21.5 that overall the volume of exports has increased slightly more than the volume of imports. The problem is, of course, that we have been able to achieve this result only because of a fall in our terms of trade, i.e. a fall in the price of exports relative to imports.

Table 21.5
The Volume of the Visible Trade of the United Kingdom
(1970 = 100)

	Imports	*Exports*
1965	76.6	75.3
1966	78.1	78.0
1967	84.9	77.6
1968	93.6	87.3
1969	94.4	95.9
1970	100.0	100.0
1971	104.2	106.7
1972	116.7	107.1
1973	133.8	122.2
1974	136.2	131.2
1975	126.4	125.6
1976	134.2	135.9

Source: *Economic Trends* (H.M.S.O., Sept. 1977).

Invisibles
The main items comprising the invisible balance are shown in table 21.6. This table shows that the private sector earns a sufficiently large surplus to outweigh the public sector's deficit. Also, within the private sector, every single year saw an increase in the surplus earned on the 'services and transfers' item, which includes the earnings of financial institutions, insurance companies, and transport companies.

Table 21.6
The Current Balance of the United Kingdom (£mn)

	1965	*1966*	*1967*	*1968*	*1969*	*1970*
Private services and transfers	208	250	340	528	585	688
Government services and transfers	−446	−470	−462	−466	−467	−486
Interest, profits and dividends:						
Private sector	567	543	546	563	822	813
Public sector	−132	−156	−168	−230	−324	−257
Invisible balance	197	167	256	395	616	758
Visible balance	−223	−66	−554	−667	−156	−25
Current Balance	−26	101	−298	−272	460	733

	1971	*1972*	*1973*	*1974*	*1975*	*1976*
Private services and transfers	831	871	1,021	1,360	1,607	2,639
Government services and transfers	−527	−566	−797	−879	−1,025	−1,556
Interest, profits and dividends:						
Private sector	693	692	1,591	1,755	1,494	1,725
Public sector	−193	−141	−208	−363	−545	−639
Invisible balance	804	856	1,598	1,873	1,531	2,169
Visible balance	280	−702	−2,334	−5,220	−3,204	−3,592
Current Balance	1,084	154	−736	−3,347	−1,673	−1,423

Source: *Economic Trends*.

The Current Balance

When we add to the invisible balance shown in table 21.6 the visible balance (as shown in table 21.3), we obtain the current balance. Taking the period 1965 to 1973 as a whole we earned a cumulative surplus of £1,200 million on current account. However deficits in excess of this figure were earned in each of the next three years.

We showed in Chapter 15 that an adverse current balance was likely to have unfavourable repercussions on the external value of sterling, and that the depreciation of sterling has important implications for prices and living standards in the U.K. We also showed that the consequences of a particular current deficit depends upon the behaviour of other components of the balance of payments, and we now examine the behaviour of the balance of payments accounts as a whole.

The Balance of Payments Accounts

Table 21.7 shows a simplified version of the U.K. balance of payments accounts for three years. We have chosen for inclusion in the table years in which the U.K.'s experience differed substantially. (See also Chapter 15.)

In 1971, as we saw in table 21.6, the U.K. had a surplus on current account. To this was added a substantial inflow on the 'investment and other capital flows account' to give a balance of payments surplus of £3,146 million, to which was added an allocation of Special Drawing Rights (see Chapter 15). This surplus allowed the U.K. to repay foreign borrowings of £1,817 million, to the I.M.F., central banks, etc., and to add £1,536 million to the official reserves.

By contrast in 1974 we had a substantial – indeed a record – current account deficit. Roughly half of this was covered by investment and other capital flows. To meet the remainder of the deficit the government borrowed heavily abroad, so heavily indeed that we were able to make a modest addition to our official reserves.

Finally in 1976 our current balance was again adverse, although the deficit was much smaller than in 1974. Unfortunately investment and other capital flows were strongly negative – due partly to the outflow of money deposited by the O.P.E.C. countries in earlier years, and partly to the operation of leads and lags (see Chapter 15). The combination of adverse current and capital flows led to an unusually heavy

Table 21.7

Balance of Payments of the United Kingdom, Selected Years (£mn)

	1971	1974	1976
Current balance	1,084	−3,380	−1,423
Investment and other capital flows	1,817	1,681	−1,938
Balancing item and other capital flows	245	53	−267
Balance for official financing	3,146	−1,646	−3,628
Allocation of S.D.Rs.	125	—	—
Total	3,271	−1,646	−3,628
Official financing:			
Drawings on (+)/additions to (−) official reserves	−1,536	−105	2,775
Other transactions (net)*	−1,735	1,751	853
Total official financing	−3,271	1,646	3,628

* Net transactions with overseas monetary authorities, and other foreign currency borrowing by H.M. government and by the public sector.
Source: *Economic Trends.*

balance for official financing. We had to dig deeply into our reserves, which fell to a dangerously low level. In addition we borrowed large sums from the I.M.F. and overseas central banks.

These borrrowings, together with an improvement in our visible balance – due largely to the development of North Sea oil – led to a growth in confidence in sterling. The capital outflow was reversed, and by October 1977 the U.K.'s reserves of gold and foreign currencies reached $20.2bn., nearly five times the total at the beginning of the year (see figure 21.7).

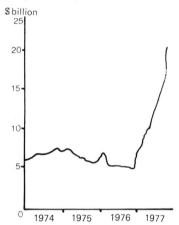

Figure 21.7 The U.K.'s Official Gold and Currency Reserves

The Distribution of Income and Wealth

The Reports of the Royal Commission on the Distribution of Income and Wealth, published at various dates during the 1970s, have revealed a steady, if slow, process of redistribution. For example table 21.8, taken from the Commission's first Report, indicates a redistribution of personal income, most notably in terms of a fall in the share of after-tax income accounted for by the top 5 per cent of income earners.

Table 21.8

Percentage Shares of Total Personal Income, after Income Tax

Share owned by:	1949	1959	1964	1967	1972–3
Top 1%	6.4	5.3	5.3	4.9	4.4
2–5%	11.3	10.5	10.7	9.9	9.8
6–10%	9.4	9.4	9.9	9.5	9.4
11–20%	14.5	15.7	16.1	15.2	15.8
21–50%	31.9	34.0	32.8	33.7	33.9
51–100%	26.5	25.1	25.2	26.8	26.7

Source: *Royal Commission on the Distribution of Income and Wealth.*

As we noted in Chapter 14, the compression of the range of after-tax incomes became more pronounced in the mid 1970s, and this led to suggestions that the redistribution of income had proceeded far enough, at least for the present. (This suggestion would, of course, be denied by some observers, and especially, perhaps, by those on the left wing of the Labour Party.)

Redistribution of wealth has also occurred, although distribution remains much more unequal than in the case of incomes. The Royal Commission estimated that, after making allowances for such things as house ownership and accrued pension rights, the top 1 per cent owned just over one quarter of personal wealth and the bottom 80 per cent just over 40 per cent of wealth.

Changes in the Pattern of Economic Activity
Expenditure
Having examined the changes that have occurred in a number of broad economic aggregates we now narrow the focus somewhat and consider changes in particular sectors of the economy. We discuss the factors which have contributed to these changes, and it is convenient to begin with government expenditure since, as we noted above, this is subject to a somewhat different set of influences from other forms of expenditure.

Government Expenditure
In table 21.9 we give a different breakdown of government expenditure from that presented earlier. A functional analysis shows the major sectors of the economy that have benefited from government expenditure, which here includes government consumption of goods and services, investment expenditure and transfer payments.

Table 21.9
Functional Analysis of Government Expenditure (per cent)

	1966	1975	1976
Defence and external relations	17.3	11.5	12.4
Roads, transport, communication	5.8	6.0	4.7
Industry and trade	9.2	12.0	8.8
Housing and environmental services	10.7	12.5	12.4
Justice, law enforcement	2.6	3.1	3.4
Social services	40.9	42.7	45.0
Debt interest	10.1	8.2	9.3
Other	3.4	3.9	4.0
Total	100	100	100

Source: *National Income and Expenditure* (H.M.S.O., 1977).

If we compare first the position in 1975 with that in 1966 we see quite substantial changes in the share of the various sectors. Especially noticeable is the relative decline in spending on defence and external relations, due largely to a reduction in the U.K.'s military commitments overseas.

The two sectors which show the largest increases during this period are industry and trade, and social services. The increased spending on industry and trade reflects increasing attention given to three areas of government policy – regional, manpower and, of course, industrial, all of which have been discussed in previous chapters. The increased spending on social services may partly reflect an increased acceptance of the state's responsibility towards the less fortunate members of community; it also reflects an increase in the number of citizens, such as retirement pensioners, qualifying for particular forms of assistance. The changes in relative shares shown in table 21.9 can therefore be seen as the result of a mix of economic, political, social and demographic forces. As we have seen, government expenditure can best respond to these forces over a longish time period. However a considerable response is possible even from one year to the next, as can be seen from a comparison of the figures for 1975 and 1976. The increase in the share of the social services continues, whereas spending on industry and trade is cut back drastically – mainly because of a reduction in subsidies and grants to producers.

Consumers' Expenditure

Although absolute spending on all major categories of products normally increases with income, some categories respond more strongly than others. Categories which respond strongly, i.e. those with a high income elasticity of demand (see Chapter 23), include alcoholic drink, durable household goods and services. Categories with a lower income elasticity of demand include food, fuel and light and clothing and footwear.

It can be seen in table 21.10 that as national income rose between 1971 and 1973 the share of spending accounted for by the products in the first category rose at the expense of the products in the second category. Subsequently, as national income fell between 1973 and 1976, this trend was partially reversed. The share of spending accounted for by food increased, while falls occurred in the shares of durable goods and services.

Table 21.10

Consumers' Expenditure

	1971	1973	1976
Housing	13.1	13.7	14.6
Fuel and light	4.6	4.2	4.9
Food	19.8	18.7	19.4
Alcoholic drink	7.3	7.6	8.2
Tobacco	4.8	4.3	4.2
Clothing and footwear	8.5	8.7	8.2
Durable household goods	8.9	9.2	8.0
Other goods	15.1	15.4	15.7
Other services	17.8	18.2	16.7
Total	100	100	100

Source: *Monthly Digest of Statistics* (H.M.S.O., Sept. 1977).

Products with a high income elasticity of demand are sometimes known as luxuries, and other products as necessities. While this is a useful shorthand expression it should be emphasized that the distinction is valid only in broad terms. As society becomes richer views change as to what are luxuries.

Furthermore, spending patterns are influenced by many factors in addition to income. So the fall in the relative importance of spending on tobacco is probably due largely to the evidence linking smoking with various forms of ill health.

The operation of the various factors which influence demand can be seen more clearly when expenditure on particular products is considered. In figures 21.8–21.10 we show changes in the volume of expenditure on three groups of products. We noted above that foodstuffs as a whole tend to have a low income elasticity of demand. Within this group, however, we find considerable differences in behaviour. The volume of expenditure on staple products such as bread and cereals has fallen steadily. Expenditure on dairy products has risen equally steadily (might the 'Drinka Pinta' advertising campaign have been important here?). Finally other products, such as meat and bacon, have shown no clear trend in either direction.

When a housewife spends more on one product she may decide to spend less

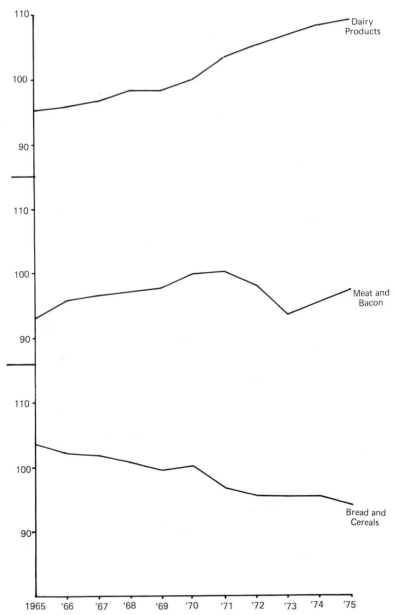

Figure 21.8 Consumers' Expenditure on Selected Foodstuffs (1970=100, constant prices)

on others, i.e. there is a *substitution effect*. It seems unlikely that there would be much substitution among the three food products shown in figure 21.8. On the other hand there is likely to be a very strong substitution effect among the three forms of fuel and light shown in figure 21.9. Expenditure on coal and coke has declined as consumers have switched to gas and electricity, attracted perhaps, by the convenience and cleanliness of these fuels.

Finally in figure 21.10 we can see evidence of both income and substitution

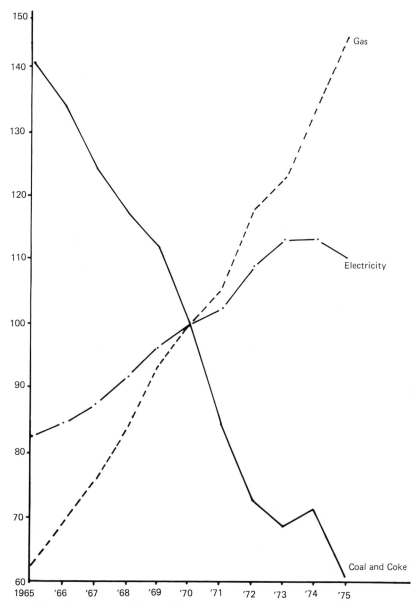

Figure 21.9 Consumers' Expenditure on Fuel and Light (1970=100, constant prices)

effects.* Higher incomes allow more people to buy cars and hence there is less demand for other forms of personal transport. Especially hard hit has been travel by bus, coach and tram, whose convenience is often much less than that of car travel.

*These concepts are discussed in greater detail in Chapter 23.

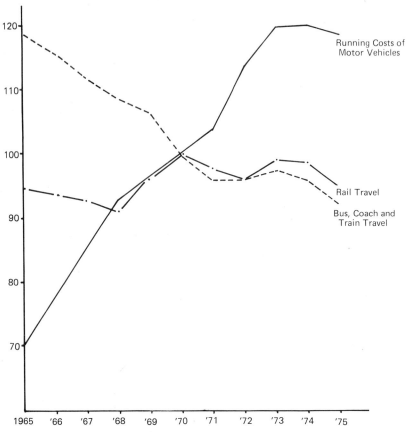

Figure 21.10 Consumers' Expenditure on Travel (1970 = 100, constant prices)

The Influence of Producers on Expenditure
We suggested above that one reason for the continued growth in expenditure on dairy products might be the promotional activities of suppliers. Gas has also bene-fited from promotional activities (especially the 'Hi-Speed Gas' campaign), and from the success of producers in discovering supplies of natural gas which gave gas a price advantage over competing fuels. Producers can also influence the pat-tern of expenditure by introducing new products.

This last factor is especially important in household durable products. As all the households who wish to possess a particular product achieve their desire, the demand for that product falls, the remaining sales being mainly for replacement purposes. Consequently, in order to maintain their sales, manufacturers have to introduce improved versions of these products and/or entirely new products. So in the U.K. in the post-war period we have seen attention given in turn to washing machines (twin-tub and fully automatic), television sets (monochrome and colour), record players, cassette players, music centres and music systems, refrigerators and freezers, dish-washers, etc.

Output
Changes in real expenditure are reflected in changes in output (although the corre-spondence is not exact because of changes in imports and exports and in the level

Table 21.11
Index Numbers of Output, Selected Industries (constant factor cost, 1970 = 100)

	1966	1975
Mining and quarrying	115	86
Manufacturing	89	101
Insurance, banking, finance and business services	82	131
Professional and scientific services	89	120

Source: *Annual Abstract of Statistics* (H.M.S.O., 1977).

of stocks). So in table 21.11 we see that the output of the service sector has increased more rapidly than that of manufacturing, while output in mining and quarrying, which is mainly coal-mining, has declined.

Using data from the index of industrial production, figure 21.11 presents information on seven market sectors, four consumer goods industries at the top, and three investment goods industries at the bottom. Looking first at the consumer goods industries we see a much steadier pattern in the output of 'necessities' – food, drink and tobacco, clothing and footwear – than of 'luxuries' – cars and other durables. Over the period as a whole, however, the production of 'other durables' increased more rapidly than the production of necessities. The fact that the production of cars did not also increase was due to a loss in market share to overseas producers and, after 1972, a decline in the total market due to a rise in the price of oil and petrol.

We showed in Chapter 6 that the demand for investment goods may be rendered less stable than the demand for consumer goods because of the operation of the accelerator. Figure 21.11 shows that there is a cyclical pattern in the production of all three categories of investment goods. The amplitude of the fluctuations, i.e. the change in output between peak and trough, is not, however, as great as might perhaps have been expected. Producers are able to smooth out fluctuations in demand by altering the length of their order books and even in some instances by producing for stock. This smoothing effect in the engineering industries can be seen clearly in figure 21.12.

Figure 21.12 also shows that over the period as a whole electrical engineering fared better, in terms of new orders and sales, than the other two branches of engineering. A major reason for this is the changes in technology which have led to some substitution of electrical for mechanical devices in many industries. Changes in technology have influenced demand and output in other industries. For example, between 1966 and 1976 output in chemicals and allied industries increased by 52 per cent, as compared to an increase of only 14 per cent for all other manufacturing industries.

Output in Retailing
Changes in consumers' expenditure are, of course, reflected in changes in the sales or 'output' of retailers. So we see in figure 21.13 that the increase in the volume of sales has been greatest in durable goods shops and least in food shops, with clothing and footwear shops coming between. We also see, however, that the fluctuations in sales have been greatest in durable goods shops and least in food shops.

Another important change in retailing relates to the share of trade accounted for by shops in different forms of organization. As can be seen from table 21.12 independent retailers, i.e. those having less than ten shops, although still the most

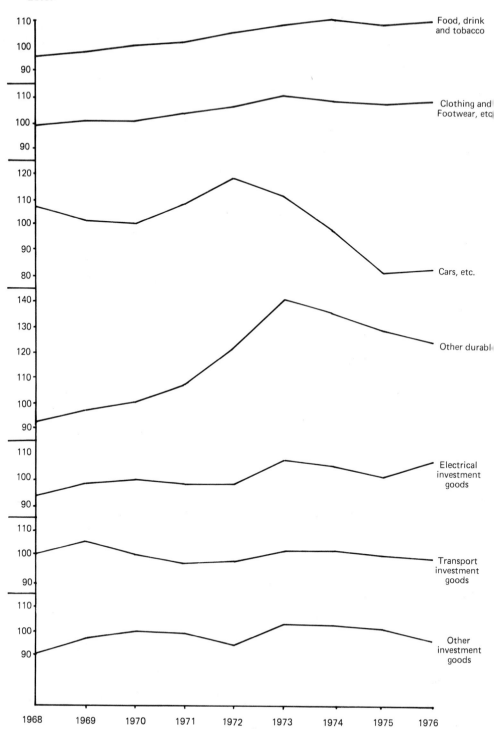

Figure 21.11 Index of the Industrial Production: Market Sector Analysis (1970 = 100)

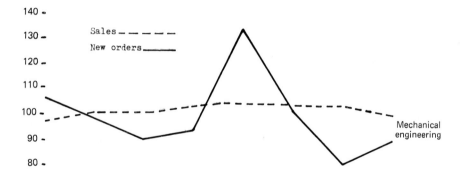

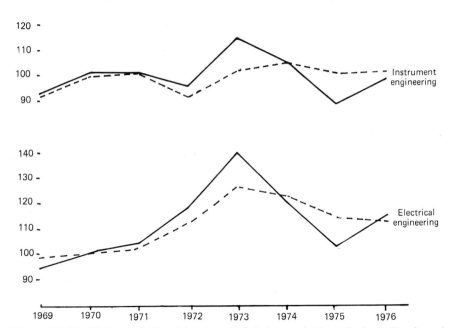

Figure 21.12 Volume Index Numbers of Sales and New Orders, Engineering (1970 = 100)

Table 21.12

Share of Retail Trade Held by Different Types of Shop

	1966	1971	1975
Independents	50.2	47.4	43.7
Multiple retailers	32.8	36.7	39.6
Co-operative societies	8.7	7.1	7.0
Department stores	4.6	4.9	4.9
Mail order businesses	3.7	3.9	4.7

Source: *Annual Abstract of Statistics* (H.M.S.O., 1977).

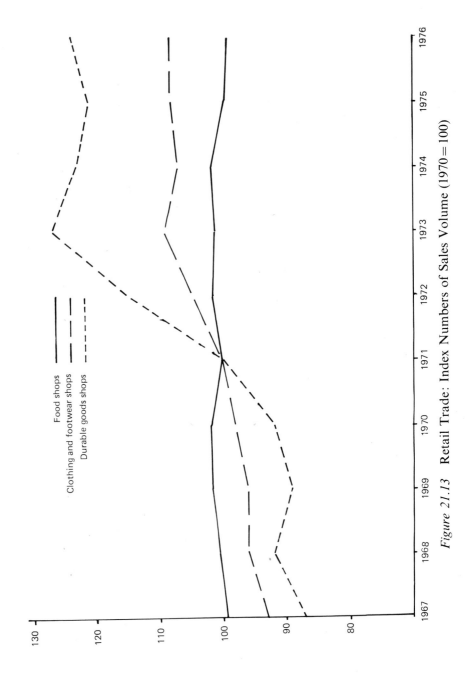

Food shops
Clothing and footwear shops
Durable goods shops

Figure 21.13   Retail Trade: Index Numbers of Sales Volume (1970=100)

important, have lost considerable ground to the multiple retailers. These multiples have been able to take advantage of economies of scale, including bulk purchasing, and the 'technology' of self-service. By passing on cost savings in the form of lower prices they have been able to attract more custom.

Employment and Productivity
As changes in demand are reflected in changes in output, so these changes are in turn reflected in changes in employment. Again, however, the correspondence is not exact. Increases in labour productivity mean that employment as a whole rises less rapidly than output. Indeed the increase in output since 1966 has been achieved despite a fall in the number of people at work, as shown in table 21.13.

Table 21.13
Employment and Productivity, United Kingdom (1970=100)

	Total employed labour force	Output per person employed	
		Whole economy	Manufacturing
1966	100.2	89.0	86.9
1967	100.9	91.6	90.0
1968	100.4	95.9	97.0
1969	100.4	97.8	99.3
1970	100.0	100.0	100.0
1971	98.3	103.3	103.0
1972	99.0	105.6	109.2
1973	101.0	109.3	117.7
1974	101.4	107.9	114.5
1975	100.8	106.3	112.6
1976	100.1	108.0	117.7

Source: *Economic Trends.*

It can be seen from table 21.13 that output per person employed increased each year until 1974. The decline that occurred in that and the following year was probably due mainly to the reluctance of employers to reduce their labour force in line with the fall in output, as mentioned above.

The experience of these years illustrates the dilemma posed by increases in labour productivity. We showed in Chapter 2 that in the long term increases in productivity are an important source of economic growth and therefore of improvements in living standards. However this conclusion holds good only insofar as demand increases at a rate sufficient to absorb the additional output. If this does not happen, an increase in productivity will lead to an increase in unemployment. The extreme situation would be where demand remained constant. In this situation an increase of productivity of, say, 3 per cent would result in a fall in employment of 3 per cent. Overall, the productivity of the total working population – including the unemployed – would be unchanged.

Various studies of international differences in productivity have suggested that the U.K. lags behind her major competitors. For example, having studied the operations of British Leyland and Chrysler (U.K.) in connection with the proposed provision of government assistance, the Central Policy Review Staff concluded that 'British productivity per man is far below the levels in the E.E.C. It has not changed in the last decade, while our competitors have improved their productivity and will continue to do so. We are particularly bad in assembly, where the labour requirements for assembling the same car, even with identical capital equipment, are nearly double. In engines it is 50 per cent to 60 per cent more.'

One of the principal findings of a N.E.D.O. report on the site performance of the engineering construction industry,* was that 'With very few exceptions the U.K. projects took longer both on total project time and on construction time on site than comparable projects abroad.' Moreover there was an even greater discrepancy in the amount of labour used. On most projects productivity in the U.K. was only a half to three quarters of the level abroad.

Finally, a study by the European Coal and Steel Community found that in 1973 productivity in the British iron and steel industry was the lowest of seven countries, being 58 per cent of the German industry, less than 50 per cent that of the U.S.A., and only just over one third of that of Japan.

There may well be some industries in which productivity is higher in the U.K. than in her major competitors. But there is no doubt that overall we have been slipping further and further behind these competitors as shown in figure 21.14,

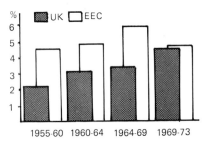

Figure 21.14 Annual Increases in Output per Person Employed in Manufacturing

taken from the National Institute's Review of August 1976. The consequence of this has been the slower rate of growth in GDP in the U.K. that was shown in table 21.1.

The Pattern of Employment

The pattern of employment is also affected by changes in labour productivity, since productivity changes at different rates in different industries. Nevertheless, despite this fact, the changes in the patterns of expenditure and output that we discussed in earlier sections are reflected in employment. So we see in table 21.14 that the number of employees in employment has risen in the service sector but has fallen in all the other major sectors of the economy. Even if one allows for the fact that the recession experienced in the 1970s might have affected services less than other industries it is clear that there has been a long term swing towards employment in the service sector. We noted in Chapter 20 that concern has been expressed by some economists at the growth of this sector, and especially at the increase in the number of workers employed in the production of non-marketed services.

Changes in the occupational pattern of employment are due partly to changes in the industrial pattern, shown in table 21.14, and partly to changes in the organization of work. Technological developments, including the spread of automation, have led to a reduction in the demand for manual workers. On the other hand there has been an increased demand for non-manual workers at many levels. levels.

A final important change in employment has been the very substantial increase in the proportion of females in the labour force, a development that has been

*N.E.D.O., Engineering Construction Performance (London: 1976).

Table 21.14
Industrial Distribution of the Total Working Population, United Kingdom (000s)

	1966	1975	% Change
Employees in employment:			
Agriculture, forestry and fishing	582	401	−31
Mining and quarrying	569	352	−38
Manufacturing	8,584	7,488	−13
Construction	1,645	1,313	−20
Gas, electricity and water	432	353	−18
Transport and communication	1,623	1,518	−6
Distributive trades	2,921	2,761	−5
Financial, business, professional and scientific services	3,409	4,659	+37
Catering, hotels, etc.	720	826	+15
Miscellaneous services	1,348	1,376	+2
National government service	585	650	+11
Local government service	837	1,005	+20
Total employees in employment	23,253	22,707	−2.3
Employers and self-employed	1,681	1,925	
H.M. Forces	417	336	
Unemployed	281	866	
Total working population	25,632	25,834	+0.8

Source: *Annual Abstract of Statistics* (H.M.S.O., 1977).

especially marked in the post-war period. This development is a result of a combination of factors.

First, an increased demand for certain products, and especially services, has led to an increased demand for female labour. Second, as the opportunities for female workers increased, the various factors limiting their supply have declined in importance. Labour-saving devices have reduced the amount of time spent on housework. A reduction in the size of the average family has reduced the number of years during which it is difficult for the mother to work. Finally, social attitudes have changed considerably; it is no longer so widely accepted that 'a woman's place is in the home'.

Table 21.15 indicates the extent to which increasing output in the post-war period has depended upon the contribution of married women. It also indicates that their contribution is expected to become even more important. However,

Table 21.15
Changes in Female Employment, Great Britain

Year	Females as Percentage of Labour Force	Married Females as Percentage of Females in Labour Force
1921	29.5	12.9
1931	29.8	15.2
1951	30.8	38.2
1961	32.5	50.2
1966	35.7	57.1
1971	36.6	63.1
Official projections:		
1981	38.1	70.3
1991	38.8	75.5

Source: Department of Employment.

although supply constraints may continue to decline, equal pay legislation may lead to a decline in the demand for female workers. Indeed the fact that the unemployment rate has increased more rapidly among young female than young male workers may be an indication that this has already begun to happen.

Summary and Conclusions

The discussion, in the first part of the chapter, of the behaviour of the major economic aggregates suggested that the recent performance of the British economy has not been entirely satisfactory. Although during the past decade we have achieved a significant improvement in our living standards, the improvement has been less than that achieved by most other industrialized nations. Moreover the U.K. has performed less well than many other nations in terms of other economic indicators – changes in prices, productivity, employment, the balance of payments, etc.

In the second part of the chapter we examined changes in particular sectors of the economy. We discussed the experience of different sectors in terms of changes in expenditure, output and employment. All these changes are specific indicators of a more general process, namely a re-allocation of resources. This process is the central theme explored in the remainder of this book.

ESSAY QUESTIONS

1 Discuss the recent performance of the British economy with reference to any three criteria you choose.
2 What problems may arise in trying to compare the economic performance of different countries?
3 Outline, and discuss the main determinants of, the major changes in the pattern of economic activity in the U.K. in recent years.
4 How would you explain the recent changes that have occurred in the pattern of consumers' expenditure?
5 Explain why, in a given economy, trends in the volume of output of particular products may differ from trends in the value of consumption of those products.
6 How would you explain the recent changes that have occurred in the pattern of employment in the U.K.?
7 'Higher labour productivity in the U.K. would mean that unemployment would be higher than it is at present.' Discuss.

EXERCISES

21.1 Question 21.1 refers to table 21.16. (i) 'Mining and quarrying declined from 1964 to 1969, since when it has gradually revived.' Would you agree with this statement? (ii) What is the major difference between the methods of calculating GDP in manufacturing and public administration and defence? (iii) Outline what you consider to be the main changes in the structure of the U.K. economy, and discuss the implications of these changes for our standard of living.

21.2 Table 21.17 shows the U.K.'s total domestic expenditure at constant market prices. (i) Which data do you consider gives the best indication of changes in standards of living in the U.K.? (You may choose either a single item or a combination of items.) Justify your choice in a few sentences. (ii) It is often

Table 21.16

Gross domestic product by industry (£mn)

	1966	1967	1968	1969	1970	1971	1972	1973	1974	1975	1976
Agriculture, forestry and fishing	1,061	1,106	1,101	1,174	1,242	1,359	1,518	1,881	2,136	2,575	3,116
Mining and quarrying	689	675	670	611	698	683	835	860	1,050	1,673	2,458
Manufacturing	11,003	11,194	12,003	13,051	14,300	15,562	16,884	19,078	21,694	26,343	30,464
Construction	2,261	2,391	2,562	2,728	2,874	3,192	3,853	5,094	5,977	6,960	7,793
Gas, electricity and water	1,069	1,145	1,299	1,389	1,378	1,574	1,745	1,921	2,324	3,028	3,905
Transport	2,079	2,087	2,349	2,506	2,727	3,018	3,329	3,909	4,448	5,721	6,624
Communication	703	753	813	930	1,045	1,190	1,458	1,712	2,216	2,970	3,691
Distributive trades	3,756	3,911	4,053	4,240	4,522	5,246	6,046	6,618	7,230	8,838	10,379
Insurance, banking, finance and business services	1,929	2,137	2,416	2,535	2,974	3,582	4,356	5,471	5,628	6,430	7,717
Ownership of dwellings	1,535	1,693	1,861	2,073	2,372	2,636	3,011	3,552	4,485	5,732	6,723
Public administration and defence	2,095	2,246	2,403	2,614	2,930	3,463	3,908	4,414	5,436	7,288	8,458
Public health and educational services	1,646	1,779	1,929	2,086	2,359	2,757	3,314	3,721	4,812	7,163	8,055
Other services	4,037	4,391	4,799	5,081	5,642	6,139	6,899	7,680	8,718	11,522	13,417
Total	33,863	35,508	38,258	41,018	45,063	50,401	57,156	65,911	76,154	96,243	112,750
Adjustment for financial services	−943	−988	−1,104	−1,182	−1,338	−1,518	−1,892	−2,579	−3,284	−3,661	−4,702
Residual error	163	357	236	−498	−357	268	−306	160	782	496	982
Gross domestic product at factor cost	33,083	34,877	37,390	39,338	43,368	49,151	54,958	63,492	73,652	93,078	109,080

Source: *National Income and Expenditure* (H.M.S.O., 1977).

Table 21.17

U.K. Domestic Expenditure at Market Prices (£mn, 1970 prices)

	Total	Consumers' expenditure	General government consumption	Gross fixed investment	Stock building
1965	53,973	28,705	8,357	7,900	616
1966	55,088	29,255	8,595	8,097	420
1967	56,964	29,876	9,075	8,780	368
1968	59,330	30,627	9,103	9,182	504
1969	60,352	30,826	8,960	9,216	468
1970	62,123	31,644	9,095	9,453	442
1971	64,035	32,597	9,344	9,682	99
1972	66,684	34,440	9,725	9,862	39
1973	71,625	36,003	10,123	10,283	1,127
1974	71,798	35,590	10,328	10,124	602
1975	69,905	35,234	10,797	9,991	−680
1976	71,452	35,290	11,057	9,556	−2

Source: *Economic Trends* (H.M.S.O., Sept. 1977).

Table 21.18

Retail Trade, Great Britain, Index Numbers of Volume and Value (1971 = 100)

Volume	1967	1968	1969	1970	1971	1972	1973	1974	1975	1976
Food shops	100	101	102	102	100	102	101	102	99	99
Clothing and footwear shops	93	96	96	98	100	105	109	107	108	108
Durable goods shops	87	92	89	92	100	115	127	123	121	124
Other non-food shops	92	96	96	99	100	109	118	117	115	114
All retailers	95	97	97	99	100	106	111	110	108	108
Value										
Food shops	77	81	87	92	100	109	123	145	175	204
Clothing and footwear shops	78	82	85	92	100	112	128	149	172	190
Durable goods shops	72	79	79	87	100	118	136	143	166	186
Other non-food shops	73	79	84	91	100	111	125	145	174	199
All retailers	75	80	85	91	100	112	127	147	175	200

Source: *Annual Abstract of Statistics* (H.M.S.O., 1977).

Table 21.19

Employees in Employment (000s)

	1966	1975
Agriculture, forestry, fishing	582	401
Mining and quarrying	569	352
Manufacturing	8,584	7,488
Construction	1,645	1,313
Gas, electricity and water	432	353
Transport and communication	1,623	1,518
Distributive trades	2,921	2,763
Financial, business, professional and scientific services	3,409	4,659
Catering, hotels, etc.	721	826
Miscellaneous services	1,347	1,376
National government service	585	650
Local government service	837	1,005
Total	23,253	22,707

Source: *Annual Abstract of Statistics* (H.M.S.O., 1977).

said that the U.K.'s relatively slow rate of growth is due to inadequate investment. Comment upon this hypothesis in the light of the above data. (iii) What factors help to explain the changes in the relative importance of general government consumption? (iv) Why does the value of stock building (changes in stocks and work in progress) fluctuate far more than the value of the other items? (v) What adjustments to the 'total' figure are required in order to arrive at gross national product at factor cost?

21.3 (i) Discuss and account for the major changes in the pattern of retail trade shown in table 21.18. (ii) Which category of shop had (a) the biggest (b) the smallest average price rise during this period?

21.4 (i) What factors account for the changes in employment shown in table 21.19? (ii) What other information would have helped you to answer (i)? (iii) Does the table reveal any trends that might be considered to be undesirable?

CHAPTER TWENTY-TWO

The Allocation of Resources

Introduction

IN the second half of the previous chapter we outlined the major changes that have occurred in the pattern of economic activity in the U.K. in recent years. We discussed changes in output and employment in particular industries and occupations, and we outlined some of the factors which might have led to these changes. In this and the succeeding chapters we shall explore these factors, these causal mechanisms, in greater detail.

During this discussion our illustrations are mainly drawn from the U.K. economy. However we also refer to other economies. It is, therefore useful to preface this discussion with a brief outline of alternative economic systems.*

Alternative Economic Systems

We can broadly classify economies as market, planned or mixed economies. The basic factor underlying this classification is the extent to which economic resources are allocated by means of the price mechanism. In a fully *planned economy* resources are allocated by administrative means. Decisions relating to a wide range of economic variables – the quantities of various products to be supplied, the methods of production to be used, and the rewards to be obtained by the various factors of production – are taken by the authorities responsible for constructing and implementing the plan. Advocates of such a system have sought to justify it either in ideological terms, e.g. that such a system is 'fair', or in economic terms, e.g. that resources can be channelled into the production of those goods that are required for economic growth.

Unplanned economies are of the two types. In primitive societies, where individuals have a high degree of self-sufficiency, *barter* may be the main form of exchange. More advanced societies have *market economies*, in which resources are allocated through the price mechanism. A market economy has also been justified on both economic grounds – the price mechanism is said to provide a constant incentive to meet the requirements of consumers as efficiently as possible – and ideological grounds, in that personal freedom of choice is maximized. (Critics of this system have pointed out that the freedom of choice enjoyed by particular consumers is very much influenced by the distribution of income and, as we have seen, reallocation of wealth and income is now generally accepted as a legitimate government activity.)

In a *mixed economy* the price mechanism continues to operate, but its operation is modified by the activity of the government or state in its role as consumer and producer.

Various aspects of market and mixed economies are discussed in this and the following chapters. (In the final chapter a more detailed comparison with planned

* The following section is a resumé of part of Chapter 2.

economies is made.) As the first stage in this discussion we outline the operation of the price mechanism.

The Operation of the Price Mechanism
In order to explain how resources are allocated through the price mechanism we utilize demand and supply curves. A demand curve indicates the various quantities of a product (or input) that would be demanded at various prices in a given time period. In figure 22.1 the demand curve D indicates that at price P_1 quantity Q_1

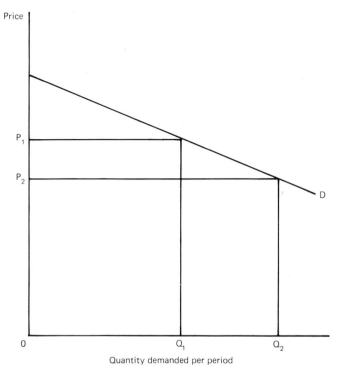

Figure 22.1 A Demand Curve

would be demanded. At the lower price P_2 a higher quantity Q_2 would be demanded. (Incidentally the shape of the demand curve shown in figure 22.1 is only one of many possible shapes, as we show below).

A supply curve indicates the various quantities of a product (or input) that would be supplied at various prices in a given time period. In figure 22.2 the supply curve indicates that at price P_1 quantity Q_1 would be supplied. At the lower price P_2, a smaller quantity, Q_2, would be supplied. (Again we should emphasize that the curve shown in figure 22.2 is only one of many possible alternatives.)

The Equilibrium Price
The equilibrium, or market clearing, price is that at which the quantity demanded in a given period equals the quantity supplied in that period. In figure 22.3 the initial demand and supply curves, D_1 and S, intersect at X, indicating an equilibrium price P_1 at which quantity Q_1 is traded.

Given the supply curve S, an increase in demand, represented by a shift of the

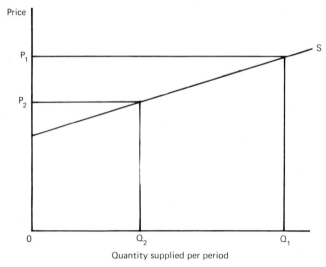

Figure 22.2 A Supply Curve

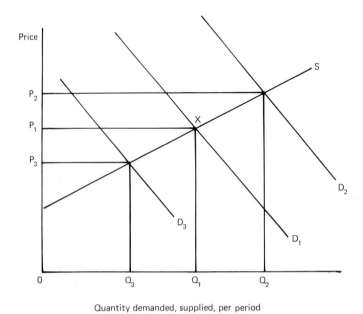

Figure 22.3 A Change in Demand and Equilibrium Price

demand curve to the right (D_2), causes the equilibrium price to rise to P_2, at which Q_2 (per period) is traded. Conversely a fall in demand, i.e. a shift of the demand curve to the left (D_3), causes the equilibrium price to fall to P_3, Q_3 being traded.

Figure 22.4 shows the effect of a change in supply, demand being given. The original equilibrium price is again P_1, Q_1 being traded. An increase in supply, i.e. a shift of the supply curve to the right (S_2), leads to a fall in the equilibrium price to P_2 and an increase in the amount traded to Q_2. Conversely a fall in supply, i.e. a shift of the supply curve to the left (S_3), leads to an increase in equilibrium price to P_3, and a fall in the quantity traded to Q_3.

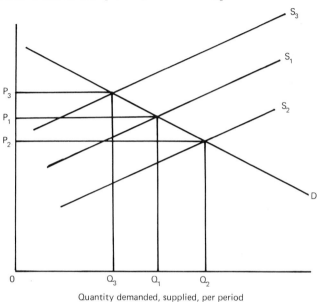

Quantity demanded, supplied, per period

Figure 22.4 A Change in Supply and Equilibrium Price

We can summarize these results as follows:

Change in Condition	Price	Quantity Traded
Demand increases	Rises	Increases
Demand decreases	Falls	Decreases
Supply increases	Falls	Increases
Supply decreases	Rises	Decreases

However it must be remembered that these particular responses will occur only if the demand and supply conditions are as indicated by the curves in figures 22.3 and 22.4. As we indicated above these conditions do not always apply, and it is appropriate to briefly consider some of the alternatives.

Figure 22.5 shows a demand curve which has the normal shape within the range of prices down to P_1, but which begins to slope backwards as price falls below P_1. Such a curve might arise if the product is a Giffen good, if consumers see the price of the product as an indicator of its quality, or if consumers buy the product for snobbish motives ('conspicuous consumption').* With a demand curve of this

---

* As we show in Chapter 23, some writers prefer to treat these last two instances as examples of a shift in the demand curve rather than of products with a backward sloping demand curve.

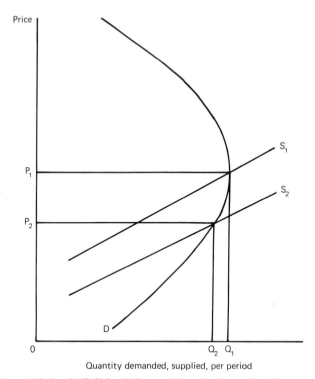

Figure 22.5 A Fall in Price and in the Quantity Demanded

nature an increase in supply, from S_1 to S_2, causes a fall in price, as before. However this now causes a decrease in the quantity traded.

In figure 22.6 the supply curve has a backward sloping portion; such a supply curve might apply to labour when workers have a target income. As the demand for labour increases from D_1 to D_2 the price (in this case the wage-rate) rises. However this results in a fall in the amount of labour traded (the number of man-hours worked), indicating that workers have attained their target income.

In figure 22.7 the supply curve slopes down to the right, indicating the existence of economies of scale (see Chapter 24). An increase in demand results in a fall in price and an increase in the quantity traded.

Summary and Conclusions
The main feature which distinguishes one type of economic system from another is the extent to which resources are allocated through the price mechanism. In many (although not all) markets, conditions are such that an increase in demand leads to an increase in price and thus to an increase in the quantity of the product supplied. This in turn implies an increase in the resources utilized in the supply of this product. A fall in demand leads, via a fall in price, to a reduction in the quantity supplied (and thus in resources utilized). Similarly, changes in supply conditions lead, via a change in price, to changes in the quantity demanded.

In the following chapters we examine in greater detail the many factors affecting demand and supply. We begin in Chapter 23 with a discussion of demand.

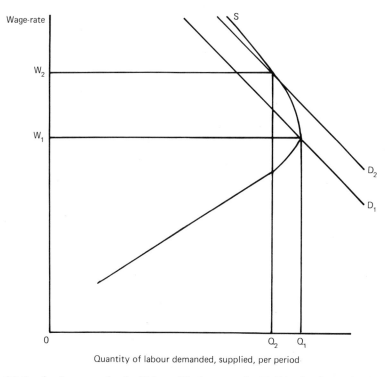

Figure 22.6 An Increase in the Price of Labour and a Fall in the Quantity Supplied

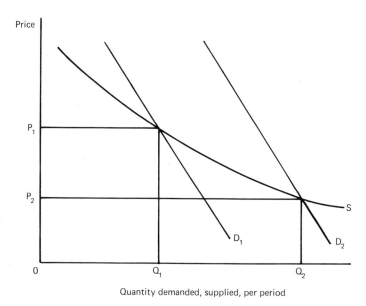

Figure 22.7 A Fall in Price and an Increase in the Quantity Traded

ESSAY QUESTIONS

1 Define demand and supply curves and show how they may be used in the analysis of resource allocation.
2 Explain the term 'equilibrium price' and discuss the factors which may cause the equilibrium price to change.
3 Discuss the conditions under which an increase in demand may *not* lead to an increase in price.
4 Explain why some demand curves may slope up from left to right and discuss the significance of this fact.

EXERCISES

22.1 What factors might help to explain the pattern of change in house prices, shown in table 22.1?

Table 22.1
Indices of House Prices and Building Costs (Great Britain, 31.12.70 = 100)

Quarter ended	New properties	Second-hand properties Modern	Older	Building costs	Index of retail prices	Average earnings
30.6.71	108	108	106	107	106	105
30.6.72	142	144	141	110	113	117
30.6.73	192	186	179	148	124	134
30.6.74	203	198	199	177	143	152
30.6.75	221	213	217	227	178	195
30.6.76	243	234	240	264	207	233
30.6.77	269	253	259	293	244	257

N.B. The house price indices are based on the purchase price of properties on which loans were approved by the Nationwide Building Society. Modern properties are those built within the preceding 40 years to modern standards of construction. Older properties are those which compare unfavourably with modern houses by virtue of their older design.

22.2 Exercise 22.2 is based on the operations of the Stock Exchange. The shares of most companies which are quoted on the Stock Exchange are distributed among a very large number, often thousands, of investors. These investors will have different views about the future prospects of any particular company in which they hold shares, and therefore about the price for which they would be willing to sell these shares. Let us take as a hypothetical example the shares of the Vestas Pottery Co. Sixty thousand Vestas shares have been issued, and the holders of these shares would be willing to sell at the following prices:

Supply Schedule for Vestas Pottery Co. Shares
Price (£)	No. of Shares Offered for Sale
1.60	60,000
1.50	40,000
1.40	25,000
1.30	15,000
1.20	7,000
1.10	2,000

At a price of £1.60 all of the existing holders would be willing to sell their shares. At a price of £1.10, only 2,000 shares would be offered for sale, and below this price no shares would be offered.

There are also many potential buyers of Vestas shares, again with different views about the company's prospects. The views of these investors can be summarized as follows:

Demand Schedule for Vestas Pottery Co. Shares

Price (£)	No. of Shares Demanded
1.50	2,000
1.40	7,000
1.30	15,000
1.20	25,000
1.10	40,000
1.00	60,000

Investors buy and sell shares through stockbrokers who transmit the instructions of their clients to jobbers who undertake the actual trading.

(i) Draw the demand and supply curves corresponding to the above schedules.

(ii) Given that on any one day stockbrokers receive buying and selling instructions as indicated by the above demand and supply schedules, how many shares will change hands?

(iii) At what price will these shares be traded?

(iv) Show by means of diagrams, how the shares traded would differ from that indicated in (i) if the following changes were to take place:

(a) The existing shareholders receive a statement from the company's chairman, which has not yet been released to members of the general public, indicating that profits are likely to be considerably greater than he had forecast at the last annual general meeting.

(b) A financial journalist with a very large following amongst investors writes an article about Vestas in which he forecasts a doubling of profits in the current year.

(c) Several very large potential buyers of Vestas Shares are advised by a reliable contact within the company that the company's sales are well below target.

(d) An extensive fire destroys the company's main factory, which is discovered to be considerably under-insured.

CHAPTER TWENTY-THREE

Demand

Introduction

IN this chapter we discuss the various factors which influence demand, developing the analysis presented in the previous chapter. In that chapter we showed that a demand curve, which indicates the various quantities of a product (or input) that would be demanded at various prices in a given time period, has two important aspects. The *shape* of the curve indicates how the quantity demanded would change in response to a change in price. The *position* of the curve indicates the quantity that would be demanded at any given price. (When we draw a demand curve we assume, of course, that we know both its shape and its position.)

In the first part of the chapter we examine the determinants of the shape of the demand curve. In the second part we examine the determinants of its position, referring to many of the changes that we have discussed in earlier chapters.

The Determinants of the Shape of the Demand Curve

Several alternative theories have been advanced which purport to explain the shape of the demand curve. We consider three of these alternatives, beginning with the marginal utility theory.

The Marginal Utility Theory

This theory is based on the proposition that products are bought because of the satisfaction or utility they yield to the purchaser. Marginal utility is the additional satisfaction obtained from the consumption of one additional unit of a product. The *law of diminishing marginal utility* states that, within any given period, the marginal utility of any product declines as the quantity consumed increases, the consumption of other products remaining constant.

Consider a housewife deciding how many potatoes she should buy each week for the family. She might decide that if she were to buy two kilos the family would obtain more satisfaction than if she bought only one kilo, but that their satisfaction would not be doubled. Again, if she were to buy three kilos there would be a further increase in satisfaction, but the additional satisfaction would be less than would be yielded by the second kilo. Finally, if she were to buy four kilos total satisfaction would decline as the members of the family would have to eat more potatoes than they would wish, i.e. the marginal utility of the fourth kilo would be negative. This relationship between utility and the quantity consumed is shown in figure 23.1. It will be noticed that total utility is maximized at the point at which marginal utility is zero, i.e. at a weekly consumption of between three and four kilos.

In order to explain the overall equilibrium position of the consumer or household we have to take into account the relative prices of all the products that might be bought. If the consumer is to maximize his (or her) utility, his pattern of con-

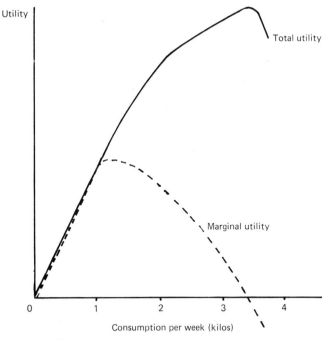

Figure 23.1 Total and Marginal Utility

sumption must be such that he equalizes the ratios of the marginal utilities of each product to their prices. Using symbols this condition can be expressed as follows:

$$\frac{MU_a}{P_a} \cdots = \cdots \frac{MU_n}{P_n}$$

where $a \cdots n$ represents the range of products purchased.

To illustrate this point let us assume that the consumer derives utility from a pair of products, say carrots and beans, as shown in table 23.1. If we assume that

Table 23.1

A Hypothetical Utility Schedule

Beans			Carrots		
Quantity bought per week (kg)	*Total utility (Utils)*	*Marginal utility (Utils)*	*Quantity bought per week (kg)*	*Total utility (Utils)*	*Marginal utility (Utils)*
1	100	100	1	50	50
2	180	80	2	90	40
3	230	50	3	120	30
4	270	40	4	140	20
5	300	30	5	150	10
6	320	20	6	150	0

beans are twice as expensive as carrots, e.g. 30p and 15p a kilo, we know that for the consumer to be in equilibrium the ratio of the marginal utilities must also be 2:1. There are, in fact, two alternative combinations that would fulfil this condition. If the consumer purchased 2 kilos of beans and 2 kilos of carrots a week we would have:

$$\frac{MU_B}{P_B} = \frac{MU_C}{P_C} \quad \text{or} \quad \frac{80}{30} = \frac{40}{15}$$

Alternatively if she purchased 4 kilos of beans and 4 kilos of carrots we would have:

$$\frac{MU_B}{P_B} = \frac{MU_C}{P_C} \quad \text{or} \quad \frac{40}{30} = \frac{20}{15}$$

Note that we have described the relationship between the relative prices of various products and the relative quantities purchased. We have not explained how much of a given product would be bought. Indeed we have shown that at 30p a kilo the consumer might buy either two kilos or four kilos of beans a week. In order to determine the actual quantities bought we would need to know not only the prices of each product but also the consumer's income. In other words the marginal utility theory does not enable us to determine the *position* of the consumer's demand curve.

The theory does, however, enable us to predict the way in which the consumption of a product will change as its price changes. To illustrate this let us assume that the price of beans falls to 15p a kilo, i.e. the ratio of the prices of beans to carrots becomes 1:1. At the previous patterns of consumption the condition for the consumer's equilibrium would no longer be fulfilled. In order to restore equilibrium the consumer must increase her consumption of beans relative to that of carrots. For example, if she previously purchased 2 kilos of beans a week (and 2 kilos of carrots) she may now purchase 4 kilos of beans (and 2 kilos of carrots), i.e.:

$$\frac{MU_B}{P_B} = \frac{MU_C}{P_C} \quad \text{or} \quad \frac{40}{15} = \frac{40}{15}$$

Alternatively, if she previously purchased 4 kilos of beans (and 4 kilos of carrots) she may now purchase 6 kilos of beans (and 4 kilos of carrots), i.e.:

$$\frac{MU_B}{P_B} = \frac{MU_C}{P_C} \quad \text{or} \quad \frac{20}{15} = \frac{20}{15}$$

Whichever of these combinations of purchases we start from, a fall in the price of beans leads to an increase in the quantity bought, i.e. the demand curve slopes downwards from left to right.

It is sometimes claimed that the marginal utility theory may help us to predict the (price) elasticity of demand, i.e. the extent to which the quantity demanded changes in response to a change in price.* This claim is usually justified by reference

---

*As noted in Chapter 7, the elasticity of demand, or more precisely the point elasticity of demand, is defined as follows:

$$\frac{\Delta Q}{Q} \div \frac{\Delta P}{P}$$

where Q is the initial quantity demanded
     P is the initial price, and
     Δ denotes a small change in the variable

to a situation such as that portrayed in figure 23.2, where two alternative marginal utility curves for a given product are shown.

We start from a situation where the consumer is in equilibrium with a marginal utility of U_1 derived from this product. This implies a consumption of Q_1 with marginal utility curve M_1, and of R_1 with curve M_2. Let us assume that, the prices of all other products remaining equal, the price of this product now doubles. In order to restore equilibrium consumption is reduced to the point where marginal

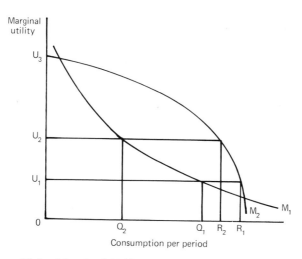

Figure 23.2 Marginal Utility and Changes in Consumption

utility is doubled, from U_1 to U_2. With curve M_1 this implies a fall in consumption from Q_1 to Q_2, i.e. a reduction of about one half. With M_2 it implies a fall in consumption from R_1 to R_2, or about one tenth.

It seems then that demand is far more elastic with marginal utility curve M_1 than M_2. However we must remember that this conclusion refers only to the particular ranges of consumption considered here. It need not apply when other ranges are considered. Indeed we would reach a different conclusion if we started from, say, the level of marginal utility U_3. This is an extremely important qualification, since, as we have already shown, we cannot predict what levels of consumption will be associated with given prices.

The concept of marginal utility also helps us to understand why a given product can command very different prices in different circumstances. A very dramatic, if somewhat unreal, example is the different prices that might be offered for a glass of water by a man dying of thirst and another who was in danger of drowning. More realistic is the difference in the relative value of an additional gallon of water during the drought experienced in the U.K. in the summer of 1976 and in the very wet winter which followed.

The marginal utility approach has the advantage of simplicity. On the other hand it makes an assumption that some economists find difficult to accept. This is that consumers can apply a *cardinal* measure to utility, i.e. can give an *absolute* value to the utility derived from a product. Dissatisfaction with this assumption has led to the development of theories which utilize the weaker assumption that consumers can apply an *ordinal* measure to utility. This implies that consumers can rank products in order of preference, although they may not be able to say by how much they prefer one product (or one combination of products) to another. This assumption is utilized in indifference theory.

Indifference Theory

In figure 23.3 the indifference curve I indicates the various combinations of two products, beans and carrots, that would give the consumer an identical amount of satisfaction. (The consumer would be indifferent as between any of the combinations represented by the curve.)

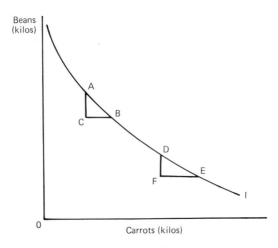

Figure 23.3   An Indifference Curve

Although it is sometimes claimed that in principle it would be possible to derive a consumer's indifference curve by experimentation, in practice the shape of the curve in figure 23.3 is based upon the assumption that the less a consumer has of one product the less of that product he would be willing to give up in exchange for one additional unit of another product. If he were at E he would be willing to give up 2 kilos of carrots (EF) in exchange for one kilo of beans (FD), whereas if he were at B he would be willing to exchange only one kilo of carrots (BC) for one kilo of beans (CA). This concept of a *declining (or diminishing) marginal rate of substitution* is clearly analogous to the proposition that marginal utility changes with the amount consumed per period, or the rate of consumption.

In order to show the effect of a change in price on the quantity demanded we introduce the concept of a budget constraint, a concept which relates both to the relative prices of products and the consumer's income. In figure 23.4 we show a 'family' of indifference curves, representing different levels of satisfaction. The highest level of satisfaction is represented by curve I_1. However the consumer cannot reach this level. His income is only sufficient to allow him to buy the various combinations represented by the budget line AB. The highest level of satisfaction that he can attain is indicated by point X, where the budget line is tangential to I_2. This shows that he is in equilibrium when he purchases Q kilos of beans and R kilos of carrots per week.

This equilibrium will be disturbed by any change in the consumer's budget line. Let us consider first a change in income, the prices of all products remaining unchanged. An increase in income would be represented by an outward shift of the

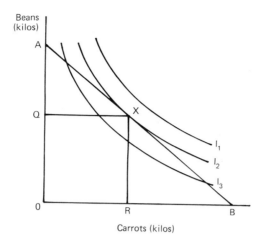

Figure 23.4   The Equilibrium of the Consumer

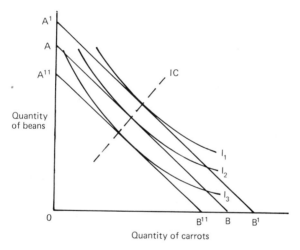

Figure 23.5   A Change in Income and in the Equilibrium of the Consumer

budget line, from AB to A¹B¹ in figure 23.5. (The two lines are parallel because the relative prices of beans and carrots are unchanged.) A fall in income would be represented by an inward shift of the budget line, from AB to A¹¹B¹¹.

As income changes, a change occurs in the combinations of products available to the consumer, and he moves to a new equilibrium position. In each instance the equilibrium position is given by the point of tangency of the budget line to an indifference curve.* These points of tangency, these equilibrium positions, may be joined to form an income-consumption line, designated IC in figure 23.5. The path traced by IC indicates that an increase in income leads to an increase in the consumption of both beans and carrots, i.e. both are normal goods (see p. 23.13).

---

* At any point of tangency $\dfrac{P\,\text{beans}}{P\,\text{carrots}} = \dfrac{MU\,\text{beans}}{MU\,\text{carrots}}$

The other factor which will cause a change in the consumer's equilibrium position is a change in the relative prices of products. In figure 23.6 we illustrate the effect of a change in the price of carrots, the price of beans being unchanged.

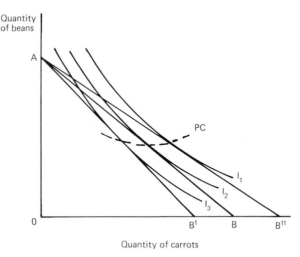

Figure 23.6 A Change in Price and in the Equilibrium of the Consumer

The initial budget line AB corresponds to that shown in figure 23.4. Since both the consumer's money income and the price of beans remain unchanged, the consumer could, if he wished, continue to buy A kilos of beans. However the change in the price of carrots changes the quantity of carrots that he could buy. As carrots become dearer, the budget line pivots to AB^1. Conversely, as carrots become cheaper the budget line pivots to AB^{11}.

Equilibrium is again determined by the points of tangency of the budget line to the indifference curves. In this instance the equilibrium points may be joined to form a price-consumption curve, designated PC in figure 23.6. The path traced by PC indicates that as the price of carrots falls the quantity purchased increases. This has clear implications for the shape of the demand curve for carrots, and we return to this point below. But first we consider the consumption of beans.

The path of PC indicates that a fall in the price of carrots may lead to either an increase or a decrease in the quantity of beans purchased. The reason for this is that the change in the price of carrots has two conflicting effects. The first is the *substitution effect*. As carrots become less expensive relative to beans, consumers substitute carrots for beans. But second, the fall in the price of carrots leads to an increase in the consumer's real income. As we saw above, if beans are a normal good, the *income effect* will be positive – an increase in real income will lead to an increase in consumption.

Since, as far as the consumption of beans is concerned, the substitution and income effects conflict, it is impossible to say a priori what the net effect will be. However some ground rules can be established. The substitution effect will obviously be greater the more likely it is that consumers will substitute one product for another. We would expect a change in the price of carrots to have a greater effect on the consumption of beans than on the consumption of a less close substitute, such as oranges.

The magnitude of the income effect depends upon two factors. The first is the extent of the change in the consumer's real income. This in turn depends upon both the proportion of the consumer's income spent on the product whose price changes and the magnitude of the price change. The second factor is the value of the income elasticity of demand for the product in question. (See p. 23.13).

Let us now consider further the consumption of the product whose price changes – in this instance carrots. Here the substitution and income effects normally work in the same direction. A fall in the price of carrots will cause consumers to substitute carrots for beans, while the increase in real income will also encourage an increase in the consumption of carrots.

As we said above, this analysis has clear implications for the shape of the demand curve. However we must extend the analysis a little further. A demand curve is drawn on the assumption that only the price of the product in question changes, i.e. that the prices of *all* other products, and the consumer's money income, are unchanged. This situation is illustrated in figure 23.7.

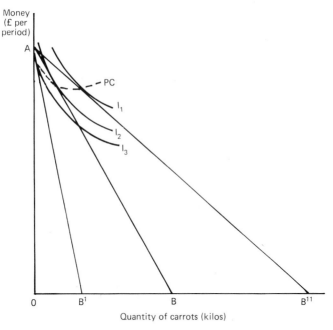

Figure 23.7   A Change in Price, Real Income and the Equilibrium of the Consumer

The initial budget line AB indicates that if the consumer were to spend all of his income on carrots he could buy B kilos per period. At the other extreme, if he bought no carrots, he would retain £A per period which he could spend on other goods. His equilibrium position is denoted by the point of tangency of AB to I_2.

As before, a change in the price of carrots causes the budget line to pivot – to AB^1 as carrots become dearer, or to AB^{11} as they become cheaper. Also as before, the points of equilibrium may be joined to form a price consumption curve PC. The path of PC indicates that the quantity of carrots increases as the price falls, i.e. that the demand curve slopes down from left to right. This again can be explained in terms of a combination of substitution and income effects, although now the substitution effect refers to the substitution of carrots for all other products.

Indifference theory suggests that the substitution effect always operates so as to increase the quantity bought when price is reduced. It follows from this assumption that if a reduction in price results in a fall in consumption, this must be due to a negative income effect outweighing the substitution effect.

This is illustrated in figure 23.8. The initial budget line AB is tangential to I_1

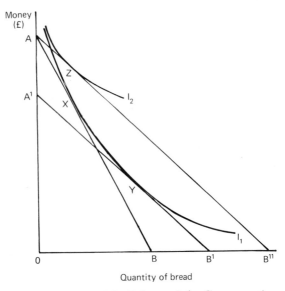

Figure 23.8   A Fall in Price and in Consumption

at point X. A fall in the price of bread causes the budget line to pivot to AB^{11} and leads to a new equilibrium position Z, where AB^{11} is tangential to I_2.

This change in the equilibrium position is due to both an income and a substitution effect. In order to separate the two effects we first cancel out the income effect. We draw an 'adjusted' budget line A^1B^1. This is drawn parallel to the new budget line AB^{11} to take account of the fall in the price of bread. It is also drawn tangential to I_1, indicating that the consumer is able to attain his initial level of satisfaction. However the point of tangency to I_1 is now Y. This change in the equilibrium position from X to Y would occur because the consumer would substitute bread for other products. Since the equilibrium of the consumer actually changes from X to Z, we can conclude that the movement from Y to Z represents a negative income effect.

As we have noted above, products for which the income effect is negative, i.e. products with a negative income elasticity of demand, are known as inferior goods (see p. 23.13). When the negative income effect is sufficient to outweigh the substitution effect, as here, the product is known as a *Giffen good*. Giffen goods are named after Sir Robert Giffen who observed in the nineteenth century that when the price of bread rose, its consumption by certain groups in society also rose.

We noted in the previous chapter that a Giffen good is one of the types of product whose demand curves slope upwards from left to right, or at least have an upward sloping portion. The other types of product which may have a similar shape of demand curve are those whose price is taken by consumers as an indicator of quality, and those which are brought for the purpose of conspicuous consumption. In these instances the shape of the demand curve can be explained by a substitution effect different from usual. As a result of the lower price, consumers will be disposed to buy less of that product and more of substitute products. If this substitution effect is sufficiently strong to outweigh any positive income effect, consumption of that product will fall as its price is reduced.*

The Revealed Preference Theory

This approach attempts to explain the relationship between price and quantity demanded without recourse to any assumptions about consumers' motivations, i.e. without introducing the concepts of utility or satisfaction. However it does assume that consumers are rational and behave consistently. From this assumption it follows that if it can be observed that a consumer buys more of a product when his income increases, he will buy more of that product when its price falls, since the reduction in price increases his real income.

In figure 23.9, with a budget line AB the consumer is observed to buy R kilos

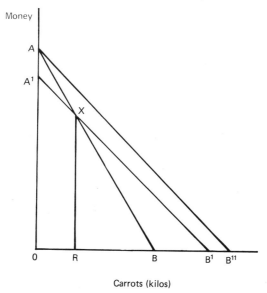

Figure 23.9 The Revealed Preference Approach to the Equilibrium of the Consumer.

of carrots per week. If the consumer acts rationally we can assume that no other attainable combination would have given him more satisfaction, i.e. there is no other point within the triangle OAB that he would have preferred to point X.

---

* The reactions of consumers to changes in the price of such a product might be interpreted as indicating a change in tastes. It would not, however, be possible to use a single demand curve to demonstrate this effect, since a demand curve is drawn on the assumption that the conditions of demand, including consumers' tastes, are unchanged.

Assume now that the price of carrots falls, giving a new budget line AB^{11}. This reduction in price has both an income and a substitution effect. In order to isolate the substitution effect we cancel the income effect. We do this by drawing an adjusted budget line A^1B^1 parallel to the new budget line AB^{11} and passing through X. This indicates that the consumer could, if he wished, continue to purchase the combination of carrots and other products represented by X. (Note that the adjustment is not quite the same as that made as part of indifference theory.)

Since the consumer previously chose X to any other point within the triangle OAB he will not now, if he is consistent, choose any point on the line A^1X. Any move away from X *must* be in the direction of a greater consumption of carrots. Since the income effect, here cancelled, would also move the consumer towards a greater consumption of carrots we can conclude that price, and quantity demanded are inversely related, i.e. that the demand curve slopes down from left to right. (This conclusion may not apply, of course, where the income effect is negative.)

The situations noted above, where the price of a product is seen as an indicator of its quality or where a product is bought for the purpose of conspicious consumption, would probably be seen as examples of irrational behaviour by the proponents of the revealed preference approach. Such behaviour is certainly inconsistent with the basic prediction of the theory, that the substitution effect can never cause a reduction in the consumption of a product whose price falls. Rational behaviour is an exceedingly slippery concept which we cannot explore here. However we should point out that there is considerable evidence to support the view that consumers' purchasing decisions are frequently influenced both by the view that the price of a product is an indicator of its quality, and by a desire for conspicuous consumption.

The Three Approaches Compared

The purpose of this section is not for the author to suggest a 'best buy' from among the competing approaches – indeed experience suggests that some students are likely to be happier with one approach and other students with another – but to review the criteria against which the different approaches might be evaluated.

As we noted when discussing the controversies between the Keynesians and the monetarists, some economists take the view that the predictive value of a theory is the most important (and perhaps the only valid) criterion. Unfortunately this does not get us very far in this instance since the same prediction emerges from all three approaches, namely that a fall in the price of a product will normally lead to an increase in the quantity demanded. The only distinction that we could make on this score is that the marginal utility approach has not provided an explanation as to why for some products (Giffen goods) price and quantity are positively related.

Again, although each approach leads to the conclusion that the demand curve slopes down from left to right, none of them enables us to draw conclusions about the precise shape of the curve, i.e. about its elasticity. We showed that certain tentative conclusions could be drawn about elasticity on the basis of alternative marginal utility schedules or curves. The price–consumption curves derived by indifference theory are also an indicator of demand elasticities. The ability to apply the analysis in this way might be considered to be an advantage of these two approaches. However, the utility schedules and the indifference curves that we presented were hypothetical; indeed no empirical evidence relating to either concept has ever been presented. This is, in fact, simply one example of the deductive nature of all three approaches. Each approach starts from certain assumptions about consumers' motivations and preferences, and derives conclusions about behaviour from these assumptions. (By contrast estimates of demand elasticities, such as those presented in table 23.2, are derived from observation of actual expenditure patterns.)

Table 23.2
Estimated Price Elasticities of Demand

Product	Price elasticity of demand
Beef and veal	−1.02
All carcass meat	−0.89
All meat (incl. poultry, bacon and chicken)	−0.45

Source: National Food Survey Committee study, based on data for 1962–7.

This might suggest that another possible criterion is the extent to which the assumptions of the different approaches accord with a common-sense view of the world. This is a very big issue, so let us simplify it by considering one central concept from each approach – diminishing marginal utility, the diminishing marginal rate of substitution, and rationality and consistency of behaviour. All of these concepts contain an important element of truth, so that again there would seem to be little to choose among the three approaches.

Finally we might wish to evaluate a theory in accordance with the extent to which it aids one's understanding of economic processes. The application of indifference theory enables both the income and substitution effects of a price change to be explored in detail. The author believes this to be an advantage of this approach. However he would understand why others might consider this advantage to be outweighed by the greater simplicity of the alternative approaches.

The Position of the Demand Curve

We now move to the second major topic covered in this chapter, namely the factors which influence the position of the demand curve. Referring to figure 23.10, we are concerned with factors which result in either an increase in demand (a shift from D_1 to D_2), or a decrease in demand (a shift from D_1 to D_3).

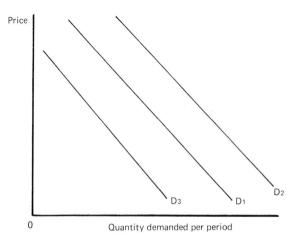

Figure 23.10 A Change in Demand

*The Conditions of Demand**
A shift of the demand curve – in either direction – indicates a change in the conditions of demand. It would be impossible to discuss all the factors which might influence demand, i.e. all the conditions of demand. However, we examine the most important, beginning with income.

INCOME
A change in real national income is likely to affect the demand for almost every product. However, the response of demand to a change in income varies from product to product. A precise measure of this response is the income elasticity of demand (IED), defined as:

$$\frac{\Delta Q}{Q} \div \frac{\Delta Y}{Y}$$

where Q is the quantity demanded per period
     Y is national income, and
     Δ denotes a small change in the variable
In table 23.3 where it is assumed that national income (Y) increases by 10 per

Table 23.3
Income Elasticity of Demand

Product	Quantity Demanded Period t	Period t+1	I.E.D.
A	100	120	2.0
B	100	105	0.5
C	100	100	0.0
D	100	95	−0.5.

cent between periods t and t+1, IED is calculated for four hypothetical products. Goods for which IED is positive, i.e. products A and B, are called *normal goods*. Within this category, if IED exceeds one – product A – demand is said to be income elastic. If IED is between zero and one – product B – demand is said to be income inelastic. If demand does not change following a change in income – product C – IED is zero. Finally, goods whose IED is negative – product D – are called *inferior goods*.

We showed in Chapter 21 that as the national income of the U.K. increased, the volume of sales of most products increased. This would suggest that normal goods are more common than inferior goods, i.e. that in figure 23.10 a change in income is most likely to result in a shift from D_1 to D_2. However it is important to remember that demand is influenced by many factors in addition to income, and we cannot draw any definite conclusions about elasticity from the sales and output figures given in Chapter 21. In order to estimate IED such figures have to be adjusted to take account, as far as possible, of the influence on demand of these other factors. The technique most commonly used for this purpose is multiple regression analysis. Table 23.4 gives estimates of IED that have been derived by means of this technique.

---

*Some writers differ from the approach that we have adopted in that they treat price as one of the conditions of demand.

Table 23.4
    Estimated Income Elasticities of Demand

Product	Income elasticity of demand
Refrigerators	0.96
Washing machines	0.74
Motor cars	0.69
Television sets	0.50

Source: J. S. Cramer, *The Ownership of Major Consumer Durables* (Cambridge: Cambridge University Press, 1962).

It should be emphasized that these values of IED relate only to the periods studied. Other periods might yield different values. Indeed there are strong reasons for believing that this is so. We showed in Chapter 21 that the demand for consumer durables in the U.K. appears to have grown more rapidly than the demand for foodstuffs. But we also pointed out that eventually the market for a particular durable product, say a cooker, will become saturated – all households who want a cooker have one. Thereafter demand is mainly for replacement purposes. Clearly IED is likely to fall once this point has been reached.

Indeed one can find examples of products whose IED becomes negative after a certain point, i.e. the good changes from being a normal to an inferior good. This is especially likely to happen when a more expensive substitute exists which more people are able to afford as income increases. In the U.K. the demand for bicycles increased for some time with increasing income, but then fell as many people switched to motor-cycles and cars.

We have been concerned in this section with changes in aggregate national income. But a given change in national income might, of course, take many different forms. The implications of this are discussed in the following section.

THE DISTRIBUTION OF INCOME

The distribution of income may change as national income changes or while national income remains constant. The relative incomes of different sectors may alter, e.g. the share of the national income going to wage and salary earners may rise while that going to companies falls. This is likely to alter the demand for both consumer and investment goods. Or the change may occur within a sector, e.g. the share of the wage and salary bill going to the lowest paid may rise while that going to the highest paid falls. Different income groups have different consumption patterns, as shown in figure 23.11 which is based on data from the 1975 Family Expenditure Survey. Consequently a change in income distribution will cause a change in the overall pattern of consumption.

CHANGES IN POPULATION

A change in total population usually leads to a change in national income, with the consequences discussed above. In addition, even if total population is constant, changes may occur in its structure, with important implications for the pattern of demand. For example an increase in the proportion of children leads to an increase in the demand for baby food and clothes and subsequently for pop records, cosmetics, etc. Conversely, an increase in the proportion of elderly citizens may lead to an increase in the demand for false teeth, hearing aids, bungalows, etc.

THE INTRODUCTION OF NEW PRODUCTS

We noted in Chapter 21 that the rapid increase in the demand for consumer

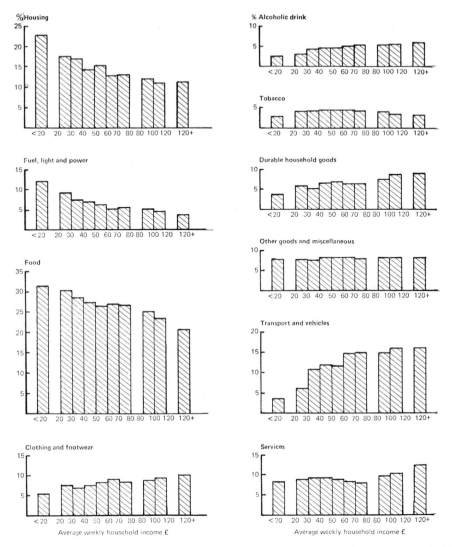

Figure 23.11 Expenditure on Product Group as Percentage of Total Household Expenditure

durables was partly due to the fact that manufacturers have introduced a large number of new and improved products. Other illustrations can be drawn from other product fields. For example the demand for frozen foodstuffs as a whole has been influenced by extensions in the range supplied by manufacturers. Many manufacturers started with such basic products as peas and fish fingers and subsequently introduced complete dinners, dishes of foreign origin, etc.

The introduction of new products and improved versions of existing products means that one has to be very careful in applying demand analysis. In principle, a series of demand curves for different periods should relate to a given product with unchanged characteristics; in practice this requirement may be difficult to fulfil.

THE PRICE AND AVAILABILITY OF SUBSTITUTES

As noted in the first part of the chapter, the demand for a product is influenced by the price and availability of substitutes. The effect of a change in price is measured by the cross elasticity of demand, which relates the percentage change in demand for one product to the percentage change in price of another product:

$$\text{Cross elasticity of demand} = \frac{\Delta Q_A}{Q_A} \div \frac{\Delta P_B}{P_B}$$

where A and B are two products
　　Q and P denote the initial quantity demanded and price, and
　　Δ denotes a small change in the variable.

Some estimated values of cross elasticity of demand are presented in table 23.5. The bigger the value, the closer substitutes the two products are considered to be.

Table 23.5
Estimated Cross Elasticity of Demand for Butter

Cross elasticity with respect to price of:	
Flour	−0.23
Margarine	0.10
Cakes and biscuits	0.59
Carcass meat	0.56

Source: R. Stone, *Measurement of Consumers' Expenditure and Behaviour in the United Kingdom, 1920–1938* (Cambridge: Cambridge University Press, 1954).

The availability of substitutes is especially important in relation to the introduction of new products. For example the introduction of colour television sets led to a fall in the demand for monochrome sets. (Incidentally it is interesting to note that some manufacturers responded by introducing an improved range of smaller, portable televisions, with the result that the total demand for all monochrome sets actually increased for some time.) Taking an example from a different market, the decline of the traditional fish and chip shop has been hastened by the extension of alternative quick-food outlets, serving hamburgers, chicken, Chinese food, etc.

THE PRICE AND AVAILABILITY OF COMPLEMENTS

Here the reverse process applies. Complementarity is said to exist when an increase in the quantity of one product sold leads to an increase in the demand for another product. The effect of a change in price can again be measured by the cross elasticity of demand, although a fall in the price of A (and hence an increase in the quantity bought) now leads to an increase in the quantity of B demanded.

The greater the degree of complementarity, the higher the value of the cross elasticity of demand. Examples of pairs of complementary products are bread and butter, cricket bats and balls, shoes and shoe laces, cars and petrol.*

---

*Some writers use the term joint demand as being synonymous with complementary demand, while others reserve the term for products, or factors, which must be used together.

THE PROMOTIONAL ACTIVITIES OF SUPPLIERS

A wide variety of activities can be included under this heading, including advertising, personal visits by salesmen and, possibly, some forms of packaging. The promotional activities whose success in stimulating demand come most readily to mind are, perhaps, the long-running advertising campaigns such as 'Drinka-Pinta-Milka-Day', and 'Guinness is Good for You'. But other activities less visible to the general public may be just as effective. Much of the promotional activity devoted to ethical pharmaceutical products comprises expenditure on communication to doctors, including visits by professionally qualified representatives.

THE TASTES OF CONSUMERS

Considerable fluctuations in the demand for some products result from changes in consumers' tastes. When mini-skirts were in fashion the demand for cloth decreased but the demand for nylon tights increased. Subsequently, as hem-lines dropped, the demand for cloth increased and the demand for tights decreased. (There was clearly a substitution effect here.) There has been a long-standing controversy as to whether or not the tastes of consumers can be changed by the promotional activities of suppliers, and especially by advertising. Fortunately we need not enter into this controversy since we have included both factors in our list of determinants of demand.

THE DEMAND FOR INVESTMENT GOODS

Many of the factors listed above can affect the demand for investment or capital goods. However, as we indicated in Chapter 6 during our discussion of the acceleration principle, a change in demand for investment goods often originates in a change in demand for consumption goods.

INTER-INDUSTRY FLOWS

The likely effect of a change in the output of one industry on other industries can be estimated from an input-output table or matrix. An extract from such a matrix is shown in table 23.6. If we look first at the rows of the matrix we see that the food industry is by far the most important customer of the agricultural industry, accounting in 1972 for almost half of the value of its sales. Consequently a fall of 10 per cent in the output of the food industry would imply that, other things remaining equal, the demand for agricultural products would fall by about 5 per

Table 23.6

Industry by Industry Input–Output Matrix (1972, £mn)

Sales by	Agriculture	Mining	Food	Purchases by Mineral oil refining	Chemicals	Total output
Agriculture	+	0	1,387	0	8	2,886
Mining	4	+	1	2	22	1,293
Food, etc	578	1	+	1	75	6,775
Mineral oil refining	54	21	51	+	148	1,305
Chemicals	193	36	103	44	+	3,311
Total inputs of goods/ services	1,466	587	4,695	1,141	1,908	

Source: *Economic Trends.*

cent. Furthermore if the agricultural industry were then to reduce its demand for inputs by 5 per cent this would imply a fall in demand for the output of other industries, especially food and chemicals.

Observation of the columns of the matrix allows us to identify the likely effects on one industry of an increase in the price (or an interruption in supplies) of the products of another industry. For example, almost 8 per cent of the total cost of goods and services purchased by the chemicals industry in 1972 comprised expenditure on mineral oil, while the corresponding figure for the food industry was only just over 1 per cent. The rapid increase in the price of oil after 1972 clearly had more serious implications for chemicals than for food manufacturing.

The Demand for Factors of Production

Since factors of production are demanded not for their own sake, but in order that suppliers may be able to meet demands for goods and services, the demand for factor inputs is known as derived demand.

The basic determinants of the demand for inputs are, of course, the various factors which determine the demand for the goods and services in whose production the inputs are utilized. The impact on factor markets of a change in demand in a product market depends mainly upon the proportion of the factor that is engaged in the production of that product. If we look at the market for labour we see that a very high proportion of miners in the U.K. are employed in the coal mining industry. Consequently the decline in the demand for coal that occurred in the U.K. was translated more or less directly into a reduced demand for miners. On the other hand unskilled workers are employed in a much wider range of industries. Consequently a decline in any one industry will have much less impact on the demand for such workers. These differences in impact can also be found in other factor markets.

In addition to the forces transmitted from product markets, there are two other major influences on the demand for factor inputs. The first is the productivity of a factor, i.e. the volume of output per unit of input. The importance of productivity can again be illustrated most easily with reference to labour, although the same principle applies to other inputs. Let us examine first the possible consequences of a fall in labour productivity, i.e. a rise in the cost of labour per unit of output.

Two separate situations may exist. The first is where the employer is unable to vary the proportions of the various inputs employed, i.e. where the technical coefficients of production are fixed. In this situation an increase in labour cost will lead to an increase in the cost and price of the product. Less of the product will be demanded and therefore the employer will reduce his demand for labour and for all other inputs.

The second situation is where it is possible to vary the proportions of the various inputs. Here the employer will replace labour, whose cost has risen, by other inputs. Therefore the demand for labour will fall because of a substitution effect. Of course the employer may still find that his total cost per unit of output rises. If this happens there will be a further reduction in the demand for labour transmitted from the product market. The demand for other inputs will also be reduced. However in the case of these other inputs we cannot say whether this effect will outweigh or be outweighed by the substitution effect.

This process can also operate in reverse. A fall in the cost of an input may induce a producer to substitute this input for others. At the same time a reduction in his total cost per unit, and hence in the price of his product, may lead to an increase in demand for the product. If this effect outweighs the substitution effect, the demand for all inputs will increase; if it does not, demand will increase only for the input whose cost has fallen.

The ultimate in the process of substitution in factor markets is where technical change results in the demand for an input disappearing entirely. Such dramatic changes normally occur only when 'input' is defined very narrowly, e.g. one metal may be replaced by a newly discovered substitute having superior qualities. Even here substitution in all uses would usually occur only over a long period.

Summary and Conclusions

We began this chapter by examining various models which indicate how consumers might respond to a change in the relative prices of products. We showed that although the models use different techniques and concepts they all arrive at the conclusion that in most instances demand curves slope down from left to right. Since these models are deductive, their conclusions about behaviour depend upon the assumptions built into the model. Moreover, these conclusions remain general. Specific measures of demand, such as values of elasticity, must be derived from observation of purchasing behaviour. Some examples of these measures were presented at the end of the first part of the chapter.

The labour theory of value is yet another approach to the explanation of relative prices. We have not explored this approach since it has one very great deficiency. It fails to explain why a commodity with a given cost of production may be sold at different prices under different demand conditions. Readers who wish to acquaint themselves with this theory will find it discussed in a number of elementary textbooks.*

In the second part of the chapter we discussed the most important influences on the position of the demand curve,–income, population, tastes of consumers This discussion was illustrated by additional empirical data, drawn mainly from the U.K. economy.

ESSAY QUESTIONS

1 State the law of diminishing marginal utility and show how it can help to explain the shape of demand curves.

2 Using indifference theory analyse the effect on the quantity of a product demanded of a change in (a) income, (b) the price of the product, (c) the price of a substitute.

3 Discuss the relative advantages and disadvantages of any two theories which attempt to explain the shape of demand curves.

4 Define price elasticity of demand and illustrate its relevance to decisions taken by (a) producers, (b) the government.

5 What types of decision might be improved by information concerning the value of each of the following: price, income and cross elasticity of demand?

6 What factors might you expect to cause a reduction in the demand for the following products: bread, ice-cream, gas, petrol, public transport?

7 'The most important influence on the current pattern of demand is the activity of producers, past and present.' Discuss.

8 'The demand for factors of production can be explained in exactly the same way as the demand for final products.' Discuss.

9 'The test of a theory's validity is its usefulness in illuminating observed reality.' Discuss this statement with reference to theories of demand.

*There are, for example, several references in P. A. Samuelson, *Economics* (New York: McGraw-Hill, 1975).

EXERCISES

23.1 *A hypothetical utility schedule*

Apples		Pears	
Quantity Bought per week (kilos	Total Utility (Utils)	Quantity Bought per week (kilos)	Total Utility (Utils)
1	100	1	100
2	175	2	175
3	225	3	225
4	265	4	265
5	300	5	300
6	325	6	325
7	320	7	320

(i) Which combinations of apples and pears would be consistent with the maximization of the consumer's utility when (a) a kilo of apples cost the same as a kilo of pears, (b) a kilo of apples cost twice as much as a kilo of pears? (ii) How many apples and pears would be consumed if they were free? (iii) Explain carefully what, if anything, can be deduced from the answers to question (i) about (a) the shape and (b) the position, of the individual's demand curves for apples and pears.

23.2 Calculate the income elasticity of demand of products A and B given the following information:

Year	National income	Sales of A	Sales of B
1976	£25 billions	100,000	500,000
1977	£26 billions	105,000	400,000

23.3 You are told that the income elasticity of demand for a certain product is unity, and that its current level of sales is 20,000 units a year. Further, it is expected that in 10 years time national income will be 50 per cent above the present level. What would you expect the annual sales of this product to be in 10 years time?

23.4 The following data relates to the quantity sold of a number of products in each of two years. Given that national income rose by 10 per cent between years 1 and 2, for which of these products is IED elastic, unity, inelastic, zero and negative?

Year				Sales of Product			
	A	B	C	D	E	F	G
1	18,000	900	650	9,000	750	910	500
2	19,000	1,000	730	9,000	825	900	525

23.5 (i) Discuss, with reference to table 23.7, 'the conditions of demand for foodstuffs'. (ii) What changes in trends in food consumption might you expect to occur over the subsequent decade?

23.6 Outline what you would consider to be the major determinants of the changes in production in each of the industries shown in table 23.8.

23.7 Calculate the price elasticity of demand for the following products:

	Product A		Product B		Product C	
	Price	Demand	Price	Demand	Price	Demand
Period 1	£1.00	100,000	£8	640	£1.00	1,000
Period 2	£0.99	102,000	£9	480	£0.99	1,010

Table 23.7

Estimated Food Consumption by all Households in Great Britain
(ounces per person per week)

	1965	1968	1971	1974	1975	1976
Cheese	3.20	3.41	3.63	3.74	3.79	3.79
Butter	6.10	6.14	5.53	5.61	5.63	5.16
Margarine	3.04	2.81	3.15	2.60	2.60	3.06
Sugar	17.56	16.35	15.80	13.03	11.29	12.20
Beef and veal	8.08	7.76	7.96	7.41	8.32	7.62
Pork	2.80	2.53	3.04	3.20	2.73	2.89
Poultry and cooked chicken	3.51	4.81	4.92	5.18	5.73	6.00
Fish, fresh and processed	4.34	4.02	3.61	2.76	2.76	2.67
Fish and fish products, frozen	0.65	0.81	0.91	0.96	1.05	1.26
Potatoes	53.24	51.92	49.18	45.66	43.90	35.30
Apples	7.36	6.39	7.80	7.08	6.77	7.44
Bread	40.60	38.31	35.76	33.50	33.67	33.17
Cakes and pastries	4.85	4.68	4.04	3.51	3.12	2.85
Tea	2.61	2.59	2.39	2.24	2.18	2.21
Instant coffee	0.26	0.36	0.44	0.51	0.50	0.51

Source: *Annual Abstract of Statistics* (H.M.S.O., 1977).

Table 23.8

Index Numbers of Production at Constant Factor Cost

	1968	1969	1970	1971	1972	1973	1974	1975	1976
Consumer goods industries:									
Cars, etc.	106.8	100.9	100.0	108.3	118.5	110.8	97.1	80.2	82.2
Other durables	92.6	96.9	100.0	106.6	121.8	141.0	134.9	125.6	123.5
Clothing and footwear, etc.	99.1	100.3	100.0	103.8	105.9	111.2	108.3	107.9	108.2
Food, drink and tobacco	96.0	98.5	100.0	110.7	105.1	109.3	110.6	109.0	110.2
Investment goods industries:									
Electrical	93.3	97.3	100.0	99.7	98.1	109.1	105.3	107.5	106.5
Intermediate goods industries:									
Fuels	97.6	98.7	100.0	103.0	102.0	109.9	106.2	108.9	94.2
Materials	97.8	100.5	100.0	97.8	100.6	109.5	105.1	113.2	99.3

Source: *National Income and Expenditure* (H.M.S.O., 1977).

23.8 For which of the following products is demand (a) price elastic, (b) price inelastic?

	Product A		Product B		Product C		Product D	
	Price	Demand	Price	Demand	Price	Demand	Price	Demand
Period 1	£20	100	£70	110	£0.05	70	£1.10	700
Period 2	£40	70	£63	123	£0.06	70	£0.99	800

23.9 Mr. Greave is managing director of a prominent engineering firm which makes vast quantities of three basic products – springs, clips and bolts. Worried by increases in his costs of production he wished to increase his prices, and favoured an across-the-board price increase of about 5 per cent on all three products. However the company's chief economist, John Slater, to whom Greave turned for advice, was rather unhappy about this proposal. An examination of the firm's sales records suggested that the sales of some products were far more sensitive than others to changes in price. He estimated price elasticities to be as follows: springs 0.2, clips 1.0, bolts 1.5. What modification would you suggest to Mr. Greave's proposal?

23.10 The following figures relate to estimates of demand elasticities for butter for the period 1921–38, derived by Professor Stone:

Income elasticity	0.37
Price elasticity	−0.43
Price elasticity with respect to:	
Flour	−0.23
Margarine	0.10
Cakes and biscuits	0.59
Carcass meat	0.56

(a) How would you explain the values obtained by Stone? What differences might you expect to find if the values were re-calculated for the post-war period?

23.11 Butter consumption increased from 372,000 tons to 402,000 tons a year between 1963 and 1967. It marked time in 1968, fell to 392,000 in 1969 and held at this level in 1970. Conversely a downward trend in margarine which began in 1964 was reversed in 1969, and held steady in 1970 at 203,000 tons, or 3.5 per cent above the 1968 level.

One factor which may affect consumption of these products is the level of income. An indication of the influence of income is given by figures from the 1969 Family Expenditure Survey, showing the average weekly expenditures on butter and margarine by families of two adults and one child, with different income levels.

Weekly Expenditure (pence)	£10 and under £20	£20 and under £25	£25 and under £30	£30 and under £40	£40 or more
Butter	15.5	15.0	16.8	16.2	19.5
Margarine	5.5	4.5	4.0	4.5	3.0

Household weekly income

N.B. The original figures have been converted into decimal equivalents.

A second important influence on the relative shares of the total market accounted for by butter and margarine is their respective prices. Since the two products are made from different raw materials their prices do not usually change in line. Take, for example, the 12 months from October 1970. At the beginning of this period the average butter price was 15p–16p a pound, or about 5p above average margarine prices. Within these averages, however, there was a grey area where some margarine and butter prices overlapped. Both prices then began to move up with butter showing the greater rise. By October 1971, with average butter prices around 25p a pound, and margarine prices averaging 12p, the differential had more than doubled. Even the cheapest butter was about 7p a pound above the most expensive margarine prices – the grey area had vanished.

An important recent development in this market was the introduction of soft margarine in tubs. The pioneer was Blue Band, first sold in its new form in 1967, and launched nationally in 1968. The success of the new product can be judged from the fact that whereas in 1966 old-style Blue Band accounted for probably less than 10 per cent of all margarine sales, by 1970 the new version had captured around 24 per cent of the margarine market. Similar products have been introduced by Kraft and the Co-op, and there is now a lengthening list of soft margarines appearing under distributors' own labels.

Soft margarines have the advantage that they can be spread 'straight from the refrigerator', thus gaining an innovative edge over butter. Furthermore, this has enabled them to lose, at least in the eyes of many consumers, the image of being an imitative or second-best product. Prior to the arrival of new Blue Band the best-selling margarine was Stork, which had relied for decades on its 'Can't tell the difference' message, followed by Summer County, which reassured people that it contained 10 per cent butter. Since then Summer County has seen its share of the margarine market shrink to around 5 per cent, while Stork, admittedly still the best seller, has lost a good 7 percentage points.

The soft margarines are being successfully sold as luxury products. The heavy advertising which surrounds Blue Band, for instance, depicts a wealthy American housewife using it – she could obviously afford to buy butter.
Source: Turvey R. *Demand and Supply* (Allen and Unwin); K. van Musschenbrock (*Financial Times*, 5.6.71).

On the basis of the above discussion, evaluate the most important determinants of the demand for butter and margarine.
23.12 With reference to tables 23.9 and 23.10, discuss (i) 'Substitution in the energy market', (ii) 'the derived demand for coal'.

Table 23.9
Inland Energy Consumption (mn. tons of coal or coal equivalent)

	1971	1972	1973	1974	1975	1976
Coal	137	121	131	116	118	120
Petroleum	149	160	162	150	134	132
Natural gas	28	40	44	52	55	58
Nuclear energy	10	11	10	12	11	13
Hydroelectricity	2	2	2	2	2	2
Total	326	333	348	332	320	325

Source: *Monthly Digest of Statistics* (H.M.S.O., Sept. 1977).

Table 23.10
Inland Consumption of Coal (weekly averages, 000 tons)

	1971	1972	1973	1974	1975	1976
Collieries	30	26	26	24	23	21
Power stations	1,379	1,262	1,454	1,269	1,412	1,473
Coke ovens	446	387	414	349	361	367
Gas works	35	11	10	2	—	—
Other conversion industries	85	86	68	72	77	65
Total fuel producers	1,975	1,772	1,972	1,716	1,873	1,926
Industry	300	221	229	210	183	170
Domestic	326	276	275	259	220	205
Public admin., commerce, etc.	66	57	49	47	37	39
Total final users	692	554	553	516	440	414
Grand total	2,667	2,326	2,525	2,232	2,313	2,340

Source: *Monthly Digest of Statistics* (H.M.S.O., Sept. 1977).

OBJECTIVE TEST QUESTIONS: SET 7

1 A demand curve indicates the

   A   quantities that were demanded in past periods
   B   quantities that were demanded at various prices in past periods
   C   quantities that would be demanded at various prices
   D   quantities that would be demanded at various prices in a given period
   E   quantities that would be demanded at various prices in different periods.

2 If the demand curve slopes down and the supply curve slopes up to the right, a fall in demand causes

   A   an increase in both price and quantity traded
   B   an increase in price and a fall in quantity traded
   C   a fall in price and an increase in quantity traded
   D   a fall in both price and quantity traded
   E   a fall in quantity traded, price being unchanged.

3 In order to maximize his satisfaction from a given level of income a consumer should spend his income in such a way that the

   A   total utility derived from each product is equalized
   B   marginal utility derived from each product is maximized
   C   marginal utility derived from each product is equalized
   D   marginal utility derived from each product is zero
   E   ratios of the marginal utilities to the prices of each product are equalized.

4 In drawing a demand curve we make all of the following assumptions except that the

   A   prices of all substitutes remain unchanged
   B   prices of all complements remain unchanged
   C   availability of both complements and substitutes remain unchanged
   D   consumer's real income remains unchanged
   E   consumer's money income remains unchanged.

5 The shift in the demand curve from D_1 to D_2 in figure 23.12 is *least* likely to have been caused by

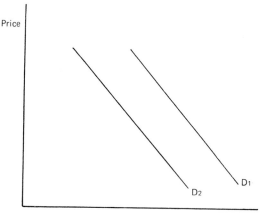

Quantity demanded per period

Figure 23.12

A a fall in national income
B a fall in the price of substitutes
C an increase in the price of complements
D an increase in population
E a redistribution of income from low to high income groups.

6 In figure 23.13 the demand curve for peas is *least* likely to have shifted from
   D_1 to D_2 because of

A an increase in the price of beans
B a fall in the price of peas
C an increase in population
D an increase in national income
E an increase in advertising by firms selling canned peas.

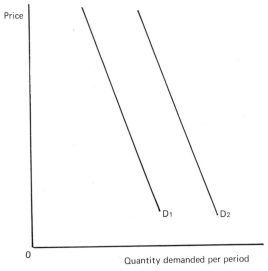

Figure 23.13

7 Some resources are allocated by means of the price mechanism in a

1 fully planned economy
2 mixed economy
3 market economy.

8 A demand curve might slope down from right to left if

1 consumers see the price of the product as an indicator of its quality
2 the purchase of the product represents conspicuous consumption
3 the product is a Giffen good.

9 The consumption of a product whose price is zero will be such that the

1 marginal utility derived from the product is zero
2 total utility derived from the product is at a maximum
3 marginal utility derived from the product equals the marginal utility derived from all other products.

10

Product X		Product Y	
Consumption (units)	*Marginal utility* (utils)	*Consumption* (units)	*Marginal utility* (utils)
1	100	1	60
2	60	2	50
3	30	3	30

If product X cost twice as much per unit as product Y, which of the following combinations of purchases would be consistent with the maximization of the consumer's utility?

1   3 units of X plus 3 units of Y
2   2 units of X plus 2 units of Y
3   1 unit of X plus 2 units of Y.

11   An assumption that the consumer is able to measure utility or satisfaction cardinally is required by the theory of value which embodies

1   the marginal utility concept
2   indifference curve analysis
3   the revealed preference concept.

12   From the indifference curve shown in figure 23.14 we can conclude that the

1   combinations of products represented by points A and B yield equal satisfaction
2   marginal rate of substitution is equal at points A and B
3   combination of products represented by A yields more satisfaction than the combination represented by C.

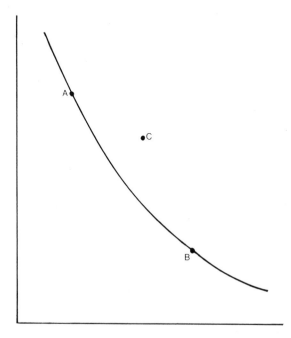

Figure 23.14

13 In figure 23.15 the movement of the budget line from AB to A¹B could have been caused by
    1 an increase in the consumer's money income
    2 a decrease in the price of pears
    3 an increase in the price of apples.

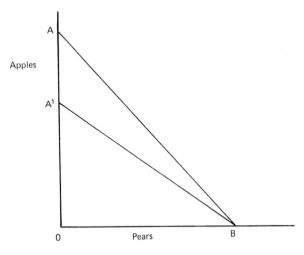

Figure 23.15

14 In figure 23.16 AB and A¹B¹ represent a consumer's budget line in two periods and IC represents his income consumption curve. From the diagram we can deduce that
    1 oranges are a normal good
    2 apples are a normal good
    3 the price of oranges relative to the price of apples remained constant from one period to the next.

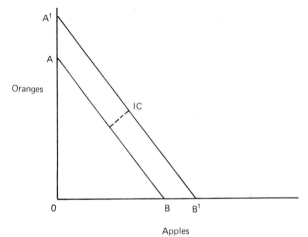

Figure 23.16

15   In figure 23.17, the shift in the demand curve for labour from D_1 to D_2 could have been caused by
  1   a fall in the productivity of labour
  2   a fall in the productivity of inputs other than labour
  3   an increase in national income.

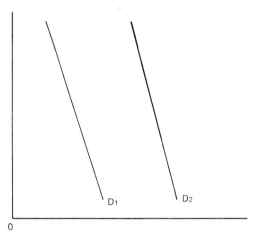

0

Figure 23.17

16   In fully planned economies barter is an important form of exchange.
    In fully planned economies resources are not allocated by means of the price mechanism.

17   An increase in demand may cause either an increase or a decrease in the quantity traded.
    The effect of a change in demand on the quantity traded depends upon the shape of the supply curve.

18   An increase in demand may cause either an increase or a decrease in price.
    The effect of a change in demand on price depends upon the shape of the supply curve.

19   Indifference analysis shows that a fall in the price of a product always leads to an increase in its consumption.
    A fall in the price of a product has both an income and a substitution effect.

20   A fall in the price of an inferior good will lead to a fall in the quantity demanded.
    The income elasticity of demand of an inferior good is negative.

TRUE/FALSE

  1   Resources are allocated entirely by administrative means in a mixed economy.
  2   A supply curve indicates the various quantities that were supplied at different prices.
  3   A supply curve always slopes up from left to right.
  4   A decrease in the price of a product may cause either a decrease or an increase in the quantity demanded.

5 Total utility is maximized where marginal utility is zero.
6 An ordinal measure of utility implies that a consumer can say by how much he prefers one combination of products to another.
7 All Giffen goods are also inferior goods.
8 Products for which the income elasticity of demand is less than one are known as inferior goods.
9 The term 'derived demand' refers to the demand for factors of production.
10 An increase in the cost of one input may lead to either an increase or a decrease in the demand for other inputs.

CHAPTER TWENTY-FOUR

Supply

Introduction

WE showed in Chapter 22 that the price of a product or input is determined by the interaction of demand and supply. Having examined demand in Chapter 23 we now consider the factors influencing supply.

This chapter follows the pattern of the previous one in that we first discuss the factors which influence the *shape* of the supply curve, and subsequently examine the determinants of the *position* of the curve.

As noted in Chapter 22, a supply curve indicates the various quantities of a product (or input) that would be supplied at various prices in a given time period. Supply curves may have different shapes, as indicated in figure 24.1. In order to explain the circumstances in which the curve is most likely to assume each of these shapes we must analyse the relationship between output and cost. We consider first the situation where the scale of organization is given.

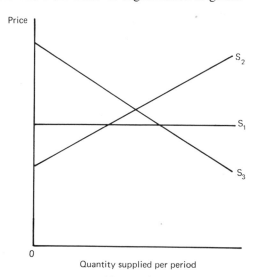

Figure 24.1 Alternative Supply Curves

The Relationship Between Output and Cost at a Given Scale of Organization

The scale of organization refers to the maximum rate of output that the firm could achieve. The larger the scale, the greater the volume of output the firm could produce in a given period – say a week or month. Whatever the scale of organization an ultimate limit to output is set by the fact that there is at least one input, one factor of production, whose quantity is limited. The longer the time period considered, the greater the opportunity for increasing the quantity of the limiting input, i.e. for increasing the scale of organization.

Some writers make a distinction between the short run, in which at least one factor is fixed, and the long-run in which all factors are variable in quantity. This distinction corresponds to our distinction between a given and a changing scale of organization. We have not used the more traditional terminology because the phrases short and long run (or short and long period) may be interpreted as referring to fixed periods of time. As we shall see, such an interpretation would not be justified. A change in the scale of organization may be accomplished far more quickly in some instances than in others.

The most likely source of the limit to output is an inability, in the given time period, to increase the quantity of capital inputs – land, factories, plant and equipment. However this is not the only possible source. A firm may have spare capacity in plant and machinery, and may be prevented from increasing its output because it is unable to recruit additional labour.

When planning its scale of organization a firm will normally take into account its expected volume of output and sales. Since these cannot be predicted precisely, firms often instal capacity in excess of their best estimate of output. In this way they reduce the possibility that, should demand turn out to be higher than expected, they may have to turn away regular customers, with a consequent loss of goodwill. Similarly they will be in a better position to gain customers from rival suppliers should the capacity of those rivals be insufficient to meet their peak demand.

Each firm has to balance these potential benefits against the costs incurred in installing the additional capacity. The balance is most likely to swing towards installing additional capacity under the following circumstances:

(a) There are no important physical differences between the products of rival suppliers, so that ability to supply becomes very important.
(b) Demand in the market is increasing, so that even if the excess capacity is not utilized in the near future, it is likely to be required eventually.
(c) There are indivisibilities in inputs; the alternative to installing capacity in excess of expected output may be to instal capacity less than expected output.

Having explored the possible relationships between capacity and *expected* output, we now examine the behaviour of costs as actual output changes. An important distinction is between the costs of those inputs whose quantity is fixed during the relevant time period and the costs of those inputs whose quantity can be varied. We deal with each of these in turn.

Fixed Cost
As we indicated above, the inputs whose quantity (and hence cost) is most likely to be fixed are land, buildings, plant and equipment. Since the total cost of these inputs is fixed, the average cost, the cost per unit produced, falls as output increases. In figure 24.2 the average fixed cost declines steadily, beyond E, the expected output, up to L, the ultimate limit. The dotted line indicates that to increase output beyond L would require an increase in the scale of organization. (As additional plant, equipment, etc., was installed, average fixed cost would rise but then decline once more as output increased.)

Variable Cost
Inputs whose quantity can usually be varied as output changes at a given scale of organization include direct labour and materials. In practice it may not be poss-

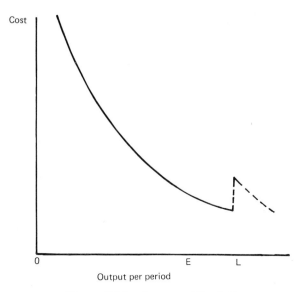

Figure 24.2 Average Fixed Cost

ible to change the quantity of these inputs, and especially labour, exactly in line with changes in output. Therefore average variable cost usually has a stepped function, as shown by the dotted line in figure 24.3. However, in order to simplify the analysis we 'smooth' the curve, as shown by the unbroken line in that diagram.

It will be noticed that average variable cost is constant over a wide range of output, but that it rises slightly as output approaches the ultimate limit. This may occur for several reasons. For example a rise in labour costs per unit of output may occur as additional, less efficient, workers are recruited in order to increase output beyond the expected level, or because of an increase in overtime working at higher wage rates. An increase in material costs may occur because of higher scrap rates resulting from increased machine speeds.

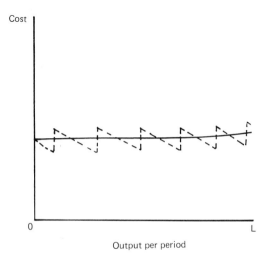

Figure 24.3 Average Variable Cost

Semi-Variable Costs
There are many inputs whose quantity can be varied, but not precisely in line with changes in output, and whose costs can therefore be classified as semi-variable. Examples are the cost of fuel and power, and of indirect materials and labour. (We have seen that even direct labour costs, normally given as an example of a variable cost, may in practice be semi-variable.)

In order to simplify the analysis we assume that semi-variable costs can be split into a fixed and a variable component. In this way we can continue to operate with two categories of cost. (Additional categories are introduced at a later stage – see Chapter 25.)

Total Cost
Since we have defined costs as either fixed or variable it follows that average total cost (ATC) at any level of output, is obtaining by adding together average fixed cost (AFC) and average variable cost (AVC). Figure 24.4 shows that at first ATC

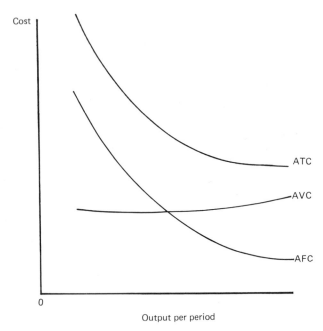

Figure 24.4   Average Fixed, Variable, Total Cost

falls as output increases. Eventually a point is reached (perhaps round about the expected level of output) beyond which ATC becomes more or less constant. This occurs because over this range of output a fall in AFC is roughly balanced by a rise in AVC.

The Relationship between Output and Cost as the Scale of Organization Changes
In figure 24.4 ATC indicates how cost is likely to vary with output at a given scale of organization. In figure 24.5 three average (total) cost curves are shown, each relating to a particular scale of organization. At any output up to M, the lowest average cost is attained with the smallest scale of organization (giving rise to AC_1). Beyond M average cost would be lower if a larger scale of organization (giving

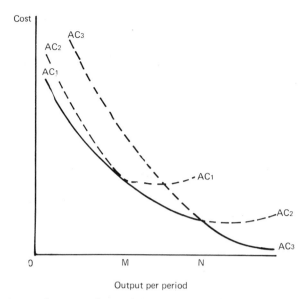

Figure 24.5 Average Cost with a Changing Scale of Organization

rise to AC_3) were adopted. Finally, beyond N average cost can be reduced by adopting an even larger scale of organization (giving rise to AC_3).

The lowest cost that could be attained at each output, given that the firm was always able to adopt the most appropriate scale of organization, is indicated by the unbroken line. Up to output M this curve slopes down because fixed factors are being utilized more fully, as discussed in the previous section. Beyond M the fall in average cost also reflects the fact that at a bigger scale of organization economies of scale arise.*

Internal Economies of Scale
These economies can be grouped into several categories.

TECHNICAL ECONOMIES
Technical economies mainly relate to the scale of the production unit. Cost savings may arise because of changes in physical dimensions. One example is where cost depends upon area, and capacity or output upon volume, e.g. gas storage, oil tankers. In these instances an increase in capacity is accompanied by a less than proportionate increase in the cost of construction (see table 24.1).

A similar example is where the capacity of an engine or motor increases more rapidly than the costs of building and operating the engine – this can apply both in factories and in transportation.

Technical economies may arise from the introduction of a different technology, such as the continuous strip mill in steel and plate-glass manufacture.

The automatic control of production processes has become increasingly common in recent years. The cost of electronic control equipment is often high, and considerable economies can be achieved by spreading this cost over a higher out-

* These internal economies can be distinguished from external economies which exist when an expansion in the scale of a whole industry results in a fall in costs in individual firms, even if the scale of these firms is unchanged, or where some operations, previously undertaken by individual firms, are carried out more efficiently by a central organization.

Table 24.1

Cost of Low Pressure Gas Storage

Holder capacity (000 cubic feet)	Capital cost (£000)	Capital cost (£ per 000 cubic feet)
10	6	600
20	8	400
40	14	350
60	17	280
100	20	200
250	32	130
500	50	100
2,250	197	90
5,000	350	70

Source: R. S. Edwards and H. Townsend, *Business Enterprise* (London: Macmillan 1959).

put. Automatic data-processing equipment, and especially the computer, has also become more widely used and again substantial reductions in the average cost of equipment can be obtained by increases in scale. In this instance, the scale of the entire organization, i.e. the company, may be more important than the scale of individual production units.

Where technical economies involve the installation of more equipment, the *division of labour* – the specialization by each worker on a narrow range of tasks – is likely to be enhanced. However the growth of a firm could lead to an increase in the division of labour quite apart from any change in technical economies. The bigger the firm the greater the opportunity for each worker to specialize in those tasks for which he is best fitted. Specialization can increase productivity because it allows two principles to come into play. The first is the principle of comparative advantage, examined during our discussion of international specialization in Chapter 7. The second is the principle that 'practice makes perfect', i.e. efficiency is increased by experience in a particular job.

Table 24.2 gives data on operating costs in two units producing plastic by an extrusion process. The differences in cost shown in that table are mainly due to technical economies of scale.

Table 24.2

Operating Costs for Plastic Extruders

Extruder capacity (lbs per hour)	135	1230
Costs per lb. (pence):		
Depreciation of machines and tools	0.59	0.13
Direct labour	0.42	0.22
Other works costs	0.96	0.57
Total operating costs	1.96	0.92

Source: C. F. Pratten, *Economies of Scale in Manufacturing Industry* (Cambridge: Cambridge Universiry Press, 1971).

MARKETING ECONOMIES

Economies may arise in selling costs, including the distribution of products from factory to customer – wholesaler, retailer or consumer. Selling in bulk may enable savings to be made in invoicing and other costs. Distribution on a larger scale may enable the firm to fully utilize larger warehouses, delivery vehicles, etc.

Furthermore, once the volume of goods to be distributed reaches a certain point, the firm may be able to reduce its costs by establishing its own distribution fleet instead of hiring transport services. Examples of economies in selling are given in table 24.3.

Table 24.3

Estimated Selling Costs of Grocery Manufacturers

Value of Consignment	£10	£40	£100	£400
Selling costs per £1 of sales (pence):				
Sales and invoicing costs	6.7	2.2	1.1	0.5
Transport costs	2.0	1.5	1.2	0.6
Depot costs	2.5	2.0	1.8	0.6
Supervision	0.7	0.2	0.1	0.0
Total	11.9	5.9	4.2	1.8

Large firms may also enjoy economies in advertising. This is especially important for firms which serve a national market, since the total cost of advertising on a nation-wide basis may be very expensive. An indication of the potential savings in advertising costs is given in table 24.4.

Table 24.4

Advertising Expenditures of Automobile Companies, U.S.A. (annual averages, 1954–7)

Company	Total ($mn)	Per car sold ($)
General Motors	80.7	26.56
Ford	49.0	27.22
Chrysler	47.0	47.76
Studebaker–Packard	7.3	64.04
American Motors	6.6	57.89

Source: L. Weiss, *Economics and American Industry* (New York: Wiley, 1961).

BUYING ECONOMIES

Some savings may be made by setting up a more efficient form of buying organization. The larger firm is more likely to be able to employ buyers who are experienced in buying particular products, whereas in a small firm the buyer may have to deal with a wider range of products. (In other words the large firm can take more advantage of the division of labour.)

Another, probably more important, advantage enjoyed by large firms is the ability to buy supplies at lower prices. In addition to being able to take advantage of the terms embodied in the quantity discount schedules operated by many suppliers, the largest buyers may be able to negotiate special terms.

The Monopolies Commission's *Report on Metal Containers* showed that Metal Box, the dominant supplier, granted a discount of up to 6 per cent on annual purchases of 200 million cans, together with additional rebates relating to the quantity of any one kind of can bought in one year. Of Metal Box's 624 customers all but 45 bought at the terms specified in the published quantity discount schedules. These 45 were able to gain additional cost-savings by special negotiations. The importance of these special negotiations can be judged from the fact that these 45 customers accounted for 88 per cent of the company's sales.

Buying economies are especially important in retailing since the cost of goods sold is by far the most important single cost. The discounts granted by manufacturers to retailers are well kept secrets. However the larger discounts obtained by multiple retailers have undoubtedly been one of the major factors enabling these retailers to undercut their small rivals and thus obtain a substantial increase in market share.*

FINANCIAL ECONOMIES

Large firms can often obtain finance more cheaply and/or more easily than smaller firms. For reasons that we discussed in Chapter 6, small firms may have to offer a higher return to investors. In addition, the costs of issuing capital do not increase as quickly as the size of the issue. Issue costs range from about 10–15 per cent of the sum raised at the lower end (say £250,000) to 3–5 per cent when the size of the issue exceeds £1 million.

RISK-BEARING ECONOMIES

A number of different advantages can be considered under this heading, but the underlying factor enabling the large firm to enjoy these advantages is that its activities are usually more diverse than those of the small firm. This means that a failure or loss in any one line of activity is less likely to endanger the viability of the whole enterprise.

Research and development is an activity whose rewards are, as matter of definition, uncertain. Substantial costs may have to be incurred before revenue, if any, begins to flow in, and large firms can best afford to take the risks inherent in this situation. A good example of the need to incur costs in advance of revenue is the conversion of oil to make protein for use as an animal food. Although the first experiments which opened up this possibility were conducted in the 1950s, the first commercial plants were not established until the 1970s by B.P. and later by I.C.I. Shell, which began conducting its own experiments in 1965, announced ten years later that although it had successfully manufactured a high protein product in trials, it was to delay the construction of a full-scale experimental plant until it had re-examined the economics of the operation. One of the events that had occurred since trials began was, of course, the steep rise in the price of oil, the primary raw material. This illustrates the risks that are inherent in developments that have a very long gestation period.

Another example is the market for new smoking materials (N.S.M.) introduced in the U.K. in 1977. The link between cigarette smoking and ill-health led a number of companies to begin research in the 1950s and 1960s into possible substitutes for tobacco. The two major areas of uncertainty facing these companies were first the attitude of the health authorities towards such substitutes, and second the reactions of consumers towards any substitutes that might be approved by the authorities. This uncertainty no doubt limited the number of companies initially undertaking research, and subsequently caused some of these pioneers to re-think this strategy.

---

* Large retailers may sometimes use their buying power to obtain higher profit margins. In 1976 the Secretary for Prices limited the discounts granted by bread manufacturers to retailers to 22½ per cent. It was thought that discounts of up to 30 per cent had previously been granted, but that the extra discounts had not been passed on to consumers in the form of lower prices. In 1977 the Monopolies Commission was asked to investigate the discounts given by suppliers to retailers, in order to determine how far they are related to cost savings and whether they are in the public interest.

The failure in Western Germany in 1975 of two cigarette brands containing a tobacco substitute led at least two companies – Bayer in Germany and Polystrep in Switzerland – to reduce their R. and D. expenditure. In the U.K. expenditure was halted by Courtaulds and the Scottish Co-operative Wholesale Society when the Hunter committee published its guidelines outlining the programme of testing required of manufacturers before being able to market their products. Courtaulds, which had already spent about £1 million on R. and D. over the previous ten years, estimated that it would cost a further £2 to 3 million to fulfil these requirements. In addition a further investment of £10 to 20 million would be required before production could begin – all of this without any guarantee of acceptance of the new product by the consumer.

In view of the uncertainty surrounding the new product it was, perhaps, not surprising that only two companies – the Celanese Corporation of U.S.A. and a company formed jointly by two U.K. giants – I.C.I. and Imperial Tobacco – entered the U.K. market in 1977.*

For a risk-bearing economy of a very different kind we turn to the travel industry. One of the products of that industry which increased in popularity in the 1960s and 1970s was the package tour holiday. It is normally to the advantage of the tour operator to sell tours well in advance of the holiday dates. However when exchange rates are floating this policy carries the risk that, having obtained payment in sterling, the operator may subsequently incur foreign currency costs greater than he anticipated when setting the price for the tour.

One way of minimizing this risk, adopted by a number of operators, is to impose a surcharge – which the customer must pay before departure – to compensate for a decline in the value of sterling. This is in effect making the customer bear at least some of the risk, and as such may lead to a loss of goodwill. With this in mind some operators began to offer 'firm-price' holidays, i.e. to bear the whole of the risk. It was noticeable that the operators who led this development were mostly large firms with extensive interests outside the package tour market, e.g. Thomsons, Thomas Cook and British Airways.

Even if research and development costs are negligible, the introduction of a new technology may involve substantial risks which the bigger firm will usually be in the best position to bear. The same applies to the introduction of new products, a point discussed further below.

Finally, a large firm may need to keep proportionately less spare machinery and parts in case of breakdown, and to stockpile proportionately less raw materials in case of interruptions of supply. This saving is due to the operation of the 'law of large numbers' or the 'principle of massed reserves' and is *not* dependent upon the firm having a diverse range of activities. It could, in fact, be seen either as a risk-bearing or a technical economy.

MANAGERIAL ECONOMIES

This term is given to a miscellaneous group of economies pertaining to the administration of the enterprise. It includes the ability to offer the high rewards needed to attract highly talented staff in various fields – personnel, purchasing, marketing, etc. It also includes the ability to utilize administrative procedures which might be too costly for the smaller firm.

---

* At the time of writing the success of the venture is by no means assured. In October one producer announced that it was to scrap one million cigarettes because demand had not been as great as expected and N.S.M. goes stale more quickly than tobacco.

Although the ability to hire expertise is clearly important we should note that it may not be as necessary for small firms to do so, nor to introduce elaborate administrative procedures. Indeed some people would claim that such procedures are required in order to prevent the emergence of managerial or administrative diseconomies.*

Having analysed the various types of scale economy, we make four final points in order to link the analysis to the previous discussion of the behaviour of costs – in particular as shown in figure 24.5.

In order to make the first point we assume that the reduction in average cost which that diagram shows to be possible at an output greater than M would involve the installation of more expensive machinery embodying a superior technology. In other words we assume that technical economies of scale can be attained. If, this new equipment having been installed, output subsequently fell below M, average cost would be higher at the new, larger, scale of organization than it would have been if the smaller scale had been retained. It might be possible for the organization eventually to revert to the smaller scale, but only after a considerable time-lag.

In this respect technical economies are rather different from other types. In these other instances an increase in the scale of organization is less likely to involve changes which are difficult to reverse. Consequently there is less likelihood that, if output turns out to be lower than expected, average cost will continue to be higher than it would have been at a smaller scale of organization.

Second, figure 24.5 relates to the alternatives that are available at a given point in time, i.e. it shows the various alternative relationships between cost and output with a given state of technical knowledge. It does *not* show changes in costs due to technological progress. Indeed, although technological progress frequently increases the scope for economies of scale, in some instances it has the reverse effect – it reduces the disadvantages of a small scale organization.

Third, some advantages of large scale operation are not fully encompassed in the behaviour of costs, and therefore cannot be represented in figure 24.5. As noted above, advertising and other marketing activities may lead to an increase in the volume of sales. In addition, or alternatively, they may make it easier for the firm to increase its prices.

Again, if expansion takes the form of an increase in the range of products offered by a company, an increase may be achieved in the sales of both the new and existing products. This is especially likely in service industries where customers often require a 'package' of services. An example of such a package is given in figure 24.6 which shows the range of services that is offered by one of the major U.K. clearing banks, and those 'bought' by one of its clients, Bejam Ltd. (denoted by an asterisk).†

Finally, although figure 24.5 does not show any tendency for average cost to rise at the largest scale of organization it is feasible that it might do so. If an increase in scale were associated with an increase in average cost we would say that diseconomies of scale existed. It seems that the most likely cause of diseconomies is the difficulty of managing or administering very large firms. One manifestation of this difficulty may be the greater incidence of strikes in larger plants, shown

---

* There is clearly an overlap between managerial and other types of scale economy. In fact the main justification for creating this additional category is related to the analysis of diseconomies of scale, discussed below.

† Source: *Financial Times* 25.6.76.

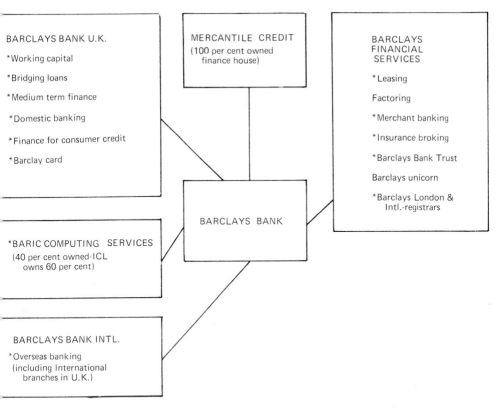

BARCLAYS BANK U.K.

*Working capital

*Bridging loans

*Medium term finance

*Domestic banking

*Finance for consumer credit

*Barclay card

MERCANTILE CREDIT
(100 per cent owned
finance house)

BARCLAYS
FINANCIAL
SERVICES

*Leasing

Factoring

*Merchant banking

*Insurance broking

*Barclays Bank Trust

Barclays unicorn

*Barclays London &
Intl.-registrars

BARCLAYS BANK

*BARIC COMPUTING SERVICES
(40 per cent owned-ICL
owns 60 per cent)

BARCLAYS BANK INTL.

*Overseas banking
(including International
branches in U.K.)

Figure 24.6 Services Provided by the Barclays Bank Group

in table 24.5. (This table might also be interpreted as indicating that the high degree of specialization that is often found in large plants may have disadvantages – boredom and dissatisfaction – as well as the advantages referred to earlier.)

Table 24.5
Incidence of Stoppages by Size of Plant (annual average 1971–3, manufacturing industry, Great Britain)

Plant size (no. of employees)	No. of stoppages per 100,000 employees	No. of working days lost per 100,000 employees
11–24	8.0	14.8
25–99	19.2	72.4
100–199	23.0	155.0
200–499	25.4	329.1
500–999	29.7	719.4
1,000 or more	28.7	2,046.1

Source: *Department of Employment Gazette 1976.*

The Direction of Growth, Economies of Scale, and Other Advantages
A firm may grow in several alternative directions, each direction having different implications and consequences.

HORIZONTAL GROWTH involves an expansion of the firm's existing activities. An example would be a car assembler which started to assemble more cars (internal expansion) or which merged with another car assembler (horizontal integration). Horizontal growth is likely to give rise to most of the economies that we considered above, although not to those risk-bearing economies which depend upon a diversified range of activities. In addition, if horizontal growth leads to an increase in market share, the firm may be able to exert more control over prices, as shown below. Although an increase in market share may result from growth either by integration or internal expansion, it is more likely to result from the former. This helps to explain why, as shown in Chapter 18, legislation has been passed to control mergers but not internal growth.

VERTICAL GROWTH involves an extension of the firm's activities into another stage of the production and distribution process. If the extension is towards the beginning of the process, it is known as backward integration, e.g. a car assembler might begin the manufacture (or might take over a manufacturer) of components which it had previously bought. If the extension is towards the end of the process it is known as forward integration, e.g. a car assembler might establish (or take over) a distribution network in order to sell the cars that it produces.

Vertical growth may give rise to some of the economies of scale associated with the size of the firm, e.g. the full utilization of elaborate data-processing facilities. But in general a more important motive for vertical growth is additional security. Backward integration gives security of supplies, and is most likely to occur when specialist sources of supply are limited. For example in U.K. there were at the end of the war more car assemblers than firms making car bodies. Gradually these manufacturers of bodies were taken over by the assemblers and there is now no major independent body manufacturer.

Forward integration guarantees outlets for the firm's products and enables the manufacturer to control the conditions under which its products are sold. Considerable capital expenditure is required to establish a distribution network, especially at the retail level, and it is often difficult for a manufacturer to provide the range of products which would justify such an investment. Manufacturers of beer have succeeded in doing so, whereas manufacturers of foodstuffs have not.

If a firm is faced by a dominant supplier or purchaser in the markets in which it deals, vertical expansion may enable it to obtain inputs at a lower cost and sell its output at a higher price. (However, any firm which has the financial resources to expand vertically is usually able to obtain reasonable terms from suppliers or purchasers. This helps to explain why a large retailer such as Marks and Spencer has not felt it necessary to develop its own manufacturing facilities.)

DIVERSIFIED GROWTH involves an extension of the range of products handled by the firm. For example a car assembler might begin to assemble lorries or motor bikes. Most of the scale economies discussed above are likely to arise, although to a lesser degree in some instances. For example quantity discounts may be less than they would be if a narrower range and bigger quantities of materials and components were bought. On the other hand, diversified growth is more likely to give rise to risk-bearing economies.*

Costs and the Supply Curve

Having examined the relationships between output and costs, we now discuss how the behaviour of cost may be reflected in the supply curve. For this purpose it

* Risk-bearing economies may be the only important type when growth involves the production of dissimilar products.

is convenient to make a distinction between two types of market. In the markets for many manufactured goods and services, cost-based pricing is practiced. These markets are discussed in the remainder of this chapter and in Chapter 25. Raw materials and agricultural products are usually sold in open markets, where the influence of cost on supply is much less pronounced. Price determination in open markets is discussed in Chapter 26.

Cost-Based Pricing
Since considerable trouble and expense may be involved in changing prices, firms prefer to set and maintain a price for a given period. The length of this period varies. At one time there was in many markets an annual pricing cycle or season. Since then more rapid rates of inflation have meant that prices are revised more frequently, perhaps every three or six months.

Whatever the length of the season, a price is set which relates to the average cost at the expected level of output during that period. In figure 24.7 the firm expects to produce quantity E at an average cost of EF. It adds the profit margin FG and sets price P (OP=EG).*

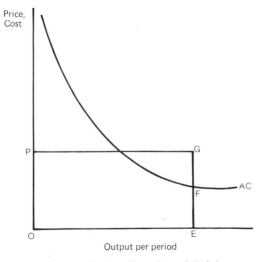

Figure 24.7   Cost-Based Pricing

Two very important questions now arise. First, what determines the size of the profit margin added by the firm? Second what happens to price if the firm's expectations are not fulfilled, i.e. if E is not sold at price P? We consider these two questions in turn.

The Determinants of the Profit Margin
This question involves two important sets of factors – the motivations of producers and the structure of the market.

The Motivations of Producers
The following conclusions should be seen as a summary of what is an extremely complicated issue. First, profitability is normally the primary objective of private

* The firm's estimate of output takes account of the price. What we have described as a process with two distinct stages is in practice a single process in which several alternative combinations of price and output are usually considered.

sector producers since unless the firm earns adequate profits it will not survive – it may be taken over by another firm or may go out of business. Second, although profitability is important it may mean different things to different firms. Some firms aim to maximize profitability, some to earn an 'adequate' profit, and some, between the two, to earn not less than and preferably more than in previous years. Third, other objectives may be very important – in particular an increase in the volume of sales or in market share. (This may in turn contribute to further objectives such as an increase in the assets of the firm and in the number of employees.) An increase in the volume of sales often implies an increase in profitability, but this is not always so, and firms sometimes compromise, aiming to increase the volume of sales provided this does not cause profitability to fall below a minimum, adequate, level.

The Structure of the Market

Whether or not a firm is able to attain its objectives depends very much upon its economic environment, an important aspect of which is the structure of the market supplied by the firm. Three aspects of market structure are especially important in this context.

THE NUMBER OF SUPPLIERS AND THE DISTRIBUTION OF MARKET SHARES
The first aspect is the number of suppliers and the distribution of market shares; there is considerable evidence to suggest that the smaller the number of suppliers the more control they can exercise over prices. Moreover, given the number of suppliers, the control of prices is usually greatest when a large share of the market is in the hands of a few firms. (The control is, of course, mainly exercised by the large firms; the small firms may have little or no influence.)

Table 24.6

Profitability and the Concentration Ratio (1950–60 U.S.A.)

Industry	Average rate* of return	Industry	Average rate of return
	Concentration ratio above 70 per cent		
Automobiles	15.5	Steel	10.8
Chewing gum	17.5	Soap	13.3
Cigarettes	11.6	Farm machinery and tractors	8.8
Ethical drugs	17.9	Copper	11.5
Flat glass	18.8	Glass containers	13.3
Liquor	9.0	Tyres and tubes	13.2
Nickel	18.9	Rayon	8.5
Shoe machinery	7.4	Gypsum products	14.4
Sulphur	21.6	Metal containers	9.9
Aluminium reduction	10.2	Cement	15.7
Biscuits	11.4	Average	13.3
	Concentration ratio below 70 per cent		
Petroleum refining	12.2	Beer	10.9
Shoes	9.6	Baking	11.0
Canned fruit and vegetables	7.7	Bituminous coal	8.8
Meat packing	5.3	Textile mill products	6.9
Flour	8.6	Average	9.0

* Net income as a percentage of net worth.
Source: H. M. Mann, 'Seller Concentration, Barriers to Entry, and Rates of Return in Thirty Industries, 1950–60' (Review of Economics and Statistics, 1966).

Incidentally, it is not always easy to identify the boundaries of a particular market, especially where producers attempt to differentiate their products from those of competitors. If these attempts are successful, a market may in effect be split into a number of separate sub-markets each having very few suppliers.

One of the results of the ability to control prices is that profitability tends to be higher in concentrated than in less concentrated markets or industries. Table 24.6, which relates to a sample of thirty industries studied by Professor Mann, shows that the average profitability of the dominant firms in the more highly concentrated industries was almost 50 per cent higher than the profitability of the dominant firms in less highly concentrated industries. (The measure of concentration used in this study was the share of the industry sales accounted for by the leading eight firms).

The conclusions derived from Mann's study are similar to those derived from most other studies carried out in different periods and with different samples of firms. There seems to be a distinct link between the level of concentration and profitability. However the link is by no means automatic. As can be seen in table 24.6, profitability was higher in some of the less concentrated industries such as petroleum refining and banking, than in some of the more highly concentrated industries such as shoe machinery and rayon manufacturing. Moreover, there were often substantial differences in the profitability of different firms within a given industry. For example the rate of return of 15.5 per cent in automobiles was an average of the 21.5 per cent earned by General Motors, 14.5 per cent by Ford and 10.5 per cent by Chrysler.

BARRIERS TO ENTRY
The second aspect of market structure is the existence or absence of barriers which make it difficult for new firms to enter the market (or sub-market). Table 24.7 refers to the twenty one industries that were identified in table 24.6 as being highly concentrated. It can be seen that the dominant firms in industries with very high barriers earned substantially higher profits than the dominant firms in industries with less high barriers. (Although there was again a considerable range of profitability within each group.) The more difficult it is for new firms to enter a market, the greater is the opportunity for existing firms to set prices which result in above average profits.

Among the most important barriers to entry are:

(a) the capital cost of establishing production and distribution facilities – this barrier is especially important if substantial economies of scale are enjoyed by existing firms;
(b) absolute cost advantages arising from the control over some vital input such as a raw material or skilled labour;
(c) scientific or technological know-how arising from a sustained research and development programme and perhaps protected by patents;
(d) marketing activities leading to a high degree of consumer loyalty, a well regarded brand-name, etc.

THE CONCENTRATION OF BUYING POWER
Both of the above aspects of market structure relate to the supply side of the market. The third aspect relates to the demand side; the larger the share of output bought by a few firms – i.e. the more concentrated is buying power – the less control will suppliers have over prices.

Table 24.7

Profitability and Barriers to Entry (1950–60 U.S.A)

Industry	Average rate of return
Very High Barriers	
Automobiles	15.5
Chewing gum	17.5
Cigarettes	11.6
Ethical drugs	17.9
Flat glass	18.8
Liquor	9.0
Nickel	18.9
Sulphur	21.6
Average	16.4
Substantial Barriers	
Aluminium reduction	10.2
Biscuits	11.4
Steel	10.8
Soap	13.3
Farm machinery and tractors	8.8
Copper	11.5
Cement	15.7
Shoe machinery	7.4
Average	11.1
Moderate to Low Barriers	
Glass containers	13.3
Tyres and tubes	13.2
Rayon	8.5
Gypsum products	14.4
Metal containers	9.9
Average	11.9

Source: H. M. Mann, op cit.

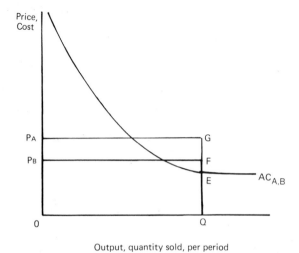

Figure 24.8 Alternative Profit Margins and Prices

The Supply Curve With a Given Scale of Organization

We have seen that the profit margin added to average cost is influenced by a wide range of factors, and that different margins are likely to be added in different circumstances. For example let us consider two firms, A and B, facing very different market conditions. We assume that both firms have the same average cost curve, AC, as shown in figure 24.8, and that both expect to produce output Q. Firm A, a dominant firm in a highly concentrated market expects to be able to sell this output at price P_A and thus to obtain a profit margin of EG. Firm B, on the other hand, as one of a large number of suppliers of a different product, faced by a single large purchaser, expects that to sell this output he will need to set a lower price P_B, yielding a lower profit margin EF.

Point G represents one point on firm A's supply curve (and F one point on firm B's supply curve). In order to ascertain other points on the supply curve, i.e. to discover the shape of the curve, we need to know what would happen if the firm's expectations were not fulfilled, i.e. if they were able to sell either more or less than they expected at the initial price.

The Response to an Unexpected Level of Demand

To some extent this response will depend upon the adequacy of the initial profit margin. However, in order to simplify the analysis we assume for the moment that the margin is adequate – if the firm were to sell its expected output at the initial price, it would meet whatever target it might have set. We also assume that the firm is representative of all the firms in the market or industry in terms of the rate of profit required to meet its objective, and also in terms of its cost and demand conditions. That is to say that each firm in the industry has identical cost and demand curves. Finally the demand curves are drawn on the assumption that all firms charge the same price. Given these assumptions the various situations which might face our representative firm are shown in figure 24.9.

If demand turns out as indicated by D_E the expectations of the firm are fulfilled, and Q_E is sold at price P_E. (Market supply at P_E will be $n(Q_E)$, where n is the number of suppliers.) If demand is higher than expected, D_H, the firm may choose

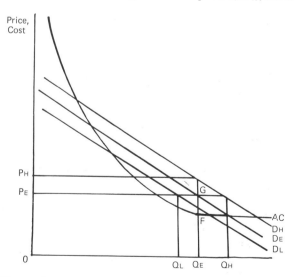

Figure 24.9 Changes in Demand, Price and Output

to sell Q_E at a higher price P_H, Q_H at price P_E or an output between Q_E and Q_H at a price between P_E and P_H.

There are several reasons for believing that of these alternatives the firm is most likely to choose to maintain price P_E and increase sales to Q_H. First, as we have seen, an increase in the volume of sales is often an important objective. Second, firms incur certain additional costs whenever they change price. Third, the lower the price the less likely it is that new firms will attempt to enter the market. These considerations would have less weight if profits were reduced following the increase in output – as might happen if a steep rise were to occur in average cost. However it can be seen that average cost does not rise and that profit margins are maintained. Consequently total profits, and profit expressed as a rate of return on capital employed, will increase.

Let us now consider the situation where demand turns out to be less than expected, at D_L. If the firm maintains its price at P_E it will sell only Q_L, and its profitability will be less than expected – first because it sells less than expected and second because its profit margin is reduced by the increase in average cost. Faced with this unsatisfactory profit position the firm will consider changing its price.

One possibility would be to increase its price in order to restore its profit margins. However the danger of this policy is clearly that sales would be further reduced and that total profits might fall further. An increase in price is likely to increase profits only under certain conditions.

The first condition relates to the elasticity of market demand. If demand is inelastic an increase in price by all suppliers would result in an increase in revenue and thus in profits. If demand is elastic an increase in price would result in a fall in revenue. But as output falls there will also be a fall in total cost, so that it is possible that total profits would rise even when demand is elastic. However when demand is below the expected level demand is likely to be highly elastic in response to a price increase. This implies that an increase in price would cause a loss of revenue far in excess of the reduction in cost.

The second condition relates to the elasticity of demand for the output of a single firm. As we saw in the previous paragraph, the elasticity of market demand *may* be such that an increase in price would result in an increase in total profits. Since we have assumed that all firms have identical cost and demand conditions, it follows that in this situation the profits of each firm would be increased provided that all firms were to increase their prices by the same amount.

In practice this condition is most unlikely to be fulfilled. As we showed in Chapter 18, formal agreements on prices are now very difficult to justify in law. In the absence of an agreement, each firm will be afraid of increasing its price in case it loses customers to competitors which do not follow its lead. This fear always exists, but will be particularly strong when demand is depressed. (The demand curves in figure 24.9 were drawn on the assumption that all firms charge the same price. If one firm raised its price and others did not follow, that firm's demand would be far more elastic than shown in figure 24.9.)

An alternative response to the fall in demand is to reduce price below P_E in an attempt to maintain sales at the expected level. Again the elasticity of market demand must be taken into account – the more elastic the demand the more likely it is that profits will increase following a reduction in price. If only one firm were to reduce its price, demand might be very elastic. However if, as is likely to happen, the reduction was matched by other firms, demand would be less elastic. Again therefore there are strong pressures discouraging a change in price following a failure of demand to reach the expected level.

We can conclude then that where firms initially set a price which includes an adequate profit margin, price is likely to be held stable over quite a wide range of output, both greater and less than expected. In other words the supply curve will be horizontal over that range of output. Let us now consider briefly how the behaviour of price might be modified if the original profit margin was not considered to be adequate.

When demand is less than expected the response is likely to be very similar in the two situations. However when demand turns out to be greater than expected (D_H in figure 24.9), suppliers are likely to take the opportunity to improve their profit margins. Since they may also wish to increase their sales volume, the most likely response is to set a price between P_E and P_H, at which price their output will be between Q_E and Q_H.

However, this response will occur only if a firm which is considering raising its price feels confident that its rivals will follow. If a price increase were not followed, demand would be more elastic than indicated in figure 24.9. As we noted above, firms are likely to be most confident about rivals' responses, i.e. to be able to exercise control over price, in highly concentrated industries.

Costs, Profitability and the Supply Curve
The discussion in the above section is summarized in figure 24.10. S_1 represents the market supply curve when the original price was considered satisfactory. S_2

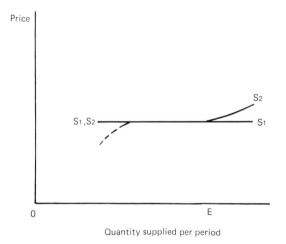

Figure 24.10 Alternative Supply Curves with a Given Scale of Organization

refers to the situation where the firms felt obliged to set an original price that they considered to be too low, and which they subsequently raised when demand turned out to be higher than expected.

We showed that initially price is unlikely to fall in response to a fall in demand. However if the fall in demand is prolonged and substantial, prices will eventually weaken. Once one firm breaks out of line, others will follow and a cumulative series of price reductions may ensue. This process is represented in figure 24.10 by the dotted portion of the supply curves, which might apply to both S_1 and S_2. The ultimate floor to the price reductions is set by average variable cost, or by opportunity cost should this be greater (see Chapter 25).

The Supply Curve with a Changing Scale of Organization

When the analysis is extended to encompass changes in scale, the supply curve may assume shapes other than those discussed above. If economies of scale arise, producers may wish to pass on the reduction in costs in the form of price reductions – this is most likely if demand is highly elastic and if an increase in sales is an important objective. Moreover, even if producers would prefer not to reduce their prices they may feel obliged to do so. Very large buyers may be able to insist on being given at least a share of the cost savings. If prices are reduced as economies of scale arise, the supply curve will be downward sloping as shown by S_1 in figure 24.11.

Figure 24.11 Alternative Supply Curves with a Changing Scale of Organization

Alternatively the supply curve may slope upwards, as shown by S_2. The main cause of an upward sloping supply curve (with a changing scale of organization) is as follows. As output increases, the additional demand for factor inputs – labour, raw materials, etc. – causes an increase in their price. (As we shall see in later chapters, the prices of such inputs is much more sensitive to changes in demand than are the prices of the products considered in this chapter.) In order to compensate for the increase in their costs, producers increase their prices.

This effect of an increase in output is likely to be most pronounced when the economy as a whole is operating near full capacity, so that producers have to offer higher prices in order to try to attract resources away from other uses. Even if resources are not fully employed, the costs of a particular industry may rise as output increases if that industry is a major purchaser of a particular input. Incidentally an increase in output may lead to an increase in factor prices, and hence in product prices, even when the scale of organization is unchanged. But the effect is clearly likely to be greater over a longer period when the scale of organization can change, since there is then scope for a bigger increase in output.

Cost Differentials and the Supply Curve

We have assumed so far in this chapter that the cost conditions of all the firms supplying a given market are identical. In many markets this is not so, and in this section we examine briefly how prices are likely to be determined when substantial differences exist in cost conditions.

In order to simplify the analysis we can consider two firms, one being representative of high cost producers and the other of low cost producers. We make the further simplifying assumption that both firms have the same scale of organization, and that the cost differences persist at all levels of output. Such cost differences could be due to differences in labour productivity, to different prices paid for inputs, etc. Finally we assume that both firms have identical demand curves whose elasticity is the same as the market demand curve. This may occur because the products are identical (homogeneous). Alternatively it may occur because, although the products are differentiated with some consumers preferring one 'brand' and other consumers another, the preferences of consumers as a whole are divided equally among all the brands.

This situation is illustrated in figure 24.12. It is extremely likely that the lead in setting prices will be taken by B, the lower cost firm. B has basically two choices.

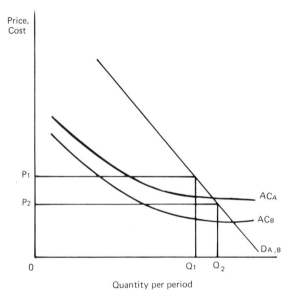

Figure 24.12   Alternative Prices of the Dominant Firm

It can set a price P_1 which yields adequate profits to firm A (and also, of course, firm B). Alternatively it can set a lower price P_2, designed to drive A out of the market. Although B's profits during this period would be lower with price P_2 than P_1, this might be compensated by higher profits in future periods, if and when A had left the market. (If A left the market, B's demand curve would shift to the right.) B would be most likely to earn higher profits if, as it expanded its output to meet the additional demand from A's former customers, it gained economies of scale. Moreover if B forced some competitors out of the market, it might subsequently be able to raise its price above P_2.

If B chooses the first alternative we can apply the analysis of the earlier sections in explaining the shape of the supply curve. At price P_1 the quantity supplied is $Q \times n$, where n is the number of suppliers. This gives us one point on the supply curve. The location of the other points on the curve will be influenced by all the factors considered above. If, on the other hand, B set price P_2 it becomes impossible to derive a supply curve, because we do not know how quickly high cost firms will leave the market. Nor do we know what price B would set once these firms have left the market.

A similar choice faces the firms in an industry in which there are substantial entry barriers. In figure 24.13 AC_B represents the cost curve of an existing firm, and AC_A refers to a potential entrant. The difference in costs between the two firms constitutes a barrier to entry.

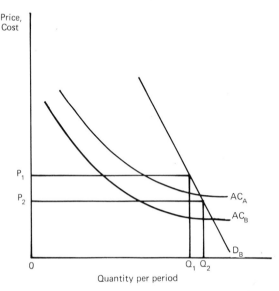

Figure 24.13   Barriers to Entry and Alternative Prices

If B set price P_1 it would earn much higher current profits than if it set price P_2. However P_1 may encourage new firms to enter the industry whereas P_2 will deter entry. If new entry occurs, prices in future periods may be forced down below P_2. Consequently B must weigh up the benefit of higher current profits against the possibility of lower profits in the future.

As we noted above, the demand curves in figure 24.12 are drawn on the assumption that all firms set the same price. If this condition does not hold, the demand curves will have quite a different shape. In order to simplify the analysis we confine our attention to the situation facing the high cost firm A. We have suggested that if B were to set price P_1, A would be happy to follow this price since it yields adequate profits. However let us now consider the situation where B sets a lower price, P, in figure 24.14. Although, if A were to sell Q at this price it would earn a profit, it would not feel this profit to be adequate. A might, therefore, consider setting other prices.

If, in order to increase its profit margin, A were to set a higher price, it would probably find that demand was highly elastic, as consumers switched to the cheaper alternatives offered by B. On the other hand, if A were to reduce its price in the hope of increasing its profits via a large increase in the volume of sales, it would probably be frustrated, finding demand inelastic. The reason for this is that B would match A's price cut in order to avoid losing sales. As the lower cost firm, B is likely to be in a better position than A to withstand a price war. Consequently A is most unlikely to institute price competition. He is more likely to accept the price set by B. We can therefore say that B acts as a *price leader* and A as a *price follower.* Alternatively we can say that B acts as a *price maker* and A as a *price taker.*

There are many recorded examples of firms which, when faced with the prospect of unsatisfactory profits, have successfully sought to reduce their cost of production, and have thus achieved more satisfactory profits. This process has been termed 'price-minus costing' by some commentators.

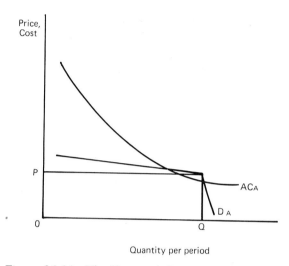

Figure 24.14 The Demand Curve of a Price Follower

THE SUPPLY OF FACTORS OF PRODUCTION
We have already indicated that an increase in price is often required to bring forth an increase in the quantity of inputs supplied, i.e. that the supply curve is likely to slope upwards, and we discuss this point further in the following chapters.

The Position of the Supply Curve
So far in this chapter we have been concerned with the shape of the market or industry supply curve. We now turn our attention to the factors which influence the position of the curve. We have seen that supply curves may have numerous alternative shapes. For our purposes in this section it is sufficient to take one of these various alternatives. We choose a curve with a gentle upward slope from left to right, as shown in figure 24.15. We shall consider what might cause supply to increase, i.e. the supply curve to shift from S_1 to S_2, or to decrease, i.e. to shift from S_1 to S_3. In other words we examine the effects of changes in the conditions of supply.

The Conditions of Supply
A CHANGE IN THE COSTS OF PRODUCTION
The most important condition of supply is the cost of production and distribution. As a general rule we can say that an increase in average cost will cause a decrease in supply, i.e. the market supply curve will shift to the left. Conversely a fall in average cost will cause an increase in supply, i.e. the supply curve will shift to

the right.* The basic causes of changes in average cost are changes in the prices of inputs and in productivity.

It is important to distinguish between *autonomous* changes in input costs, and changes which occur because of a change in output (discussed above). Autonomous changes in cost cause a shift in the position of the supply curve. Output-induced changes in cost are encompassed in the shape of the curve.

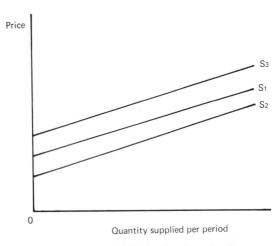

Figure 24.15 A Shift in the Supply Curve

Supply conditions may also be affected by technological change. Technological change normally reduces average cost, i.e. causes the supply curve to shift to the right. The same effect follows from an increase in the efficiency with which production is organized.

A CHANGE IN PROFIT MARGINS

If suppliers set their prices so as to achieve a constant profit per unit under all circumstances, a change in average cost is directly reflected in a shift of the supply curve. In figure 24.16 a reduction in average cost of MN causes the supply curve to shift from S_1 to S_2. If, on the other hand, suppliers decided not to pass on all of the cost reduction, the curve would shift less. For example, if they increased their profit margin by NP, the supply curve would shift to S_3.

Suppliers may decide to change their profit margins without a change occurring in other supply conditions. In figure 24.17 an increase in profit margins causes the supply curve to shift from S_1 to S_2.

As we noted above, firms usually take account of demand conditions when deciding upon their profit margins, and thus their price. The shift from S_1 to S_2 in figure 22.17 might indicate that producers had begun to take a more favourable view of future demand prospects. (We also saw above that experience of demand conditions during a pricing season might cause some producers to change their profit margins and thus their price. Changes in price which are linked to changes in output affect the *shape* of the supply curve.)

---

*A shift of the supply curve to the left could also be described as an upward shift, and a shift to the right as a downward shift.

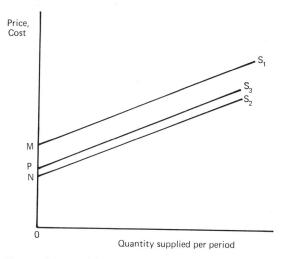

Figure 24.16 Alternative Shifts in the Supply Curve

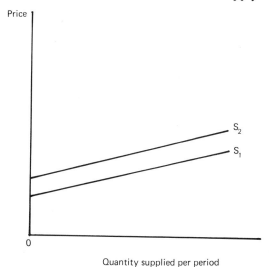

Figure 24.17 An Increase in the Profit Margin and a Shift in the Supply Curve

A CHANGE IN OPPORTUNITY COST

A firm's profit margin on one product may be influenced by the (maximum) profits that it could earn by producing other products, i.e. by the opportunity cost of the present use of its resources. If prospective profitability in other markets rose, i.e. if opportunity cost increased, the firm might require higher profits from its existing markets. This higher target profit would cause the supply curve to shift to the left. (We could also explain this leftward shift in terms of an increase in the (opportunity) costs of the firm.)

A CHANGE IN THE NUMBER OF PRODUCERS

An increase in the number of producers will cause an increase in supply, a fall in the number of producers a decrease in supply. The precise nature of the change in supply will depend upon the change that occurs in the overall cost conditions of producers.

The number of producers may change for various reasons. But especially important is a change in profitability in this market as compared to prospective profitability in other markets. (Such a change may itself be due to a wide variety of factors.) A change in entry barriers – both in this and other markets – may also be important.

INDIRECT TAXATION

As far as the producer is concerned, the imposition of an indirect tax on a product is equivalent to an increase in that product's cost of production. It is a further expense which must be covered by the product's price. In figure 24.18 we illustrate

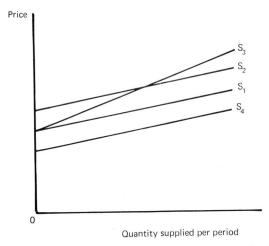

Figure 24.18 Indirect Taxes and the Supply Curve

the effect of two different types of indirect or expenditure tax. (We assume that in each case the imposition of the tax is fully reflected by the shift in the supply curve.)

The original supply curve is S_1. After the imposition of a *specific tax*, i.e. a tax of a fixed amount per unit, the supply curve shifts to S_2. After the imposition of an *ad valorem* tax, i.e. a tax whose rate varies in accordance with the price of the product, the supply curve shifts to S_3. Finally note that a (specific) subsidy causes the supply curve to shift downward to S_4. A subsidy is, in effect, a negative tax.

Summary and Conclusions

We have examined the many factors that influence both the shape and position of the supply curve. We showed that the shape of the supply curve is influenced by the motivations of producers, by various aspects of market structure and by the length of the time period under consideration. The position of the curve may change because of a change in the costs of production, profit margins, opportunity cost, the number of producers and indirect taxation.

Both the shape and the position of the supply curve are, of course, relevant to the determination of price. The shape of the curve determines the response of price to a change in demand. In figure 24.19, with an initial supply curve S_1 an increase

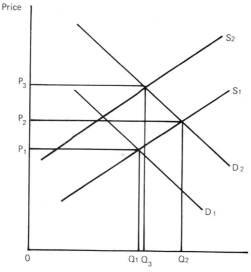

Figure 24.19 Changes in Demand, Supply, Price and Quantity Traded

in demand from D_1 to D_2 results in an increase in price from P_1 to P_2. A shift of the supply curve usually causes a change in price, the extent of the change depending upon the shape of the demand curve. In figure 24.19, with demand D_2, a shift from S_1 to S_2 results in an increase in price from P_2 to P_3. These shifts of the demand and supply curves also cause changes in the quantity traded.

ESSAY QUESTIONS

1 How would you explain the fact that, despite the widespread existence of economies of scale, many small firms survive?
2 Explain the reasons for believing that average total cost is often constant over quite a wide range of output, and discuss the significance of this fact.
3 Outline the various possible forms of internal growth and discuss the types of scale economy most likely to be associated with each form.
4 Discuss the advantages and disadvantages of internal growth as compared to growth by merger.
5 Why do so many firms adopt a policy of cost-based pricing?
6 'Cost-based pricing ensures that adequate profits are earned.' 'Cost-based pricing is a certain road to bankruptcy.' Comment.
7 Examine the factors which might determine the margin added to cost in arriving at a firm's target price.
8 'The response of price to a change in demand is likely to depend upon the time period under consideration.' Discuss.
9 'The greatest problems facing a firm which is considering changing its price arise from uncertainty concerning the reactions of its rivals.' Explain this statement and show how a firm may try to reduce the degree of uncertainty.
10 Examine the alternative policies open to a price leader and discuss the relative merits of each policy.

11 Explain the circumstances in which a policy of 'price-minus costing' is most likely to be adopted.
12 What factors will a firm take into account in deciding whether or not to change its prices following (a) an increase (b) a decrease in average cost?

EXERCISES

24.1 The Fishburn Machine Co. was about to begin the manufacture of a new type of metal fastener which they had not made before. Two machines suitable for making this fastener were on the market. Machine A, the cheaper of the two, had a rated capacity equivalent to an output of 400 units a day. It was in fact possible to increase output beyond this point by running the machines more quickly. However this required additional labour, since each worker could look after fewer machines. Moreover it had been found that there was an appreciable increase in the scrap rate, and hence in material costs.

Machine B had a greater capacity and, being fitted with more automatic devices, required fewer workers to operate it. Unfortunately, it was more expensive than machine A.

Using its usual method of depreciation, the company estimated its fixed costs would be £50 a day with machine A, and £100 a day with machine B. It estimated its variable cost to be as follows:

Daily output	Material costs (£ per unit)		Labour costs (£ per unit)	
(units)	Machine A	Machine B	Machine A	Machine B
100	0.25	0.25	0.40	0.30
200	0.25	0.25	0.40	0.30
300	0.25	0.25	0.40	0.30
400	0.25	0.25	0.40	0.30
500	0.30	0.25	0.50	0.30
600	0.35	0.25	0.60	0.30

(i) Draw the average total cost curves for both types of machine and indicate the single curve that would apply if the company could always choose the scale of organization appropriate to each level of output.
(ii) While the firm expects to sell 400 units a day, it realizes that sales could either exceed or fall short of this level. Examine the arguments in favour of installing each type of machine.

24.2 Each of 10 manufacturers of a certain product has the following cost schedule:

Output (000s)	Average cost (pence)	Average variable cost (pence)
1	80	30
2	55	30
3	47	30
4	43	30
5	40	30

Each firm expects to produce 5,000 units, and sets a price of 60 pence in order to achieve a target profit of £1,000.

Below are three alternative market demand schedules for this product.

| Price (pence) | Demand (000 units) | | |
	I	II	III
30	65	55	50
40	60	50	40
50	55	45	25
60	50	30	10

(i) Calculate each firm's total profit with demand schedule I.
(ii) With demand schedule II calculate each firm's total profit if they:
  (a) maintain price at 60 pence;
  (b) reduce price to the level of average cost at the output initially expected.
(iii) With demand schedule III calculate each firm's total profit if they:
  (a) maintain price at 60 pence;
  (b) reduce price to the level of average cost at the output initially expected.
(iv) Calculate each firm's total contribution in situations (iii) (a) and (b).
  (Contribution = sales revenue minus variable cost.)

24.3 The demand schedule for a certain product, currently priced at 50 pence, is as follows:

Price (pence)	Quantity demanded
50	10,000
55	9,000
60	8,000
65	7,000
70	6,000
75	5,000

Demand is distributed equally among 10 suppliers. At an output of 1,000 units, the average variable cost of each firm is 40 pence, and the average total cost 60 pence.

(i) Calculate (a) the total profit, and (b) the total contribution, currently earned by each firm.
(ii) Since demand shows no sign of improving, two firms leave the market. The remaining firms find that output is insufficient to meet demand at the existing price. They therefore increase price to the level at which demand and output are equal. Calculate (a) the total profit and (b) the total contribution, being earned by each firm.
(iii) The level of profit continuing to be unsatisfactory, a further three firms leave the market. The remaining firms again maintain the same level of output and raise price to the level at which output is just sufficient to meet demand. Calculate (a) the total profit and (b) the total contribution now earned by each firm.

24.4 The sales of a certain product are shared equally among three firms, each of which has the following cost schedule.

Output (000 units)	Average cost (pence)
1	70
2	50
3	40
4	40
5	45

The market demand schedule is as follows:

Price (pence)	Quantity demanded (000 units)
40	10.0
50	9.0
60	7.5
70	6.0
80	1.0

(i) In the absence of an agreement to co-ordinate their pricing decisions, each firm feels it wise to set a price which includes a reasonable profit margin of 25 per cent of average cost. Given that each firm expects to produce between three and four thousand units, calculate the total profit that will result from this pricing policy.

(ii) If the firms were able to co-ordinate their pricing decisions, and they wished to obtain the highest profit possible, what price should they set? By how much would the profit of each firm exceed that in situation (i)?

24.5 During the summer of 1971 a long spell of hot weather made it increasingly difficult for some brewers to keep up with demand, despite record levels of production.

In London, Courage was unable to meet the full demand for draught Harp Lager. 'The supply of new containers has been speeded up, but the demand for keg Harp is rising every week at a rate higher than new containers can be produced,' commented a spokesman, who added that draught Harp sales were 150 per cent up on those of the previous year.

Whitbread's keg beer, Tankard, was also in short supply in the West Country as the peak demand was aggravated by a fire at the Tiverton brewery and depot. Whitbread's nearest supply points were already at full stretch, so equipment was brought out of retirement at the Chiswell Street City brewery to cope with the situation. Police-escorted beer tanker fleets went from London to Devon on two nights in some weeks and once a week subsequently.

Britain's two largest brewers, Bass Charrington and Allied Breweries, both admitted to being at full stretch but claimed that no pub had gone short of supplies. Unfortunately for these brewers, although the boom pushed production units to full capacity and thus helped profits, the overall effect was not very dramatic. The low margin of profit on beer is costed very carefully, and normal wage rates are used in the calculation. Margins took a knock as production and distribution staff were put on overtime to cope with the demand.

Draw diagrams to illustrate the behaviour of demand and supply of (i) Harp lager in London, (ii) Tankard in the West Country, (iii) the beers of Bass Charrington. Explain your diagrams in not more than 300 words.

24.6 In the early part of the 1960s the fruit-squash market fell into two clearly defined parts, the main proprietary brands selling at around 2/3d to 2/9d (approximately 11p–14p) a bottle, and the rapidly growing private-label business, at 3d to 4d (1.25p–1.67p) a bottle less.

Then in June 1965 cyclamates were officially cleared for use in soft drinks. This gave the opportunity for a considerable saving in production costs, since cyclamates are some 30 times sweeter than sugar, and also obviate the need for expensive sugar-boiling equipment. Furthermore they enable squashes to be concentrated to a much greater degree than is possible with sugar. Finally, cyclamates enhance the flavour of citrus fruits, which account for by far the largest proportion of all squash flavours.

However the companies which took the earliest advantage of this new opportunity were not the manufacturers of the major brands, but a number of smaller companies, and in particular Rachelle and K.C. Developments, who brought out drinks, under both their own and retailers' private labels, at around 1/6d ($7\frac{1}{2}$p) a bottle.

When Rachelle went public it revealed that its sales had risen from £147,000 in 1965, to £343,000 in 1967 and £667,000 in 1968, as its proprietary brand, Sunice, drew level and then forged ahead of its private-label business. KCD, as a private company, did not need to reveal its sales figures, but claimed to be as big as Rachelle.

The success of these very cheap products finally provoked a response from some of the major manufacturers. For instance Schweppes brought out its New Kia Ora, and Robinsons introduced a Super Value squash range.

However competition from all such products finally came to an end when the government banned the use of cyclamates in soft drinks. The effect on the fortunes of those manufacturers who relied on price as their main selling point was just as dramatic as had been the effect of the decision to permit the use of cyclamates four years earlier, and the profits of both KCD and Rachelle slumped.

What light does the above case throw on:
(a) The effect of technological change on price competition:
(b) The nature of barriers to entry in the fruit squash market.

24.7 An analysis of U.S. data for the period 1936–40 by Professor Bain revealed that in industries in which the largest eight sellers accounted for at least 70 per cent of sales, the average rate of return on capital employed of the largest firms was 11.8 per cent, while the corresponding figure for industries with a lower concentration ratio was 7.8 per cent.

A later study by H.M. Mann showed that in the period 1950–60 in the industries where the largest eight sellers supplied at least 70 per cent of the market the average rate of return of the largest firms, at 13.3 per cent, was significantly higher than the comparable rate, 9.0 per cent, in less concentrated industries.

However, Professor Stigler showed that during the 1950s, while highly concentrated industries had the higher rates of return when the economy was relatively depressed, they tended to have the lower rates of return when the economy was booming.

(i) Why do you think large firms earned higher rates of return in more highly concentrated industries than in less concentrated industries in the periods 1936–40 and 1950–60? (ii) Why do you think there may be a tendency for higher rates of return to be earned in less concentrated industries when the economy is booming? (ii) In order to decide whether high levels of concentration are desirable, what factors should be taken into account in addition to relative rates of return?

24.8 It is clear that in one sense price leadership must restrict 'competition'. For if this is defined as fully independent action, then price leadership must restrain it. But if by competition is meant the bringing into existence of prices and costs that correspond with the requirements of efficient supply (i.e. the same as would emerge in a market with many sellers competing independently) then barometric price leadership is a device for creating these conditions, and therefore a means of making price competition effective where it would otherwise be hampered. For if there were fully independent pricing there would either be a tendency towards price rigidity or a 'price war' which might reach the point of price cutting aimed at mutual elimination. The first is clearly inefficient because it paralyses the price mechanism which is the means of attracting scarce resources into the uses where they can best satisfy customers' wants. And the second is also undesirable because in cut-throat 'price wars' prices may no longer correspond with costs but fall below them, and the end-result may be the survival not of the most efficient supplier but of the firm with strongest financial resources. Even if the process stops short of this stage, resource allocation will still be distorted because prices and profits will fall below the level which correctly reflects the requirement of resources to meet customers' wants (i.e. the effect of interdependence in oligopoly will have been to force prices below the level that would emerge in independent competition between many small suppliers).

Source: G. and P. Polanyi, *Parallel Pricing: a Harmful Practice* (Moorgate and Wall Street, Spring 1974), p. 59.

(i) What is the justification for the statement that 'if there were fully independent pricing there would either be a tendency towards price rigidity or a price war'? Do you agree with this statement? (ii) Comment upon the authors' conclusion that interdependence in oligopoly is undesirable if its effect is to force prices below the level that would emerge in independent competition between many small suppliers.

CHAPTER TWENTY-FIVE

Price Differentials

Introduction

IN the previous chapter we assumed that a supplier charged the same price to all purchasers of a given product. We made this assumption in order to simplify the explanation of how supply curves are derived. However in practice many suppliers charge different prices to different purchasers, and in this chapter we discuss the circumstances in which this is most likely to happen. We discuss first the charging of different prices when the cost of supplying different customers is identical, a situation that can be defined as price discrimination.

Price Discrimination

When a producer sells a given product in two (or more) distinct markets he will obtain greater profits by setting different prices in the different markets than he would by setting the same price, providing the following conditions apply:

(1) The different markets have different price elasticities of demand.
(2) There is no 'leakage' between the markets. This implies that
   (a) customers are unable to benefit by buying in one market and reselling in another;
   (b) customers are unable to transfer from one market to another. (This condition assumes particular importance in markets for services.)

We can demonstrate that price discrimination increases profits where demand elasticities differ, by reference to figure 25.1. We start from a position where the firm sets the same price, P, in both markets and in order to simplify the analysis we assume that quantity Q is sold in both markets, i.e. the two demand curves coincide at point X.

The firm now increases its price in the less elastic market B, and reduces its price in the more elastic market A. In order to further simplify the analysis we assume that the price adjustments are such as to leave total output unchanged. Since we have assumed that the average cost of supplying both markets is the same, total cost will also be unchanged. However it can be seen that total revenue, and therefore total profit, has increased:

$$[OP_B EQ_B + OP_A FQ_A] > [2(OPXQ)]$$

The Sub-Division of Markets

We now consider the various ways in which a market might be differentiated, i.e. divided into sub-markets. The most obvious basis is probably geographical (differentiation by space). In large countries, such as the U.S.A., differentiation between regional markets may be practical. Producers in smaller countries may be restricted to differentiation between home and export markets.

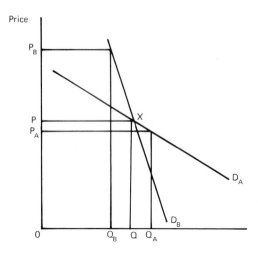

Quantity per period

Figure 25.1   Price Discrimination

A second basis is differentiation by time. Consumers may put different values on a product which is made available at different times. If, as a result, demand elasticities differ at different times, profits will be increased by price discrimination. So we find that telephone calls are cheaper in the evening, early morning and at weekend; railway travel is cheaper at off-peak times; and cinema and theatre tickets are sometimes cheaper for matinee performances.

The final basis for differentiation that we consider is the type of customer. In some instances this is tied up with another form of differentiation. For example *some* price concessions to retirement pensioners, females or children are available only for off-peak purchases. Again a price discount offered by a manufacturer to a wholesaler might be partly due to the fact that, as a wholesaler, the purchaser undertakes certain functions that are helpful to the manufacturer and that are not undertaken by other types of customer. But the discount may also take into account the quantity of the product bought by the purchaser. In other instances price differentials may be made purely on the basis of the type of customer, – whether he is a child or an adult, a manufacturer, wholesaler or retailer, etc.

Price Discrimination and the Supply Curve
As we said at the beginning of this chapter, the assumption that a producer charges the same price to all purchasers helps to explain how a supply curve is derived. Where price discrimination is practised between clearly defined sub-markets, a common price exists within each sub-market. In other words the producer has a separate supply curve for each sub-market. The overall supply curve for each sub-market is derived in the usual way by aggregating the supply curves of individual suppliers to that sub-market.

Price and Cost Differentials
In the introduction we defined price discrimination as the charging of different prices to different customers when the cost of supplying those customers is identical. It follows that if differences in prices reflect differences in cost, this does *not*

constitute price discrimination in an economic sense (although customers who are charged the higher price may feel that they are being discriminated against).

It is not difficult to think of reasons why costs may differ. The costs of supplying two different geographical markets may differ because of differences in transport costs or because the two markets are supplied from two factories which have different levels of efficiency. The cost per unit of a large order may be less than of a small order because of the economies of a large production run. The cost of supplying services at different times may differ because of the need to pay workers premium rates for 'unsocial' hours of work.

In some of these cases the analysis is straightforward. Two different average cost curves and therefore two different supply curves exist for the two markets. The analysis becomes more complicated when it is not possible to make a clear distinction between the costs that are incurred in supplying one market (or sub-market) and those incurred in supplying another. In order to analyse this situation we must refer to certain cost concepts that have not so far been required.

Additional Cost Concepts
INCREMENTAL COST
Incremental cost is the additional cost that results from an increase in output. A small increase in output may require an increase only in the quantity of direct materials used, since spare capacity may exist in other inputs. Larger increases in output are likely to require an increase in more inputs and even, perhaps, an increase in the scale of organization.

MARGINAL COST*
Marginal cost is a similar concept to incremental cost, but it refers to a change in output of one unit. Although in principle such a change *could* require an increase in the scale of organization it is most unlikely to do so in practice. Consequently marginal cost normally relates to a change in the cost of variable inputs, such as direct labour and materials.

ESCAPABLE COST
Escapable cost is the opposite of incremental cost. It is the reduction in cost that occurs when output falls. The reduction may apply to any input, e.g. less labour may be employed, fewer raw materials may be bought, machines may be scrapped. If the reduction in output refers to a single unit, the term marginal cost can be applied to the reduction in cost.

SUNK COST
A sunk cost is a cost that has already been incurred, and is therefore not affected by a change in output. If a machine has already been purchased the purchase price represents a sunk cost – only the operating costs would be saved by scrapping the machine. This is an extremely important point, since many of the fixed costs that we considered in the previous chapter are in fact sunk costs. In order to explain the connection between these two cost concepts we need to explore briefly the meaning and purpose of depreciation.

DEPRECIATION
When capital equipment is purchased the firm usually tries to recover its cost, not in the year of its purchase, but over a number of years, – perhaps five or ten for

* See also the appendix to this chapter.

machinery, longer for a factory. For example, if a firm purchased for £100,000 a machine which it expected to use for 10 years its annual cost would be considered to be £10,000. (If the firm used a replacement cost rather than a historical cost basis of depreciation, and it expected a new machine to cost £120,000 in ten years time, its annual cost would be £12,000.) The spreading of the initial, fixed, cost over a number of years is known as depreciation.*

The firm would hope and expect to charge a price that would cover this annual cost (together with the cost of all other inputs). However it might not always be able to do so. It might find that its customers would accept a price above variable cost but below total cost. As we said above, most fixed costs are usually sunk costs. If we make the simplifying assumption that all fixed costs are sunk we reach the conclusion that the firm would be better off, i.e. its *cash flow* would be greater, if it sold its output at a price above variable cost than if it did not produce at all.

Alternative Cost Concepts and Pricing Decisions

In order to link these concepts with the analysis presented in the previous chapter consider figure 25.2. Since average variable cost (AVC) is constant up to output

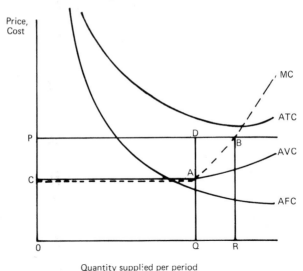

Figure 25.2 Average Total, Fixed, Variable and Marginal Cost

Q, marginal cost (MC) equals AVC up to that point. Then as AVC begins to increase, MC rises above AVC. As we noted above, marginal cost refers to a change in output of one unit. So the marginal cost of increasing output by one unit to Q is QA. Similarly the marginal cost of increasing output by one unit to R would be RB. It follows that the incremental cost of increasing output from Q minus one unit (Q−1) to R, is the area under the relevant part of the marginal cost curve, i.e. QABR.

Escapable cost is found by moving down the marginal cost curve. The reduction in marginal cost resulting from a reduction in output by one unit to R is RB, and by one unit to Q is QA. The escapable cost of reducing output from R plus one

* The number of years over which equipment and other assets are depreciated or written-off may, of course, differ from that assumed here.

unit $(R+1)$ to Q is again area RBAQ. If the firm were producing output Q the escapable cost if it were to cease production would be the area QACO.

If the firm sold quantity Q at price P it would fail to cover its total cost. Nevertheless it would be better to sell at this price than to cease production. If it ceased production its revenue would fall by QDPO whereas, as we have seen, its cost would fall by only QACO. In this decision the firm ignores sunk, or fixed, cost.*

The above conclusion depends, of course, upon the assumption that the firm could not use its assets in a more profitable way. If it believes that the maximum revenue that it could obtain in a given time period is OQDP, and if it could sell up, withdraw its resources from this market and invest them in an alternative use that would yield more than OQDP per period, it would pay it to redeploy its resources. We say that the opportunity cost of resources is greater than OQDP.

We can summarize by saying that the ultimate 'floor price' is equal to average variable cost (or opportunity cost if this is greater). However it is important to remember that when the time period is sufficiently long to enable the scale of organization to be changed, all inputs and costs become variable. As the existing machinery wears out new machinery must be bought (unless the firm is willing to move to a smaller scale). Consequently it is not possible for firms to permanently maintain price below average total cost. If the firm is unable to cover total cost and to earn a satisfactory profit at any scale or organization, it will eventually leave the market.

Price Differentials

In the shorter period, if the firm is unable to sell its output at its target price, it may still be able to sell part at this price and part at lower prices. (Alternatively, if it is unable to sell any at the target price, it may offer smaller reductions to some customers than others.)

It might appear that such a policy would represent price discrimination. But further exploration of the meaning of 'cost' may lead to a different conclusion. In order to simplify the analysis we assume in figure 25.3 that average variable cost is constant over the relevant range of output, and so is equal to marginal cost. We omit the average fixed cost curve from the diagram, since this is not relevant to the decisions considered here.

The current pattern of orders might suggest that during the present 'season' the firm will be able to sell output Q at price P_1. This price is lower than the firm hoped to obtain, and does not yield a satisfactory profit. The firm then has the opportunity to sell an additional amount QR at a price P_2. The revenue from this order would be QWVR. The cost would be QTSR. Consequently the additional profit from the order, i.e. the incremental profit, would be TWVS.

It will probably now be clear why it is not easy to decide whether taking this order would represent price discrimination. Although the price is below that charged to other customers, it yields a profit over the costs incurred in meeting that order. In deciding whether to accept the order the firm must take into account the factors outlined above. It must ensure that there is no leakage between the markets, i.e. that the purchaser will not resell the output QR to customers who would otherwise have purchased from the producer at price P_1. It must also ensure that these other purchasers do not realize that sales have been made at P_2 and demand a similar reduction in price on their purchases. Finally it must consider the opportunity cost of devoting resources to the production of goods for sale

*Sunk and fixed cost are in fact seldom identical, but we are justified in treating them as so in an elementary textbook.

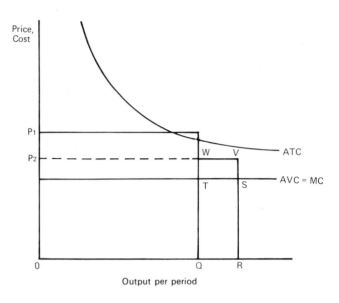

Figure 25.3 Differential Pricing

at price P_2. If it is sure that its orders from other customers will not exceed Q, the opportunity cost of the resources required to produce QR may be negligible. However if there is a chance that additional orders may be obtained at a price P_1, the firm may decide against using its resources to produce goods to be sold at P_2. (The potential opportunity cost exceeds the actual 'cash' cost of these resources.)

In the above example we have assumed that only two different prices are charged, but in some instances a producer may charge many different prices to different customers in a given season. In such situations it becomes difficult to envisage a supply curve of the type that we have considered so far. In fact if we wish to retain the concept of a supply curve, it must be interpreted as indicating the *average* prices at which given quantities would be supplied, it being understood that there might be a considerable spread of prices around this average.

The Pricing of Services

The principles discussed in the above sections may be applied to markets for both goods and services. But services have certain characteristics which often make price differentials especially appropriate. The most important of these characteristics is that services cannot be 'stored'. If a person wishes to travel by public transport at 8.00 a.m. or to attend the theatre at 8.00 p.m., the facilities must be made available at those times.

This has a very important implication if demand has an uneven pattern over time, as often occurs in service markets. If sufficient facilities are provided to meet the peak demand, excess capacity will occur at other times. Consequently, marginal or incremental cost in off peak periods is likely to be relatively low. For example whereas an increase in the peak demand for railway travel might require an increase in capacity, e.g. the purchase of more rolling stock, an increase in off-peak demand may simply mean that seats previously unoccupied are now occupied. One of the purposes of price concessions at off-peak times is to encourage the utilization of excess capacity.

The elasticity of demand is, of course, also relevant to pricing decisions. In many service markets demand is likely to be far less elastic at peak than at off-peak times. This again would suggest that a system of differential pricing would be likely to increase total revenue (see figure 25.1).

Moreover, even if some transfer of custom occurs from the high to the low price market, leading to a reduction in total revenue, price differentials may still increase profitability because of the favourable compensating effect on cost. If the peak demand falls the producer needs less capacity, and this reduction in 'capacity costs' may outweigh the loss of revenue. This is an especially important consideration in markets in which demand is growing overall, where the need to increase capacity, and hence incur additional capacity costs, would be reduced.

The Pricing Policies of the Nationalized Industries

Guidelines for pricing policies were laid down in a White Paper (Cmnd. 3437) issued in 1967. The major guidelines were as follows:

(a) '... nationalised industries' revenues should normally cover their accounting costs in full'.

(b) '... pricing policies should be devised with reference to the costs of the particular goods and services provided. Unless this is done, there is a risk of undesirable cross-subsidisation and consequent misallocation of resources'.

(c) '... in addition to recovering accounting costs, prices need to be reasonably related to costs at the margin and to be designed to promote the efficient use of resources within industry. Where there is spare capacity ... or excess demand, short run marginal costs are relevant. ... In the long run, the main consideration is ... long run marginal costs.'

If an industry supplied only one product to a single market, guidelines (a) and (c) *might* be compatible. Figure 25.4 refers to an industry in which average cost, and therefore marginal cost, is constant over the range of output Q_1Q_2. Over this

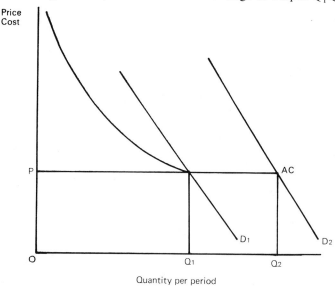

Figure 25.4   Revenue Covers Accounting Costs

range price P equals average (and marginal) cost. Consequently with demand within the range $D_1 D_2$ revenue covers 'accounting costs in full'.*

However some industries may not have the cost conditions illustrated in figure 25.4. In figure 25.5 we show an industry whose average cost continues to fall as output increases. In this situation, at price P_1 revenue covers average cost but the price exceeds marginal cost. Conversely, although price P_2 equals marginal cost, revenue does not cover average cost. In other words it is impossible in this situation, (whatever the demand conditions) to set a price which meets both guidelines (a) and (c).

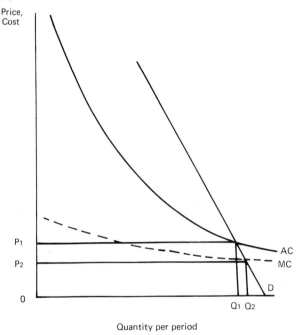

Quantity per period

Figure 25.5 Nationalized Industry Pricing with Falling Average Cost

In figure 25.6 we show an industry in which, beyond a certain point Q, average cost rises as output increases. In this instance there *is* a price, P, which may equal marginal cost and also yield a revenue sufficient to cover 'full accounting costs'. However this occurs only if demand is as shown. If the demand curve is either to the left or right of D (as is likely) a loss will result if price is set at P.

In practice all nationalized industries supply more than one product. Moreover each product is supplied to several different markets or sub-markets. This would suggest that differential pricing policies should be adopted. This is, in fact, recognized in the guidelines, especially in (b) which refers to 'the costs of particular goods and services provided', and also in (c) which refers to the relevance of short run marginal costs where there is excess capacity.

It is not clear whether the White Paper intended to advocate a system of differential prices based on costs or a policy of price discrimination. The guidelines could

* This phrase was not precisely defined in the White Paper. Average cost should be interpreted here to include an allowance for a surplus which is required for the financing of future capital expenditure. We showed in Chapter 19 that the nationalized industries are usually expected to finance some of their capital expenditure from retained earnings.

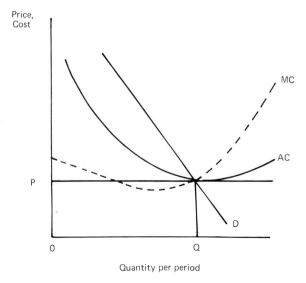

Figure 25.6 Price Equals Average and Marginal Cost

be interpreted in either way. In fact, as we showed above, the difficulties of defining the costs of particular goods and services may be such that it is impossible to decide whether a system of differential prices does or does not represent price discrimination.

When the National Economic Development Office examined in 1975 the pricing policies adopted by the nationalized industries, they found that overall each industry had attempted to cover its full costs, although, as noted in Chapter 19, this policy was sometimes modified following government intervention. NEDO also found considerable evidence of pricing differentials, especially in industries such as the British Steel Corporation and British Rail which faced substantial competition from other producers or products. Moreover these differentials were often determined in the light of demand conditions, which could indicate that price discrimination was practised.

Summary and Conclusions
In this chapter we have been concerned with pricing decisions when a producer supplies two or more different markets or sub-markets. When identical costs are incurred in supplying different markets, a system of price differentials constitutes price discrimination.

Price discrimination yields higher profits than would a policy of uniform pricing provided that the different markets have different price elasticities of demand, and that there is no 'leakage' between the markets. These conditions must be fulfilled whatever the basis on which the market is differentiated or sub-divided, whether by space, time or type of customer. (The only exception to this requirement is where a loss of revenue due to leakage is outweighed by a reduction in total cost.)

In some instances it is not clear whether or not price differentials constitute price discrimination, since 'cost' is by no means a simple concept. Furthermore, even if price discrimination can be shown to exist, it does not follow that its consequences are necessarily undesirable. Indeed it can be shown that in some circumstances both producers and consumers would be worse off in the absence of discrimination.

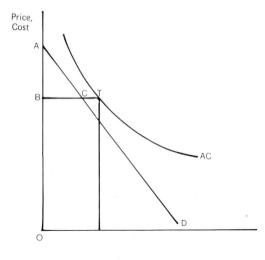

Figure 25.7 Cost and Revenue under Perfect Price Discrimination

In figure 25.7 the producer would be unable to cover his costs at any price that might be uniformly applied. He would therefore eventually leave the market. On the other hand, if he were able to practice perfect price discrimination, i.e. charge each consumer what he would be prepared to pay, he could make a profit and remain in business. At output Q total revenue would be OQRA, which exceeds total cost OQTB. (This can be clearly seen since ΔABC > ΔCTR.)

Appendix   The Marginal Analysis
In this and the previous chapter we have presented models of price determination which approximate closely to actual business behaviour. Many textbooks present an alternative series of models based on the marginal analysis. These models assume that firms wish to maximize their short run profits, and they show that in order to attain this objective the firm should produce to the point at which marginal cost equals marginal revenue. (More precisely they should produce to the point at which the marginal cost curve cuts the marginal revenue curve from below.)

Table 25.1 shows the relationship between total, average and marginal cost. In the main body of the chapter we defined marginal cost as the change in total cost that occurs as a result of a change in output of one unit. In table 25.1 marginal cost is constant at £4 per unit.

Table 25.1

Total, Average and Marginal Cost

Output	Fixed cost	Variable cost	Total cost	Average cost	Marginal cost
(units)	(£)	(£)	(£)	(£)	(£)
1	10	4	14	14	4
2	10	8	18	9	4
3	10	12	22	7.3	4
4	10	16	26	6.5	4
5	10	20	30	6	4

Marginal revenue is the change in total revenue that occurs as a result of a change in output of one unit. Table 25.2 shows that marginal revenue declines as output increases. This happens because a reduction in price is required in order to increase the volume of sales, i.e. the demand curve is less than perfectly elastic.* Consider for example, the consequences of reducing price from £10 to £9. Sales increase by one unit, which increases revenue by £9. However the lower price has also to be offered to the customer who would have been prepared to pay £10. Consequently there is a loss of potential revenue from this customer of £1. The overall change in revenue as a result of the increase in output, i.e. the marginal revenue, is therefore £8 (£9 – 1).

Table 25.2

Total, Average and Marginal Revenue

Price (=average revenue)	Output	Total revenue	Marginal revenue
(£)	(units)	(£)	(£)
10	1	10	10
9	2	18	8
8	3	24	6
7	4	28	4
6	5	30	2

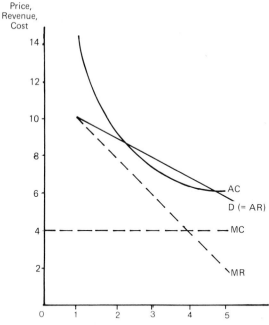

Figure 25.8 Marginal Analysis and the Profit Maximizing Price

The application of the rule for profit maximization to the data in tables 25.1 and 25.2 indicates that the firm should set a price of £7 and sell 4 units. A diagrammatic representation of this situation is presented in figure 25.8. The marginal cost curve cuts the marginal revenue curve from below at an output of 4 units.

The profit maximizing position is, of course, that at which the excess of total

* A perfectly elastic demand curve is examined in Chapter 26.

revenue over total cost is greatest. This position could be shown diagrammatically by drawing total revenue and cost curves. It can also be derived from the data in tables 25.1 and 25.2. A comparison of the total revenue and total cost columns confirms that profits are maximized at an output of 4 units, where revenue exceeds cost by £2. It appears that profits would also be maximized at an output of 3 units. In fact the marginal analysis interprets cost as including an element of profit ('normal profit'). Since total cost, and therefore normal profit, is greater at an output of 4 than of 3 units, total profit (normal plus abnormal or supernormal) would also be greater with an output of 4 units.

The marginal analysis can also be used to explain profit maximization when price discrimination is practised. In figure 25.9 the firm supplies two markets with

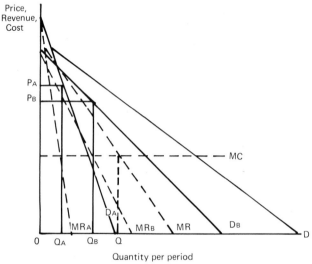

Figure 25.9   Marginal Analysis and Price Discrimination

different elasticities, as shown by the demand curves D_A and D_B. If it follows the profit maximizing rule, the firm will equate marginal cost and marginal revenue in each market. In the less elastic market A, Q_A is sold at price P_A. In the more elastic market B, Q_B is sold at the lower price P_B. (Note that at any price, total demand equals the sum of the demand in the two markets, i.e. $D = D_A + D_B$. Similarly $MR = MR_A + MR_B$. The equilibrium output Q $(= Q_A + Q_B)$ occurs at the intersection of MC and MR.)

A Critique of the Marginal Analysis
Models incorporating marginal analysis are able to present an apparently simple rule for profit maximization, an advantage that should not be dismissed lightly. However this simplicity is attained only by making the very dubious assumption that the firm wishes to maximize its *short run* profits. We believe that in the markets that we have considered in this and the previous chapter, i.e. the markets for manufactured goods and services, suppliers are likely to have a longer time horizon. They are interested in building up a market position which will guarantee their profitability, and hence their survival, in future years.

This is a very important distinction, since – as we showed during our discussion of new entry in the previous chapter – higher profits today may mean lower profits tomorrow.

Moreover, even if the analysis is confined to the short run, the models presented in this appendix assume a much greater degree of certainty about demand conditions than usually exists in practice. One could take the view that the demand curves shown in the diagrams represent the firm's best estimate of market conditions, and that firms take price and output decisions in the light of these estimates. However this is an unsatisfactory assumption. Many firms are so uncertain about the reactions of their rivals that it would not be meaningful to think of a demand curve on the basis of which marginal adjustments to price and output could be made. Instead firms usually prefer to set a price for a season and to adjust output, but not price, if demand conditions are not as expected.

This does not mean that marginal principles are of no account. Indeed we have shown that firms may face many decisions to which incremental analysis – which embodies marginal principles – can be applied. However these decisions often cannot be satisfactorily analysed in terms of models which assume the existence of distinct markets or sub-markets, each having clearly defined demand and cost schedules or curves.

ESSAY QUESTIONS

1   State and illustrate the conditions that must be fulfilled if profits are to be increased by price discrimination.
2   Describe the various ways in which a market might be sub-divided by a firm practising price discrimination.
3   Explain why it may not be easy to decide whether the existence of price differentials indicates that price discrimination is being practised.
4   Illustrate the types of decision for which the following cost concepts are relevent: marginal cost, incremental cost, escapable cost, opportunity cost.
5   It has been suggested that the nationalized industries should adopt a policy of 'marginal cost pricing'. Discuss the meaning of this term and explain what problems might arise if such a policy were adopted.
6   'Price discrimination can benefit both producers and consumers'. Discuss.
7   Show how marginal analysis can help to identify the profit maximizing price. Explain why firms may *not* apply this analysis to their pricing decisions.
8   'Empirical studies reveal that very few firms attempt to produce the output at which marginal cost equals marginal revenue. This indicates that marginal analysis is of very little practical value.' Discuss.
9   'Charging half price fares to school children at peak periods indicates that bus companies are motivated by considerations of equity rather than profitability.' Discuss.

EXERCISES

25.1 Exercise 25.1 is based on the following cost data, relating to the production of a certain piece of industrial equipment:
     The cost of raw materials is £3 per unit of output, regardless of the number of units produced. The cost of labour is £2 per unit of output, regardless of the number of units produced. The monthly depreciation charge is constant at £600 for any output up to and including 110 units. However a larger output would require the installation of additional machinery, which would result in the monthly depreciation charge rising to £700. This additional machinery would raise the capacity to a maximum output of 150 units; however if the

firm should ever want to have it taken out, the cost of removal would just about equal its scrap value.

Calculate:

(i) The average total cost, with a monthly output of (a) 100 units, (b) 120 units, (c) 140 units.

(ii) The additional cost incurred when output is increased from 100 to 101 units. (What do we call this cost?)

(iii) The incremental cost when output is increased from (a) 100 to 110 units, (b) 100 to 120 units.

(iv) The escapable cost when output is reduced from 120 to 110 units.

25.2 The Road-Ready Tyre Company is a small company producing re-tread tyres. It normally produces about 1,000 tyres a week at a unit of cost of £2.50, which are sold under its own brand name to wholesalers at a price of £3.50. The company has an unexpected opportunity to sell additional tyres under private labels to three retail outlets. Able's Auto Accessories offers to buy 1,000 tyres at £3.25; Baker's Car Accessories offers to buy 1,000 tyres at £3.00, and Charlie's Motor Spares offers to buy 1,000 tyres at £2.75.

The company has sufficient machine capacity to meet these orders. However it will need to introduce overtime working, which will increase the level of costs. It estimates that the unit cost for the first additional 1,000 tyres will be £2.60, for the next 1,000 £2.70 and for the next 1,000 £2.80.

Which, if any, of these three orders should Road-Ready accept?

25.3 An engineering company which usually makes the major components used in the various machines that it manufactures wished to increase its weekly output of one particular component from 200 to 300 units. On this occasion it decided that it should seek a quotation from outside suppliers, and found that the best terms that it could obtain were:

$$100 \text{ units a week} - £1.00 \text{ per unit}$$
$$200 \text{ units a week} - £0.90 \text{ per unit}$$
$$300 \text{ units a week} - £0.80 \text{ per unit}$$

The company estimated its own cost of producing this component as follows:

Direct cost (labour and materials)	£0.50
Factory overhead (100% of direct cost)	£0.50
General overhead (20% of direct cost)	£0.10
Total cost per unit	£1.10

The factory overhead mainly comprised the depreciation of plant and equipment. Since this plant and equipment was used in the manufacture of a large number of different types of component it was not feasible to calculate a precise charge per unit of each component made. Instead factory overhead was levied as a proportion of direct cost. The same principle was applied to the allocation of general overhead, which mainly comprised central administrative expenses.

How many, (if any), components should the company buy from the outside supplier if (a) it has sufficient excess capacity to allow it to increase production to 300 units a week, (b) in order to increase production it would have to enlarge its factory and install additional machinery?

25.4 The Johnson Leisurewear Co. makes a wide range of sports and leisure wear –

anoraks, ski-pants, sweaters, etc. There is a high fashion content in the company's products, which are usually priced towards the top end of the market. Because of the high reputation of its products, Johnson obtains a high volume of pre-production orders, and on the basis of these orders it is usually able to make a fairly accurate estimate of the total demand for any particular article over the forthcoming season. If any articles remain unsold at the end of the season it will dispose of them at a discount; however the accuracy of its forecasting methods has meant that it has not usually had to make significant markdowns.

At the company's annual showing of the following year's range of products, a new style of anorak was shown, which utilized a new material, designed to give added warmth with no extra weight. This new material also enabled a printing technique to be used which could print in various five-colour combinations.

The new anorak was very well received by the buyers for the stores through which Johnson made most of its sales, and a pre-production order for 25,000 anoraks was placed. The anoraks were to retail at £27, and would cost the retailer £18. This was the largest pre-production order for anoraks ever received, and Johnson decided to make 30,000 articles. However sales in the shops were by no means as good as has been expected, the main complaint of customers being that the multi-coloured patterns were too 'busy'. None of the retailers who had placed pre-production orders reordered, and other retailers bought only a further 2,000 garments. This left the company with 3,000 unsold garments, which had cost £15 each to manufacture. The marketing manager estimated that sales during the rest of the season, at various prices, would be as follows:

If price to retailer were	Estimated number sold
£18.00	200
£16.50	500
£15.00	600
£13.50	1,000
£12.00	1,300
£10.50	1,700
£9.00	1,900
£7.50	2,500
£6.00	3,000

At what price should Johnson offer the remaining anoraks?

25.5 The Delight Chocolate Co. makes a range of specialist chocolate and sugar confectionery goods, liqueur chocolates, fondants, bon-bons, etc. The company restricts the distribution of its products to a limited number of 'high-class', independent retailers, whose image is consistent with the quality image of the 'Delight' brand name, which the company wishes to foster.

As a very expensive brand, a high proportion of Delight sales are for the gift market. This results in a strong seasonal pattern of sales, with about one-half of orders from retailers coming in the October–December period. This is in turn reflected in a seasonal pattern of production; although the company tries to even out the fluctuations by producing for stock, there is a limit beyond which it feels it would be unwise to go in this respect, since the product has a limited shelf-life. Consequently, during the first half of the year the company operates at below full capacity.

In February of one year, when Delight's level of activity was at about its lowest point, the company was approached by the buyer of a large chain store, which offered to buy a large quantity of one of Delight's major lines, at a price of £1.00 a box. The boxes would be labelled not with the Delight brand, but with the brand name of the store, and delivery would be made during May and June.

Delight normally sold this line to retailers at a price of £1.25 a box, the usual retail price being around £1.60. The average cost of production of this line based on the normal volume of sales was calculated as follows:

Direct material and labour	£0.90
General administration and overheads	£0.16
Selling and advertising	£0.04
Total cost per box	£1.10

Profit levels in the industry during the previous few years had on the whole been unsatisfactory, mainly because of a fall in the consumption of chocolate and sugar confectionery. Delight had been one of the few companies which had succeeded in maintaining its profits, and this was felt to be due largely to the fact that it produced only high quality, expensive lines.

The general view in the industry was that these recent trends were likely to continue.

Should Delight take the order from the chain store?

25.6 A manufacturer of regulators, thermostats and switches had a system of quantity discounts whereby purchasers were given discounts in accordance with the number of articles of one type ordered at any one time. The scale of discounts was as follows:

Quantity ordered	Discount from list price
1–5	Nil
6–10	5%
11–20	10%
21–100	20%
101–500	30%
501–1,000	40%
1,000+	50%

In order to try to assess the effectiveness of this discount structure, the company took a sample of its customers' accounts, and calculated the cost of supplying, and the revenue derived from, these customers. Two of these customers, C and D, bought a standard type of switch. During the previous year, firm C placed 24 orders for a total of 580 switches; the average discount given was 20 per cent on the list price of £1.40 per switch. Firm D placed 8 orders for a total of 10,660 switches, and received an average discount of 50 per cent. The manufacturing company handles several thousand sales orders per year; the average cost of processing each order (total cost of order processing – personnel, equipment, forms, postage, etc. – divided by the number of orders) was £18.60. The particular switch ordered by C and D is produced continuously on a large scale at a cost of £0.40 per unit.

Calculate the total cost (manufacturing plus order processing) and total revenue attributable to customer C and customer D during the year. If firm C is unwilling to order in larger quantities, should the manufacturer stop seeking its business?

25.7 Schedule of net prices of sparking plugs.

	Price (cents per plug)
Purchaser	
1. Automobile manufacturers	
(a) For original equipment	6
(b) For replacement parts	24
(c) Average prices to one automobile manufacturer	13 to 15
2. National distributors	
(a) Largest service-station group buyer	23
(b) Large oil-company	23
3. Distributors who sell branded products to dealers and garages	27.1
4. Mail-order houses and other large private-brand sellers	18
5. Secondary jobbers and fleet owners in purchases of 1,000+	29
6. Retailers and garages (who buy from secondary jobbers), recommended price:	
(a) Quantity:1–99	39
(b) Quantity: 100–299	36
(c) Quantity: 300+	32
7. Car owner, recommended prices:	
(a) Quantity: 1 plug	65
(b) Quantity: set of 6 or 8 plugs	59

Source: J. Dean, *Managerial Economics* (Englewood Cliffs, N.J.: Prentice Hall, 1951), p 521.

What factors might help to explain the pattern of prices set out in the schedule above?

25.8 Inflation-weary travellers planning this summer's vacation in the U.S. can relax with the comforting thought that prices in at least one important area will be well down on last year's levels. After more than two years during which U.S. air fares have been pushed sharply higher, the trend has now been reversed in rounds of fare discounting designed to offset the impact of the recession and fill increasingly empty aircraft.

By any standards it has been a bleak winter for the airline industry. Since last November, passenger air traffic has been steadily declining, in sharp comparison with the surprisingly and totally unexpected gains seen in late 1973 and early 1974 as the petrol shortage forced cars off the road. Over the first three months of this year, revenue passenger miles (the best measure of passenger traffic) fell 5 per cent in what the Civil Aeronautics Board (C.A.B.) described as the worst slump in the industry's history.

The real dimensions of the slump are better measured by the airline's load factor – the all-important percentage of seats occupied by paying passengers. During the first three months of 1975 virtually every domestic airline saw its load factor down from 1974's profitable levels of around 60 per cent to about 50 per cent which is below the breakeven point.

The current level of discounting had quite modest beginnings. In January American Airlines' introduction of a special (25 per cent off) excursion fare for passengers flying over 1,500 miles was approved, and quickly copied by other carriers. This scheme, like its successors, bore conditions designed to ensure that the business traveller, who would be flying whatever the rate, could not benefit from the cut price. A 14-day advance ticket purchase was required, together with a return booking and a guaranteed one to two week length of stay.

The discounts have steadily grown bigger and the required conditions less restrictive as each carrier introduced its own 'unique' scheme. The result has been a bewildering array of different fares and other expensive promotion gimmicks. Continental has recently re-introduced its luxury coach lounges and is now showing 1940s in-flight films, while American Airlines offers passengers a closed-circuit television view of the pilot at work.

It was, perhaps, last April when discounting really got going, with National Airlines' introduction of its 'no frills' fare for north–south East Coast travel. The special 'third-class' fare ('no frills' passengers sat in special tail-end seats and could buy neither food nor liquor) was 35 per cent below the scheduled rate and, perhaps most surprisingly, was cheaper than rail and bus fares on the same route.

National scored a major promotional triumph and immediately regained most of its share of the New York to Florida market lost during its 1974 strike. While National's competitors on the route – Delta and Eastern – were less than convinced about the profit potential of the scheme, they not only followed suit but went one step further. Within a matter of weeks, the scheme was extended to include non-wide-bodied aircraft and passengers were able to buy spirits and food 'at special prices'.

The above passage is based on an article in the *Financial Times*, 23.6.75. Evaluate the policy of discounting from the viewpoint of (a) suppliers, (b) consumers, (c) overall economic welfare.

25.9 In 1975 the retail petrol market was characterized by price cutting on a scale not previously encountered – some garages sold petrol at 12p a gallon below the recommended price. Eventually, following talks with the Minister for Prices and Consumer Protection, the major oil companies agreed to reduce the discounts that they had been granting to some retailers, one of the sources of the reductions in retail prices. (Subsequently the majors successfully applied to the Price Commission for an increase in the recommended retail price).

However in January 1976 Esso announced that they were re-introducing major discounts to selected retailers in certain areas – mainly in North and East England. The lead given by Esso was followed almost immediately by the other major oil companies. Esso stated that they had been forced to re-introduce these special discounts because of competition from three sources: (a) garages selling petrol imported from continental refiners at low prices; (b) garages selling petrol obtained from I.C.I., who produce petrol as a by-product of chemical processes; (c) garages owned by ASDA, a prominent supermarket chain, and located on supermarket sites. While competition, from these sources certainly existed, the fact that the other major companies followed Esso's lead so quickly was seen by certain commentators as an indication of a concerted effort by the majors to force the smaller independent producers out of the market.

(i) Why do you think I.C.I. (a) was able and (b) decided, to sell petrol so cheaply? (ii) Why do you think ASDA (a) was able and (b) decided, to sell petrol so cheaply? (iii) would you agree that the fact that all the other majors followed Esso so quickly in re-introducing special discounts was an indication of a concerted strategy? What alternative explanation of this policy might be advanced? (iv) In 1975 the majors withdrew special discounts after discussions with a government minister. This implies that the public might suffer some disadvantages as a result of these discounts. What might these disadvantages be?

25.10 To the Scotch whisky industry a 'parallel exporter' is someone who operates outside the normal channels. And those normal channels mainly involve the U.K. producers selling to sole importers in individual overseas markets.

In 1975, parallel exports really began to make an impact on the industry because the export price for Scotch had moved way above the U.K. market price. The difference was as much as £2 for a case of 12 bottles.

International supermarket groups found that they could buy their Scotch in the U.K., ship it to the Continent and either take the extra profit or sell the whisky at cut prices far below anything which could be offered by the local sole importer. Distillers Company, which owns brands like Haig, Vat 69, Black and White and Dewar's as well as Johnnie Walker, the world's best-selling Scotch, was faced with irate agents who were threatening to withdraw financial support for the brands they handled because their profits had suffered so badly.

Glenlivet Distillers, recently traced the path of 300 cases of its eight-year-old Glen Grant malt whisky which were sold to a U.K. wholesaler who in turn sold them to a supermarket chain in the West Country. The following week the Scotch turned up in Liverpool with many other brands ready for shipment overseas. Glenlivet discovered this and bought back from the Liverpool wholesaler its own Scotch at £16 a case compared with the £12 paid by the original wholesaler-customer. Glenlivet was £1,200 down on the deal but it had prevented some of its Scotch going out via the parallel market.

'Sales by parallel importers are not made because there is an unfulfilled demand which the accredited distributors are unable to meet. They are made because parallel importers, having no obligation to advertise or promote brands, or to ensure their availability throughout the market, are able to undercut the distributors' prices. The sales made by parallel importers are possible only by the efforts that the distributors have made over the years to make the brand widely known and to ensure its acceptance. The main interest of the parallel importer is to make a quick sale to a particular customer. The accredited distributor has a long-term interest in the success of the brand', says Distillers.

The above passage is based on an article in the *Financial Times*, 31.1.77. (i) What light does the passage throw on the conditions for successful price discrimination? (ii) Comment on Glenlivet's policy of buying back its own whisky at a loss. (iii) One 'parallel exporter', who was refused supplies by the Distillers Company, asked the Office of Fair Trading to investigate what he considered to be a restrictive practice. Do you think that Distillers should be allowed to refuse to supply potential customers?

25.11 When the cost of a monthly rail ticket from Brighton to London was £42.70 the cost of an annual ticket was £443.00. (i) Calculate the saving resulting from the purchase of an annual ticket as compared with 12 monthly tickets. (ii) In what circumstances would you advise a commuter to buy (a) an annual ticket, (b) 12 monthly tickets? (iii) What information should British Rail take into account in fixing the differential between the price of annual and monthly tickets?

25.12 The Post Office Act 1969 lays down that 'it shall be the duty of the Post Office so to exercise its powers as to secure that all its revenues are not less than sufficient to meet all charges properly chargeable to revenue account, taking one year with another.' But also that 'If it appears to the Minister that the Post Office is showing undue preference to, or is exercising discrimination against, any person or persons of any class or description in the charges or other terms and conditions applicable to services provided by it ... he may ... give it directions ... to secure that it ceases to do so'.

Comment on these guidelines.

25.13 The most common method of 'pricing' water used by U.K. domestic consumers is to fix an annual water rate which is proportional to the rateable value of the premises being supplied. This annual payment is fixed regardless of the actual quantity of water taken by the particular premises. The water rate is such that the total revenue from all consumers covers the total cost of the water provided by the supplier. Different rates are charged by different supplying authorities. However within the area supplied by a given authority all domestic consumers occupying premises of a given rateable value pay the same amount.

(i) What are the economic advantages and disadvantages of this method of pricing water? (ii) What other methods might be adopted? (iii) What would be the advantages and disadvantages of these other methods?

OBJECTIVE TEST QUESTIONS: SET 8

1 The best definition of a supply curve is that it shows the

A relationship between average cost and price
B relationship between price and the quantity supplied
C quantity supplied at various prices
D quantity that would be supplied at various prices
E quantity that would be supplied at various prices in a given period

Questions 2 to 7 are based on figure 25.10 which relates to the market for bauxite (aluminium ore). The unbroken lines are the initial demand and supply curves and the broken lines are the demand and supply curves which might arise as a

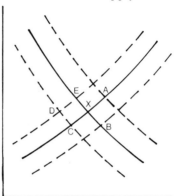

Figure 25.10

result of the various changes listed below. Starting each time from the original equilibrium position X, indicate the new equilibrium position A, B, C, D or E. Each letter may be used once, more than once, or not at all.

2 The price of copper, a substitute for aluminium, falls.

3 The cost of transporting bauxite increases.

4 An increase occurs in the price of electricity, used in the process of transforming bauxite into aluminium.

5 New low-cost deposits of bauxite are discovered.

6 The demand for aluminium goods falls; a strike by bauxite miners reduces supplies from low-cost mines.

7 The government places a tax on copper goods; an increase occurs in real national income.

8 Which of the following could *not* explain why a firm's average total cost decreased as its output increased at a given scale of organization? (AFC= average fixed cost; AVC=average variable cost.)

A both AFC and AVC decreased
B AVC decreased while AFC remained constant
C AFC decreased while AVC remained constant
D the decrease in AFC outweighed the increase in AVC
E AVC decreased more rapidly than AFC.

9 If a grocery wholesaler took over a retail grocery chain this would be an example of

A horizontal growth
B backward integration
C backward growth by internal expansion
D forward integration
E forward growth by internal expansion.

10 The shift of the supply curve from S_1 to S_2 in figure 25.11 could have been caused by any of the following except

A the imposition of a specific indirect tax
B the imposition of an ad valorem indirect tax
C an increase in the price of inputs
D technological progress
E a fall in labour productivity.

Figure 25.11

Questions 11–13 relate to the table below which refers to a product whose fixed cost is £1,000, and whose average variable cost is constant at all levels of output.

Output	Average Cost (£)
2	520
3	353.3
4	—
5	220

11 The average total cost at an output of 4 units would be (£)

A   300
B   286.7
C   280
D   270
E   250

12 The incremental cost of an increase in output from 2 to 5 units would be (£)

A   300
B   100
C   80
D   60
E   20

13 The marginal cost at all levels of output is (£)

A   300
B   100
C   80
D   60
E   20.

14 Assuming a given scale of organization, a producer will cease production if there is no output at which revenue equals or exceeds

A   total cost
B   fixed cost
C   variable cost
D   sunk cost
E   escapable cost.

15 If a firm were certain that its cost and revenue conditions were as shown in figure 25.12, and if it wished to maximize its short run profits, what output would it produce – A, B, C, D or E?

16 The shift in the supply curve from S_1 to S_2 in figure 25.13 could have been due to

1   economies of scale being attained as output increased
2   a fall in the cost of production at all levels of output
3   the granting of subsidies to producers.

17 If demand is inelastic an increase in price must result in an increase in

1   total revenue

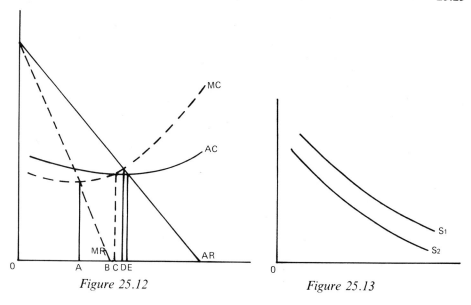

Figure 25.12   Figure 25.13

2   total profits
3   profit margins (profit per unit sold).

18 Profits will increase as a result of price determination provided that
    1   there is no leakage between markets
    2   all markets have the same elasticity of demand
    3   price differences reflect differences in costs.

19 With a given scale of organization, if average total cost increases as output
    increases, we can conclude that average variable cost also increases.
        With a given scale of organization, average fixed cost falls as output in-
    creases.

20 If demand is elastic an increase in price may result in either a rise or a fall
    in total profits.
        If demand is elastic an increase in price results in an increase in revenue.

TRUE/FALSE

1   The limit to a firm's output is always set by the inability to increase the
    quantity of capital inputs.
2   If demand is inelastic an increase in price will lead to an increase in both
    revenue and profits.
3   If demand is elastic a decrease in price will lead to an increase in both revenue
    and profits.
4   If one firm reduces its price its demand will be less elastic if competitors reduce
    their prices than if their prices are unchanged.
5   When the supplier of a given product sets different prices that do not reflect
    cost differences he is said to practice price discrimination.
6   A firm which obtained greater economies of scale than other firms would have
    lower average costs than these other firms at all levels of output.

7 Technical economies of scale are more likely to result from a process of horizontal than diversified growth.

8 A cost that has already been incurred and is not affected by a change in output is known as a sunk cost.

9 The nationalized industries usually set a price equal to marginal cost.

10 The reduction in cost that occurs as output is reduced is known as incremental cost.

CHAPTER TWENTY-SIX

Price Determination in Open Markets

Introduction

IN the previous two chapters we discussed how prices are determined when cost is taken as the starting point in the pricing decision. We showed that the profit margin added to cost, and also the way in which cost is defined, may vary in different circumstances. Nevertheless, despite these differences, the price set in a market or sub-market is related to the firm's expected costs. The only exception is the price-taker who accepts the price set by the dominant firm. Even here the price in the market is related to the costs of the dominant firm, the price-maker.

By contrast, in open markets price is set by the interaction between aggregate (market) demand and aggregate (market) supply. No individual supplier can influence price. In fact we can say that in open markets all suppliers are price takers. It follows that cost is a much less important influence on price than in the markets we have discussed so far. However we shall see that the influence of cost is not completely absent.

Open Markets

Many mineral and agricultural products are sold in open markets. Probably the best example of such a market is the sale by auction of a perishable product such as fish or tomatoes. In such instances the pricing season is extremely short, lasting only as long as the auction – normally less than one day. Price is determined by the interaction between demand and supply on that day. Demand is subject to the usual influences, and the quantity demanded varies in accordance with the price. Supply, on the other hand, is completely inelastic, i.e. a given quantity is supplied whatever the price. The quantity supplied at a fish auction will depend upon the catches made by boats landing on the day of the auction; at an auction of tomatoes supply will depend upon the deliveries made by farmers on that day.

In figure 26.1 the quantity supplied is Q, the supply curve being vertical at that point. Given this supply, price is determined by demand. With demand at D_1 price is P_1; with demand at D_2, price is P_2. At both prices the quantity traded is, of course, Q.

The Influence of Cost

Although prices in open markets are often said to be 'demand determined', cost may still influence price in several ways. First, continuing our previous example, let us assume that fishermen wish to insure themselves against the fluctuations in price, and hence in revenue, which characterize auction markets. Rather than allow all their fish always to be sold by auction for human consumption, they might seek an alternative market to which supplies could be diverted if the price at auction were unsatisfactory. The manufacturers of pet food might provide such an alternative market. (The revenue obtainable from the pet food manufacturers would constitute the opportunity cost of supplying fish to the auction market.)

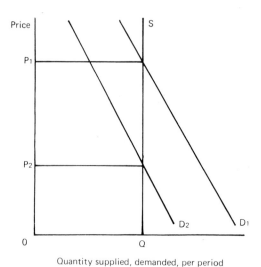

Quantity supplied, demanded, per period

Figure 26.1 Equilibrium Price in an Open Market

Since the manufacturers guarantee to pay a given price, and thus give suppliers the additional security they require, this price will obviously be below the average price expected in the auction market over a long period. In figure 26.2 the average, expected, price is designated as P_E, and the guaranteed, floor, price as P_F. With demand at D_E the entire supply would be sold at auction at price P_F. On the other hand if demand on a given day were to fall to D_A, the agreement with the manufacturers would be activated. Quantity R would be sold at auction, and RQ to the manufacturers – the price being P_F in both instances.

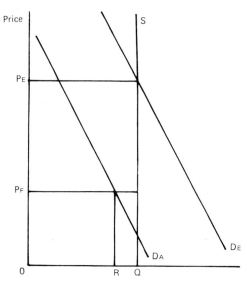

Quantity supplied, demanded, per period

Figure 26.2 A Floor Price in an Open Market

The floor price might also be reached because the quantity supplied is very large on a particular day. In figure 26.3 S_E is the expected supply. When supply is at S_A, quantity Q is sold at auction and QR to the manufacturers.

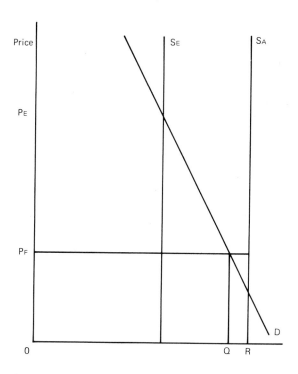

Figure 26.3   A Floor Price when Supply Exceeds the Expected Level

Similar agreements might be made by the suppliers of other perishable products such as fruit and vegetables. In addition the amount of produce that farmers bring to the market on any given day may be influenced by the price that they obtained on previous days. This influence will be particularly strong where prices fall to a level at which the variable cost of 'harvesting' and bringing the crop to market is not covered. If farmers expect these demand conditions to continue they will withdraw from the market. The effect of this withdrawal is shown in figure 26.4.

On day 1 quantity Q_1 is sold at price P_1, which is below the average variable cost. As some farmers withdraw from the market on the following day supply falls. The remaining farmers supply Q_2 and, if demand is unchanged, this quantity is sold at price P_2. It is impossible to predict exactly what the change in supply and hence price will be, since this depends upon the decisions of many individual farmers, some of whom will have a more optimistic view than others about future demand conditions. However it is clear that pressure for a reduction in supply will continue as long as price is below average variable cost. Therefore AVC can be seen as tending to put a floor to price.

Average variable cost is even more likely to constitute a floor to price in markets such as those for metals and minerals, where producers are not faced with the need to sell a stock of perishable commodities within a very short period.

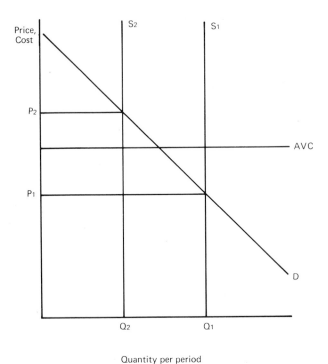

Figure 26.4 Changes in Daily Supply and Price in an Open Market

Moreover variable cost is likely to be greater in these industries since it encompasses a greater part of the total production process than in agriculture or horticulture where, as we saw, it may relate only to the cost of harvesting and transporting produce.

Changes in the Scale of Organization
When the time period is extended to encompass the possibility of a change in the scale of organization, suppliers will be concerned with the relationship between price and average total cost. (It will be remembered that all costs now become variable.) If prices have not been high enough to yield an adequate profit, some producers may withdraw from the market.

The greater the opportunity cost, i.e. the more profitable the alternative uses for resources, the more likely is it that suppliers will withdraw, and that supply will fall. A fall in supply in response to inadequate profits will be relatively slow in fishing, since it is difficult to find alternative uses for most of the capital equipment employed in the industry. Much greater opportunities for the redeployment of resources exist in agriculture – land can usually be used for growing several different crops or keeping several different types of animal.

Where constant switching of resources takes place, constant fluctuations in price may result. This is illustrated in figure 26.5, which we assume refers to the market for cucumbers. In this diagram we ignore the fluctuations in demand, supply and price which may occur during a given year; the demand and supply curves relate to the year as a whole. (The price which results from the interaction of demand and supply should be interpreted as the average price for the year.)

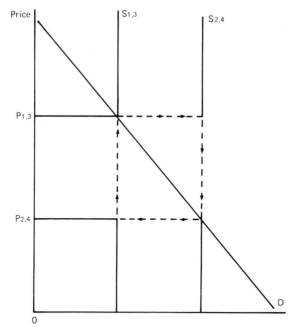

Figure 26.5 The Cobweb: Price Fluctuations in an Open Market

In year 1 price is P_1 which we assume yields a higher rate of return than was obtained from the growing of other crops such as lettuces. Consequently in year 2 some land is taken out of lettuce production and used for growing cucumbers. This results in an increase in supply (S_2). With an unchanged demand, price falls to P_2 at which the returns are less than those obtained from other crops. Consequently in year 3 supply decreases (S_3) with the result that price rises (P_3). In year 4, with supply S_4, price is P_4.

The path traced by price via the changing supply curves, is shown by the dotted line in figure 26.5. Because of the configuration of this path this process has been called the cobweb. There is no reason why price fluctuations should not continue indefinitely, since the actions of suppliers are uncoordinated. Although each supplier who considers entering the market may recognize that if sufficient suppliers enter, the price may fall to an unacceptable level, he cannot tell, until after his own decision is made, what other suppliers have decided to do.

Figure 26.5 shows that price fluctuates between two points. This follows, of course, from the assumption that supply fluctuates between two levels. But in practice supply, and therefore price, may behave in other ways. If fluctuations in supply increased over time, i.e. if S_3 lay to the left of S_1 and S_4 to the right of S_2, price fluctuations would become greater. (This is known as a divergent cobweb). Conversely if fluctuation in supply decreased (if S_3 lay to the right of S_1 and S_4 to the left of S_2) price fluctuations would decrease and eventually disappear (a convergent cobweb.)

We have shown that even in open markets cost influences price, since unless firms earn adequate profits, i.e. unless the relationship between revenue and cost is satisfactory, resources will be withdrawn from the market – either temporarily or permanently. Nevertheless, during a pricing season firms act as price takers, except in extremely adverse circumstances when a price floor – related in some way to cost – operates.

Price taking is characteristic of firms in perfectly competitive markets, a market form discussed in many textbooks. It is therefore useful to examine briefly the conditions that might apply in such a market.

Price Determination in Perfectly Competitive Markets

It is assumed that producers aim to maximize their short-run profits, i.e. the profits earned during the current period. Profit maximization requires a level of output such that marginal cost equals marginal revenue. So in figure 26.6 the producer (who is one of many) accepts the market price P and produces output Q.

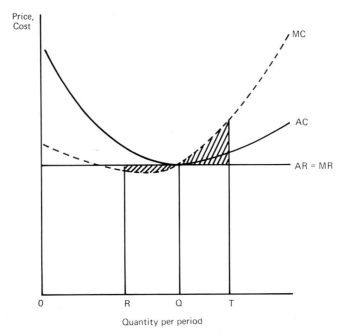

Figure 26.6 Equilibrium in a Perfectly Competitive Market

Since this producer can sell any quantity that he is capable of producing at price P his demand or average revenue curve is horizontal. Consequently his average and marginal revenue curves coincide. (For example if the market price is 10p, the revenue that he obtains from every additional unit sold, i.e. his marginal revenue, is 10p.) In order to maximize his profits he produces to the point at which the marginal cost curve cuts the marginal revenue curve from below. This occurs at output Q. His average cost curve is assumed to include an allowance for 'normal' profit. Since average cost equals average revenue at output Q, normal profit is earned.

In order to show why profits are maximized at this output we can consider two alternative levels of output. If he produced less than Q, say R, he would forego profits indicated by the shaded area lying beneath the marginal revenue curve and above the marginal cost curve. Conversely if he produced more than Q, say T, his profits would be reduced by the shaded area lying above the marginal revenue and below the marginal cost curve.

Open and Perfectly Competitive Markets

It would take far too long to make a comprehensive comparison between models of open and perfectly competitive markets, but three points may be made.

First, on the one hand there is common ground between the models in that in both the product is homogeneous, and price is determined by the interaction of aggregate demand and supply. Similarly, in both models the individual producer is seen as making a decision on output in the light of this price.

Second, on the other hand there is a divergence of view about the nature of this output decision. In models of perfectly competitive markets it is assumed that a producer can vary his supply by infinitely small amounts in arriving at the profit maximizing position. In models of open markets it is assumed that such small adjustments are rarely possible. Indeed it may be impossible to adjust supply at all (supply is fixed) during the pricing season. Moreover – and this is an even more important difference – in many open markets output decisions are often made in ignorance as to what demand conditions will be when the production process is completed, and therefore of the price at which output will be sold.

Finally, despite the lack of descriptive realism of the perfect competition model, some writers would advocate more extended treatment of it than we have presented, on the grounds that it provides 'a bench mark to appraise the efficiency of an economic system'.* The present author would, not, however, agree with this claim since it is difficult to reconcile the assumptions of perfect competition with the conditions required for the introduction of new products and improved methods of production.† There is, therefore no reason to think that an economy comprised entirely of perfect markets would be more efficient than one in which some imperfections exist. (However imperfections may sometimes reduce efficiency.)

Summary and Conclusions

Prices in open markets are demand determined in the sense that supply is often fixed during the pricing season so that price is very sensitive to changes in demand.

Since price is determined by aggregate (market) demand and supply, the individual supplier normally acts as a price taker. However he may set a floor price below which he will refuse to supply. With a given scale of organization the floor price may be related to average variable cost, or to opportunity cost if this is greater.

Over a longer period producers will expect to obtain a price which covers their total costs and yields an adequate profit. If they are not able to do so, some producers are likely to withdraw from the market. The consequent reduction in supply will enable the remaining producers to obtain higher prices.

ESSAY QUESTIONS

1   Explain what is meant by the statement that in open markets prices are demand determined.

* P. A. Samuelson, *Economics* (New York: McGraw Hill, 9th edn., 1973), p. 631.
 † See G. B. Richardson, *Information and Investment* (London: Oxford University Press, 1960).

2 Discuss the factors which might determine the floor price in an open market and discuss the likely relationship between this price and the expected average price.
3 Explain why many open markets are characterized by price fluctuations.
4 Analyse the conditions of demand and supply which may give rise to (a) a convergent cobweb, (b) a divergent cobweb.
5 'Firms are assumed to act as price takers in both open and perfectly competitive markets.' Discuss.
6 Compare and contrast models of open and perfectly competitive markets.
7 'In perfectly competitive markets demand conditions make it easy for producers to apply marginal analysis, but supply conditions make it very difficult to do so.' Discuss.

EXERCISES

26.1 A group of market gardeners had for many years sent their tomatoes to be sold at the weekly market in Littledale. However the Littledale Council decided to ban the parking of cars in all the streets surrounding the market, with the result that the number of people shopping in the market decreased substantially. At first the farmers continued to send their tomatoes to Littledale in the hope that trade might pick up again. However eventually those farmers living furthest away switched their supplies to Fulbrook where conditions for shopping were more favourable.

Show by means of one diagram, the demand and supply position in Littledale:

(i) Before the ban on parking was introduced.
(ii) Immediately after the ban on parking was introduced.
(iii) A considerable time after the ban on parking was introduced.

26.2 Early in 1970 the major oil companies were just about in balance in terms of the stock of and demand for tanker space. Then in anticipation of the usual drop in summer freight rates they allowed their stocks to diminish.

Instead of a freight fall, however, they were confronted with a political situation which put the market into turmoil. The closure of the Tap Line, supplying Middle East oil to the East Mediterranean ports, meant a large amount of extra oil had to be shipped round the Cape. Then the Libyan Government cut down on exports and production in order to obtain a higher price for its oil. This came at a time when demand in Europe and Japan was running considerably higher than predicted.

Faced with these difficulties the companies naturally covered themselves. They wanted to be in a position to have enough shipping to transport the oil from alternative sources if the Tap Line remained closed and the Libyan government shut off supplies.

As it happened these problems were resolved: the oil companies finalized an agreement with the Libyans (although production still remained restricted), and the Tap Line was re-opened. By this time, however, the oil companies had chartered every available tanker, the competition sending the rates to very high levels.

A generally mild winter throughout the northern hemisphere aggravated the position with consumption nothing like as heavy as the oil companies had budgeted for.

The effect of these factors on freight rates can be judged from the tanker charter index, based on Worldscale rates. From a point of less than Worldscale 100 in April 1970 the index rose to a high point of 298 in August 1970, and then slumped to Worldscale 65 by the end of June 1971.

To take an example in monetary terms, the rate at the top of the peak in 1970 for a single voyage between the Persian Gulf and Rotterdam would have been about $27.51 per ton (Worldscale 300). In July 1971 the comparable rate was about $2.75 (30W), at which rate owners of a 70,000 or 80,000 ton vessel would lose money. (Although the loss would be less than if the vessel were allowed to be idle in port.)

(i) Draw a demand/supply diagram to illustrate the situation in the summer of 1970.
   (a) as it actually was;
   (b) as the oil companies expected it to be early in the year.
(ii) Draw a demand/supply diagram to illustrate the situation in the first part of 1971
   (a) as it actually was:
   (b) as the oil companies expected it to be in the summer of 1970.

CHAPTER TWENTY-SEVEN

Factor Markets

Introduction

IN several previous chapters we have referred to the factors of production. In particular the demand and supply analysis presented in Chapters 23 to 26 included illustrations taken from factor markets. However it is appropriate to devote a separate chapter to pricing in factor markets in order to emphasize the special characteristics of these markets. Consequently in this chapter we draw together the references made in previous chapters, and considerably extend the analysis, particularly with respect to the labour market.

The Demand for Factors of Production

Factors of production, or inputs, are required not for their own sake but because they can be utilized in the production of goods and services, i.e. the demand for inputs is a derived demand. In many instances the chain of derived demand is very elaborate. For example the services of coalminers are demanded because there is a demand for coal; coal is itself demanded partly because there is a demand for electricity; one of the uses of electricity is to drive machinery used in the production of a wide range of products.

The Marginal Productivity Theory

The individual firm is often unaware of the full complexity of this chain, and of changes that may be occurring in it. Its demand for a particular input depends upon the value of the contribution made by that input to the firm's output – the higher the value of the contribution, the greater the demand for the input. If a change in the volume of output could be achieved by a change in the quantity of only a single input, it would be possible precisely to determine the contribution made by that input. That is to say, it would be possible to measure the marginal physical product of the input. This is illustrated in figure 27.1, where MPP shows the changes in the volume of output that would occur as the quantity of the input is varied. As we saw in previous chapters the term marginal denotes a change of a single unit. So for example we see from figure 27.1 that an increase from nine to ten units of the factor would lead to an increase of five units in the volume of output, while the employment of a further unit of the factor would increase output by a further four units. The MPP of the tenth unit of the input is 5; that of the eleventh unit is 4. MPP would generally be expected to fall as more of one factor is employed in conjunction with a given quantity of other factors.

To convert a marginal physical product curve into a marginal revenue product curve we multiply the change in the volume of output by the price of output. In figure 27.2 two marginal revenue product curves are drawn which might relate to the MPP curve of figure 27.1. MRP_1 is drawn on the assumption that the price of the product does not change as output changes – the shape of the curve is the

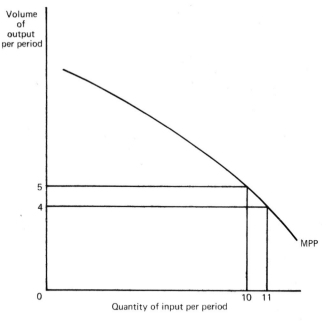

Figure 27.1   Marginal Physical Productivity

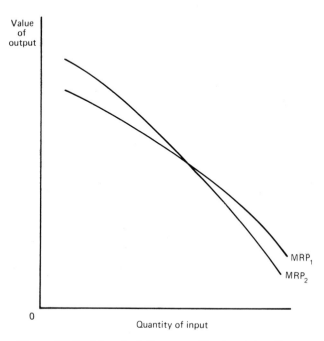

Figure 27.2   Marginal Revenue Productivity Curves

same as the shape of the MPP curve. MRP_2 assumes that price falls as output increases – the gradient of MRP_2 is steeper than that of MPP.

As we said above, these curves are drawn on the assumption that a change in output requires a change in the quantity of only a single input. In practice this assumption is most unlikely to be fulfilled. The technical conditions of production usually require the quantities of two or more inputs to be changed at the same time. An increased amount of raw material is likely to require an increase in labour to work that raw material, an increase in the power used to drive machinery, and so forth.

Moreover, even if technical factors did not make it necessary to vary the employment of two (or more) factors together, the firm might wish to do so, in order to prevent the marginal productivity of one factor declining in the way indicated in figures 27.1 and 27.2. Since the price of the factor is unlikely to fall as more is employed, a fall in productivity implies an increase in the cost of the factor per unit of output.

The Supply of Factors of Production

Whereas a common framework, utilizing the concepts of derived demand and marginal productivity, can be used in analyzing the demand for inputs, the supply of the various inputs or factors of production must be discussed separately, since the supply of each factor is subject to a different set of influences.

Land

As we saw in Chapter 1 land can be defined in several slightly different ways. If it is defined as the surface area of the planet, including oceans, lakes and rivers, we can treat it as being fixed in supply. Again, if it is defined as the area of dry land, it is virtually fixed in supply. On the other hand, if the quality of the land, its suitability for economic use, is taken into account, supply is more elastic. As we indicated in Chapter 1, the amount of land suitable for agriculture can be increased by good practices, such as irrigation and the application of fertilizer; or decreased, for example, by too intensive farming leading to dust bowls. Land can also be made more suitable for non-agricultural purposes. Marshes can be drained and the terrain made more suitable for the building of factories and offices. (Note that when defined in this way, land includes the result of the application of labour and capital, which makes it difficult to measure the productivity of land alone.)

Finally, under an even wider definition, land would include the natural resources found on or under the surface – minerals, metals, etc. An area of increasing debate in recent years has been the danger of exhaustion of certain natural resources. This danger is clearly greater if we consider only the resources still remaining in the land and sea than if we take into account the recycling of waste or used resources. (This point is discussed further in the following chapter.)

Capital

Capital is a man-made factor of production which, in principle if not always in practice, can be distinguished from natural resources. We showed in Chapter 6 that an increase in the stock of capital goods is known as net investment, defined as gross investment minus depreciation. We also showed that net investment in any period is influenced by a wide range of factors, including technological conditions, and the volume of resources *not* required for consumption and other purposes.

Labour

As we showed in Chapter 1, the most important determinant of the supply of labour in the long term is the size of the population. Over shorter periods the number of workers is determined by the age and sex structure of the population and also by such institutional factors as the minimum school-leaving age, the age at which retirement pensions are paid, regulations concerning, and social attitudes towards, the employment of females, etc. The supply of labour is also determined by the number of hours worked per year by each worker. This depends upon the number of holidays and the average length of the working week. It may also be affected by the structure of taxation, as shown in Chapter 11.

The Supply of Factors of Production to Particular Uses

All factors of production have alternative uses. Because of differences in demand these alternative uses normally offer different rewards. There will be a tendency for factors to move out of the uses which offer the lowest rewards and into those uses which offer the highest rewards. Equilibrium is established, i.e. such movement ceases, when the rewards to be obtained from different uses are equalized, rewards being defined so as to include both monetary and non-monetary components. Note that the non-monetary components may be positive – e.g. status, an interesting job, the ability to control the pace of one's work – or negative – e.g. dangerous or dirty working conditions.

How quickly a system moves towards equilibrium depends partly upon the pace of change on the demand side, and partly upon factor mobility. We briefly discuss the main determinants of the mobility of each factor in turn.

MOBILITY OF LAND

Although land is physically the least mobile factor it is often highly mobile as between different uses. This is especially true of agricultural land where the farmer can normally choose from among a wide range of alternative crops at the beginning of each planting season. (The implications of this were discussed in Chapter 26.)

Mobility is lower when land has been built upon. Changes in use do occur. Factories are demolished and offices and shops are built. Again, open-cast coal mining stops and the land is returned to agriculture. However such changes take a much longer time and are usually much more costly than is a switch from one crop to another.

MOBILITY OF CAPITAL

The mobility of capital depends upon several factors. The first is the number of different uses to which the particular plant or equipment can be put. For example a machine for cutting at the coal face has a very specific use, whereas a computer can be used for a wide variety of data processing operations. The second factor is the number of different industries in which the equipment can be used. Although a lorry may be used only for carrying goods, it may be used by firms in many different industries. Finally, physical or geographical mobility is important. Contrast the mobility of a tractor with that of a power station.

Although mobility is clearly a complex matter, there is no doubt that much capital equipment, once built and installed, is highly immobile, i.e. the opportunity cost of such equipment is likely to be low. We discussed in Chapter 25 the implications of this fact for the pricing of goods and services. We examine below the implications for factor prices.

MOBILITY OF LABOUR

The ability of an individual to enter a particular occupation depends upon the extent to which his (or her) abilities, experience and training match the requirements of that occupation. The ability required might be strength, intelligence, steadiness of hand, etc. The training might involve an apprenticeship, an extended period in an educational institution, a probationary period 'on the job', etc.

The distribution of abilities in the population is such that the potential supply of labour to different jobs differs. These 'natural' differences in supply may be accentuated by the unwillingness of some potential entrants to meet the cost of education and training. Of the people who have the ability to become doctors only a small proportion apply for admission to medical school, one of the reasons being the very long training period involved. Even if the cost of training is met by the state, the training is not costless to the individual. There may be a substantial opportunity cost in terms of the additional income (salary minus grant) foregone during the training period.

In addition to these natural and self-imposed barriers, man-made or institutional barriers to mobility may be imposed. Let us consider further the education and training of doctors. In the U.K., as in many other countries, there are sufficient places for only a minority of those who apply for entry to medical school. The decision on the number of places to be made available is taken by the government – not surprisingly in view of the fact that the cost of the facilities is largely met by the state.

In its decision the government relies heavily upon the advice of civil servants concerning the country's need for doctors. It also receives advice from many other bodies, not all of whom define 'need' in the same way. For example the Patients Association, one of the representatives of the consumer, is likely to have a different view from that of the spokesmen of the doctors, such as the British Medical Association. One of the objectives of the B.M.A. is the protection and improvement of doctors' incomes. This might help to explain why in the mid 1970s the B.M.A. suggested that the entry to medical schools should be restricted in order to avoid the danger of an 'over-supply' of doctors.

Institutional restrictions on entry are frequently imposed directly by professional organizations and trade unions. Although such barriers may help to maintain the quality of labour, and thus benefit the employer and consumer, the protection of members' interests is usually a more important aim of these restrictions.

If we consider the labour force as a whole, mobility depends to a considerable extent, especially over the longer term, on the movements of those people who leave and enter the labour force. Mobility is enhanced if, upon retirement, people leave contracting occupations while those entering the labour force go into expanding occupations. If it is felt that the mobility arising from this 'natural' process is inadequate, governments may intervene in one way or another. As we saw in Chapter 17, U.K. governments have been concerned in the post-war period to increase the level of training and re-training. A major aim of these policies was to increase the flow of workers into expanding, and out of contracting, occupations.

The Determination of Price in Factor Markets

Having discussed the major influences on the demand for and the supply of factors of production we can now examine how the prices of factors are determined.

In figure 27.3 the demand and supply curves relate to a given factor market, such as that for a given type of labour. The demand curves indicate the demand for this type of labour by a group of firms engaged in making a particular range

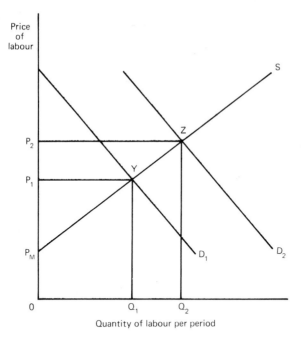

Figure 27.3   An Increase in the Demand for Labour

of products. The supply curve indicates the supply of labour to those firms. With demand D_1 and supply S, Q_1 labour is employed at price P_1.

With demand and supply curves of this shape, the price of the factor will change as a result of a change in either demand or supply. For example an increase in demand to D_2 causes an increase in price to P_2 and an increase in the quantity employed to Q_2. Demand might increase (or fall) for several reasons.

A Change in Demand

As we noted above, the demand for factors is a derived demand, and the first reason why demand may increase is that the demand for the firms' products increases, i.e. the shift in the demand curve in the factor market parallels that in the product market.

Second, the demand for one factor may increase because it is substituted for another factor whose price has risen. However, as we showed in Chapter 24, the ease with which one factor can be substituted for another depends very much upon the technical conditions of production and the time scale involved. For example if the wage rates of bus drivers and conductors increased it might be possible to reduce cost (or at least minimize the increase) by introducing one-man-operated buses, i.e. by substituting capital for labour. However should a further rise in labour costs occur it would not be possible to reduce the labour content further. Moreover, the increase in the cost of one factor may, even after substitution, cause the average cost of production to rise. If this increase in cost results in higher product prices, the volume of sales may fall. If this 'price effect' outweighs the substitution effect the demand for *all* factors (including the factor that has become relatively cheaper), is likely to fall.

The third possible reason for an increase in the demand for a factor is an increase in its productivity. If we again take labour as an example this increase in productivity could be due to harder or more efficient working or to a change in some other factor, e.g. the installation of improved machinery.

TRANSFER EARNINGS AND ECONOMIC RENT

In figure 27.3 P_M indicates the minimum price that would have to be offered in order to attract any of this factor to this particular use. This minimum price is known as the *transfer earnings* of the factor, i.e. the income that the factor could obtain if it transferred to another use or occuption (a suitable adjustment being made for any non-monetary rewards in the two uses).

The fact that the supply curve slopes upwards indicates that the transfer earnings of different units of the factor differ. As higher rewards are offered in this market additional resources – resources with higher transfer earnings – are attracted. The total transfer earnings at any point would be given by the area under the relevant portion of the supply curve. For example if Q_1 units were employed, transfer earnings would be OQ_1YP_M. If Q_2 units were employed, transfer earnings would be OQ_2ZP_2.

The income obtained by a factor over and above its transfer earnings is known as *economic rent*. With Q_1 units employed, economic rent would be P_MYP_1. An increase in demand to D_2 would cause an increase in economic rent to P_MZP_2. It is not difficult to understand why changes in demand will have a greater effect on a factor's income the less elastic the supply of that factor, and why a greater proportion of the change in income will comprise a change in economic rent.

The Effect of a Change in Supply

A change in the equilibrium price in a factor market may also occur because of a change in supply conditions. Figure 27.4 shows that an increase in supply would

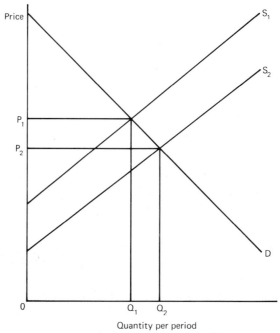

Figure 27.4   An Increase in the Supply of a Factor of Production

result in more of the factor being employed at a lower price. An increase in supply might occur for several reasons. For example an increase in the population of working age might lead to an increase in labour supply, new discoveries of mineral deposits to an increase in the supply of raw materials, and technological progress to an increase in the supply of capital goods. In addition to such influences on the total supply of a given input, the supply in one market will be influenced by conditions in other markets. For example if the demand for postmen declines this will lead to an increase in supply to certain other occupations, such as porters and drivers.

The Elasticity of Supply

The elasticity of supply is defined as the percentage change in the quantity supplied (per period) divided by the percentage change in price. Using symbols this can be expressed as follows:

$$E_S = \frac{\Delta Q}{Q} \div \frac{\Delta P}{P}$$

where Q represents the quantity of the factor supplied per period
P represents its price, and
Δ denotes a small change in the variable.

The shapes of the supply curves in figures 27.3 and 27.4 indicate that the elasticity of supply of the factor is positive. An aggregate supply curve of this shape would be characteristic of many inputs, and especially of raw materials. However we have seen that the supply of a particular factor to a particular market may be subject to many influences, and it is therefore appropriate to consider the implications of alternative supply curves.

Figure 27.5 shows a completely (or perfectly) inelastic supply curve, such as

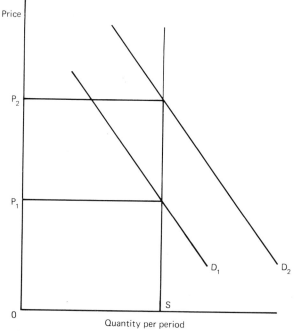

Figure 27.5 A Completely (or Perfectly) Inelastic Supply Curve

might arise if the supply of newly qualified people entering an occupation just matched the number leaving through retirement and death. An increase in demand from D_1 to D_2 would have a much greater effect on the income of workers in these circumstances than it would if supply were less inelastic. (The same would also apply, of course, to a fall in demand.)

In practice the supply of labour is unlikely to be completely inelastic, because of the alternative jobs which are open to most people. However the supply curve for a highly specialized occupation may well have a vertical portion, especially at the upper end in the short term. For example an increase in the demand for airline pilots would be unlikely to cause an increase in the quantity supplied for some time. (Note that in these circumstances the increase in the earnings of existing pilots would entirely comprise economic rent.)

As we showed in Chapter 26, the many raw materials which are traded in open markets tend to have an inelastic supply in the short term. This means that their prices are highly sensitive to changes in demand. An indication of the magnitude of these price fluctuations is given in figure 27.6. This relates to a period when an increase in the demand for raw materials was suddenly and dramatically reversed.

The main reason for this reversal was the industrial recession in leading consuming countries which followed the steep rise in the price of OPEC oil. The fall in

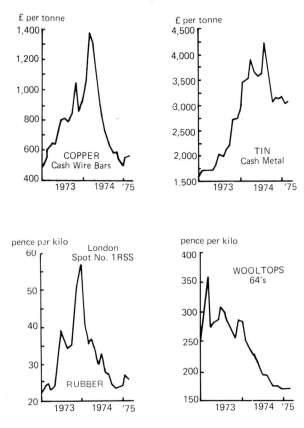

Figure 27.6 Fluctuating Raw Material Prices

commodity prices, triggered by this recession, was probably accentuated by buyers' expectations. When prices are rising, buyers often increase their orders in order to build up stocks ahead of future price rises. Once prices begin to fall buyers run down their stocks and reduce their demands, thus putting further downward pressure on price.

In figure 27.7 we show a supply curve whose elasticity is positive up to price

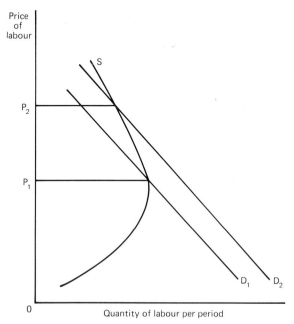

Figure 27.7 Supply of a Factor with a Target Income

P_1, but negative at higher prices. As we indicated in Chapter 22 such a curve could indicate that the factor, labour, has a target total income. Once this income is achieved, an increase in the price per unit causes less of the factor to be supplied. It has been observed that in dirty or dangerous occupations such as mining, or monotonous jobs such as car assembly, increases in wage-rates have sometimes been followed by increases in absentee rates, a pattern of behaviour consistent with this hypothesis.

A consequence of such supply conditions is that once wage rates have reached the level which yields the target income, employers are unable to persuade existing workers to work longer hours by increasing wage rates. (Increases in wage rates may, however, increase the number of workers willing to work for those employers, i.e. in total, supply would continue to be positively related to price.)

Finally, the supply of a factor may be completely elastic at a given price. This might occur in the market for capital goods where manufacturers' costs are constant at all levels of output, and where the price is fixed for a season. (See Chapter 24.)

The concept of a pricing season can also be usefully applied to the market for labour. In numerous occupations minimum wage rates are fixed following central negotiations between representatives of employers and trades unions. In figure 27.8 S_N represents the minimum wage for the ensuing period, below which no labour would be supplied. This minimum wage may be supplemented by amounts negotiated at local or plant level. Plant bargaining is sensitive to conditions in the local labour market. The higher the demand for labour, the greater is likely to be the gap between the nationally negotiated minimum rate (S_N) and the locally negotiated rate (S_L), as shown in figure 27.8.

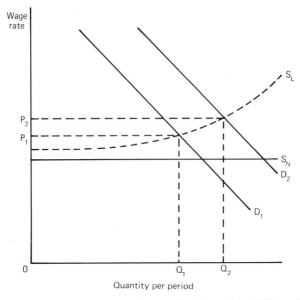

Figure 27.8   Nationally and Locally Negotiated Wage Rates

Trade Unions and Labour Markets

Trades unions and professional associations may seek to influence labour markets in a number of ways. First, as noted above, they may lay down requirements that must be fulfilled by their members, e.g. in terms of education and training. Such requirements permanently reduce the supply of labour. The result of this reduction, represented in figure 27.9 by the shift of the supply curve from S_1 to S_2, is that fewer workers are employed but at a higher wage rate.

Second, as noted above, trades unions may centrally negotiate wage rates. In figure 27.10 the free market supply curve, S_F, indicates what supply would be in the absence of central negotiations. With demand D_1, this would yield an equilibrium wage rate P_F. The wage rate negotiated by the union, P_N, is above the free market rate. (We ignore any local negotiations in order to simplify the analysis). Consequently the number of workers employed falls from Q_F to Q_N.

Is figure 27.10 realistic? Would a trade union push wage rates to the point where the employment opportunities of its members were reduced? Our answer to this question will depend very much upon the assumptions that we make about the negotiation process, and in particular about the information available to the union.

One reason why the union might negotiate a wage rate P_N is that it might misjudge the state of the labour market, believing the demand to be stronger than it actually is. (It must be remembered that wages are often negotiated on an annual

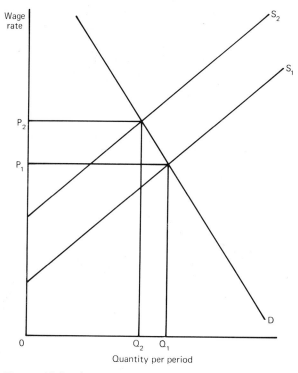

Figure 27.9 A Restriction on the Supply of Labour

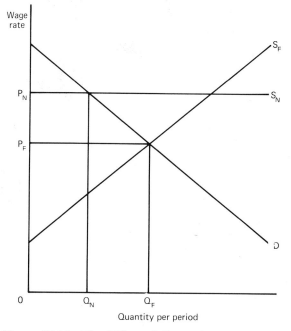

Figure 27.10 The Effect of Central Wage Bargaining

basis, so that the negotiators have to try to look up to twelve months ahead.) This may happen, for example, because union and employers fail to foresee a change in government policy designed to reduce the pressure on resources and because central bargaining may cause the market to respond less flexibly to the unforeseen circumstances.*

A rather more cynical explanation would be that the union was aware that the higher wage rate might lead to lower employment opportunities but that it was willing to accept this. It might do so if it believed that the reduction in employment opportunities would affect only potential entrants or recent entrants who had little influence within the union.

Finally the above two lines of argument can be combined in an explanation that appears to be quite plausible. Drawing the demand curve as a single line, D_1, as we have done in figure 27.10, suggests that the factor's marginal revenue productivity, which forms the basis of the demand curve, can be precisely measured. In practice, as we noted earlier in the chapter, this may not be possible, if only because a firm seldom varies the employment of a single factor only. Moreover the quantity of a factor employed is seldom varied by only a single unit. Consequently it may be more realistic to think of the demand curve as a band, bounded by D_1 and D_2. (This would, of course, imply that there might be more than one equilibrium position.)

Given this area of uncertainty the union may believe a claim for higher wages to be in its members' best interests. It may hope that the employer will grant an increase in wages to P_N without reducing employment.

Leaving aside the effect of uncertainty concerning the productivity of labour, let us consider the conditions under which an increase in wage rates is least likely to result in a reduction in employment opportunities for a group of workers, such as the members of a particular union.

First, employers may be earning profits in excess of their target profits. This is most likely to happen when competition in the product market is restricted, e.g. in those highly concentrated markets in which the dominant firms have a high degree of pricing discretion. In such instances a wage increase may result in some of the excess profits being transferred from companies to employees.

Second, workers may be able to push up wages at the expense of profits even where these are not initially in excess of the target. Although employers would clearly not be happy with such a situation they may accept it rather than risk a prolonged strike which would hit their profitability even harder. In taking this decision employers will be influenced by the power of the union, not only to impose higher wages but also to fight redundancies. This power will depend upon such factors as the proportion of the work-force in the union, the financial resources available to the union for the payment of 'strike money' to their members, and the financial resources of their members.

However, although the balance of power between unions and employers may have a crucial effect in the short term, other considerations are likely to be more important in the longer term. If profits remain depressed, companies' investment expenditure is almost certain to fall, as we showed in Chapter 11. This fall in investment will in turn reduce employment opportunities as companies become less competitive in national and/or international markets.

The third situation is where employers concede higher wages in the belief that

---

* This is a particular example of a general tendency for central bargaining to introduce elements of rigidity into the labour market.

they can pass these on in the form of higher prices. If such a belief were justified, an increase in wage rates would be followed by a shift to the right in the demand curve so as to leave the equilibrium employment unchanged. Employers may take this view if they believe that the government is committed to a policy of full employment and to monetary and fiscal policies designed to bring this about. However, although these circumstances may make it easier for unions to negotiate higher *money* wages, these are unlikely to be reflected in higher *real* wages. All employers are likely to take a similar view of the economic conditions and all product prices are likely to rise, thus cancelling out the effect of the rise in money wages.

Finally, unions may be able to increase wages without a loss of employment opportunities in the short term if technical conditions make it impossible to substitute other factors for labour. But again there is likely to be a bigger effect in the long term, since technical conditions are more likely to change so as to increase the scope for factor substitution.

Wage and Salary Differentials

Having discussed the various factors which might influence wages and earnings, we now briefly examine the earnings in different occupations in the U.K.

Table 27.1 shows the average weekly earnings for men over twenty one in a

Table 27.1

Average Gross Weekly Earnings
(Men over 21)

	April 1976		April 1970	
	£	(Ranking)	£	(Ranking)
Academics	107.1	(1)	44.2	(2)
Professional electrical engineers	98.5	(2)	38.6	(3)
Managers (marketing and sales)	97.3	(3)	53.1	(1)
Teachers	90.3	(4)	35.9	(4)
Coalminers	80.7	(5)	25.4	(13)
Policemen	78.5	(6)	29.4	(7)
Train drivers	74.5	(7)	28.9	(8)
Skilled welders	74.1	(8)	31.3	(5)
Non-electrical fitters	72.9	(9)	30.4	(6)
Bus drivers	71.6	(10)	26.3	(10)
Heavy goods vehicle drivers	67.5	(11)	27.7	(9)
Postmen	67.4	(12)	25.5	(12)
Motor mechanics	61.5	(13)	26.6	(11)
Packers etc.	59.3	(14)	24.0	(14)
General labourers	56.3	(15)	22.0	(15)
Farm workers	46.8	(16)	17.6	(16)
All manual	65.1	—	26.2	—
All non-manual	81.6	—	35.7	—
All occupations	71.8	—	29.4	—

Source: *Department of Employment Gazette*, 1976.

sample of occupations in 1970 and 1976. We see that overall the earnings of non-manual workers were some 25 per cent above those of manual workers in 1976. (In 1970 the differential was 36 per cent, and the reduction is mainly due to the existence over much of this period of income policies in which 'flat-rate' wage increases were an important component.)

The higher earnings in non-manual occupations are partly explained by the longer periods of training and education which restrict the supply of labour to these occupations. This factor is especially important in the professions, and we find academics, managers, professional engineers and teachers at the top of the earnings table.

Within the manual occupations, earnings tend to be higher for skilled than for non-skilled occupations (although the percentage differentials have again been eroded by flat-rate increases). Here again, greater skill and longer training are associated with higher rewards. However the correlation is by no means perfect. Of the three worst paid groups, farm labourers are at least as skilled as packers and general labourers, and yet they have substantially lower earnings. This may be due partly to the greater non-monetary advantages enjoyed by farm labourers, partly to the lack of alternative employment opportunities in rural areas, and partly to lower union bargaining power (minimum wage rates are set by agricultural wages boards).

The importance of trade union power can be seen in the move up the earnings league of coalminers. During the 1960s the earnings of miners improved less than those of many other industrial workers. As the demand for coal fell, employment in the industry was substantially reduced and the union was probably reluctant to take any action which would hasten this reduction. Furthermore the government at times put pressure on the N.C.B., together with other public sector employers, to resist wage claims, as part of the attempt to control inflation.

Eventually, however, the miners took action to reverse this trend. Early in 1974 a strike was called which led to the introduction in other industries of the 'three-day-week' and eventually to the defeat of the Conservative government. The demands of the miners were largely met by the incoming Labour government, and they moved up considerably in the earnings table, as shown in table 27.1.

On the other hand, earlier in the period covered by table 27.1 a national strike did not enable postmen to achieve their demands, and they have continued to occupy a position towards the bottom of the earnings table. The users of the official postal services were able to turn to substitutes, particularly the telephone service, and private local letter services that were introduced during the strike. This contrasts with the fact that when the supply of coal was restricted it proved impossible to find adequate substitute fuels to maintain the normal level of economic activity.

The Effect of Demand on Earnings

The contrasting experience of the miners and the postmen shows that the power to raise wages possessed by a union is strongly influenced by the current demand conditions pertaining to the goods or services produced by the members of that union. Wages and earnings can also be influenced by *changes* in demand. Studies undertaken by Phelps, Brown and Browne, by Reddaway and by the O.E.C.D. all found evidence of a tendency for earnings to rise faster in expanding than in contracting industries.*

Summary and Conclusions

The prices of factors of production can be explained in terms of demand and supply analysis. Demand for factors is a derived demand, and changes in product markets

---

* For a summary of the evidence see A. R. Prest and D. J. Coppock (eds.), *The U.K. Economy* (London: Weidenfeld and Nicolson, 6th ed., 1976), ch. 5.

are reflected in changes in factor markets. The concept of marginal productivity helps to explain the demand for factors, although in practice it is difficult to measure marginal productivity since firms normally change the quantity employed of two or more factors at the same time.

Incidentally, further problems of measurement arise in non-traded goods such as the education and health services, where it is not clear how output should be defined. As we saw in Chapter 5, in the absence of a satisfactory measure of output, these services are valued at their cost of production. But such a measure is clearly of no use when we wish to measure productivity, since this is a relationship between outputs and inputs.

Supply conditions vary considerably from one factor to another. Since we dealt with material inputs at some length in earlier chapters, we concentrated in this chapter on labour. We showed that the supply of labour to different occupations can be affected by a wide range of factors, including differences in natural aptitudes and institutional factors, of which the activities of trades unions and professional institutions are especially important.

We showed that trades unions may seek to influence labour markets in several different ways. Since one of their objectives is to increase the real wages of their members, we explored the conditions which were most conducive to this end. We saw that technical conditions, the availability of substitutes in both factor and product markets, the government's macro-economic policy and changes in the pattern of demand may all be important. The power of a particular union may also have an influence, especially in the short term. Indeed, as we saw in Chapter 14, it has been suggested that differences in power between one union and another, and between unionized and non-unionized workers, may constitute a justification of an incomes policy.

ESSAY QUESTIONS

1 Assess the usefulness of the marginal productivity theory as an explanation of the demand for factors of production.
2 Why do different wage rates exist in different occupations?
3 Analyse the possibile effects of an increase in labour productivity on the demand for (a) labour, (b) other factors.
4 How would you expect a fall in demand for coal to affect the incomes of (a) coal miners, (b) secretarial staff employed in the mining industry?
5 Explain the relationship between the elasticity of supply of a factor and economic rent.
6 'The earnings of pop stars are almost entirely economic rent.' Discuss.
7 Analyse the relationship between technological progress and the demand for capital goods.
8 Discuss the ways in which trade unions can influence the supply of labour.
9 In what circumstances are trade unions most likely to be able to achieve an increase in the total real incomes of all their members?
10 'Trade unions can increase the wage rates of their members only at the expense of a reduction in employment.' Discuss.

EXERCISES

27.1

No. of workers	Expected yield (tonnes)
1	100
2	150
3	180
4	205
5	220
6	225

The above table shows the yield of wheat expected from a farm if different numbers of workers were employed. (i) If the farmer expected to obtain a price of £100 per tonne of wheat, how many workers would he employ at an annual wage of (a) £1,000, (b) £2,000? (ii) How many would he employ in each case if he expected the price of wheat to be £50 a tonne?

27.2 A beet sugar factory extracts sugar from beet by slicing the beets and washing them in large vats of circulating water. The water is subsequently evaporated, leaving the residue of sugar. The more water used, the greater the quantity of sugar obtained from a given quantity of beet, as shown in the table below

Water used (000 gallons)	Sugar recovery (%)
500	70
540	71
585	72
635	73
695	74
770	75
860	76
970	77
1100	78

The factory uses 20 tonnes of beet per day, the sugar content of which is estimated at 1 per cent by weight. The value of the raw sugar extracted is £5,000 per tonne. Given that water costs 2p per thousand gallons, and that the fuel cost for evaporation etc. is 8p per thousand gallons, calculate (a) how much water per day the factory should use; (b) how much sugar per day will be produced.

27.3 In figure 27.11 the line labelled 100 indicates the various combinations of two factors, X and Y, which would be required to produce 100 units of a certain product. The price of factor X divided by the price of factor Y is equal to OA/OB. (i) How would you account for the shape of line 100? (ii) Given the existing prices, profit maximization requires an output of 100 units. Reproduce the diagram, and show what combination of the two factors will be employed. (iii) The prices of the factors remaining unchanged, a change in demand results in an increase in the profit maximizing output to 200 units. Indicate what combination of the two factors will now be employed. How would this combination have been affected had factor Y become more expensive and factor X less expensive?

27.4 In a report issued in 1974 the Pay Board recommended that the London allowances paid to public sector employees should be substantially increased. The recommended allowances – £400 a year in Inner London and £200 in Outer London – were designed to compensate for two factors. The first was the

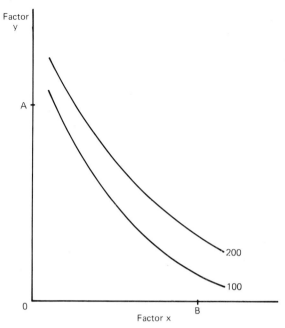

Figure 27.11   Factor Combinations

additional financial costs incurred, mainly on housing and travel, in London. The second was the non-financial costs, e.g. the additional 'wear and tear' of travelling. The Board recommended that the new allowances should be paid to all public employees, regardless of income or occupation. It also hoped that the new scale of allowances would be paid by private sector employers with national wage and salary structures.

(i) Discuss the merits and demerits of paying a London allowance to employees in (a) the public sector, (b) the private sector. (ii) Assuming that it has been decided that a London allowance should be paid, discuss the relative merits of fixing a scale which is designed to (a) compensate for the additional financial costs incurred by working in London, (b) compensate for the additional financial and non-financial costs, (c) counteract labour shortages in given occupations.

27.5 The Department of Employment provides data on changes in basic wage rates and in average earnings. Basic wage rates are hourly or weekly rates of pay set by national collective agreements, wage councils or boards, and largely reflect the minimum or standard rate of pay for manual workers. The index is based on information on wage settlements concerning 14 million workers in 80 industries. Average earnings include overtime and piece work payments, bonuses and any other premium over minimum wage rates. This index is based on the earnings of 12 million workers employed by 11,500 large firms and organizations. Between July 1975 and July 1976 the index of weekly wage rates increased by 17.7 per cent, while the index of average earnings increased by 13.7 per cent.

What factors might account for the difference in the behaviour of the two indices during this period?

27.6 (i) How would you account for the changes in the relative earnings of skilled workers, semi-skilled workers and labourers, shown in table 27.2? (ii) Discuss the likely consequences of these changes.

Table 27.2
Index of Average Hourly Earnings of Adult Male Manual Workers
(Earnings of labourers at June of each year = 100)

	1963	1967	1971	1975	1976
Mechanical engineering					
Skilled	139.9	142.3	139.1	128.3	127.0
Semi-skilled	115.0	117.4	117.9	116.4	115.3
Electrical engineering					
Skilled	144.6	146.3	144.3	134.6	131.3
Semi-skilled	115.6	118.4	119.6	117.0	114.6

Source: *Department of Employment Gazette.*

OBJECTIVE TEST QUESTIONS: SET 9

Questions 1 to 7 are based on figure 27.12. Indicate which of the five curves A to E is referred to in each instance. Each curve may be referred to once, more than once, or not at all.

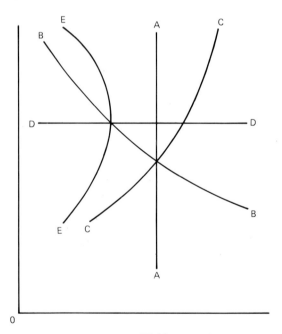

Figure 27.12

1   A supply curve for labour when workers have a fixed target income.

2   A supply curve for wool sold by auction.

3   A supply curve for a product whose producer enjoys substantial economies of scale.

4   A supply curve when producers maintain a given price regardless of demand conditions.

5   A market demand curve for a Giffen good.

6   A market demand curve for a normal good.

7   A firm's demand curve in a perfectly competitive market.

Questions 8–11 are based on figure 27.13, in which the unbroken lines represent the initial conditions of demand and supply in the market for postmen. The broken lines represent new demand and supply conditions that might apply after the changes listed below have occurred. Starting each time from the initial equilibrium position X, indicate the new equilibrium position A, B, C, D or E (Each letter may apply once, more than once, or not at all.)

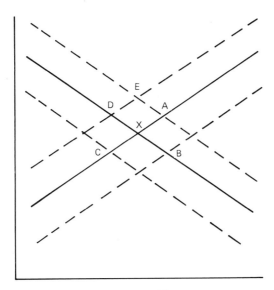

Figure 27.13

8   An increase occurs in the number of letters posted.

9   Employers offer higher wages in other jobs that could be filled by postmen.

10 The official age of retirement for men is reduced.

11 The number of letters posted remains constant despite an increase in postal charges.

Questions 12 and 13 relate to figure 27.14 in which D indicates the demand for, and S the supply of, a factor of production.

12 The economic rent obtained by this factor is

   A   ORTQ
   B   OPXT
   C   RPXT
   D   RPX
   E   RXT.

27.21

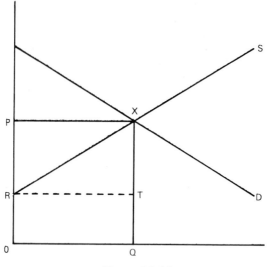

Figure 27.14

13 The transfer earnings of the factors are

    A ORTQ
    B OPXT
    C RPXT
    D RPX
    E RXT.

14 Figure 27.15 shows the marginal revenue productivity of labour in a certain firm in two time periods. The shift from MRP_1 to MRP_2 could have been due to the fact that the

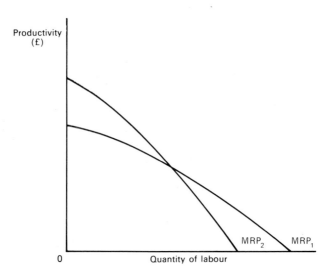

Figure 27.15

1   firm substituted capital for labour
2   efficiency of labour increased at all levels of output
3   demand for the firm's products became less price elastic.

15 An increase in the demand for one factor of production could arise following

1   an increase in the productivity of that factor
2   an increase in the price of the products made by that factor
3   a fall in the price of other factors.

16 The supply curve for labour shown in figure 27.16 could reflect the fact that

1   workers have a fixed target income
2   leisure and income are complementary goods
3   higher wages leads to higher productivity.

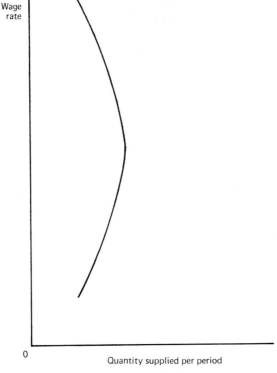

Figure 27.16

17 The marginal physical productivity of a factor depends upon both the volume of output and the price at which that output is sold.
      The marginal physical productivity of a factor normally falls as more of the factor is added to fixed quantities of other factors.

18 An increase in the price of one factor can never cause the demand for another factor to fall.
      A change in the relative prices of factors usually has a substitution effect.

19 If the total rewards of a factor of production remained unchanged an increase in its transfer earnings would imply a fall in its economic rent.

The total rewards of a factor of production comprise transfer earnings plus economic rent.

20 In a perfectly competitive market the firm's marginal revenue curve is horizontal.

In a perfectly competitive market, market demand is completely elastic.

TRUE/FALSE

1 In open markets cost has no influence on price.
2 When a given quantity is supplied regardless of the price, supply is said to be completely inelastic.
3 The demand for all factors of production is a derived demand.
4 The more elastic the supply of a factor the greater will be the change in economic rent following a change in demand for that factor.
5 Price fluctuations increase over time in a divergent cobweb.
6 Models of open and perfectly competitive markets both assume that price is determined by the interaction of aggregate demand and supply.
7 Models of open and perfectly competitive markets both assume that producers can vary output by infinitely small amounts.
8 A change in the cost of a factor will affect its marginal revenue product but not its marginal physical product.
9 Economic rent denotes the highest reward that a factor could obtain in an alternative use.
10 In order to determine the marginal productivity of a factor it is necessary to vary the quantity of that factor employed, while the quantity of other factors remains unchanged.

CHAPTER TWENTY-EIGHT

Some Additional Aspects of the Price Mechanism

Introduction

IN the previous six chapters we have discussed various aspects of the price mechanism as it operates in product and factor markets. We have shown that in market and mixed economies the price mechanism plays an important role in the allocation of resources. However we have also noted that the price mechanism may have undesirable consequences, and that this may lead governments to intervene in order to influence or modify the operation of the mechanism.

Intervention may occur at the macro or the micro level. By intervening at the macro level the government seeks to influence the behaviour of broad economic aggregates such as consumption and investment. In this way the government may indirectly influence the demand and supply conditions in all industries and markets.

Intervention at the micro level implies intervention in particular industries or markets. This may take two forms. First the state may assume responsibility for the production of goods and services, the 'producer' being central government, local government or a public corporation. This will involve a modification of the price mechanism if price and output decisions differ from those in the private sector. Second, production may remain within the private sector but the state may modify the operation of the price mechanism in various ways, e.g. by imposing price controls.

The various forms of intervention at the macro level were examined during our discussion of macro economic policy. Consequently we confine our attention in this chapter to intervention at the micro level. Moreover, since we have already discussed the activities of public sector producers we shall concentrate on the second form of micro intervention – the modification of the operation of the price mechanism in those markets supplied by private sector producers.

Government intervention clearly implies a belief that the free play of market forces may have undesirable consequences, and when we examine specific types of intervention, we indicate what these alleged consequences may be. However it is useful to begin by briefly considering the advantages of the price mechanism. In order to do this we present a (highly simplified) account of how resources are allocated in a market and in a fully planned economy.

The Meaning of Equilibrium

It is convenient to start by considering again the meaning of the term equilibrium as it applies in a product market. As we have said earlier, an equilibrium position is that at which the quantity demanded by consumers in a given period equals the quantity that producers are willing to supply in that period. In principle an equilibrium position can be attained in either a market or a planned economy, but it is important to recognize that the term means different things in the two instances.

In figure 28.1 we show demand and supply curves similar to those shown in earlier chapters. If this diagram is taken as referring to a free market we would say that with the supply curve S and the demand curve D_1 the equilibrium price is P. By this we mean that provided that no change occurs in supply conditions, producers would be happy to continue supplying in each period a quantity Q at price P, i.e. their profitability is satisfactory. Similarly with unchanged demand conditions, consumers would continue to purchase Q at price P.

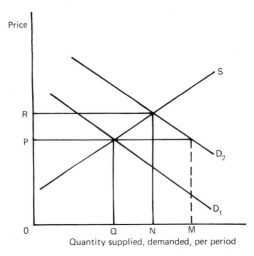

Figure 28.1   The Response to an Increase in Demand

If figure 28.1 is taken as referring to a planned economy, it would indicate that producers have been allocated an output quota Q per period, that it has been centrally decided that this output should be sold at price P, and that these deicisions have coincided with consumers' decisions as to the quantity of that product they would wish to buy at that price.

These differences in interpretation may not seem to be important while the market is in equilibrium. However they become more important when we consider disequilibrium positions. It is necessary to study such positions since there is, of course, no guarantee that a market will be in equilibrium whatever the type of economic system.

The Response to Disequilibrium
One disequilibrium position would be where the quantity demanded exceeded the quantity supplied at a given price. For example if in figure 28.1 demand shifted to D_2, there would be an excess demand QM at price P. In both market and planned economies producers would notice an increase in the volume of orders, and in each instance the immediate consequence would probably be the formation of 'queues' and the lengthening of order books. However the ultimate response might be different under the two systems.

As we have seen, producers in market economies are strongly motivated by a desire to expand their sales and profits. Consequently they will react to lengthening order books by increasing their output. In order to do this they will need to employ more resources. This may involve expansion by existing producers and/or the entry of new producers into the market. In either case the demands of consumers are translated, via the producers, into additional output and the employment of additional resources. (With the upward sloping supply curve, S, the equilibrium price is R, and the equilibrium output N. With a perfectly elastic supply, i.e. a horizontal supply curve, price would remain at P and output would increase to M.)

In a planned economy producers would have less incentive to increase output in order to satisfy the additional demand, since they have fulfilled their quota by producing output Q. Moreover even if producers wished to increase output they would find it difficult to do so if resources had been allocated to them on a quota basis, as occurs in a fully planned economy. If output and price remain unchanged, equilibrium will not be restored; consumers will continue to queue, waiting lists to lengthen. The situation may eventually be corrected, the planners may increase production quotas, but the response is likely to be much slower than in a market system.

As an alternative to increasing output, an official system of rationing may be introduced. This *could* be portrayed as shifting the demand curve to the left so that Q is once more demanded at price P. But demand would not now have the same meaning as in a market economy. Moreover, far from overcoming the fundamental disequilibrium, such a response actually perpetuates it.

A disequilibrium position may also arise because the quantity demanded at a given price, is less than producers are willing to supply at that price. This is illustrated in figure 28.2, where demand is not D_1, as expected, but D_2. Producers

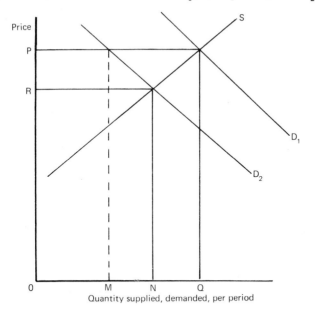

Figure 28.2 The Response to a Fall in Demand

find that at price P they can sell not Q but M. The initial response is likely to be an increase in stocks (inventories). However eventually output will be reduced and resources will be released from this market or industry. With the supply curve S, the new equilibrium price would be R, and the equilibrium output N.

In a planned economy, since the managers of production units are evaluated in terms of their success in meeting production quotas, there is less incentive to react to the fall in demand by reducing output below Q. Consequently stocks of unsold goods will continue to grow and too many resources will continue to be employed in this market. Again, while the situation may eventually be corrected, the speed of response is likely to be slower than in a market economy.

This brief comparison suggests that the allocation of resources is likely to adjust to changes in demand more quickly in a market than in a planned economy. This greater flexibility would generally be considered an advantage. However this might not always be so. It is conceivable that a certain degree of 'stickiness', a delay in the response to a change in demand, might be desirable where changes in demand are temporary and where the resources released from particular industries cannot be utilized in other industries.

Having briefly examined the advantages of the price mechanism, we now consider a number of measures taken to modify its operation. As we noted above, intervention implies that the operation of the price mechanism has some disadvantages, and some of the measures that we discuss are designed to limit the role of the price mechanism. However in other instances intervention has the opposite purpose – it is intended to improve the operation of the price mechanism and thus extend its role.

The Control of Price in Open Markets

We showed in Chapter 26 that large price fluctuations are far more likely to occur in open markets than in markets in which individual producers have a greater measure of influence on price. These extreme price fluctuations are undesirable for several reasons.

First, many of the products traded in open markets are important sources of revenue, and of foreign exhange, for underdeveloped countries. Since living standards in some of these countries are very low, a reduction in revenue in one year may have very serious consequences in terms of ill-health and death.

Second, fluctuations in the prices of raw materials add to the uncertainty faced by customers in planning their operations. In order to reduce the level of uncertainty they may turn to alternative products whose prices are more stable. This is, of course, most likely to happen when the price of a raw material rises above that of a substitute. For example when in 1974 the price of sisal exceeded $1,000 a tonne many customers substituted the synthetic material, polypropylene. Producers of polypropylene responded to the increase in demand by substantially increasing their capacity, bringing about such a drastic change in the balance between demand and supply that by the middle of 1976 the price of sisal had fallen to $400 a tonne. In other words the high prices enjoyed by sisal producers in earlier years led not only to much lower prices, but also to a loss of market share, in subsequent years.

As we saw in Chapter 15 numerous attempts have been made, on a national or international level, to prevent – or at least moderate – price fluctuations. We now consider the various forms that intervention might take, beginning with buffer stock schemes.

Buffer Stock Schemes
FLUCTUATIONS IN SUPPLY
A buffer stock scheme is operated by a central agency, national or international. This agency enters the market – as a buyer or seller – in order to maintain the target price, denoted by P_T in figure 28.3. Given the consumers' demand, D, the target price would be achieved with an output of Q. If output is above Q, say T, the

equilibrium price would fall to P_L. To prevent this happening, the central agency will buy QT at price P_T, and add this to the buffer stock. Conversely if, when output is R, the agency wishes to prevent price from rising to P_H it will release from the buffer stock RQ, which it will sell at P_T.

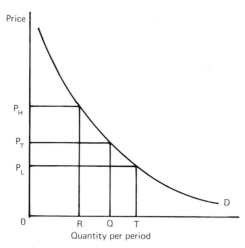

Figure 28.3 The Stabilization of Price

Considerable difficulties may arise in operating a buffer stock scheme. If, as we have assumed so far, the only purpose of the scheme is to eliminate price fluctuations, the agency must be able to forecast what the average free market price would be over a number of years. This average is the target price set by the agency. Unless it sets an appropriate target price, the agency's sales and purchases will not balance out over the years.

In practice, the elimination of price fluctuations may *not* be the only purpose of a buffer stock scheme. There is considerable evidence to suggest that a target price may be set above the average free market price. This implies that purchases by the agency will exceed sales, i.e. that the size of the buffer stock will gradually rise. For example the target prices set by the E.E.C. led to an output of milk and milk products in excess of demand at those prices. The result was a 'butter mountain' and increasing stocks of dried milk. In order to try to reduce these stocks the E.E.C. resorted to a variety of tactics, including selling butter at a substantial loss to countries outside the E.E.C., a proposal to raise taxes on substitutes for butter, and the introduction of regulations requiring the use of dried milk as an animal feedstock in preference to cheaper alternatives.

While a buffer stock scheme of the type illustrated in figure 28.3 eliminates fluctuations in price, it does not eliminate fluctuations in producers' income. Indeed, if price is maintained at a constant level regardless of output the producers' income will change in line with output.

In order to reduce fluctuations in income following changes in output, the elasticity of demand must be brought closer to unity. Indeed if demand is of unitary elasticity revenue is the same at all prices. A demand curve having this property is a rectangular hyperbola, shown as D_1 in figure 28.4. Revenue at output Q (OQCA) equals revenue at output R (ORDB). If, without the buffer stock scheme, the demand curve had been D_2, revenue at output R (OREF) would have been greater than at output Q (OQGH).

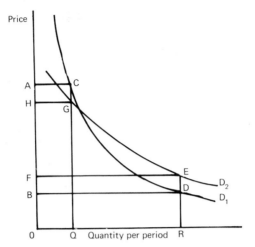

Figure 28.4 Stabilization of Producers' Income

FLUCTUATIONS IN DEMAND

The schemes considered above were designed to modify fluctuations in prices or incomes arising from fluctuations in supply. Fluctuations in supply frequently characterize agricultural markets, especially foodstuffs. In markets for many industrial raw materials the main cause of fluctuations in price are fluctuations in demand.

Since open markets are sometimes supplied by a large number of small producers, it may be very difficult to adjust supply in line with demand. Figure 28.5 illustrates the extreme case where, in the absence of intervention, there would be

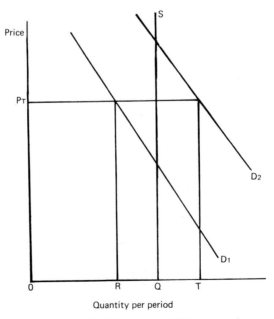

Figure 28.5 Stabilization of Price and Income

no adjustment of supply, i.e. Q would be supplied regardless of the state of demand. If consumers' demand were at D_1, then in order to maintain the target price, P_T, the agency would be required to buy RQ, thus reducing the quantity supplied to the market to R. Conversely with demand at D_2 the agency would be required to release QT from stock, increasing the amount supplied to the market to T. (Note that in this instance, since the quantity supplied by producers is constant from one period to the next, stabilization of price also implies stabilization of producers' income.)

Other Forms of Intervention

If the market demand is inelastic producers may agree to restrict their output and raise their price in order to increase their revenue. The most successful example of this policy in the post-war period was the increase in the price of oil imposed by the members of the Organization of Petroleum Exporting Countries. In addition to the necessary condition that demand should be price inelastic, several other conditions explain the success of the O.P.E.C. policy. Although oil is produced from a large number of production units (oil wells), the bulk of the output is controlled by a small number of governments. (This suggests that the oil market is not an open market.) Co-operation among these producers was enhanced by the fact that most of them had a common political interest, namely opposition to the state of Israel. Moreover the average cost of producing oil in the O.P.E.C. countries was substantially less than elsewhere, so there was little chance that an increase in price would lead to a substantial loss of sales to other producers. In other words not only was the *total* demand for oil price inelastic (as noted above), but the demand for O.P.E.C. oil was also inelastic within a considerable price range. Furthermore, even if the volume of sales declined, as other sources of supply such as the North Sea were developed and as some consumers switched to substitute fuels, it seemed likely that most of the O.P.E.C. countries would continue to earn sufficient revenue to foster their desired economic development. A final important consideration was the fact that oil is a non-renewable resource. Thus a reduction in current output means that reserves will be exhausted less quickly.

It can be seen, therefore, that conditions were particularly propitious for the formation of a successful cartel, and are unlikely to be repeated in other markets. Nevertheless, encouraged by the example of O.P.E.C., producers of bauxite, iron ore, copper, tungsten, uranium and various other products have tried, with varying degrees of success, to co-ordinate their output decisions.

Land Banks

Another way of trying to restrict supply and hence bring about an increase in price is by reducing the capacity of the industry. In agriculture this means reducing the land under cultivation, either by government edict or by paying compensation to farmers. The expense of compensation payments has meant that this policy has been mainly confined to richer countries such as the U.S.A.

The justification advanced for the adoption of this policy in the U.S.A. is that higher prices are required to improve the living standards of the poorer farmers – usually those owning small farms. While the policy may have this effect, it is likely to be of even greater benefit to the richer farmers with big farms. They have more land to withdraw from cultivation and therefore qualify for bigger compensation payments. Lee and McNown quote the finding of C. L. Schultze that in the late 1960s 40 per cent of the additional income received by farmers as a result of government intervention went to only 7 per cent of the farms. In 1970 nine farms received subsidy payments of more than $1 million each. The average income of these recipients was, of course, substantially above that of the taxpayers who ultimately met the cost of the compensation payments.*

The Stabilization of Demand for Industrial Products
Stabilization schemes for industrial products are relatively rare since fluctuations in the balance between demand and supply tend to be much less pronounced than in the markets for primary products. Nevertheless fluctuations do occur – especially in demand – and the consequences of these fluctuations have sometimes led to government intervention.

In the U.K. one of the components of the government's industrial policy has been the provision of financial assistance for investment projects that are undertaken earlier than they would have been otherwise. One of the major objectives of this assistance has been to reduce unemployment. But in addition it was hoped that by helping to reduce fluctuations in the demand for capital goods, the policy might encourage firms in that sector to increase their capacity. A lack of capacity cut short economic growth in earlier 'boom' periods.

A different form of intervention in capital goods markets occurred in 1977 when the European Commission imposed a minimum price for certain types of steel bars produced by E.E.C. manufacturers. This event led one commentator to observe that 'The crisis of the European steel industry has prompted the Commission to move towards a quota and price cartel, thus extending the principle of regulation so far reserved for agriculture into the area of industry.'†

Intervention was clearly designed to protect the income of the steel producers. Further arguments in favour of intervention might be that the protection of producers' income would encourage investment which would in turn lead to greater efficiency and employment. While such a chain of events is possible it must be remembered that the action of the Commission would probably not have been allowed under U.K. legislation – and indeed the legislation of some other European countries – had it been taken by a group of private producers (see Chapter 18).

The forms of intervention discussed above are designed to put a floor to price and, in some instances, to raise price above the free market level. Intervention may also occur in order to put a ceiling to price and/or to bring prices down below the free market level. The two main ways of achieving these objectives is via subsidies and price controls. We consider examples of each of these in turn.

Subsidies: the Market for Medical Services
Medical services are a good example of a merit good, i.e. a good whose consumption the government wishes to encourage. In the U.K. the major form of encouragement is the provision of medical facilities at zero or very low prices. The effects of this policy are illustrated in figure 28.6. (In practice there are, of course, many different medical services, and figure 28.6 can be interpreted as relating to a 'representative' service).

If we assume that private producers would add to the average cost a profit margin CP_1, giving the supply curve S_1, the free market price would be P_1. With demand

*D. R. Lee and E. F. McNown, *Economics in Our Time: Concepts and Issues* (Chicago: Science Research Associates, 1975), ch. 3.

†A. H. Hermann 'Competition bows out to regulation in the E.E.C.' (*Financial Times*, 11.5.77.).

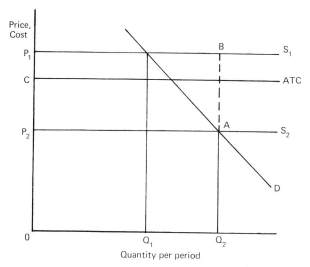

Figure 28.6 A Subsidized Merit Good

at D, quantity Q_1 would be bought. If the government set the lower price P_2, Q_2 would be bought.*

The lower price affects resource allocation in a number of ways. First, and most obviously, the quantity of resources employed in the industry increases. (This assumes that demand and cost conditions would be the same whether medical services were provided by the public or the private sector. This assumption could, of course, be challenged.) It follows that fewer resources will be available for employment in other industries.

Second, the total amount spent by consumers on medical services will be affected. The effect will depend upon the size of the subsidy and the elasticity of demand for the product. Consequently we cannot say a priori whether total expenditure will increase or decrease. However it seems likely that the very low price charged in the U.K. has the effect of reducing expenditure by consumers. This means that the consumers of medical services will have more money to spend on other products.

On the other hand the cost of the subsidy, amounting in figure 28.6 to $P_2 P_1 BA$, must be met by taxation of one form or another (including national insurance contributions). The effect of taxation is, of course, to reduce disposable income. Overall, therefore the subsidy will cause a redistribution of real income and of expenditure.

Whether this redistribution is desirable depends upon the nature of the good or service, upon the form of the subsidy and finally, of course, upon one's political and ethical views. In the particular example that we have chosen here the arguments in favour of subsidization are fairly straightforward. In terms of equity it can be argued that some people require more medical services than others – because of accidents or because they are less healthy constitutionally – and that it is unfair that their ability to obtain these services should depend upon their income. It can also be argued that a healthy community is likely to be more productive – in other words that the provision of medical facilities is a form of investment and that the

* In the U.K. medical services are mainly provided by the public sector below cost. In principle, a similar result could be achieved by giving subsidies to private sector producers. A price P_2 implies a subsidy of $P_2 P_1$ per unit.

maximum benefit will be obtained from the investment by making the facilities available free or at low prices.

The critics of subsidies might make a number of points in reply to the above arguments. First, while recognizing that the cost of certain medical facilities, such as those involved in major operations, might be beyond the capacity of some citizens, they would point out that it is possible to subscribe to medical insurance schemes. Under these schemes the benefit payable (and hence the cost of the treatment that can be obtained) is linked to the contributions paid. It is then up to each citizen to decide how he should allocate his income as between medical insurance and other goods and services. To the criticism that the incomes of some citizens might be inadequate to permit them to contribute to a medical insurance scheme, the advocates of the free market approach would probably reply that their incomes should be raised by means of a reverse or negative income tax. It might also be necessary to protect the interests of those citizens who were not earning – the unemployed, the retired and children – perhaps by paying contributions on their behalf.

With regard to efficiency, while acknowledging the link between health and productivity, the critics of subsidies might point out that there is no reason to think that a subsidized health service would lead to the consumption of medical facilities required to maximize economic efficiency. Indeed it is possible that better facilities would be provided under a free market system. This is an extremely complex issue to which a whole chapter, and indeed a whole book, might be devoted. We can do no more here than point to the fact that in some areas of the British health service in recent years an increase in spending appears to have been accompanied by an increase in administrative costs but not to an improvement in the service provided to patients.

Price Controls: the Market for Housing
Controls on the price of housing are usually justified on the grounds that housing is a basic necessity, and that everyone should be able to enjoy at least a minimum standard. In an uncontrolled market an excess of demand over supply will cause prices to rise and houses to become 'too expensive'.

While one may agree with the moral sentiments expressed in the above paragraph it does not follow that price controls are the best solution to the 'housing problem'. In fact it seems entirely possible that controls will make the problem worse. The imposition of controls implies that the profitability of suppliers will be reduced, and this will tend to reduce the supply of houses. So we find that in 1969 in New York City, about five times as many apartment units were abandoned by landlords as were built or rehabilitated in that year.*

It is clearly possible that the benefit derived by some tenants from rent controls was outweighed by the distress of prospective tenants who could not obtain accommodation.

The U.K. housing market has had a not dissimilar experience. The control of privately rented accommodation is probably the main reason for the decline in the number of rented dwellings from $7\frac{1}{2}$ millions (55 per cent of the housing stock) in 1945 to 2.6 millions (14 per cent of the stock) in 1972.

This situation is illustrated in figure 28.7. In the absence of controls the equilibrium price would be P_1, Q_1 houses being bought and sold. If the government imposes a price ceiling P_2 only Q_2 houses will be made available for sale, leaving an unsatisfied demand of Q_2Q_3.

*D. R. Lee and R. F. McNown, op. cit., ch. 3.

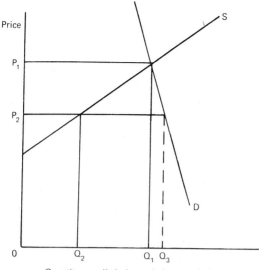

Figure 28.7 The Effect of Price Control

It may be possible to fill the gap left by private builders or landlords by expanding the activities of the public sector – in the U.K. this means mainly the local authorities. However the provision of council houses is by no means an unmixed blessing. There is no guarantee that public housing will always be allocated to those in greatest need. Indeed subsidized rents provide an incentive to existing occupiers to stay put, even when their family and financial circumstances have become far more favourable than those of people on the authorities' 'waiting lists'.

It is conceivable that a better solution to the housing problem might be to improve the financial position of those people who cannot afford accommodation at free market prices. This might be done by altering the pattern of assistance available from the building societies, in such a way as to favour first-home buyers more strongly. Another solution might be to improve the incomes of the lowest paid by means of a negative income tax. (We could not, of course, ensure that the additional disposable income would be spent on housing. Indeed a negative income tax is usually proposed as a solution, not to a specific problem such as housing, but to the general problem of low incomes.)

Minimum Wage Legislation
Intervention is not confined to product markets. It has been extended to factor markets and especially to labour markets. As noted in Chapter 27, wage rates are determined by the interaction of a large number of forces. In most economies (including planned economies) these forces result in a wide spread of wage rates and earnings between occupations. In order to try to reduce the spread of differentials some countries have introduced legislation specifying minimum wage rates. However there are reasons for believing that this attempt to protect the lower-paid from the consequences of the operation of market forces may not succeed.

One possible outcome is that higher-paid workers may negotiate pay rises which restore the differentials vis-à-vis the lower paid. If producers pass on the increased costs in the form of higher prices, the real incomes of the lower-paid will not have been improved.

Alternatively, if the lower paid do obtain an increase in real incomes this may be at the expense of the number of such workers employed. This is most likely to happen if the wage differentials are due to differences in productivity. If the wages of the lower paid workers are increased, and there is not a corresponding increase in productivity, employers will dismiss workers, preferring to use more skilled workers or to substitute capital for labour.

Moreover, this response may occur even when there is a 'non-economic' reason for the differential. For example if employers have a prejudice against coloured workers they will employ such workers only if they are allowed to pay them lower wages than white workers. Legislation which prevents this may lead employers to substitute white for coloured labour. In 1959 the minimum hourly wage in the U.S.A. was raised from 75 cents to $1. Subsequently a Department of Labor survey of twelve industries affected by the new minimum found that employment had decreased in all but one. The workers whose employment prospects were most affected by the legislation were black teenagers.*

This process is illustrated in figure 28.8. In the absence of government inter-

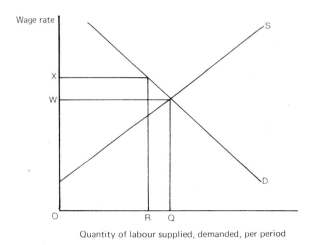

Figure 28.8 The Effect of Minimum Wage Legislation

vention the equilibrium wage would be W, Q workers being employed. If the government imposes a minimum wage of X, the number employed falls to R. (We showed in the previous chapter that a wage increase might not always lead to a reduction in employment, especially when a trade union can prevent redundancies. However we suggested that a reduction in employment was likely to occur, especially in the longer term.)

Cost Benefit Analysis
We have shown in earlier chapters that the prices of products reflect, to a greater or lesser extent, the cost of producing those products (private costs). Prices do not, however, reflect costs which production may impose on the community at large (external costs). Similarly prices reflect only the benefits obtained by the purchasers or users of the products in question (private benefits). They do reflect any

* D. R. Lee and R. F. McNown, op. cit., ch. 3.

benefits obtained by non-users of the products (external benefits). Cost benefit analysis attempts to measure these external costs and benefits and so to arrive at a 'price' which would reflect total or social costs and benefits.*

COST BENEFIT ANALYSIS AND INVESTMENT DECISIONS

Cost benefit analysis has two main applications. First, it can be used in investment decisions. It is possible that a decision which would not yield a satisfactory return at market prices would do so if all the external effects were taken into account. If a private producer is involved in the decision, the state might provide a subsidy to the investment. (Examples of such subsidies were considered during our discussion of regional and manpower policy.)

If the investment is undertaken by a public sector producer the shortfall on revenue† may be made up from the revenue obtained from that producer's other activities, or by a government subsidy. As an example consider the decision to build the Victoria Line on the London underground system. This line was not expected to yield a private profit. However an analysis undertaken after the decision had been made, suggested that the building of the line would increase total welfare, i.e. that a 'social profit' would result when external effects were taken into account. These effects included benefits both to users – which were not reflected in higher prices, and to non-users, such as a reduction in road congestion as some drivers and passengers switched from road to rail.‡

Some potential public sector investment projects, such as the building of a motorway, have no private benefits as measured by prices, since the 'product' is supplied free. In these instances cost benefit analysis attempts to measure external benefits, to compare these with total cost, and thus to arrive at a social rate of return.

Sometimes cost benefit analysis may suggest that an investment project which would yield a satisfactory private profit ought not to be undertaken because of the external costs that would be involved. These costs might include a risk to health or life, pollution of various kinds and congestion. (These costs are considered further below.)

Finally, cost benefit analysis may be applied to alternative investment projects, such as the siting of the third London airport. The Roskill Commission, set up to advise the government, evaluated the costs and benefits attaching to four alternative sites.§ The costs examined again related both to users (in particular the time taken to get from the airport to central London) and non-users (especially aircraft noise).

COST BENEFIT ANALYSIS AND PRICES

The second application of cost benefit analysis is to prices. As we noted above, market prices may be either too high or too low when considered in the light of the total costs and benefits attaching to the product. We gave medical services

---

* This definition of social costs (benefits), as the sum of private and external costs (benefits), is the most common. However some writers use social costs or benefits in the sense of external costs or benefits.

† The investment may yield a profit below the target, or it may even fail to cover its cost.

‡ C. D. Foster and M. E. Beesley 'Estimating the social benefits of constructing an underground railway in London' (*Journal of the Royal Statistical Society*, Series A, 1963).

§ The Report of the Commission on the Third London Airport (London: H.M.S.O., 1971). The government finally decided not to proceed with the project, allegedly because of changes in the pattern of demand for air travel and in the technology of air transportation.

as an example of a product which is supplied in the U.K. at a price well below the free market price, and we suggested that one justification for this is the external benefit derived from the consumption of medical services, namely the increase in the productivity or efficiency of the work force.

As an example of underpricing we can consider pollution. Two important resources, air and the waterways, are frequently used for the disposal of waste products at no cost to the user – but possibly at a very considerable cost to non-users. This underpricing occurs basically because it is not feasible to establish private ownership rights in these resources. Without ownership rights the price mechanism cannot operate.

Since the disposal of waste products frequently gives rise to external costs, governments may assume ownership rights over the resources used for their disposal, and then control their use in one way or another. They may impose charges (which may vary in accordance with the amount of pollution caused). If control or rationing via the price mechanism is felt not to be feasible or desirable, the government may impose direct controls. For example they may require firms to instal plant for the treatment of the waste products.

The Time Dimension of the Price Mechanism

In market and mixed economies resources are allocated in response to the signals provided by the price mechanism, and the speed of response is generally believed to be one of the main advantages of these types of economy. However doubts have been expressed concerning the ability of these economies to anticipate and adjust to future changes. It is argued that the price mechanism may not give sufficient advance warning of these changes and that the adjustment process may therefore begin later than would be desirable. These doubts have been expressed most frequently in connection with energy supplies.

ENERGY SUPPLIES

A feature which distinguishes sources of energy from most other material resources is that the resources from which energy is obtained cannot generally be recycled. (Some nuclear fuels are an exception to this generalization.) This might suggest that governments would be justified in seeking to control, or at least influence, the rate at which these resources are utilized.

Particular concern has been expressed about the possible exhaustion of oil supplies. A number of reports have been issued containing projections of the demand for and supply of oil. Two such projections are shown in figure 28.9. These were given in a report published in 1977* and correspond fairly closely to projections contained in other studies such as that undertaken by O.E.C.D.

The projections are subject to a wide range of influences, including the rate of economic growth, the price of oil relative to other fuels and the quantity of oil supplied each year. However the report showed that most assumptions lead to the conclusion that the supply of oil is likely to be outstripped by demand before the end of the century. Even if these forecasts turn out to be pessimistic, such a situation will arise sooner or later. It is, therefore, worth considering the implications for government policy.

One possibility is that governments should try to depress the rate of economic growth so as to delay the point at which demand for oil outstrips supply. This

---

Energy: Global Prospects 1985–2000, Report of the Workshop in Alternative Energy Strategies (W.A.E.S.) (New York: McGraw-Hill, 1977).

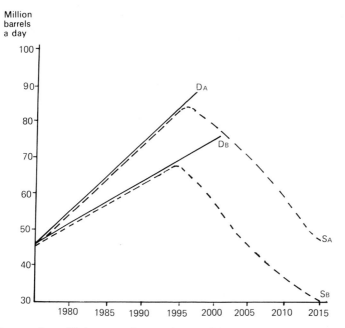

D_A, S_A–Assumptions: High economic growth rate, rising energy price, vigorous government response, coal as principal replacement fuel, gross additions to oil reserves of 20 billion barrels per year.
D_B, S_B–Assumptions: Low economic growth rate, constant energy price, restrained government response, nuclear as principal replacement fuel, gross additions to oil reserves of 10 billion barrels per year.

Figure 28.9 World Oil Production and Consumption (excluding Communist countries).

would seem to be a counsel of despair, and is unlikely to commend itself to under-developed countries who are desperately trying to increase their growth rates in order to obtain more of the material benefits enjoyed by other countries.

A more feasible alternative would be to discourage the use of oil products by rationing or by fiscal measures. Two fiscal measures suggested by President Carter in the U.S.A. in 1977 were higher taxes on petrol (which was much cheaper in the U.S.A. than in many other countries) and a differential tax on cars, designed to discourage the use of cars with a heavy petrol consumption. It may take five years to design new models with lower fuel consumption, and ten years to change the country's stock of cars. Consequently, although the imposition of taxes might reduce petrol consumption to a limited extent in 1977, its full effect would not be felt until the 1980s. This illustrates the point made earlier, that it may be desirable for the government to modify market prices in order to hasten the process of resource reallocation.

Governments may also need to take more positive steps to encourage the development of alternative fuels – again the market might not signal the need for such development as early as would be desirable. The W.A.E.S. report estimated that in principle coal production in the non-Communist world could expand three fold by the end of the century. However this would require 'major and early' investment in mines, coal-handling equipment, coal transport systems, and in new systems to use the coal either as fuel or as feedstock for substitute petroleum fuels.

Government initiative and financial support might be required in order to ensure that the required investment was undertaken.

Even greater investment over a longer time period is likely to be required for the development of less conventional sources of energy such as solar, geothermal and tidal power. For example a government report issued in 1977 estimated that building a barrage across the Severn Estuary in order to generate electricity from tidal power would cost between £3 and 4 billions. Since the total construction period for the barrage would be about twenty years government involvement would clearly be inevitable.

CONSERVATION OF OTHER RESOURCES

Concern has also been expressed about the possible exhaustion of other resources. It is sometimes claimed that resources will be used up more quickly, i.e. that conservation will be less likely, under a system of private than of collective property rights. The validity of this argument depends very much upon the form in which the collective rights exist. If they are vested in the government it will certainly have the *power* to control the utilization of resources, although it is by no means certain whether or how it will use this power.

If collective rights are not vested in a central authority, it seems that resource utilization and depletion are likely to occur *more* quickly than when there are private ownership rights. For example if a forest is privately owned the owner will take into account the cost of depleting the forest and is likely to try to regenerate it by planting new trees as mature ones are felled. If, on the other hand, the forest is collectively owned each person will exercise his rights as fully as possible. Furthermore he will have little interest in regeneration since he cannot be sure that a private cost to him (planting new trees) will result in a private benefit, since these trees may be felled by someone else.

CONSERVATION, SUBSTITUTION AND RECYCLING

The fear that, in the absence of government intervention, certain resources might soon become exhausted is sometimes expressed in very strong terms. Note, for example, the following passage: 'Present reserves of all but a few metals will be exhausted within fifty years if consumption rates continue to grow as they are'. Further, 'if current trends are allowed to persist ... the breakdown of society and the irreversible disruption of the life support systems on this planet are inevitable'.*

While the increase in the world's population and in the level of economic activity have certainly led to a tremendous increase in the rate of utilization of resources, statements such as these appear to give too little weight to certain fundamental aspects of the price mechanism.

First, if the pressure of demand causes an increase in the price of resources, producers will have an additional incentive to search for new supplies. A good example of this process is the impetus given to the development of North Sea oil by the increase in the price of O.P.E.C. oil. (Estimates of reserves at a given point in time normally refer to 'proven' reserves, and may be far below the absolute level.)

Second, as one resource becomes more expensive, there is an incentive to develop substitutes. Sometimes the source of the substitute may be most unlikely. For example in textiles we have seen natural fibres such as wool, cotton, flax and jute, supplemented by a range of artificial fibres produced by the chemical industry.

Finally, as reserves in the ground dwindle it becomes more worthwhile to recycle

* E. Goldsmith (ed.), *Blueprint for Survival* (Harmondsworth: Penguin, 1973).

material that would previously have been wasted. The increasing importance of recycling can be judged from the fact that in the U.K. in 1973 recovery of various materials, as a percentage of consumption, was as follows: ferrous metals 82 per cent, lead 62 per cent, copper 36 per cent, aluminium 30 per cent, paper 29 per cent, glass 25 per cent, and rubber 17 per cent.

This does not mean, of course, that we should be complacent about the possible exhaustion of reserves. But it does suggest that the economic system may be able to adjust to potential shortages rather more easily than is sometimes suggested. There are two areas in which intervention to modify or supplement the price mechanism is most likely to be required. The first, as noted above, is where there is a long lead time in the process of design and production. The second is where there are important economies of scale, including economies of information and standardization. For example the government may facilitate an increase in recycling by providing the physical facilities, by bringing together suppliers and potential users of recycled materials, and by establishing technical specifications designed to encourage standardization of product.

Summary and Conclusions

In this chapter we have examined the reasons which might lead the government to modify the operation of the price mechanism. We showed that intervention might be designed to increase, decrease or stabilize prices, and we examined the various forms which intervention might take in order to achieve these objectives.

In all instances intervention implies that the market price is inappropriate in one sense or another. For example it may act as a rationing device in markets in which it is felt other methods of allocation are more appropriate. While recognizing that the existing distribution of some products might not be appropriate, we showed that interfering with the operation of the price mechanism does not necessarily lead to a better distribution – indeed it might act to the detriment of those people whose interests intervention was designed to protect.

We also considered examples of government intervention designed to introduce the price mechanism where it did not operate previously, e.g. in order to reduce pollution. However we saw that other methods of control, such as physical control over the offending activities, might be introduced as an alternative.

Finally we examined the possibility that the price mechanism might not send out signals about future changes in the balance between demand and supply sufficiently early to allow all the necessary adjustment processes to be put into effect.

The extent to which the price mechanism should be modified has long been debated by both economists and politicians. Given the mixed results which we have shown intervention to have, given the changing nature of economies, and finally given the changes which occur in people's objectives, it is clear that the debate will continue for many years to come.

ESSAY QUESTIONS

1 What reasons are there for thinking that a situation of disequilibrium will be corrected more rapidly in a free market economy than in a planned economy? In what circumstances may a rapid adjustment *not* be desirable?
2 Explain why price control has often been felt to be more necessary in open than in other markets.

3 Show how buffer stocks may be used to stabilize (a) prices, (b) producers' incomes.
4 Discuss the conditions required for a successful price stabilization scheme.
5 Evaluate the case for the provision by the state of (a) free education, (b) subsidized medical services, (c) subsidized television sets for retirement pensioners.
6 Discuss the possible consequences of a government policy which controlled the rents of private rented accommodation and subsidized the rents of council houses.
7 Analyse the possible consequences of the introduction into the U.K. of minimum wage legislation.
8 Explain the statement that cost–benefit analysis may be used to adjust for imperfections in the market mechanism and discuss the factors which are likely to limit its application.
9 How would you expect a market system to adjust to the approaching depletion of a natural resource? Under what circumstances might government intervention in the adjustment process be justified?
10 Explain with examples the statement that government intervention may be designed to increase, decrease or stabilize the price of particular products.
11 'Changes in market prices are signals which lead to the re-allocation of resources in the public interest.' Discuss.
12 Explain the distinction between private cost and social cost and show how these concepts may be applied to traffic congestion.

EXERCISES

28.1 In figure 28.10 the two demand curves indicate the demand for the current output of a product, (a) when a buffer-stock scheme exists, (b) when there is no interference with market forces.
   (i) Indicate which demand curve applies in each situation. (ii) Use the diagram to show the possible effects of the buffer-stock scheme on (a) fluctuations in price, (b) fluctuations in producers' income. (iii) Indicate the range of output

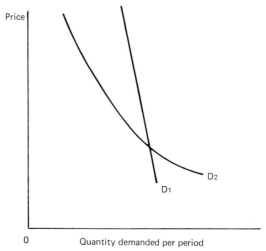

Figure 28.10   Alternative Demand Curves

which would cause the size of the buffer stock to increase, and discuss the problems which would arise if this level of output were maintained.

28.2 'Further evidence that the whole future of raw material supplies and prices is entering a new era of control by producers, which could be similar to O.P.E.C. in oil, has been provided recently in both the copper and tin markets. Rio Tinto-Zinc, the British-based international mining group, has been acting on behalf of a number of leading copper producing countries to deal with the problem of surplus supplies, especially in Japan, depressing copper prices to a level which is below the cost of production for many mines.

'The basic idea is to organize a financial consortium to take over, and effectively remove from sale at current prices, the huge surplus of copper supplies in Japan – estimated at some 250,000 tonnes – and also to obtain world-wide agreement to cut back production levels more suited to the present low demand.

'It was the export of surplus copper by Japanese smelters, who refine ore concentrates into copper, when domestic demand plummeted after the oil crisis, that was the major influence in the collapse of world copper prices last year from a peak of £1,400 to £500 a tonne in the space of a few months.

'The Japanese Government, bowing to requests from developing countries dependent on copper for the bulk of their export earnings, banned further exports in November. Since then, however, it has been faced with surplus stocks piling up and threatening to bankrupt the smelters.'

The above passage was extracted from an article in the *Financial Times*, 21.4.75.

(i) How would you explain the fact that copper prices had fallen to a level 'below the cost of production for many mines'? (ii) Can selling copper at this price ever be a sensible policy? (iii) Assuming that a consortium could be formed which would buy up the surplus supplies of copper, what factors would influence the extent to which such a policy would be commercially successful? (iv) Indicate in two or three sentences the basis on which a reasonable target price might be determined.

28.3 'Over-production of dairy products for the world as a whole is expected to continue in 1976, especially in the E.E.C., according to a report by the Food and Agriculture Organisation of the U.N. issued to-day.

'World milk production, which virtually stagnated this year at about 425 m. tons, is expected to increase somewhat in 1976. Although demand for milk and milk products should gradually recover from this year's drop, the report stated that the imbalance between supplies and commercial outlets is likely to persist in 1976, especially in the E.E.C.

'Skim milk powder stocks are estimated to total 1.8 m tons in developed countries – more than double their level at the beginning of the year. Prospects of a recovery of skim milk powder prices, which dropped more than 50 per cent in 18 months to about $500 a ton, were considered poor.

'Butter stocks have risen over levels of a year earlier, but were not yet considered excessive. However, the report warned of a possible accumulation of a "butter mountain" unless Eastern European countries and the U.S.S.R. bought larger quantities.'

'Animal feed prices would rise by 6 per cent, if the E.E.C. Commission's proposal for the compulsory use of 2 per cent skim milk powder in all compound rations was adopted, Europe's feed manufacturers said yesterday.

'The Commission's proposal in its farm price package is designed to reduce the 1 m. tonne skim milk powder "mountain" in Common Market intervention stores.

'In a letter to Mr. Pierre Lardinois, the Agricultural Commissioner, Mr. Ken Arnott the president of the European Federation of Feed Manufacturers, said the proposal was a "quite unacceptable interference in the formulation of our products. As a matter of principle it seems to us utterly wrong that the compound industry should have to suffer the consequences of the past policies over which it is in no way responsible" he wrote.

'Although there would be some subsidising of the powder, feed prices would rise by about £4.50 a tonne, or about 6 per cent. This was "a harsh penalty on the dairy farmer, but it is manifestly unjust that the feeder of pigs and poultry should be obliged to subsidise a sector with which he is not concerned".'

The above items appeared in the *Financial Times*, 16.12.76 (i) Why do you think that 'the imbalance between supplies and commercial outlets' arose in 1975? (ii) Comment on the proposed method of solving the problem of the skim milk mountain. (iii) What other solutions might be adopted?

28.4 Tea, a commodity whose demand is believed to be price inelastic, is produced by a relatively small number of countries. The 'traditional' producers are mainly in Asia, e.g. India, Sri Lanka, Bangladesh, while the 'new' producers are mainly in Africa. Large areas of virgin land, higher labour productivity than in the traditional tea producing areas and younger, and therefore more productive, tea bushes all imply that production costs are lower in the African than in the Asian tea-producing countries.

Show which of the various factors mentioned in the passage above would (a) help, and (b) hinder, attempts to co-ordinate action designed to raise the price of tea.

28.5 A government Green Paper issued in 1977 gave details of households' spending on housing (net of rates) as a proportion of household disposable income. It showed that this proportion stood at 8 per cent in 1967, rose to 8.8 per cent in 1972 and fell back to 8 per cent in 1975. If there had been no tax relief on interest payments on mortgages taken out by owner-occupiers or subsidies to council house tenants, the proportion would have been 9.5 per cent in 1967 and 11.3 per cent in 1975. (The rise in this proportion is due partly to the fall in the number of people living in unsubsidized private rented accommodation and partly to increases in tax relief and subsidies.) The Green Paper also showed how the cost of housing changed – in comparison with the retail price index – for (a) owner-occupiers, (b) council-house tenants paying 'full' (but subsidized) rents, (c) council-house tenants paying rebated rents. (See figure 28.11.)

In the light of this information evaluate the policy of (a) giving tax relief to owner occupiers, (b) subsidizing the rents of council houses, (c) giving rent rebates to low-income council-house tenants.

28.6 Among the major points of a policy statement on oil issued by President Carter in 1977 were the following:

A three-stage tax to bring the price of all oils produced in the U.S. up to the world price by 1980. Alaskan oil and newly discovered oil will be treated separately.

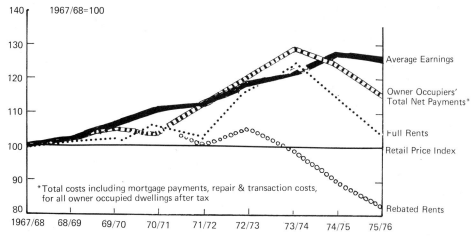

140 ┐ 1967/68=100

130

120

110

100

90

80

*Total costs including mortgage payments, repair & transaction costs,
for all owner occupied dwellings after tax

Average Earnings

Owner Occupiers'
Total Net Payments*

Full Rents

Retail Price Index

Rebated Rents

1967/68 68/69 69/70 70/71 71/72 72/73 73/74 74/75 75/76

Figure 28.11 Changes in the Cost of Owning and Renting a House

A graduated tax designed to penalize buyers of large petrol-eating cars and encourage a switch to smaller ones.

A new tax on petrol which would increase by 5 cents for each year in which petrol consumption fails to fall 1 per cent below the consumption of petrol in an agreed year.

A combination of new taxes and investment credits to persuade industry to switch from oil and natural gas to coal and the expansion of coal production to over 1 bn. tonnes by 1985.

An automatic uniform tax rebate – the precise details of which have yet to be worked out – for all Americans of about $25 to $30 a year to offset the deflationary effect on the economy of the 10 bn. that the new taxes may be taking out of it once they are in effect.

Tax credits to encourage insulation in both industry and the home and to encourage the switch to solar energy.

A major expansion of research into more efficient ways of using coal.

Explain why it was thought that a new policy was needed, and discuss the merits and demerits of the various measures.

28.7 The Meteorological Office provides a wide range of information about future weather conditions. Some of this information is provided virtually free, e.g. the forecasts included in newspapers and on the radio. In other instances, when information is provided for a specific 'audience', a charge is levied. For example at a cost of £42 a day North Sea oil operators can obtain forecasts of wind and sea conditions which they use in planning their operations. For about £150 information will be supplied about the various alternative routes which can be taken by an ocean-going vessel. For a 'few hundred pounds' a civil engineering contractor can obtain a year's forecasts for any large building site in Britain.

(i) Would you consider the information provided by the Meteorological Office to be a public good? (ii) How would you justify the provision of free information by the Office? (iii) How would you justify levying a charge for information? (iv) On what basis should the charge for information be calculated?

OBJECTIVE TEST QUESTIONS: SET 10

1 Of three goods A is substitute for, and B complementary to the third good, C. A rise in the price of C, following an increase in the cost of production, will cause the quantity traded of
   A all three goods to fall
   B A and C to fall
   C A to rise and B to fall
   D C to fall, the quantity of A being unaffected
   E C to fall, the quantity of B being unaffected.

2 If consumers have budgeted a fixed amount of money to buy a certain commodity, and within a range of prices will spend neither more nor less than this amount on it, then their demand for this commodity, within this price range, is said to be
   A in equilibrium
   B of zero elasticity
   C perfectly inelastic
   D perfectly elastic
   E of unitary elasticity

3 Which of the following cannot be true? As output increases, the scale of organization remaining unchanged,
   A average variable cost rises
   B average total cost rises
   C total cost rises
   D average fixed costs rises
   E marginal cost rises.

Questions 4–8 refer to figure 28.12 which represents the conditions of demand and supply in the market for home-produced beef. The unbroken lines are the initial demand and supply curves. The broken lines are new demand and supply curves which might apply after the various changes, indicated below, have taken place.

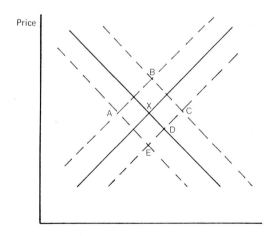

Quantity supplied, demanded, per period

Figure 28.12

Starting each time from X, the initial equilibrium position, indicate the new equilibrium position A, B, C, D, or E. (Each letter may apply once, more than once, or not at all.)

4 The real income of consumers increases; a large part of the nation's stock of cattle is destroyed by foot and mouth disease.

5 The price of pork and lamb falls; the introduction of more intensive forms of cattle-rearing lowers the cost of producing beef.

6 An advertising campaign increases consumers' preferences for beef; the cost of transporting cattle to the market increases.

7 A dock strike holds up imports of frozen beef; the government introduces a subsidy to British farmers of £10 per head of cattle reared.

8 The cost of animal food-stuffs rises; the government increases the level of income tax.

9 The demand for labour is least likely to increase following
   A   an increase in the size of the budget deficit
   B   an increase in the marginal propensity to consume
   C   an increase in the level of tariffs on imported goods
   D   a reduction in the level of corporation tax
   E   an increase in the standard rate of income tax.

10 Suppose that on the day before Christmas the local florist has a number of cut Christmas trees for sale which he will throw away (at no cost to himself) if they are not sold that day. Each tree cost the florist 50p. What price should he set if he wants to maximize his profits? A price
   A   which gives the greatest profit per tree sold
   B   just low enough to make sure that all the trees will be sold
   C   which maximize total receipts
   D   greater than 50p
   E   of 50p.

Items 11–12 relate to the following factors
   A   a rise in national income
   B   an increase in value added tax on new cars
   C   a rise in railway fares
   D   a cut of 50 per cent in the excise duty on petrol
   E   the imposition of more severe penalties on people convicted of driving unroadworthy cars.

11 Which of the above factors would *not* tend to lead to an increase in the price of second-hand cars?

12 Which of the above factors would be likely to contribute to an increase in the demand for second-hand cars but not for new cars?

13 If we denote the elasticity of demand for exports as EE and the elasticity of demand for imports as EI then devaluation will lead to an improvement in the country's balance of payments on current account if

A   EI > EE
B   EE > EI
C   (EE + EI) > 1
D   (EE + EI) = 1
E   (EE + EI) < 1.

14   If value added tax is imposed upon a product for which demand elasticity is zero the price will rise by the full extent of the tax if

A   the supply curve slopes up to the right
B   the supply curve is horizontal
C   the supply curve slopes down to the right
D   the supply curve has any of these shapes
E   none of these will apply (i.e. the price could not rise by the full extent of the tax).

15   In a situation of very low unemployment and rapidly rising prices, which of the following government policies would be appropriate?

1   increasing the level of Special Deposits
2   reducing the standard rate of income tax
3   increasing the level of government expenditure.

16   Which of the following statements is/are true?

1   the elasticity of demand is influenced by the availability of substitutes
2   if revenue falls when price increases, demand is elastic
3   a change in price will leave the quantity sold unchanged only if the elasticity of demand is less than one.

17   In which of the following ways can a private company obtain finance for expansion?

1   obtaining a loan from a bank
2   issuing shares to members of the general public, to be traded on the stock exchange.
3   issuing debentures to members of the general public, to be traded on the stock exchange.

Questions 18 and 19 refer to the following three factors

1   a doubling of the U.K.'s foreign aid programme
2   an increase in the number of overseas visitors taking holidays in the U.K.
3   a reduction in the U.K.'s imports of machinery.

Which of the above is/are likely to lead to

18   A worsening of the U.K.'s balance of payments.

19   An improvement in the U.K.'s balance of visible trade.

20   The reserve assets of the commercial banks include

1   Special Deposits
2   money at call
3   Treasury bills.

TRUE/FALSE

1   Any measure which reduces fluctuations in the price of a commodity will also reduce fluctuations in the incomes of the producers of that commodity.

2   Any measure which brings the price elasticity of demand for a commodity closer to unity will reduce fluctuations in producers' incomes arising from changes in supply.

3   Cost benefit analysis can help in the evaluation of the external costs, but not the benefits, of an investment project.

4   The market price of a product may either exceed, or be exceeded by, the total benefit derived from a unit of that product.

5   Collective agreements to fix prices are prohibited by the Restrictive Trade Practices Act.

6   If a commodity is reduced in price and more is then bought for a smaller total expenditure the demand for the product is said to be elastic.

7   Only those products which are sold are included in the calculation of the national income.

8   An increase in the level of Special Deposits tends to reduce the overall level of spending by the commercial banks.

9   The elasticity of demand for a product will tend to be greater the greater the number of close substitutes.

10   When average cost begins to increase as output increases, the scale of organization being unchanged, it does so because fixed costs account for an increasing proportion of total costs.

Index